A Dictionary of
Computing

FOURTH EDITION

Oxford   New York

OXFORD UNIVERSITY PRESS

OXFORD

UNIVERSITY PRESS

Great Clarendon Street, Oxford OX2 6DP

Oxford University Press is a department of the University of Oxford.
It furthers the University's objective of excellence in research, scholarship,
and education by publishing worldwide in

Oxford New York

Auckland Bangkok Buenos Aires Cape Town Chennai
Dar es Salaam Delhi Hong Kong Istanbul Karachi Kolkata
Kuala Lumpur Madrid Melbourne Mexico City Mumbai Nairobi
São Paulo Shanghai Taipei Tokyo Toronto

Oxford is a registered trade mark of Oxford University Press
in the UK and in certain other countries

Published in the United States
by Oxford University Press Inc., New York

First published 1983
Second published 1986
Third edition 1990
Fourth edition 1996

British Library Cataloguing in Publication Data

Data available

Library of Congress Cataloging in Publication Data

Data available

ISBN 0-19-280046-9

10

Printed in Great Britain by
Clays Ltd, St Ives plc

Preface

The world of computing continues to expand and to cross new frontiers of public awareness. Jargon grows apace, and confusion abounds as the field moves from the domain of specialists into general knowledge. In preparing the Dictionary of Computing, we have recognized the need for clear explanations of the concepts that affect more and more aspects of life and the terminology that accompanies them. The dictionary is aimed mainly at students and teachers of computing but should also be of value to professional and amateur computer users.

The fourth edition of the dictionary contains nearly 6000 entries and a comprehensive cross-reference system. Almost 1700 new entries have been added and many of the existing entries have been extensively updated. This reflects recent advances in all aspects of computing, especially in personal computing, multimedia, and graphics, networking and the Internet, artificial intelligence, and computer security.

The principal areas of interest include:
- computer applications, for example in industry, the office, science, education, and the home;
- the means of achieving these applications in terms of hardware, software, computer organization, telecommunications, and user interaction;
- security, safety, and legal aspects of computing;
- the world of computing – the major computer manufacturers and organizations;
- underlying concepts and theories of computing and where appropriate of electronics, mathematics, and logic.

We would like to express our thanks and appreciation to all those involved in the preparation of the new edition. Over thirty-five practitioners in diverse branches of computing and associated fields produced the new and updated entries. The dictionary has been compiled and prepared for computer typesetting by Market House Books Ltd.

February 1996   *Valerie Illingworth*
Ian Pyle

Consultant editor

I. C. Pyle MA, PhD, FBCS, FIEEE, CEng

General editor

Valerie Illingworth BSc, MPhil

Major contributors

P. P. Aslin BSc, MEng, AMIEE

David Aspinall MSc, PhD, FBCS, CEng, FIEE

R. C. Backhouse MA, PhD

David W. Barron MA, PhD, FBCS

Frank Bott MA, CEng, MBCS

Alan Bradley MA, MIEE, MBCS

Alan Bundy BSc, PhD

C. T. Burton BA, MSc, PhD

B. K. Daniels BSc, CEng, FIEE, MBCS, MInstMC, FSaRS

Jonathon A. Dell BSc, CEng, MIEE, MIEEE

David A. Duce BSc, PhD, CEng, MBCS

W. Fawcett BSc, PhD, MIEE, CEng

Robert P. Fletcher BA, DPhil

William Freeman BSc, MBCS, MACM, MIEEE

A. M. Frieze BA, MSc, PhD

Paul E. Garner BSc

Edward L. Glaser AB, DrSc, FIEEE, MNAE

G. Hall BA, PhD

J. Hamilton-Fey CEng, MIMechE

C. J. Higley MA, PhD, CEng, MBCS

F. Robert A. Hopgood MA, Dr-IngEh, CEng, FBCS

Martin G. Hopkins BSc

John J. Illingworth BSc, MSc

Ken Jackson MSc, CEng, MBCS

Alistair Kelman BSc, AMBCS, Barrister at Law

P. J. H. King DSc, CEng, FBCS

P. R. Kirk BSc, MIEE, CEng

Mark H. Lee PhD, CEng, FIEEE, FRSA

Thaddeus Lipinski BSc

I. D. MacArthur CEng, MIMechE

Andrew D. McGettrick BSc, PhD, MBCS

G. P. McKeown BSc, PhD, AFIMA

J. Norbury BSc

Patrick Olivier BA, MA, CompDip, MBCS

V. J. Rayward-Smith MA, PhD, AFIMA, MBCS

P. D. Roberts BA, MBCS, MACM, LIMA

G. J. S. Ross BA, DipMathStats, FSS

David Sayers BSc, MSc, PhD, GradIMA

Edel Sherratt BSc, PhD

V. Stenning BSc, DPhil, MBCS

J. V. Tucker BA, MSc, PhD

Colin J. Tully MA, FBCS

Raymond Turner BSc, PhD, MBCS

Michael Wells MA, PhD, FBCS

Jack Williams BTech, DPhil

J. V. Woods MScTech, PhD, AMIEE

P. Worsdale BTech

Guide to the dictionary

Alphabetical order in this dictionary ignores spaces, punctuation, and numbers in the entry titles. Greek letters in an entry title are spelt out. Entry titles that consist only of numbers appear at the beginning of the dictionary.

Synonyms and generally used abbreviations are given either in brackets immediately after the relevant entry title, or occasionally in the text of the entry with some additional information or qualification.

An asterisk (*) used before a word or group of words indicates to readers that they will find at the entry so marked further information relevant to the entry that is being read. The asterisk is not used before all the words in an article that are themselves entry titles as this would lead to an unhelpful proliferation of asterisks.

Some entries simply cross-refer the reader to other articles. These may be synonyms or abbreviations or terms more conveniently discussed under the article referred to. In the latter case, the relevant term will appear in the entry in italic type.

A distinction is made between an acronym and an abbreviation: an acronym can be pronounced while an abbreviation cannot. The entry for an acronym usually appears at the acronym itself whereas the entry for an abbreviation usually appears at the unabbreviated form, unless the abbreviation is in common use.

Some terms listed in the dictionary are used both as nouns and verbs. This is usually indicated in the text of an entry if both forms are in common use. In many cases a noun is also used in an adjectival form to qualify another noun. This occurs too often to be noted.

Typography and character set

The typefaces and characters used in the dictionary entries follow normal conventions for printing mathematical and technical texts (rather than the more rigorous styles used in some specialist computing texts).

The special characters shown in the table have been used to express specific logic, set theory, and mathematical operations; for further information, see relevant entry. Letters of the Greek alphabet also occur in some entries.

operation, etc.	symbol
AND operation, conjunction	$\wedge \cdot$
OR operation, disjunction	$\vee +$
NOT operation, negation	$' \neg \sim$
NAND operation	$\mid \triangle$
NOR operation	$\downarrow \nabla$

For set S and/or set T:

x is a member of S	$x \in S$
x is not a member of S	$x \notin S$
S is a subset of T	$S \subseteq T$
S is a proper subset of T	$S \subset T$
complement of S	$S' \sim S \; \overline{S}$
union of S and T	$S \cup T$
intersection of S and T	$S \cap T$
Cartesian product of S and T	$S \times T$
relation	R
function of x	$f(x)$, etc.
function f from set X to set Y	$f : X \to Y$
inverse function	f^{-1}
inverse relation	R^{-1}

operation, etc.	symbol
sum, with limits	$\sum_{i=1}^{n}$
integral, with limits	$\int_{b}^{a} dx$
elements of matrix A	a_{ij}
transpose of matrix A	A^{T}
inverse of matrix A	A^{-1}
equivalence	$\leftrightarrow \equiv$
biconditional	$\leftrightarrow \equiv$
conditional	$\to \Rightarrow$
general binary operation	$\circ$
universal quantifier	$\forall$
existential quantifier	$\exists$
greater than	$>$
greater than or equal to	$\geq$
less than	$<$
less than or equal to	$\leq$
approx. equal to	$\approx$
not equal to	$\neq$
infinity	∞

Greek alphabet

alpha	α, A	eta	η, H	nu	ν, N	tau	τ, T
beta	β, B	theta	θ, Θ	xi	ξ, Ξ	upsilon	υ, Y
gamma	γ, Γ	iota	ι, I	omikron	o, O	phi	ϕ, Φ
delta	δ, Δ	kappa	κ, K	pi	π, Π	chi	χ, X
epsilon	ϵ, E	lambda	λ, Λ	rho	ρ, P	psi	ψ, Ψ
zeta	ζ, Z	mu	μ, M	sigma	σ, Σ	omega	ω, Ω

386 *See* Intel.

486 *See* Intel.

80386, 80486 *See* Intel.

68000 *See* Motorola.

A* algorithm A member of the class of *best-first *heuristic search techniques that attempt to find a "best" path from a given start node to a designated goal node in a problem *graph. An *evaluation function is used to estimate the cost of the (unknown) distance from the current node being explored to the goal and this is then added to the (known) cost of the shortest path from the start node to the current node to give a figure of merit for the current node. At each iteration the node with the best cost figure is used to pursue the search. The operation of the algorithm displays a behavior that is a mixture of *depth-first and *breadth-first searching.

abduction An *inference process widely used in *artificial intelligence, particularly in *expert systems and *rule-based systems. In diagnosis, for example, there may be a rule like "if measles then red spots" so that, when the symptom red spots occurs, we may use the rule in reverse to conclude that measles is present. However, unlike *deduction, abduction is not logically sound because of inherent uncertainty that can lead to false conclusions – note that measles is not the only cause of red spots. Abduction is an example of a *plausible-reasoning technique.

abelian group (commutative group) *See* group.

ABI *Abbrev. for* application binary interface. Definition of the binary-level interface between application programs and the operating system, including the format of executable files. Compiled binary applications can be ported between systems with the same ABI.

ablative An optical recording technique in which the heat generated by the recording beam melts or vaporizes a small area of the recording medium, leaving the underlying layer (with a different reflectivity) exposed.

abnormal termination A termination to a *process brought about by the operating system when the process reaches a point from which it cannot continue, e.g. when the process attempts to obey an undefined instruction. In contrast, a process that reaches a successful conclusion terminates normally by issuing a suitable supervisor call to the operating system. It is common practice to inform the initiator of the process as to whether the termination was normal or abnormal.

abort (of a process) To undergo or cause *abnormal termination. Abortion may be a voluntary act by the process, which realizes that it cannot reach a successful conclusion, or may be brought about by the operating system, which intervenes because the process has failed to observe system constraints. Thus, computationally, the term has a rather similar meaning to its medical meaning of spontaneous or induced fetal death.

absolute address A unique number that specifies a unique location within the *address space where an operand is to be found/deposited, or where an instruction is located. It generally specifies a memory location but in some cases specifies a machine register or an I/O device. In the case of a binary machine, it is an n-bit number specifying one of 2^n locations. The result of calculating an *effective address is usually an absolute address.

absolute code Program code in a form suitable for direct execution by the central processor, i.e. code containing no symbolic references. *See also* machine code.

absorption laws The two self-dual laws

$$x \vee (x \wedge y) = x$$
$$x \wedge (x \vee y) = x$$

(*see* duality) that are satisfied by all elements x, y in a *Boolean algebra possessing the two operations $\vee$ and $\wedge$.

abstract computabilty theory The theory

of functions that can be computed by algorithms on any *algebra. Its aim is to explore the scope and limits of computation on any kind of data. It is a generalization to arbitrary many sorted algebras of the theory of the effectively calculable or recursive functions on the natural numbers.

Abstract computability theory starts with an analysis and classification of many models of computation and specification that apply to algebras. This reveals the essential features of methods, and results in a *generalized* *Church–Turing thesis* that establishes which functions on an *abstract data type are programmable by a *deterministic programming language. Comparisons can be made between computations on different algebras, modeling data types and their implementations. The theory also provides a foundation for new theories of computation for special data types, such as algebras of real numbers, which can be used in applications.

The *while programming language is a simple example of a method for computing functions on any many-sorted algebra A (that possesses the Booleans). On the natural numbers it can compute all *partial recursive functions. Computation is based on the operations of the algebra – sequencing, branching, and iteration – and has available a limited means of searching A. However, a vital missing component is the capacity to compute with finite sequences of data from A. On the natural numbers finite sequences can be simulated using pairing functions, but it is not possible to simulate finite sequences on an algebra A. Finite sequences and operations for every data set in A are therefore added to A to make a new algebra A^*. It turns out that while programs on A^* (i.e. while programs equipped with finite sequences) have all the essential properties of the computable functions on A. This class of functions is the subject of the generalized Church–Turing thesis.

Most of the main results in the theory of computability on the natural numbers can also be proved for abstract computability theory on any finite generated *minimal algebra.

abstract data type A *data type that is defined solely in terms of the operations that apply to objects of the type without commitment as to how the value of such an object is to be represented (*see* data abstraction).

An abstract data type strictly is a triple (D,F,A) consisting of a set of domains D, a set of functions F each with range and domain in D, and a set of axioms A, which specify the properties of the functions in F. By distinguishing one of the domains d in D, a precise characterization is obtained of the *data structure that the abstract data type imposes on d.

For example, the natural numbers comprise an abstract data type, where the domain d is

$$\{0,1,2,\ldots\}$$

and there is an auxiliary domain

$$\{TRUE,FALSE\}$$

The functions or operations are ZERO, ISZERO, SUCC, and ADD and the axioms are:

$$ISZERO(0) = TRUE$$
$$ISZERO(SUCC(x)) = FALSE$$
$$ADD(0,y) = y$$
$$ADD(SUCC(x),y) =$$
$$SUCC(ADD(x,y))$$

These axioms specify precisely the laws that must hold for any implementation of the natural numbers. (Note that a practical implementation could not fulfill the axioms because of word length and overflow.) Such precise characterization is invaluable both to the user and the implementer. Sometimes the concept of function is extended to procedures with multiple results.

The Ada programmer can obtain many of the benefits of abstract data types by defining *packages.

abstract family of languages (AFL) There are many useful types of *formal language, and classes often have similar properties. An AFL is a class of formal languages that is closed under all the following operations: *union, *concatenation, Kleene-plus (*see* Kleene star), *intersection with *regular set, Λ-free homomorphic image, and inverse homomorphic image (*see* homomorphism). An AFL is *full* if it is also closed under Kleene star and homomorphic image. The motivation for the concept of an AFL is to investigate properties of classes of languages that follow merely from the assumption of these *closure properties. Each member of the *Chomsky hierarchy is an AFL; all except for the class of context-free languages are full.

abstraction The principle of ignoring those aspects of a subject that are not relevant to the current purpose in order to concentrate solely on those that are. The application of this principle is essential in the development and understanding of all forms of computer system. *See* data abstraction, procedural abstraction.

abstract machine A machine can be thought of as a collection of resources together with a definition of the ways in which these resources can interact. For a real machine these resources actually exist as tangible objects, each of the type expected; for example, addressable storage on a real machine will actually consist of the appropriate number of words of storage, together with suitable address decoders and access mechanisms. It is possible to define an abstract machine, by listing the resources it contains and the interactions between them, without building the machine. Such abstract machines are often of use in attempting to prove the properties of programs, since a suitably defined abstract machine may allow the suppression of unneeded detail. *See* virtual machine.

abstract reduction system (abstract rewrite (or replacement) system) A general characterization of the process of deriving or transforming data by means of rules. It is an abstraction based primarily on examples of *term rewriting systems: it is simply a reflexive and transitive binary relation $\rightarrow_R$ on a nonempty set A. For $a, b \in A$, if $a \rightarrow_R b$ then a is said to *reduce* or *rewrite* to b.

Using this abstraction, it is easy to define a range of basic notions that play a role in computing with rules.

(1) An element $a \in A$ is a *normal form* for $\rightarrow_R$ if there does not exist b, different from a, such that $a \rightarrow_R b$.

(2) The reduction system $\rightarrow_R$ is *Church–Rosser* (or *confluent*) if for any $a \in A$ if there are $b_1, b_2 \in A$ such that $a \rightarrow_R b_1$ and a

$\rightarrow_R b_2$ then there exists $c \in A$ such that $b_1 \rightarrow_R c$ and $b_2 \rightarrow_R c$.

(3) The reduction system $\rightarrow_R$ is *weakly terminating* (or *weakly normalizing*) if for each $a \in A$ there is some normal form $b \in A$ so that $a \rightarrow_R b$.

(4) The reduction system $\rightarrow_R$ is *strongly terminating* (or *strongly normalizing* or *Noetherian*) if there does not exist an infinite chain

$$a_0 \rightarrow_R a_1 \rightarrow_R \cdots \rightarrow_R a_n \rightarrow_R \cdots$$
of reductions in A wherein

$$a_i \neq a_{i+1} \text{ for } i = 0, 1, 2, \ldots$$

(5) The reduction system $\rightarrow_R$ is *complete* if it is Church–Rosser and strongly terminating.

(6) A reduction system is Church–Rosser and weakly terminating if, and only if, every element reduces to a *unique* normal form. Let $\equiv_R$ denote the smallest equivalence relation on A containing $\rightarrow_R$. If $\rightarrow_R$ is a Church–Rosser weakly terminating reduction system then the set $NF(\rightarrow_R)$ of normal forms is a transversal for $\equiv_R$, i.e. a set that contains one and only one representative of each equivalence class.

abstract specification A specification for software expressed in a (mathematically) *formal language such that the specification is completely independent of, and does not imply, any design and implementation method and languages. It does not normally express the constraints that the final software must satisfy. *See also* formal specification.

A-buffer A buffer used with a *Z-buffer to hold information concerning the visible transparent surfaces to be considered at each *pixel of an image. The A-buffer originated in an *anti-aliased *hidden-surface removal algorithm developed by Loren Carpenter around 1984. It resolves visibility among an arbitrary collection of opaque, transparent, and intersecting objects. The algorithm was developed for the REYES system at Lucasfilm Ltd. Road to Point Reyes was a famous image produced by the system.

acceleration time (start time) The time taken for a device to reach its operating speed from a quiescent state.

accept (recognize) a formal language. *See* automaton, finite-state automaton.

acceptable use policy (AUP) The set of

rules governing the use that can be made of a network. All network users are expected to conform to any existing legislation, and to any commercial conditions that form part of any contract for the use of commercial networks. In the case of academic or research networks there are also likely to be constraints on using the network to carry commercial traffic, and these will be embodied in the AUP.

acceptance testing *See* testing. *See also* review.

access 1. The reading or writing of data, with the connotation that the content of the reading or writing is taken into account. The word is most commonly used in connection with filed information and is often qualified by an indication as to the types of access that are to be permitted. For example, read-only access means that the contents of the file may be read but not altered or erased.
2. The right or opportunity to read or write data or programs. The UK *Computer Misuse Act 1990 states that "a person secures access to any program or data held in a computer if by causing a computer to perform any function he alters or erases the program or data, copies or moves it to any storage medium other than that in which it is held or to a different location in the storage medium in which it is held, uses it or has it output from the computer in which it is held (whether by having it displayed or in any other manner)".
3. To gain entry to data, a computer system, etc. In the US, to access strictly means to instruct, communicate with, store data in, retrieve data from, or otherwise obtain the ability to use the resources of a computer or any part thereof.

Access *Trademark* A relational database management system for personal computers from Microsoft.

access control A *trusted process that limits access to the resources and objects of a computer system in accordance with a *security model. The process can be implemented by reference to a stored table that lists the *access rights of subjects to objects, e.g. users

to records. Optionally the process may record in an *audit trail any illegal access attempts.

access method Any algorithm used for the storage and retrieval of records from a *data file or *database. Access methods are of two kinds: those that determine the structural characteristics of the file on which it is used (its *file organization) and those that do not (as in secondary indexing (*see* indexed file) and *data chaining). In the first case essentially the same algorithm is used for the retrieval of a record as was used for its original physical placement, whereas in the second these algorithms are quite distinct. Hence in the first case the same term may be used interchangeably (and loosely) for both the access method and the file organization (*see* random access (def. 2), sequential access).

access path The name given to the set of names of devices, *directories, *subdirectories, and a specific *file, by means of which the file-management system is able to reach the specified file. Depending on the details of the file-management system actually in use, the access path may start with the name of a physical or logical device, which holds a number of directories that associate the identity of an object with its location on the device; these objects may in turn be further directories (usually then known as subdirectories) or they may be files containing end-user data. The complete set of intermediate objects, in the order in which they are used, is the access path.

access rights (access privileges) A classification of the modes of access to an object granted to particular subjects, or groups of users. Thus, the owner of a file will typically have rights to read, write, or delete the file. Some or all these rights may also be granted to other users on the system. *See* access control.

access time The time taken to retrieve an item of information from storage. The access time may be counted in nanoseconds for a semiconductor device, in milliseconds for a magnetic disk, or in minutes if the file containing the required data is on magnetic tape.

In the case of disk storage, the access time

is the average time taken for a disk drive to provide the first byte of data, measured from the time the host issues a read command. To a good approximation, the average access time is the sum of the average *seek time, the command overhead, and the average *latency. *See also* memory hierarchy.

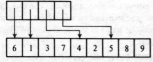

6

1   3   7

4   2

5   8   9

row-ragged array

| 6 | 1 | 3 | 7 | 4 | 2 | 5 | 8 | 9 |

representation using an access vector

Access vector

access vector A vector that is used in the representation of a *ragged array. For example, the elements of a row-ragged array, A, would be stored row by row in a vector B. The ith element of the access vector would then point to the position in B where the first element of the ith row of A was stored (*see* diagram). A column-ragged array would be similarly represented using an access vector referring to the beginning of columns and a listing of the elements column by column.

accountable file A file that will be taken into account when evaluating system usage. An example is a user's permanent file holding the text of a program. Files that have only a transient existence, for example to hold spooled files, will not be accountable.

accounting file A file that contains records of the resources used by individual jobs. These records are required both to regulate the amount of resource used by a job and, in a commercial environment, to manage the charging for use of the system. As each job is started, an entry is opened in the accounting file into which records concerning system

utilization are written as the job is processed. *See also* system accounting.

accumulator A *register that is implicitly specified by one-address format instructions and is used to contain the results of an operation performed by the *ALU. It can normally be one of the inputs to the ALU, thus the results of a number of successive operations may be built up – hence the name. In addition to holding results, the accumulator commonly has the ability to perform the various *shift and *circular shift instructions. It may be part of the *processor status word.

accuracy *See* precision.

ACE *Acronym for* Automatic Computing Engine. An electronic stored-program computer designed in 1945–46 by Alan Turing while he was at the National Physical Laboratory (NPL), near London. The prototype version *Pilot ACE* was built at the NPL, ran its first program in 1950, and was in full-time use in 1952. The final version was working by 1957.

ACIA *Abbrev. for* asynchronous communications interface adapter. An integrated circuit that can be used in serial data communication interfaces. The function of the device can be varied by signals applied to its control inputs.

ACK The "acknowledge" control character. *See* acknowledgment.

Ackermann benchmark A use of the *Ackermann function to provide a *benchmark for computer performance. Typically in excess of 100 000 recursive calls to the function are made and the number of completed calls per second measured. The benchmark gives a good indication of the overhead associated with procedure and function calls.

Ackermann function The *function A defined inductively on pairs of nonnegative integers in the following manner:
$$A(0,n) = n + 1$$
$$A(m+1,0) = A(m,1)$$
$$A(m+1,n+1) = A(m,A(m+1,n))$$
where $m,n \geq 0$. Thus
$$A(1,n) = n + 2$$
$$A(2,n) = 2n + 3$$
$$A(3,n) = 2^{n+3} - 3$$
The highly recursive nature of the function

makes it a popular choice for testing the ability of *compilers or computers to handle *recursion. Named for W. Ackermann, it provides an example of a function that is general *recursive but not *primitive recursive because of the exceedingly rapid growth in its value as m increases.

The Ackermann function may also be regarded as a function Ack of a single variable:

$$Ack(n) = A(n,n)$$

where A is defined as above.

acknowledgment 1. A message that describes the status of one or more messages sent in the opposite direction. A *positive acknowledgment (ACK)* confirms that the previous messages were received correctly. A *negative acknowledgment (NAK)* indicates that the previous messages were not received correctly and should be retransmitted. In some *protocols, acknowledgments are also used as a simple form of *flow control: sending an ACK implies that another message may be sent in the same direction as the message being acknowledged.

Different layers of a protocol hierarchy may have their own acknowledgment systems operating simultaneously. For example, an end-to-end transport protocol may be used to send a message reliably from one host to another in a packet switching network. When the message reaches its destination, an acknowledgment will be generated and sent in the opposite direction. Both the original message and its acknowledgment will cause data link layer acknowledgments to be generated as they travel from node to node in the network. *See also* backward error correction. **2.** Output to the operator or user of a graphics system that indicates that some input has been received. *See also* prompt, echoing, feedback.

ACM Association for Computing Machinery, a US organization founded in 1947 and dedicated to the development of information processing as a discipline, to the exchange of information about the subject, and to the responsible use of computers in an increasing diversity of applications.

acoustic coupler A type of *modem that converts serial digital data into a *frequency shift keyed sound signal in the audio range for transmission down telephone lines, and decodes similar incoming sound signals. The connection between the acoustic coupler and the telephone system is made by means of a small microphone and loudspeaker held close to the earpiece and mouthpiece of an ordinary telephone handset in a sound-absorbent enclosure.

This system is ideal for connecting portable terminals or data-capture devices to remote computers using any convenient telephone. The lack of any electrical connection between terminal and phone lines is of benefit when obtaining the approval of the PTT for the use of such a device. The quality of ordinary switched voice circuits normally limits the speed of transmission to 300 baud or less.

acoustic delay line *See* delay line.

acoustic memory *See* delay time.

active *Another term for* running.

active filter A combination of operational amplifiers and reactive elements that performs a variety of *filtering functions.

active-matrix LCD *See* LCD.

active star A network topology in which the outer *nodes connect to a single central node that processes all messages in the network, including messages that it forwards from one outer node to another. A failure of the central node causes the entire network to fail. *See also* passive star, star network, network architecture.

active transition of a clock signal. *See* clock.

active vision A subfield of *computer vision where controlled movement of the viewpoint of the imaging camera is an integral part of the image-processing task. Previously in computer vision research, in order to reduce the enormous complexity of visual data, fixed camera geometry and static images have been beneficial in constraining and simplifying the image-processing tasks. Active vision takes a different approach and, by analogy with animal vision, does not avoid movement but gains information from the dynamics of changing viewpoints to resolve ambiguities, gain depth information, and establish relationships between visual sensing and action.

active widget A *widget that both displays its current value and achieves the relevant action.

activity network (activity graph) A graphical method for showing dependencies between tasks (activities) in a project. The network consists of *nodes connected by arcs. Nodes denote events and represent the culmination of one or more activities. Arcs represent activities and are labeled with the name of the activity and have an estimated time to complete the activity. Dummy unlabeled arcs with zero completion time are used to fan out from one event to other dependent events. Before progress can be made from one event to another, all activities leading to that event must have been completed. The longest path through the activity network gives the completion time for the project represented by the network. *See also* critical path method, PERT chart.

Actor An *object-oriented language used to develop applications for Microsoft Windows. Confusingly it is not an *actor language.

actor language An *object-oriented language in which objects exist as concurrent processes (*see* concurrency).

actors An early message-passing model of concurrent computation in artificial intelligence. The model has many features that relate to *object-oriented programming and conceptual similarities with the language *Smalltalk. *See also* actor language.

actual parameter Information passed to a *subprogram at the *call. *See also* parameter, argument.

actuator of a disk drive. The mechanism that causes the head carriage and heads to be moved to the desired track. The *voice coil* actuator gains its name because its operating principle is similar to that of a moving-coil loudspeaker. This type of actuator invariably forms part of a closed loop servosystem. The reference information may be provided by a disk with a dedicated servosurface: the servohead positions itself symmetrically between two servotracks by sensing positioning information from both tracks (di-bits) and moving in such a way that the amplitudes of the two signals are equal. A second method records the servo information in a fixed number of equiangular "spokes"; this technique is known as *embedded servo.* Dedicated servo drives suffer head stack and/or disk stack tilt, due to temperature variations – especially after being powered-on. This causes heads located further away from the servo head to be misaligned from the corresponding data track centerline. Accordingly, these drives must interrupt the data flow to the host system to carry out regular calibrations. Embedded servo drives do not need to interrupt the data flow and so are better suited to applications that must provide a continuous data stream, e.g. video-on-demand systems. As track densities increase (currently around 4000 tracks per inch) more manufacturers are turning to embedded servo techniques.

acyclic graph A *graph possessing no *cycles; when the term is applied to directed graphs the direction associated with the edges must be taken into account. *See also* tree.

Ada *Trademark* A programming language developed at the behest of the US Department of Defense for use in *real-time systems containing *embedded computers. The name commemorates Augusta Ada King, Countess of Lovelace, who assisted Charles Babbage and has some claim to be the world's first programmer.

The original version (now known as *Ada 83*) was designed by international competition, published in 1980, and adopted as an ANSI standard in 1983 and as an ISO standard in 1987. It incorporated ideas of *modular programming, *concurrent programming, and separate compilation to support the development of large programs. It also introduced the idea of a programming support environment (*APSE) whereby program development tools are specified along with the language as an integral whole. However, the absence of agreement on specific tools has led to a number of different and incompatible support environments for Ada.

From 1986 use of Ada was made mandatory for US military applications (unless the contractor could show "good cause" for a waiver), and several European countries have followed suit.

The language was revised in the early 1990s (when it was called *Ada 9x*) and adopted by ISO in 1995; the new version is now known as *Ada 95*. In spite of differences in presentation, Ada 95 is virtually a superset of Ada 83, so almost all Ada-83 programs are valid Ada-95 programs. The core of Ada 95 includes facilities for *object-oriented programming and facilities for synchronized access to shared data (protected objects). There are annexes for distributed systems, informations systems, real-time systems, systems programming, safety and security, numerics, and interfaces to other languages.

Ada 95, Ada 83 *See* Ada.

Adams methods *See* linear multistep methods.

adaptive channel allocation A process by which the capacity of a communication channel is multiplexed (shared) among several sources depending upon their relative requirements. The resource distribution varies with time to match changing requirements. *See* multiplexing.

adaptive compression (adaptive compaction) A *compression technique that chooses between different techniques depending on the information to be compressed. *See also* statistical compaction.

adaptive-control system An automatic (process) control system that uses adaptation as part of its prediction of process behavior in order to optimize the control. *See* adaptive process.

adaptive interface A human–computer interface (*see* HCI) that adjusts to user skill.

adaptive maintenance *See* software maintenance.

adaptive meshing Meshing an area where each element of the *mesh can be independently subdivided to ensure a desired effect is achieved. For example, *finite-element calculations will require more detailed meshes where there are rapid changes in the structure or the parameter of interest is changing rapidly.

adaptive process The process of performing computations on a set of measured or presented data (believed to be) from a physical, i.e. natural, source in such a way as to develop a "best" parametric model of that physical source, i.e. one that best fits the observed data according to some error criterion. *See also* adaptive-control system, self-organizing system.

adaptive quadrature *See* numerical integration.

adaptive ray tracing *See* ray tracing.

ADC *Abbrev. for* analog-to-digital (A/D) converter.

ADCCP *Abbrev. for* advanced data communication control procedure. A bit-oriented *data link control protocol developed by ANSI and similar to *SDLC and *HDLC.

A/D converter (ADC) *Short for* analog-to-digital converter. A device that can accept an analog, i.e. continuous, signal whose amplitude lies within a given range, and produce an equivalent digital signal, i.e. an n-bit parallel binary word that represents this analog signal. The analog signal is "examined" at discrete fixed intervals of time by means of a *sampling process in order to produce the digital signal. Analog signals originating from devices such as analog sensors or tachogenerators may thus be converted into a form that can then be processed by, say, a microprocessor.

The *resolution* of an A/D converter gives the smallest change in analog input that can be discriminated by the device. If the resolution of an n-bit A/D converter is ΔV, then its range is either

$$0 \text{ to } \Delta V(2^n - 1)$$

or

$$\pm \Delta V(2^{n-1} - 1)$$

according as it is *unsigned or *signed. In practice, the value of n is usually 8, 10, 12, 14, or 16. Since the resolution is finite, the conversion process introduces quantization noise (*see* discrete and continuous systems). A/D converters are available in integrated circuit form. *See also* D/A converter.

adder In its simplest form, a digital electronic device that performs the operation of addition on two binary digits, the *augend* and the number to be added, the *addend*. It is therefore also known as a *binary adder*. This operation is exemplified by the truth table shown in the diagram, where Σ is the sum and C_o is the carry. From this it can be seen that binary addition may generate a carry to subsequent stages.

A	B	Σ	C_o
0	0	0	0
0	1	1	0
1	0	1	0
1	1	0	1

Truth table of binary half-adder

A *full adder* has provision for inputs of addend, augend, and a carry bit and is capable of generating sum and carry outputs. These adders may be cascaded when it is desired to add binary words greater than one bit in length by connecting together the carry inputs and outputs of adjacent stages.

A *half-adder* is an implementation of an adder that has provision only for input of addend and augend bits and is capable of generating sum and carry outputs. These devices cannot directly be cascaded as can full adders but may be made to perform a similar function by including additional logic gating.

See also parallel adder, serial adder, carry lookahead.

add-in card (add-on card, expansion card) A *printed circuit board that plugs into an *expansion slot in a computer to provide some extra facility. The sockets normally connect to a *bus, and the type of connector and the use to which each contact is put are strictly defined to ensure compatibility between the card and the computer. Cards are available that provide extra memory, communications interfaces, sound I/O capabilities, device interfaces to extra disks or tape backup devices, for instance, or perhaps extra processors in multiprocessor systems. *See also* PCMCIA.

address 1. The term most generally used to refer (in some way) to a location within the computer memory; the word *location* is actually used as a synonym. Such reference is usually made for the purpose of retrieving or storing some information at that location. The reference may be explicit (*see* direct addressing) or it may be made in any of a number of ways for convenience or brevity (*see* addressing schemes). In some architectures the registers in the CPU and/or the I/O devices are also addressed.

The word address is also used as a verb: to specify a location.

2. In communications, *see* addressing.

addressability of a display device. *See* resolution.

addressable location A location whose position in a storage medium is precisely defined and can be accessed. As a safeguard it is usual to arrange that not all memory locations are addressable by all programs.

address bus A *bus that is dedicated to passing address information. It may be a set of conductors that are physically separate from other dedicated buses or it may be a subset of a system bus. The number of conductors is often the same as the maximum allowable number of bits in the address.

address calculation sorting A form of *sorting that uses extra storage space to improve upon a *straight insertion sort. One method employs n *list heads, corresponding to n different ranges of the sortkey, together with a *link field on each record.

address format *See* instruction format.

addressing The method used to identify the location of a participant in a *network. Ideally, addressing specifies where the participant is located rather than who they are (*see* name) or how to get there (*see* routing). This is true for *flat addressing*, in which addresses are assigned independently of each other and carry no internal structure. More common, however, is *hierarchical addressing*, in which addresses are grouped to reflect relationships among the addressed entities. Often the grouping reflects the physical topology of the network, so addressing and routing are interrelated. Sometimes the grouping reflects administrative or functional relationships (*logical addressing*), so addressing and naming are interrelated.

In a system employing layered protocols (*see* seven-layer reference model), different forms of addressing may be used at different levels. The data link level may use addresses that identify specific stations on a multidrop line. The network level uses addresses that identify the source and destination hosts associated with a packet. Higher protocol layers may use addresses that distinguish different connections or processes.

Addresses may be fixed-length or extensible. In *fixed-length addressing* all addresses occupy a fixed number of digits. An example is the Ethernet protocol, which uses 48-bit addresses. In *extensible addressing* the length of an address may vary from case to case. For example, in X121 "international data numbers" are defined and these may be from 3 to 14 decimal digits in length.

addressing schemes The wide variety of schemes developed in order to provide compact or convenient *address references in cases where the *absolute address is too large to be accommodated in an instruction (*see* instruction format) or where it is not possible or even necessary to assign an explicit address. *Augmented, *indirect, *implied, *immediate, and *relative addressing schemes provide compact references. *Indexed, relative, and *symbolic addressing schemes provide convenient references. In the absence of any of these addressing schemes *direct addressing is used.

address mapping Use of one of the *addressing schemes to convert an address that is specified in an instruction into an *absolute address. *Virtual memory and *cache memory use forms of address mapping for additional memory-management functions.

address mark The special code on a magnetic disk track that occurs just prior to the address information of a *sector. In the case of an MFM drive (*see* disk format), the encoding rules for MFM are broken so that the code is unique. The purpose of the address mark is to bring the drive control electronics into byte synchronization with the header data.

The *data mark* fulfills the same function with respect to data as the address mark to the address.

address register A *register in which an *address is stored. *See also* control unit.

address-relative Having or involving a relative address or relative addresses. *See* relative addressing.

address space The number of distinct locations that may be referred to with the *absolute address. For most (i.e. binary) machines it is equal to 2^n, where n is the number of bits in the absolute address. The address space is often larger than the number of physical or real addresses that are present in the system, and some mapping scheme is necessary to obtain the physical address from the specified address. The physical address space embraces the primary memory, the I/O devices, and, in some cases, the registers in the CPU.

address table sorting A form of *sorting that is useful when the information records are long. A table of addresses that point to the records is formed and these addresses, rather than the records themselves, are manipulated.

add-subtract time The time required by a computer to find the sum or difference of two numbers; it may or may not include the time required to obtain the numbers from memory. This was once used as one form of (speed) figure of merit for computers. *See also* computer power.

adequacy theorem A theorem about a logical system L and a semantics S stating that if a formula is valid in the semantics S then it is provable in the logic L. An adequacy theorem confirms that the logic can express and derive all properties that are valid according to the semantics. *See also* completeness theorem.

adjacency list *Another name for* adjacency structure.

adjacency matrix (connectivity matrix; reachability matrix) A *matrix used as a means of representing an *adjacency structure, which in turn represents a *graph. If A is the adjacency matrix corresponding to a given graph G, then

$$a_{ij} = 1$$

if there is an edge from vertex i to vertex j in G; otherwise

$$a_{ij} = 0$$

If G is a directed *graph then

$$a_{ij} = 1$$

if there is an edge directed from vertex i to vertex j; otherwise

$$a_{ij} = 0$$

If the vertices of the graph are numbered $1,2,...m$, the adjacency matrix is of a type $m \times m$. If

$$A \times A \times ... \times A \ (p \text{ terms}, p \leq m)$$

is evaluated, the nonzero entries indicate those vertices that are joined by a *path of length p; indeed the value of the (i,j)th entry of A^p gives the number of paths of length p from the vertex i to vertex j. By examining the set of such matrices,

$$p = 1,2,...,m-1$$

it can be determined whether two vertices are connected.

It is also possible for adjacency matrices to be formed from *Boolean matrices.

adjacency structure (adjacency list) A means of representing a *graph. The adjacency structure corresponding to a *path G is the set

$$\{\text{Adj}(v) \mid v \text{ is a vertex in } G\}$$

If G is an undirected graph, then a vertex w is in $\text{Adj}(v)$ if and only if there is an edge in G between v and w; if G is a directed graph, then w is in $\text{Adj}(v)$ if and only if there is an edge in G directed from v to w.

ADP *Abbrev. for* automatic data processing. *See* data processing.

affine mapping (affine transformation) A mapping from one coordinate system to another under which parallel lines remain parallel and ratios of collinear points are preserved. An affine mapping can be decomposed into linear transformations (rotation, scaling, and shear) and translation.

AFIPS American Federation of Information Processing Societies, founded in 1961 to provide a structure for professional societies with a primary interest in information pro-

cessing to join together in order to advance the state of the art. AFIPS was dissolved in 1990. In 1991 its two principal members, the *ACM and the *IEEE Computer Society, formed a joint committee known as *FOCUS* (Focus on Computing in the US), which represents the US in *IFIP.

AFL *Abbrev. for* abstract family of languages.

agenda mechanism A control scheme often used in *knowledge-based systems and *blackboard systems to order the sequence of action execution. While the system is running, inference processes may examine the agenda and manipulate it by the dynamic addition, removal, and reordering of items.

agent An autonomous system that receives information from its environment, processes it, and performs actions on that environment. Agents may have different degrees of intelligence or rationality, and may be software, hardware, or both.

Software agents operate in symbolic environments, and perceive and act upon strings of symbols; examples include personal assistant agents that enhance and customize facilities for computer users, and *data mining agents that search for interesting patterns in large databases. In a *distributed system, the agent for a *remote procedure call is in a different computer from the caller; its environment is the network and the procedure body. A robot (*see* robotics) is an example of an agent that perceives its physical environment through sensors and acts through effectors.

AGV *Abbrev. for* autonomous guided vehicle.

AI *Abbrev. for* artificial intelligence.

Aitken's Δ^2 process A method to convert any convergent sequence $\{x_n\}$ into a more rapidly convergent sequence $\{x_n{}'\}$. For linearly converging sequences the formula is:

$$x_n{}' = x_n - (x_{n+1} - x_n)^2 / (x_{n+2} - 2x_{n+1} + x_n)$$

AIX An IBM version of *UNIX.

ALARP principle A principle that is associated with the design and development of safety systems, and captures the notion that the risk to individuals, society, and the environment should be *As Low As Reasonably Possible*. *See also* safety-critical system, safety-related system.

aleph null *See* cardinality.

algebra 1. The investigation of mathematical properties of data, such as numbers, and of operations on data, such as the addition and multiplication of numbers.

2. A collection of *sets together with a collection of *operations over those sets. Many examples involve only one set, such as the following:

(a) the set $N = \{0,1,2,...\}$ of natural numbers together with, for example, the operations of addition, subtraction, and multiplication;

(b) the set $B = \{\text{TRUE, FALSE}\}$ of Boolean truth values together with the operations AND, OR, and NOT (*see also* Boolean algebra);

(c) the set of all finite strings over a set of symbols together with the operation of *concatenation;

(d) a set of sets together with the operations of *union, *intersection, and *complement (*see also* set algebra).

In computer science, however, it is natural to consider algebras involving more than one set. These are called *many-sorted algebras*, in contrast to *single-sorted algebras* with only one set. For example, in programming languages there are different *data types such as Boolean, integer, real, character, etc., as well as user-defined types. Operations on elements of these types can then be seen as giving rise to a many-sorted algebra. By stating axioms that define properties of these operations, an *abstract data type can be specified. *See also* algebraic structure, signature.

algebraic abstract data type An *abstract data type whose behavior is defined in algebraic terms using sets, mappings, functions, relations, morphisms, and categories.

algebraic language *Another name for* context-free language.

algebraic model *See* algebraic structure.

algebraic semantics A refinement of *denotational semantics that stresses the algebraic structure on both syntactic and semantic entities. Typically syntactic and semantic entities are expressed as elements of some *algebra, and the mapping from syntax to semantics is then a *homomorphism. The syntax and semantics of expressions and simple languages invariably have obvious and natural algebraic structures. Any context-free language has the structure of an algebra of *terms over a *signature. *Equations and *initial algebras play a fundamental role in algebraic semantics. A feature of this approach is that it seeks, as far as possible, to study properties of programs subject only to some precisely stated axiomatic assumptions about the range of possible semantic algebras.

algebraic specification A special type of axiomatic specification in which the axioms are *equations or *conditional equations. *See also* module specification.

algebraic structure An alternative expression for an *algebra. Sometimes there is a technical difference: algebras are always sets with constants and functions; algebraic structures are sometimes algebras to which are added relations. A common term for this latter case is *algebraic system* (or *model*).

algebraic surface A surface specified by *patches in an algebraic form rather than a parametric or geometric one.

algebraic symbol manipulation language A programming language in which the data are algebraic expressions in symbolic form, and the operations are the operations of algebra. The operations provided usually include multiplying out brackets, simplification, factorization, polynomial division, and differentiation with respect to one or more variables. Such languages are now rare, their function being subsumed into *algebra systems.

algebraic system *See* algebraic structure.

algebra system An interactive system that performs the operations of algebra (simplification, factorization, multiplying out brackets, etc.) on algebraic expressions typed in by the user. These systems are increasingly used in "mathematical assistants", particularly in the field of general relativity. Popular systems include MACSYMA, MAPLE, MATHEMATICA, and REDUCE. *See also* algebraic symbol manipulation language.

Algol *Acronym for* algorithmic language. The generic name for a family of high-level languages of great significance in the development of computing. In 1958 the Association for Computing Machinery (ACM) in the US and the Gessellschaft für Angewante Mathematik und Mechanik (GAMM) in Europe set up a joint committee to define an *international algorithmic language (IAL)*. The language that was designed became known as Algol, and was later called *Algol 58* to distinguish it from later versions. Algol 58 was not intended to be a viable language, and in 1960 an augmented committee was convened to devise the second iteration, which was published as the language *Algol 60. See also* JOVIAL.

Algol 60 was much more popular in Europe than in the US, probably due to the dominance of IBM and Fortran in the North American market. It introduced many new concepts, notably block structure (*see* block-structured languages), nested scopes, modes of parameter passing to procedures, and the definition of the language introduced the now classic *BNF notation for describing syntax. The influence of Algol 60 can be seen in all succeeding languages, and it stands as a milestone in the development of programming languages.

In the years following the publication of the Algol 60 Report, a working group of the International Federation for Information Processing was set up to consider the definition of a successor to Algol 60. There were many dissensions within the group, and eventually a minority report was issued proposing the language *Algol 68*. The first implementation of Algol 68, named ALGOL 68R, was produced at the Royal Signals and Radar Establishment in the UK. ALGOL 68R demonstrated that Algol 68 was a viable language (not at the time a self-evident proposition).

Although Algol 68 introduced many novel concepts of great theoretical interest and significance, its practical application was almost nil. One of the most notable features of Algol 68 is its formal specification using a *two-level grammar. Although a very precise definition, it is very difficult to understand, and this difficulty partly accounts for the low acceptance of the language. One of the most significant effects of the split in the Algol 68

working group is that it led indirectly to the development of *Pascal.

algorithm A prescribed set of well-defined rules or instructions for the solution of a problem, such as the performance of a calculation, in a finite number of steps. Expressing an algorithm in a formal notation is one of the main parts of a *program; much that is said about programs applies to algorithms, and vice versa. An *effective algorithm* is one that is effectively computable (*see* effective computability). The study of whether effective algorithms exist to compute particular quantities forms the basis of the theory of algorithms.

Save for the simplest of algorithms it is difficult to *prove* that an algorithm is correct (*see* program correctness proof), or even to specify the effect it is intended to achieve. In practice it is usually necessary to be content with *algorithm validation*. This process certifies, or verifies, that an algorithm will perform the calculation required of it. It involves testing the routine against a variety of instances of the problem and ensuring that it performs satisfactorily for these test cases. If the test set is chosen sufficiently well there can then be confidence in the algorithm.

Algorithm analysis is the study of the performance characteristics of a given algorithm. One branch of this study, *average-case analysis*, examines the average behavior of the algorithm. *Worst-case analysis* studies the behavior when all circumstances are as unfavorable as possible. Algorithms can be analyzed in terms of their *complexity and efficiency, where *algorithm efficiency is characterized by its *order.

algorithm analysis *See* algorithm.

algorithm efficiency A measure of the average execution time necessary for an algorithm to complete work on a set of data. Algorithm efficiency is characterized by its *order. Typically a *bubble sort algorithm will have efficiency in sorting N items proportional to and of the order of N^2, usually written $O(N^2)$. This is because an average of $N/2$ comparisons are required $N/2$ times, giving $N^2/4$ total comparisons, hence the order of N^2. In contrast, *quicksort has an efficiency $O(N \log_2 N)$.

If two algorithms for the same problem are of the same order then they are approximately as efficient in terms of computation. Algorithm efficiency is useful for quantifying the implementation difficulties of certain problems.

algorithmic language A language or notation used to express clearly an algorithm. It is usually part of a programming language.

aliasing A distorting effect caused by *sampling an image at too low a rate. When a signal is undersampled, high-frequency components cannot be distinguished from lower-frequency components. Thus the higher frequencies assume the alias (or false identity) of the lower frequencies. Some common computer-graphics artefacts due to aliasing are jagged lines, small objects missing from a scene, and jerky motion. Aliasing effects can be removed or subdued by *anti-aliasing. Fine detail, such as mesh curtains, can be totally lost or distorted without anti-aliasing. Aliasing effects are even more prominent in animated images.

allocation routine A routine that is responsible for the allocation of resources to a *process. *See* resource allocation.

Alpha AXP *Trademark* A 64-bit *RISC *scalable processor family from *Digital Equipment Corporation, designed for applications from PCs to large systems. Alpha is not biased toward any particular operating system and there are implementations of *VAX/VMS, OSF/1 (a form of *UNIX; *see* OSF) and Microsoft *Windows NT. Alpha became available in 1992 and the architecture has a projected 25 year life.

alphabet An ordered *character set. *See also* formal language, Latin alphabet.

alphabetic code A code whose target alphabet contains only letters and/or strings of letters from the Roman alphabet.

alpha buffer A plane in a *frame buffer that contains information concerning the *transparency of each object in a scene, just as a *Z-buffer contains information about depth. It may be implemented as an associated resource rather than be part of the frame buffer itself.

alphamosaic Graphics characters used by *videotex. To produce the overall graphic required, the screen is divided into small areas (say, 40×28), each of which contains a specific character.

alphanumeric character Any letter of the English alphabet, upper or lower case, or any of the decimal digits, 0 to 9.

alphanumeric code A code whose target alphabet contains *alphanumeric characters and/or strings thereof.

alpha test *See* beta test.

ALU *Abbrev. for* arithmetic and logic unit. A portion of the *central processor that generally forms functions of two input variables and produces a single output variable. These functions usually consist of the common *arithmetic operations, the common *logic operations, and *shift operations. Associated with the ALU is a *condition-code register that holds certain properties of the last output variable (*see also* program status word).

Alvey Programme A five-year program of precompetitive collaborative R&D, started in the UK in 1983 as a result of the government-initiated Alvey Report, in response to the Japanese *fifth generation project. The four "enabling technologies" addressed by the Alvey Programme were *VLSI, *software engineering, *knowledge-based systems, and the *human-computer interface. Since 1988 the Alvey Programme has been succeeded by other initiatives but the scope and scale of funding have been progressively diminished.

ambient light The background illumination applied to all objects in a scene. The *lighting model assumes an imaginary light hits each point of every object in the scene with the same color and intensity. Ambient light approximates the overall diffuse interreflections in the scene. Ambient light does not need to be specified if the lighting model takes account of the *diffuse reflection of light between surfaces.

ambiguous grammar A *context-free grammar that derives the same word by different *derivation trees, or equivalently by different *derivation sequences. A familiar programming language example is:

    S → if C then S else S
    S → if C then S

where S and C stand for statement and condition. This grammar is ambiguous since the following compound statement

    if c1 then if c2 then s2 else s1

has two interpretations, corresponding with two derivation trees, as shown in the diagram. *See also* inherently ambiguous language.

Two derivation trees in an ambiguous grammar

amplitude *See* signal.

amplitude modulation (AM) *See* modulation.

amplitude quantization *See* discrete and continuous systems, quantization.

analog computer A computer that performs computations (such as summation, multiplication, integration, and other operations) by manipulating continuous physical variables that are analogs of the quantities being subjected to computation. The most commonly used physical variables are voltage and time. Some analog computers use mechanical components: the physical variables become, for example, angular rotations and linear displacements. *See also* discrete and continuous systems.

analog signal A smoothly varying value of voltage or current, i.e. a signal that varies continuously in amplitude and time. It often represents a measured physical quantity. *See also* A/D converter, D/A converter, discrete and continuous systems.

analog-to-digital converter (ADC) *See* A/D converter.

analysis of variance (ANOVA) A technique, originally developed by R. A. Fisher, whereby the total variation in a vector of numbers $y_1 \ldots y_n$, expressed as the sum of squares about the mean

$$\sum_i (y_i - y)^2,$$

is split up into component sums of squares ascribable to the effects of various classifying factors that may index the data. Thus if the data consist of a two-way $m \times n$ array, classified by factors A and B and indexed by

$$i = 1, \ldots, m \qquad j = 1, \ldots, n$$

then the analysis of variance gives the identity

$$\underset{\text{Total}}{\sum_{ij} (y_{ij} - y_{..})^2} \equiv \underset{\substack{\text{A} \\ \text{main effect}}}{\sum_{ij} (y_{i.} - y_{..})^2} +$$

$$\underset{\substack{\text{B} \\ \text{main effect}}}{\sum_{ij} (y_{.j} - y_{..})^2} + \underset{\substack{\text{A.B} \\ \text{interaction}}}{\sum_{ij} (y_{ij} - y_{i.} - y_{.j} + y_{..})^2}$$

where dots denote averaging over the suffixes involved.

Geometrically the analysis of variance becomes the successive projections of the vector *y*, considered as a point in *n*-dimensional space, onto orthogonal hyperplanes within that space. The dimensions of the hyperplanes give the *degrees of freedom* for each term; in the above example these are

$$mn-1 \equiv (m-1) + (n-1) + (m-1)(n-1)$$

A statistical model applied to the data allows mean squares, equal to (sum of squares)/(degrees of freedom), to be compared with an error mean square that measures the background "noise". Large mean squares indicate large effects of the factors concerned. The above processes can be much elaborated (*see* experimental design, regression analysis).

Analytical Engine The logic design for a mechanical computer conceived by Charles Babbage around 1833, but never built. The design envisioned a memory of a thousand 50-digit numbers. The machine, which could do addition, subtraction, multiplication, and division, was to be controlled by programs punched into loops of cards; the machine was thus to be directed through a variety of computations, and alternative paths could be taken depending on the values of intermediate results. It was to have included a printer to obtain the results. The design was remarkable in anticipating so many elements of modern computers.

analyzer A program, such as a parser, that determines constituents in a string; the word is rarely used except in the combinations syntax analyzer and lexical analyzer. *See also* static analysis.

ancestor of a node in a *tree. Any node on the unique path from the root of the tree to the node in question. A *proper ancestor* of a node, A, is a node, B, such that B is an ancestor of A and $A \neq B$. *See also* parent.

AND gate An electronic *logic gate whose output is logic 1 (true) only when all (two or more) inputs are logic 1, otherwise it is logic 0 (false). It therefore implements the logical *AND operation on its inputs and has the same *truth table. The diagram shows the usual circuit symbol and the truth table of a two-input gate.

inputs	A1	0	0	1	1
	A2	0	1	0	1
output	B	0	0	0	1

Two-input AND gate, circuit symbol and truth table

P	F	F	T	T
Q	F	T	F	T
$P \wedge Q$	F	F	F	T

Truth table for AND operation

AND operation The logical *connective combining two statements, truth values, or formulas P and Q in such a way that the outcome is true only if both P and Q are true; otherwise the outcome is false (*see* table). The AND operation is usually denoted by $\wedge$, and occasionally by . or by juxtaposition, as in PQ. It is one of the dyadic operations of *Boolean algebra and is both *commutative and *associative.

When implemented as a basic machine operation on computers, the AND operation is usually generalized to operate on complete words. Then the operation described above is applied to the corresponding bits in each word. In this context AND is often used for *masking purposes, i.e. to select parts of words, such as the address field.

AND/OR graph A form of *graph or *tree used in problem solving and problem decomposition. The nodes of the graph represent states or goals and their successors are labeled as either AND or OR branches. The AND successors are subgoals that must all be achieved to satisfy the parent goal, while OR branches indicate alternative subgoals, any one of which could satisfy the parent goal.

animation *See* computer animation.

ANN *Acronym for* artificial neural network.

annotation Explanation added to a program to assist the reader. This may take the form of manuscript additions to the program listing, but more often takes the form of *comments included in the program text.

anonymous FTP A mechanism that allows a user to take copies of files from a network *file server, without having a named account on the server. The user "anonymous" is allowed to log into the server, and has limited privileges allowing him or her to initiate an outgoing file transfer. *See also* file transfer protocol.

ANOVA *Acronym for* analysis of variance.

ANSI American National Standards Institute, an organization, founded in 1918, that establishes US industrial standards. It accredits organizations to write these standards following the rules established by ANSI. It is the US representative to *ISO (International Organization for Standardization). ANSI determines hardware-related and software standards.

anti-aliasing Taking specific action to remove or subdue *aliasing effects. *Supersampling or smoothing the image by *filtering are techniques often used to reduce aliasing.

antisymmetric relation A *relation R defined on a set S and having the property that

whenever $x \, R \, y$ and $y \, R \, x$

then $x = y$

where x and y are arbitrary members of S. Examples include "is a subset of" defined on sets, and "less than or equal to" defined on the integers. *See also* asymmetric relation, symmetric relation.

any-time algorithms A class of algorithms intended for use in *real-time systems, in which, after a specified minimum period, a result is always available. The accuracy of the result increases with the time the algorithm has been running.

APA mode *Abbrev. for* all points addressable mode, usually applied to printers that can display graphical data. A mode of operation in which the printout is not constrained to rows of characters.

API *Abbrev. for* application programming interface. An interface that is defined in terms of a set of functions and procedures, and enables a program to gain access to facilities within an application. A typical example would be a *CASE tool that provides an API to enable users to develop special programs to utilize the information within the CASE tool's internal database. The use of such facilities enables users to customize the application for their own purposes and to integrate the application into a customized development environment.

APL *Acronym for* a programming language. Originally devised by Iverson as a mathematical notation in the mid-1960s, and only later implemented as a programming language, APL had a meteoric rise in popularity. The main feature of APL is that it provides a rich set of powerful operators for handling multi-dimensional arrays, together with the capability for users to define their own operators. The built-in operators are mainly represented by single characters using a special character set. Thus APL programs are very concise and often impenetrable.

APP *Abbrev. for* application portability profile.

Apple Computer Inc. A US-based producer of Macintosh ("Mac") personal computers and peripherals. It pioneered the *desktop and *windows metaphors for the user interface and was an early market leader in the field. The first commercial *spreadsheet, VisiCalc, was developed for its machines. As well as running Apple's own software, the

computers can also run Microsoft *Windows and the PC applications it supports. Apple is number 10 in terms of revenue in the list of the world's top IT suppliers (1993 figures).

application A particular role or task to which a computer system can be applied, or, more usually, the software used for such a purpose. *See* application package, applications program.

application binary interface *See* ABI.

application generator A program – a *software tool – that is capable of creating a range of application programs in a particular domain. The generated program will be configured by information provided by the person using the application generator. Domains in which application generators are frequently encountered include simulation, process control, and user interface software. *See also* fourth-generation language.

application layer of network protocol function. *See* seven-layer reference model.

application package (software package) A collection of programs or modules that is directed at some generic application and can be tailored (perhaps with some additions) to the needs of a specific instance of that application.

application portability profile (APP) A statement of the characteristics of a computer program that defines the facilities (of the *programming language, *operating system, *APIs, etc.) which it utilizes. This profile then defines the minimum set of facilities that must be available on any computer system to enable that program to be executed.

application programming interface *See* API.

applications program (or application program) Any program that is specific to the particular role that a given computer performs within a given organization and makes a direct contribution to performing that role. For example, where a computer handles a company's finances a payroll program would be an applications program. By contrast, an *operating system or a *software tool may both be essential to the effective use of the computer system, but neither makes a direct contribution to meeting the end-user's eventual needs.

applications programmer A person who specializes in writing *applications programs. *Compare* systems programmer.

applications software Collective term for *applications programs.

application terminal A combination of input and output devices configured into a unit to meet the requirements of a particular type of business activity and environment. They usually have some built-in processing capability and are connected to a controlling processor via a data communication link. Examples include *point-of-sale (POS) terminals and automated teller terminals (*ATMs).

applicative language *Another name for* functional language.

approximation theory A subject that is concerned with the approximation of a class of objects, say F, by a subclass, say $P \subset F$, that is in some sense simpler. For example, let

$$F = C\,[a,b],$$

the real continuous functions on $[a,b]$, then a subclass of practical use is P_n, i.e. polynomials of degree n. The means of measuring the closeness or accuracy of the approximation is provided by a metric or *norm*. This is a nonnegative function that is defined on F and measures the size of its elements. Norms of particular value in the approximation of mathematical functions (for computer subroutines, say) are the *Chebyshev norm* and the *2-norm* (or *Euclidean norm*). For functions

$$f \in C\,[a,b]$$

these norms are given respectively as

$$\|f\| = \max_{a \leqslant x \leqslant b} |f(x)|$$

$$\|f\|_2 = (\int_a^b f(x)^2 \, \mathrm{d}x)^{1/2}$$

For approximation of data these norms take the discrete form

$$\|f\| = \max_i |f(x_i)|$$

$$\|f\|_2 = (\sum_i f(x_i)^2)^{1/2}$$

The 2-norm frequently incorporates a weight function (or weights). From these two norms the problems of *Chebyshev approximation* and *least squares approximation* arise. For example, with polynomial approximation we seek

$$p_n \in P_n$$

for which

$$\|f - p_n\| \text{ or } \|f - p_n\|_2$$

are acceptably small. Best approximation problems arise when, for example, we seek

$$p_n \in P_n$$

for which these measures of errors are as small as possible with respect to P_n.

Other examples of norms that are particularly important are *vector* and *matrix norms*. For n-component vectors

$$x = (x_1, x_2, \ldots, x_n)^{\mathrm{T}}$$

important examples are

$$\|x\| = \max_i |x_i|$$

$$\|x\|_2 = (\sum_{i=1}^n x_i^2)^{1/2}$$

Corresponding to a given vector norm, a subordinate matrix norm can be defined for $n \times n$ matrices A, by

$$\|A\| = \max_{\|x\| \neq 0} \frac{\|Ax\|}{\|x\|}$$

For the vector norm

$$\|x\| = \max_i |x_i|$$

this reduces to the expression

$$\|A\| = \max_i \sum_{j=1}^n |a_{ij}|$$

where a_{ij} is the i,jth element of A. Vector and matrix norms are indispensible in most areas of numerical analysis.

apps *Short for* applications.

APSE *Acronym for* Ada programming support environment. The *PSE that was intended to be used for software development using *Ada.

arc of a graph. *See* graph.

architectural design (high-level design) *See* program decomposition, program design, system design.

architecture The specification of a (digital) computer system at a somewhat general level, including description from the programming (user) viewpoint of the instruction set and user interface, memory organization and addressing, I/O operation and control, etc. The *implementation of an architecture in members of a given *computer family may be quite different, yet all the members should be capable of running the same program. Implementation differences may occur in actual hardware components or in subsystem implementation (e.g. *microprogramming as opposed to wired control), generally in both. Different implementations may have substantially different performances and costs. An implementation feature – such as a cache memory – that is *transparent to the user does not affect the architecture. Common architecture provides *compatibility from the user's viewpoint.

In the context of engineering and hardware design, the term architecture is used to describe the nature, configuration, and interconnection of the major logic organs of a computer (and is thus closer to the general meaning of the word). These devices would normally include the memory and its components, the control unit and the hardware components designed to implement the control strategy, the structure, range, and capability of the ALU, and the interconnection of the input/output – such as whether star or bus connected – and the nature and capabilities of any channel controllers. A detailed block diagram or schematic of the actual (as distinct from the virtual) machine would normally form part of, or even be central to, such a description.

archive A repository for information that the user wishes to retain, but without requiring immediate access. (The word is also used as a verb: to transfer into the archive system.) There are three quite different activities that must be distinguished:

(a) the routine taking of *backup copies, initiated by the system manager, to protect users and system managers against *corruption of stored information;

(b) the autonomous transferring of information from a higher-performance to a lower-performance storage system, initiated by the *operating system, to achieve economies in the total cost to the system manager of information storage;

(c) the voluntary transferring of a file between normal file storage and archive stor-age, initiated by the user, to achieve economies in the total costs to the user of information storage.

Most systems retain information that the user can alter on magnetic disk. (Information that the user cannot alter may either be held on a nonwriteable form of storage such as a *CD-ROM, or on a writeable form but with some form of hardware or system write-inhibit control.) Magnetic disks offer high performance, but the user may be prepared to use a slower medium such as magnetic tape, which has lower unit costs for storage. Users may do this on their own behalf by attaching a magnetic-tape subsystem to their workstation, and overseeing the transfer of files to the magnetic tape and their subsequent recovery when the information is required again. Alternatively, in a large multiuser multiserver environment, there may be a *server set aside specifically for the purpose of allowing users to transfer their information onto shared magnetic-tape devices. This server will also cooperate with the system's file-access software in maintaining the modified directory entries that allow the overall system to keep track of the information held on the magnetic tapes, and to oversee its recovery on behalf of the user. *See also* memory hierarchy.

Arden's rule A *formal language can be specified by means of equations, based on operations on languages. Arden's rule states that $A^* B$ is the smallest language that is a solution for X in the linear equation

$$X = AX \cup B$$

where X, A, B are sets of strings. (For notation, *see* union, concatenation, Kleene star.) $A^* B$ is furthermore the only solution, unless A contains the empty string, in which case $A^* B'$ is a solution for any subset B' of B.

Although simple, Arden's rule is significant as one of the earliest fixed-point results on equation solving in computer science. In conjunction with the normal process of eliminating variables, it can be used to solve any set of simultaneous linear equations over sets of strings. *See also* Kleene's theorem (on regular expressions).

area coherence The constancy of a property

over an area. Computer-graphics algorithms often take advantage of area coherence, *image compression being an example.

area filling Painting a defined area with a specific color or pattern. If the area is defined by a set of boundary *pixels, there are specific algorithms for area filling starting from a seed pixel inside the boundary.

argument A value or address passed to a procedure or function at the time of call. Thus in the Basic statement

$$Y = SQR(X)$$

X is the argument of the SQR (square root) function. Arguments are sometimes referred to as *actual parameters*.

arithmetic and logic unit *See* ALU.

arithmetic instruction An instruction specifying that one of the *arithmetic operations is to be carried out by the computer.

arithmetic/logic unit *See* ALU.

arithmetic operation An operation that forms a function of two variables. This function is usually one of the class of operations: add, subtract, multiply, and divide. These operations may be carried out as operations on integers, fractional numbers, or floating-point numbers. The operation is normally performed in the *ALU. *See also* floating-point notation.

arithmetic operator A type of *operator appearing in an expression denoting one of the operations of arithmetic, e.g. +, −, * (multiplication), / (divide).

arithmetic shift *See* shift.

arithmetic unit (AU) *Short for* arithmetic and logic unit. *See* ALU.

arity of an operator. The number of operands to which the *operator applies. *See also* operation.

arm To bring a device to a state of readiness.

ARMA *Abbrev. for* autoregressive moving average. *See* time series.

ARPA Advanced Research Projects Agency (known for a time as *DARPA). An agency of the US Department of Defense responsible for research and technical development in areas where no single service (Army, Navy, Air Force, Marine Corps) has a clear jurisdiction or interest. It is perhaps most famous for the network technology development that led to the *ARPANET.

ARPANET *Acronym for* Advanced Research Project Agency Network. The ARPANET was initiated as a four-node network in Dec. 1969, and has evolved via DARPANET into the present *Internet.

The impetus for the ARPANET came from a small group of workers in universities and private research laboratories in the USA, who were funded by the US Department of Defense Advanced Research Project Agency to create a data network that was capable of continuing to function even when parts of the network were destroyed. The solution proposed relied on the use of *packet switching, which was implemented by small dedicated computers called interface message processors (IMPs), and used a distributed routing algorithm to manage the movement of self-contained *packets of data between their source and destination.

ARPANET pioneered many of the network concepts now in current use, including the use of layered *protocols. Each protocol governs the transfer of information for a range of associated applications, and delegates the control of the traffic flow to cooperating processes located either at the end-user applications, or, for the lower layers of the protocol, to processes located in the switching nodes.

array 1. An ordered collection of a number of elements of the same type, the number being fixed unless the array is *flexible. The elements of one array may be of type integer, those of another array may be of type real, while the elements of a third array may be of type character string (if the programming language recognizes compound types).

Each element has a unique list of *index values that determine its position in the ordered collection. Each index is of a discrete type. The number of dimensions in the ordering is fixed.

A one-dimensional array, or *vector, consists of a list of elements distinguished by a single index. If v is a one-dimensional array and i is an index value, then v_i refers to the ith element of v. If the index ranges from L through U then the value L is called the *lower bound* of v and U is the *upper bound*. Usually in mathematics and often in mathematical computing the index type is taken as integer and the lower bound is taken as one.

$$\begin{bmatrix} a_{11} & a_{12} & \cdots & a_{1n} \\ a_{21} & a_{22} & \cdots & a_{2n} \\ \vdots & \vdots & & \vdots \\ a_{m1} & a_{m2} & \cdots & a_{mn} \end{bmatrix}$$

Two-dimensional array

In a two-dimensional array, or *matrix, the elements are ordered in the form of a table comprising a fixed number of rows and a fixed number of columns. Each element in such an array is distinguished by a pair of indexes. The first index gives the row and the second gives the column of the array in which the element is located. The element in the ith row and jth column is called the i,jth element of the array. If i ranges from L1 through U1 and j ranges from L2 through U2 then L1 is the *first lower bound* of the array, U1 is the *first upper bound*, L2 is the *second lower bound* and U2 is the *second upper bound*. Again it is common practice to take the indexes as integers and to set both L1 and L2 equal to one. An example of such a two-dimensional array with U1 = m, U2 = n is given in the diagram.

In *three-dimensional arrays* the position of each element is distinguished by three indexes. Arrays of higher dimension are similarly defined.

2. *Short for* disk array. *See also* RAID.

array management software *See* disk array.

array processor A computer/processor that has an architecture especially designed for processing *arrays (e.g. matrices) of numbers. The architecture includes a number of processors (say 64 by 64) working simultaneously, each handling one element of the array, so that a single operation can apply to all elements of the array in parallel. To obtain the

same effect in a conventional processor, the operation must be applied to each element of the array sequentially, and so consequently much more slowly.

An array processor may be built as a self-contained unit attached to a main computer via an I/O port or internal bus; alternatively, it may be a *distributed array processor* where the processing elements are distributed throughout, and closely linked to, a section of the computer's memory.

Array processors are very powerful tools for handling problems with a high degree of parallelism. They do however demand a modified approach to programming. The conversion of conventional (sequential) programs to serve array processors is not a trivial task, and it is sometimes necessary to select different (parallel) algorithms to suit the parallel approach.

See also vector processing.

arrow keys (direction keys) Four keys on a computer keyboard with arrows engraved on the keycaps pointing up, down, left, and right. They can be separate keys, usually found to the right of the typewriter keys, or combined with other keys. A 102-key PC keyboard has separate arrow keys as well as arrow keys on the numeric keypad. A laptop keyboard will often have the arrow keys combined with the typewriter keys and activated by a special shift key. The action performed by arrow keys is under program control, but usually involves moving the cursor or some part of the display in the indicated direction.

articulation point *Another name for* cut vertex.

artificial intelligence (AI) A discipline concerned with the building of computer programs that perform tasks requiring intelligence when done by humans. However, intelligent tasks for which a *decision procedure is known (e.g. inverting matrices) are generally excluded, whereas perceptual tasks that might seem not to involve intelligence (e.g. seeing) are generally included. For this reason, AI is better defined by indicating its range. Examples of tasks tackled within AI are: game playing, inference, learning, *natural-language understanding, plan formation, *speech understanding, *theorem proving, and *computer vision.

Perceptual tasks (e.g. seeing and hearing) have been found to involve a lot more computation than is apparent from introspection. This computation is unconscious in humans, which has made it hard to simulate. AI has had relatively more success at intellectual tasks (e.g. game playing and theorem proving) than perceptual tasks. Sometimes these computer programs are intended to simulate human behavior (*see* cognitive modeling). Sometimes they are built for technological application (*see* expert systems, robotics). But in many cases the goal is just to find any technique for doing some task, or to find a technique that does the task better than hitherto.

Computational techniques that have been invented in AI include *augmented transition networks, *means/ends analysis, *rule-based systems, *resolution, *semantic networks, and *heuristic search.

artificial life A research field in *artificial intelligence that aims to understand the principles underlying the behavior of natural living systems. Experiments with software simulations are used to synthesize self-organizing self-replicating dynamic models of phenomena from the living world.

artificial neural network (ANN) *Formal name for* neural network.

ASCC *Abbrev. for* Automatic Sequence Controlled Calculator. *See* Harvard Mark I.

ASCII (or Ascii) *Acronym for* American standard code for information interchange. A standard character encoding scheme introduced in 1963 and used widely on many machines. It is a 7-bit code with no parity recommendation, providing 128 different bit patterns. The character set is shown in the table, together with the control characters (*see also* ISO-7).

International 8-bit codes that are extensions of ASCII have been published by ISO in the series of ISO 8859. In addition to several *Latin alphabets covering English and various other European languages, there are also Cyrillic, Arabic, Greek, and Hebrew code tables.

See also character set.

ASF *Abbrev. for* aspect source flag.

ASIC *Acronym for* applications specific integrated circuit. An integrated circuit designed to carry out one or more specific functions and implemented on a single semiconductor chip in order to reduce the size of a system, reduce the number of interconnections that are required at printed circuit board level, and to reduce the number of components that, at a lower level of integration, might otherwise be used to implement the function. ASICs are economic where production runs in the high hundreds are required and have become viable due to advances in VLSI design, layout, and fabrication technology. *See also* semicustom.

ASM *Abbrev. for* algorithmic state machine. A technique, based upon annotated charts, used in the design of computer hardware.

aspect The characteristic that changes the appearance of a graphical output primitive. Typical aspects are color, line width, and line style. Aspects define the property but not how it is bound to an output primitive. *See also* attribute.

aspect ratio The ratio of width to height for a specified rectangular area such as a display surface or window.

aspect source flag (ASF) A flag associated with a graphical output primitive to define whether an *aspect associated with the primitive (color, etc.) is defined by a value specified globally or for a specific device.

assembler 1. A program that takes as input a program written in *assembly language and translates it into *machine code or *relocatable code.

2. *Colloquial* An assembly language.

assembly language A notation for the convenient representation of machine-code programs in human-readable terms. An assembly language allows the programmer to use alphabetic operation codes with mnemonic significance, to use personally chosen symbolic names for memory registers, and to specify *addressing schemes (e.g. indexing, indirection) in a convenient way. It also allows the use of various number bases (e.g. decimal, hexadecimal) for numerical con-

b7 b6 b5 →				0 0 0	0 0 1	0 1 0	0 1 1	1 0 0	1 0 1	1 1 0	1 1 1
b4	b3	b2	b1	column→ / row↓ 0	1	2	3	4	5	6	7
0	0	0	0	0	NUL	DLE	space	0	@	P	`	p
0	0	0	1	1	SOH	DC1	!	1	A	Q	a	q
0	0	1	0	2	STX	DC2	"	2	B	R	b	r
0	0	1	1	3	ETX	DC3	#	3	C	S	c	s
0	1	0	0	4	EOT	DC4	$	4	D	T	d	t
0	1	0	1	5	ENQ	NAK	%	5	E	U	e	u
0	1	1	0	6	ACK	SYN	&	6	F	V	f	v
0	1	1	1	7	BEL	ETB	'	7	G	W	g	w
1	0	0	0	8	BS	CAN	(	8	H	X	h	x
1	0	0	1	9	HT	EM	)	9	I	Y	i	y
1	0	1	0	A	LF	SUB	*	:	J	Z	j	z
1	0	1	1	B	VT	ESC	+	;	K	[	k	{
1	1	0	0	C	FF	FS	,	<	L	\	l	|
1	1	0	1	D	CR	GS	-	=	M	]	m	}
1	1	1	0	E	SO	RS	.	>	N	^	n	~
1	1	1	1	F	SI	US	/	?	O	_	o	DEL

ASCII code chart with binary and hex equivalents

NUL	null character	DLE	data link escape
SOH	start of header	DC1	device control 1
STX	start of text	DC2	device control 2
ETX	end of text	DC3	device control 3
EOT	end of transmission	DC4	device control 4
ENQ	enquiry	NAK	negative acknowledge
ACK	acknowledge	SYN	synchronous idle
BEL	bell	ETB	end of transmission block
BS	backspace	CAN	cancel
HT	horiz. tabulation	EM	end of medium
LF	line feed	SUB	substitute
VT	vert. tabulation	ESC	escape
FF	form feed	FS	file separator
CR	carriage return	GS	group separator
SO	shift out	RS	record separator
SI	shift in	US	unit separator
		DEL	delete

ASCII control characters

ASCII character set

stants, and allows the user to attach *labels to lines of the program so that these lines can be referenced in a symbolic manner from other parts of a program (usually as the destination of a control transfer or jump).

assertion A Boolean formula whose value is claimed to be true. The following are all examples:

$$4 + 5 = 9$$
$$4 \text{ is even and 5 is odd}$$
$$x \text{ is even or } y \text{ is odd}$$
$$x - y > 15$$
$$\text{for all relevant } i, x[i] < x[i+1]$$

The last assertion states that the array x is sorted into ascending order, with no repeated values.

Assertions are employed extensively in proofs of *program correctness, where they are used to characterize program states.

assertion checker An automated system for checking whether *assertions attached to the text of some program are consistent with the *semantics of that program as given by some formal semantic definition of the programming language. *See also* mechanical verifier.

assignment-free language A programming language that does not include the concept of assigning values to variables. Common examples are *functional languages.

assignment statement A fundamental statement of all programming languages (except *declarative languages) that assigns a new value to a variable. The typical form in Algol-like languages is

$$\text{variable} := \text{expression}$$

where := is read as "becomes"; the symbol suggests a left-pointing arrow to signify the conveyance of a value to the variable on the left. Other languages (particularly Basic, C, and Fortran) use = as the assignment operator, e.g.

$$a = b + c$$

This leads to problems in expressing the concept of equality. Basic, being an unsophisticated language, is able to use = for both purposes; C uses == for equality and Fortran uses .EQ.

associative addressing A method of addressing a location by virtue of its data content rather than by its physical location.

An access specifies something about the contents of the desired location rather than a normal address. An *associative memory (or content-addressable memory) provides a search mechanism to match on the whole or on partial memory contents for a word that satisfies the match. In some applications it may be permissible for more than one word to be found. The desired data will be in close association or proximity, possibly as an additional field of the retrieved word. An *associative processor exploits the parallel-access facility of associative memory to achieve a form of parallel processing.

associative law *See* associative operation.

associative memory (content-addressable memory, CAM) A memory that is capable of determining whether a given datum – the *search word* – is contained in one of its addresses or locations. This may be accomplished by a number of mechanisms. In some cases parallel combinational logic is applied at each word in the memory and a test is made simultaneously for coincidence with the search word. In other cases the search word and all of the words in the memory are shifted serially in synchronism; a single bit of the search word is then compared to the same bit of all of the memory words using as many single-bit coincidence circuits as there are words in the memory. Amplifications of the associative memory technique allow for *masking the search word or requiring only a "close" match as opposed to an exact match. Small parallel associative memories are used in *cache memory and *virtual memory mapping applications.

Since parallel operations on many words are expensive (in hardware), a variety of stratagems are used to approximate associative memory operation without actually carrying out the full test described here. One of these uses *hashing to generate a "best guess" for a conventional address followed by a test of the contents of that address.

Some associative memories have been built to be accessed conventionally (by words in parallel) and as serial comparison associative memories; these have been called *orthogonal memories. See also* associative addressing, associative processor.

associative network *Another name for* semantic network.

associative operation Any *dyadic operation ∘ that satisfies the law

$$x \circ (y \circ z) = (x \circ y) \circ z$$

for all x, y, and z in the domain of ∘. The law is known as the *associative law*. An expression involving several adjacent instances of an associative operation can be interpreted unambiguously; the order in which the operations are performed is irrelevant since the effects of different evaluations are identical, though the work involved may differ. Consequently parentheses are unnecessary, even in more complex expressions.

The arithmetic operations of addition and multiplication are associative, though subtraction is not. On a computer the associative law of addition of real numbers fails to hold because of the inherent inaccuracy in the way real numbers are usually represented (*see* floating-point notation), and the addition of integers fails to hold because of the possibility of *overflow.

associative processor (content-addressable parallel processor) A processor having parallel processing capabilities by virtue of the parallel memory manipulation properties of *associative memory. The ability to interrogate and write to selected bits in each word of associative memory in parallel makes possible word-parallel bit-serial operations, which are efficient for the manipulation of large data sets.

assurance A measure of the confidence that (a) a system complies with its *security policy or (b) a feature of a system complies with its security requirement. Assurance may be increased by the use of rigorous design techniques and/or by *security evaluation.

A-stability *See* stability.

astable An electronic circuit that has no stable output state and whose output therefore oscillates between two voltage levels. As a result it functions as a square-wave oscillator or a pulse generator. *See also* multivibrator.

asymmetric relation A *relation R defined on a set S and having the property that

whenever $x \, R \, y$

then it is never the case that

$$y \, R \, x$$

where x and y are arbitrary elements of S. The usual "is less than" ordering defined on the integers is an asymmetric relation. *See also* antisymmetric relation, symmetric relation.

asymptotic Denoting a (usually simpler) value that in the limit gets closer and closer, indeed arbitrarily close, to a given value; for example,

$$n * n + 4$$

is asymptotic to $n * n$ as n tends to infinity.

asymptotic analysis The analysis of a situation under limiting conditions, frequently involving *asymptotic expansions.

asymptotic expansion A series

$$A_0 + A_1/z + A_2/z^2 + \ldots + A_n/z^n + \ldots,$$

that may either converge for large values of $|z|$ or diverge for all values of z, is called an asymptotic expansion of the function $F(z)$, valid in a given range of values of arg z, if, for every fixed value of n, the expression

$$z^n \left(F(z) - A_0 - A_1/z - A_2/z^2 - \ldots - A_n/z^n \right)$$

tends to zero as $|z| \rightarrow \infty$, while arg z remains in the given range.

asynchronous Involving or requiring a form of computer control timing protocol in which a specific operation is begun upon receipt of an indication (signal) that the preceding operation has been completed, and which indicates to a subsequent operation when it may begin. The rate at which operations proceed is determined by the time required by individual operations. *See also* interrupt, glitch. *Compare* synchronous.

asynchronous bus A bus that interconnects devices of a computer system where information transfers between devices are self-timed rather than controlled by a synchronizing clock signal. A connected device indicates its readiness for a transfer by activating a request signal. A responding device indicates the completion of this transfer by activating an acknowledge signal. The time required to complete the transaction is determined by the response times of the devices and the delays along the interconnecting bus and may vary for different devices.

asynchronous circuit An electronic logic circuit in which logic operations are not performed under the control of a clock signal with the result that logic transitions do not occur (nominally) simultaneously. In asynchronous circuits transitions may follow one another with minimum delay, but at some cost in circuit complexity and risk of incorrect operation.

asynchronous interface A set of signals that comprises the connection between devices of a computer system where the transfer of information between devices is organized by the exchange of signals not synchronized to some controlling clock. A request signal from an initiating device indicates the requirement to make a transfer; an acknowledging signal from the responding device indicates the transfer completion. This asynchronous interchange is also widely known as *handshaking.

asynchronous TDM See time division multiplexing.

asynchronous transfer mode See ATM.

asynchronous transmission A method of data transmission in which data is transmitted in small fixed-size groups, typically corresponding to a character and containing between five and eight bits, and in which the timing of bits within the group is not directly determined by some form of clock. The standard practice is to precede each group of data by a *start bit*, whose duration indicates the expected duration of each subsequent bit within the group, and to follow the group by a *stop bit* whose duration is at least one and a half times that of the start bit. The presence of the start and stop bits necessarily reduces the rate of sending genuine data bits. Asynchronous transmission is normally used only for relatively slow data rates, up to say 2400 bps. See also synchronous transmission.

Atanasoff–Berry computer (ABC) The first known attempt at an electronic digital computer, designed in 1936–38 by John Atanasoff, a mathematics professor at Iowa State College, primarily for the solution of linear algebraic equations. It was built by Atanasoff and his assistant Clifford Berry, using vacuum tubes (valves) as the logic elements, but was never fully operational and was abandoned in 1942.

AT&T American Telephone and Telegraph Company. In 1991, AT&T merged with NCR to produce a company that is now number seven in terms of revenue in the list of the world's top IT suppliers (1993 figures). Its major revenues come from data communications, peripherals, maintenance, and services, but it is an important supplier of computers of all sizes, with a particular emphasis on *UNIX-based machines, and of software. Following a merger with Teradata Corp., the company now has products in the area of massively parallel database machines.

ATL *Abbrev. for* automated tape library.

Atlas The first computer to incorporate many features now considered standard, including: a virtual (logical) address space larger than the actual (physical) address space; a *one-level memory using core backed by drum; an architecture based on the assumption of a software operating system, with hardware features to assist the software (e.g. extracodes). The design commenced in 1956 under Tom Kilburn at the University of Manchester, UK, and the project was supported from 1958 by Ferranti Ltd. The prototype was operating in 1961 and production models appeared in 1963. See also virtual machine.

ATM 1. *Abbrev. for* asynchronous transfer mode. A form of *switching system designed to minimize the magnitude of switching times. In most switching systems an entire *packet must be received and checked for accuracy before the software within the switch will initiate the onward transmission of the packet to the next switch or to the final destination. By using a simple fixed structure for the data, ATM can reduce the time needed to recognize and process packets as they move through a switch.

In common with other systems, data to be transmitted in ATM is subdivided into a number of small units that are transmitted in sequence and reassembled at the receiving end. ATM uses a very small fixed-length *cell, with each cell having an identical format. The format of the cell guarantees that the addressing information for each cell is always found in a fixed position and format. This allows the actual switching operation for each cell to be implemented in table-driven firmware, which in turn allows a very short switching time for each cell so that very large numbers of cells can be switched each second.

An ATM cell is made up of a *header*, holding 5 bytes, and a *body*, holding 48 bytes. The header holds all the addressing, routing, and control information and is transmitted as the first part of the cell, followed immediately by the body, which contains the user's data. The accuracy of the header is checked by a single parity bit forming part of the header. As soon as the header is received and verified as having the correct parity, the software in the switch will immediately initiate the onward transmission of the complete cell, attaching it to a queue of outgoing cells on the appropriate connection. The overall effect is that the onward transmission of the cell may well overlap the receipt of the body of the cell, being started shortly after the receipt of 5 bytes (i.e. the end of the header) rather than after 53 bytes (i.e. the receipt of the entire cell). The switching algorithms used are also very simple, relying on the creation of a *virtual circuit before the actual transmission of user data, with the identity of the virtual circuit embedded in the header and serving to define the switching action by what is in effect a table lookup. This simple algorithm can be implemented largely as *firmware.

The intention is that ATM can be used as a low-level *bearer, capable of carrying a variety of different packet formats. However, unlike some other low-level bearers, ATM does not define the actual bit-rate at which signals are carried, hence the description "asynchronous". ATM products operating at a wide range of bit rates – from 34 Mbps up to 2.48 Gbps – are already proposed.

2. *Abbrev. for* automated teller machine. A computer-controlled device that dispenses cash, and may provide other services, to customers who identify themselves with a *pin.

atom A value that cannot be decomposed further. In *LISP an atom is a representation of an arbitrary string of characters or the special atom NIL, i.e. nothing. The word is also used as a predicate in LISP-like languages to determine whether an arbitrary value is or is not an atom:

(atom (cons(h, t)))

always yields FALSE but

(atom, NIL)

and

(atom, "word")

evaluate to TRUE.

atomic action An indivisible sequence of primitive operations that must complete without interruption (or that can be expected to do so), or can be considered as instantaneous.

atomic formula *See* propositional calculus.

atomicity A term used in connection with the extent to which a resource can be subdivided. For some resources the amount allocated to a process can be completely arbitrary; an example is processor time (outside *critical sections). For other resources allocations must be in terms of a smallest allowable amount; an example might be memory, which may only be allocated in multiples of, say, 1024 bytes.

attach To make a device available for use by a system. On simple systems this may be achieved by simply engaging the appropriate plug and socket of the interface and putting the device into a state of readiness. In more complex systems it is often necessary to make the operating system aware of the type of device and the address of the connector to which it is attached. It is also necessary to ensure that the operating system has available the appropriate utility program for that device. In some designs the operating system can itself determine the type and address of all the peripherals that are electrically connected. *See also* install.

attenuation The reduction in amplitude of a *signal when it passes through a medium that dissipates its energy. It is usually measured in decibels (attenuation then being negative while *gain* is positive).

attribute A defined property of an entity, object, etc. In computer graphics it is a particular property that applies to a graphical output primitive; lines have attributes such as line width, color, and line style. *See also* ERA model, inheritance.

attribute grammar A *context-free grammar that has been augmented with attribute evaluation rules or conditions enabling non-context-free aspects of a language to be specified. Associated with each symbol of the grammar is a finite set of attributes or conditions. Rules for evaluating the attributes are associated with the productions of the grammar. Using these rules the attributes of each node in a *parse tree may be evaluated. The attributes may either be *inherited*, meaning that their values are a function of the attribute of their parent node in the parse tree, or *synthesized*, meaning that their values are a function of the attributes of their children in the parse tree.

The concept of an attribute grammar was introduced by D. E. Knuth who suggested that the semantics of a program could be specified by the attributes of the root node in its parse tree.

audio card *Another name for* sound card.

audio response unit An output device that can give a spoken response. The message may be prerecorded phrases, a collation of prerecorded words, or synthesized from digital data. The range of applications includes prompts to operators of application terminals and acknowledgment of input via a telephone keypad.

audit trail 1. A record showing the occurrence of specified events relevant to the security of a computer system. For example, an entry might be made in the audit trail whenever a user logs in or accesses a file. Examination of the audit trail may detect attempts at violating the security of the system and help to identify the violator.
2. The external file that contains the sequential flow of information between the application and a graphics system.

augmented addressing (augmenting) A method of expanding a short specified address by concatenating the specified address (as low-order address bits) with the contents of the *augmented address register* (as high-order bits) to produce an *absolute address. *See also* addressing schemes.

augmented reality *See* virtual reality.

augmented transition network A generalization of *finite-state automata that is used to represent natural-language grammars and hence to parse and generate natural-language text (*see* parsing, natural-language understanding). The grammar is represented as a set of labeled directed *graphs whose labels are word categories, or recursive calls to itself or other graphs, or calls to update or access a set of registers. Procedures can be associated with the arcs to build a *parse tree or a semantic representation, or to generate text, etc.

AUI *Abbrev. for* attachment unit interface. An interface connecting an *Ethernet transceiver to the controller.

AUP *Abbrev. for* acceptable use policy.

authentication A process by which subjects, normally users, establish their identity to a system. This may be effected by the use of a *password or possession of a physical device, e.g. a coded token. In *reverse authentication*, the object is required to authenticate to the subject, e.g. to establish confidence in a user before sensitive information is entered into a system.

authentication code An appendage to a message that indicates to the recipient whether the message has been tampered with during transit. Authentication codes can be derived cryptographically as a function of the message and a secret key held by the sender and recipient. *See also* cryptography.

authoring language A *high-level language used for creating CAL (*computer-assisted learning) and other educational and training software packages.

autobaud *Colloquial expression for* automatic baud rate detection. A feature of some communication systems that automatically detect and adapt to the transmission speed of incoming data.

autochanger *Short for* automatic disk changer. A device in which a single read head is linked to a *caddy containing several *CD-ROMs. The head is moved to select the required disk.

autocode The generic name given to the precursors of modern high-level programming languages. The term is now obsolete.

autodump *See* autoload.

autoload 1. A facility provided on some tape transports whereby a tape reel is automatically located and clamped on the hub and the tape is then automatically threaded.
2. A facility in a magnetic tape subsystem whereby a single unqualified command from the host causes a quantity of data from the tape mounted on a transport, selected according to predetermined rules, to be read and transferred to the host. The function is provided to assist in initial program loading. The corresponding process in which data is written to tape is known as *autodump*.

autoload cartridge *See* magnetic tape cartridge.

automated disk library *See* optical disk library.

automated tape library (ATL) A peripheral device in which a large number of cartridges or reels of magnetic tape are stored in cells in a storage matrix. Any chosen cartridge can be transferred mechanically to a tape transport where it can be accessed by the host system, and then returned to the same or another cell. The device also contains one or more *drawers* that can also be reached by the transfer mechanism: these are accessible to an operator so that cartridges can be introduced to or removed from the library.

automatic coding A term used in the early stages of development of computers to signify the use of a primitive high-level language or *autocode, as contrasted with the more usual "hand coding".

automatic data conversion The conversion of data from one form to another without any direct action by the programmer, e.g. decimal integers on input to stored form of integer. Such facilities are commonly available for individual items of data in modern programming languages. Many database input systems carry out more complex transforma-tions of the data, and at the extreme may translate data from the format of one database system to another.

automatic data processing (ADP) *See* data processing.

automatic programming 1. The use of a high-level programming language. The term in this sense is now obsolete.
2. Generation of programs automatically from a nonprocedural description of their desired effect. Thus in artificial intelligence we describe the required actions of a robot, and the system generates a program that will cause the required movements to take place. In commercial data processing we describe the various documents – orders, invoices, delivery notes, etc. – and the relationship between the quantities involved, and the system generates a suite of programs to do the required processing. The term is falling into disuse. *See also* generator.

automaton A general term for a device that mechanically processes an input string with the aim either of deciding whether it belongs to some set of strings (i.e. to a *formal language) or of producing an output string.

There are two senses in which an automaton A is said to *recognize* (or *accept*) a language *L*: for any input string *w*,

(a) A halts and indicates that it *accepts* or *rejects w*, corresponding with whether or not $w \in L$;

(b) A halts if $w \in L$ and fails to halt otherwise.

In the case of *Turing machines, the languages recognizable in sense (a) and the weaker sense (b) are the *recursive sets and the *recursively enumerable sets, respectively.

Turing machines are a particular kind of automaton. Other kinds include the *finite-state automaton, *pushdown automaton, and *linear-bounded automaton. *Sequential machines are automata that produce an output string. According to the *Church–Turing thesis, if a language is recognizable (in either of the above senses) by *any* kind of automaton, it is so recognizable by a Turing machine.

automorphism An *isomorphism from an *algebra to itself.

autonomous guided vehicle (AGV) A form of mobile robot that can transport goods and materials from one place to another in a constrained environment, usually in manufacturing industries. *See also* mobile robotics.

autoregression *See* time series.

autothread A facility provided on some open-reel tape transports whereby magnetic tape is automatically threaded from the file reel through the tape path and secured to the hub of the take-up reel (*see also* autoload). The first autothreading transports required the tape reels to be manually mounted on the transport hub. More recent types only require the tape reel to be "posted" through a slot in the transport housing.

auxiliary memory *Another name for* backing store.

availability **1.** The probability that a system will be capable of functioning according to specification at any point in time throughout a stated period of time. *Compare* reliability. **2.** The ratio of *available time to total time for a system in a given period.

available list (free list) A list of the unallocated parts of a sharable resource. Some resources, such as processors, are shared by being allocated in their entirety to a *process for a period of time. Other resources consist of a number of functionally similar units, e.g. pages within memory, and the resource is shared by units of the total resource being allocated to a process. This allocated share remains with the process until the process releases it. The available list provides the resource controller with a convenient record of which parts of the resource are not allocated to a process. *See also* free-space list.

available time The amount of time in a given period that a computing system can be used by its normal users. During available time the system must be functioning correctly, have power supplied to it, and not be undergoing repair or maintenance. Available time is comprised of *productive time* and *idle time*. Productive time is the amount of time in a given period that a system is performing useful work for the users. Idle time is the amount of time in a given period that a system is performing no useful function. It usually occurs when waiting for completion of some I/O function or backing-store transfer.

average-case analysis *See* algorithm.

AVL tree (height-balanced tree) A *binary search tree such that for each node the *heights of the left and right subtrees differ by at most one. Thus the *balance of each node is −1, 0, or +1. During insertion or deletion, a node in an AVL tree may become *critical* or unbalanced and then the tree has to be reorganized to maintain its balanced property. The tree is named for its originators, Adel'son-Vel'skii and Landis.

AWK An interpreted language for manipulating textual data. Programs take the form of a collection of patterns expressed as *regular expressions, with associated actions in a C-like syntax to be performed if the pattern appears in the input. The name is derived from the initials of the authors − Aho, Weinberger, and Kernighan.

axiom In logic, a statement that is stipulated to be true for a particular chain of reasoning. *See* deduction.

axiomatic semantics An approach to defining the *semantics of programming languages in which the meaning of a language is given by describing the true statements that can be made about programs in that language using axioms and proof rules. Typically the statements are written in some suitable formal notation, such as *predicate calculus or *modal logic, and concern the states before and after running the program. For example, the formula

$$\{p\}\ S\ \{q\}$$

expresses: if a state satisfies property p then there is an output state after executing program S, and it satisfies property q. This assertion is called a *total correctness assertion*; another type is a *partial correctness assertion*.

The approach grew out of the early work of R. W. Floyd and C. A. R. Hoare. Though originally intended as methods for *program correctness proofs (in particular as an alternative notation for the *Floyd method), it was observed that *Hoare logic could also be viewed as an axiomatic semantics for a very simple programming language, namely the *while language. The approach was consequently extended to the description of practically useful languages.

axiomatic specification A particular approach to writing *abstract specifications for programs, modules, or data types. What distinguishes this approach is the fact that specifications are expressed purely in terms of the effects of operations characteristic of the system, and not in terms of their implementations or of the particular representation of any data involved. A specification in this style consists of a collection Σ of operation names, together with a collection T of axioms that express how these operations combine with each other. The operation names can be thought of as comprising a *signature, and the axioms are written in a formal logical language over the signature, such as first-order logic; thus T could be a first-order theory over Σ. An implementation of the operation names can be thought of as an *algebra over that signature, satisfying the axioms. *See also* formal specification. *Compare* constructive specification.

axonometric projection A *projection where the view plane is perpendicular to the direction of projection and the major axes of the object do not coincide with the direction of projection.

B

b (or **B**) *Symbols for* byte.

B A programming language derived from *BCPL, developed in 1970 as an implementation language for the PDP-11 version of the *UNIX operating system. Like BCPL, B was a type-free language: it was soon superseded by *C, the main difference being the addition of types.

Babbage A machine-oriented high-level language (*MOHLL) for the GEC 4080 series machines and their derivatives. Particularly noteworthy is the fact that it was supplied by the manufacturer and entirely replaced the assembler for these machines.

backbone network (bearer network) The underlying *nodes of a multilevel distributed network, providing communication services for the rest of the network (the hosts). The backbone network usually consists of dedicated packet, message, or circuit switches connected by high-capacity trunk circuits, along with some special diagnostic and control equipment.

Backbone networks must be extremely reliable. For this reason they are usually built out of homogeneous (essentially similar) processors and run by a centralized administration, although the rest of the network may be highly heterogeneous and under distributed authority. Distributed procedures are often used to control the operation of the backbone network in order to reduce the possibility that a single failure might disrupt the entire network. When a central control system is used, there is usually a standby system ready to take over when the active system fails.

Backbone networks are often characterized by distributed traffic patterns. *Packet switching may be used internally by backbone networks to take advantage of these traffic patterns, even though the backbone network may present a *circuit-switching appearance to external hosts (*see* virtual circuit). Traffic-pattern analysis may be used to construct backbone networks that minimize certain network parameters, such as average delay, circuit costs, etc. Backbone networks may themselves be multilevel, incorporating low-capacity terrestrial links, high-capacity terrestrial links, and satellite links.

back-end processor A processor that is used for some specialized function such as database management, or a special-purpose ALU. *Compare* front-end processor.

back-face detection Determination of whether a face of an object is facing backward and therefore invisible. The usual test is whether the surface normal points into the screen or not. Special attention is needed for faces on the silhouette of the object.

background processing Processing without the opportunity for interaction with the user, within a system that provides for interaction by *foreground processing. The jobs are submitted by users from terminals but are not processed immediately. They are placed into a *background queue* and are run off as resources become available.

backing store (auxiliary memory; bulk memory; secondary memory) The memory on which information is held for reference but not for direct execution. Backing store is the lower part of the *memory hierarchy, in which the speed of access to the information stored is matched to the requirements of the system so as to achieve the greatest economy. The term may be used either in an absolute sense, in which case it usually refers to a disk, or it may be used in a relative sense to refer to the device next down in the memory hierarchy.

backplane A hardware device that may be considered as the physical "plane" by means of which a computer or similar device communicates with its various peripherals. Normally a backplane consists of a series of multiway sockets that are wired in parallel and are connected to the internal wiring, or *buses, of the computer. Peripherals may then be attached to the computer simply by inserting compatible interface cards into any one of these sockets.

back plane A plane parallel to the *view plane and on the opposite side to the point of projection in a viewing system. Objects behind the back plane are not displayed.

back propagation A supervised learning procedure for training feed-forward *neural networks to learn from test samples. A series of test cases, known as the *training set*, are presented to the net, one at a time. The errors between the actual and desired output of the net are propagated backward to the internal layer(s) in order to adjust the connection weights in proportion to their contribution to the error. The least mean squares of the errors is often used as the optimizing criterion.

backtracking A property of an algorithm that implies some kind of tentative search for a goal, and the possibility that any search path may turn out to be a dead end; the algorithm then retreats back down the search path to try another path. The technique is generally suitable for solving problems where a potentially large but finite number of solutions have to be inspected. It amounts to a systematic tree search, bottom-up.

backup A resource that is, or can be used as, a substitute when a primary resource fails or when a file has been corrupted. The word is also used as a verb, to *back up*, i.e. to make a copy in anticipation of future failure or corruption. Thus a *dump forms a backup to be used in cases where a user's file has become unusable; the taking of the dump can be regarded as backing up the version on disk.

Backus normal form, Backus–Naur form *See* BNF.

backward chaining A strategy for controlling inference procedures, or goal selection, during problem solving. In the case of a *rule-based system, a rule whose consequent part matches the desired goal can be used to generate subgoals from the rule's antecedent part. The subgoals then become target goals and the process is repeated recursively until all subgoals have been satisfied. Backward chaining is also known as *goal-directed processing*, in contrast to data-driven processing (i.e. *forward chaining).

backward compatibility *See* compatibility.

backward error analysis *See* error analysis.

backward error correction (backward correction) Error correction that occurs in a channel through the detection of errors by the reciever: the receiver responds to any errors in a *block by requesting the transmitter to retransmit the affected block. Backward correction requires a *return channel, by contrast with *forward error correction.

There are two ways in which the return channel can be used to indicate errors: *positive acknowledgment* and *negative acknowledgment*. With positive acknowledgment, the receiver returns confirmation of each block received correctly, and the transmitter is prepared to retransmit a block that is not acknowledged within an appropriate time.

With negative acknowledgment, the receiver returns a request to retransmit any block received erroneously, and the transmitter is prepared to retransmit such a block (implying that the transmitter retains a copy of every block sent, indefinitely).

Since the return channel itself may be prone to errors, and to limit the amount of storage necessary at the transmitter, the positive acknowledgment and retransmission (PAR) technique is generally preferred. *See also* error-detecting code.

backward error recovery A mechanism that, on discovery of an error, restores a system to an earlier state (a *recovery point) by undoing the effects of operations that have been performed since that earlier state was last current. This is achieved by saving *recovery data during the execution of operations.

badge reader A device designed to read information encoded into a small plastic card. It is often part of a data collection system in which each operator can be identified by the badge they present to the machine. It can also be used to control access to areas associated with electrically operated door locks, and when built into keyboards and other parts of information systems it can control access to information. The badge is usually of plastic, or paper laminated between plastic, and may contain a photograph and other information in addition to what is encoded. The encoding takes many forms, some of which are proprietary and complex to achieve greater security.

bag (multiset) 1. An unordered collection of items where more than one instance of the same item is allowed.
2. Any data structure representing a bag. Representations are similar to those used for *sets. In a set, however, it is only necessary to represent the presence (or absence) of an element whereas in a bag it is also necessary to represent the number of times it occurs.

balance of a node in a *binary tree. A measure of the relative size of the left and right subtrees of the node. Usually, the balance is defined to be the height of the left subtree minus the height of the right subtree (or the absolute value thereof). However, formulas are also used that measure balance in terms of

the total number of nodes in the left and right subtrees.

balanced (height-balanced; depth-balanced) Denoting a tree that has *height (and thus *depth) approximately equal to the logarithm of the number of nodes in the tree. This property is usually achieved in a binary tree by ensuring every node is balanced according to some measure. *See also* AVL tree, B-tree.

band 1. A set of adjacent tracks on a magnetic or optical disk.
2. A section of the frequency spectrum lying between limits that are defined according to some requirement or to some functional aspect of a given signal or transmission channel. When used as a suffix the word is a contraction of *bandwidth, as in narrowband, wideband.

band-limited channel A transmission channel with finite *bandwidth. All physically realizable channels are band-limited. *See also* channel coding theorem, discrete and continuous systems.

band matrix A *sparse matrix in which the nonzero elements are located in a band about the main diagonal. If A is a band matrix such that
$$a_{ij} = 0 \text{ if } j - i > p \text{ or } i - j > q$$
where p and q are the distances above and below the main diagonal, then the *bandwidth* w is given by
$$w = p + q + 1$$

band-pass filter A *filtering device that permits only those components in the *Fourier transform domain whose frequencies lie between two critical values to pass through with little attenuation, all other components being highly attenuated.

band printer (belt printer) A type of *impact *line printer in which the font – characters and timing marks – is etched on a steel band. The operating principle, involving horizontal movement of the font, is similar to that of the earlier *chain printer and *train printer. Although demonstrated in the mid-1960s it was 1972 before machines with satisfactory print quality and band life were available. Band printers have price/performance advantage over *drum (or barrel) printers; any mistiming of the impact on a horizontal-font machine results in a change in the space between characters, which is less noticeable than the vertical displacement that occurs with mistiming in a drum printer.

The majority of new impact line printers from the late 1970s onward have been band printers. Machines are available at speeds from 300 lpm to 2500 lpm, the higher-speed printers using a 64 character repertoire. Designs for the lower-speed machines often time-share a print hammer between adjacent print positions.

band-reject filter *Another name for* band-stop filter.

band-stop filter (band-reject filter) A *filtering device that permits only those components in the *Fourier transform domain whose frequencies lie below one critical value or above another (higher) critical value to pass through with little attenuation; all components whose frequencies lie between the critical values are highly attenuated.

If the two critical values are very close together, the device is called a *notch filter*. Notch filters are used, for example, in *modems in order to prevent certain components of the data signal from interfering with equipment in the telephone system.

bandwidth 1. of a transmission *channel. A measure of the information-carrying capacity of the channel, usually the range of *frequencies passed by the channel. This will often consist of a single *passband, but may instead consist of several distinct (nonoverlapping) passbands. Each passband contributes to the bandwidth of the channel a quantity equal to the difference between its upper and lower frequency limits; the sum of all such differences gives the total bandwidth.

In these cases bandwidth is measured in frequency units, i.e. hertz (Hz). If the bandwidth is considered in a transform domain other than frequency (such as *sequency) then it is measured in the appropriate units.

There are several loose classifications of frequency bandwidths employed for con-

venience of description in various areas of technology; one classification is as follows:

narrowband (up to 300 Hz)
voiceband (300–3000 Hz)
wideband (over 3000 Hz)

See also band-limited channel, channel coding theorem (for Shannon–Hartley law), Nyquist's criterion.

2. *See* band matrix.

bank switching A technique for *memory management commonly used in microcomputer systems that require more memory than the microprocessor can directly address. In a bank-switched system, different *banks* of memory are selected by writing different bit patterns to a specified output port. Bank switching is similar in concept to memory segmentation (*see* segment) but does not require the use of a processor that knows about a segmented address space.

bar code (or barcode) A printed machine-readable code that consists of parallel bars of varied width and spacing. The application most commonly observed is the coding on food and other goods that is read at the checkout and translated into a line of print on the bill showing product and cost. The information is also used to update stock records and provide sales statistics.

In the US the code used for this purpose is the *Universal Product Code (UPC)* and in Europe it is the *European Article Numbering (EAN) code*. The UPC decodes initially into two five-digit numbers. The first five identify the supplier and the next five are the item number within that supplier's range of goods. From this information the checkout terminal can access the details to be printed on the bill. The EAN code has a two-digit number to indicate country of origin, then the two five-digit numbers, followed by a check digit. The EAN arrangement simplifies the allocation of codes to suppliers. Only the two-digit code and the format need to be agreed internationally.

Other codes are used for shop-floor data collection, library systems, and monitoring the circulation of confidential documents. The advantage of bar codes is that they can be produced and read by relatively simple equipment. Codes used for these purposes are Code 39, Codabar, and "2 of 5". *See also* bar code scanner.

bar code scanner A device for scanning a *bar code. It may take the form of a hand-held *wand, a *holographic scanner, a laser beam deflected by an oscillating mirror, a telescope with a sensor, or a slot containing a sensor.

Barker sequence In data communications, a sequence of symbols (binary or *q-ary) that, when embedded in a string of randomly chosen symbols (from the same alphabet), has zero autocorrelation except in the coincidence position. Barker sequences are used to check, and if necessary to correct, the synchronization and framing of received data.

barrel printer *UK name for* drum printer.

base 1. *Another name for* the radix of a positional number system. Hence decimal numbers are base 10 numbers and binary numbers are base 2 numbers. *See* number system. **2.** *See* base-bound register, relative addressing.

10base5, 10base2 *See* thick wire.

base addressing *See* relative addressing.

baseband networking Communication in which a digital signal is placed directly on the transmission medium without requiring a carrier, i.e. without modulation. Only one signal may be present on the baseband channel at a time. This type of signaling, *baseband signaling*, is also called *d.c. signaling* because in some baseband networks a continuous d.c. voltage is present when the data does not change. Baseband networks may use twisted pair, coaxial cable, or optical fiber for data transmission. *Compare* broadband networking.

baseband signaling *See* baseband networking.

base-bound register (base-limit register) Hardware used for *virtual-memory allocation. A base-bound register is associated with each *segment of data or code and defines the position in physical memory of word zero for that segment, the so-called *base*, and the number of words available to that segment, the so-called *bound* or *limit* (or alternatively the physical memory address of the next word after the end of the segment, in which case it is a *bounds register). Whenever a process attempts to access the memory segment, the hardware of the system checks that the address of the word lies within the range

$$0 \le \text{word address} < \text{bound}$$

and then adds the address to the value contained in the base register to give the physical address. A restriction on this system is that the storage for the segment must be allocated in a contiguous area of memory (*see* best fit, first fit).

The *base register*, used in the construction of relative addresses, should not be confused with the base of a base-bound system; the result of modifying an address by a base register's contents is still an address within virtual memory space of the process, and is not necessarily a physical address.

base field *See* polynomial.

base-limit register *See* base-bound register.

base register *See* relative addressing.

Basic (or BASIC) *Acronym for* beginners' all-purpose symbolic instruction code. Originally a simple programming language developed in the mid-1960s for use in education in order to exploit the then novel capability of using a computer interactively from a remote terminal. The language could be learned very quickly, and the Basic system incorporated a simple program editor, so that the user was insulated from the complexities of the underlying operating system. At first only numeric variables were provided, but later Basic was extended to handle string variables, and was provided with a set of procedures for simple string manipulation that has become a de facto standard.

The simplicity of Basic made it a natural choice of programming language for the early microcomputers, and incompatible dialects proliferated, despite the production of an ISO standard. As microcomputers evolved into more powerful desktop computers, new versions of Basic appeared that incorporated modern control structures; the latest of these, Microsoft *QuickBasic*, has much the same functionality as Pascal.

Important recent developments have been

the introduction of *Visual Basic as a means of prototyping and developing applications for Microsoft Windows, and the adoption of Basic as the underlying language for control of Microsoft applications software, first in the form of *Word Basic and later in the form of *Visual Basic for Applications (VBA). *See also* Turbo languages.

batch control Correctness checks built into *data-processing systems and applied to batches of input data, particularly in the data-preparation stage. There are two main forms of batch control: *sequence control* involves numbering the records in a batch consecutively so that the presence of each record can be confirmed during *data validation; *control totals* involve establishing record counts, or totals of the values in selected fields within each record, and checking these totals during data validation. Control totals may be "meaningful", in the sense that they may have a use (for instance to an auditor) that is additional to their function within the system. Most commonly, however, they are meaningless totals (e.g. of employee numbers), often referred to as *hash totals.

The scope of batch control may extend beyond the data validation stage for as far into the system as batches retain their separate identities. In particular, they may be used to check that incorrect records, rejected during data validation, are resubmitted before a batch is released for further processing.

Batcher's parallel method (merge exchange sort) A form of *sorting by selection that chooses nonadjacent parts of sortkeys for comparisons. The sequence of comparisons was discovered by K. E. Batcher in 1964. It is particularly appropriate for *parallel processing.

batch learning (one-shot learning) *See* machine learning.

batch processing 1. Originally, a method of organizing work for a computer system, designed to reduce overheads by grouping together similar jobs. One form avoided reloading *systems software. The jobs were collected into batches, each batch requiring a particular compiler, the compiler was loaded once, and then the jobs submitted in sequence to the compiler. If a job failed to compile it took no further part in the processing, but those jobs that did compile led to the production on magnetic tape or other backing store of an executable binary. At the end of the batch of compilations those jobs that had produced an executable binary form were loaded in sequence and their data presented to the jobs. Another form avoided the time taken to read cards and print on paper by offline processing, having a batch of jobs on magnetic tape.

The term has also come to be applied to the *background processing of jobs not requiring intervention by the user, which takes place on many multiaccess systems.

2. A method of organizing a *data processing system in which *transactions are input in a batch, sorted, and sequentially processed to update and/or query a *master file. This is the only possible method if magnetic tape is used as backing store; there are applications where it is the most efficient method even using disks. *See also* transaction processing.

baud rate The number of times per second that a system, especially a data transmission *channel, changes state. In the particular case of a binary channel, the baud rate is equal to the bit rate, i.e.

1 baud = 1 bit per second

For a general channel,

1 baud = 1 digit per second

1 baud = 1 symbol per second

or whatever the states of the system represent. The rate was named for J. M. E. Baudot.

Bayesian network *See* Bayes's theorem.

Bayesian statistics *Statistical methods that make use of assumed prior information about the *parameters to be estimated. The methods make use of a theorem of Rev. T. Bayes, measuring the change in *probability attributed to observational data. The use of Bayesian statistics is sometimes regarded as controversial.

Bayes's theorem A theorem used for calculating the conditional probability of an event, where conditional probability, $\text{Prob}(x\,|\,y)$, is the probability of x while y holds.

This is a method in *probabilistic reasoning where Prob(causes | symptoms) can be computed from knowledge of Prob(symptoms | causes), i.e. if we know statistical data on the occurrence of symptoms associated with a disease we can find the probability of those symptoms correctly indicating the disease. A classic application of Bayes's theorem is found in the Prospector *expert system, which successfully predicted the location of valuable mineral deposits.

The combinatorial number of conditional probabilities that have to be computed by the method can be significantly reduced by using *Bayesian networks*, where arcs between propositions define causal influences and the independence of relations.

BBS *Abbrev. for* bulletin board system.

BCD *Abbrev. for* binary-coded decimal.

BCD adder A 4-bit binary *adder that is capable of adding two 4-bit words having a BCD (*binary-coded decimal) format. The result of the addition is a BCD-format 4-bit output word, representing the decimal sum of the addend and augend, and a carry that is generated if this sum exceeds a decimal value of 9. Decimal addition is thus possible using these devices.

BCH code *Short for* Bose–Chaudhuri–Hocquenghem code.

BCPL A systems programming language that incorporates the control structures needed for *structured programming. Its main distinguishing feature is that it is type-free, i.e. the only type of data object that can be used is a word made up of bits (hence the suitability for systems programming). BCPL has been implemented on many machines, and programs written in the language are readily portable, but it is now little used. *See also* CPL, B, C.

BCS British Computer Society, a national source of advice to government and industry on all issues affected by computing. It is the UK member of IFIP.

BDF methods *See* linear multistep methods.

beam deflection Deflection of the electron beam in a *cathode-ray tube. It is controlled either by means of two pairs of magnetic coils mounted around the tube (*electromagnetic beam deflection*) or by two pairs of plates mounted inside the tube (*electrostatic beam deflection*). Electromagnetic deflection is nonlinear with respect to the applied current, causing *pincushion distortion of the image; this has to be compensated for by circuitry. Electrostatic deflection tends to be more expensive than electromagnetic deflection but is more accurate.

bearer The means by which data is carried in a network. The term may either refer to a simple physical device such as a cable or optical fiber, or may describe a complete service designed to transport individual data items.

bearer network *Another name for* backbone network.

behavioral animation *See* computer animation.

behavior-based systems A recent alternative approach to symbolic *artificial intelligence, whereby autonomous *agents are designed to be driven by goal-seeking processes, called *behaviors*, implemented in low-level reactive architectures rather than symbolic cognitive structures. The behavior-based approach has close links with *mobile robotics.

belief systems Belief can be viewed as unsupported fact, i.e. data that are believed to be true (or false), in contrast to knowledge, which is often considered to be known to be true (or false). Partial knowledge thus indicates missing or incomplete data, but partial belief implies a degree of doubt about some given data. Methods for representing degrees of belief have been developed in *probabilistic reasoning. Other techniques include reason-management systems, which record dependencies between data and thus act as justifications that support beliefs (*see* truth-maintenance systems).

In *distributed artificial intelligence, the local collections of belief of individual agents in a multiagent environment are called *belief spaces*.

Bell Telephone Laboratories The research and development laboratories for *AT&T (American Telephone & Telegraph Company), jointly owned by AT&T and Western Electric Corporation (the manufacturing arm of AT&T). The products of Bell Labs include Shannon's seminal work on information theory, the transistor, and the UNIX operating system.

belt printer *Another name for* band printer, used to describe the early versions of those machines, but also used to describe printers in which the font is carried on plates or fingers attached to a flexible belt. The operating principle is similar to that of the *chain printer but the font carrier is lower in cost.

benchmark (benchmark problem) A problem that has been designed to evaluate the performance of a system (hardware and software). In a *benchmark test* a system is subjected to a known workload and the performance of the system against this workload is measured. Typically the purpose is to compare the measured performance with that of other systems that have been subject to the same benchmark test; the performance is then said to be *benchmarked*.

Examples of benchmark programs include the *Ackermann benchmark, *debit-credit benchmark, *pi benchmark, *Ramp-C benchmark, and *whetstone benchmark.

best-first search A search of a directed *graph or *tree in which a set of "best yet" nodes are maintained. As nodes are visited an *evaluation function is used to estimate their value (in terms of a problem solution), and the search proceeds by exploring the node with the best value from the set of best yet nodes. The A* algorithm is an example method.

best fit A method of selecting a contiguous area of memory that is to be allocated for a segment. The available areas are examined in order of increasing size; the area that exceeds the request by the smallest amount is taken and the request met by allocating the amount requested from this area.

beta *Short for* beta release. A version of a software product in the final stages of development, released to selected users for field testing. *See* beta test.

Beta An *object-oriented language featuring *concurrency.

beta reduction *See* lambda calculus.

beta test A test of a packaged software product in a small number of normal working (as opposed to development) environments. The beta test is usually performed at carefully selected customer sites. A beta test is carried out following acceptance *testing at the supplier's site (*alpha test*) and immediately prior to general release of the software as a product. It is a confidence-building exercise that also limits the costs of correcting faults revealed when new or upgraded software is first exposed to its normal working environment and workload.

Bézier curve A *spline approximation developed by Pierre Bézier and widely used in computer-aided design. An nth-degree Bézier curve is an nth-degree polynomial defined by $n + 1$ control points, $r_0 \ldots r_n$. The Bézier curve is defined by

$$r(u) = \sum_{i=0}^{n} r_i B_i^n(u)$$

where $B_i^n(u)$ is the Bernstein polynomial of degree n defined by

$$B_i^n(u) = n!/(i!(n-i)!) \times u^i(1-u)^{n-i}$$
$$\text{if } 0 \leq i \leq n,$$
$$\text{or} = 0 \text{ otherwise.}$$

Bézier curves have a number of important properties. For example, the curve passes through the first and last control points and is completely contained within the polygon that forms the *convex hull of the control points; the gradient at each of the end points is the same as the gradient of the line joining the end point to its immediate neighbor; the control points exert a pull on the direction of the curve which is clamped by the slope at the end points.

Bézier patch A *patch defined in the same way as a *Bézier surface.

Bézier surface A surface swept out by a moving *Bézier curve of constant degree. Each control point of the original Bézier curve also moves through space on a Bézier curve and the curves on which the control points move all have the same degree.

Suppose the initial curve is a Bézier curve of degree m,

$$\mathbf{r}^m(u) = \sum_{i=0}^{m} \mathbf{r}_i B_i^m(u),$$

and let each $\mathbf{r}_i$ traverse a Bézier curve of degree n,

$$\mathbf{r}_i = \mathbf{r}_i(v) = \sum_{j=0}^{n} \mathbf{r}_{ij} B_j^n(v),$$

then the point $\mathbf{r}^{m,n}(u,v)$ on the surface is given by

$$\mathbf{r}^{m,n}(u,v) = \sum_{i=0}^{m} \sum_{j=0}^{n} \mathbf{r}_{ij} B_i^m(u) B_j^n(v)$$

bias 1. The d.c. component of an a.c. signal.
2. The d.c. voltage used to switch on or off a *bipolar transistor or *diode (*see* forward bias, reverse bias), or the d.c. gate-source voltage used to control the d.c. drain-source current in a *field-effect transistor. The word is also used as a verb: to switch.
3. In statistical usage, a source of error that cannot be reduced by increasing sample size. It is systematic as opposed to random error.

Sources of bias include (a) bias in *sampling, when members of the sample are not fully representative of the population being studied; (b) *nonresponse bias* in sample surveys, when an appreciable proportion of those questioned fail to reply; (c) *question bias*, a tendency for the wording of the question to invite an incorrect reply; (d) *interviewer bias*, a problem of personal interviewing when respondents try to reply in the way the interviewer is thought to expect.

A narrower definition of bias in statistical analysis (*see* statistical methods) is the difference between the mean of an estimating formula and the true value of the quantity being estimated. The estimate

$$\sum_i (x_i - \bar{x})^2 / n$$

for the variance of a population is biased, but is *unbiased* when n is replaced by $(n-1)$.
4. **(excess factor)** *See* floating-point notation.

biased exponent *Another name for* characteristic. *See* floating-point notation.

bicomponent algorithm A *depth-first search with the addition of tests to check whether a vertex in the tree is a *cut vertex, i.e. to make sure a particular path is not searched twice, which could happen if a vertex could be reached in two different ways.

biconditional A logical statement combining two statements, truth values, or formulas P and Q in such a way that the outcome is true only if P and Q are both true or both false, as indicated in the table.

P	F	F	T	T
Q	F	T	F	T
$P \equiv Q$	T	F	F	T

Truth table for biconditional

The biconditional *connective can be represented by

$$\equiv \quad \leftrightarrow \quad <\!-\!> \quad \text{or} \quad <\!=\!>$$

and is read as "if and only if" or "iff". or "is equivalent to". Note that $P \equiv Q$ has the same truth table as the conjunction

$$(P \rightarrow Q) \wedge (Q \rightarrow P)$$

where $\rightarrow$ denotes a simple *conditional. The biconditional connective itself is also known as the biconditional.

biconnected graph A *graph G, either directed or undirected, with the property that for every three distinct vertices u, v, and w there is a path from u to w not containing v. For an undirected graph, this is equivalent to the graph having no *cut vertex.

Two edges of an undirected graph are said to be related either if they are identical or if there is a *cycle containing both of them. This is an *equivalence relation and partitions the edges into a set of *equivalence classes, $E_1, E_2, \ldots E_n$, say. Let V_i be the set of vertices of the edges of E_i for $i = 1, 2, \ldots n$. Then each graph G_i formed from the vertices V_i and the edges E_i is a *biconnected component* of G.

bidirectional reflection distribution A *reflectance model for producing realistic images of rough surfaces by means of computer graphics developed by Robert Cook in 1981. Reflectance models describe both the color and the spatial distribution of reflected light. The bidirectional reflection model predicts the directional distribution and spectral composition of the reflected light. This is split into two components that represent the light reflected from the surface of the material and a diffuse component that is dependent on the nature of the surface. Bidirectional reflection distribution was one of the first models to render images that could look plastic or metallic depending on the parameters of the surface.

bifurcation A splitting in two. The term can be applied in computing in various ways.

1. Bifurcation is the generic name for a collection of algorithms that initially convert a *decision table into a *tree structure, which can then be systematically encoded to produce a program.

The *bifurcation method* involves choosing some condition C and eliminating it from the decision table to produce two subtables, one corresponding to the case when C is true and the other to when C is false. The method is then applied recursively to the two subtables. From this approach a *decision tree can be built, each node of the tree representing a condition and subtrees representing subtables; leaf nodes identify rules.

2. *Bifurcation theory* is the theory of equilibrium solutions of nonlinear differential equations; an equilibrium solution is a steady solution, a time periodic, or a quasi-periodic solution. Generally *bifurcation points* are points at which branches and therefore multiple solutions appear.

big-endian Denoting an addressing organization whereby the section of a memory address that selects a byte within a word is interpreted so that the smallest numerical byte address (e.g. 00) is located at the most significant end of the addressed word. *See also* little-endian.

bijection (one-to-one onto function) A *function that is both an *injection and a *surjection. If

$$f : X \to Y$$

is a bijection, then for each y in Y there is a unique x in X with the property that

$$y = f(x)$$

i.e. there is a one-to-one correspondence between the elements in X and the elements in Y. The sets X and Y will have the same number of elements, i.e. the same *cardinality. There will be a unique function

$$f^{-1} : Y \to X$$

such that f and f^{-1} are *inverses to each other; f^{-1} will also be a bijection.

binary adder *See* adder.

binary chop *Informal name for* binary search algorithm.

binary code A *code whose alphabet is restricted to $\{0, 1\}$. In general, any *q-ary code has the important special case $q = 2$. *See* binary system.

binary-coded decimal (BCD) A code in which a string of binary digits represents a decimal digit. In the *natural binary-coded decimal (NBCD)* system, each decimal digit 0 through 9 is represented by the string of four bits whose binary numerical value is equivalent to the decimal digit. For example, 3 is represented by 0011 and 9 is represented by 1001. The NBCD code is the *8421-code such that the weighted sum of the bits in a codeword is equal to the coded decimal digit. *See also* EBCDIC, packed decimal.

binary-coded octal The representation of any octal digit by its three-bit binary equivalent.

binary counter *See* counter.

binary digit *See* bit, binary system.

binary encoding **1.** The representation of symbols in a source alphabet by strings of binary digits, i.e. a *binary code. The most commonly occurring source alphabet consists of the set of *alphanumeric characters. *See* code.

2. The encoding of a number into a binary string in which the ith bit from the end carries weight 2^i. For example, 13 is represented by 1101. This encoding of natural numbers can be extended to cover signed integers and fractions. *See also* radix complement, fixed-point notation, floating-point notation.

3. of a set A. Any assignment of distinctive bit strings to the elements of A. *See also* character encoding, Huffman encoding.

binary-level compatibility *Compatibility that exists when a program in executable binary form may be executed on different computer systems without recompilation. This will normally only be possible between systems with the same operating system and with processors or *emulations of processors capable of executing the same instruction set. *See also* ABI, source-level compatibility.

binary logic *Digital logic employing two states. *See also* logic circuit, *q*-ary logic.

binary notation *See* binary system.

binary number A *binary encoding of a number.

binary operation 1. **(dyadic operation)** defined on a set *S*. A *function from the domain $S \times S$ into S itself. Many of the everyday arithmetic and algebraic operations are binary, including the addition of two integers, the union of two sets, and the conjunction of two Boolean expressions.

Although basically functions, binary operations are usually represented using an infix notation, as in

$$3 + 4, U \cup V, P \wedge Q$$

The operation symbol then appears between the left and right operand. A symbol, such as °, can be used to represent a generalized binary operation.

When the set *S* is finite, *Cayley tables and sometimes *truth tables are used to define the meaning of the operation.
2. An operation on binary operands.

binary relation A *relation defined between two sets.

binary search algorithm (logarithmic search algorithm; bisection algorithm) A *searching algorithm that uses a file in which the sortkeys are in ascending order. The middle key in the file is examined and, depending upon whether this is less than or greater than the desired key, the top or bottom part of the file is again examined. Continuing in this way the algorithm either finds the desired record or discovers its absence from the file. Thus the algorithm treats the file as though it were a *binary search tree.

IF   t is empty THEN *v* not present
ELSE   case 1: t = root ⇒ *v* present
        case 2: t < root ⇒ search left subtree
        case 3: t > root ⇒ search right subtree

Binary search tree, search algorithm

binary search tree A *binary tree in which the data values stored at the nodes of the tree belong to a *well-ordered set, and the value stored at any nonterminal node, A, is greater than the values stored in the left subtree of A

and less than the values stored in the right subtree of A. To search a binary search tree, t, to see if the value, *v*, is present, the recursive search algorithm shown in the figure is used.

In data-processing applications, the data values stored at the nodes of a binary search tree will be key values with an associated link to the record to be retrieved. The same principle is used in the *binary search algorithm. The concept can be generalized to a *multiway search tree. *See also* AVL tree, optimal binary search tree.

binary sequence A sequence of binary digits. Such a sequence, produced randomly or pseudorandomly (*see* random numbers) and generally of known statistical properties, may be employed either as a model of noise affecting a binary channel or as a means of controlling synchronization between transmitter and receiver.

binary signal *See* digital signal.

binary space-partitioning tree (BSP tree) A description of a scene obtained by recursive binary splitting. The BSP tree formed the basis of an algorithm developed by Henry Fuchs et al in 1980 to generate realistic images of scenes composed of polygons (planes) where many images of the same static environment are required. The BSP tree's root node defines a chosen polygon in the image. The two subtrees define the set of polygons on either side of the root plane. At each level, this process is repeated. If polygons straddle the specified plane at any stage, the polygon is split into two parts. Node polygons are chosen to minimize the number of polygons that are split.

binary symmetric channel (BSC) A binary communication channel in which the random errors are such that substitution of a 0 for a 1 occurs with the same probability as substitution of a 1 for a 0. Much of the theory of *error-correcting and *error-detecting codes assumes a BSC.

binary synchronous communications *See* BISYNC.

binary system Usually, the binary number system, i.e. the positional *number system

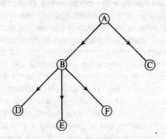

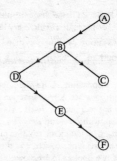

A tree and its binary representation

with base 2. This is the number system most commonly used in computers. A *binary digit* (or *bit*) is either 0 or 1. The representation of numbers by binary digits is called *binary notation*.

The term binary system is also used to describe any system in which there are just two possible states. For example, each of the elements comprising the memory of any computer is a binary system, one of whose states is used to denote the binary digit 0 and the other to denote the binary digit 1. It is customary to refer to such a storage element, or to the unit of information in any binary system, as a *bit*.

binary tree 1. A *tree in which each node has at most two subtrees, called the *left* and *right subtrees* of the node. At *level h of a binary tree there is a maximum of 2^h nodes. A binary tree of *depth d thus has at most $(2^{d+1} - 1)$ nodes and one with n nodes has a minimum depth of $\log_2 n$.

The term binary tree is also used to describe any (ordered) tree of *degree two.
2. Any data structure used to represent a binary tree. Each node is usually represented by pointers to the left and right subtrees as well as to the data value associated with the node. The binary tree can then be represented as a pointer to its root node.

binary-tree representation 1. A binary tree constructed to represent a tree of arbitrary *degree. For any node, the root of the left subtree in the binary-tree representation is the eldest child of the node in the original tree and the root of the right subtree is the next eldest sibling (*see* diagram).

2. *See* binary tree (def. 2).

bind To resolve the interpretation of some *name used in a program for the remaining lifetime of that instance of the program. For example, upon invocation of a procedure the formal parameters are bound to the actual parameters that are supplied for that invocation, and this binding remains in force throughout the lifetime of that invocation. Similarly, at some time the variables in a program must be bound to particular storage addresses in the computer, and this binding typically remains in force for as long as the variable continues to exist. In a *virtual memory system, there is further binding between the virtual addresses used in the program and the physical addresses of the hardware.

For an *abstract specification, the implementation will involve *binding* to a language. For example, the *PCTE specification is available in *C and *Ada language bindings, each having a binding to *UNIX.

binding *See* bind.

binding occurrence *See* free variable.

binomial distribution The basic discrete *probability distribution for data in the form of proportions. An event, E, can occur with *probability p. In a sample of n independent trials the probability that E occurs exactly r times is

$$^nC_r \, p^r(1 - p)^{n-r}$$

(*see* combination). The distribution is discrete, taking only the values 0, 1, 2,..., n. The mean of the binomial distribution is np and the variance is $np/(1 - p)$.

BIOS *Acronym for* basic input/output system. The *firmware permanently resident in microcomputer systems that is responsible for performing input and output operations when so directed. The BIOS is usually called from the operating system, but can be called directly from applications. Calling the BIOS directly can result in performance gains and loss of portability.

bipartite graph A *graph *G* whose vertices can be split into two *disjoint sets, *U* and *V*, in such a way that the only edges of *G* join a vertex in *U* and a vertex in *V*. Bipartite graphs tend to provide a convenient graphical representation of *relations and therefore *functions.

biplot A graphical technique for displaying the results of *multivariate analysis in which both the measured variables and the observed units are displayed on one plot. Units with similar values of the measured variables appear close together, and variables closely associated with particular units appear among those units. The original methods are due to K. Gabriel.

bipolar integrated circuit *See* integrated circuit.

bipolar signal A signal whose signaling elements consist of both positive and negative voltages. Bipolar signals are used in data-communication systems. *Compare* unipolar signal.

bipolar transistor A semiconductor device having three electrodes: *emitter, base*, and *collector*. It is effectively a sandwich of two types of doped *semiconductor, usually p-type and n-type silicon, and so contains two p-n *junctions. When the region common to both junctions is p-type, an *npn transistor* is formed; when it is n-type a *pnp transistor* is formed. This central region forms the base electrode.

Bipolar transistors are so named because both charge carriers, i.e. electrons and holes, contribute to the flow of current. Current flow between collector and emitter is established by applying a *forward bias between base and emitter. In linear (i.e. *nonsaturated*) operation, the magnitude of this current is proportional to the input current drawn at the base. The current flow is in opposite directions in npn and pnp transistors.

If the base current is increased but the collector current is restrained, so that the transistor effectively receives more base current than it would seem to require, the transistor is driven into a state of *saturation*. It then behaves as a very efficient switch since the base-collector junction becomes *reverse-biased and, in saturation, the collector-emitter voltage can fall as low as 20 millivolts. The device thus seems virtually a short circuit. Bipolar transistor switches, working into saturation, are the basis of *TTL circuits. Saturated transistors do however have a fairly low switching speed. The much higher switching speeds of *Schottky TTL and *ECL circuits are achieved by using a non-saturated mode of operation.

biquinary code (quibinary code) A seven-bit *weighted code, two bits of which are used to indicate whether the encoded number (a decimal digit) is or is not at least 5 in value, the remaining five bits comprising four zeros and a single one whose position is used to determine the number completely. Thus from left to right the weights of the bits are 5, 0, 4, 3, 2, 1, and 0. The weighted sum gives the value of the encoded decimal digit; for example, 3 is represented by

$$0101000$$

and 9 is represented by

$$1010000$$

Birkhoff's completeness theorem Equational logic is a formal system for reasoning with *equations. It has simple rules for manipulating equations, based on the reflexivity, symmetry, transivity of equality and the substitution of equal terms into equations. Birkhoff's completeness theorem says that an equation *e* is provable in equational logic from the equations in a set *E* if and only if *e* is true in all *algebras that satisfy the equations in the set *E*. Related to the theorem is the fact that a class of algebras is definable as the class of all models of some set of equations if and only if the class is closed under constructing subalgebras, homomorphic images, and direct products. These results were proved by G. Birkhoff in 1935. *See also* equational specification, term rewriting system.

bis *See* CCITT.

B/ISDN *See* ISDN.

bisection algorithm *Another name for* binary search algorithm.

bistable An electronic circuit, usually an integrated circuit, whose output has two stable states to which it is directed by the input signal or signals. It is more usually known as a *flip-flop. *See also* multivibrator.

BISYNC (BSC) *Abbrev. for* binary synchronous communications (protocol). A *line protocol created by IBM for synchronized communication between mainframe computers and remote job-entry terminals. BISYNC is a character-oriented protocol: it uses special control characters to mark the beginning and end of a *message, to acknowledge previous messages, to request retransmission of missing or damaged messages, etc. The BISYNC protocol may be used with the 6-bit Transcode, 7-bit ASCII, or 8-bit EBCDIC character codes, and multidrop or point-to-point communication lines.

The protocol is inherently half duplex: a message is sent, a reply is sent, the next message is sent, etc. Thus BISYNC communication usually uses half duplex communication lines and modems. Full duplex communication lines and modems may be used but most of the additional capacity is wasted.

BISYNC has been largely replaced in computer communications by newer data link control protocols, such as *SDLC and *HDLC. BISYNC's retransmission and acknowledgment scheme does not work efficiently over connections with long delay times. This is particularly important in the US and other areas where the telephone system is converting to satellite transmission systems for voice and data traffic.

bit *Short for* binary digit. 1. Either of the two digits 0 and 1 in the binary number system. Bits are used in computing for the internal representation of numbers, characters, and instructions. The bit is the smallest unit of storage and hence of information in any *binary system within a computer.

2. The fundamental unit of information used in *information theory. It is the quantity of information required to distinguish between a pair of equiprobable events.

bit-block transfer *See* bitblt.

bitblt (pronounced bitblit) *Short for* bit-block transfer. An operation that, in its simplest form, can rapidly change the contents of a *bitmap and thus the displayed image. Such operations are frequently required by window management systems. It can also be used for graphical operations such as *area filling and image rotation.

The operation has three operands – source, destination, and pattern – that are each rectangular arrays of bits. The pattern operand is usually smaller and is used periodically to create an operand of the same size as the other two. First the pattern and destination operands are combined by a bitblt operator. The result is combined with the source operand by a second bitblt operator and replaces the destination. The two bitblt operators may be any one of the 16 possible *logic operations between two Boolean variables. The bitblt function is usually implemented in hardware with fast parallel circuitry.

The *pixelblt function extends the bitblt to shaded and color displays.

bit density The number of bits stored per unit length or area of a magnetic recording medium. The figure is usually calculated as the maximum density achieved, i.e. it does not take account of the unrecorded areas between blocks, tracks, sectors, etc.

bit handling The facility provided in some programming languages to manipulate the individual bits of a byte or word. Operators provided usually include bitwise "and" and "or" between two bytes (or words), bitwise "not" (inversion) of a single byte (or word), and circular shifts. Many of the programming operations traditionally regarded as bit handling can be achieved in Pascal by use of sets, at some cost in efficiency.

bitmap An array of bits that map one to one to the monochrome image on a *raster display. If a color or gray-level image is required, needing many bits to define each *pixel in the display, a *pixmap is required.

bit matrix A two-dimensional *array in which each element is equal to 0 or to 1. *Compare* Boolean matrix.

Bitnet *Acronym for* because its time network. A system established as a *message switching network, originally linking IBM mainframe systems located in North America and with backing from IBM. Bitnet operates in a store-and-forward mode, in which each complete message is transmitted from one mainframe system to the next until the destination is reached. The network has been substantially extended to other parts of the world, usually on a region-by-region basis, and has been implemented on other hardware platforms. Bitnet and its associated networks elsewhere are now fully self-supporting.

bitpad A device for digitizing the position of a pen. *See* digitizer.

bit rate The number of bits transmitted or transferred per unit of time. The unit of time is usually one second, thus giving rise to bits per second, bps. *See also* baud rate.

bit-slice architecture A computer architecture or design, used especially for microprocessors, in which the CPU is constructed by concatenating a number of high-performance processing units. Each of these "slice" elements represents a limited width (commonly 2, 4, or 8 bits) of an ALU and CU section; a parallel computer of any desired word size can therefore be constructed. Specific system customization is accomplished by *microprogramming. This form of architecture permits the use of standard (thus low-cost) VLSI elements to produce different computer systems.

bits per pixel The number of bits used to define the gray-scale value or color value of a *pixel. Modern color systems often have 24 bits per pixel giving 256 possible values for each of the red, green, and blue components (*see* RGB model).

bit string A *string of bits.

bit stuffing 1. A means of providing synchronization in a *data link control protocol such as HDLC where, for example, a 0 is automatically inserted whenever a predetermined number of 1s is present in a data stream at the sending end of the link. The receiving equipment automatically deletes the extra 0s before delivering the received message to the receiving terminal.
2. A means of inserting and deleting bits on multiply connected high-speed digital transmission links that are not synchronously clocked.

blackboard system An architecture for building problem-solving systems. A series of separate processes, i.e. expert systems, databases, or other sources of expertise in the application domain, communicate through a central global database known as the *blackboard*. Partial solutions are built up on the blackboard, which effectively coordinates the problem-solving process. A blackboard system has the characteristics of parallel, incremental, opportunistic operation. An *agenda mechanism is frequently used as the main control mechanism to schedule the flow of activity in the system.

black-box testing A style of *testing that considers only the inputs, the outputs, and the relationships specified between them to derive test inputs that will demonstrate that the required outputs occur. Usually the term is applied to software, but is also used for any system component (hence "box") for which no knowledge of the internal structure or processing is used to derive the test (hence "black"). *Compare* glass-box testing.

black Ethernet *Another name for* thin Ethernet. *See* thick wire.

blank Empty, i.e. not containing meaningful data. In a memory, blank cells may contain a particular bit pattern that has no assigned value.

blank character A character that creates a blank space when displayed or printed. *Compare* space character.

blend A surface introduced between two existing surfaces to smooth out the join between them. The blend may be a different type of surface from the two that it blends between.

blending The process of constructing *blends.

blink An attribute that causes a character to be intermittently displayed on a screen at a regular rate, usually in the range 1–10 Hz. *Compare* flicker.

blobby model A model where objects have a basic shape that can be perturbed by interactions with neighbors or the environment. Such objects are described as *soft* and include muscles and the human body. *See also* metaballs.

block 1. A collection of data units such as words, characters, or records (generally more than a single word) that are stored in adjacent physical positions in memory or on a peripheral storage device. A block can therefore be treated as a single unit whereby data can be (and usually is) transferred between storage device and memory, using one instruction. Blocks may be fixed or variable in size.

A stream of data to be recorded on magnetic tape is divided into blocks for convenience of handling and particularly for *error recovery. (The equivalent on disks is *sectors.) Successive blocks are usually separated by interblock gaps and often also by control signals introduced by the magnetic tape subsystem and invisible to the host (*see* tape format). It is usual but not essential for the block length to be the same for all blocks of data within a volume or at least within a file, though this may not apply to *labels; where the end of a file occurs partway through a block, the remainder of the block may be filled with *padding characters*.

The choice of block length is largely dependent on *error management considerations. The minimum length of the interblock gap is defined by the standard for the tape format in use; the maximum length is usually undefined, except that a very long stretch (typically 25 feet) of blank tape is taken to mean that there is no more data on the volume. To avoid wastage of tape the gap written is usually fairly close to the minimum but it may be elongated in some circumstances, e.g. by error recovery actions or to leave space for the *editing* of a file (which in

this context means its replacement by a new version of the same length).

In conventional magnetic tape subsystems the division of data into blocks is carried out by the host. However some buffered tape subsystems, particularly streaming cartridge tape, accept a continuous data stream from the host, and the subsystem itself divides the data into blocks (in this case often called *blockettes*) in a manner that is not visible to the host. In these subsystems the interblock gap may be very short or absent.

2. In coding theory, an ordered set of symbols, usually of a fixed length. The term is generally synonymous with word or string, but with the implication of fixed length.

3. *See* block-structured languages.

4. In parallel programming, to prevent further execution of one sequence of instructions until another sequence has done whatever is necessary to unblock it. *See also* blocked process.

block cipher A cipher in which a fixed-length block of data is encrypted, or decrypted, at each iteration of the algorithm: each block is input, encrypted, and output, with no memory (to retain message-dependent information) between blocks (*compare* stream cipher). Nevertheless, it is possible to use a block cipher as a component within a more complex system that effects a stream cipher. *See also* cryptography.

block code A type of *error-correcting or *error-detecting code in which a fixed number (conventionally k) of digits are taken into the encoder at a time and then output in the form of a *codeword* consisting of a greater number (conventionally n) of digits. It is often specified as an (n, k) *code*, with block length k and codeword length n. The corresponding decoder takes in n digits, and outputs k digits, at a time. Since the codewords are longer than the input words, the possible received words are no more numerous. The codewords are only a selection of all possible words of their length: the selection method gives any code its particular properties. *See also* code.

block compaction *Another name for* memory compaction.

block diagram A diagram that represents graphically the interconnection relationships between elements of an electronic system, e.g. a computer system. These elements may range from circuits to major *functional units; they are described as labeled geometric figures. The whole block diagram may represent any level of computer description from a compound circuit to an overall computer complex.

blocked process A *process for which a process description exists but which is unable to proceed because it lacks some necessary resource. For example, a process may become blocked if it has inadequate memory available to it to allow the loading of the next part of the process.

blockette See block.

blocking factor The number of records, words, characters, or bits in a block.

block length 1. See block (def. 1).
2. The input word length, k, of an (n, k) *block code. The term is also applied to the codeword length, n, of an (n, k) block code.
3. The input word length (i.e. the *extension of the source) used in a *variable-length code.

block retrieval Fetching a block from backing store as part of a *memory-management process.

block-structured languages A class of high-level languages in which a program is made up of *blocks* – which may include *nested blocks* as components, such nesting being repeated to any depth. A block consists of a sequence of statements and/or blocks, preceded by declarations of variables. Variables declared at the head of a block are visible throughout the block and any nested blocks, unless a variable of the same name is declared at the head of an inner block. In this case the new declaration is effective throughout the inner block, and the outer declaration becomes effective again at the end of the inner block. Variables are said to have *nested scopes*.

The concept of block structure was introduced in the *Algol family of languages, and block-structured languages are sometimes described as *Algol-like*. The concept of nested scopes implicit in block structure contrasts with Fortran, where variables are either local to a program unit (subroutine) or global to several program units if declared to be COMMON. Both of these contrast with Cobol, where all data items are visible throughout the entire program.

Blue Book 1. The *coloured book that defines the file transfer protocol used by the UK academic networking community. See also NIFTP.
2. Part of the defining documentation for the *ISDN standards, which further refines the definitions appearing in the earlier *Red Book.

Blum's axioms Two axioms in complexity theory, formulated by M. Blum. Let
$$M_1, M_2, \ldots, M_n, \ldots$$
be an effective *enumeration of the Turing machines and let f_i be the *partial recursive function of a single variable that is computed by M_i. (For technical reasons it is simpler to think in terms of partial recursive functions than set (or language) recognizers.) If
$$F_1, F_2, \ldots, F_n, \ldots$$
is a sequence of partial recursive functions satisfying
axiom 1:
$f_i(n)$ is defined if and only if $F_i(n)$ is defined,
and axiom 2:
$F_i(x) \leq y$ is a recursive predicate of i, x, and y,
then $F_i(n)$ is a computational complexity measure and can be thought of as the amount of some "resource" consumed by M_i in computing $f_i(n)$. This notion represents a useful abstraction of the basic resources – time and space. Several remarkable theorems about computational complexity have been proved for any measure of resources satisfying the two axioms (see gap theorem, speedup theorem).

BM algorithm See Boyer–Moore algorithm.

BMP Short for bitmap format. A Microsoft Corp. protocol for storing raster images in an uncompressed form.

BNF Abbrev. for Backus normal form, Backus–Naur form. The first widely used formal notation for describing the *syntax of

$$\langle\text{digit}\rangle ::= 0 \mid 1 \mid 2 \mid 3 \mid 4 \mid 5 \mid 6 \mid 7 \mid 8 \mid 9$$

$$\langle\text{integer}\rangle ::= \langle\text{digit}\rangle \mid \langle\text{digit}\rangle \langle\text{integer}\rangle$$

$$\langle\text{fractional number}\rangle ::= \langle\text{integer}\rangle \mid \langle\text{integer}\rangle . \langle\text{integer}\rangle$$

$$\langle\text{number}\rangle ::= \langle\text{integer}\rangle \mid \langle\text{fractional number}\rangle$$

$$\langle\text{signed number}\rangle ::= \langle\text{number}\rangle \mid + \langle\text{number}\rangle \mid - \langle\text{number}\rangle$$

Production rules of a BNF grammar

a programming language; it was invented by John Backus. BNF was introduced as a defining mechanism in the Algol 60 Report (editor Peter Naur) to describe the syntax of Algol 60. BNF is capable of describing any *context-free language, and variants of it are still in use today.

A BNF grammar consists of a number of *production rules*, which define syntactic categories in terms of other syntactic categories, and of the *terminal symbols* of the language. Examples are shown in the diagram. The name of the syntactic category that is being defined is placed on the left, its definition on the right; the two are separated by the symbol ::=, read as "is defined to be". The names of syntactic categories are enclosed by angle brackets. The symbol | is read as "or".

See also extended BNF.

body (payload) The part of a *cell or *packet in a network that holds the information supplied by the end-user for transmission from the sender to the receiver.

boilerplate A frequently used section of text, such as a heading or a standard paragraph, kept on a permanent online storage medium, such as a hard disk, and retrieved as a whole into a document that is being created or edited, usually by a *word processing program.

book A term used in connection with the organization of files in Algol 68. A file is regarded as one or more books, each book being composed of numbered pages; within a page data is organized into lines made of individual characters. It is important to distinguish "page" in this context from a *page in memory management systems.

Boolean algebra An *algebra that is particularly important in computing. Formally it is a *complemented *distributive lattice. In a Boolean algebra there is a *set of elements B that consists of only 0 and 1. Further there

will be two *dyadic operations, usually denoted by $\wedge$ and $\vee$ (or by . and +) and called *and* and *or* respectively. There is also a *monadic operation, denoted here by $'$, and known as the *complement operation*. These operations satisfy a series of laws, given in the table, where x, y, and z denote arbitrary elements of B.

There are two very common examples of Boolean algebras. The first consists of the set

$$B = \{\text{FALSE, TRUE}\}$$

with the dyadic *AND and *OR operations replacing $\wedge$ and $\vee$ respectively, and the *NOT operation producing complements. Thus 1 and 0 are just TRUE and FALSE respectively. This idea can be readily extended to the set of all n-tuples

$$(x_1, x_2, \ldots, x_n)$$

where each x_i is in B. The AND and OR operations are then extended to operate between corresponding pairs of elements in each n-tuple to produce another n-tuple; the NOT operation negates each item of an n-tuple.

The second common example of a Boolean algebra is the set of subsets of a given set S, with the operations of *intersection and *union replacing $\wedge$ and $\vee$ respectively; set *complement fills the role of Boolean algebra complement.

Boolean algebras, named for George Boole, the 19th-century English mathematician, are fundamental to many aspects of computing – logic design, logic itself, and aspects of algorithm design.

Boolean expression (logical expression) An expression in *Boolean algebra, i.e. a well-formed formula of Boolean variables and constants linked by *Boolean operators. An example is

$$a \wedge (b \vee \neg c)$$

Any *combinational circuit can be modeled

directly and completely by means of a Boolean expression, but this is not so of *sequential circuits.

Boolean function (logical function) A *function in *Boolean algebra. The function is written as an expression formed with binary variables (taking the value 0 or 1) combined by the dyadic and monadic operations of Boolean algebra, e.g.

$$f = (x \wedge y) \vee (x' \wedge z)$$

For any particular values of its constituent variables, the value of the function is either 0 or 1, depending on the combinations of values assigned to the variables. A Boolean function can be represented in a *truth table. It can also be transformed into a *logic diagram of logic gates. *See also* product of sums expression, sum of products expression.

Boolean matrix A two-dimensional *array in which each element is either TRUE or FALSE. *Compare* bit matrix.

Boolean operation (logical operation) An operation on *Boolean values, producing a Boolean result (*see also* Boolean algebra). The operations may be *monadic or *dyadic, and are denoted by symbols known as *Boolean operators. In general there are 16 Boolean operations over one or two operands; they include *AND, *OR, *NOT, *NAND, *NOR, *exclusive-OR, and *equivalence. Boolean operations involving more than two operands can always be expressed in terms of operations involving one or two operands.

In *constructive solid geometry, Boolean operations are the three set operations *union, *set difference, and *intersection.

Boolean operator (logical operator) Any one of the logical connectives of *Boolean expressions, i.e.

$$\neg \quad \wedge \quad \vee \quad \bar{\wedge} \quad \bar{\vee} \quad \equiv \quad \neq$$

or, in another notation,

NOT AND OR NAND NOR
EQUIV XOR (or NEQUIV)

See also Boolean operation.

Boolean type (type Boolean; logical type) A *data type comprising the Boolean values TRUE and FALSE, with legal operations restricted to *logic operations.

Boolean value (logical value) Either of the two values TRUE and FALSE that indicate a truth value.

boom An input device consisting of a long shaft whose end can be moved in three dimensions, so allowing three-dimensional input.

boot To invoke a *bootstrap, especially to read from backing store the operating system of a computer and load it into the empty memory.

boot sector virus *See* virus.

bootstrap 1. In general, a means or technique for causing a system to build up from some simple preliminary instruction(s) or information. The preliminary instruction may be hardwired and called by the operation of a switch. The word is used in a number of contexts.

For example, a bootstrap can be a short

idempotent laws:
$$x \vee x = x$$
$$x \wedge x = x$$

associative laws:
$$x \vee (y \vee z) = (x \vee y) \vee z$$
$$x \wedge (y \wedge z) = (x \wedge y) \wedge z$$

commutative laws:
$$x \vee y = y \vee x$$
$$x \wedge y = y \wedge x$$

absorption laws:
$$x \vee (x \wedge y) = x$$
$$x \wedge (x \vee y) = x$$

distributive laws:
$$x \wedge (y \vee z) = (x \wedge y) \vee (x \wedge z)$$
$$x \vee (y \wedge z) = (x \vee y) \wedge (x \vee z)$$

identity laws:
$$x \vee 0 = x$$
$$x \wedge 1 = x$$

null laws:
$$x \vee 1 = 1$$
$$x \wedge 0 = 0$$

complement laws:
$$x \vee x' = 1$$
$$x \wedge x' = 0$$

Laws of Boolean algebra

program, usually held in nonvolatile memory, whose function is to load another longer program. When a computing system is first powered-on, the contents of its memory are in general undefined except for those parts that are fabricated from read-only memory or for the contents of nonvolatile memory. The bootstrap routine is stored in ROM and is capable of reading from backing store the complete operating system, which is loaded into the empty memory. The computer is then said to be *booted* or *booted up*.

A bootstrap is also a method by which a compiler is transferred from one machine to another, and which depends on the compiler being written in the language it compiles. To transfer from machine A to machine B, given a compiler that runs on machine A, it is first necessary to make the compiler generate B's machine code. The source code of the compiler is then compiled by this modified compiler, so generating a version of the compiler for machine B. In practice it is usually necessary to recode some machine-dependent portions of the compiler by hand to complete the transfer.

The term originates from a story told by Baron Munchausen who boasted that finding himself trapped and sinking in a swamp, he lifted himself by the bootstraps and carried himself to safety on firm ground.

2. (statistical bootstrap) A family of techniques introduced by B. Efron in which empirical *distributions of estimators are obtained by intensive resampling from a given data set. Bootstrap estimators make few assumptions about the theoretical distribution of errors in a statistical model. The *mean, *variance, and *confidence intervals of quantities of interest may be computed, and the empirical *histogram plotted.

Borland International Inc. A US-based producer of PC software. Its best-known offerings are Quattro Pro (acquired by Novell in 1994) and Paradox; it also produces Turbo Pascal and similar development systems. In 1991 it bought Ashton-Tate and thus acquired dBASE.

Bose–Chaudhuri–Hocquenghem codes (BCH codes) An important family of

*binary *linear *error-correcting *block codes. They are reasonably efficient and have reasonably good error-correcting abilities, but their importance lies in their ease of encoding (by means of *shift registers) and of decoding. They can be regarded as a generalization of *Hamming codes, and as a special case of *Reed–Solomon codes. BCH codes can be arranged to be *cyclic.

BOT marker *Short for* beginning of tape marker. A physical feature of a magnetic tape by which the tape transport senses on the tape the start of the volume into which data can be recorded, or has been recorded. When the transport senses the marker it commences the logical sequence of recording or reading data. The marker may be, for example, a rectangular strip of reflective material adhering to the tape, a transparent part of the tape, or a hole in the tape, according to the type of tape and transport. The distance of the marker from the physical beginning of the tape allows the tape to be loaded, threaded through the transport, and wound on to a point at which data will be reliably recorded. This distance, and the form of the marker, are defined by the standard pertaining to the type of tape. *See also* EOT marker. *Compare* tape mark.

bottom-up development An approach to program development in which progress is made by composition of available elements, beginning with the primitive elements provided by the implementation language and ending when the desired program is reached. At each stage the available elements are employed in the construction of new elements that are more powerful in the context of the required program. These new elements will in turn be employed at the next stage in the construction of still more powerful elements, and so on until the available elements can be employed directly in the construction of the desired program.

In practice, "pure" bottom-up development is not possible; the construction of new elements must always be guided by a look-ahead to the requirements of the eventual program, and even then it will often be discovered at a later stage that some earlier construction sequence was inappropriate, leading to a need for iteration. *Compare* top-down development.

bottom-up parsing (shift-reduce parsing)
A strategy for *parsing sentences of a *context-free grammar that attempts to construct a *parse tree beginning at the leaf nodes and working "bottom-up" toward the root.

Bottom-up (or shift-reduce) parsers work by "shifting" symbols onto a stack until the top of the stack contains a right-hand side of a production. The stack is then "reduced" by replacing the production's right-hand side by its left-hand side. This process continues until the string has been "reduced" to the start symbol of the *grammar.

The string of symbols to be replaced at each stage is called a *handle*. Bottom-up parsers that proceed from left to right in the input string must always replace the leftmost handle and, in so doing, they effectively construct a rightmost *derivation sequence in reverse order. For example, a rightmost derivation of the string *abcde* might be

$$S \Rightarrow ACD \Rightarrow ACde \Rightarrow$$
$$Acde \Rightarrow abcde$$

A bottom-up parser would construct this derivation in reverse, first reducing *abcde* to *Acde*, then to *ACde*, then to *ACD*, and finally to the start symbol *S*. The handle at each stage is respectively *ab*, *c*, *de*, and *ACD*.

See also LR parsing, precedence parsing.

bounce *Informal* The return of an e-mail message to the original sender when it is not possible to deliver the message, usually because the name of the putative recipient of the e-mail is not known to the receiving system.

bound *See* lower bound, upper bound.

boundary protection *See* bounds registers.

boundary representation A description of a solid object in terms of the faces that bound it. Faces can be either planar or curved although some algorithms for manipulating boundary representations are limited to planar faces. Information about faces, edges, and vertices are stored as part of the representation.

boundary-scan testing A technique used to facilitate effective testing of the digital ICs,

and their interconnections, on high-density *printed circuit boards in the factory and in the field. Extra logic is included and this intercepts the logic signals at each functional pin of the logic components. The extra logic is transparent in normal operation but can be configured as a long *shift register in a special test mode. The shift registers on each component are connected into a daisychain so that all the logic circuits can be accessed through a special group of test connections brought out to the *edge connector. This structure is used to feed predefined information to the input pins and collect the results from the output pins, thus enabling several types of test to be performed (function and interconnect).

boundary-value problem *See* ordinary differential equations, partial differential equations.

bounded delay A term used to describe a network in which the total delay experienced by data traversing the network can be guaranteed not to exceed some predetermined value. This is especially important where the network is used to carry speech, as the human ear is very intolerant of breaks in speech. *See also* network delay.

bound occurrence *See* free variable.

bounds registers Two registers whose contents are used to denote an area of memory for which there is *access control. The area may be defined by beginning and ending addresses, or by the beginning address and the area length – in which case it is a *base-bound register. The use of bounds registers is a form of hardware security, and is sometimes known as *boundary protection*. *See also* memory protection.

bound variable A variable with a bound occurrence in an expression. *See* free variable.

Box–Jenkins forecasting techniques *See* time series.

boxplot A simple display of an observed *frequency distribution in which the main body of the data between the 10th and 90th *percentile are displayed as a rectangular box, divided at the *median, while the lower and upper portions are indicated by lines drawn to the extreme values of the range.

Boyer–Moore algorithm (BM algorithm) A string search developed by R. Boyer and J. Moore in 1975. This search compares characters at the end of the pattern rather than at the beginning, until a match is found.

bpi *Abbrev. for* bits per inch.

bps *Abbrev. for* bits per second. *See also* bit rate.

bpt *Abbrev. for* bits per track.

branch 1. A *control structure in which one of two or more alternative sets of program statements is selected for execution. The selection is achieved during execution by means of a *branch instruction*; this instruction thus breaks the normal sequential program flow. (Branch instruction is usually regarded as synonymous with jump instruction.) *See also* jump, if then else statement, case statement, GOTO statement.
2. The set of instructions selected for execution as a result of a branch instruction.
3. To perform such a selection.

branch and bound algorithm An organized and highly structured search of all possible solutions to a problem. It is a general form of the *backtracking methods, and is used extensively in artificial intelligence and operations research.

branching factor The average number of *branches* (successors) from a (typical) node in a *tree. It indicates the bushiness and hence the complexity of a tree. If a tree branching factor is B, then at depth d there will be approximately B^d nodes.

branch instruction (jump instruction) *See* branch.

branch testing A test strategy seeking to choose test data values that lead to the testing of each *branch in a program at least once (branching occurring at each decision point). It is equivalent to finding a set of paths through the *control-flow graph whose union covers all the arcs of the graph. Branch testing normally requires more tests than *statement testing but fewer than *path testing. *See also* test coverage.

breadboard An easily adapted *circuit board on which experimental arrangements of electronic components may be realized. Access to the individual components is simple and hence the overall arrangement may be readily modified. Breadboards are used mainly for the development of prototype circuit designs.

breadth-first search A technique of searching through a tree whereby all nodes in a tree at level k are searched before searching nodes at level $k + 1$. *Compare* depth-first search.

breakpoint *See* debugging.

Bresenham's algorithm An algorithm that efficiently calculates the *pixel positions needed to define a specified line using only integer arithmetic.

BRI *Abbrev. for* basic-rate ISDN. *See* ISDN.

bridge A unit that supports a low-level link of two regions of a single network. In networks using a broadcast *protocol, in which all network nodes receive all messages, it is helpful to subdivide the network into a number of regions in which the majority of traffic is between pairs of nodes within that region, with only a small amount of traffic leaving the region. A bridge can be inserted between two such regions: it allows interregion traffic to cross the bridge but will not forward into the second region traffic that is addressed to a destination in the same region as the sender. To achieve this, a bridge must be capable of interpreting the sender and receiver addresses in the data. It must therefore be capable of interpreting the network protocol, and will almost certainly need to store an entire packet before forwarding it. The bridge will be designed so as to function at the lowest possible level within the protocol stack, consistent with achieving correct partitioning of the network.

Despite the complexity of the unit, and the delay it introduces, large networks almost invariably include bridges since their presence greatly reduces the total network traffic. A bridge may be *adaptive*, determining the addresses in each region by examining the contents of the address fields of the packets. A bridge may operate as a *filtering bridge*, with a fixed set of node identities that will be allowed to send packets across the bridge, providing a limited form of safeguard against unwanted attempts to connect to a sensitive system. *See also* router, firewall.

bridgeware Any software or hardware that eases the transition from use of one computer system to use of another not entirely compatible one. Bridgeware is normally supplied by a computer manufacturer when a new range of machines does not offer complete upward *compatibility from some previous range. Typically the bridgeware will permit programs developed for the previous range to be executed (perhaps after minor modifications) on the new range of machines.

broadband coaxial systems Communication systems that use *broadband networking techniques on coaxial cable. The 300 megahertz (MHz) bandwidth of a coaxial cable is divided into multiple channels through *frequency division multiplexing. The channels can transmit signals at different data rates, allowing diverse applications to share the cable by means of dedicated channels. Channel bandwidth may range from a few kilohertz to several megahertz. A single cable may carry both digital data and analog data (voice, television) simultaneously. Access to the cable is provided through radio-frequency *transceivers (modems) assigned to a particular channel. *Frequency-agile modems* may be used to communicate on different bands at different times.

There are two classifications of broadband coaxial systems. In a one-way system signals travel in only one direction in the cable. This kind of system is common in cable TV (CATV) systems. In a two-way system signals can travel in both directions on the cable. All traffic that originates from network nodes travels on the inbound channels to the *headend*. The headend is the origin of all traffic on the outbound channels, routing all messages on inbound channels to the proper outbound channel to reach their destination. Network nodes transmit messages on inbound channels and receive messages on outbound channels.

Two-way systems fall into *midsplit* or *subsplit* categories. Midsplit systems divide the cable bandwidth equally between inbound and outbound channels. Subsplit systems put inbound traffic in the 5–30 MHz bands and outbound traffic in the 54–100 kHz bands. This format is the easiest way to retrofit onto a one-way CATV system, and leaves the VHF TV channels on their normal "off-the-air" frequency assignments.

broadband ISDN *See* ISDN.

broadband networking 1. Communication using a modulated carrier (*see* modulation) to apply a data signal to a transmission medium in analog form. Multiple signals can be present simultaneously using *frequency division multiplexing. Different bandwidths may be allocated to different signals, and different kinds of traffic (digital data, analog voice, television) may be carried at the same time. *See also* broadband coaxial systems. *Compare* baseband networking.
2. A term sometimes used for wideband networking, i.e. networking with wideband channels (*see* bandwidth).

broadcasting A message-routing algorithm in which a *message is transmitted to all *nodes in a network. Some data-communication media, such as the *Ethernet, are inherently broadcast in nature. *Address filtering* is used to restrict the set of messages that any one host actually reads. The network service that delivers the message is known as *broadcast service* and is implemented using a special address, which all stations are prepared to accept. Other communication systems may require that a copy of the message be separately addressed to each possible recipient in order to implement broadcasting.

Broadcasting may be used for a variety of purposes. For instance, to find the shortest path to a destination, a message can be broadcast to all intermediate nodes repeatedly until the destination node is reached. If path information is recorded as the message traverses the network, the same path can be used for future messages to the same destination node. As a second example, in local area networks with a tree-like topology, or in satellite communication links with multiple ground stations within a beam radius, broadcasting can be used to simplify addressing. This allows certain messages, such as request for a bootstrap, to be sent to all hosts with the expectation that at least one host will be able to satisfy the request. Thirdly, a broadcast message may be one that carries general information of potential interest to all nodes on the net.

brother *Another name for* sibling, now rarely used.

brouter *Informal* A unit in a network that combines the functions of a *bridge and a *router.

browse To examine the contents of a large data set, especially when locating and retrieving information with a search strategy that cannot be predicted at the outset, or possibly with no search strategy at all. *See also* browser, gopher.

browser A utility program that allows a user to locate and retrieve information from networked information services. Netscape Navigator and Microsoft Internet Explorer are examples of *World Wide Web browsers.

BSC 1. *Abbrev. for* binary symmetric channel. **2.** *See* BISYNC.

BSI British Standards Institution, founded in 1901 and now the recognized authority in the UK for the preparation and publication of national standards for industrial and consumer products. Collaborating closely with the *ISO, it represents the UK at ISO and European standards meetings.

B-spline A piecewise polynomial function, defined over a knot sequence, that has local support and is nonnegative (*see* spline). The B-spline of order n (degree $n-1$) is zero everywhere except over the n successive spans

$$x_{i-n} < x_{i-n+1} < \ldots < x_i$$

The importance of B-splines is that any spline can be expressed as a sum of multiples of B-splines, and if a spline of degree $n-1$ is expressed in terms of B-splines, then changing the coefficient of one of the B-splines alters precisely n spans of the curve without affecting its continuity properties.

B-spline patch A surface *patch defined by *B-spline curves in the same way that a *Bézier patch is defined by *Bézier curves. Given a characteristic polygon defined by

vertices r_{ij}, $i = 0,1,\ldots p$, $j = 0,1,\ldots q$, the B-spline patch is defined by

$$r(u,v) = \sum_{i=0}^{p} \sum_{j=0}^{q} r_{ij} B_{\rho,i+1}(u) B_{\rho,j+1}(v)$$

where B is the B-spline basis function of degree ρ.

BSP tree *Short for* binary space-partitioning tree.

B-tree (or b-tree) 1. (balanced multiway search tree) of *degree n (≥ 2). A *multiway search tree of degree n in which the root node has degree ≥ 2, every nonterminal node other than the root has degree k, where $n/2 \leq k \leq n$, and every leaf node occurs at the same level. Originally defined by R. Beyer and E. McCreight, the data structure provides an efficient dynamic retrieval device.

An extension to a B-tree is a *B+ tree*, which is used as a primary index to an *indexed file. It comprises two parts: a sequential index containing an entry for every record in the file, and a B-tree acting as a multilevel index to the sequential index entries. B+ trees are used in *VSAM.

2. A binary tree with no nodes of degree one.

B+ tree *See* B-tree.

BTron *See* Tron.

bubble jet A type of *inkjet printer.

bubble memory *See* magnetic bubble memory.

bubble sort (exchange selection) A form of *sorting by exchanging that simply interchanges pairs of elements that are out of order in a sequence of passes through the file, until no such pairs exist. The method is not competitive with *straight insertion.

bucket 1. A subdivision of a *data file, serving as the unit within which records are located. Buckets are specially used in connection with *hashing techniques, and with indexing techniques (*see* index) where index entries point to groups of records. In these circumstances, hashing or indexing will yield the address of the start of the bucket; the location for storage or retrieval within the bucket will then be found by searching.

2. A capacitor whose electric charge is used as a form of dynamic *RAM. A fully charged bucket, or *full* bucket, is equivalent to a logic 1; an uncharged or *empty* bucket is equivalent to a logic 0. The charge may be passed through an array of capacitors and associated electronics, which together form a *bucket brigade*.

bucket sort An external sort in which the records to be sorted are grouped in some way, and each group stored in a distinct *bucket. Different buckets will probably be stored on different storage devices. If searching is to be performed on the data, then each bucket should contain records with the same hash value (*see* hashing). In this way all the records that might contain the required key may be fetched from the external memory at once.

buddy system A method of implementing a *memory management system. The available memory is partitioned into blocks whose sizes are always exact powers of two. A request for m bytes of memory is satisfied by allocating a block of size 2^{p+1} where
$$2^p < m \le 2^{p+1}$$
If no block of this size is available then a larger block is subdivided, more than once if necessary, until a block of the required size is generated. When memory is freed it is combined with a free adjacent block (if one exists) to produce a larger block, always preserving the condition that block sizes are exact powers of two.

buffer 1. A temporary memory for data, normally used to accommodate the difference in the rate at which two devices can handle data during a transfer. The buffer may be built into a peripheral device, such as a printer or disk drive, or may be part of the system's main memory. *See* buffering.
2. A means of maintaining a short but varying length of magnetic tape between the reels and the *capstan and head area of a tape transport, in order that the acceleration of the tape at the reels need not be as great as that of the tape at the capstan. There are two principal types of buffer: *tension arm* and *vacuum column*. In the first, the tape passes over a series of rollers, alternate rollers being fixed in position and the rest being attached to a sprung pivoted arm, so that a variable length of tape is taken up in the resulting loops; in the second, the tape is drawn by a difference of pressure into a chamber whose width is

just that of the tape. Vacuum column transports are more expensive and noisier but can handle higher tape speeds.
Streaming tape transports and many types of cartridge drives do not use buffers and are therefore limited to lower accelerations of the tape in the area of the head and (if there is one) capstan.
3. Any circuit or device that is put between two others to smooth changes in rate or level or allow asynchronous operation. For example, line *drivers can be used to isolate (or buffer) two sets of data lines.

buffering A programming technique used to compensate for the slow and possibly erratic rate at which a peripheral device produces or consumes data. If the device communicates directly with the program, the program is constrained to run in synchronism with the device; buffering allows program and device to operate independently. Consider a program sending output to a slow device. A memory area (the *buffer) is set aside for communication: the program places data in the buffer at its own rate, while the device takes data from the buffer at its own rate. Although the device may be slow, the program does not have to stop unless the buffer fills up; at the same time the device runs at full speed unless the buffer empties. A similar technique is used for input. *See also* double buffering.

buffer register A storage location or device for the temporary storage of information during the process of writing to or reading from main memory. It generally has a capacity equivalent to one byte or one word.

bug An error in a program or system. The word is usually used to mean a localized implementation error rather than, say, an error introduced at the requirements or system-design stage. *See also* debugging.

bug seeding *See* seeding.

bulk memory *Another name for* backing store.

bulletin board (BBS) A *teleconferencing system often run on a dedicated computer for use by enthusiasts who can connect their personal computers by means of *modems and telephone lines or network connections. The bulletin board allows its users to post notices that they wish seen by other users on a variety of topics, to read the notices left by previous users, and to *download software and information for use on their own systems. This latter activity is one of those blamed for the spread of computer *viruses.

bump mapping A method of rendering realistic shading on bumpy surfaces without actually rendering a full three-dimensional model of the bumps. The surface is treated as smooth for the purpose of visible surface determination. The appearance of bumps or roughness is created by perturbation of the surface normals. *See also* displacement mapping.

bundle To sell the hardware and software components of a computer system as one indivisible package. *See also* unbundling.

bundled attributes *Attributes of a graphical output primitive that are defined in a device-dependent table pointed at by an index associated with the primitive.

burster A mechanism for separating continuous fan-folded paper used in line printers and some page printers into separate sheets. Frequently it also performs the function of separating out interleaved carbon and sorting the multicopy output into sets. It may also trim the edges to remove the sprocket holes and the ragged edge left by the perforations between sheets. Generally this is done offline but some versions can be linked directly to the output printer.

burst error (error burst) An error pattern, generally in a binary signal, that consists of known positions where the digit is in error ("first" and "last"), with the intervening positions possibly in error and possibly not. By implication, digits before the first error in the block and after the last error in the block are correct.

burst mode Usually, dedicated use of a multiplexer *channel for a single I/O device, thus permitting that device to operate at high (burst) speed. A number of data characters or words are transferred as one group rather than character by character.

bus A signal route to which several items of a

computer system may be connected in parallel so that signals can be passed between them. A bus is also called a *trunk* in the US, and a *highway* in the UK. The signals on a bus may be only of a particular kind, as in an *address bus or *data bus, or they may be intermixed. To maximize throughput, the number of lines in the bus should equal the sum of the number of bits in a data word, the maximum address, and the number of control lines. As this is expensive to implement, a *multiplexed bus may be used.

There are a number of widely used proprietory bus systems, such as Digital Equipment's *Unibus and Intel's *Multibus. There is also a widely used instrumentation bus standard, referred to as *IEEE–488 or as GPIB, general-purpose interface bus. For microprocessors there are a number of standardized bus systems, one of the most widely used being the *VME bus.

bus arbitration The procedure in bus communication that chooses between connected devices contending for control of the shared bus; the device currently in control of the bus is often termed the *bus master*. Devices may be allocated differing priority levels that will determine the choice of bus master in case of contention. A device not currently bus master must request control of the bus before attempting to initiate a data transfer via the bus. The normal protocol is that only one device may be bus master at any time and that all other devices act as *slaves* to this master. Only a bus master may initiate a normal data transfer on the bus; slave devices respond to commands issued by the current bus master by supplying data requested or accepting data sent.

bus driver *See* driver.

bused interface *Another name for* daisychain.

bus hierarchy An interconnection system used when a single system bus cannot provide the degree of *connectivity required. Devices are connected using multiple buses that are themselves then interconnected to form a hierarchical connection system.

business graphics Computer graphics related to business, commerce, industry, and non-scientific applications. Examples include pie charts, graphs, and clip art.

bus master *See* bus arbitration.

bus terminator An electric circuit connected at the end of a bus to hold it at a predetermined signal level when it is not active, and also to ensure impedance matching and thus avoid unwanted reflections of signals. It is often available as a single package for mounting onto a printed circuit board.

It is important to ensure that the electric impedance of a bus carrying high-frequency signals does not have any abrupt changes. If the ends of the conductors are not terminated, the signals see an almost infinite impedance and are reflected back along the conductor. A fast switching circuit connected to an unterminated bus could detect both the signal and the reflection and so give rise to errors.

busy signal A signal from a device indicating that it cannot accept any new commands or data for the time being. *Compare* ready signal.

button An area on a screen that when activated by means of a *pointing device or predetermined key sequence causes an action to be initiated. Buttons can be any shape or size and need not be visible. The commonest form is a small rectangular area shaded to give the appearance of protruding slightly from the screen and labeled with text that indicates its function ("close", "ok", "print", etc.) or with an *icon. When the button is activated or "pressed", its appearance will normally change so that it appears recessed. A horizontal or vertical row of buttons is called a *button bar*.

byte A fixed number of *bits that can be treated as a unit by the computer hardware. It is a subdivision of a *word, and almost always comprises 8 bits although 6, 7, or 9 bits are occasionally encountered.

The letters B and b are commonly used as symbols for byte, as in MB (megabyte), and GB (gigabyte), although the word is often written in full in such cases, as in Mbyte.

See also character.

bytecode *See* Java.

byte machine *See* variable word length computer.

Byzantine Generals problem The problem of devising an algorithm that will decide whether a collection of generals, who communicate using messages some of which may be lost due to deficient transmission, agree to carry out an attack on a target. This is a reformulation in familiar terms of a problem that occurs in the design and development of distributed computer systems.

C

C A programming language originally developed for implementation of the *UNIX operating system. C is the preferred language for systems software development in the UNIX environment, and is widely used on personal computers. It combines the control and data structures of a modern high-level language with the ability to address the machine hardware at a level more usually associated with assembly language. The terse syntax is attractive to professional programmers, and the compilers generate very efficient object code. C is derived from *BCPL, via a short-lived predecessor *B. *See also* Turbo languages.

C++ A programming language derived from *C. C++ is a superset of C that adds type checking, operator overloading, abstract data types, and classes to the original language. It thus combines the power of *object-oriented programming with the efficiency and notational convenience of C. C++ has become the language of choice for implementing applications to run under Microsoft *Windows.

C^2, C^3, C^4 *See* command and control.

cable A physical medium for carrying signals. *Fiber optics requires specially prepared optical fibers to carry light signals. Electric cable is usually insulated copper wire encountered in various forms depending on the intended application; common forms include *twisted pair (unshielded and shielded), *coaxial cable, and *ribbon cable.

An electric circuit must always contain an outward and a return path. For low-frequency signals the outward path can consist of a single conducting wire, with the return path carried by a common ground (earth) return, which can be shared by many different circuits. At higher frequencies this system is no longer effective, and it is necessary to provide both an outward and a return conductor. At still higher frequencies, the two conductors need to be kept close to one another, as in twisted pair, so that the outward current in one conductor is balanced by the corresponding inward current in the other; this reduces the amount of energy lost by radiation. *Screened cable* is a multipath electric cable with a surrounding screen usually formed from an interwoven fine wire mesh, and used for example in shielded twisted pair; the screen provides some isolation from external sources of electrical interference. *Multicore cable* is a multipath cable frequently containing a mixture of screened and single conductors; sometimes one or more coaxial cables are included to provide paths for high-frequency or other special signals.

cache (cache memory) A type of memory that is used in high-performance systems, inserted between the processor and memory proper. The *memory hierarchy on a system contains registers in the processor, which are the highest-speed storage, and, at a slightly lower level of accessibility, the contents of the main memory. The cache is intended to reduce the discrepancy in accessibility between these two types of unit, and functions by holding small regions that map the contents of main memory. The formal behavior of the cache corresponds closely to that of the *working set in a *paging system.

Some magnetic disk *controllers have a cache. The working of the cache is not visible to the main CPU, but again provides a mapping of the current contents of part of the disk units in order to provide improved performance.

Some magnetic tape units have built-in cache memory. In this case the aim is to allow a *streaming tape transport to emulate the behavior of a (more expensive) start-stop unit so that it can be attached to a system designed

to support only the latter without substantial software modification. The arrangement was introduced by Cipher in the early 1980s.

See also disk cache.

CAD *Abbrev. for* computer-aided design.

CADCAM *See* computer-aided design.

caddy A form of *cartridge used specifically for *CD-ROM optical disks. Unlike most cartridges, the operator can readily remove the disk and replace it with another.

CADMAT *See* computer-aided design.

CAE 1. *Abbrev. for* computer-aided engineering. **2.** *Abbrev. for* common application environment.

CAFS *Abbrev. for* content-addressable file system. A development by ICL of *associative memory.

CAI *Abbrev. for* computer-aided instruction. *See* computer-assisted learning.

CAIS–A *See* PCTE.

CAL *Abbrev. for* computer-assisted learning.

calculator A small electronic device by means of which arithmetic operations can be performed on numbers entered from a keyboard. Final solutions and intermediate numbers are generally presented on *LCDs. Calculators range from very cheap simple devices capable of performing the basic arithmetic operations to those whose capabilities extend to sophisticated mathematical and statistical manipulation and that may be programmed with large numbers of steps. Add-on memory modules containing sets of specialist programs for particular fields – engineering, navigation, or business for example – may be purchased as accessories to the more expensive calculators, as can small printers.

The dividing line between sophisticated calculators and small personal computers, such as *notebooks and *pocketbooks, is becoming less clear-cut; there are significant overlaps in both price and power.

call To transfer control to a *subroutine or *procedure, with provision for return to the instruction following the call at the end of execution of the subroutine/procedure.

call by name *See* parameter passing.

call by reference (call by address) *See* parameter passing.

call by value *See* parameter passing.

calling sequence The code sequence required to effect transfer of control to a subroutine or procedure, including *parameter passing and the recording of the return address. Uniformity of calling sequences is vital if it is required to call procedures written in a different language from the calling program.

call instruction An instruction that saves the contents of the *program counter before branching to a *subroutine or *procedure. *Compare* return instruction.

CAM *Abbrev. for* 1. computer-aided manufacturing, 2. content-addressable memory, 3. cellular automata machine.

CAMAC A standardized multiplexing intermediate interface. It does not usually connect directly to a processor or a peripheral, but provides a standardized interface to which a number of peripheral interface adapters and a single computer interface controller can be connected.

The peripheral adapters may each have different functions (e.g. digital to analog converter, level changers, parallel to serial converter), and thus have different interfaces facing outward from the CAMAC. Similarly the controller module connects to the CAMAC interface but the outward-facing interface can be chosen to suit the available computer. The name CAMAC was chosen to symbolize this characteristic of looking the same from either direction. The adapters are typically a single printed circuit card that plugs into the internal 86-way connector. The outward-facing connections are usually mounted on a panel attached to the circuit card or may be made via a second connector mounted above the 86-way CAMAC connection. The interface is widely used for connecting instruments and transducers to computers.

CAMAC was proposed as a standard by the UK Atomic Energy Authority and further development and documentation was done by the European Standards of Nuclear Electronics (ESONE) and the Nuclear Instrument Module Committee of the US. The parallel interface is documented in IEC-522 and the modular construction is in IEC-516.

Cambridge Ring A pioneering high-speed *local area network, originally developed at Cambridge University, UK. It used a *minipacket* of 40 bits: 16 bits held 2 bytes of data, two groups of 8 bits specified the addresses of the source and destination nodes, and the remaining 8 bits were used for control purposes. A master station controlled the interbit time and the gap between packets, so that the ring circulated an exact number of packets and gaps. Each packet contained a single-bit indicator as to whether it was full (i.e. the packet contained useful data) or empty (i.e. the packet data had been received by the destination node, and the packet had completed a circuit of the ring back to the original source node). The Cambridge Ring was thus an example of an "empty slot" ring. *See also* token ring.

campus-wide information service *See* CWIS.

cancellation The loss of significant digits in subtracting two approximately equal numbers. This is a frequent cause of poor accuracy in numerical results but it can usually be avoided by some reorganization of the calculation. Consider, for example, the quadratic equation

$$ax^2 + bx + c = 0$$

The formula for the roots of a quadratic is

$$(-b \pm \sqrt{(b^2 - 4ac)})/2a$$

If b^2 is large compared with $4|ac|$ severe cancellation occurs in one of the roots. This root can be computed from the fact that the product of the roots is c/a.

C&C *See* command and control.

Capability and Maturity Model (CMM) A five-level model for assessing the capability and maturity of software development organizations. It was developed by Watts Humphrey at the *Software Engineering Institute and the first version was released in 1987. The level of an organization is assessed in terms of key process areas and key practices.

Level 1, the *initial* level, is characterized

by lax procedures and lack of management appreciation of software issues. At level 2, the *repeatable* level, basic procedures are defined and there is sufficient discipline to enable earlier successes to be repeated; there is, however, no framework for improvement and the risks associated with new and different developments are high. The *defined* level, level 3, is the level at which all software development projects in the organization use a documented and approved version of the organization's process for developing and maintaining software; in addition, there are procedures in place for maintaining the process model. At level 4, the *managed* level, detailed measurements of process and product quality are collected and analyzed, so that the causes of changes in process performance can be identified. The last level is the *optimizing* level, characterized by steady process improvement arising from the feedback obtained from the projects.

When the model was first introduced, 80% of the organizations looked at were found to be at level 1 and none had reached level 4. The existence of the model has spurred organizations into improving their development process and a few are now judged to have attained level 5.

capability architecture An architecture that extends across both the hardware and the (operating system) software of a computer system. It is intended to provide better protection features to facilitate both multiprocessing and computer security. In this form of architecture there are two types of words in memory: data (including programs) and *capabilities*. Capabilities can only be manipulated by privileged portions of the system. The capability descriptor tells where data is and what sorts of access to that data are permitted.

Examples of systems with capability architecture are the Plessey 250 and the Cambridge CAP. *Object-oriented architecture is an extension of this concept.

capability list The list of permitted operations that a subject can perform on an object. *See* object-oriented architecture, capability architecture.

capacity 1. The amount of information that can be held in a storage device. The amount may be measured in words, bytes, bits, or characters.
2. The maximum range of values that can be held in a register.
3. of a transmission channel. *See* channel coding theorem.

CAPM *Abbrev. for* computer-aided production management.

CAPP *Abbrev. for* computer-aided process planning.

caps lock A mode of keyboard operation whereby the alphabetic characters produced by a keyboard are constrained to be in upper case. This mode does not affect numeric characters. *See also* shift lock.

capstan The component of a tape transport that transmits motion (sometimes indirectly) to the magnetic tape and controls the speed of its motion past the head; the motion of the tape reels is usually separately controlled. *Streaming tape transports often have no capstan.

CAR The *LISP function that when applied to a list yields the *head of the list. The word was originally an acronym for contents of address register. *Compare* CDR.

card *See* magnetic card, smart card, add-in card, punched card.

card cage A framework in which *circuit boards can be mounted. It comprises channels into which the boards can be slid and sockets and wiring by means of which they are interconnected.

cardinality A measure of the size of a *set. Two sets S and T have the same cardinality if there is a *bijection from one to the other. S and T are said to be *equipotent*, often written as $S \sim T$. If the set S is finite, then the cardinality of S is the number of elements in the set. For an infinite set S, the idea of "number" of elements no longer suffices. An important fact, discovered by Cantor, is that not all infinite sets have the same cardinality. The two most important "grades" of infinite set can be illustrated as follows.

If S is equipotent to the set of natural numbers

{1,2,3,...}

then S is said to have cardinality $\aleph_0$ (a symbol called *aleph null*).

If S is equipotent to the set of real numbers then S is said to have cardinality $\mathbf{C}$, or cardinality of the *continuum*. It can be shown that in some sense

$$\mathbf{C} = 2^{\aleph_0}$$

since the real numbers can be put in bijective correspondence with the set of all subsets of natural numbers.

card punch An obsolete machine formerly used to punch a pattern of holes in a *punched card. The pattern had a coded relationship to the data passed to the machine from another data-processing machine or an operator at a keyboard.

card reader A machine that senses the data encoded on a card and translates it into binary code that can be transmitted for further processing (*see also* magnetic card, smart card, punched card).

The *magnetic card* (or *magnetic stripe*) *reader* can have a power-driven transport that will draw the card into the machine and move it past the read head. In some designs there are cleaning brushes before the read head. The direction of travel is reversed after the card has been read and thus the card is returned to the operator. In designs used with automatic cash dispensers, the direction of travel may not reverse if the card and/or the associated identification number are not valid.

A *slot reader* is a relatively simple device for reading badges or plastic cards. The badge or card is manually moved along a slot that guides it past a sensing station. The data to be read may be encoded magnetically or printed in *bar code or a machine-readable font. Since the rate of movement past the read head is not controlled by the device, the sensing head and electronics are generally designed to work over a range of speeds. Compared to a reader with a powered transport the device is much cheaper and quicker. Some designs for use with bank teller terminals can read the printed encoding on checks and the magnetic encoding on plastic cards.

The *smart card reader* has a guide and a connector that engages contacts on the card.

When the machine senses that the card is in place and the related code has been keyed in, the memory device embedded in the card can be read.

carriage return (CR) A control code that is used in the formatting of printed or displayed output. It indicates that the next data character is to appear in the leftmost position on a line. In some serial printers, the CR code may cause a physical movement of the printing carriage to the leftmost print position. In other types of printer the characters will be correctly positioned on the line although they may be printed in some other sequence or even simultaneously. Some operating systems use CR to terminate a line of input and often an implied *line feed is added.

carrier 1. *See* modulation.
2. of an algebra. *See* signature.

carry lookahead A method that is used in multibit *parallel adders whereby the carry into an individual element of the adder can be predicted with a smaller delay than that required for the carry to be produced by rippling through previous adder stages as a result of adding the less significant addend and augend bits. Logic to achieve this examines, in parallel, each pair of addend and augend bits and infers whether carries generated in previous stages will be propagated to the carry input of each adder stage.

Carry lookahead affords a considerable improvement in performance over, say, ripple-carry adders since the carry is generated in parallel at all stages of addition rather than sequentially, as in the ripple adder. Adders using the lookahead technique are thus often described as high-speed adders.

Cartesian product of two *sets S and T. The set of all *ordered pairs of the form (s,t) with the property that s is a member of S and t is a member of T; this is usually written as $S \times T$. Formally,

$$S \times T = \{(s,t) \,|\, (s \in S) \text{ and } (t \in T)\}$$

If R denotes the set of real numbers, then $R \times R$ is just the set of points in the (Cartesian) plane or it can be regarded as the set of complex numbers, hence the name.

The concept can be extended to deal with the Cartesian product of n sets,

$$S_1, S_2, \ldots, S_n$$

This is the set of ordered n-tuples

$$(s_1, s_2, \ldots, s_n)$$

with the property that each s_i is in S_i. In the case where each S_i is the same set S, it is customary to write S^n for

$$S \times S \times \ldots S \ (n \text{ terms})$$

Cartesian structure Any data structure where the number of elements is fixed and linearly ordered. The term is sometimes used as a synonym for *record.

cartridge A container used to protect and facilitate the use of various computer-related media such as *magnetic tape, *magnetic disk, *optical disk, integrated circuitry, or printer ink *ribbon. It is usually designed so that the medium remains permanently within the cartridge or at least attached to it, and the medium itself is not touched by an operator. *See* magnetic tape cartridge, disk cartridge, ROM cartridge, caddy.

cartridge drive Either a tape transport for handling cartridge tape, or a disk drive for handling disk cartridges.

cartridge font *See* font cartridge.

cartridge tape Tape carried in a *magnetic tape cartridge.

cascadable counter An individual counter element, usually containing a number of *flip-flops in a chain of such elements. Each element has facilities for a count input and is capable of generating an overflow (or carry) output. The counter elements may typically have count lengths of integer powers of 2 (binary counters) or integer powers of 10 (decimal counters). Cascading a counter that has a count length of 4 with one having a count length of 10 will give a counter that has a count length of 40.

Since cascadable counters are available as integrated-circuit blocks or modules, cascadable counters are also called *modular counters*. *See also* counter.

cascade A configuration in which the output of one electronic device drives the input of another.

cascaded windows *See* tile.

CASE *Acronym for* computer-assisted software engineering. A marketing term, used to describe the use of *software tools to support *software engineering. There are two distinct classes of CASE, referred to as *lower* CASE and *upper* CASE. Lower CASE generally supports the programming aspects of the development life cycle and here the term is synonymous with programming support environment (*PSE). Upper CASE is used to describe tools that support methods used earlier in the life cycle to elicit or record user requirements, software (or system) requirements, and design.

case-based reasoning A technique from *artificial intelligence that attempts to solve new problems by using past experience. The main task involves matching problem details against a library of previous cases. The cases are stored together with solutions so that when the nearest case is located the corresponding solution can be adjusted to suit the current problem. There are many different approaches to the design of the matching process, the storage of the cases, and methods for modifying the retrieved solution to fit the current problem.

case grammar A theory of grammar, originally devised by Charles Filmore within the general orientation of *generative grammar, that regards *deep cases as the grammatical primitives in terms of which sentences are constructed.

case-sensitive Requiring or making a distinction between upper- and lower-case letters. In any situation where a computer program is reading characters, a decision has to be made whether to treat upper- and lower-case letters the same or differently. In some cases, such as *word processor or *text editor input, case must be preserved, while when performing an alphabetic sort, case might be ignored. In some areas there is no consensus; for example, *UNIX commands are case-sensitive whereas *MS-DOS commands are not.

case statement A conditional *control structure that appears in most modern programming languages and allows a selection to be made between several sets of program statements; the choice is dependent on the value of some expression. The case statement is a more general structure than the *if then else statement, which allows a choice between only two sets of statements.

cassette *Nominally another name for* cartridge; in practice the term is normally reserved for the type of cassette originally introduced by Philips for audio purposes under the trademark *Compact Cassette*. For computer use, more robust drives and higher precision cassettes are available.

The digital audio tape cartridge is sometimes referred to as a cassette.

CAT *Abbrev. for* computer-aided testing.

CAT-3 *Short for* category-3. One of two sets of standards, the other being *CAT-5* (category-5), that together govern the details of the *twisted-pair cabling, and the cabling installation, for cables intended to carry data at multimegabit rates over distances of the order of a hundred metres. As a guide, CAT-3 cabling supports up to 10 Mbps, CAT-5 cabling supports up to 100 Mbps.

CAT-5 *See* CAT-3.

catastrophic code A *convolutional code that is prone to *catastrophic error propagation*, i.e. a situation in which a finite number of *channel errors causes an infinite number of decoder errors. Any given convolutional code is or is not a catastrophic code.

catastrophic error propagation *See* catastrophic code.

category A collection of *objects* A, together with a related set of *morphisms* M. An object is a generalization of a *set and a morphism is a generalization of a *function that maps between sets.

The set M is the *disjoint *union of sets of the form [A,B], where A and B are elements of A; if α is a member of [A,B], A is the *domain* of α, B is the *codomain* of α, and α is said to be a morphism from A to B. For each triple (A,B,C) of elements of A there is a *dyadic operation ∘ from the *Cartesian product

$$[B,C] \times [A,B]$$

to [A,C]. The image β∘α of the ordered pair (β,α) is the *composition* of β with α; the composition operation is *associative. In addi-

tion, when the composition is defined there is an *identity* morphism for each A in A.

Examples of categories include the set of *groups and *homomorphisms on groups, and the set of *rings and homomorphisms on rings. *See* functor.

cathode-ray tube (CRT) A display device in which a beam of electrons (cathode rays), emitted by an electron gun, is focused and deflected to a series of specific positions on the phosphor-coated screen of the display. The image is generated as the electron beam moves over the screen (*see also* raster-scan display, vector display, beam deflection). Electrons striking a spot of phosphor on the screen increase the phosphor's energy state so that it becomes excited. The excited phosphor emits light as it returns to its ground state, thus creating a small area of the image. As the light is only emitted for a short period, it is necessary to provide some mechanism for continually redrawing, or *refreshing, the display if a constant image is required. Different phosphors emit different colored light. By coating the screen with small areas of red, green, and blue phosphors and having three electron guns, it is possible to produce a color display (*see also* RGB color model, shadow-mask cathode-ray tube).

The CRT is the most widely used computer display device, with at least 200 million in use worldwide. It is also used in TV sets (whose numbers are not included in the above figure).

Catmull–Clark surfaces A class of recursively generated *B-spline surfaces on arbitrary topological meshes that converge to a surface.

causal reasoning A form of reasoning that is used in *artificial intelligence and is based on a causal model of the problem. A causal model attempts to represent the underlying principles in the domain or device being modeled and frequently takes the form of rules, which express causes (actions or events) and their effects.

caustic In optics, light focused by reflection from or refraction through a curved object. For example, when a magnifying glass is used to burn a piece of paper, the intense point of focused light at the paper's surface forms a caustic. *Ray-tracing algorithms in computer graphics typically have difficulty correctly detecting and handling this phenomenon. An example might be the form of the sunlight on the bottom of a swimming pool when there are ripples on the surface of the water that focus the light into caustics.

CAV *Abbrev. for* constant angular velocity. A mode of operation used for magnetic disks and some optical disks in which the disk is rotated at a steady speed. *Compare* CLV, MCAV, MCLV.

	right operand			
○	1	−1	*i*	−*i*
1	1	−1	*i*	−*i*
−1	−1	1	−*i*	*i*
i	*i*	−*i*	−1	1
−*i*	−*i*	*i*	1	−1

left operand (for rows 1, −1, *i*, −*i*)

Cayley table

Cayley table (composition table; operation table) A tabular means of describing a finite *group, first used by the 19th-century mathematician Arthur Cayley. To illustrate, the set

$$\{1,-1,i,-i\}$$

forms a group under the *dyadic operation ○ as described by the Cayley table shown in the diagram. The value of −1○*i*, for example, is −*i*. The name composition table is usually used when the group operation is *composition of functions.

CBC *Abbrev. for* Cipher Block Chaining. *See* Data Encryption Standard.

CBL *Abbrev. for* computer-based learning. *See* computer-assisted learning.

CBR *Abbrev. for* constant bit rate.

CBT *Abbrev. for* computer-based training.

CCD *Abbrev. for* charge-coupled device. A semiconductor device that has the structure of a *MOSFET with an extremely long channel and many gates, perhaps 1000, closely spaced between the source and drain electrodes. A MOS capacitor is formed between each gate and the substrate; since this capacitor is capable of storing a charge, CCDs can be used as memory devices. The CCD essentially acts as a long (high-density) *shift register since, by manipulating the voltages applied to the gates, charge can be transferred from one MOS capacitor to its neighbor, and so on along the channel.

The physical structure of the device and the way in which the gate voltages are manipulated determines the number of gates needed to store one bit of information, typically two or three gates being required. Since the stored charge leaks away, CCDs must be continuously clocked, typically at a frequency of one megahertz. CCD memories are particularly suited to applications where memory contents are accessed in a serial manner, as in *refresh memories for CRT terminals. They are slower than comparable RAMs but faster than magnetic backing store.

CCDs are also manufactured in arrays and as they are sensitive to light they are widely used in video cameras, where they replace the vidicon tube used previously, and in other sensing applications. Both monochrome and color arrays are available.

CCITT Comité Consultatif Internationale de Télégraphique et Téléphonique (International Telegraph and Telephone Consultative Committee), an agency of the International Telecommunications Union (ITU), itself an agency of the UN. The CCITT acts as a worldwide coordinating agency for telephone and data communications systems, dealing with regulatory matters and with technical standards. The voting members of the CCITT include the national telecommunications administrations such as the *FCC and the *PTTs in Europe, and recognized private administrations such as AT&T and BT. Nonvoting members include scientific and industrial organizations and standards bodies such as ISO.

The CCITT produces definitive versions of the standards to be used in both national and international telecommunications. CCITT standards are categorized by an initial letter, which indicates the broad topic area for the material, and a decimal number, which identifies the particular standard.

Standards specifically relating to data transmission have the letter V (over analog circuits (*see* V)) or X (over digital circuits (*see* X)); standards relating to *ISDN have the letter I while standards for monitoring and controlling communications systems have the letter M. Where there have been major revisions of standards that have been in use for some time, the number will be followed by either *bis* or *ter*, indicating a second or third version of the standard.

CCS *Abbrev. for* calculus of communicating systems. A mathematical treatment of the general theory of *concurrency and *synchronization derived by R. J. Milner. *See also* process calculus.

CCTA The Government Centre for Information Systems (originally the Central Computing and Telecommunications Agency), part of the UK government's Office of Public Service and Science (OPSS).

CDC Control Data Corporation, a long-established US manufacturer of mainframes intended primarily for scientific and engineering applications. It has lost ground in recent years but is still a force in the supercomputer field. Ranked nine in terms of revenue among the world's mainframe suppliers, its revenue from this source is less than 1% of that of IBM, the largest company in the sector (1993 figures).

CD-DA (or **CD-A)** *See* CD-ROM format standards.

CDDI *Abbrev. for* copper distributed data interface. A high-speed network system that uses the same protocols and signaling conventions as FDDI, but is designed to operate over *CAT-5 twisted-pair cabling rather than an optical fiber. *See* fiber distributed data interface.

CD-I CD interactive, a CD-ROM format that allows the interleaving of data, sound, and images on the same disk. *See also* CD-ROM format standards.

CDIF *Abbrev. for* CASE data interchange format. A format for encoding data gathered by *CASE tools so that the data can be moved from one CASE tool to another. Work is progressing on the definition of an international standard definition for CDIF.

CDOS (concurrent DOS) A version of *DOS that supports multitasking, allowing a user to initiate several applications that run together.

CD-PROM A *rewritable optical disk designed to be readable by systems that can read CD-ROM disks. A specific commercial implementation is *CD-THOR. *See also* CD-ROM format standards, PROM.

CDR The *LISP function that when applied to a list yields the *tail of the list. The word was originally an acronym for contents of decrement register. *Compare* CAR.

CD-R CD-recordable, a *write-once optical-disk format designed to be readable by systems that can read CD-ROM disks. *See also* CD-ROM format standards.

CD-ROM CD read-only memory, a means of providing read-only access to a large amount of data for use on computer systems; the term applies to the medium in general and to a particular instance. Based on the 120 mm diameter audio CD, CD-ROMs are the predominant form of *optical disk.

A *CD-ROM drive* must be used with the computer system to read the information from disk. Most drives can also play CD audio disks, but audio disk players cannot handle CD-ROMs. A standard CD-ROM, like the standard audio CD, is capable of holding about 640 Mbytes of data. The first CD-ROM drives moved the disk at the same speed as the audio product, both using *CLV, and had a much lower rate – about 180 Kbytes per second – than hard magnetic disks (although higher than floppy disks). Double-speed and quad-speed drives are now the norm, with a proportionate increase in the data rate; most can also run at the standard speed.

The data on CD-ROMs is encoded in the form of a spiral of minute pits impressed into one surface of the disk at the time of manufacture, and cannot normally be rewritten (*but see* CD-R, CD-PROM). The data may be in any form – text, sound, static or video images, or binary data, or a mixture (*see* multimedia); various *CD-ROM format standards exist to handle these.

CD-ROM is widely used for the distribution of data, images, and software. Many commercial databases and indexes are available on CD-ROM, often as an alternative to an online service. CD-ROM is also being used increasingly, especially in personal computing, as an alternative to multiple floppy disks for the distribution of software, clip art, and fonts. For situations where frequent access to several different CD-ROMs is needed, automatic disk changers (*autochangers) or CD-ROM *jukeboxes are available.

CD-ROM was first announced in 1983, but did not become a mass-market medium until the mid-1990s. Newer technology has been developed that would allow a disk of the current size to have much better capacity and performance, but the investment in drives to suit the present format probably ensures the dominance of this read-only format for some time. A drawback of the format is that the drive will not fit the 3½ inch footprint that is now standard for personal computer disk drives. A smaller disk of similar capacity (based on a consumer product) is available but is as yet little used.

CD-ROM drive (CD-ROM transport) *See* CD-ROM.

CD-ROM format standards The *formats of *CD-ROMs are defined by standards. They can be divided into two groups: firstly the basic standards, now followed by nearly every CD-ROM disk, which define how data files are recorded on disk regardless of what kind of data is contained in the files; secondly, more specialized standards for the handling of data of various types, such as sound, image, or text, or a mixture of these (*multimedia). The standards in the first group are intended to apply to all hardware and software configurations that handle CD-ROM disks. The remaining standards may need more specific configurations.

There are three standards in the first group. The first is a proprietary standard known as the "Red Book" (formerly *CD-DA*), which defines those features that are common to CD-Audio and CD-ROM. It includes a measure of error correction that is adequate for audio disks. The second standard, the international standard ISO 10149, defines the additional features (including more powerful error correction) needed to allow data to be held on the disk, i.e. for recording on CD-ROM; it supersedes the proprietary "Yellow Book" standard. The third standard, ISO 9660 (developed from the earlier *High Sierra* standard), defines how a data file is represented on the disk in such a way that it can be accessed by different operating systems.

The second group of format standards is more diverse. An important subgroup, including *DVI (digital video interactive) and *CDTV*, is concerned with providing TV-quality video (i.e. moving images). Because of the low data transfer rate of CD-ROM drives, this involves powerful *data compression, which can also be used for still images; however, video and still *bitmapped images do not normally require the additional error correction that is needed for digital data.

The *CD-I* format is defined by the proprietary standard known as the "Green Book". This sets down a method of interleaving text, sound, images, and a limited form of video on the same CD-ROM disk, but is aimed at interactive domestic CD players rather than computers. The Green Book defines not only the disk format but also the hardware to support it. *CD-ROM XA* is a standard similar to CD-I but is aimed at personal computers.

The *CD-R* format is regulated by the proprietary standard known as the "Orange Book". This defines a recordable (*write-once) disk that is closely compatible with CD-ROM; systems that can read CD-ROM disks can also read the CD-R format. Systems designed to read recordable disks must be *multisession compatible* if the disk is written in several separate sessions rather than recorded in one session (i.e. at one time, with a single table of contents); most modern systems (and all that support CD-ROM XA) comply. *Photo-CD is a proprietary format for the recording of scanned color photographs on CD-R disks.

Two less frequently used format standards are *CD-V*, which allows a suitable player to read both CD-ROM and *videodisk, and

CD+G, which allows an audio CD to carry a few graphic images; both are intended for consumer products rather than computers. Other formats are likely to emerge in the future.

As the Red Book standard is common to all CD disks, most CD-ROM drives can play standard audio CD disks on which sound is recorded in the simple Red Book format and not interleaved with data or images.

CD-ROM library (CD-ROM jukebox (*informal*)) *See* optical disk library.

CD-ROM XA *See* CD-ROM format standards.

CD-THOR *Trademark* A *rewritable optical-disk format based on *dye-polymer media, designed to be readable by systems that can read CD-ROM disks. It is thus a form of *CD-PROM. *See also* CD-ROM format standards.

CDTV *See* CD-ROM format standards.

ceiling If x is a real number, then ceiling(x), also written as $\lceil x \rceil$, is the smallest integer greater than or equal to x.

cel *Short for* celluloid transparency, used in traditional animation to superimpose one object relative to another.

cell 1. An address, a location in memory, or a register, usually one capable of holding a binary number. It is sometimes a location capable of holding one bit.
2. The basic unit of a *spreadsheet or some other table of text, formed by the intersection of a row and column. It contains a label, value, or formula with attributes such as size, font, and color.
3. The name given to a *packet in one version of a packet switching system. Packet switching systems subdivide the data to be transmitted into a number of packets. In contrast to many systems, a cell is short – for instance 53 bytes in the case of an *ATM cell – and its internal structure is fixed. Small size and fixed structure allow the cell to be switched using a very simple algorithm; the processing time required for switching is thus reduced, with a corresponding increase in the number of cells switched in a given time.

cellar *Another name for* stack, rarely used.

cell array A computer-graphics output primi-

tive defined by a rectangular grid of equal-size rectangular cells each having a single color.

Cello A utility that allows a user at a networked workstation to access information on the *World Wide Web. *See also* Mosaic.

cell relay A form of switching in which the individual packets, or *cells, have a fixed length and a fixed internal structure; in many cases the cells are also deliberately kept to a small size, typically a few tens of bytes. Once the initial decision on cell routing has been made, typically at the time of creating a *virtual circuit, it is possible to realize the actual switching activity almost entirely in table-driven hardware, rather than invoking a software implementation, allowing very short switching times. The large number of cells into which even a short message is subdivided increases the ratio of overheads to useful payload. *See also* ATM, frame relay.

cellular automata machine (CAM) A *multiprocessor machine based on an array of *cellular automata*. Each automaton is usually a simple processor capable of simple computational tasks. In a normal architecture, each of these processing nodes can interchange data only with its immediate neighbors and all processing nodes carry out the same computational operation. Although the operations available at each node are quite simple, the aggregated effect of many such nodes can exhibit complex behavior and can rapidly model quite complex dynamic systems.

CEN/CENELEC European Committee for Standardization (CEN) and European Committee for Electrotechnical Standardization (CENELEC), voluntary associations of *ISO/*IEC members that in effect represent federations of all the national standards-making institutes of the European Union. CEN/CENELEC aims to harmonize members' national standards and adopt new European standards, including those for computing.

centralized structure store (CSS) The conceptual workstation–independent storage area for structure networks in *PHIGS.

central processor (CPU; central processing unit) The principal operating part of a computer. It is usually defined as the *ALU (arithmetic and logic unit) and the *control unit (CU). It must be joined to a *primary memory to form the processor-memory pair of the basic *von Neumann machine.

Centronics interface A de facto standard plug-compatible *parallel interface for printers, first used in printers manufactured by Centronics Corp.

CEPIS Council of European Professional Informatics Societies.

CERT *Acronym for* computer emergency response team.

certainty factor A device used in *rule-based systems to assign weight to facts or pieces of knowledge. The weights express the perceived certainty of a fact being true: usually –1 indicates certainly false, +1 indicates definitely true, and intermediate values represent varying degrees of certainty, with 0 meaning unknown. The medical *expert system MYCIN used uncertainty factors, with conjunctions of rules taking the minimum value. The use of certainty factors is similar to *probabilistic reasoning but is less formally related to probability theory.

certification 1. A formal demonstration that a system or component complies with its specified requirements and is acceptable for operational use.
2. A written guarantee to this effect.
See also quality management system, conformance testing.

CFB *Abbrev. for* Cipher Feedback. *See* Data Encryption Standard.

CFF *Abbrev. for* critical flicker frequency. The *refresh frequency of a displayed image at which *flicker is perceived by the operator. It depends upon the brightness of the display, the angle subtended at the eye, and on the persistence of the phosphor. This frequency varies between individuals, but for typical cathode-ray tubes flicker is generally accepted as being perceptible to less than 5% of users when the CFF exceeds 80 hertz.

CGA *Abbrev. for* color graphics adapter. A general-purpose *graphics adapter formerly used in IBM-compatible PCs but now superseded. It could generate a 320 × 200 four-color screen and a 640 × 200 two-color screen.

CGI *Abbrev. for* computer graphics interface – the ISO/IEC 9636 standard, Interfacing Techniques for Dialogues with Graphical Devices. A device-independent interface standard between a graphical input or output device and a graphics utility program (*see* graphical device interface). The initial (ANSI) name of the interface was *VDI* (*abbrev. for* virtual device interface).

CGM *Abbrev. for* computer graphics metafile – the ISO 8632 standard, Metafile for the Storage and Transfer of Picture Description Information. A standardized file format for transmission and storage of two-dimensional pictures. It is widely used in the computer industry for exchanging information between different systems and for transmitting graphical information to a remote printer.

chad The pieces of material that are removed when holes are punched in a data medium, such as those produced from the tractor holes in continuous form paper.

chain 1. A *singly linked linear *list.
2. *See* directed set.

chain code 1. A method of describing contours by a succession (chain) of symbols representing a discrete set of directional vectors. It is used in computer graphics and pattern recognition for description of line drawings (including characters).
2. *Another name* (*chiefly UK*) *for* simplex code.

chained file A file that uses *data chaining.

chained list *Another name for* linked list.

chaining 1. An extension of *pipelining in which the results of the operations are used in the operations that follow within the next clock cycle. The delay associated with the storing and subsequent reaccess of a result for the next operation is bypassed.
2. *Short for* data chaining.

chaining search A search in which each item contains the means for locating the next.

chain printer An obsolete type of *solid-font

*line printer in which the font was etched or engraved on small plates linked together to form a chain. The chain was connected around two sprocket wheels so that the straight part of the chain between the wheels ran parallel to the paper and spanned the line to be printed. This was one of the first types of computer printer to use the *hit-on-the-fly* principle, developed in the mid-1950s: the chain carrying the type font moved continuously at high speed relative to the paper, and the characters were printed by briefly impacting the paper and an inked ribbon against the moving type font. The chain printer was superseded by the *train printer.

change dump (differential dump) An output, usually printed, that lists the content of all memory locations that have changed subsequent to a defined event. This is usually the result of a routine that is written and used as an aid to debugging a program.

channel 1. A specialized processor that comprises an information route and associated circuitry to control input and/or output operations. It normally provides for formatting and buffering and has the necessary control to meet the timing requirements of an I/O device. In an interface that has a number of parallel channels, each is usually separately dedicated to the passing of a single type of information such as data.

Several different I/O devices may be connected to one channel and the control circuitry within the channel directs the data streams to or from the appropriate device. If the I/O devices have a relatively slow data rate, e.g. line printers, displays, document readers, then a *multiplexer channel* is used to connect them to the processor. The transfers to or from the separate devices are multiplexed, i.e. interleaved, character by character, such that several devices can work simultaneously.

When a number of devices with high data rates, e.g. magnetic disk and tape, are to be connected, a *selector channel* is used. This will transfer a complete record to or from a device before reselecting. Usually the selection of a device remains stable for the passage of more than one record. While the selector channel

is dealing with one device, the other devices connected to it cannot transfer information but they may still be active, e.g. in a search or rewind mode.

A channel is often a *wired-program processor. As channels have become more elaborate they have tended to become programmed computers (*I/O processors*) in themselves. *See also* peripheral processor.

2. (transmission channel; communication channel) An information route in data transmission. *See also* Shannon's model.

3. A link (physical or virtual) to a *host computer in a communication network.

channel capacity *See* channel coding theorem.

channel coding The use of *error-detecting or *error-correcting codes in order to achieve reliable communication through a transmission *channel. In channel coding, the particular *code to be used is chosen to match the channel (and especially its *noise characteristics), rather than the source of the information. *See* channel coding theorem, Shannon's model. *Compare* source coding.

channel coding theorem In *communication theory, the statement that any channel, however affected by *noise, possesses a specific *channel capacity* – a rate of conveying *information that can never be exceeded without error, but that can, in principle, always be attained with an arbitrarily small probability of error. The theorem was first expounded and proved by Claude Elwood Shannon in 1948.

Shannon showed that an *error-correcting code always exists that will reduce the probability of error below any predetermined level. He did not, however, show how to construct such a code (this remains the central problem of *coding theory), although he did show that randomly chosen codes are as good as any others, provided they are extremely long.

Among Shannon's results for specific channels, the most celebrated is that for a *power-limited continuous-amplitude channel subject to *white *Gaussian noise. If the signal power is limited to P_S and the noise power is P_N, the capacity of such a channel is

$$C = \tfrac{1}{2}\nu \log_2(1 + P_S/P_N) \text{ bit/s}$$

If it is a discrete-time channel, ν is the number of *epochs per second; if it is a continuous-time channel, ν is the minimum number of samples per second necessary to acquire all the information from the channel. In the latter case, if ν is to be finite, the channel must be *band-limited; if W is its *bandwidth (in Hz), then, by *Nyquist's criterion,

$$C = W \log_2(1 + P_S/P_N) \text{ bit/s}$$

This is sometimes called the *Shannon–Hartley law*, and is often applied, erroneously, in circumstances less restricted than those described. This and other expressions for the capacity of specific channels should not be confused with the channel coding theorem, which states only that there is a finite capacity (which may be zero) and that it can be attained without error.

See also Shannon's model, source coding theorem.

channel controller The control unit for an I/O *channel. *See also* I/O processor.

channel error An error, in a signal arriving at the *decoder in a communication system, whose occurrence is due to *noise in the channel. By contrast, a *decoder error* is an unsuccessful attempt by the decoder (of an *error-correcting code) to correct a channel error.

channel switching 1. A means of communicating on or switching between several different communication channels.
2. *Another name for* circuit switching.

channel time response *See* convolution.

chaos The phenomena of apparently random behavior generated by simple deterministic systems. An essential hallmark of chaos in nonlinear systems is the extreme sensitivity of the system to initial conditions.

character 1. An element of a given *character set.
2. A subdivision of a *word in a machine, usually comprising 6, 7, or 8 bits. This is sometimes called a *byte*.
3. The smallest unit of information in a *record.

character cell *See* text mode.

character encoding An encoding, normally a *binary encoding, of a given *character set. Examples include ASCII and EBCDIC.

characteristic (biased exponent) *See* floating-point notation.

characteristic function of a *subset S of a *universal set U. A *function that indicates whether or not an element is a member of the subset S. It is the function

$$f: U \to \{0,1\}$$

defined as follows:

$$f(x) = 1 \quad \text{if } x \in S$$
$$f(x) = 0 \quad \text{if } x \notin S$$

The codomain might also be given as {true,false} or {1,2}.

characteristic vector 1. A *vector of bits representing a set in a finite universe. If the universe has n elements $a_1, a_2, ..., a_n$ then any set, A, can be represented by a vector of n bits where the ith bit is 1 if and only if $a_i \in A$.
2. *English form of* eigenvector. *See* eigenvalue.

character machine *See* variable word length computer.

character mode *Another name for* text mode.

character recognition A process in which a machine senses and encodes printed characters that are also readable by a person. The characters may be printed using a special magnetic ink and/or a special style of character, but modern machines can read good-quality typewritten or equivalent standard of print, in a variety of type fonts. *See* MICR, OCR, ICR.

character representation A representation of a character as a distinctive bit string that is defined by some *character encoding.

character set The set of characters that is handled by a specified machine or allowed by a given programming language or protocol. The set usually includes the *alphanumeric characters, special characters, and operation characters (*see* table), all of which are *graphic characters*, and various *control characters. Graphic characters thus denote a printed mark or a space while control characters produce some particular effect.

Two of the widest used character sets are *ASCII (American standard code for information interchange) and *EBCDIC (extended binary coded decimal interchange code).

special characters	operation characters
space	+ −
, ; : . ? !	* /
( ) [ ] { }	> = <
$ % # & @ ~	
| \ ' ' ↑ →	

Character set

EBCDIC is used primarily on IBM machines while ASCII, introduced in 1963, is in more general use. International 8-bit character sets are defined in ISO 8859, which covers Latin-based languages, Cyrillic, Arabic, Greek, and Hebrew. *See also* Latin alphabet.

character string A *string of elements from a given *character set.

character type (type character) A *data type whose members can take the values of specified *characters and can be operated on by character operations, such as *concatenation. *See also* ASCII.

charge-coupled device *See* CCD.

chassis In general, a mechanical system that is designed to provide a supporting and/or enclosing medium for an item of electronic equipment. The system may be equipped with supporting structures to carry standard-sized *circuit boards in addition to a *motherboard or *backplane into which the boards are inserted and connected via sockets. Alternatively the individual components may be hardwired onto tag strips attached to the chassis.

For safety reasons the metal parts of a chassis should be permanently connected to a local zero-voltage reference or ground. In some equipment, however, it is more convenient (but potentially dangerous) to connect the chassis to one side of the a.c. or d.c. line (mains) supply; the equipment is then said to have a *hot chassis*. The chassis may also be left unconnected or floating.

CHDL *Abbrev. for* computer hardware description language. A formal language with a lexicon that enables the nomination of the individual logical or physical elements of a computer. It has a syntax to enable a description of the way such elements are interconnected and the way they behave to provide the structure that is capable of performing a computation. The behavior of these elements is described as the sequence in which they change their state to enable the structure to perform the function. CHDLs in use include *VHDL. *See also* register transfer language, ISP, CONLAN.

Chebyshev approximation, norm *See* approximation theory.

check Some means or process of validating the accuracy of a segment of data, the result of a computation, or completion of a successful message transmission (across a network or to an I/O device).

check box A small square in a *dialogue box with an option given alongside, allowing the option to be *selected or cleared. With multiple check boxes, as many options as needed may be selected.

check character A character, or more generally some element of specified size ranging from a single bit to a few bytes, that contains the result of a check computation performed on a segment of data.

check digit *Another name for* check character.

checkers-playing programs The game of checkers (*draughts* in the UK) has been automated up to a very high level of performance, as with chess-playing programs (*see* computer chess). The classic work of Arthur Samuel still provides inspiration and many important game-playing techniques can be found in his work.

checking program A program that examines other programs or data for certain classes of error, usually relatively straightforward ones such as syntax errors in the source text of a program.

checkout 1. All activities concerned with bringing a program to the state where it produces some results (as distinct from, say, failing to compile or terminating abnormally) so that *testing can begin. Such activities might include *desk checking*, i.e. checking by human inspection, and use of a special "checkout" mode of compilation and execution that provides extensive information on erroneous use of the programming language or abnormal program termination.

2. The action of taking a configuration item from a repository prior to making changes to it. The act of removal usually locks the item so that nobody else may check it out until it has been formally returned.

checkpoint A point in a process or job at which a *dump check is taken (and hence also referred to as a *dump point*), and the point from which a subsequent *restart will be effective.

checksum (modulo-n check, residue check) A simple error detection method that operates on some set of information (usually data or program). If this information is in units that are *m* bits wide, a sum is taken modulo *n*, where $n = 2^m$, and appended to the information. At a later time or different location the check may be recomputed and most simple (all single) bit errors will be detected. A *parity check is the simplest version of this check with $m = 1$ and $n = 2$.

chief programmer team A programming team in which responsibility for program design and implementation rests entirely with one highly skilled member, the *chief programmer*. The other team members provide various forms of support. A typical team could consist of the chief programmer, a backup programmer, librarian, administrator, and secretary: the backup programmer assists the chief programmer and is able to take over that role if necessary; the librarian maintains all technical documents on the project, such as design documents, source modules (in all versions), and test histories; the administrator relieves the chief programmer of all administrative duties on the project. Various other services might be obtained from outside the team as needed.

This team organization has been advocated for the production of large programs: a single highly skilled programmer, when properly supported, can produce programs more quickly and more reliably than a team of less talented programmers working as

equals. In particular, the problem of communication within the team is minimized.

The approach was pioneered in the early 1970s by the Federal Systems Division of IBM, particularly by Harlan D. Mills. Successful results have been reported from various projects, including some that produced more than 100 000 lines of source code.

child Any node in a *tree, except the root. Every child thus has a *parent.

CHILL *Acronym for* CCITT high-level language. A programming language developed by *CCITT and adopted as the standard language for the programming of computer-based telecommunication systems and computer-controlled telephone exchanges. CHILL is a *real-time language, bearing a substantial resemblance to *Ada.

Chinese remainder theorem Let
$$m_1, m_2, \ldots, m_r$$
be positive integers that are relatively prime to one another, and let their product be *m*:
$$m = m_1 m_2 \ldots m_r$$
Let $n, u_1, u_2, \ldots, u_r$ be integers; then there is exactly one integer, *u*, that satisfies
$$n \le u < (m + n)$$
and
$$u \equiv u_j \text{ (modulo } m_j) \text{ for } 1 \le j \le r$$

chip 1. A small section of a single crystal of *semiconductor, usually silicon, that forms the substrate upon which is fabricated a single semiconductor device or all the individual devices comprising an *integrated circuit.

2. *Informal name for* integrated circuit.

chip card *Former name for* smart card.

chip set A set of integrated circuits that when connected together form a single functional block within an electronic system.

chip socket A device that allows easy replacement of chips (*integrated circuits) on a *printed circuit board. The chip socket is soldered to the circuit board; the chip is pushed into the socket, which has a small hole for each of the chip's legs. With larger chips care is needed to avoid bending the legs of the chip on insertion.

chi-squared distribution An important *probability distribution with many uses in *statistical analysis. Denoted by the Greek symbol χ^2, it is the distribution of the sum of squares of f independent *random variables, each being drawn from the *normal distribution with zero mean and unit variance. The integer f is the number of *degrees of freedom. Critical values of the probability distribution are widely available in tables, but exact calculations involve the incomplete gamma function. The most common applications are

    (a) testing for interactions between different classifications of data using *contingency tables;

    (b) testing *goodness-of-fit;

    (c) forming *confidence intervals for estimates of *variance.

choice A type of input to a graphics system that provides a choice between a small number of possibilities. Choice devices are *logical input devices and are most likely to be implemented by menus.

Cholesky decomposition *See* LU decomposition.

Type	Grammar	Automaton
0	arbitrary	Turing machine
1	context-sensitive	linear-bounded
2	context-free	pushdown
3	regular	finite-state

Chomsky hierarchy

Chomsky hierarchy A series of four classes of *formal languages whose definition in 1959 by Noam Chomsky marked the beginning of formal language theory, and that have ever since remained central to the subject. In increasing complexity they are called *type 3*, *type 2*, *type 1*, and *type 0*, each one a subclass of the next. Each type can be defined either by a class of *grammars or by a class of *automata, as indicated in the table. Type 0 consists of all *recursively enumerable languages. Type 1 is a subclass of the languages recognizable by *primitive recursive functions. Languages in types 2 and 3 can be recognized by a *Turing machine in cubic and linear time, respectively.

Chomsky normal form A restricted type of *context-free grammar, namely one in which each production has the form

$$A \rightarrow BC \text{ or } A \rightarrow d,$$

i.e. each right-hand side consists of either two nonterminals or one terminal. Any context-free language is generated by such a grammar, except that derivation of the empty string, Λ, requires the additional production

$$S \rightarrow \Lambda$$

chromaticity The color quality of light that is defined by its dominant wavelength and purity.

chromaticity coefficient The ratio of any one of the *chromaticity values of a three-component color to the sum of the three values. *See also* color model.

chromaticity diagram A triangle where the vertices represent the specified primary colors in a *color model (no combination of two primary colors can create the third). A color is defined by a point within the triangle. The relative contribution of each primary to the color is defined by the triangular area from the point to the other two vertices.

chromatic number *See* coloring of graphs.

chunk of data. *See* RAID.

Church–Rosser (confluent) Admitting an appropriate version of the *Church–Rosser theorem. *See also* abstract reduction system.

Church–Rosser theorem A theorem, proved jointly by A. Church and J. B. Rosser, concerning Church's *lambda calculus. It states that if a lambda-expression x can be reduced in two ways leading respectively to expressions y_1 and y_2 then there must be an expression z to which both y_1 and y_2 can be reduced. The choice of ways to reduce an expression arises from the possibility of separately reducing different "parts" of the expression. The Church–Rosser theorem shows that either part can be worked on first, without the loss of any possibilities obtainable from starting with the other part. A corresponding theorem exists for combinatory logic. More generally, any language for which there is a notion of reduction for expressions within the language is said to have the *Church–Rosser property*, or to be *confluent*, if it admits an appropriate version of the Church–Rosser theorem. The property plays an important role in *term rewriting with equations.

Church's thesis The hypothesis, put forward by Alonzo Church in 1935, that any function on the natural numbers that can be computed by an algorithm can be defined by a formula of the *lambda calculus. *See also* Church–Turing thesis.

Church–Turing thesis The proposition that the set of functions on the natural numbers that can be defined by algorithms is precisely the set of functions definable in one of a number of equivalent models of computation. These models include *Post production systems, Church's *lambda calculus, *Turing machines, Kleene's mu-recursion schemes, Herbrand–Gödel equational definability, Shepherdson–Sturgis register machines, the while programming language, and flow charts. The proposition is a scientific hypothesis, subject to empirical and theoretical confirmation rather than mathematical proof. The evidence that it is true is roughly the following.

First, a large number of disparate methods (e.g. those listed above) for computing functions have been shown to be equivalent in power when computing on the natural numbers. Second, there has been a failure to find a function and a convincing method of computing it that has not been computable by one of the known models of computation. Third, philosophically distinct notions – mechanical computability, digital and analog computability, definability in a formal calculus, definability in an algorithmic language – have been investigated and interrelated. Fourth, a generalization of the theory of computable functions to an *abstract computability theory for *algebras has revealed new connections and distinctions between models, but confirmed the primary nature of the features of the computation theory on the natural numbers.

The Church–Turing thesis leads to a mathematical theory of digital computation that classifies what data can be represented, what processes simulated, and what functions computed (*see* computable algebra). It provides a scientific foundation for a discussion of the scope and limits of computable processes in the physical and biological sciences, and hence attracts the attention of philosophers, scientists, and engineers.

CICS *Acronym for* customer information control system. A *transaction processing system widely used on IBM mainframes.

CIE *Abbrev. for* Commission Internationale de l'Éclairage. The body responsible for making recommendations with regard to photometry and *colorimetry.

CIE color model A *color model developed by the *CIE and based on a standard observer whose color vision is representative of the human population having normal color vision. The first CIE color model was published in 1931. A color is specified by a triad of numbers (X, Y, Z). These *tristimulus values give the amount of each of three hypothetical supersaturated primaries in the color. The Y value gives the *luminance of the object and the primaries are chosen such that the perceptible colors are defined by positive values.

In 1964, the model was updated and based on data with a wider viewing angle and correcting the Y primary, which was found to be slightly in error. Two new specifications, *CIELAB* and *CIELUV*, were defined in 1976. The CIELAB model represents colors on subtractive media, where light is absorbed by inks, dyes, and other pigments; the CIELUV model represents colors on additive color media such as emissive phosphor displays and colored lights. The lightness scale for both is the same and is based on the cube root of luminance, which gives a linear scale.

CIELAB, CIELUV *See* CIE color model.

CIM 1. *Abbrev. for* computer-integrated manufacturing.
2. *Abbrev. for* computer input (on) microfilm, i.e. the process, or the input itself; it is not widely used. Input devices that have been produced have relied on optical character recognition (*OCR) to recode alphanumeric data on microfilm or have read special microfilm on which the data was recorded as binary code. *See also* COM.

Cineon format An image file format for storing 35 mm motion-picture images at a resolution of 4096 by 3112 with 10 bits for each color per pixel. The Walt Disney film 'Snow White and the Seven Dwarfs' was digitized and enhanced frame by frame using this process.

cipher 1. An *algorithm employed for *encryption, or, in its *inverse form, for *decryption. *See* cryptography. 2. An encrypted message.

ciphertext The result of enciphering plaintext. *See* cryptography.

CIR *Abbrev. for* current instruction register.

circuit 1. The combination of a number of electrical devices and conductors that, when interconnected to form a conducting path, fulfill some desired function. *See also* logic circuit, integrated circuit, printed circuit. 2. A physical (electrical) connection used for communication. *See also* circuit switching, virtual circuit. 3. of a graph. *Another name for* cycle.

circuit board A single rigid board of insulating material on which an electric circuit has been built. It often has an *edge connector at one end for making all the connections to other circuits so that the board may be plugged into a piece of equipment. Circuit boards come in a variety of sizes, some of which are standardized. The term *circuit card* is often used synonymously but is sometimes considered smaller than a circuit board. *See also* printed circuit, backplane.

circuit card *See* circuit board.

circuit switching A method of communications that is used in telephone systems and requires a physical transmission path – a *circuit* – to exist between the two devices wishing to communicate. The end-to-end path must exist before data can be sent. The only delay to which the data is subject is the propagation delay along the transmission medium (6 microseconds per 100 km for copper telephone lines). Since the path is reserved during the entire connection, any unused bandwidth is wasted. *Compare* message switching, packet switching, virtual circuit.

circular list A *linked list in which the last item contains a link to the first. This allows access to all of the list from any starting

point. Circular lists are most useful if the pointer to the list links to the last node, allowing easy access to both ends of the list. *See also* ring.

circular shift (end-around shift) *See* shift.

circulating register A *shift register in which quantities (data) shifted out at one end are entered into the other end. This accomplishes a *circular shift and may be performed in either direction.

CISC *Acronym for* complex instruction set computer. A conventional computer in which the *instruction set has evolved to satisfy the needs of high-level languages and system software to enable generation of compact efficient *object code, often in a time-sharing environment governed by an *operating system. *Compare* RISC.

Cix *Acronym for* computerlink information exchange. A commercial agency offering bulletin board and conferencing services as well as general access to the Internet. Cix is a member of CIX.

CIX *Acronym for* commercial Internet exchange. An organization whose members are commercial agencies that offer access to the Internet and have agreed to exchange traffic.

CKD *Abbrev. for* centre for key distribution (in *data security).

clamp An electronic circuit that is designed to return the d.c. voltage level at a given point in the circuit to a fixed reference value at fixed points in time, often in response to an externally generated clamp pulse.

class A facility introduced in the programming language *SIMULA. The class provides a form of *abstract data type. It is also the basis of the concept of *object that underlies Smalltalk and other object-oriented languages.

classifier systems Programs in *artificial intelligence that partition sets of data into different classifications on the basis of specified features in the data. Techniques from *machine learning are used when the classification structure is to be constructed by the system. *See also* decision surface, concept learning.

clear An *instruction or *microinstruction that causes a designated variable, register, or counter to be set to the all-zero state (i.e. cleared).

Clear A language for writing formal *specifications, first described by R.M. Burstall and J.A. Goguen in 1977. The language provides a formalism for expressing a complex specification hierarchically as a combination of simpler ones. This formalism can be given a precise semantics using ideas familiar from *algebra and *category theory.

CLI *Abbrev. for* command-line interface.

click To press and release a button on a *mouse or similar device, or (as a noun) the action of pressing and releasing a button. This will be interpreted by the current program as a request for some action to be performed. Most mice have one, two, or three buttons, so the prefixed forms *left click, right click, middle click* are often used. The *double click* consists of two clicks of the same button in quick succession; when performed too quickly or too slowly then the user's intention is misunderstood. To *click and drag* involves holding a button down while moving the mouse; this technique is often used first to select (click) and then to move (drag) an object on the screen.

click and drag *See* click.

client In general, someone or something receiving a service of some kind. Within computing the term frequently refers to one element of a *client/server system, typically an *application, that communicates with the end-user by means of a *server.

client/server (c/s) In general terms a client receives a service of some sort from a server. As applied to computing, the relationship between the *clients and the *servers is formalized so as to allow different aspects of a computational task to be subdivided among a server, which acts as an agent on behalf of the end-user, and a collection of clients for the service(s) offered by that server. Each client needs to bring about the completion of a set of activities that represent components of a complete computational task; the client achieves this by requesting services from the collection of servers for each separate activity. Clearly it may be necessary to complete some activities before others can be started, while it may be possible to allow some activities to be run in any order or to be run all at the same time. When a client calls on a server to perform a service, the client will indicate the service to be carried out and the details of the way in which the server should respond to the client when the service is completed. The response from the server may indicate successful conclusion, together with the value of the result, or may indicate some form of failure. The role of the client is to combine the responses from the servers, and to ensure that the separate subactivities are run in such a way as to observe any necessary constraints on the order in which they are initiated or completed.

It is not necessary for the clients and the servers to be running on the same computer system. Indeed, the use of client/server systems is especially effective where many users on a network require a range of different services, which can be best supplied by the use of a specialized hardware configuration provided at a small number of locations on the network.

Many of the ideas underlying client/server computing were first given a firm definition in the *X Windows system. *See also* interprocess communication, remote procedure call.

clip art Simple drawings held in digital form on a computer. These items are often supplied in large libraries of files that can easily be incorporated into word processor or presentation graphics documents. They are either supplied as a component of a software package, such as a word processing package, or as a separate product. The individual pictures are often line drawings of a single object, free of background material.

clipboard A temporary storage location where a section *cut or *copied from displayed textual or graphical information is held until it can be *pasted into another location. The technique can be used within a text editor or word processor session to move or copy within a given document, or in a *graphical user interface to move items between one application and another. For instance, part of a spreadsheet display could be copied into the clipboard and then inserted into a word processor document.

clipping The process in computer graphics of removing part of an object outside a specified region. Only that part within the specified region is passed on for further processing.

CLNS *Abbrev. for* connectionless network service.

clock An electronic device, generally a stable oscillator, that generates a repetitive series of pulses, known as the *clock signal*. The *pulse repetition frequency is accurately controlled.

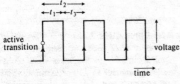

Clock signal

The *clock rate* is the frequency, expressed in *hertz, at which *active transitions* of a given clock signal occur. The active transition may be from a low to a high voltage level, or vice versa, but will always be followed after a fixed time by an opposite *inactive transition*. The clock signal is thus formed as a series of fixed-width pulses having a fixed repetition frequency (*see* diagram). The pulse width, t_1, is often 50% of the pulse repetition period, t_2, i.e. $t_1 = t_3$. The clock rate is $1/t_2$ hertz. A *clock cycle* is considered to be one complete cycle of the clock signal and will always contain one active transition of the clock. For the clock signal illustrated, a clock cycle occurs in t_2 seconds.

Because of its constant rate, a clock signal is used to initiate actions within a *sequential logic circuit and to synchronize the activities of a number of such circuits. These circuits are said to be *clocked*. The *primary* clock rate controls the fastest parts of a computer while slower components are timed by numerous submultiples of the basic frequency.

clock cycle *See* clock.

clocked flip-flop *See* flip-flop.

clocking 1. In synchronous communication networks, the use of a single time standard to control all bit transmissions and switching throughout the network. *See* synchronous transmission.
2. In modem-terminal interconnection, the use of a timing signal to indicate when data can be properly transferred between the modem and the terminal device. The signal is usually from the modem to the terminal, although in some cases it can be the reverse.

clock rate *See* clock.

clock signal *See* clock.

clock skew *See* skew.

clone A computer or other system that is claimed by its manufacturer or supplier to behave in exactly the same way as a system from another company, i.e. it will produce identical results from an identical program. A whole industry exists to produce *PC clones*, computers that behave like one of IBM's personal computer range.

CLOS An *object-oriented programming system based on *Common LISP.

close To instruct an application that a file is no longer required. When a file is closed, any changes that have been made can be committed to disk, and the file may be released so that other applications can use it. In some cases an entirely new version of the file will be created and the previous version discarded, or renamed in such a way as to make clear that it is a *backup version. *See also* open.

closed A term applied to a *set S on whose elements a *dyadic operation ∘ is defined and that possesses the property that, for every (s,t) in S, the quantity $s ∘ t$ is also in S; S is then said to be closed under ∘. A similar definition holds for *monadic operations such as ~. A set S is closed under ~ provided that, when s is in S, the quantity $~s$ is also in S.

The set of integers is closed under the usual arithmetic operations of addition, subtraction, and multiplication, but is not closed under division.

closed loop A term used in the early development of programming to describe the repetition construct now known just as a *loop.

(Since a loop is necessarily closed, the short term suffices.)

closed semiring A *semiring S with two additional properties:

(a) if $a_1, a_2, \ldots, a_n, \ldots$ is a *countable sequence of elements of S then

$$a_1 + a_2 + \ldots + a_n + \ldots,$$

exists and is unique; the order in which the various elements are added is irrelevant;

(b) the operation • (*see* semiring) distributes over countably infinite sums as well as finite sums.

A special unary operation called *closure* can be defined on closed semirings. Given an element a in S, powers can be defined in the expected manner:

$$a^0 = 1$$
$$a^n = a \cdot a^{n-1} \text{ for all } n > 0$$

Then the closure $a^\star$ can be defined as follows:

$$a^\star = 1 + a + a^2 + \ldots + a^n + \ldots$$

The properties of a semiring imply that

$$a^\star = 1 + a \cdot a^\star$$

Closed semirings have applications in various branches of computing such as automata theory, the theory of grammars, the theory of recursion and fixed points, sequential machines, aspects of matrix manipulation, and various problems involving graphs, e.g. finding shortest-path algorithms within graphs.

closed shop A method of running a computing facility such that the design, development, writing, testing, and running of programs is carried out by specialist computing staff and not by the originators of the problem. *Closed shop operation* is the operation of a computing system, excluding terminals, by specialist computer operators and not by other computing staff or computer users. *Compare* open shop.

closed subroutine *See* subroutine.

closed term (ground term) *See* term.

closed-world assumption An approach for dealing with incompleteness in *artificial intelligence. In a logic knowledge base, all facts are taken to be either true or false. Any items that have unknown truth values cannot be represented without awkward modifications. The closed-world assumption deals

with this by assuming that anything that is not contained within the knowledge base is false; in other words, unknown is equivalent to false.

closure *See* closed semiring. *See also* Kleene star.

	closed under complement	closed under intersection
3	yes	yes
2	no	no
1	unknown	yes
0	no	yes

Closure properties for Chomsky hierarchy

closure properties A class L of *formal languages is *closed* under an operation f if the application of f to languages in L always yields a language in L. For example, if, for any L_1 and L_2 in L,

$$L_1 \cup L_2$$

is also in L, then L is closed under union. Typical operations considered are:

*union, *intersection, *complement, intersection with *regular set;

*concatenation, *Kleene star;

image under *homomorphism, inverse homomorphism, *substitution;

*gsm-mapping, etc.

Most familiar classes of languages are closed under these operations. The detailed picture for the *Chomsky hierarchy is given in the table. Certain classes of languages, e.g. *regular languages, can be uniquely characterized by their closure properties.

CLP *Abbrev. for* constraint logic programming.

cluster 1. A group of similar devices, such as processors, storage units, or peripheral devices, brought together to provide enhanced performance, security, or resilience to failure.

2. A unit of storage, usually on a disk, that comprises a contiguous area made up from a number of basic units of storage.

3. *See* concept learning.

cluster analysis Any statistical technique for

grouping a set of units into clusters of similar units on the basis of observed qualitative and/or quantitative measurements, usually on several variables. Cluster analysis aims to fulfill simultaneously the conditions that units in the same cluster should be similar, and that units in different clusters should be dissimilar. It is not usually possible to satisfy both conditions fully, and no single method can be recommended as best for all sets of data. Among other desirable properties of clusters are that some variables should be constant for all units within a cluster, which makes it possible to provide a simple scheme for identification of units in terms of clusters.

Most cluster analysis methods require a *similarity* or *distance* measure to be defined between each pair of units, so that the units similar to a given unit may be identified. Similarity measures have been proposed for both quantitative (continuous) variables and qualitative (discrete) variables, using a weighted mean of similarity scores over all variables considered. The term distance comes from a geometric representation of data as points in multidimensional space: small distances correspond to large similarities.

Hierarchical cluster analysis methods form clusters in sequence, either by amalgamation of units into clusters and clusters into larger clusters, or by subdivision of clusters into smaller clusters and single units. Whichever direction is chosen, the results can be represented by a *dendrogram* or family tree in which the units at one level are nested within units at all higher levels.

Nonhierarchical cluster analysis methods allocate units to a fixed number of clusters so as to optimize some criterion representing a desired property of clusters. Such methods may be iterative, involving transfer of units between clusters until no further improvement can be achieved. The solution for a given number of clusters need bear little relation to the solution for a larger or smaller number.

Cluster analysis is often used in conjunction with other methods of *multivariate analysis to describe the structure of a complex set of data.

clustering In computer graphics, the collecting of nearby objects into groups so that their effect in a *radiosity calculation with another well-separated group can be approximated by a single interaction.

CLV *Abbrev. for* constant linear velocity. A mode of operation used for an *optical disk in which the rotation rate is varied according to the radius of the track accessed so that a constant data transfer rate corresponds to a constant bit density along the track. This allows an increase in capacity as compared to *CAV, but the access time is also increased. CLV is used in the *CD-ROM disk drive (as in the Compact Audio product on which it is based) and in some other optical disk drives. *See also* MCLV.

CM *Abbrev. for* configuration management.

CMI *Abbrev. for* computer-managed instruction. *See* computer-assisted learning.

CMM *Abbrev. for* Capability and Maturity Model.

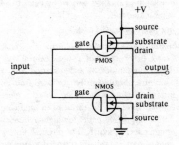

CMOS inverter

CMOS *Acronym for* complementary metal oxide semiconductor. A family of logic circuits that uses pairs of complementary *MOSFETs, i.e. PMOS plus NMOS, to implement the basic logic functions. The complementary transistors are arranged so that there is no direct current flow through each pair of PMOS and NMOS. In the circuit of the CMOS inverter (*see* diagram), the PMOS conducts when the input is logic 0 and the NMOS conducts (to ground) when the input is logic 1.

By scaling down the dimensions of the MOS devices, higher switching speeds and larger packing densities are possible; these devices are often termed *HMOS.

CMS *See* VM/CMS.

CMY color model A *color model that specifies colors by the three parameters cyan (C), magenta (M), and yellow (Y), which define the amount of light subtracted in each case. The model is used for defining colors on output devices such as plotters.

CMYK color model A *color model that specifies colors by the three parameters cyan (C), magenta (M), and yellow (Y) plus black (indicated by K). The model is used in the four-color printing process. Black is used in place of equal amounts of cyan, magenta, and yellow.

CNC *Abbrev. for* computer numerical control.

CNF *Abbrev. for* conjunctive normal form. *See* conjunction.

CNF satisfiability *See* P=NP question.

Coad–Yourdon An object-oriented software development method devised by Peter Coad and Ed Yourdon.

coax *Short for* coaxial cable.

coaxial cable (coax) A form of electric *cable that consists of a single central conductor surrounded by and insulated from a concentric sheath usually fabricated from an interwoven fine wire mesh. One or more coaxial cables may be included in multicore *cable to provide paths for high-frequency or other special signals. The physical dimensions of coax are usually arranged to present a particular characteristic impedance (50 ohms or 75 ohms) to electric signals. *See also* broadband coaxial systems, Ethernet.

Cobol (or **COBOL**) *Acronym for* common business-oriented language. A programming language that was developed by *CODASYL and is a de facto standard for commercial data processing. Cobol first came into use in 1960; the current version Cobol 85 is an ANSI standard adopted by ISO and replaces the earlier standards Cobol 74 and Cobol 68.

A Cobol program is divided into four divisions, of which the most important are the DATA division and the PROCEDURE division. In the DATA division the programmer defines the working storage and the files to be used by specifying their record structure. The PROCEDURE division is made up of statements, grouped into sentences, paragraphs, and sections. These statements define manipulation of data from the current record(s) of one or more files. The notation is English-like, e.g.

IF X = Y MOVE A TO B;

IF GREATER ADD A TO Z;

OTHERWISE MOVE C TO D.

File input-output is defined in terms of complete records, so the typical program reads a record from its input file, processes it, and writes a record to its output file, repeating this sequence until the whole file is processed. A powerful feature allows the data definition to specify editing that will take place as a side-effect of output, such as suppressing nonsignificant zeros. There are also facilities for handling VDU terminals.

cocktail shaker sort A refinement of the *bubble sort in which alternate passes go in opposite directions.

CoCom Coordinating Committee on Multilateral Export Controls. The export of various technologies, including computing systems, networking, hardware, and software, is restricted where this might enhance the military capability of the other country or place at risk the technology advantage of the exporting country. CoCom is the committee, with representatives from the 15 western nations in the NATO alliance plus Japan, that specifies the technology for which (CoCom) export approval is required.

COCOMO (or **CoCoMo**) *Acronym for* constructive cost model. An algorithmic software *cost estimation model devised by Barry Boehm. The basic model is intended to give an order of magnitude estimate of cost based on three classes of project: *organic mode, semidetached mode, embedded mode*. For each class an estimate for effort and duration can be calculated as a function of thousands of delivered source instructions (kdsi).

Organic mode projects require relatively small teams working in familiar environments on familiar projects. Semidetached mode projects have a mixture of experienced and inexperienced staff, with limited experience of the application type and probably unfamiliar with some of the aspects of the project. Embedded mode projects have tight time constraints, strong coupling between software, hardware, regulations, and operational procedures. Variations in specifications are usually impracticable, and validation is rigorous. Project team members are usually inexperienced in the particular application.

The intermediate COCOMO model applies a series of multipliers to the basic estimates for effort and time. There are 15 modifiers in four groups of attributes: *Product attributes* are required software reliability, database size, product complexity; *computer attributes* are execution time constraints, storage constraints, virtual machine volatility, computer turnaround time; *personnel attributes* are analyst capability, application experience, virtual machine experience, programmer capability, programming language experience; *project attributes* are modern programming practices, software tools, required development schedule.

Each attribute multiplier may be selected from points on a qualitative scale. The modifier value for modern programming practices also varies with the estimated kdsi size of the delivered software. The combined effect of all modifiers leads to a maximum multiplier of 84.6, and a minimum of 0.0076, for the basic estimates for each mode.

The COCOMO models essentially estimate cost to deliver, which may be a small proportion of the total software life-cycle cost. Boehm also provides models to estimate maintenance effort.

CODASYL An organization dedicated mainly to the development of the data processing language *Cobol and associated software. It originated at a meeting, the Conference on Data Systems Languages, called in the Pentagon by the US Department of Defense in 1959 to consider both the desirability and feasibility of establishing a common language for data processing. The acronym for that conference, CODASYL, became the name of the continuing organization. The initial version of the language, COBOL-60, was published the following year, subsequent versions being COBOL-61, COBOL-65, and the Cobol ANSI standards in 1968, 1974, and 1985, adopted by ISO.

During 1965–67 CODASYL established a Database Task Group (DBTG) to investigate and develop proposals for a common database management system to be used in association with Cobol as the host language (*see* database language). In 1969 a report giving a specification was published and widely discussed. A revised report published in 1971 allowed also for other languages to be used as the host programming language. IDMS is the leading product based on these proposals. *See* CODASYL network model.

CODASYL network model The *data model proposed by the CODASYL DBTG (*see* CODASYL) in which data is organized into records of different types and records are organized into sets of different types, both record and set types being named. A particular set type is defined as having an *owner* record type and one or more *member* record types. An instance of a set type consists of a single instance of its owner record type and zero, one, or more instances of each of its member record types. A member record instance may not occur in more than one instance of a particular set type.

In practice sets usually have only one member record type when, in effect, the CODASYL network model provides for a one–many relationship between the two types of records to be maintained, modeled as an isomorphism between the owner record instances and the elements of a disjoint partition of the member record instances. A set is said to be *mandatory* if this partition is constrained to be a complete cover and *optional* if it need not be. A common way of implementing database systems based on this model is by pointers embedded in the records, but pointers and this implementation technique are not inherent to the model, which is formulated in terms of abstractions.

code 1. A rule for transforming a message from one symbolic form (the *source alphabet*) into another (the *target alphabet*), usually without loss of information. The process of transformation is called *encoding* and its converse is called *decoding*. These processes are carried out by an *encoder* and a *decoder* respectively; the encoder and decoder may be implemented in hardware or software, the encoding and decoding processes being algorithmic in nature. The term "an encoding" is sometimes used synonymously with "a code".

From a more formal viewpoint, a code is a one-to-one *homomorphism h from the set of Σ-words, Σ_1^*, to the set Σ_2^*, where Σ_1 and Σ_2 are alphabets (*see* word, formal language). Since h is one to one, $h(w)$ may be "decoded" to obtain w for any w in Σ_1^*.

See also fixed-length code, variable-length code, error-correcting code, error-detecting code, channel coding theorem, source coding theorem, cryptography.

2. Any piece of program text written in a programming language (as opposed to a data structure or algorithm illustrated by a diagram or flowchart, or a program specified or sketched out in natural language prose). The term sometimes implies executable code as opposed to declarations or tables, but this is by no means always the case. *See also* coding. **3.** The particular language in which some code is written, e.g. *machine code, *source code.

8421 code A *weighted code in which each decimal digit 0 through 9 is represented by a four-bit codeword. The bit positions in each codeword are assigned weights, from left to right, of 8, 4, 2, and 1. *See also* binary-coded decimal, excess-3 code, biquinary code.

codec *Short for* coder-decoder. A device that converts an incoming *analog signal into an encoded representation as a digital *stream (the coder), and converts an incoming stream of digital signals into an analog signal (the decoder). Codecs are used in both telephone and video systems to convert an analog speech or video signal into a digital form, which can then be treated as a stream of data for the purposes of transmission and switching; the advantages are that digitally encoded signals can be transmitted at higher data rates, with lower error rates, and are more readily switched using *packet-switching

means than can be achieved by *circuit switching.

All codecs operate by sampling the analog signal at a sufficiently high rate (of the order of twice the frequency of the highest Fourier component that is to be transmitted). At the transmitting end, the sampled signal is converted by an *analog-to-digital converter to a digital form with the necessary precision, and the resulting bit stream is transmitted across the network to the receiver's codec. At the receiving end each sample is converted by a *digital-to-analog converter to recreate an approximation to the original analog signal. These same techniques can be applied to the storing of a signal for later replaying.

A standard telephone codec operates at 8000 samples per second, and generates an 8-bit digital value for each sample, giving a total data rate of 64 000 bps. This is adequate for the realistic reproduction of speech, with a nominal frequency response up to 4 kilohertz and with a nominal accuracy of 0.4%. For broadcast-quality or high-fidelity audio transmissions, higher sampling rates and greater precision are used, giving a signal with a higher bit rate. It is also common to add redundancy to the digitally encoded signal to allow error recovery. For example, a normal compact-disk system uses two channels, each sampled approximately 44 000 times per second with 16-bit precision, giving a total data rate of 176 Kbytes/second.

A video codec must handle much higher sampling rates, and a variety of techniques are used. Rather than simply digitizing a standard broadcast composite video signal, which includes one or more audio channels as well as synchronization information, it is common practice to treat the video line and frame synchronization separately, and to isolate the audio from the video. It is also common to apply a considerable amount of *data compression, in the digital domain, to reduce the overall bandwidth of the digital output. For *videoconferencing the codec produces an encoded output at 128 Kbps, which can be transmitted over two B-channels of *ISDN; the result gives a high-grade audio signal but with noticeable degradation of the colored video image, especially where the scene includes rapid movement. Other systems use higher data rates, typically 2 Mbps, achieving correspondingly improved video quality. For broadcast-quality video very high sampling rates are required, with a resulting high bandwidth for the digital signal.

code inspection A *review technique carried out at the end of the coding phase for a module. A specification (and design documentation) for the module is distributed to the inspection team in advance. M. E. Fagan recommends an inspection team of about four people. The module programmer explains the module code to the rest of the team. A moderator records detected faults in the code and ensures there is no discussion of corrections. The code designer and code tester complete the team. Any faults are corrected outside the inspection, and reinspection may take place subject to the quality targets adopted.

code length In an encoder, the number of symbols output when an encoded operation takes place. Usually the number of symbols input to the encoder is fixed; the number output may or may not vary, depending on whether the encoder is designed to give a *variable-length code or a *fixed-length code.

code of conduct A recommendation or guideline produced by a professional or trade body regarding the operation of a type of business particularly with regard to ethical and moral considerations. Codes of conduct have no statutory effect but can have legal consequences: e.g. a code of conduct for the handling of personal data in a particular trade may be referred to by a court in determining whether there is a prima facie case of misuse of data under the Data Protection Act 1984 in determining, as an issue, whether the business has acted fairly.

coder-decoder *See* codec.

codeword, codeword length *See* block code.

coding The transformation of a detailed design into a program. Use of the term coding generally implies a straightforward activity – simply expressing an existing design in some formal programming language – and

that any decisions made during the activity (such as the choice among arbitrary locations for particular variables) would not be classed as design decisions since they are of a relatively trivial nature. *See also* software life cycle.

coding bounds A variety of inequalities that apply, generally or specifically, to *error-detecting and *error-correcting codes, setting bounds to their performance as expressed by parameters such as the number of codewords (*see* block code), minimum *Hamming distance, codeword length, and efficiency. Of the many bounds that are known, the most important are the *Hamming bound and the *Gilbert–Varshamov bound.

coding standards *See* programming standards.

coding theorems *See* source coding theorem, channel coding theorem.

coding theory The branch of *communication theory that deals with the mathematical study of *codes with a view to their employment in *communication systems, usually for the purpose of increasing their efficiency and reliability. *See* source coding, channel coding.

codomain *See* function, relation, category.

cognitive modeling An approach taken by psychologists in which models of human behavior are developed in order to explain or engineer systems involving human components. This is important in areas where an operator is an essential part of the system, for example a pilot or chemical-plant operator.

cognitive science A multidisciplinary research field involving artificial intelligence, cognitive psychology, linguistics, neuroscience, and philosophy. The goal is to understand the phenomena of thinking and the relationship between brain and mind. Progress depends upon work on computer simulations, perception, language, mental states, and consciousness.

cohesion (functional cohesion) A measure of the degree to which parts of a program module are closely functionally related. High cohesion means that each part is directed toward and essential for that module to perform its required function, and that the module performs only that function. Low cohesion might be due to convenience grouping of functions that are unrelated by function, timing, logic, procedure, or by sequence.

Temporal cohesion occurs where a module contains several functions that must be performed at the same time, but are not closely related by function.

Logical cohesion is where several logically related functions are placed in the same module. For example a unit may handle all input to a program irrespective of its source being from disk, communications port, keyboard, etc.

Procedural cohesion is where functions that must be performed in a certain order are grouped together in the same module.

Sequential cohesion occurs when the output from one part of a module is the input to the next part, but if the module is not constructed for functional cohesion it is possible that not all the related parts will occur in the one module.

High functional cohesion might be seen as one characteristic of good design. *See also* coupling.

cold boot (cold restart) A method of starting a computer or other equipment either from a switched-off state, or in a way that has the same effect as switching it off and on again. *See also* warm boot.

collating sequence An ordering of the internal character set, used in alphabetic and alphanumeric sorting.

collision detection *See* Ethernet.

collocation methods An important approach to the numerical solution of *ordinary differential and *integral equations. Approximations are obtained on the basis that the equation is satisfied exactly at a particular set of points in the given problem range. For example, for
$$y'' = f(x, y, y'), \ a \le x \le b,$$
an approximation
$$P(x) = \sum_{i=1}^{n} \alpha_i \phi_i(x)$$
can be obtained from a suitable set of orthog-

onal functions $\phi_i(x)$ by choosing the coefficients α_i for which
$$P''(x_j) = f(x_j, P(x_j), P'(x_j)),$$
for some set of collocation points
$$a \le x_1 < x_2 < \dots < x_n \le b$$
Initial conditions and boundary conditions may also be incorporated into the process (*see* boundary-value problem).

color display A device capable of displaying pictures in color.

color gamut The range of colors that can be produced on a particular device or by a particular process.

colorimetry The branch of physics that defines colors in a quantitative way.

coloring of graphs An assignment (of colors) to the vertices of a *graph in such a way that adjacent vertices are assigned different colors. The minimum number of colors needed to color a graph is known as the graph's *chromatic number*.

color model A coordinate system in which colors can be specified and measured. In a *trichromatic* color model, a color is defined in terms of three components. *See also* CIE color model, CMY color model, CMYK color model, HLS color model, HSV color model, RGB color model.

color printer A printer, such as an *inkjet or *laser printer, that is able to render colored images.

color space A means of defining colors precisely by their position in a multidimensional space, usually three-dimensional. An example is the RGB color space with points normalized to the range (0,1) in each dimension.

Colossus An electronic special-purpose digital "computer" that was built in great secrecy by the Post Office Research Station in London and began useful work at the government establishment at Bletchley Park, Buckinghamshire, in late 1943. It contained 1500 vacuum tubes (valves) and could operate at high speed. The strategy or "program" was controlled from patchboards and switches. The faster Mark II machines, operating by mid-1944, contained 2500 tubes. Both versions were used for code-breaking purposes during the war.

coloured book The UK academic networking community was one of the earliest to attempt to devise a complete set of *open systems interconnection (OSI) standards for all aspects of its networking requirements, and to make a concerted effort to apply these to the entire community. A main thrust of the approach was the definition of *protocols for each of the major networking requirements, each protocol being issued in a different colored binder. The important protocols were:

Yellow Book   defining a transport service, roughly equivalent to layer 4 of the ISO *seven-layer reference model.

Green Book   defining a terminal connection protocol.

Blue Book   defining a file transfer protocol.

Grey Book   defining an electronic mail service.

Red Book   defining a job transfer and submission protocol.

Pink Book   defining a transport service to run over an ISO OSI *CSMA/CD service.

Orange Book   defining a network service running over a *Cambridge Ring.

Colors have been used to identify various other standards, including *CD-ROM format standards.

column-major order One way of mapping the elements of a two-dimensional *array onto a vector, e.g. for representation in memory. If a two-dimensional array, A, with m rows and n columns is mapped in column-major order onto a vector b with $m \times n$ elements then
$$a_{ij} = b_k$$
where $k = m(j - 1) + i$
See also row-major order.

column-ragged *See* ragged array.

column vector *See* matrix.

COM *Acronym for* computer output (on) microfilm. Output recorded in miniaturized form on microfilm, either on a reel of film or on card-sized sheets of film known as *microfiche*. The term COM also applies to the techniques used to produce this form of output. Special optical viewers must be used to enlarge the information on the microfilm for reading purposes. The facility has been available since the early 1960s and currently most COM devices are run offline. Computer-assisted retrieval of information stored on microfilm usually involves the interrogation of an index, maintained on disk, of the documents stored on the microfilm. *See also* CIM.

COMAL *Acronym for* common algorithmic language. A programming language that was developed for use in schools in Denmark and enjoyed a brief vogue in the UK. It was defined as a set of extensions to *Basic, combining modern control structures such as *if...then...else and *do...while with the traditional simplicity and familiarity of Basic. Modern dialects of Basic provide these structures, and COMAL has consequently fallen into disuse.

combination 1. A *subset of a finite set of elements. The number of combinations of n distinct objects taken k at a time is
$$^nC_k = n!/[k!(n-k)!]$$
2. A method of combining *functions in a parallel manner (*compare* composition). For functions f and g,
$$f : S \to T \text{ and } g : U \to V$$
the combination $f \times g$ is such that
$$f \times g : S \times U \to T \times V$$
where $S \times U$ and $T \times V$ are *Cartesian products, and
$$(f \times g)(s,u) = (f(s),g(u))$$
(*see* ordered pair).

combinational circuit A *logic circuit whose outputs at a specified time are a function only of the inputs at that time. In practice, any physically realizable combinational circuit will have a finite transit time, or delay, between the inputs changing and the outputs changing; the intention of the term combinational is to include algebraic elements (*AND gates, *OR gates, etc.) and preclude memory elements (*flip-flops, etc.). Analysis and synthesis of combinational circuits is facilitated by *Boolean algebra and *Karnaugh maps. *Compare* sequential circuit.

combinational logic *Digital logic restricted to the description of *combinational circuits. *See also* Boolean expression.

combinator A *lambda expression containing no *free variables. While this is the most general definition, the word is usually understood more specifically to refer to certain combinators of special importance, in particular the following four:

$$I = \lambda x \,.\, x$$
$$K = \lambda x \,.\, \lambda y \,.\, x$$
$$S = \lambda x \,.\, \lambda y \,.\, \lambda z \,.\, x(z)(y(z))$$
$$Y = \lambda f \,.\, (\lambda u \,.\, f(u(u)))\,(\lambda u \,.\, f(u(u)))$$

The combinators I, K, and S were introduced by Schönfinkel and Curry, who showed that any λ-expression can essentially be formed by combining them. More recently combinators have been applied to the design of implementations for *functional languages. In particular Y (also called the *paradoxical combinator*) can be seen as producing *fixed points, since $Y(f)$ reduces to $f(Y(f))$.

combinatorial circuit *Another (UK) name for* combinational circuit.

combinatorial explosion The exponential growth rate experienced in many *search problems. For example, in the game of chess the number of choices at each level increases by the *branching factor, which may typically multiply the options by 20 or more at each move. Although in theory it should be possible to analyze the game of chess from start to finish, the number of states to be examined is so enormous that it is completely impractical, not only at present but for any conceivable computer in the future. (To appreciate this, consider an example: if one million game states can be examined each second and the branching factor is 10, then to analyze 6 moves ahead takes 1 second, to analyze 12 moves takes 11 days, and to cover 18 moves takes nearly 32 000 years.)

One of the main thrusts of *artificial intelligence work has been to find ways, such as *heuristic search, to circumvent the combinatorial explosion.

combinatorics The branch of mathematics concerned with the counting problems and enumeration problems associated with such topics as *combinations, *permutations, number theory, arithmetic, and the theory of *graphs, *groups, and other *discrete struc-

tures. *Induction, *recursion, and *recurrence relations tend to play a significant role in much of this work. In computational combinatorics the underlying theory is applied to algorithms of any kind.

combinatory logic A version of *lambda calculus in which all expressions are constructed out of certain basic *combinators.

command 1. *See* job-control language.
2. *Obsolete name for* instruction or statement, i.e. the elementary unit from which a program is built up.

command and control (C&C, C²) A term referring to a system for military (or quasimilitary) operational decision-making. The term *command, control, and communications* (C^3) is intended to convey further complexity, and this is sometimes extended to the form C^4.

command control language A programming language designed for the implementation of *command control programs. The earliest such language was *JOVIAL; the latest is *Ada.

command control program A program that controls some piece of equipment, especially in the military context. Such programs are now more usually called embedded systems.

command file *Another name for* script.

command language *Another name for* job-control language.

command-line interface (CLI) An interactive system where user input is achieved through lines of text. The user learns these commands by consulting an online *help system or a reference manual. Users familiar with the interface may use abbreviations or mnemonic commands to speed access and reduce the number of keystrokes required for a given command.

comment Part of a program text included for the benefit of the reader and ignored by the compiler. Each language has its own syntax for comments, usually a form of bracketing, e.g.

$$\{.....\} \quad \text{in Pascal,}$$
$$/* ..... */ \quad \text{in C.}$$

Some languages, including Ada, prefer "end-of-line" comments, which are introduced by a characteristic symbol and are automatically terminated at the end of a line. Older languages such as Basic and Fortran restrict comments to be whole lines and do not allow them to be appended to a line of code.

common application environment (CAE) The set of services available to an application program on a Macintosh computer, defined in such a way that these services can be implemented on a different platform.

COMMON area In Fortran, an area of storage accessible from more than one program unit (subroutine). Data is local to the subroutine in which it is defined unless it is declared to be in a COMMON area. There is one anonymous COMMON area, called "blank COMMON", and any number of other areas, which are named ("labeled COMMON").

common carrier In the US, a private business or corporation that offers to the public general communication services such as telephone or intercomputer communications. Common carriers are regulated by the Federal Communications Commission (FCC), and all services offered must charge according to tariff schedules filed with and approved by the FCC.

common instance *See* unification.

Common LISP A version of *LISP that integrates the facilities of FranzLisp and MACLisp, adopted as an informal standard by the major users and suppliers of LISP systems.

common-sense reasoning Most reasoning in *artificial intelligence concerns higher-level functions, such as game playing, language processing, and symbolic problem solving. Common-sense reasoning is concerned with the understanding and manipulation of information about the everyday world of objects and their interactions. Deciding that a pile of objects is unstable or that a vehicle will not get through a red light in time are examples of common-sense reasoning. Unfortunately this is surprisingly difficult to automate as the problem domain is so ill defined and open-ended; for example, the *closed-world assumption is invalid. One

approach is to provide large amounts of domain knowledge (*see* CYC project), while others concentrate on reasoning about materials, physics, space, and time (*see* naive physics, imprecision). The topic has also stimulated research into philosophical and logical issues in a search for formal structures.

common user access *See* CUA.

comms (or **coms, com**) *Short for* communications, as in datacomms, telecomms, comms equipment, and comms link.

communicating sequential processes *See* CSP.

communication channel *See* Shannon's model.

communication interface A computer *interface designed to allow connection to other digital equipment. This may be by way of a modem and telephone lines or through a high-performance computer network as in workstation environments. *See also* communication port.

communication network *See* communication system, network.

communication port (com port) Any external socket on a computer that can be connected to a communication line and used to exchange information with other computers or electronic systems. Communication ports can be *serial ports such as *RS232C, *parallel ports such as the *Centronics or *SCSI interfaces, or ports for networks such as *Ethernet or *token ring. Each type of port has strictly defined connector types and pin assignments as well as electronic and logical signal protocols.

communication processor A specialized *I/O processor that is used to control a number of communication lines and/or communication devices. These lines/devices operate slowly in comparison to computing speeds so that one communication processor is usually multiplexed across a large number of lines/devices. Communication processors are used for the handling of data (in blocks, packets, messages, datagrams, etc.) for purposes of protocol, error checking and correction, acknowledgment, buffering, and also for encryption and decryption. They are now (mostly) programmed computers; earlier generations tended to be less general wired-program systems.

Communication processors are sometimes called concentrators, transmission control units, or front-end processors.

communication server *Another name for* gateway. *See also* server.

communication subnetwork (subnet) The dedicated processors and trunk circuits that are responsible for communication functions in a distributed network. *See* backbone network.

The term is sometimes used to refer to the communication circuits in a computer network, exclusive of any switching equipment.

communication system Any system whereby a source of information is enabled to convey that information, with due regard for efficiency and reliability, to a destination. Such a system may contain more than one source and/or more than one destination, in which case it is called a *communication network*. Communication systems are usually studied with *Shannon's model in mind.

communication theory The study of *communication systems through mathematical models of their operation. It is broadly divided into *information theory (the entropy formulation of sources and channels) and *coding theory (source coding and channel coding).

commutative diagram A method for displaying equations between *functions. For example, suppose that there is a function φ
$$\phi : X \to Y$$
and what is needed is to represent or code the data in X and Y, and the function, by means of the data sets A and B, respectively. Functions α and β are chosen where
$$\alpha : A \to X \text{ and } \beta : B \to Y$$
and a function $f : A \to B$ is defined to be a representation or function for φ on the code sets A and B if, for all $a \in A$, the following equation holds:
$$\phi\alpha(a) = \beta f(a)$$
This equation is depicted by the commutative diagram shown in the figure.

Commutative diagram

Equations and commutative diagrams of this form play an important role in relating different levels of abstraction, and are used to formulate the correctness of data-type implementations, compilers, and machine architectures. As equations grow in complexity, commutative diagrams become essential. *See also* computable algebra.

commutative group (abelian group) *See* group.

commutative law *See* commutative operation.

commutative operation Any *dyadic operation ∘ that satisfies the law
$$x \circ y = y \circ x$$
for all x and y in the domain of ∘. The law is known as the *commutative law*. The usual addition of integers is commutative but subtraction is not.

commutative ring *See* ring.

commutative semiring *See* semiring.

compaction 1. Any of a number of methods to reduce unused or unusable space in primary, secondary, or other memory. *See* memory compaction.

2. Removal of redundant data from a record. Many systems work with fixed-length records as a convenient method of handling files. This has the disadvantage that all records must be capable of holding the longest record, giving uneconomic use of storage. The fixed-length records can be processed (compacted) into a variable-length form. One method involves the removal of trailing spaces; another involves the replacement of long strings of identical characters by a *flag that indicates the occurrence of such a string, together with a count of the number of characters and a single instance of the character. Compaction will require CPU time when the record is stored and again when it is unpacked to fixed-length form, but the consequent saving in storage may justify this.

3. *See* data compaction.

Compaq Computer Corporation A US manufacturer of PC *clones. An early and successful entrant into the *portable computer market, Compaq is second only to IBM in terms of revenue from the microcomputer market and number 13 in the world list of top IT companies (1993 figures).

comparator 1. A piece of hardware or software that checks the outputs of a system while that system is operational. For a single channel system (i.e. no redundancy or diversity), the comparator might check across several outputs to see that only valid combinations are produced. The comparator may deal only with binary signals, usually termed *voting logic*, or may compare analog signals.

2. A piece of software that, for example, compares the contents of two text files and highlights any differences between the contents. It is often used in *word processing or editing of program source files and as a *software quality assurance tool in *configuration management.

comparison counting sort A sorting algorithm that stores, for each sortkey, the number of keys less than the given key. If N_j denotes the number of keys less than the jth key then (assuming that keys are unique) the jth record should be in position $N_j + 1$ in a file sorted into ascending order of the keys. This is a simple but inefficient algorithm.

compartmentalization (compartmentation) The process of keeping resources with differing access attributes in separate groupings.

compatibility 1. of hardware. The ability of a subsystem (e.g. memory) or an external device (e.g. a terminal) to be substituted for the originally designated equipment. To designate that one manufacturer's hardware can be connected to another manufacturer's hardware, the terms *plug-to-plug compatible*, or *plug-compatible*, are used. The ability of new hardware to handle interfaces of previous generations is called *backward compatibility*.

2. of software. The ability of a computer to directly execute program code that was compiled, assembled, or written in machine language for another computer. Generally this occurs for successive computers in a given manufacturer's line. Since later computers are usually more capable (i.e. have a larger instruction set and/or more memory), the ability to run the program of a less capable machine is usually called *upward compatibility* or *backward compatibility*. *See also* portable, emulation.

3. of a new piece of software. The ability to reproduce the behavior of its predecessor, in particular to accept the same input formats.

compilation time The time at which a high-level language program is translated into some other representation, such as machine code, so that the program can subsequently be executed by some computer system. *Compare* run time.

compiler A program that translates high-level language into *absolute code, or sometimes into *assembly language. The input to the compiler (the source code) is a description of an algorithm or program in a problem-oriented language; its output (the object code) is an equivalent description of the algorithm in a machine-oriented language.

compiler-compiler A program that accepts the syntactic and semantic description of a programming language and generates a *compiler for that language. The syntax is expressed in *BNF or a derivative thereof, and must conform to the rules dictated by the parsing technique to be used in the generated compiler. The semantics of the language are usually described by associating a code-generation procedure with each syntactic construct, and arranging to call the procedure whenever the associated construct is recognized by the parser. Thus the user still has to design the run-time structures to be used, and decide how each syntactic construct is to be mapped into machine operations. Then he/she has to write the code-generating procedures. A compiler-compiler is therefore a useful tool to aid the compiler writer, but nothing more.

Strictly speaking a compiler-compiler includes a parser generator as a component part, but the two terms are often used synonymously. *See also* LEX, YACC.

compiler validation *See* conformance testing.

complement 1. of a *set, S, with respect to some universal set U. The set consisting of elements that are in U but not in S; it is usually denoted by S', $\sim S$, or $\overline{S}$. Formally,

$$S' = \{x \mid (x \in U) \text{ and } (x \notin S)\}$$

The process of taking complements is one of the basic operations that can be performed on sets.

The *set difference (or *relative complement*) of two sets S and T is the set of elements that are in S but not in T; it is usually written as $S - T$. Thus

$$S' = U - S$$

See also operations on sets.

2. *See* Boolean algebra.

3. of a *subgraph G', with vertices V' and edges E', of a *graph G, with vertices V and edges E. The subgraph consisting of the vertices V and the edges in E but not in E'.

4. *See* radix-minus-one complement. *See also* radix complement, complement number system.

complementary logic *See* negative logic.

complemented lattice A *lattice in which there are identity elements 0 and 1 and in which each element a has at least one complement b, i.e.

$$a \wedge b = 0 \text{ and } a \vee b = 1$$

It will also be the case that b is a complement of a and that 0 and 1 are the complements of each other.

complement number system An alternative representation of numbers in a fixed-radix *number system. In a complement system each positive integer is represented in its usual form in the given radix system except that it is prefixed by at least one leading zero. Each negative number is then represented by the complement of the corresponding number. For example, in both the ten's complement system and the nine's complement system any number with leading digit 9 rep-

resents a negative number. *See also* radix complement, radix-minus-one complement.

complete graph A *graph G in which there is an edge joining every pair of distinct vertices; every vertex is adjacent to every other vertex. If G contains n vertices then the number of edges is $n(n-1)/2$.

complete lattice A *set D on which there is a *partial ordering and in which every subset of D has both a least *upper bound and a greatest *lower bound in D. By contrast, the weaker notion of *lattice requires only that finite subsets have least upper bounds and greatest lower bounds.

completeness The property or state of being logically or mathematically complete. In logic, an inference procedure is complete if it can derive every possible valid conclusion from the given axioms. A knowledge-based system can be considered *incomplete* if missing data hinders its operation or corrupts the results.

completeness theorem A theorem about a logical system L and a semantics S stating that a formula is provable in the logic L if and only if it is valid in the semantics S. A completeness theorem consists of a *soundness and an *adequacy theorem: it confirms that the logic is expressing and deriving precisely the properties that are valid according to the semantics.

complete term rewriting system *See* term rewriting system.

complete tree Any tree constructed from a *full tree of depth k by deleting some of the leaf nodes and the arcs leading to them. In a complete binary tree, the deleted nodes are often constrained to be the rightmost terminal nodes.

The term is also sometimes used as a synonym for full tree.

complex algebra The rules for performing operations on *complex numbers in a way that forms a useful and effective model for many scientific and engineering processes.

complex instruction set computer *See* CISC.

complexity The "ease" or "difficulty" of solving computational problems, measured in terms of some resource consumed during computation. The resource can be an abstract measure, or something specific like space or time. The analysis of the complexity of computational problems is a very active and large area of research at present and has important practical implications. *See also* complexity classes, complexity measure.

complexity classes A way of grouping algorithms, computable functions, or specifications according to their computational *complexity. Computable functions that have the same complexity according to some measure are placed in the same complexity class; functions in the same class are equally difficult to compute with respect to the measure.

The classification is most thoroughly done for *formal languages that can be recognized by *Turing machines. If L is a formal language that can be recognized by a deterministic Turing machine program M, and the time complexity (*see* complexity measure) for M is a function $T_M(n)$ of the length n of the input string, then L is classified according to the nature of $T_M(n)$. If $T_M(n)$ is bounded (e.g. by a polynomial or exponential function) then there exists a bounding function $S(n)$ such that for all n,

$$T_M(n) \leq S(n)$$

For a particular function $S(n)$ there is consequently a class of languages for which the above bound on time holds. This class is denoted by

$$\text{DTIME}(S(n))$$

Thus $\text{DTIME}(S(n))$ is the class of languages recognizable within time $S(n)$.

There is a similar definition of a class of languages

$$\text{DSPACE}(S(n))$$

in terms of the space complexity (*see* complexity measure).

There are various known relations between complexity classes. For example, if for two bounding functions S_1 and S_2

$$\lim_{n \to \infty} S_1(n)/S_2(n) = 0$$

then there is a language in $\text{DSPACE}(S_2(n))$ that is not in $\text{DSPACE}(S_1(n))$. Note that this applies if S_1 is polynomial and S_2 is exponential. There are similar results for time complexity classes.

Complexity classes can also be defined for nondeterministic *Turing machine programs. Thus a language L is in

$$\text{NSPACE}(S(n))$$

if there is some nondeterministic Turing machine program that recognizes L and such that on an input string of length n none of the possible computations uses more than $S(n)$ tape squares. Time complexity classes, NTIME, can be similarly defined. It is known for example that

$$\text{NSPACE}(S(n)) \subseteq \text{DSPACE}(S(n)^2)$$

complexity function If A is an algorithm for solving a particular class of problems and n is a measure of the size of a particular problem in this class, then a complexity function $f_A(n)$ is a function of n giving an upper bound on the maximum number of basic operations that algorithm A has to perform to solve any problem of size n. For example, n might be the number of records in a file and $f_A(n)$ the maximum number of comparisons required to sort the file. There are many algorithms and problems where the number of basic operations depend on the data rather than the size of the data (e.g. Euclid's algorithm for greatest common divisors). *See also* complexity measure.

complexity measure A means of measuring the resources used during a computation. A general definition is contained in *Blum's axioms. In the special case of *Turing machines, during any Turing machine computation various resources will be used, e.g. space and time. These can be defined formally as follows.

Given a Turing machine program M and an input string x, then $\text{Time}(M,x)$ is defined as the number of steps in the computation of M on x before M halts. Time is undefined if M does not halt on x. The *time complexity* of M is defined to be the integer function T_M where

$$T_M(n) = \max(\text{Time}(M,x): |x| = n)$$

for nonnegative integer n.

$\text{Space}(M,x)$ is similarly defined as the number of tape squares used by M on x, and the *space complexity* S_M is defined by

$$S_M(n) = \max(\text{Space}(M,x): |x| = n)$$

However, in order to distinguish the space

required for working as opposed to the space for the input string x, the machine is sometimes considered as having a read-only input tape, and Space(M,x) is defined as the number of squares used by M on x.

The more general measures of complexity share many of the common properties of time and space (*see* Blum's axioms).

An algorithm for which the complexity measure $T_M(n)$ or $S_M(n)$ increases with n no more rapidly than a polynomial in n is said to be *polynomially bounded*; one in which it grows exponentially is said to be *exponentially bounded*.

See also complexity classes.

complex number A number that, for mathematical convenience, is regarded as being composed of two *scalars (called the *real* and *imaginary parts* of the complex number), and is subject to a standard set of operations according to the rules of *complex algebra.

In engineering, and especially control engineering and electrical and electronic engineering, complex numbers and *complex operations are an essential tool without which calculations would be much more difficult to express and understand. Consequently, support for complex numbers and operations is an important consideration in the design of programming languages and packages for use in engineering applications.

complex operation One of a number of *operations (addition, subtraction, multiplication, etc.) defined on ordered pairs of *scalars according to the conventions of *complex algebra. Many programming languages provide complex operations as standard language features, or make them available in standard packages. *See also* complex number.

com port (or **comm port**) *Short for* communication port.

composition 1. (relative product) A method of combining *functions in a serial manner. The composition of two functions

$$f : X \to Y \text{ and } g : Y \to Z$$

is the function

$$h : X \to Z$$

with the property that

$$h(x) = g(f(x))$$

This is usually written as $g \circ f$. The process of performing composition is an *operation between functions of suitable kinds. It is *associative, and *identity functions fulfill the role of units.

If R denotes the set of real numbers and

$$f : R \to R, f(x) = \sin(x)$$
$$g : R \to R, g(x) = x^2 + 3$$

then $f \circ g$ is the function h:

$$h : R \to R, h(x) = \sin(x^2 + 3)$$

The idea of composition of functions can be extended to functions of several variables.

2. A subdivision of a positive integer n into parts $a_1, a_2, \ldots a_k$ in which the ordering is significant and in which

$$n = a_1 + a_2 + \ldots + a_k$$

where each a_i is a positive integer. It is thus similar to a partition (*see* covering) but in a partition the ordering is not significant. In general the number of compositions of n is 2^{n-1}.

3. A particular form of association between entities found in object-oriented approaches. The association is used to indicate a hierarchy of objects such that objects lower in the hierarchy are part of objects higher in the hierarchy. Thus the hierarchy indicates a component structure.

composition table *See* Cayley table.

compound document A document that contains sound or video components as well as text.

compression Reduction of the space needed to define an entity using one of the many techniques available. The *compression factor* is the ratio of the storage size of an uncompressed representation to that of the compressed representation. *See also* data compression, image compression, speech compression.

compression factor *See* compression.

CompuServe A US-based commercial agency offering e-mail, conferencing, bulletin board, and publishing facilities, as well as general access to the Internet.

computability *See* effective computability. *See also* computable algebra.

computable *See* Turing machine,

Church–Turing thesis, effective computability.

computable algebra An *algebra that can be faithfully implemented or represented on a computer, in principle. The notion is made mathematically precise using the theory of the effectively computable functions on the set of natural numbers (and the *Church–Turing thesis).

An algebra is computable if
(a) there is a mapping $\alpha : \Omega \to A$, called a *numbering*, that uses a *recursive set Ω of natural numbers to represent, or code, the set A of elements of the algebra;
(b) there are *recursive functions on numbers that track the operations of the algebra in the set Ω of natural number codes;
(c) there is a recursive function that can decide whether or not two numbers in Ω code the same element of A.

The idea in (b) of tracking operations in the code set is formulated by a *commutative diagram depicting an equation: for each operation
$$\sigma : A^k \to A$$
of the algebra there is a recursive function
$$f : \Omega^k \to \Omega$$
such that
$$\sigma(\alpha(x_1), ..., \alpha(x_k)) = \alpha(f(x_1, ..., x_k))$$
for all $x_1,...,x_k \in \Omega$. The idea of deciding equality in A is formulated by the relation
$$n \equiv_\alpha m \Leftrightarrow \alpha(n) = \alpha(m)$$
for $n,m \in \Omega$

A closely associated concept is that of a *semicomputable algebra*; this satisfies properties (a) and (b) above, and a third condition, weaker than (c), that whether or not two numbers in the set Ω code the same element of A is *recursively enumerable, rather than recursively decidable.

The concepts of computable and semicomputable algebras are used to establish the scope and limits of digital computation. Some fundamental completeness theorems link these algebras with *equational specifications and their properties:
(1) an algebra is semicomputable if and only if it can be defined uniquely by a finite set of equations, possibly involving extra or hidden functions and sorts, and using initial-algebra semantics;

(2) an algebra is computable if and only if it can be defined uniquely by a finite set of equations (possibly using hidden functions) whose associated *term rewriting system has the Church–Rosser and strong termination properties.

computable function A *function
$$f : X \to Y$$
for which there exists an algorithm for evaluating $f(x)$ for any element x in the domain X of f.

computable real number *See* real numbers.

computable set *See* recursive set.

computational geometry 1. The mathematical representation, manipulation, analysis, and synthesis of shape information in a computer. (This definition is taken from the seminal paper in this field by Robin Forrest, published in 1971.)
2. The study of algorithms for solving geometric problems on a computer. (This is a more restrictive definition, reflecting the way in which the term is more commonly used nowadays.)

computational psychology A discipline lying on the border between *artificial intelligence and psychology. It is concerned with building computer models of human cognitive processes and is based on an analogy between the human mind and computer programs. The brain and computer are viewed as general-purpose symbol-manipulation systems, capable of supporting software processes, but no analogy is drawn at a hardware level. *See* cognitive modeling, cognitive science.

computation, model of A method for computing sets and functions. *See* Church–Turing thesis, abstract computability theory.

computer A device or system that is capable of carrying out a sequence of operations in a distinctly and explicitly defined manner. The operations are frequently numerical computations or data manipulations but also include input/output; the operations within the sequence may depend on particular data values. The definition of the sequence is called the program. A computer can have either a *stored program or *wired program.

A stored program may exist in an alterable (*read-write or *RAM) memory or in a non-alterable (*ROM) memory. *See also* digital computer, analog computer, von Neumann machine.

computer-aided design (CAD) The application of computer technology to the design of a product, or the design itself. Computer-aided design is used especially in architecture and electronic, electrical, mechanical, and aeronautical engineering. A computer-aided design uses as inputs both the appropriate technical knowledge of individuals who enter design criteria, edit results, and otherwise test and modify the design, and also accumulated information from libraries of standards for components, element sizes, regulations, etc., such as standard ICs for a digital design system or standard pipe lengths and fittings for a hydraulic or piping system.

Processing of the data from the inputs takes place in at least two phases:

(a) certain interactive programs are invoked by the technical designer during the design process, these results being generally displayed on a VDU;

(b) programs are applied that may take considerable periods of running time to analyze tolerances, clearances, electrical characteristics, etc., the results of these runs being displayed back to the technical designer.

Output from a computer-aided design system consists of printouts of specifications and other information, and machine-readable files that are passed to *computer-aided manufacturing (CAM) systems and *computer-aided testing (CAT) systems. Examples of output to a CAM system are computer-produced artwork for printed circuit boards, or computer-produced tapes for automatic component insertion and board drilling. The combined process of computer-aided design and manufacture is known as *CADCAM*. The whole procedure – design, manufacture, and testing – is often referred to as *CADMAT*. There is an ISO standard (*STEP) for the exchange of product model data, including CAD data.

computer-aided engineering (CAE) An umbrella term that covers all uses of computers in engineering applications. Thus computer-aided design, computer-aided planning, and computer-aided manufacturing, are all branches of computer-aided engineering. The subject area is not usually taken to include software engineering.

computer-aided instruction (CAI) *See* computer-assisted learning.

computer-aided manufacturing (CAM) A set of techniques which integrate various subtechniques that can be used in computer control or *process control for various forms of manufacturing. Computer-aided manufacturing implies the integration of all aspects of manufacturing systems within the factory, i.e. the use of computer techniques not only for process control but also for aspects such as automatic ordering of materials, predicting material usage, factory scheduling, inventory control, predicting machine changeover, and projecting manpower requirements. Computer-aided manufacturing is particularly important as it follows naturally from *computer-aided design. *See also* computer-integrated manufacturing, numerical control, computer-aided testing.

computer-aided process planning (CAPP) The use of computer facilities to construct, manipulate, and analyze plans for an industrial process.

computer-aided production management (CAPM) The use of computer facilities to monitor, regulate, or optimize an industrial production process.

computer-aided testing (CAT) The application of computers to control either analog or digital test techniques in order to evaluate the quality of components and products. Computer-aided testing is used to check that the component parts, subassemblies, and full systems are within specified tolerances and also perform up to specification. Note that performance to specification may require that the unit or system operates under stressful conditions that would not be encountered in normal use. The parameters (test criteria) for computer-aided testing are often derived from *computer-aided design and *computer-aided manufacturing systems.

computer animation The introduction of the time dimension into computer graphics to manipulate objects and create the illusion of animated movement. *Facial animation*, for example, is aimed at modeling precisely the muscular structure and surface of the human face. *Behavioral animation* is based on the behavior patterns of animals (birds flock for protection, fish swim in schools).

computer architecture *See* architecture.

computer-assisted learning (CAL) Any use of computers to aid or support the education or training of people. CAL can test attainment at any point, provide faster or slower routes through the material for people of different aptitudes, and can maintain a progress record for the instructor.

Computer-assisted learning is one of several terms used to describe this application of computers. Other terms include *computer-aided* (or *-assisted*) *instruction*, *CAI*, *computer-based learning*, *CBL*, and *computer-managed instruction*, *CMI*.

computer-assisted software engineering *See* CASE.

computer-based learning (CBL) *See* computer-assisted learning.

computer-based training (CBT) The use of computers to provide or supervise staff training. The term emphasizes the need for practice in the acquisition of skills.

computer chess The development of computer game playing methods to produce high-quality chess playing programs. Most programs are based on *search techniques with sophisticated enhancements (*see* minimax). Theoretical work on search has benefited from computer-chess experience – for example, through experiments on *heuristics. Commercial and research systems of very high performance are now available.

computer emergency response team (CERT) A team established by the administrative authority for a network to act as a focal point for reporting security violations and to disseminate advice and coordinate action to counter such *threats to networked systems. A particular CERT usually serves a particular community, often the group of sites con-

nected to a *wide area network. In addition the separate CERTs cooperate where there is evidence that a threat crosses community boundaries.

computer family A group of (digital) computers that are successive generations of a particular computer system. They will tend to have similar but not identical *architectures.

computer fraud Any technique aimed at manipulating information within a computer system for the purpose of illicit, usually financial, gain.

computer games Recreational computer programs. Computers have been used to play games from the very start, and as the computers have become more powerful and cheaper, the games have become more sophisticated, particularly in their appearance and sound. Much computer game playing is done on purpose-made computers called *games consoles*. The serious side of games is in the algorithms underlying them, many of which have become important in other areas of computing. Equally games have inherited techniques from industrial and military simulators. Currently *virtual reality is becoming more important in games, while networks have made the multiuser game popular. *See also* computer chess.

computer graphics The creation of, manipulation of, analysis of, and interaction with pictorial representations of objects and data using computers. The information may be a simple histogram, a complex map or engineering design with textual annotation, or a photorealistic rendered scene. The output may be via a transient display such as a *cathode-ray tube or as a permanent record via a printer or plotter. Input devices range from *digitizers to *spaceballs. Interaction with the displayed image is possible.

Output-only computer graphics was used as early as the late 1950s. The first interactive graphics system that defined a number of the current paradigms was *Sketchpad*, devised by Ivan Sutherland at MIT Lincoln Laboratory and published in 1963.

computer hardware description language *See* CHDL.

computer-integrated manufacturing (CIM) The use of computers to control equipment used in manufacturing systems. The term covers systems constructed from machine tools, and *robotics, and includes parts distribution and handling, automated storage of raw materials, work in progress, and finished goods. *See also* computer-aided engineering, computer-aided manufacturing, computer-aided production management.

computer logic The basic organization, design, and wiring used to realize a particular computer *architecture. Someone involved with computer logic is therefore concerned with the design of building blocks or components, both logical and physical, and with the logic design involved in realizing a particular set of machine-code instructions; this may include the provision of facilities such as *microprogramming whereby the set of basic instructions can be altered.

computer-managed instruction (CMI) The use of computers (usually offline) to produce lesson prescriptions based on student history and test performance. Components comprising each lesson unit are selected in accordance with learners' needs, as indicated by test performance on previous units, academic history, etc.

Computer Misuse Act 1990 The act that criminalized hacking in the UK by creating two new offenses and that created the offense of unauthorized modification of computer material. The basic hacking offense in Section 1 of the Act is "unauthorized access to computer material" and a person is guilty of this offense "if he causes a computer to perform any function with intent to secure access to any program or data held in any computer" knowing at the time that the access is unauthorized (*see* access def. 2). The intent a person has to have need not be directed at any particular program or data. This offense is targeted at computer hackers who simply gain access to see what information the computer holds without the intention to commit any other serious act. However the offense is so widely drafted that it could cover unauthorized driving of a motor car with a microprocessor-controlled igni-

tion, unauthorized making of telephone calls from a computerized PBX, and unauthorized use of a microprocessor-controlled washing machine. The maximum penalty under Section 1 is six months imprisonment.

Section 2 of the Act creates the second hacking offense: unauthorized access with intent to commit or facilitate the commission of further offenses. It does not matter if the further offense is committed at the time of the hack or on a later occasion. The maximum penalty under Section 2 is five years imprisonment.

Section 3 of the Act provides that an offense will be committed by a person who, acting with intent, causes an unauthorized modification of the contents of any computer. The term modification is defined in Section 17 to include the addition of data or its alteration or erasure. A modification will be regarded as unauthorized if the person causing it is not authorized so to act or does not possess the consent of a person who is so entitled.

computer numerical control (CNC) *See* numerical control.

computer power A figure-of-merit for a computer system, sometimes defined in terms of performing a specific set of computations. It is described/measured by a number of methods: *cycle time, *mips, *flops, *throughput, and the results of *benchmarks are among the most common ones.

computer science The study of computers, their underlying principles and use. It comprises topics such as: programming; information structures; software engineering; programming languages; compilers and operating systems; hardware design and testing; computer system architecture; computer networks and distributed systems; systems analysis and design; theories of information, systems, and computation; applicable mathematics and electronics; computing techniques (e.g. graphics, simulation, artificial intelligence, and neural networks); applications; social, economic, organizational, political, legal, and historical aspects of computing.

It is not a science in the strict sense of

being a discipline employing scientific method to explain phenomena in nature or society (though it has connections with physics, psychology, and behavioral science), but rather in the looser sense of being a systematic body of knowledge with a foundation of theory. Since however it is ultimately concerned with practical problems concerning the design and construction of useful systems, within constraints of cost and acceptability, it is as much a branch of engineering as it is a science.

Computer Services Association A UK trade association founded in 1975 to promote the interests of computer service companies in the UK.

computer-supported cooperative working (CSCW) The use of computers to allow people to cooperate in the execution of a task at a distance. It often involves audio and video links between the users and the ability to share documents interactively.

computer vision Research on computer vision continues in *artificial intelligence but commercial vision systems are now widely available and provide flexible systems for users' image-processing needs. A typical small computer-vision system consists of a camera, a *frame-grabber card that plugs into a personal computer to capture images, and a suite of software that allows the user to experiment with image-processing operators and develop application systems.

computer word *See* word.

compute server A system specifically designed to undertake large amounts of computation, usually but not necessarily in a *client/server environment.

concatenated code The effective compound code (comprising an inner code followed by an outer code) employed in a *concatenated coding system, or a code designed for use in such a system, either as the inner code or as the outer code.

concatenated coding systems *Communication systems in which messages are encoded by means of an *inner code* before being passed through a channel and then being decoded according to the inner code;

this entire inner encoder-channel-decoder system is itself regarded as a channel (it is hoped less noisy than the original channel), and therefore has a further encoder and decoder placed before and after it; these implement an *outer code*. Alternatively, such a system may be considered as a channel with a compound encoder before it and a compound decoder after it, the compound encoder and decoder implementing a *factorable code.

To a good approximation, the inner code should be designed to correct any *channel errors arising in the original channel, while the outer code should be designed to cope with decoder errors occurring in the inner decoder. Since these decoder errors tend to occur in bursts, the outer code is usually a burst-error-correcting code: the *Reed–Solomon codes are often used for this purpose. The inner code is often a *convolutional code.

concatenation The operation of joining two *strings to form a longer string. The concatenation of the strings

$$u = a_1,\ldots,a_m \text{ and } v = b_1,\ldots,b_n$$

is the following string of length $m + n$:

$$a_1,\ldots,a_m b_1,\ldots,b_n$$

Common notations for referring to it include uv and $u<>v$, but others are also used.

The term concatenation is also generalized to an operation on sets of strings (i.e. *formal languages). Let K and L be two sets of strings. Then they can be combined into the following set by concatenating strings from K with strings from L in all possible ways:

$$\{uv \mid u \in K, v \in L\}$$

This set is usually written KL. The phrase *language concatenation* is sometimes used to distinguish this from simple concatenation of strings. Both string concatenation and language concatenation gives rise to *monoids, the identity elements being Λ and $\{\Lambda\}$ respectively (where Λ is the *empty string).

concatenation closure *Another name for* Kleene star.

concentrator A communication device that combines input lines whose total *bandwidth is higher than that of the output line; the process is known as *concentrating* or *concentration*. A concentrator is used when the actual traffic of each of the input lines is below its potential traffic. It is possible for the concentrator to become overloaded and to lose data. A common method used by concentrators to combine (multiplex) the input lines is asynchronous *time division multiplexing. *See also* communication processor.

concept learning A major topic in *machine learning that addresses the problem of classifying a series of data instances as equivalent on the basis of some given properties. The idea is to locate *clusters* within sets of data, using methods of *induction, so that the clusters define and distinguish salient features within the data. The clusters represent "concepts" and their descriptions define a class of data that fits a particular conceptual cluster.

conceptual graphs A representation formalism, designed by John Sowa, that combines logic-based features with the expressibility and flexibility of *semantic networks. Conceptual graphs provide a unifying framework for modeling many of the other *knowledge representation techniques.

conceptual schema *Another name for* logical schema.

concurrency The progressing of two or more activities (processes, programs) in parallel. It is a term that describes the general topic of parallelism in computer systems, specifically *multiprocessing systems. Specification of concurrency, and the consequent problems of *interlock and *synchronization, requires special features in the programming language, and is a feature of the class of *real-time languages.

The usual method of describing parallelism is *Flynn's classification*, which does so in terms of parallelism in the *instruction stream and in the *data stream of a system. Thus there are four categories:

SISD   single instruction, single data;
SIMD   single instruction, multiple data;
MISD   multiple instruction, single data;
MIMD   multiple instruction, multiple data.

The first of these, *SISD*, is the conventional serial processor. The third of these, *MISD*,

does not really occur in current systems. The other two are of most interest in multiprocessor systems. The *SIMD* is suited to operating upon data of the sort that exists in vectors and matrices by taking advantage of the inherent parallelism in that data. Thus the *array processor is one such system. Another is represented by the *supercomputer with parallel and different arithmetic units that *overlap arithmetic operations. The *MIMD* system represents a wide range of architectures from the large symmetrical multiprocessor system to the small asymmetrical minicomputer/DMA channel combination.

Shared-memory systems form a distinct group within the MIMD category. They are general-purpose multiprocessor systems that share common memory, and are thus also called *closely coupled* or *tightly coupled* systems. *Distributed systems – *wide area, *metropolitan area, and *local area networks – form another MIMD group, sometimes referred to as *loosely coupled* systems.

concurrent assignment An *assignment statement of the form

$$x_1, ..., x_n := t_1, ..., t_n$$

in which the value of the terms $t_1, ..., t_n$ over some *signature Σ are evaluated and assigned in parallel as the new values of the variables $x_1, ..., x_n$. For example, the concurrent assignment

$$x, y := y, x$$

simply swaps the values of x and y.

concurrent DOS *See* CDOS.

concurrent programming A near-synonym for *parallel processing. The term is used both to describe the act of creating a program that contains sections to be executed in parallel as well as its subsequent execution.

condensation *See* connected graph.

conditional 1. Taken account of in some but not all circumstances.

P	F	F	T	T
Q	F	T	F	T
$P \rightarrow Q$	T	T	F	T

Truth table for conditional

2. A logic statement of the form
$$P \rightarrow Q \text{ or } P \supset Q \text{ or } P \Rightarrow Q$$
that should be read as "if P is true then Q follows", although its meaning in logic only partly resembles its usage in English (*see* table).

conditional equation An expression of the form
$$e_1 \& \dots \& e_n \rightarrow e,$$
which means that if the equations $e_1, \dots, e_n$ hold then the equation e holds. Conditional equations have many properties in common with *equations; in particular, sets of conditional equations possess *initial algebras and generalizations of *Birkhoff's completeness theorem.

conditional jump (conditional branch) A *jump that takes place only if a specified condition holds, e.g. specified register contents zero, nonzero, negative, etc.

condition-code register (qualifier register) A set of *indicators that records the status or condition of the last result to be output from the *ALU. It forms part of the *program status word.

condition number A number that gives a measure of how sensitive the solution of a problem is to changes in the data. In practice such numbers are often difficult to compute; even so they can play an important part in comparing algorithms. They have a particularly important role in *numerical linear algebra. As an example, for the *linear algebraic equations
$$Ax = b,$$
if b is changed to $b + \Delta b$ (simulating, for example, errors in the data) then the corresponding change Δx in the solution satisfies
$$\frac{\|\Delta x\|}{\|x\|} \leq \text{cond}(A) \frac{\|\Delta b\|}{\|b\|}$$
where $\text{cond}(A) = \|A\| \|A^{-1}\|$ is the condition number of A with respect to solving linear equations. The expression bounds the relative change in the solution in terms of the relative change in the data b. The actual quantities are measured in terms of a vector norm (*see* approximation theory). Similarly the condition number is expressed in terms of a corresponding matrix norm. It can be

shown that $\text{cond}(A) \geq 1$. If $\text{cond}(A)$ is large the problem is said to be *ill-conditioned* and it follows that a small relative change in b can lead to a large relative change in the solution x. This means that the accuracy of a computed approximation must be interpreted accordingly, taking into account the size of the possible data errors, machine precision, and errors induced by the particular algorithm.

Similar ideas apply to other problem areas and condition numbers feature in a measure of eigenvalue sensitivity in the matrix *eigenvalue problem.

cone of influence The volume within which a spot light influences the rendering of objects.

conferencing *See* teleconferencing, videoconferencing.

confidence interval A range of values about a *parameter estimate such that the *probability that the true value of the parameter lies within the range is some fixed value, α, known as the *confidence level*. The upper and lower limits of the range are known as *confidence limits*. Confidence limits are calculated from the theoretical *frequency distribution of the estimating function. The concept may be generalized to several parameters. A *confidence region* at level α contains the true values of the parameters with probability α.

configuration 1. The particular hardware elements and their interconnection in a computer system for a particular period of operation. *See also* reconfiguration.
2. In *configuration management, the functional and physical characteristics of hardware or software as set out in documentation or achieved in a product.

configuration management (CM) Ensuring throughout its lifetime that a product put to some usage is properly constituted for that usage – for example that the correct procedures have been followed in creating the product, that the appropriate version of each individual component has been selected, that any required tests have been performed, that the product represents a complete and consistent whole, and that all known problems in any way pertinent to the product have been properly considered. As an illustration, a relatively simple configuration management activity might ensure that the individual components of a software system are the appropriate ones for the particular hardware on which the system is to run. A rather more complex activity might be to assess the impact on all software systems of a newly discovered problem with some version of a compiler, and to initiate any necessary corrective action.

The problems of configuration management can be complex and subtle, and for many projects effective configuration management can be crucial to overall success. Approaches to configuration management fall into two broad classes. One approach attempts to retain control over the product as it evolves, so that configuration management is viewed as a continuous activity that is an integral part of product development. The other approach views configuration management as a separate activity; it is a distinct milestone when the product is first placed under configuration management, and each new revision of the product is subject to the configuration management process, but configuration controls are not imposed during periods of development.

configured-in, -off, -out Terms used to detail the *configuration of a system, or changes (*reconfigurations) therein.

confluent *See* Church–Rosser theorem, abstract reduction system.

conformance testing Testing carried out to show that a product meets the requirements of a relevant standard. Typically conformance testing is carried out for compilers (thus *compiler validation*), and for products that implement interface specifications such as for *OSI or *EDI. The testing will usually be carried out by a third-party organization approved by the appropriate national body, will use an approved *conformance test suite* and *conformance test procedure*, and will result in the issue of a *conformance certificate* for the product. Usually a certificate will be of limited duration, typically one year, when retesting will be required. If a product is altered in any way retesting will also be required.

congruence relation 1. An equivalence rela-

tion defined on the integers in the following manner. Let m be some given but fixed positive integer and let a and b be arbitrary integers. Then a is congruent to b modulo m if and only if $(a - b)$ is divisible by m. It is customary to write this as

$$a \equiv b \ (\text{modulo } m)$$

One of the most important uses of the congruence relation in computing is in generating random integers. A sequence

$$s_0, s_1, s_2, \ldots$$

of integers between 0 and $(m - 1)$ inclusive can be generated by the relation

$$s_{n+1} \equiv as_n + c \ (\text{modulo } m)$$

The values of a, c, and m must be suitably chosen.

2. An *equivalence relation R (defined on a set S on which a *dyadic operation $\circ$ is defined) with the property that whenever

$$x \ R \ u \text{ and } y \ R \ v$$
$$\text{then } (x \circ y) \ R \ (u \circ v)$$

This is often referred to as the *substitution property*. Congruence relations can be defined for such *algebraic structures as certain kinds of *algebras, *automata, *groups, *monoids, and for the integers; the latter is the congruence modulo m of def. 1.

conjunction A logical expression of the form

$$a_1 \wedge a_2 \wedge \ldots \wedge a_n$$

where $\wedge$ is the *AND operation. A particular conjunction of interest is the *conjunctive normal form* (*CNF*) of a Boolean expression involving n variables, $x_1, x_2, \ldots, x_n$. Each a_i is of the form

$$(y_1 \vee y_2 \vee \ldots \vee y_n)$$

where $\vee$ is the *OR operation and y_i is equal to x_i or the complement of x_i. Reducing expressions to conjunctive normal form provides a ready method of determining the *equivalence of two Boolean expressions. *See also* propositional calculus. *Compare* disjunction.

conjunctive normal form (CNF) *See* conjunction.

CONLAN *Acronym for* consensus language, a consensus hardware description language. The aim of CONLAN is to provide a common formal syntactic and semantic base for all levels and aspects of hardware and firmware description, in particular for descriptions of system structure and behavior. *See also* CHDL, VHDL.

connected graph A *graph in which there is a *path joining each pair of vertices, the graph being undirected. It is always possible to travel in a connected graph between one vertex and any other; no vertex is isolated. If a graph is not connected it will consist of several components, each of which is connected; such a graph is said to be *disconnected*.

If a graph G has e edges, v vertices, and p components, the *rank* of G, written $\rho(G)$, is defined to be

$$v - p$$

The *nullity* of G, written $\mu(G)$, is

$$e - v + p$$

Thus $\rho(G) + \mu(G) = e$

With reference to a directed *graph, a *weakly connected graph* is one in which the direction of each edge must be removed before the graph can be connected in the manner described above. If however there is a directed path between each pair of vertices u and v and another directed path from v back to u, the directed graph is *strongly connected*.

More formally, let G be a directed graph with vertices V and edges E. The set V can be partitioned into *equivalence classes V_1, $V_2, \ldots$ under the relation that vertices u and v are equivalent iff there is a path from u to v and another from v to u. Let $E_1, E_2, \ldots$ be the sets of edges connecting vertices within V_1, $V_2, \ldots$ Then each of the graphs G_i with vertices V_i and edges E_i is a *strongly connected component* of G. A strongly connected graph has precisely one strongly connected component.

The process of replacing each of the strongly connected components of a directed graph by a single vertex is known as *condensation*.

connectedness A measure of the extent to which a given graph is *connected. An undirected graph is k-connected if for every pair of vertices u and v there are at least k paths between u and v such that no vertex other than u and v themselves appear on more than one path. A *connected graph is 1-connected, a *biconnected graph is 2-connected.

connectionism A branch of *artificial intelligence that advocates the use of *massively parallel* systems based on many simple processing elements with large numbers of connections between them. Inspiration is derived from brain models, with *neural networks providing the classic example of connectionism.

The connectionist approach to *machine learning is based on the idea that all learning may be achieved through the local or global adjustment of weights that express the strength of connections between elements in the network.

connectionless network service (CLNS) A network in which each *packet of information between a source and destination travels independently of any other packets. In practice, many networks are capable of operating in either a connectionless or a connection-oriented mode, and the choice of which approach is adopted rests as much with the designer of the protocols as with the actual hardware of the network. *See also* datagram.

Connection Machine *Trademark* A parallel processor in which many processor-memory pairs – small computers – operate simultaneously. Central to the machine is a communication network that permits the small computers to exchange information in a pattern suited to the algorithm being executed. The Connection Machine marketed in 1994 could yield a sustained performance of 20 Gflops from a 512 processor configuration. Peak performance is higher but gives little guide to useful computational power. Particular areas of application include *image processing, *information retrieval, *graphics, *artificial intelligence, and fluid flow.

connection-oriented network service (CONS) A network in which a pair of remote activities that wish to communicate are required to establish some form of circuit, often a *virtual circuit, before they can exchange data. In a *circuit switching network, the connection will take the form of a physical circuit, while in a *packet switching network it is a virtual connection. *See also* datagram.

connective A logical device used for the construction of more complex statements or expressions from simpler statements or expressions. Examples in everyday use are "and", "or", and "not". Connectives also occur in *Boolean algebra, *switching theory, *digital design, *formal logic, and in *programming languages. In all these cases they are used, often as operators, in the formation of more complex logical or Boolean expressions or statements from simpler components. These simpler components inevitably have a value that is either true or false. *Truth tables describe the effect or result of using a connective, given the truth of the simpler components.

connectivity 1. of a computer network. A rather loosely defined property referring either to the extent to which sites wishing to connect to the network are actually equipped with a network connection, or to the extent to which sites with an existing connection are still able to contact other network sites in the event of a component failure.
2. of a *graph G. The minimum number of vertices (and associated edges) of G whose removal from G results either in a graph that is no longer *connected or in a trivial graph with a single vertex: at least k vertices must be removed from a graph with k-connectivity. The higher the connectivity the more edges there are joining vertices.

The quantity described above is sometimes called the *vertex connectivity* to distinguish it from the *edge connectivity*, which by analogy is the minimum number of edges whose removal from G results in a graph that is disconnected or trivial.

connectivity matrix *Another name for* adjacency matrix.

CONS *Acronym for* connection-oriented network service.

consensus In combinational logic, a condition that is said to exist when two terms of a *Boolean function have one shared variable, which in one term is true and in the other complemented. A new term can be generated by the product of the remaining literals in the two terms, with the consensus variable eliminated, without altering the value of the function. For example, if
$$f = ab + a'c$$

then, in addition,
$$f = ab + a'c + bc$$
The term bc is sometimes called an *optional product*. This operation is invaluable in the elimination of circuit static hazards. Its systematic application to a Boolean function provides the basis of a *minimization procedure that is less voluminous than the Quine-McCluskey method, since it does not require the full canonical expansion of the original function.

consistency A term used in the context of methods for ordinary and partial differential equations. A formula derived from a *discretization is consistent if the *order is at least one with respect to the stepsize, h. Consistency is a necessary condition for convergence of a discretization formula (*see* error analysis).

console The workstation from which the operation of a computer system can be monitored and controlled. In current systems the console is usually a desk-height surface supporting a keyboard and one or more VDUs and reference documents. There may also be a number of other switches and indicators mounted on a panel. In early systems the control unit at the console was often a teleprinter. As systems became larger and more sophisticated the consoles first became more complex and then much simpler as the development of operating systems advanced. Some recent medium-sized systems do not have a console.

constant 1. A quantity or data item whose value does not change.
2. A value that is determined by its denotation, i.e. a *literal.

constant bit rate (CBR) A stream of data in which the data arrives at a fixed number of bits per second. The term may also imply that there is a guaranteed upper bound on the delay experienced by the data as it is carried. As an example, a speech *codec generates an 8-bit byte at intervals of 125 microseconds; each byte contains the result of sampling an audio signal, and digitizing it as an 8-bit quantity, and the result is a signal with a bandwidth requirement of 64 Kbps. If during transmission any of the samples are lost or delayed, then the reconstructed speech signal may well be unintelligible as the human ear is very intolerant of gaps in speech. It is therefore essential to guarantee that the full 64 Kbps can always be carried, and that the transmission delay will be effectively constant. *See also* bounded delay, network delay, variable bit rate.

constant delay in a network. *See* network delay, constant bit rate.

constraint-based solid modeling Modeling of solid objects that allows specification of constraints that parts of the model have to satisfy.

constraint logic programming (CLP) A variation of logic programming (*see* logic programming languages) where *constraint satisfaction is the mechanism used to perform computations rather than *unification. Several programming languages have been developed for CLP.

constraint network, constraint propagation *See* constraint satisfaction.

constraint satisfaction The process of resolving conflicts by removing or reconciling inconsistent values in a *constraint network*. A constraint network is a system of constraint equations and inequalities that represent the structure of a given problem. A crossword is an example of a constraint problem; the row/column sizes limit the choice of possible words and the interactions of rows and columns further constrain the solution.

The first stage in constraint satisfaction is *constraint propagation*, where any dependencies between constraints are exploited to introduce more constraint and thus reduce the solution space. Then follows a search where variables are assigned values and matched against current constraints; this involves further constraint propagation and *backtracking from failures. A solution is produced when a single set of values fits the final reduced set of constraints. An overconstrained problem will have no solution and an under-constrained problem may produce many alternative solutions.

construct *See* language construct.

constructive function A *function defined (explicitly rather than implicitly) in such a way that there is a rule that describes how the effect of the function can be realized; such functions are utilized by mathematicians who adopt an intuitionist or constructionist view of their subject. For example, it is inadequate to say that cube roots can be derived by solving a cubic equation of the form $x^3 = a$. It is necessary to give guidance on how cube roots can be evaluated.

constructive solid geometry (CSG) An approach to modeling solid objects using a set of primitive solids (such as cubes, cylinders, and spheres). Instances of these are scaled, rotated, and translated, and then combined with the set operations union, difference, and intersection to define a more complex object.

constructive specification A particular approach to writing *abstract specifications for programs, modules, or data types. Systems are modeled using representations for the data items involved, in terms of basic set-theory constructs such as *sets, *functions, *relations, and *sequences. The operations involved are then defined at this level of abstraction, typically by giving preconditions and postconditions for each operation. An implementation of the specification would involve replacing the set-theory constructs by lower-level ones, while preserving the meaning expressed by the specification. Although using abstract set theory, a constructive specification does give explicit constructions for the data and explicit definitions for the operations; it therefore contrasts with *axiomatic specification, in which the representations are not prescribed. Widely used constructive specification formalisms are *VDM and the specification language *Z.

consumable resource Any resource, such as paper or ink cartridges used in printers, that is by its nature usable on only a limited number of occasions. *Compare* reusable resource.

contact bounce *See* debouncing.

contact forces The simulation of dynamic (sliding) and static (dry) friction in rigid-body animations.

content-addressable memory (CAM)
Another name for associative memory. *See also* associative addressing.

content-addressable parallel processor
Another name for associative processor.

contention A situation in which several independent activities simultaneously seek access to the same resource, as when several independent transmitters wish to send data across a single communication channel. Where contention may arise, it is necessary to provide some form of arbitration to determine which activity gains access to the resource.

context-free grammar A *grammar in which the left-hand side of each production is a single nonterminal, i.e. productions have the form

$$A \rightarrow \alpha$$

(read as rewrite A as α), where α is a string of terminals and/or nonterminals. These productions apply irrespective of the context of A. For brevity one writes

$$A \rightarrow \alpha_1 \mid \alpha_2 \mid \dots \mid \alpha_n$$

to indicate the separate productions

$$A \rightarrow \alpha_1, A \rightarrow \alpha_2, \dots, A \rightarrow \alpha_n$$

As an example, the following generates a simple class of arithmetic expressions typified by $(a + b) \times c$:

$$E \rightarrow T \mid T + E \mid (E)$$
$$T \rightarrow E \mid E \times T \mid a \mid b \mid c$$

The *BNF notation used in defining the syntax of programming languages is simply a context-free grammar.

Context-free grammars are a class of *phrase-structure grammar (PSG). GPSG represents the principal attempt at constructing context-free grammars capable of characterizing the grammars of natural language.

Compare context-sensitive grammar.

context-free language (algebraic language) Any formal language generated by a *context-free grammar or, equivalently from another viewpoint, any formal language recognized by a *pushdown automaton. It can also be characterized as the frontier of a regular *tree language, or as generated by term algebras (*see* initial algebra).

context-sensitive grammar A *grammar in which each production has the form

$$\alpha A \beta \rightarrow \alpha \gamma \beta$$

where A is a nonterminal and α, β, and γ are arbitrary *words with γ nonempty. If γ was allowed to be empty then any type 0 (equivalently, recursively enumerable) language of the *Chomsky hierarchy could be generated. To derive the empty word, a production

$$S \rightarrow \Lambda$$

must also be included, with S not occurring in the right-hand side of any production. The term context-sensitive refers to the fact that A can be rewritten to γ only in the "context" $\alpha \dots \beta$.

In a *length-increasing grammar* each production has a right-hand side at least as long as its left-hand side (apart possibly from $S \rightarrow \Lambda$). Clearly any context-sensitive grammar is length-increasing, but it can also be shown that any length-increasing grammar is equivalent to a context-sensitive one. Context-sensitive grammars are a class of *phrase-structure grammar.

Compare context-free grammar.

context-sensitive language Any formal language that is generated by a *context-sensitive grammar or, equivalently from another point of view, that is recognized by a *linear-bounded automaton.

context switch A general term covering the situation in which a *process initiates a new type of activity. Any process functions in some form of environment, which defines the currently valid *variables that the process can manipulate, and their actual values, including the "undefined" value in the case where a variable has been created but has as yet had no value assigned to it. These remarks apply equally if the process being considered is one that is being dealt with by a person rather than a machine. A context switch occurs when the environment for the currently active process is replaced by a new environment.

contingency table In statistical analysis, a *frequency distribution of sample data classified by two or more factors, each with two or more classes. A simple example is a medical clinical trial of two treatments in which the number of patients assigned to each treatment is classified according to whether improvement was observed or not. If there is no significant difference between the proportions of patients improving, there is said to be no *interaction* between the two classifications of the table. The statistical analysis of contingency tables depends on certain assumptions (random assignment to classes, absence of other relevant factors) that make the interpretation controversial, and care must be taken in applying the tests correctly. *See also* chi-squared distribution.

continuation 1. A concept in programming language semantics, allowing the meaning of program constructs to be defined in terms of the effect they have on the computation remaining to be done, rather than on the current state of the computation. This is particularly useful in giving the semantics of constructs that effect the flow of control, such as GOTOs and loop exits.

2. An approach to solving a mathematical problem that involves solving a sequence of problems with different parameters; the parameters are selected so that ultimately the original problem is solved. An underlying assumption is that the solution depends continuously on the parameter. This approach is used for example on difficult problems in *nonlinear equations and *differential equations. For example, to solve the nonlinear equations

$$F(x) = 0,$$

let $x^{(0)}$ be a first approximation to the solution. Let α be a parameter $0 \leq \alpha \leq 1$, then define the equations

$$\hat{F}(x, \alpha) = F(x) + (\alpha - 1)F(x^{(0)}) = 0$$

For $\alpha = 0$, $x^{(0)}$ is a solution;
for $\alpha = 1$,

$$\hat{F}(x, 1) = F(x) = 0,$$

which are the original equations. Hence by solving the sequence of problems with α given by

$$0 = \alpha_0 < \alpha_1 < \ldots < \alpha_N = 1$$

the original problem is solved. As the calculation proceeds each solution can be used as a starting approximation in an *iterative method for solving the next problem.

continuous function A *function from one *partially ordered set to another having the property, roughly speaking, that least *upper bounds are preserved. A function

$$f : S \to T$$

is said to be continuous if, for every *directed subset X of S, f maps the least upper bound of X to the least upper bound of the *image of X under f. Continuous functions are significant in *denotational semantics since they correspond to the requirement that a computational process produces arbitrarily close approximations to the final output, given arbitrarily close approximations to the total input.

A continuous function $f(x)$ has no breaks or instantaneous changes in value. In the hierarchy of mathematical functions the smoothest are those, such as $\sin x$, $\cos x$, that can be differentiated any number of times, always producing a continuous function.

continuous inkjet printer *See* inkjet printer.

continuous signal, system *See* discrete and continuous systems.

continuous simulation *See* simulation.

continuous stationery *See* stationery.

continuous-tone image An image, such as a photograph, where the gray levels in the image are continuous and not discrete.

contradiction *See* tautology.

contrapositive of a conditional, $P \to Q$. The statement

$$\neg Q \to \neg P$$

where $\neg$ denotes negation. The contrapositive of a conditional is therefore equivalent to the original conditional. *See also* converse, inverse.

control bus A *bus that is dedicated to the passing of control signals.

control character A character that when typed at a keyboard or sent to a peripheral device is treated as a signal to control operating functions. *See also* character set, ASCII.

control circuitry Electric circuits within a computer or peripheral that regulate its operation.

Control Data Corporation *See* CDC.

control design The design of a *control unit. Control units may be designed using *random logic or *microprogramming. Microprogramming was well suited to the control of the complex sequences of register transfers required by CISC instruction sets. Contemporary RISC processors with their emphasis on the rapid execution of simple instruction sets usually employ random logic control to optimize performance.

control flow The sequence of execution of statements in a program.

control-flow graph A *directed graph representing the sequence of execution in a program unit, in which nodes represent branching points or subprogram calls in a program, and arcs represent linear sequences of code. From the control-flow graph an analysis can show

the structure of the program,
starts and ends of program segments,
unreachable code and dynamic halts,
branches from within loops,
entry and exit points for loops,
paths through the program.

See also static analysis.

control key *See* keyboard, control character.

controlled sharing Making used resources available to more than one using resource through an *access control mechanism.

controller A subsystem that governs the functions of attached devices but generally does not change the meaning of the data that may pass through it. The attached devices are usually peripherals or communication channels. One of the functions of the controller may involve processing the data stream in order to format it for transmission or recording.

control line A conductor in a multiwire interface that conveys a control signal.

control memory *Another name for* microprogram store.

control points Points used in the specification of curves to define the general required shape.

control record A record that contains *control totals* derived by summing values from other records in a file. The totals may or may not have some sensible meaning. Their purpose is to check that none of the preceding records

has been lost or altered in some way. *See also* hash total.

control sequence A string of characters used to control the operation of a peripheral device. The composition of these strings is defined in ISO 6429. This standard does allow latitude for manufacturers to define proprietary sequences for specific purposes, and many such sequences are in use; 7-bit and 8-bit versions of the *control characters are defined. An earlier standard widely used in the US is ANSI X3.64. *See also* escape sequence.

control stack A stack mechanism that contains an instruction sequence. It is part of the control unit in a computer with stack architecture. *See* stack processing.

control structure A syntactic form in a language to express flow of control. Common control structures are

if...then...else, while...do,
repeat...until, and case.

control total *See* control record.

control unit (CU) The portion of a *central processor that contains the necessary *registers, *counters, and other elements to provide the functionality required to control the movement of information between the memory, the *ALU, and other portions of the machine.

In the simplest form of the classical von Neumann architecture, the control unit contains a *program counter, an *address register, and a register that contains and decodes the *operation code. The latter two registers are sometimes jointly called the *instruction register*. This control unit then operates in a two-step *fetch-execute* cycle. In the fetch step the instruction is obtained (fetched) from memory and the decoder determines the nature of the instruction. If it is a *memory reference instruction the execute step carries out the necessary operation(s) and memory reference(s). In some cases, e.g. a *nonmemory reference instruction, there may be no execute step. When the instruction calls for *indirect addressing, an additional step, usually called "defer", is required to obtain the indirect address from the memory. The last action during the execute step is to increment the program counter or, in some cases – e.g. a *conditional branch instruction – to set the program counter to a value determined by the instruction register, depending on the status of the *accumulator or *qualifier register.

In more complex machines and *non von Neumann architectures, the control unit may contain additional registers such as *index registers, arithmetic units to provide address modifications, registers, *stacks, or *pipelines to contain forthcoming instructions, and other functional units. Control units in supercomputers have become powerful and complex; they may contain specialized hardware that allows for parallel processing of instructions which are issued sequentially.

control word 1. A word whose contents determine actions elsewhere; it may be used to control the use of a resource.
2. A word in a microprogram. *See* microinstruction, microprogramming.

convergence of an algorithm. *See* error analysis.

conversational mode *See* interactive.

converse 1. of a conditional, $P \rightarrow Q$. The statement

$$\neg P \rightarrow \neg Q$$

where $\neg$ denotes negation. *See also* contrapositive, inverse.
2. of a binary relation. *Another name for* inverse.

convex hull The smallest convex set that contains a given set. A set is convex if for any two points in the set, the points on the straight line segment joining the two points are also contained in the set.

convolution Mathematically, the operation of combining two functions, w and f, to produce a third function, g, such that

$$g_k = \sum_{i=0}^{\infty} w_i f_{k-i}$$

(or the corresponding continuous operation). This is envisaged as a transformation of an input function f to an output function g, by viewing f through a fixed window w.

In coding theory, f is considered as a *signal and w as the response of a *linear channel; g is then the effect upon that signal (regarded as a sequence of successive elements) brought about by the time response of the linear channel. The *channel time response* is the sequence of successive elements output by the channel in response to a signal that has one element of unit amplitude and all other elements zero. The input signal sequence and the channel time response are said to be *convolved*.

The inverse process is *deconvolution*: the convolved output sequence can be *deconvolved* with the channel time response sequence to restore the original input signal sequence.

It is important, both mathematically and practically, that the convolution of discrete-time signals corresponds to the conventional multiplication of *polynomials.

See also feedback register, feed-forward register.

convolutional code A *linear error-correcting code, characterized by a $k \times n$ generator matrix,

$$G = (g_{ij}[x]),$$

whose elements $g_{ij}[x]$ are *polynomials whose highest degree, m, is called the *memory* of the code. The quantity

$$c = m + 1$$

is called the *constraint length* of the code.

The convolutional encoder operates as follows. The input stream, regarded as the coefficients of a polynomial of arbitrary degree, is cyclically distributed (i.e. demultiplexed) among the inputs of k *shift registers, all of length c: the contents of the ith shift register is serially multiplied by each of the n polynomials $g_{ij}[x]$ (using n serial multipliers in parallel). Then n output streams are formed by summing the outputs of the jth multiplier on each register. These streams are cyclically multiplexed to form the output of the encoder. All this can be carried out to base q, for q prime; such codes are usually implemented in binary form ($q = 2$). In practice, the parameter k is normally equal to 1.

The main decoding algorithms for convolutional codes are *Viterbi's algorithm* and various *sequential algorithms, of which the most important are *Fano's algorithm* and the *stack algorithm*. Viterbi's is a maximum-likelihood algorithm.

Linear *block codes can be regarded as a special case of convolutional codes with $m = 0$ and $c = 1$. Convolutional codes are often specified by the parameters (n, k) or (n, k, c), although the simple phrase (n, k) code usually specifies a block code rather than a convolutional code.

Convolutional codes are of increasing importance as they become better understood theoretically, as better decoding algorithms are found, and as it becomes increasingly economical to provide programmable decoders, the decoding algorithms being best programmed in software owing to their complexity.

Cook–Torrance model An extension of the basic *reflectance model to make objects look less like plastic. (Plastic has an uncolored substrate, thus reflected light is not significantly altered in color.) A variable is added to alter the intensity of the reflected light dependent on the solid angle of the incident beam. The specular component shifts the wavelength of reflected light depending on the angle of incidence.

Coons patch A *patch that is fitted between four arbitrary boundary curves. The patch is constructed purely from information given on its boundary and from auxiliary functions, called *blending functions*, whose effect is to blend together four separate boundary curves to give a single well-defined surface.

coprocessor A microprocessing element designed to supplement the capabilities of the primary processor. For example, several microprocessor manufacturers have coprocessors in their product lines that offer expanded mathematical processing abilities, including high-speed floating-point arithmetic and computation of trigonometric functions. The coprocessor extends the set of instructions available to the programmer. When the main processor receives an instruction that it does not support, it can transfer control to a coprocessor that does.

The variety of functions that could be implemented in a coprocessor is unlimited, and more than one coprocessor may be used in a system if the primary processor has been suitably designed. For instance, one coprocessor may provide high-speed math processing and another may provide database management primitives. An example of a coprocessor is the Intel 487, which is a math chip designed to work with the 486SX processor.

copy To produce a replica of some stored information in a different part of the store or on a different storage device. For example, a piece of text or graphical information can be copied by marking it in some way, reading it into a temporary storage area, and writing it into a new location (*compare* cut).

copyright The right to prevent copying. It is a negative right that can be exercised by a copyright holder both by means of civil proceedings and also by seeking a criminal prosecution. Copyright protects the form in which an idea is expressed but not the idea itself. It is the main legal protection for computer-based inventions. Under the GATT agreement all nations agreed to protect computer programs as literary works. Copyright law is now also used to limit the use that can be made of all digitally recorded information (programs, data, databases, etc.) to stop rental of works or use of works by multiple users without the payment of higher royalties.

There is currently a very active movement to harmonize all the national copyright laws so that a Global Information Infrastructure could be created. This process involves a union of the continental European authors' rights systems based upon The Rights of Man with the Anglo-Saxon copyright system found in the USA, UK, Ireland, and the Commonwealth. The net result of this union is increasing power to authors of copyright works who are requiring payment for rental use of their works from publishers who publish on a pay-per-view basis on the Internet.

No formalities are required to obtain copyright protection for any literary work (including computer programs) although it remains good practice to place a copyright notice in all original works.

copy synthesis A technique of analyzing an acoustic speech signal and extracting information (for example *formant frequencies and *bandwidths), which can then be used to resynthesize a version close to the original speech. *See also* speech synthesis.

CORAL A programming language loosely based on *Algol 60 and developed in the UK for military applications. Although described as a real-time language, CORAL has no built-in facilities for parallel processing, synchronization, interrupt handling, etc. These necessary facilities have to be provided in machine code, and for this purpose CORAL provides a macro facility and a convenient escape to assembler level. The most widely used version of the language is CORAL 66. The use of CORAL is declining as *Ada comes into wider use.

CORBA *Acronym for* common object request broker architecture. A *protocol for communication between *objects in a distributed system.

CORE A method with supporting tools for capturing, structuring, and expressing system and software requirements. It was originally devised by British Aerospace (BAe) in 1979 and later extended by BAe and Systems Designers in the UK. CORE supports the different roles and viewpoints of user, customer, and analyst, and provides techniques to ensure completeness, consistency, and lack of ambiguity by cross-referencing between viewpoints. The informal CORE notation provides a series of diagramming techniques and associated text descriptions.

core store A type of nonvolatile memory in which binary information is stored in an array of toroidal magnetic cores. The cores are made of a *ferrite material that has two stable magnetic states and can be switched from one to the other by imposing a sufficient magnetic flux; the flux is generated by electric currents in conductors threaded through the cores. The principle of the core store was discovered in 1949 by J. W. Forrester of MIT. Although widely used as main storage for processors from the mid-1950s to the late 1970s, core store has been displaced in modern processor design by *semiconductor memory.

coroutine A program component that allows structuring of a program in an unusual way.

A coroutine resembles a *subroutine, with one important difference. A subroutine has a subordinate position relative to the main routine: it is *called* and then *returns*. Coroutines, however, have a symmetric relation: each can call the other. Thus a coroutine is *resumed* at a point immediately following its call of another coroutine; it never returns, but terminates its operation by calling (resuming) another coroutine.

Coroutines are not commonly found in high-level languages. They are particularly useful as a means of modeling concurrent activity in a sequential machine.

corrective maintenance *Another name for* remedial maintenance. *See also* software maintenance.

correctness proof *See* program correctness proof.

correlation A measure of a tendency for two or more *random variables to be associated. The formula for r, the sample *correlation coefficient* between two variables x and y, is

$$\frac{\Sigma (x_i - \bar{x})(y_i - \bar{y})}{\sqrt{[\Sigma(x_i - \bar{x})^2 \Sigma(y_i - \bar{y})^2]}}$$

which varies between −1 and +1. Negative values or r indicate that y tends to decrease as x increases, while positive values indicate that x and y increase or decrease together. If the value of r is zero then x and y are *uncorrelated*.

Rank correlation measures the correlation between the ranks (or order numbers) of the variables, i.e. between the positions when the numbers are arranged in increasing order of magnitude.

Correlation does not imply causation. Variables may be correlated accidentally, or because of joint association with other unmeasured agencies such as a general upward trend with time. If the relationship is not linear the correlation coefficient may be misleading.

correlation coefficient *See* correlation.

correspondence analysis A method of *multivariate analysis popular in France and developed by J. Benzecri. The purpose of the technique is to rearrange the rows and columns of a *data matrix so that units and variables with similar properties appear together giving rectangular blocks of similar values. The results may also be displayed graphically.

corrupt No longer in a proper state (or, as a verb, to cause to be no longer in a proper state). The term is most commonly used in connection with data that is being stored or transmitted: *corrupt data* when recovered or received has been altered from the version that was originally stored or transmitted. Since corrupt data may either be of little use, or may be positively harmful if used, most systems that store or transmit data include mechanisms to detect the presence of corruption, and to allow the original data to be recovered.

coset of a *group G that possesses a *subgroup H. A coset of G modulo H determined by the element x of G is a subset:

$$x \circ H = \{x \circ h \mid h \in H\}$$
$$H \circ x = \{h \circ x \mid h \in H\}$$

where $\circ$ is the dyadic operation defined on G. A subset of the former kind is called a *left coset* of G modulo H or a left coset of G in H; the latter is a *right coset*. In special cases

$$x \circ H = H \circ x$$

for any x in G. Then H is called a *normal subgroup* of G. Any subgroup of an abelian *group is a normal subgroup.

The cosets of G in H form a partition of the group G, each coset showing the same number of elements as H itself. These can be viewed as the *equivalence classes of a *left coset relation* defined on the elements g_1 and g_2 of G as follows:

$$g_1 \rho g_2 \quad \text{iff} \quad g_1 \circ H = g_2 \circ H$$

Similarly a *right coset relation* can be defined. When H is a normal subgroup the coset relation becomes a *congruence relation.

Cosets have important applications in computer science, e.g. in the development of efficient codes needed in the transmission of information and in the design of fast adders.

coset relation *See* coset.

cost estimation model A mathematical model used to predict the overall cost of creating software or hardware. Usually for hardware the model comprises a database of past achieved effort/duration/costs for development and manufacture (sometimes maintenance), and support for the estimator in matching characteristics of the historic data with those of the proposed new systems (or similar parts of the systems). The estimate of cost is then formed from the historic data, from constants and parameters derived from the database, and is modified using engineering judgment and a knowledge of the risk factors and local conditions.

For software the expected size of the software (lines of code) is usually used as the main input to a cost estimation model, with other inputs characterizing the main risk factors in the development. An underlying (software estimation model) database of past projects is built up from experience in a particular company or using one software paradigm. Typical software cost estimation models are *COCOMO (Barry Boehm) and GECOMO (GEC Software, UK), PRICE S (RCA), PROMPT Estimator (LBMS, UK), and SLIM (Putnam, Norden, Rayleigh model, software from QSM Inc, US). The models make no apportionment of costs to different life-cycle phases, and generally give cost to deliver. Some models (such as COCOMO) can be used to estimate maintenance costs.

See also function point analysis.

cost function A scalar measure of a complex situation, used for optimization. *See also* weighted graph.

countable set A *set that, in some sense, is no larger than the set of natural numbers. The elements of the set can be put into order and counted. Such a set is either *finite or *denumerable*; the elements of a denumerable set can be placed in a one-to-one correspondence with the set of natural numbers. The set of rational numbers can be shown to be countable but the set of real numbers is not countable.

counter A clocked digital electronic device whose output takes up one and one only of a number, n, of distinct states upon the application of each clock pulse (*see* clock). The output thus reflects the total number of clock pulses received by the counter up to its maximum capacity, n. All n states are displayed sequentially for n active transitions of the clock, the sequence then repeating. Since n clock pulses are required to drive the output between any two identical states, counters provide a "divide-by-n action" and are thus also known as *dividers*.

A counter whose output is capable of displaying n discrete states before producing an overflow condition can also be called a *mod-n counter* (or *modulo-n counter*), since it may be considered to be counting input pulses to a base of n. The value of n is often an integer power of 2. Counters are generally formed by a cascaded series of clocked *flip-flops (see cascadable counter), each of which provides a divide-by-two action. For a counter consisting of m flip-flops, the maximum capacity of the counter will be 2^m since 2^m discrete output states are possible, i.e. n is equal to 2^m. These are known as *binary counters*.

Count lengths of other than integer multiples of two are possible. For example, a *decade counter* (or mod-10 counter) exhibits 10 separate and distinct states. To achieve this digitally requires a counter having at least four individual flip-flop elements, giving 2^4 or 16 possible output states; six of these states are prevented from occurring by a suitable arrangement of logic gates around the individual flip-flops. In *multimode counters* the number, n, of distinct states can be selected by the user.

See also ripple counter, synchronous counter, shift counter.

counting problem 1. The task of finding the number of elements of some set with a particular property. Such counting problems are usually encountered in *combinatorics.

2. The task of counting the number of solutions to a problem. For example, to find the number of *spanning trees of a given graph, there is a formula in terms of the determinant of a certain matrix that is computable in *polynomial time. However there are other problems, like counting the number of *Hamiltonian cycles in a given graph, that are expected to be difficult, because determining whether or not a graph has a Hamiltonian cycle is NP-complete (*see P=NP question). Although it is possible to determine whether or not a graph has a perfect *matching* (a set of edges that do not meet each other but meet every vertex) in polynomial time, computing the number of such matchings can be done in polynomial time only if $P=NP$.

The matching problem referred to is, in the bipartite case, the same as computing the permanent of a 0–1 matrix, for which no good methods are known.

coupled A rather vague term, used to indicate that systems which might operate separately are actually being used in some form of cooperative mode. The term is applied to hardware units, as in *cross coupled*, where a pair of inverting gates are used to form a *latch circuit: the output of each gate serves as an input to the other. It is also applied to complete processors, as in *loosely coupled* and *tightly coupled* processors: there are substantial discrepancies in usage between different users of these terms, especially with respect to the precise overtone associated with the qualifying adverb. *See also* coupling, concurrency.

coupling A measure of the strength of interconnections between modules of a program. A high coupling would indicate strong dependencies between one module and another. Loose coupling allows greater flexibility in the design and better traceability, isolation, and correction of faults. The strength of coupling depends on the number of references of one module by another, the amount of data passed (or shared) between modules, the complexity of the interface between modules, and the amount of control exercised by one module over another. Completely *decoupled* modules have no common data and no control flow interaction. *See also* cohesion, coupled.

covariance A measure of the joint variation of two random variables, analogous to variance (*see* measures of variation). If the variables are x and y then the covariance of x and y is

$$\Sigma(x_i - \bar{x})(y_i - \bar{y})$$

The *analysis of covariance* is an extension of the *analysis of variance in which the variables to be tested are adjusted to take account of assumed linear relationships with other variables. *See also* correlation.

covering 1. of a *set S. A finite set of *subsets of S whose *union is just S itself. The subsets, $A_1, A_2, ..., A_m$, are said to cover S. If the elements A_i for $i = 1, 2, ..., m$ are mutually *disjoint, then the covering

$$\{A_1, ... A_m\}$$

is called a *partition* of S.

2. A relationship between two elements of a partially ordered set S. If x and y are elements of S then y covers x if and only if $x < y$, and whenever $x \leq z \leq y$ for some element z in S, then either $x = z$ or $z = y$.

covert channel A communication path, usually indirect, by which information can be transmitted in violation of a *security policy. For example, a covert channel may exploit system flags to allow one program to send confidential information to another.

CPL *Abbrev. for* combined programming language. A language developed in the early 1960s at the Universities of Cambridge and London in the UK. Its aim, rather unusual for the time, was to provide a single language for all applications on a new computer, including those areas at that time universally thought to be the province of assembly language. Although it never came into general use, CPL is noteworthy for the fact that it anticipated many of the concepts that are now regarded as characterizing modern "advanced" languages, notably the control structures of *structured programming and the reference concept that forms a major feature of Algol 68. CPL was the direct precursor of *BCPL and thus an ancestor of *C.

CPM *Abbrev. for* criticial path method.

CP/M *Trademark* An operating system that was intended for use on microprocessor-based systems supporting a single user at any one time. It is no longer used. *See also* MS-DOS.

cps *Abbrev. for* characters per second. A rate of processing, transferring, or printing information.

CPU *Abbrev. for* central processing unit. *See* central processor.

CPU cycle Usually, the time required for the execution of one simple processor operation such as an addition; this time is normally the reciprocal of the *clock rate. The term has been used formerly for the time required for the fetching and execution of one simple (e.g. add or subtract) machine instruction; this use however is inappropriate now when most processors exploit *pipelining. The CPU cycle is one of many figures-of-merit for a computer system. *See also* computer power, cycle.

CPU time (processor time) The time for which a *process has been receiving service from the processor. *See also* system accounting.

Craig's interpolation theorem A theorem that provides an answer to the question of whether an *interpolant I exists such that given a formula $A \Rightarrow B$ then both $A \Rightarrow I$ and $I \Rightarrow B$ are valid.

crash A system failure that requires at least operator intervention and often some maintenance before system running can resume. The word is also used as a verb. *See also* recovery.

Cray Research A US manufacturer of supercomputers, primarily for the scientific and engineering fields, although it is attempting to enter more commercial fields. The original Cray-1 was launched in 1976. Cray Research is number 66 in terms of revenue in the list of the world's top IT suppliers (1993 figures).

CRC *Abbrev. for* cyclic redundancy check, or for cyclic redundancy code.

crisis time The time during which an *interrupt must be serviced, otherwise a fault, such as the loss of requested data, will occur.

criticality analysis *See* failure modes, effects, and criticality analysis.

critical path method (CPM) A project planning, management, and scheduling method that divides a project into activities, each with a statement of time and resources required, and their precedence dependencies. These activities are then connected in a graph that expresses the dependencies and the times. The *critical path* is defined as the path through the graph that requires the maximum time. Variations of this method allow for statistically distributed time and resources, time/resource tradeoffs, etc. *See also* PERT.

critical region A section of code that may only be executed by one *process at any one time. *See also* critical resource, critical section, mutual exclusion.

critical resource A resource that can only be in use by at most one *process at any one time. A common example is a section of code that deals with the allocation or release of a shared resource, where it is imperative that no more than one process at a time is allowed to alter the data that defines which processes have been allocated parts of the resource.

Where several asynchronous processes are required to coordinate their access to a critical resource, they do so by controlled access to a *semaphore. A process wishing to access the resource issues a P operation that inspects the value of the semaphore; the value indicates whether or not any other process has access to the critical resource. If some other process is using the resource then the process issuing the P operation will be suspended. A process issues a V operation when it has finished using the critical resource. The V operation can never cause suspension of the issuing process but by operating on the value of the semaphore may allow some other cooperating process to commence operation.

critical section Part of a *process that must be executed indivisibly. Originally it was thought that the indivisibility had to be absolute. Now it is considered that it is only necessary for the critical section to be uninterrupted by other critical sections of a particular set of processes, i.e. those among which there is *mutual exclusion.

cross assembler An *assembler that runs on one machine, producing an object program to run on a different machine. Rarely encountered nowadays, the technique was used in the early days of microprocessors to generate software for microcomputers that were themselves too small to support an assembler.

crossbar switch *See* mesh interconnection.

cross compiler A *compiler that runs on one machine, producing an object program to run on a different machine. Rarely encountered nowadays, the technique was used in the early days of microprocessors to generate software for microcomputers that were themselves too small to support a compiler.

cross-coupling An interconnection between two *logic gates, permitting them to form a *flip-flop.

crosstalk A signal that has leaked or "crossed" from one communication channel to an adjacent channel. This interferes with (causes errors on) the second channel. Crosstalk is usually associated with physical communication channels, such as an RS232 connection, or other buses.

cross-validation A statistical technique in which a model is tested by dividing data sets randomly into two subsets. The model is fitted to the first set and the predictions from the model are compared with the second set. The process may be repeated many times. The method is related to statistical *bootstrap estimation.

CRT *Abbrev. for* cathode-ray tube.

cryogenic memory A type of memory operating at a very low temperature by means of *superconductivity and electron tunneling.

cryptanalysis Processing of an encrypted message to derive the original message by an "attacker" lacking prior knowledge of the secret key. *Compare* decryption.

cryptogram A complete message containing *ciphertext.

cryptography The coding of messages so as to render them unintelligible to other than authorized recipients. Many techniques are known for the conversion of the original message, known as *plaintext*, into its encrypted form, known as *ciphertext*, *cipher*, or *code*.

In a simple cipher system, for example, the sender and recipient hold identical copies of a secret *key*, and also an algorithm with which they each generate identical *pseudorandom bit sequences. During encryption the sender modifies the plaintext string by combining it with the pseudorandom sequence to produce the ciphertext; the ciphertext is then transmitted. The recipient performs the reverse process with an identical pseudorandom sequence and the received ciphertext to recover the plaintext.

An alternative technique is to use a *block cipher, in which the ciphertext corresponding to each block of, typically, 64 bits of plaintext is generated algorithmically using a key. In a *symmetric* block cipher the key used for decryption is closely related to that used for encryption, and both have to be kept secret. With *asymmetric* or *public key encryption*, the decryption key cannot be deduced from knowledge of the encryption key, which can thus be publicized to all intending message senders. *See* Data Encryption Standard, RSA encryption.

cryptology The study of *cryptography.

c/s *Abbrev. for* client/server.

CSCW *Abbrev. for* computer-supported cooperative working.

CSG *Abbrev. for* constructive solid geometry.

CSL *Abbrev. for* control and simulation language, one of the earliest *simulation languages. It is now obsolete.

CSMA/CD *Abbrev. for* Carrier Sense Multi-Access/Collision Detection, the formal name for *Ethernet.

CSound A system for the programming of complex sounds and music. It has a number of different sound sources that may be combined together with a number of special effects. Typically a musician would create an orchestra file and a score file, the first defining the instruments in terms of the available sound sources and the second defining the performance of those instruments over time.

CSP *Abbrev. for* communicating sequential processes. A mathematically formal approach to the description of software that addresses the specification of a set of concurrent processes and the way in which they interact; it was developed by Tony Hoare. The means of interaction is limited to a "synchronous" protocol in which any pair of communicating processes must be simultaneously involved for communication to be achieved.

CSS *Abbrev. for* centralized structure store.

CTron *See* Tron.

CU *Abbrev. for* control unit.

CUA *Abbrev. for* common user access. A specification created by IBM that defines the keystrokes and icon usage by which conforming applications implement frequently used activities, such as invoking menus or window sizing and positioning. For example, a *menu bar near the top of a window allows access to pull-down menus, which may be activated by a mouse or by typing Alt + F for the File menu, Alt + E for the Edit menu, etc. Also certain *buttons on the screen allow the user to minimize or maximize a window, select other applications, or reposition or resize a window.

cubic spline A *spline curve of degree 3.

cull To remove objects from a complex *computer-graphics computation on the basis of a quicker test. For example, if the front faces of a cube are hidden by another object, all the geometry of the cube can be omitted from the calculation. *See also* back-face detection.

cumulative distribution function *See* probability distributions.

current address register *Another name for* program counter.

current instruction register (CIR) A register, usually in the control unit, that contains the information specifying the instruction that is being (or is about to be) performed. *See also* instruction format.

curried function A *function of one variable that is related to a function of several variables. Let f be a function of two variables, x and y. Then by considering x constant we obtain a function in y; this function depends on the value of x. We write

$$g(x)(y) = f(x, y)$$

where g is called a curried version of f. Note that $g(x)$ denotes a function rather than a plain value. Currying is often used in theoretical work to deal simply with functions of several variables, e.g. in the lambda calculus.

cursor A symbol on a display screen that indicates the active position, e.g. the position at which the next character to be entered will be displayed. The underline symbol is often used: it is made to blink or flash so that it is easily noticed and can be distinguished from an underline that is part of the text. Other symbols, such as an arrow, pointing finger, or cross, are also used. The exact shape can be used to convey status information to the user. The cursor can be moved to a new position on the screen by means of *arrow keys on the keyboard or a *pointing device such as a mouse.

curvature In nonlinear *regression analysis, measures of curvature were proposed by D. Bates and D. Watts as a means of assessing the reliability of certain linear approximations. Curvature has two components: *parameter-effects curvature*, which can be reduced by suitable transformations of the parameters, and *intrinsic curvature*, which represents the essential aspect of nonlinearity. Estimation of these measures requires the second derivatives of the *expectation functions in the model.

curve compression Techniques for reducing the space needed to define complex curves.

cut 1. To mark a piece of text or graphical information in some way, read it into a temporary storage location, and delete it from the original document. The information may then be inserted into a new location. This has the effect of moving the information from one location to another and is often called a *move* or *cut and paste* by analogy with scissors and glue techniques. *See* clipboard. *Compare* copy.
2. A mechanism used in *Prolog to limit *backtracking. Roughly speaking, the effect of a cut is to fix certain decisions that have already been made, thus preventing the system from undoing those decisions in order to perform further search for solutions to its goals. This is a way of avoiding costly search known in advance to be fruitless, or of excluding alternative solutions that are not wanted. However, writing cuts in a program makes its behavior dependent on the system's search sequence. Such dependency prevents the program from being a pure statement of logical relationships and thus goes against the spirit of *logic programming.

cut and paste *See* cut.

cutout A portion of text or a graphic that has

been marked in some way, for instance by *dragging the cursor across it, in preparation for a *cut or *copy operation.

cut set of a *connected graph *G*. A set of edges whose removal produces a disconnected graph. *See also* connectivity.

cut-sheet feed *See* stationery.

cut vertex (articulation point) of a *connected graph *G*. A vertex of *G* whose removal together with the removal of all edges incident to it results in the remaining graph being disconnected. The term can also be extended and applied to more general graphs. Then the removal of a cut vertex and all arcs incident to it increases the number of connected components of the graph. *See also* connectivity.

CWIS *Acronym for* campus-wide information service. A specific form of information service dedicated to the needs of a campus, usually a university campus.

cybercafe A cafe equipped with terminals to provide public access to the *Internet.

cybernetics A discipline concerned with control and communication in animal and machine. Cybernetics attempts to build a general theory of machines independent of the material they are made from, e.g. electronic, organic, clockwork. Cybernetics draws an analogy between brains and electronic circuits. *See also* neural networks.

cyberspace An informal word first thought to have been used by the novelist William Gibson to refer to the total data on all the computers on all the networks in the world. The word has passed into common use as a way of referring to any large collection of network-accessible computer-based data.

cycle 1. (cycle time) An interval of time in which one set of events or phenomena is completed. It is usually the time required for one cycle of the memory system – the time between successive accesses – of a computer, and is sometimes considered to be a measure of *computer power.
2. Any set of operations that is repeated regularly and in the same sequence. The operations may be subject to variations on each repetition.

3. (circuit) of a *graph. A path that starts and ends at the same vertex. A cycle is said to be *simple* provided no edge appears more than once, and is *elementary* if no vertex (other than the start) appears more than once. *See also* Euler cycle, Hamiltonian cycle.

4. A *permutation of a set that maps some subset

$$T = \{t_1, t_2, ..., t_m\}$$

of S in such a way that each t_i is mapped into t_{i+1} ($i = 1, 2,..., m-1$) and t_m is mapped into t_1; the remaining elements of S are left unaltered by the permutation. Two cycles

$$(u_1 \, u_2 \, ...) \text{ and } (v_1 \, v_2 \, ...)$$

are disjoint provided the sets

$$\{u_1, u_2, ...\} \text{ and } \{v_1, v_2, ...\}$$

are disjoint. Every permutation of a set can be expressed uniquely as the *composition of disjoint cycles.

cycle index polynomial A formal polynomial associated with a *group of *permutations on a set, indicating the decomposition of the permutations into *cycles. Such polynomials occur for example in *switching theory.

cycle stealing (data break) *See* direct memory access.

cycle time *See* cycle.

cyclic access A mode of access to stored information whereby access can only be achieved at certain times in a cycle of events. A magnetic disk is an example of a device with cyclic access.

cyclic code A *linear code in which, given that v is a codeword, then so are all the cyclic shifts of v. For example, if

abcde

is a codeword in a cyclic code, then

bcdea
cdeab
deabc
eabcd

are also codewords.

cyclic redundancy check (cyclic redundancy code; CRC) The most widely used *error-detecting code. Extra digits are appended to each *block in order to provide a means of checking the data for errors that may have occurred, say, during transmission or due to recording and readback processes:

the digits are calculated from the contents of the block on input, and recalculated by the receiver or during readback.

A CRC is a type of *polynomial code. In principle, each block, regarded as a polynomial A, is multiplied in the encoder by a generating *polynomial G to form AG. This is affected during transmission or recording by the addition of an error polynomial E, to form

$$AG + E$$

In the decoder this is divided by the same generating polynomial G to give a residue, which is examined to see if it is zero. If it is nonzero, an error is recorded and appropriate action is taken (*see* backward error correction). In practice, the code is made *systematic by encoding A as

$$Ax^r + R$$

where r is the degree of G and R is the residue on dividing Ax^r by G. In either case, the only errors that escape detection are those for which E has G as a factor: the system designer chooses G to make this as unlikely as possible. Usually, in the binary case, G is the product of $(x + 1)$ and a primitive factor of suitable degree.

A binary code for which

$$G = x + 1$$

is known as a *simple parity check* (or *simple parity code*). When applied across each character of, say, a magnetic tape record, this is called a *horizontal check*; when applied along each track of the record, it is called a *vertical check*. Simple checks (horizontal and/or vertical) are much less secure against *burst errors than a nontrivial CRC with G of degree (typically) 16. The term *longitudinal redundancy check (LRC)* usually refers to a nontrivial CRC, but may apply to a simple vertical check.

CYC project An ambitious ten-year exercise to encode part of the knowledge in the Encyclopaedia Britannica into a very large knowledge base (VLKB); "CYC" is derived from en*cyc*lopedia. Inference procedures are incorporated into the system in order to answer questions and deduce results according to user requirements. In this way, both explicit and implicit knowledge is being captured. The project is based on the premise that a very large baseline of knowledge must be acquired before intelligent behavior can emerge.

cypher *A variant of* cipher. *See* cryptography.

Cyrus–Beck clipping algorithm An algorithm for *clipping a line to an arbitrary convex region. The algorithm uses the normal vector to reliably determine whether a point is inside, on, or outside a clipping region.

D

DAC 1. *Abbrev. for* digital-to-analog (D/A) converter.

2. *Abbrev. for* discretionary access control.

D/A converter (DAC) *Short for* digital-to-analog converter. A device, usually in integrated-circuit form, that can accept a digital signal in the form of an *n*-bit parallel data word and convert it into an equivalent analog representation. Digital output signals from, say, a microprocessor may thus be converted into a form that is suitable for driving analog devices such as motors, meters, or other analog actuators. The *resolution* of a D/A converter is a measure of the change in analog output for a change of one least significant bit in the input. *See also* A/D converter.

DAI *Abbrev. for* distributed artificial intelligence.

daisychain (bused interface) A means of connecting a number of devices to a *controller, or, used as a verb, to connect by this means. A cable is connected from the controller to the nearest of the devices and then a separate cable connects the first unit to the second and the process is repeated as required. This allows a single connector on the controller to serve a variable number of devices. It also reduces cable cost and eases installation when several devices have to be connected. The *IEEE-488 interface is suitable for this sort of connection.

Daisychain connection is also used as a means to prioritize I/O interrupts. In this application there is active logic at the points of interconnection to ensure that the priority accorded to a device is directly related to its place in the chain. The device nearest to the controller has highest priority.

daisywheel printer An obsolete type of *serial *impact printer formerly widely used on word-processor systems for producing letters and documents. The font was formed on the end of spring fingers extending radially from a central hub. The font carrier was rotated by a servosystem until the correct character was opposite the printing position and a single hammer impacted it against the inked ribbon and paper. The carriage with the font and hammer – and usually the ribbon – was then moved to the next printing position in the line. The print head and paper position could generally be incremented bidirectionally by control commands, making possible proportional spacing, justification, subscript and superscript characters, etc.

The daisywheel printer was introduced by Diablo Systems Inc. in 1972 and represented a considerable improvement in speed and reduction in mechanical complexity compared to other typewriters then used as low-speed printers. The speed was initially 30 characters per second with a repertoire of 96 characters. Developments led to speeds of 65 cps for average text and up to 192 characters on the type wheel; by overprinting it was possible to form a further 250 characters. This development partially overcame the disadvantage – relative to *matrix printers – of the limited character set. By 1990, however, daisywheel printers had been superseded by faster, more flexible, and quieter *dot matrix printers and *page printers.

dangling else The ambiguity that arises if a language allows constructs of the form

  if *b1* then if *b2* then *S1* else *S2*

in which it is not clear which if is associated with the else. Algol 60 resolved the ambiguity by forbidding the use of if immediately after then; Pascal associates the else with the innermost if. Modern languages such as Ada avoid the problem by pairing each if with an explicit end if.

DANTE *Acronym for* delivery of advanced network technology in Europe. An organization that acts as a management agent for a number of cooperative projects in academic and research networking, especially in the provision of leading-edge network services on a semicommercial basis.

dark fiber An *optical fiber that is provided to a user with no additional devices attached to it for lower-level protocol handling or electrical-to-optical conversion. These services may be provided by the owner of an optical fiber as part of a managed service, for which the user may be charged.

DARPA Defense Advanced Research Projects Agency. *See* ARPA.

DASD (pronounced dazdi) *Acronym for* direct-access storage device.

DAT *Abbrev. for* digital audio tape.

data 1. *Information, in any form, on which computer programs operate. The distinction between program (instructions) and data is a fundamental one in computing (*see* von Neumann machine). It is in this fundamental sense that the word is used in terms such as *data, *data break, *data bus, *data cartridge, *data communications, *data compression, *data name, *data protection, *data subject, and *data type.

2. In a more limited sense, data is distinguished from other contrasting forms of information on which computers operate, such as text, graphics, speech, and image. The distinguishing characteristic is that it is organized in a structured, repetitive, and often compressed way. Typically the structure takes the form of sets of *fields, where the field names are omitted (this omission being a main means of achieving compression). The "meaning" of such data is not apparent to anyone who does not know what each field signifies (for example, only a very limited meaning can be attached to "1234" unless you know that it occupies the "employee number" field). That characteristic gives rise to the popular fallacy that "data is meaningless".

Terms such as *database, *data dictionary, *data hierarchy, *data independence, *data model, *data preparation, and *data processing normally carry this second sense – though not invariably; the context should

determine which sense is intended.
3. *See* statistics, statistical methods.

data abstraction The principle of defining a *data type in terms of the operations that apply to objects of the type, with the constraint that the values of such objects can be modified and observed only by use of these operations. This application of the general principle of *abstraction leads to the concept of an *abstract data type.

Data abstraction is of very considerable importance in modern programming, especially for the coarse structuring of programs. Such use yields several benefits. The abstract data type provides a natural unit for specification and verification purposes (*see* module specification). It provides some basis for high-level design, and is consistent with the principles of *information hiding. The specification of the data type in terms of available operations provides all the information needed to make use of the data type while leaving maximum freedom of implementation, which indeed can be changed if required without affecting the users. There is also the possibility of developing a "library" of useful data abstractions – stacks, queues, etc.

The typical implementation of an abstract data type within a program is by means of a multiprocedure module. This module has local data that can be used to represent a value of the type, and each procedure implements one of the operations associated with the type. The local data of the module can only be accessed by these procedures, so that the user of the data type can only access the operations and has no direct access to the representation. The implementer is therefore free to choose the representation, which remains "invisible" to the users and can be changed if required. Each instance of the abstract data type employs one instance of the local data of the module to represent its value.

Proper support for such multiprocedure modules demands that the concept be recognized by the programming language, which must, for example, allow for the clustering of modules and data and have scope rules reflecting the desired restrictions on access. The first language to provide such support was SIMULA with its CLASS. Many modern languages now offer a similar facility, e.g. the MODULE of Modula and PACKAGE of Ada. *See* package.

data acquisition Data capture and/or data collection often with some filtering of the input signal, which may, for example, recover signals in a noisy environment.

databank A system that offers facilities for the deposit and withdrawal of data to a community of users on a particular topic (e.g. biological species, trade statistics, commodity prices). While it need not be an open public facility, the usual implication is that the user community is widespread. Access to a databank may be, for instance, via a *videotex facility, or via any other form of *network, or even via the postal service. The data itself may be organized as a *database or as one or more *files.

database 1. Normally and strictly, a body of information held within a computer system using the facilities of a *database management system. All accessing and updating of the information will be via the facilities provided by this software as will be the recording of information on the *log file, *database recovery, and multiaccess control.
2. Occasionally and colloquially, a collection of data on some subject however defined, accessed, and stored within a computer system. (This nontechnical use of the term can cause confusion to the nonspecialist as in: "we don't use a database management system for our database, just straightforward VSAM files.")

database administration (DBA) *See* database administrator.

database administrator (DBA) A person or member of a group that is responsible for the specification, design, implementation, efficient operation, and maintenance of a *database. The identification of a distinct role for *database administration (DBA)* follows from the concept of *data independence, and from the realization that databases form an important and valuable corporate resource.

The DBA person or group would work with users in establishing application requirements and creating an appropriate

*data model of the information to be held in the database as part of the activity of system specification; would encode the data model as the *logical schema of the database using the appropriate data description language together with any required *user views; would specify the initial *storage schema after consideration of the relative importance of the various activities to be carried out against the database; would advise and work with programmers whose programs access the database; and would be responsible for the initial setting up and loading of the database as part of the activity of system implementation.

The activity is an ongoing one involving the monitoring of performance and any consequential modification of the storage schema to improve it, responsibility for backup and recovery, for creating further user views as required, and generally with *database integrity, *security, and efficiency. The work is usually seen as encompassing both the business modeling role at one extreme and, at the other, the day-to-day technical problems of making the database system work effectively in practice.

database integrity The condition of a database in which all data values are correct, in the sense (a) of reflecting the state of the real world – within given constraints of accuracy and timeliness – and (b) of obeying rules of mutual consistency. The maintenance of database integrity involves integrity checking, and recovery from any incorrect state that may be detected; this is the responsibility of *database administration using the facilities of a *database management system.

File integrity can be defined in similar terms. Typically, however, files are subject to less extensive integrity checking than databases.

database language A generic term referring to a class of languages used for defining and accessing *databases. A particular database language will be associated with a particular *database management system. There are two distinct classes of database language: those that do not provide complete programming facilities and are designed to be used in association with some general-purpose programming language (the *host language*), and those that do provide complete programming facilities (*database programming languages*). Some products adopting the former approach seek to minimize host-language programming by the provision of *fourth-generation language (4GL) facilities.

A database language must provide for both *logical-schema specification and modification (*data description*) and for retrieval and update (*data manipulation*). In some cases, particularly products derived from the CODASYL network database standard, these aspects are treated distinctly as the *data description language (DDL)* and the *data manipulation language (DML)*. Modification to the *storage schema is also generally separately provided.

database management system (DBMS or dbms) A software system that provides comprehensive facilities for the organization and management of a body of information required for some particular application or group of related applications. This implies some overall logical view of the database in terms of some particular *data model, and database management systems are conventionally categorized according to the data model they implement. The system will provide a *database language in which schemas and subschemas (user views) can be specified and retrieval and update programs written. There will be facilities to specify and modify the *storage schema, for logging, rollback, and recovery. A major objective of a DBMS is to provide *data independence within the constraints of its data model. More modern DBMS provide a higher degree of data independence than earlier products where significant schema modification requires the database system to cease to be operational and for the data to be reorganized and reloaded. This can be impractical for large operational systems, a main reason for them becoming out of date and requiring redevelopment.

Well-known DBMS include the relational database systems ORACLE, INGRES, SYBASE, and INFORMIX, and the earlier systems IMS, IDMS, and ADABAS, still widely used in practice. Some of these products have versions with more limited facilities for the PC environment, for which specialist products such as Access and dBASE IV have also been developed. *See also* object-oriented database.

database programming language *See* database language.

database recovery The process of restoring *database integrity once a database has been found to be incorrect. *See also* recovery log.

database system 1. *See* database (def. 1).
2. *Short for* database management system.

data break (cycle stealing) *See* direct memory access.

data bus (data path) A group of signal lines used to transmit data in parallel from one element of a computer to another. The number of lines in the group is the *width* of the data bus, each line being capable of transferring one bit of information. In a mainframe the width of the data bus is typically equal to the word length, i.e. 32, 48, or 64 bits. The data bus used to interconnect LSI components need not have the same width as is used on the chips themselves. For example, a processor with an internal data bus width of 32 bits could be designed to transmit information over an 16-bit-wide external data bus. Such processors are said to use a multiplexed data bus (*see* multiplexed bus). The wider the data bus, the higher the potential performance of the system, since more information is transmitted in parallel with a wider data bus. Narrower data buses in general degrade performance but are less costly to implement. A multiplexed data bus is often chosen to reduce the number of pins needed on an integrated circuit for the data bus.

data capture A process for achieving the extraction of relevant data while the related transaction or operation is occurring. An example is a supermarket checkout equipped with point-of-sale terminals. The transaction is primarily concerned with the sale to the customer but while the purchased items are being entered onto the bill it is usual for the machine to record, and thus capture, data that will allow calculation of stock movement and other information.

If the equipment for data capture is online to a computer system, it is part of a *data collection process and may be referred to as either data capture or data collection equipment. The term data capture is often used where a computer system monitors (and maybe controls) laboratory instruments, process parameters, etc.; in this context it is also known as *data logging*.

data cartridge A *magnetic tape cartridge, commonly the 3M-type cartridge.

data chaining Organizing a *data file so that records are linked (*see* link, def. 3). A record may belong to more than one chain. Chaining permits access to records in a number of different sequences.

data channel An information route and associated circuitry that is used for the passing of data between systems or parts of systems. In an interface that has a number of parallel channels the channels are usually separately dedicated to the passing of a single type of information, e.g. data or control information.

data cleaning *Another name for* data validation.

data collection The process of collecting data from distributed points at which it has been captured or input as a separate operation. Generally the equipment used for the process is connected to a host computer via a communication system; sometimes portable equipment is carried to each site for information to be input into its memory and then the equipment – or a disconnectable module containing the memory – is connected to the host system. *See also* data capture.

datacomms *Short for* data communications.

data communication equipment *See* DCE.

data communications The collection and redistribution of information (data) through communication channels. Data communications may involve the transmission and reception of data in analog or digital form. *Data sources* originate data while *data destinations* receive it.

data compaction Removal of redundant *information from a file or data stream. The term *data compression* is commonly used to mean the same thing, although, strictly, while compression permits the loss of information in the quest for brevity, compaction is *lossless. The effects of compaction are thus exactly reversible.

Generally, in the context of *discrete and continuous systems, the output from discrete systems, if it is to be abbreviated, is losslessly compacted. Data compaction is appropriate, by way of example, for files containing text (including source programs) and machine code. In fax transmission, the position of black *pixels is discretely encoded, and so again data compaction is employed.

Data compaction may be carried out in a *probabilistic or *statistical manner, and a particular algorithm may be suited to one or other of these. A data compaction algorithm may be more or less *effective* (in achieving a high ratio of compaction) and more or less *efficient* (in economy of time taken for *encoding and *decoding). To a large extent, these demands conflict. For example, *Huffman coding is optimally effective when unconstrained, but may require a high *extension of the source, and need the output stream to have a small *alphabet (ultimately binary, which requires bit manipulation possibly on a large scale); Huffman can thus be very inefficient. On the other hand, *Lempel–Ziv compaction is very efficient, and within given time constraints may be more effective than a similarly constrained Huffman code.

data compression 1. *Another name for* data compaction, although, strictly, data compaction is *lossless while data compression need not be (see def. 2).
2. Removal from a file or data stream of *information that may be redundant either in the sense of *information theory, or in the sense that the retention of precision, definition, or some similar measure of quality is less important than the necessity to abbreviate the data. In the former sense, the abbreviation is *lossless, while in the latter sense it is *lossy. Compression permits either or both kinds, and so its effects are not always exactly reversible.

Generally, in the context of *discrete and

continuous systems, the output from continuous systems, if it is to be abbreviated, can often be lossily compressed. This is notably the case with sound, and with halftone and colored images. *See also* image compression.

data concentrator *See* concentrator.

data contamination The alteration, maliciously or accidentally, of data in a computer system. *See also* data integrity.

data dependency A data dependency exists if an instruction is dependent on a result from a sequentially previous instruction before it can complete its execution. In high performance processors employing *pipeline or *superscalar techniques, a data dependency will introduce a gap in a processor pipeline or inhibit the parallel issue of instructions in a superscalar processor.

data description, data description language *See* database language.

data dictionary Essentially a dictionary of the names used in the specifying documentation and programs for a data-processing application or group of related applications. Against each entry there would typically be the type of object being named (that is, whether it is a data item or field, record, file, report, screen display, etc.), its precise specification, some explanatory description of its use, and a reference to all places in the documentation and programs where it is used.

Developed in the late 1960s the purpose of such a dictionary was originally simply to assist in the maintenance of large-scale data-processing systems. The idea was further developed in the 1970s with the advent of special-purpose software systems to maintain such dictionaries, having features such as the automatic regeneration of Cobol data divisions as necessary when changes were made. These systems have evolved to include databases with features such as automatic DDL generation (*see* database language).

For large-scale and complex systems a data dictionary is a vital tool for the central control of naming, and of the semantics and syntax of the system. It is a tool widely used in *database administration and increasingly to assist in the broader task of *system design, many design methodologies being founded

on the use of a data dictionary. The terms *system dictionary* and *data directory* may be used synonymously in the case of the more ambitious software-based dictionary systems.

The term data dictionary is sometimes used misleadingly by software product vendors to refer to the alphabetical listings of names automatically produced when database schema and data manipulation coding is being processed and compiled, and it is important not to confuse this use with the accepted technical meaning of the term.

data directory *See* data dictionary.

data-driven design A design method in which the structure of the software system reflects the structure of the data processed by the system. Examples of data-driven methods are *JSD and *SSADM. *Compare* functional design.

data-driven processing *Another name for* forward chaining.

Data Encryption Algorithm (DEA) *Another name for* Data Encryption Standard.

Data Encryption Standard (DES) A very widely used cipher developed by IBM and standardized by the US National Bureau of Standards in 1977. It is a *Feistel cipher employing a 64-bit data block and a 56-bit key. The shortness of the key has given rise to much controversy concerning its security.

DES can be used simply as a *block cipher, in which case its "mode of operation" is called *Electronic Codebook (ECB)*. The three other NBS-recommended modes of operation are *Cipher Block Chaining (CBC)*, *Cipher Feedback (CFB)*, and *Output Feedback (OFB)*. These increase the security of the system by using DES as a building block in a *stream cipher, and differ regarding recovery from possible errors of transmission.

The US National Security Agency announced in 1986 that it would no longer certify the algorithm, so it lapsed as an official standard. It should now properly be called the *Data Encryption Algorithm (DEA)*, although DES remains its most usual name, and it continues to be used throughout the world despite being regarded as insecure for many purposes since brute-force exhaustive key searches have become feasible in some contexts.

data entry The process in which an operator uses a keyboard or other device to input data directly into a system. The term is sometimes misapplied to the process of *data capture, where the input of data to the system is not the prime objective of the related activity.

Direct data entry (DDE) is an online process in which data is entered into a system and written into its online files. The data may be entered by an operator at a keyboard (this is the usual meaning) or by a data capture device.

data field *See* field.

data file A *file containing data, such as a file created within an applications program; for example, it may be a word-processing document, a spreadsheet, a database file, or a chart. Data files are normally organized as sets of *records with one or more associated *access methods.

dataflow 1. A form of program analysis that examines the relationship between a source of data and the repository or user of that data. Dataflow analysis may be used to show the following: undeclared variables, uninitialized variables, unused variables, use of variables, mismatch of variables across module interfaces, and frequency/density of variable usage.
2. An item on a *dataflow diagram that represents a flow of data between two functions or between a function and a data store.

dataflow diagram (DFD) A directed *graph showing processing elements and data stores with the *dataflow between them. *See also* structured systems analysis, static analysis.

dataflow machine A computer in which the primitive operations are triggered by the availability of inputs or operands. In a classical *von Neumann machine, there is the concept of sequential flow of control, and an operation (i.e. instruction) is performed as and when flow of control reaches that operation. By contrast, in a dataflow machine there is a flow of data values, from operations that produce those values to operations that "consume" those values as operands. An operation is triggered as soon as all its operands are available. Since the result of one operation can be an operand to many other operations, and hence can potentially trigger many operations simultaneously, there is the possibility of a high degree of parallelism.

Dataflow machines are one of the major examples of *non von Neumann architectures, and are of considerable research interest. They are usually programmed in a *single-assignment language or a *declarative language. Traditional *imperative programming languages, which prescribe a particular flow of control, are poorly suited to dataflow machines.

dataglove A graphical input device consisting of a glove with sensors that detect hand and finger movements. The hand position is usually determined by a sensor on the back of the glove. The finger positioning is determined by fiber optics.

datagram A self-contained package of data that carries enough information to be routed from source to destination independently of any previous and subsequent exchanges. A *datagram service* transports datagrams on a "best-effort" basis. There is a nonzero probability that any datagram will be lost or damaged before reaching its destination. The order in which datagrams are submitted by the source is not necessarily preserved upon delivery. In some networks there is the possibility that a datagram may be duplicated and delivered to the destination more than once. It is the responsibility of the application to guard against errors arising from datagram loss or duplication.

data hierarchy A hierarchical structure of *records, in which (a) a record at level i holds data that is common to a set of records at level $i + 1$ and (b) starting from the higher-level record, it is possible to access the set of lower-level records. Any record may only "own" one set of lower-level records, and may only be a member of one such set. A data hierarchy may reflect "real-world" hierarchical relationships, or may be a *user view provided by a DBMS to facilitate a purpose or activity.

data independence The facility to modify a

database schema (*logical or *storage schema) with no consequent requirement to modify *user views or programs interacting with the database nor any need to reload data. To provide data independence has been a main motivation for the development of database management software. It is a relative term and different products provide different levels of data independence. It is particularly important for large shared databases that are required to evolve in line with user needs. The provision of data independence frequently conflicts with the need for efficient (i.e. fast) processing and usually necessitates some compromise in terms of the software techniques used.

Logical data independence refers to the facility to change the logical schema and thus evolve the content of the database; *physical data independence* refers to the facility to change the storage schema and thus modify and improve performance.

data integrity Resistance to alteration by system errors of data stored in a computer. It is a condition that denotes only authorized and proper alteration of data. It is a measure of the reliability of data read from magnetic media, in terms of the absence of undetected errors (*see* error rate). However the undetected error rate perceived by the host system may be worse than that arising at the magnetic disk or tape if undetected errors can arise, e.g. from the effect of noise on connecting cables where the interface concerned has insufficient error detection capability.

From a system point of view the undetected error rate of a peripheral may be inadequate: the system can improve on it by making additional provision for checking in software.

data item The *representation of any value that can be used alone or as a component of a *data structure.

data link A physical connection between two or more devices (called *nodes* or *stations*) by a communication channel that appears "wire-like", i.e. bits arrive in the order sent. Coaxial cables, telephone lines, optical fibers, lasers, and even satellite channels can be data links. Data links are assumed to be susceptible to noise (i.e. have error properties) and have finite data rate and nonzero propagation delay.

data link control protocol A communication *protocol that converts noisy (error-prone) *data links into communication channels free of transmission errors. Data is broken into *frames, each of which is protected by *checksum. Frames are retransmitted as many times as needed to accomplish correct transmission. A data link control protocol must prevent data loss caused by mismatched sending/receiving capacities. A *flow control procedure, usually a simple sliding *window mechanism, provides this function. Data link control protocols must provide *transparent data transfer. *Bit stuffing or byte stuffing strategies are used to mask control patterns that occur in the text being transmitted. Control frames are used to start/stop logical connections over links. *Addressing may be provided to support several *virtual connections on the same physical link.

data link layer of network protocol function. *See* seven-layer reference model.

data logging A procedure that involves recording all data and interactions that pass through a particular point in a system. The point chosen is usually part of a communication loop or a data path to or from a device such as a keyboard and display on which data is transitory. If a system failure or an unexpected result occurs it is possible to reconstruct the situation that existed. Such logs are not generally archived and can be overwritten once the associated job has been completed. *See also* data capture.

data management A term normally used to refer to systems that offer users an interface that screens them from the majority of the details of the physical handling of the files, leaving them free to concentrate on the logical properties of the data.

data management system A class of software systems that includes *database management systems and *file management systems.

data manipulation, data manipulation language *See* database language.

data mark *See* address mark.

data matrix A rectangular array of data variables, which may be numerical, classificatory, or alphanumeric. The data matrix forms the input structure upon which statistical procedures for *regression analysis, *analysis of variance, *multivariate analysis, *cluster analysis, or survey analysis will operate.

data medium A material having defined properties, including a physical variable that can be used to represent data. The defined properties ensure that the medium is compatible with devices that can record or read data on the medium. Examples of data media are *magnetic tape, *magnetic disks, and *optical disks, and also paper used for printer output.

data mining The nontrivial explication or extraction of information from data, in which the information is implicit and previously unknown; an example is identification of the pattern of use of a credit card to detect possible fraud. The data is normally accessed from one or more databases, so the technique is also known as *knowledge discovery in databases* (*KDD*). It involves a number of different methods from artificial intelligence such as neural networks and machine induction, together with statistical methods such as cluster analysis and data summarization.

data model An abstract model of some real-world situation or domain of interest about which information is to be held in a *database and which the *logical schema for that database encodes. The term data model (or data modeling method) is also used for a set of logical abstractions employed in constructing such a model. *See also* relational model, hierarchical data model, CODASYL network model.

Data Module The name used by IBM to refer to their removable, hermetically sealed disk pack, incorporating the read/write heads and carriage assembly, that was used with the 3340 *Winchester technology disk drive. Current data-processing systems use fixed disk storage; however, the term data module

was once in general use and was interchangeable with the terms disk pack and storage module.

data name In data-processing languages, a symbolic name chosen by the programmer to identify a data object. *See also* variable.

data network A communication network that is devoted to carrying computer information, as opposed to voice, video, etc. It consists of a number of nodes, or stations, connected by various communication channels.

data path *Another name for* data bus, although often used in a wider context to mean any logical or physical connection between a source and destination of digital or analog information.

data preparation The process of converting data into a machine-readable form so that it can be entered into a system via an available input device. There is no interaction with the system in the course of preparation. The process has been superseded by direct *data entry systems and *data capture.

data processing (DP) A term used predominantly in the context of industrial, business, governmental, and other organizations: within that context it refers (a) to a class of computer applications, (b) to a function within the organization.

While it is hard to generalize, data-processing applications may be characterized as those that store and process large quantities of *data on a routine basis, in order to be able to produce (regularly or on request) information that is predictably needed by an organization's employees, by its customers or suppliers, by government, or by any other organization. They are often referred to broadly as *commercial applications*. Typical applications within this category include financial accounting, cost and management accounting, market research and sales forecasting, order processing, investment analysis, financial modeling, stock control, production planning and control, transport planning and control, payroll, and personnel records.

*Cobol, since its introduction in 1960, has been the most commonly used language for data processing, though it has progressively been usurped by more modern *high-level languages and by *fourth-generation languages. Data-processing systems are normally long-lived (apart from the need to redesign/rewrite them periodically, they may well last as long as the host organization), and they handle data that is large in volume and complex in structure (which leads to a major concern for the problems and costs of data input and storage).

The data-processing function within an organization is that department responsible for the development and operation of application systems (largely of the types listed above) on behalf of other parts of the organization. Its tasks normally include systems analysis and design, program development and maintenance, database administration, computer operation, data preparation, data control, and network management. The data-processing department may not, however, be responsible for all data-processing applications within an organization, especially in the face of the widespread use of individual desktop computers, and conversely it may have responsibility for some applications that are not usually thought of as data processing (e.g. industrial process control).

In recognition that a lot of clerical and unit-record tasks could be described as data processing, the terms *automatic data processing (ADP)* or *electronic data processing (EDP)* were used in the 1960s, and can still occasionally be encountered. The term *integrated data processing (IDP)* also had some limited use as it became clear that much of an organization's data was common to separately developed systems, and the effort was made to integrate or rationalize them; that effort has mainly been diverted into the growth of *databases and *database management systems.

The term data processing is used in contexts other than the one described above: for instance, scientific data processing means the fairly straightfoward processing of large quantities of experimental results, and personal data processing means an individual's use of a microcomputer to keep personal records.

Data Protection Act 1984 The Act enacted in 1984 by the UK to comply with the Council of Europe Convention. (It is described at the end of the dictionary.)

data protection legislation Legislation that has been or is being introduced all over the world to protect personal data handled in computers. The aim of the legislation is to control the immense potential for misuse of information that arises when personal data is stored in computers. Once the data has been transcribed from paper files into a form that is easily readable and accessible by computers, it is an inexpensive and easy task for the data to be extracted from one record and correlated with personal data concerning the same person from another file. This results in a synergistic combination of information that is considered to be an infringement of *privacy.

To combat the fear of misuse of data, governments have introduced legislation that, among other things, makes the following requirements of organizations that maintain personal records on computers:

to declare and/or register the use for which the data is stored;

to provide the data subject with a right of access to data concerning himself or herself on their computers;

to maintain a prescribed minimum level of electronic and physical *security in their computer installation;

not to transmit personal data to any organization that does not have similar controls over misuse of data.

This last requirement has led to fears that countries without data protection legislation on their statute books are losing contracts for the processing of data, since countries with such legislation can refuse to permit the export of data to countries where data is not adequately protected. For this reason companies that consider that the data protection fears are not borne out by real instances of misuse of data are nonetheless pressing for legislation.

In Europe a convention concerning misuse of data was signed by all member countries of the Council of Europe. The OECD (Organization for Economic Cooperation and Development) has also drafted a convention of similar effect. The USA has a Privacy Act that deals with data stored by government agencies, but it is thought by some in the legal profession that for constitutional reasons the USA could not legislate to prohibit misuse of data along the lines required by the OECD and Council of Europe conventions. The debate is rapidly getting more complicated: third world countries are now finding that data protection legislation may enable them to create a nontariff barrier around indigenous data processing companies, and hence the issues are moving out of civil rights and into economics.

In 1984 the UK enacted the Data Protection Act to comply with the Council of Europe Convention. (The Act is described at the end of the dictionary.)

In February 1995 the Council of Ministers of the European Union formally approved a common position on the "Framework" Data Protection Directive, in response to the political agreement reached on 6 February 1995. The final version of the Directive includes a 12-year transition period for noncomputerized data. Member States will also have a three-year transition period in which to implement the Directive following its adoption.

data rate *Short for* data transfer rate.

data reduction *Another name for* data compression (especially when strictly *lossy) and, sometimes, data compaction.

data retrieval The process by which data is selected and extracted from a file, a group of files, or a database.

data security system Generally, any means (technical, operational, or managerial) for keeping private the *information contained in data that are transmitted, stored, or processed in a computer system. A data security system must make information available to those authorized to receive it, without undue delay or inefficiency. Also, it must keep information secret from those not so authorized, in such a way that the cost of unauthorized disclosure would exceed the value of the information to the illegitimate recipient.

A data security system may involve physi-

cal security (safes, locks, entry cards) for access to disks and passwords, and also the techniques of *cryptography and *authentication. The specification and design of a good data security system relies on the formation of an appropriate *threat model. *See also* security.

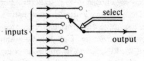

Data selector/multiplexer

data selector/multiplexer A logic circuit that may be considered as a single-pole multiway switch whose output is determined by the position of the switch wiper (*see* diagram). The wiper position is controlled by a select signal, normally digital, that indicates which of the inputs is to be connected to the output. In this way a number of channels of data may be placed sequentially on a time-shared output bus under the control of the select signal, a process known as *time-division multiplexing. Inputs to and outputs from a multiplexer may be in digital or analog form. *See also* decoder/demultiplexer.

data set 1. *Another name for* modem.
2. *Another name for* file.

data sheet A manufacturer's specification of the parameters of a device or integrated circuit, its functions, and its pin connections.

data store *See* dataflow diagram, structured systems analysis.

data stream A sequence of data elements, often packed in some manner into a sequence of words having sizes different from the size of the data elements.

data structure (information structure) An aspect of *data type expressing the nature of values that are composite, i.e. not *atoms. The nonatomic values have constituent parts (which need not themselves be atoms), and the data structure expresses how constituents may be combined to form a compound value or selected from a compound value. Thus "date" regarded as a data structure is a set containing a member for every possible day, combined with operations to construct a date from its constituents – year, month, and day – and to select a desired constituent.

An implementation of a data structure involves both choosing a *storage structure and providing a set of procedures/functions that implement the appropriate operations using the chosen storage structure. Formally, a data structure is defined as a distinguished domain in an *abstract data type that specifies the structure. Computer solution of a real-world problem involves designing some ideal data structures, and then mapping these onto available data structures (e.g. *arrays, *records, *lists, *queues, and *trees) for the implementation.

Note that terms for data structures are used to denote both the structure and data having that structure.

See also dynamic data structure, static data structure.

data subject An individual about whom information is stored in a computer-based system. *See* data protection legislation.

data sublanguage A language or part of a language concerned only with database query and update and/or database definition. *See* database language.

data summarization *See* statistical methods.

data tablet A graphical input device that returns the position of a *puck or stylus as it is moved over a flat surface. The term was originally a tradename used by Sylvania to describe a product of this type.

data terminal equipment *See* DTE.

data transfer rate The rate at which data can be moved between devices. The average rate is determined by the capability of the read or write device but the instantaneous rate is determined by the capability of the interface or transmission path. *Buffer memories are used to achieve the change in rate. For typical magnetic tape operating at 800 bytes per inch and 75 inches per second the rate is about 60 kilobytes per second. Disk storage systems can have transfer rates in excess of 3 megabytes per second. Fast serial interfaces operate up to 50 Mbps.

data transfer time The time taken for a data transfer between the drive and the host system. This time is dependent on the size of the data transfer and the rate at which it can be transmitted to/from the host.

data translation The process of converting data from the form used by one system into the form required by another. *See also* automatic data conversion.

data transmission The process of sending data (analog or digital measurements, coded characters, or information in general) from a sender to one or more receivers, i.e. from a source to one or more destinations.

data transparency 1. A property of a communication system (network) such that the output data stream delivered is the exact bit sequence presented to the input of the system without any restriction or exception.
2. A property of a communication system such that the output data stream delivered provides an output bit sequence functionally equivalent to the input bit sequence, from which the exact input bit sequence can be derived.

The second definition implies that the communication system provides protocol translation between input and output devices whereas the first definition implies that there is a compensating translation. The second definition cannot be implemented in all cases since there are functions that are supported by some terminal devices but have no equivalent in others.

data type An abstract set of possible values that an instance of the data type may assume, given either implicitly, e.g. INTEGER, REAL, STRING, or explicitly as, for example, in Pascal:

TYPE color = (red, green, orange)

The data type indicates a class of internal representations for those values.

Types may be defined in terms of other more primitive types, such as arrays of integers. Some languages consider *procedures or *functions as data types, which can also be used in the construction of more complex types.

See also abstract data type.

data validation (data vetting, data cleaning) The process of checking that data conforms to specification. It is usually the first process undertaken on *raw data. The following are among the kinds of checks that may be carried out: number and type of characters in a *data item; range of values of a data item; correctness of *check character(s); consistency between one data item and others in the same record; correctness of check totals for individual records; correctness of *batch controls.

data vetting *Another name for* data validation.

data word A word that can only, or is expected only to, contain data.

DB2 A *database management system from IBM. *See also* SQL, SQL/DS.

DBA *Abbrev. for* database administrator *and/or* database administration.

dBASE IV *Trademark. See* database management system.

DBMS (or dbms) *Abbrev. for* database management system *and* database management software.

DC *Abbrev. for* device coordinates.

DC cartridges *See* magnetic tape cartridge.

DCE 1. *Abbrev. for* data communication equipment. The side of an interface that represents the provider of a data communication in a standard such as RS232C or X25. DCEs are usually analog or digital *modems or network interface units. *Compare* DTE.
2. *Abbrev. for* distributed computing environment. A software system for UNIX, providing distributed services to applications. It is sponsored by the *OSF.

d.c. signaling *See* baseband networking.

DCT *Abbrev. for* discrete cosine transform.

DDC *Abbrev. for* direct digital control.

DDCMP *Abbrev. for* digital data communication message protocol. A *data link control protocol developed by Digital Equipment Corporation. It is similar to *SDLC and *HDLC but is character-oriented rather than bit-oriented. It allows a variety of data link characteristics: full duplex or half duplex, asynchronous or synchronous, switched or dedicated, point-to-point or multipoint, and serial or parallel. Data trans-parency is achieved using a data-length field rather than bit or byte stuffing techniques. Active NAKs are used for error control, in addition to timeouts.

DDE *Abbrev. for* direct data entry. *See* data entry.

DDL 1. *Abbrev. for* data description language. *See* database language.
2. *See* document description language.

DDP *Abbrev. for* distributed data processing. *See* distributed processing.

DEA *Abbrev. for* Data Encryption Algorithm.

deadlock 1. *Another name for* deadly embrace.
2. A specific form of *deadly embrace that arises in a *Petri net, in which some states of the net become forever inaccessible.

deadly embrace (deadlock) A situation that may arise when two (or more) separately active *processes compete for resources. Suppose that process P requires resources X and Y and requests their use in that order, and that at the same time process Q requires resources Y and X and asks for them in that order. If process P has acquired resource X and simultaneously process Q has acquired resource Y, then neither process can proceed, each process requiring a resource that has been allocated to the other process. On larger systems containing more than two processes and more than two resources, it is still possible for deadlock to develop although its detection may be more difficult.

debit/credit benchmark A *benchmark test for measuring the number of office tasks completed on a computer installation per hour. The basic feature of the test is to use a fixed number of terminals on a given computer configuration and to ramp up the number of standardized transactions per second until the system can only complete 95% of requested transactions in under one second.

debouncing A technique to avoid each reverberation of a closing switch or other electrical contact being registered as a separate event. After the detection of the initial closure a short pause is made in order to allow the reverberations of the contact, known as *contact bounce*, to die away. The contact is then sampled again to determine its final state.

DE BRUIJN DIAGRAM

Debouncing is often used in connection with the reading of keyboards.

de Bruijn diagram (de Bruijn graph) *See* Good–de Bruijn diagram.

debugging The identification and removal of localized implementation errors – or bugs – from a program or system. By contrast, *testing seeks to establish whether bugs exist but does not isolate or remove them. Program debugging is often supported by a *debug tool*, a *software tool that allows the internal behavior of the program to be investigated. Such a tool would typically offer trace facilities (*see* trace program), allow the planting of *breakpoints* (i.e. points in the program at which execution is to be suspended so that examination of partial results is possible), and permit examination and perhaps modification of the values of program variables when a breakpoint is reached.

debug tool (debugger) *See* debugging.

DEC *See* Digital Equipment Corporation.

decade counter *See* counter.

decal *Another name for* texture mapping.

de Casteljau algorithm A recursive algorithm for computing *Bézier curves from the *control points. Given control points $r_0 \ldots r_n$, set

$$r_i^r(u) = (1 - u)r_i^{r-1}(u) + ur_{i+1}^{r-1}(u)$$

for $r = 1, \ldots n$ and $i = 0, \ldots n-r$ and $r_i^0(u) = r_i$. Then $r_i^n(u)$ is the point with parameter value u on the Bézier curve of degree n.

decidable problem *See* decision problem.

decidable set *See* recursive set.

decision gate An electronic *logic gate whose output indicates whether a logical relationship is either true or false. The following are examples: an equality *comparator, indicating when two binary numbers are equal; an *odd parity checker, indicating when a binary input has an odd number of ones; a *majority element, indicating when the binary inputs have more 1 entries than 0 entries.

decision problem A computational task that for each possible input requires "true" or "false" to be output, depending on whether the input possesses a certain property. An

algorithm that produces the correct decision in each case is called a *decision procedure* for that problem. If a decision procedure exists then the problem is said to be (algorithmically) *solvable*, while an (algorithmically) *unsolvable* problem is one for which no decision procedure exists. An example is logical validity, the inputs being logical expressions, with the output "true" for valid expressions and "false" for others. This problem is solvable for *propositional logic (the construction of *truth tables being a decision procedure) but not for *predicate logic (by Church's theorem of 1936). Solvable problems can be further classified according to the efficiency of decision procedures existing for them (*see* P=NP question).

Some unsolvable problems possess a *semidecision procedure*, i.e. an algorithm that correctly outputs "true" but fails to terminate in cases where "false" should be output. This is the same as saying that the inputs requiring the output "true" form a set that is *recursively enumerable (but need not be *recursive). Alternatively it can be said that the problem corresponds to a predicate that is *semidecidable* (but need not be *decidable*).

decision procedure *See* decision problem.

decision support system (DSS) *See* management information system.

decision surface A (hyper) surface in a multidimensional *state space that partitions the space into different regions. Data lying on one side of a decision surface are defined as belonging to a different class from those lying on the other. Decision surfaces may be created or modified as a result of a learning process and they are frequently used in *machine learning, *pattern recognition, and *classification systems.

decision table A table that indicates actions to be taken under various conditions, the *decision* being the selection between the alternative actions. Conventionally a decision table has four parts that are named and laid out as shown in Fig. *a*. The *condition stub* part lists the individual inputs upon which the decision depends, while the *action stub* part lists the alternative actions that may be taken. The entry parts then show the conditions under which each action is selected. This is done by arranging the *condition entry* part into columns, where each column specifies some condition on each of the input values, and then placing a cross in the same column of the *action entry* part to indicate the particular action to be taken. All the conditions of the column must be satisfied in order for the column to be selected. Normally the complete table covers all possible combinations of input values in such a way that application of the table always selects precisely one action (*see also* ELSE rule). The example in Fig. *b* shows a table for deciding how to travel to work. A '–' symbol in the condition entry part indicates "don't care".

condition stub	condition entry
action stub	action entry

Fig. *a* Parts of a decision table

rain	N	N	Y	–	–	–
snow	N	N	N	Y	–	–
fog	N	N	N	N	Y	Y
temperature	>8	<8	–	–	>0	<0
take bicycle	×					
take automobile		×	×			
take train					×	×
stay home						×

Fig. *b* Example of a decision table

Decision tables have been used both for program specification and implementation, the latter being achieved by directly interpreting (or generating an executable program from) the decision table format.

decision tree A *binary tree where every *nonterminal node represents a decision. Depending upon the decision taken at such a node, control passes to the left or right subtree of the node. A *leaf node then represents the outcome of taking the sequence of decisions given by the nodes on the path from the root to the leaf. *See also* bifurcation.

declaration One of the two major kinds of element in a conventional program, the other being a *statement. A declaration introduces an entity for part of the program – its *scope* – giving it a name and establishing its static properties. Examples are declarations of variables, declarations of procedures, declarations of input/output ports or files.

declarative languages (nonprocedural languages) A class of programming languages. With a declarative language a program explicitly states what properties the desired result is required to exhibit but does not state how the desired result is to be obtained; any means of producing a result that displays the required properties is acceptable in implementations (*compare* imperative languages).

Since declarative languages are concerned with static rather than dynamic concepts (i.e. with what rather than how), they do not depend on any inherent notion of ordering and there is no concept of flow of control and no *assignment statement. Ideally a program in a declarative language would consist solely of an unordered set of equations sufficient to characterize the desired result. However, for reasons of implementation and efficiency, the existing languages fall somewhat short of this, either in semantics or in style of use (or both). Declarative languages are not tied to the von Neumann model of computation and typically there is scope for employing new architectures with a high degree of parallelism in obtaining the desired result.

See also functional languages, logic programming languages.

DECnet *Trademark* A network system produced by Digital Equipment Corporation (DEC) to run on their VAX proprietary systems. A number of other suppliers have products that either implement parts of the DECnet system or are able to exchange data with a DECnet system.

decoder 1. The means by which a decoding process is effected (*see* code). It may be implemented in hardware or software, the process being algorithmic in nature.
2. *See* decoder/demultiplexer.

decoder/demultiplexer A logic circuit, usually an integrated circuit, that is capable of setting one of its 2^n output lines active, i.e. at logic 1, in response to an n-bit binary code present at its input. For an n-bit device, 2^n distinct elements of a code can be input.

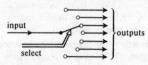

Decoder/demultiplexer

A decoder/demultiplexer may be considered as a switch that directs data from a time-shared data bus to one of several possible outputs under the control of a select signal, which is normally digital; the select signal indicates which of the outputs is to be connected to the input (*see* diagram). Individual data channels may be recovered from a time-division multiplexed input bus provided that the scanning of the select signal is made synchronous with that of the multiplexer. The input to and outputs from a decoder/demultiplexer may be in digital or analog form. *See also* data selector/multiplexer.

decoder/driver An electronic device that is capable of accepting encoded data at its input and generating unencoded data at its output. The decoding process employed may conform to an agreed standard or be user-defined. The outputs of these devices are capable of directly driving external equipment such as *LCD- or *LED-type displays.

decoder error *See* channel error.

decoding The process of reconverting a coded message to the message from which it was encoded. *See* code.

decollator A machine that can process multi-copy printed output into separate stacks of copy and used carbon paper. It is normally done as an offline activity and may be combined with a *burster that breaks the continuous forms at the perforations to give separate sheets.

decompiler A program that attempts to do for compiler output what a *disassembler does for assembler output, i.e. translate back from

machine code to something resembling the source language. The task is difficult and not often attempted.

decomposition 1. In switching theory, the realization of an n-variable switching function as a composition of functions, each of which has less than n variables. Like other *minimizations, decomposition is facilitated by *Karnaugh maps.
2. In programming, the analysis of a problem into simpler subproblems. *See* program decomposition, modular programming.

decompression Returning a compressed image or compressed data to its uncompressed form. Some compression methods lose information so that the uncompressed image or data is not equivalent to the original.

deconvolution *See* convolution.

decryption The processing of an encrypted message by an authorized recipient in order to recover the original message. *See also* cryptography. *Compare* cryptanalysis.

dedicated Committed entirely to a single purpose or device. For example, a computer system may be dedicated to the job of controlling an industrial machine tool. A dedicated device or resource may be idle for significant periods of time.

dedicated mode A processing mode in which the system is operated for a single purpose, and for only those users with sufficient *security clearance to access all the information on the system.

deduction A formal method of logical inference. Deduction is the process of applying one or more inference rules to a given set of facts (known as *axioms*) and inferring new facts. Unlike the other methods of inference, *abduction and *induction, deduction produces logically sound results, i.e. involves no uncertainty.

deep case One of a set of semantic roles that can be used as grammatical primitives in terms of which sentences are constructed. Examples of deep cases are Agent, Patient, and Theme, although the contents of comprehensive lists vary from one presentation to another. *See also* case grammar.

deep structure A notion that is central to transformational grammar's (Chomsky 1965) description of the *syntax of natural language. Deep structure is where the predicate–argument relationships are expressed, and both relates the words of a sentence to its meaning and expresses grammatical generalizations. Within the "standard theory" of transformational grammar the context-free base generates deep structures and a set of transformations that map these to the surface structure. In natural-language processing, sentences can be analyzed by either fully or partially running transformations in reverse.

default A value that is used when no other value has been supplied. Defaults may be stored in a configuration file, or they may be embedded in a program or permanently encoded into ROM, or read from the settings of a DIP switch. Nearly every application has defaults for something. For instance, word processors have default fonts, justification, and page length, World Wide Web browsers have default home pages, compilers have default optimization levels, and drawing programs have default palettes and pen thickness.

default rules A method for resolving conflicts and dealing with inconsistencies that arise in *inheritance systems and *nonmonotonic reasoning. Default rules can contain components that define normality so that exceptions do not cause conflicts. For example, knowing that birds fly and Fred is a bird is inconsistent with knowing that Fred is a penguin. Attaching a "normal" predicate to the rule that birds fly and knowing that penguins are not normal birds resolves the problem.

defect skipping A method used on obsolete disk drives by which a media defect on a magnetic disk *track was avoided such that no data were written in the vicinity of the defect.

deferral Delaying the presentation of output to the graphics screen to improve efficiency.

deferred addressing *Another name for* indirect addressing.

deferred approach to the limit (Richardson extrapolation) *See* extrapolation.

definition The fineness of spatial sampling of a digital image and hence a measure of image sharpness and contrast. It is expressed in pixels.

deflation *See* polynomial equation.

defrag *Short for* defragmentation.

defragmentation The act of consolidating the fragments of unused space in memory into a smaller number of larger areas. The requirement to do this can arise either in the allocation of *random-access memory or of *blocks on a disk. *See* fragmentation.

degree 1. of a vertex of a *graph. The number of edges incident with the vertex, i.e. that emanate from that vertex. In a directed graph, the *indegree* is the number of edges entering a vertex while the *outdegree* is the number leaving a vertex. **2.** of a node in a *tree. The number of children of that node, i.e. the number of subtrees rooted at that node. More correctly, this is the *outdegree* of the node. **3.** of a tree. The maximum degree of all the nodes in the tree. **4.** of a polynomial. *See* polynomial.

degree of precision The degree of polynomials that a given rule for *numerical integration integrates exactly. The same concept can be applied in other areas, such as the solution of ordinary differential equations. It is related to the concept of *order of approximation, and provides a measure of the approximating power of a given method.

degrees of freedom In statistical analysis, the number of independent observations associated with an estimate of variance (*see* measures of variation) or of a component of an *analysis of variance. The simplest example is in estimating the variance of a sample of n observations, where the degrees of freedom is $n - 1$, the divisor of the sum of squared deviations from the sample mean. More generally, the degrees of freedom, f, is the difference between the number of *parameters in a given model, and a special case of that model with fewer parameters. The number of degrees of freedom is required when selecting a particular instance of the *chi-squared distribution, *Student's t distribution, or *F distribution.

Dekker's algorithm An algorithm, based on a combination of successive linear *interpolation and binary search, that finds a zero of a function that changes sign in a given interval.

Delaunay triangulation A recursive algorithm for splitting an area into triangles that ensures that the circle circumscribing the vertices of a triangle contains the vertices of no other triangle within it. This avoids long thin triangles, for example. See also triangulation.

delay differential equations *Ordinary differential equations where the derivatives depend on values of the solution at the current value and several previous values of the independent variable. The simplest form is

$$y'(x) = f(x, y(x), y(x - \tau(x))),$$
$$a \leq x \leq b$$

where $\tau(x) \geq 0$. To determine a solution, $y(x)$ must be specified on an interval $a^* \leq x \leq a$ where a^* depends on the values taken by $\tau(x)$.

Most of the commonly used step-by-step methods for ordinary differential equations can be adapted to problems of this form, although they have not yet been developed to the same extent. It is necessary to incorporate an *interpolation scheme to approximate

$$y(x - \tau(x))$$

at values that will not usually coincide with a previously computed approximation.

delayed branch A *conditional branch instruction found in some *RISC architectures that include *pipelining. The effect is to execute one or more instructions following the conditional branch before the branch is taken. This avoids stalling the pipeline while the branch condition is evaluated, thus keeping the pipeline full and minimizing the effect of conditional branches on processor performance.

delay line An electronic device that produces a finite accurate time delay between a signal imposed on its input and the appearance of the same signal at its output. These devices may be used as short-term signal stores or to provide accurate delays in signal-processing circuits. In an *acoustic delay line* electrical sig-

nals are converted into a pattern of acoustic (sound) waves that travel through a medium between a transmitter and receiver.

Delay lines were the most common storage devices in *first-generation computers: this *acoustic memory* was used, for example, in EDSAC, EDVAC, pilot ACE and ACE, UNIVAC 1, and LEO 1. In EDSAC (1949), quartz crystals were used as transducers and the ultrasonic pulses were passed along a tube of mercury about 5 feet (1.5 meters) in length. The delay was approximately 1 millisecond but it enabled nearly 1000 pulses to be stored. Later acoustic memory used magnetostrictive transducers and nickel-iron wire, with the electrical signals converted into stress waves.

delay-power product A figure of merit that is frequently quoted as characteristic of a particular *logic family. It is the product of the *propagation delay (usually in nanoseconds) and the power dissipation (usually in milliwatts) of a gate typical of the family; it has dimensions of energy, the usual unit being the picojoule, pJ. The smaller the delay-power product is, the better the logic family is considered to be.

delete 1. To remove or obliterate a record or item of data, such as by overwriting data on disk or tape with new data or null characters. **2.** To remove permanently an object, such as a character, word, paragraph, or graphic, from a document, or to remove an entire document file from permanent storage. In either case there is usually a period of grace during which the decision to delete can be rescinded, and after which the action is irreversible. **3.** One of the basic actions performed on *sets that, when applied in the form

$$delete(el, S)$$

removes the element el from S; if el was not present in S the action has no effect on the membership of S. See also operations on sets.

delimiter A symbol that serves to mark the beginning or end of some programming construct, e.g. the semicolon that separates statements in Algol-like languages, the period that marks the end of a sentence in Cobol, the ENDIF that marks the end of an IF statement in Fortran 77.

delta PCM (delta modulation) *See* pulse code modulation.

demand paging A method of dealing with a situation in which a *process requires access to a *page of memory that has been written to backing store. Some systems attempt to forecast the pattern of demand for pages; other systems rely on demand paging in which no attempt is made to forecast the pattern of behavior, but pages are transferred from backing store into main memory on demand as required by the individual process.

demand reading, writing A process in which data is transferred directly between a processor and a storage device. This is a normal mode of operation for main memory but is sometimes applied to other devices.

demodulator A device that receives analog signals as input and produces digital data as output. Demodulators use the inverse of the methods used by *modulators, which encode data as analog signals. *See also* modulation, modem.

demon In some operating systems, the process that controls a peripheral device. (The word is probably a contraction of *device monitor*.) By an extension of meaning the word is sometimes used for any process within the operating system, even if the process is not actually responsible for a peripheral device.

de Morgan's laws The two laws of a *Boolean algebra that provide a method of expressing the complement of a complex expression in terms of the complements of individual components:
$$(x \vee y)' = x' \wedge y'$$
$$(x \wedge y)' = x' \vee y'$$
The pair is self-dual. The term de Morgan's laws is often used to describe instances of these laws as they apply in particular cases, e.g. to sets or to logical expressions. The laws are named for Augustus de Morgan.

demultiplexer 1. In communications, a device that performs the reverse function to a *multiplexer.
2. A *combinational circuit that converts from n inputs to 1 of m outputs, where $m \leq 2^n$.

See also decoder/demultiplexer.

dendrogram *See* cluster analysis.

denial An assertion taking the form that a particular statement is false.

denial of service The prevention of an authorized user from processing information, for example because that information has been intentionally corrupted or else because the processing unit is kept busy by spurious tasks. *See* threat.

denotational semantics An approach to the *semantics of programming languages in which the meaning of a program in a particular language is given by a valuation function that associates with each well-formed syntactic construct of the language an abstract value, e.g. a term with a number, a test with a truth value, or a command with a function on states. These valuation functions are compositional or recursive in nature: the value of a program is specified as a function of the values denoted by its syntactic subcomponents. To define valuation functions it is usually necessary to solve functional equations using *fixed-point methods.

This approach was initiated and developed by Christopher Strachey and Dana Scott to provide a semantic theory that was more abstract than *operational semantics. It is less abstract than *axiomatic semantics.

density 1. A measure of the amount of information in a given dimension of a storage medium. The density of information on a disk is almost always a fixed number of bits per sector, sectors per track, and tracks per disk. For magnetic tape it is the amount of information recorded per unit length of tape, usually in bits per inch or bits per millimeter. In general the number of flux reversals per inch (or per mm) is different because of redundancy in the coding. The density is stated for a single track. A tape transport can often read tapes with different densities under program control.
2. *See* packing density.

denumerable set *See* countable set.

deposit To place a value in a register in a processor, or in a word in memory. On many microprocessor or mini systems this can be achieved by manual operations on the control panel of the system.

depth 1. of a node in a tree. The length of the unique path from the root of the tree to the node. Thus if a node A is the root node then its depth is zero, otherwise its depth is one greater than that of its parent.

In some texts, depth of a node is synonymous with *level of a node.

2. of a tree. The maximum depth of any node in a tree. The depth of a given tree will have the same numerical value as the *height of that tree.

depth-balanced *See* balanced.

depth buffer *See* Z-buffer.

depth cueing Modeling atmospheric attenuation by rendering distant objects at a lower intensity than near ones, hence giving them the appearance of depth.

depth-first search A search of a directed *graph, and hence of a *tree, conducted as follows. An initial starting vertex u is selected and visited. Then a (directed) edge (u, v) incident upon u is selected and a visit is made to v. Let x be the most recent vertex visited. Select some unexplored edge (x, y) incident upon x. If y has not been previously visited, visit y and proceed from there. If y has been previously visited select another edge incident upon x. Having completed the search through all paths beginning at y, return to x and continue to explore the edges incident upon x.

Depth-first searches of graphs play an important part in the design of efficient algorithms on graphs, in game theory, heuristic programming, and in artificial intelligence. *See also* iterative deepening.

Compare breadth-first search.

deque *Derived from* double-ended queue. A linear *list where all insertions, removals, and accesses are made at the ends. *See also* stack.

derivation sequence In formal language theory, a sequence of *words of the form

$$w_1 \overset{*}{\Rightarrow} w_2 \overset{*}{\Rightarrow} \ldots \overset{*}{\Rightarrow} w_n$$

(for notation *see* semi-Thue system). For a *context-free grammar, such a sequence is *leftmost* (or *rightmost*) if,

for each $1 \leq i \leq n$,

w_{i+1} is obtained from w_i by rewriting the leftmost (or rightmost) nonterminal in w_i. Such sequences exist for all derivable words.

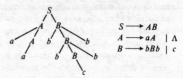

Derivation tree

derivation tree A way of indicating how a *context-free grammar derives a particular word. The *leaf nodes of the tree are terminals, the other nodes are nonterminals. For example, the tree in the diagram shows a derivation of *aabbcbb* from the grammar that is shown. Many different *derivation sequences can correspond to the same derivation tree.

derivative of a *formal language. The *left-derivative* of a language L, with respect to a word w, is

$$\{w' \mid ww' \in L\}$$

where ww' is the *concatenation of w and w'. Similarly a *right-derivative* is

$$\{w' \mid w'w \in L\}$$

DES *Abbrev. for* Data Encryption Standard.

descendant of a node, A, in a tree. Any node, B, such that A is an *ancestor of B.

descriptor Stored information that describes how other information is stored, e.g. in an array, record, or file. By referring to the descriptor, a program can interpret the other data. *See also* file descriptor, process descriptor.

design database A database concerned with design data, such as that used by *computer-aided design tools. Access to a design database will often be over a long period of time as opposed to the short processing times of *transactions in conventional databases.

design review *See* review.

desktop 1. (desktop computer, worktop) An entire computer that sits on a desk or table, a PC or Macintosh being examples. It usually consists of a *display, either color or monochrome, a *system box* containing the processor, memory, disk drives, power supply, and communication interfaces, a *keyboard, and a *pointing device, often a mouse. The system box is usually a convenient size on which to stand the display monitor (*but see* miditower). Although the desktop computer is relatively cumbersome compared with a *notebook computer of equivalent power, it currently has a significantly better power/performance ratio.

2. Part of a *graphical user interface which invites the user to imagine that some or all of the screen is an actual desktop on which actions analogous to those occurring on a physical desktop can be carried out. These include the opening and closing of manila folders, the entry and modification of text, the disposal of unwanted material into a wastebasket, and the use of communication systems analogous to telephones and mailboxes. The analogy is supposed to make life easier for office workers unused to computers.

desktop publishing (DTP) The use of a computer system or *workstation together with a *page printer to perform many of the functions of a print shop. These include page layout and design, the choice of *font, and the inclusion of diagrams and pictures. DTP software normally produces its output in a *page description language that is then interpreted by the page printer to the best of its ability. The DTP program can take its input from, for instance, text files from *word processors or *text editors, pictures from graphics programs, or digitized images from *scanners. Pagemaker, Framemaker, and Quark Express are examples of DTP software.

The distinction between DTP and *word processing is becoming less marked as each new version of word-processing software contains features formerly only available in DTP packages.

destructive read A read operation that alters the contents of the accessed memory location and must be immediately followed by a rewriting of the contents in order to preserve

them. This was the case for example with magnetic core store.

determinant A number associated with a *square matrix of numbers. The determinant of an $n \times n$ matrix A is denoted by $\det(A)$ or $|A|$ and given by

$$\sum_\sigma \text{par}(\sigma)\, a_{1\sigma_1} a_{2\sigma_2} \cdots a_{n\sigma_n}$$

where the sum is taken over all $n!$ *permutations

$$\sigma = \sigma_1 \sigma_2 \ldots \sigma_n$$

of the integers $1, 2, \ldots, n$. par(σ), the parity of σ, is either $+1$ or -1 depending on whether σ is an even permutation or an odd permutation.

deterministic Denoting an algorithm, machine, method, process, procedure, program, etc., the resulting behavior of which is uniquely determined by the inputs and initial state. *See also* nondeterminism, statistical methods, pseudorandom.

deterministic language Any *context-free language recognized by a deterministic *pushdown automaton. An example of a simple nondeterministic language is the set of all palindromes over an alphabet with two or more letters. A language is deterministic if and only if it is LR(k) for some k (*see* LR parsing).

deterministic Turing machine *See* Turing machine. *See also* nondeterminism.

development life cycle *See* software life cycle, system life cycle.

device 1. In general, any printer, storage, display, input, or output mechanism that may be attached to a computer system.

2. On some operating systems, the name "device" is also associated with a destination. The output from or input to a process may be connected to a device, file, or another process. In most computers, printers, displays, keyboards, and other input mechanisms are regarded as devices.

device coordinates (DC) A device-dependent coordinate system whose coordinates are typically in integer units (e.g. raster lines and pixels).

device driver A program, or part of a program, used to control the detailed operation of an input or output device connected to a computer system. In many cases the device drivers are embedded as part of the *operating system, and different device drivers are written to conform to an agreed set of standards governing the way in which the user's application program communicates with the device driver. This allows programs to be written in such a way as to be able to use any device for which a suitable device driver has been produced. The inclusion of the appropriate device drivers may take place when the operating system for a particular configuration is being generated. Alternatively when the system is first started it may determine what devices are connected, and incorporate the corresponding device drivers. In some cases this approach is taken even further, and attaching a new device will cause the system to locate and include the corresponding device drivers. *See also* plug-and-play.

DFD *Abbrev. for* dataflow diagram.

D flip-flop

D flip-flop A clocked *flip-flop having a single D input (*see* diagram). The flip-flop Q output will take on the current state of the D input only when a given transition of the clock signal occurs between its two logic states, i.e. from low to high voltage level (*positive-edge triggered*) or from high to low level (*negative-edge triggered*).

DFT *Abbrev. for* discrete Fourier transform.

dhrystone benchmark A program designed to be used to compare the performance of compilers for a particular high-level language (especially for Ada). The program does not compute anything useful, but it is syntactically and semantically correct. The distribution of statements is approximately 53% assignments, 32% control, and 15% procedure or function calls. This mix is considered to be representative of typical use when a high-level language is used for real programs. (The name derives as a contrast with *whetstone benchmark.)

diagnostic routine A routine within a program that is entered as a result of some error condition having been detected, and serves to analyze the cause of that error or to provide information that is subsequently used for such analysis. A typical diagnostic routine might attempt to isolate the cause of the error to a particular hardware or software subsystem, or simply record the values of the major data objects at the time that the error occurred.

diagonalization A proof technique in *recursive function theory that is used to prove the unsolvability of, for example, the *halting problem. The proof assumes (for the sake of argument) that there is an effective procedure for testing whether programs terminate. Under this assumption the method of diagonalization allows a contradiction to be derived. From this it is deduced that there is no such effective procedure.

The technique was developed by G. Cantor to prove that the *cardinality of the real numbers is greater than the cardinality of the integers. In this application the real numbers are enumerated in the form of a grid. A real number is then constructed, using the diagonal of the grid, that is not part of the original enumeration.

The technique was also used by J. Richard to generate a paradox about the namability of real numbers. This paradox (together with the "liar paradox" of antiquity) is reputed to have prompted K. Gödel to apply a similar technique of diagonalization in constructing a number-theory formula not provable in formal arithmetic. *See* Gödel's incompleteness theorems.

diagonal matrix A square matrix A in which $a_{ij} = 0$ if $i \neq j$. The *inverse of a diagonal matrix, if it exists, is particularly easy to calculate and is itself diagonal.

diagrammatic technique A style of analysis or design that relies primarily on the use of diagrams (as opposed to text or databases). The advantage is the direct appeal to users, the disadvantage the limitation to two dimensions. *See* CORE, ERA diagram, JSD, MASCOT, Nassi–Shneiderman chart, SADT, SSADM, Yourdon.

dialogue box A simple *window containing a
title bar, a message, and one or more response
*buttons. This kind of window will normally
allow no other actions to take place until a
button has been pressed. In the simplest case
a single button marked "ok" is pressed to
acknowledge the message; in other cases
there may be a choice of buttons such as
"yes" "no" "cancel" or "replace" "create
backup" "cancel". Dialogue boxes may contain more complex objects such as *radio
buttons, *pull-down menus, or *scroll bars.

dialogue management The methods and
procedures governing the way that information is exchanged between the user and the
computer system. It involves the consistent
formatting of prompts, check boxes, lists of
options, sliders, messages, and other constructs. There are *modal dialogues*, where the
user can do nothing else until the action
required to satisfy the dialogue has been
taken; this can be as simple as acknowledging
a message. Conversely, a *modeless dialogue* is
one that may be returned to after attending
to other matters. *See also* dialogue box.

dictionary Any data structure representing a
set of elements that can support the insertion
and deletion of elements as well as a test for
membership. *See also* data dictionary, symbol
table.

difference equations Equations that have
the same general form as *recurrence relations; however, the term also refers to situations in which the solution is not determined
recursively from initial conditions. Difference equations play a large part in numerical
computation. The equations are sometimes
expressed in terms of differences of function
values rather than function values themselves. The standard difference representations are:
forward difference,
$$\Delta f(x) = f(x + h) - f(x)$$
backward difference,
$$\Delta f(x) = f(x) - f(x - h)$$
central difference,
$$\delta f(x) = f(x + \frac{1}{2}h) - f(x - \frac{1}{2}h)$$
Difference equations arise in the application
of the *finite-difference method.

differential backup *See* full backup.

differential dump *Another name for* change
dump.

differential equations Equations for one or
more unknown functions involving derivatives of those functions. The equations
describe changes in a system, usually modeling some physical or other law. Except in
simple cases the solution cannot be determined analytically. *See* ordinary differential
equations, partial differential equations.

differential PCM (DPCM) *See* pulse code
modulation.

diffuse reflection Reflection due to light
being absorbed by a thin layer under the surface of an object then reradiated. The radiated light is distributed uniformly from the
point of incidence on the same side of the
surface as the incident light. The reflected
light has a spectrum equal to the product of
the spectrum of the incident light and the
absorption spectrum of the surface.
  Diffuse reflection varies between the case
when all the light is absorbed so that the surface is invisible and the other extreme when
the surface reflects back all light from the
source. Diffusely reflected light makes a surface appear dull with a matt finish that is
independent of the viewing direction. *Compare* specular reflection.

digital Operating by, responding to, or otherwise concerned with the use of digits (i.e. discrete units) to represent arithmetic numbers,
approximations to numbers from a continuum, or logical expressions/variables. *See also*
discrete and continuous systems.

digital audio tape (DAT) A *helical-scan
magnetic-tape system originally designed for
audio recording, but now adapted for computer use. The cartridge is very compact but
the recording method allows a capacity of a
gigabyte or more, depending on the precise
format used.

digital cassette A particular form of *magnetic tape cartridge.

digital circuit An electronic circuit that
responds to *digital signals and produces
digital signals as its output.

digital computer A computer that operates
on discrete quantities (*compare* analog com-

puter). All computation is done within a finite number system and with limited precision, associated with the number of digits in the discrete numbers. The numerical information is most often represented by the use of two-state electrical phenomena (on/off, high voltage/low voltage, current/no current, etc.) to indicate whether the value of a binary variable is a "zero" or a "one". Usually there is automatic control or sequencing (through a *program) of operations so that they can be carried through to completion without intervention. *See also* discrete and continuous systems.

digital copier A document copier that scans a page (*see* scanner), converts it to a digital image, and then prints it by means of a *page printer. *See also* intelligent copier.

digital data transmission Digital data uses discrete discontinuous signals to represent its meanings. In a DC (direct current) transmission system, different voltage (or current) values are used to represent the values (usually 0 and 1). A digital transmission has a very low error rate and can be sent at very high speeds. Weak signals can be regenerated with low probability of cumulative error. Since all signals are made up of 0s and 1s, signals from many sources can be readily multiplexed using digital techniques. *See* multiplexing.

Digital data can also be transmitted over AC transmission lines. Since DC signals are blocked out by AC transmission lines, a different technique is used. AC lines use analog signals to transmit data; to transform digital data to analog signals a *modulator is used. *See also* modulation.

digital design (logic design) The design of circuits and systems whose inputs and outputs are represented as discrete variables. These variables are commonly binary, i.e. two-state, in nature. Design at the circuit level is usually done with *truth tables and *state tables; design at the system level is done with *block diagrams or *digital design languages.

digital design language A high-level language, often called a *register transfer language, used to facilitate the description and manipulation of digital systems and their interconnection. *See also* digital design, CHDL.

Digital Equipment Corporation (DEC) A US computer manufacturer, founded by Ken Olsen and Harlan Anderson in 1956 to exploit the research work that had led to the development of the *Whirlwind computer at Massachusetts Institute of Technology. It is perhaps the most famous and spectacular example of the commercial exploitation of university research. Digital's PDP8 and PDP11 computers were the archetypal minicomputers of the late 1960s to the early 1980s; they were followed by the VAX range of midrange machines and, in 1992, by the Alpha line. Although it still supports its proprietary VMS operating system, Digital has committed itself to the open systems approach through its OSF/1 operating system (*see* OSF). In terms of revenue, it is the fifth largest IT company in the world (1993 figures).

digital filtering The employment of *digital signal processing techniques to effect the *filtering of a signal.

digital halftone *See* halftone.

digital image An image consisting of data (specifically a set of elements) defined on an n-dimensional regular grid that has the potential for display. These elements are referred to as *pixels. The pixels in different images may represent a variety of types of information, such as temperature, pressure, velocity, terrain height, or tissue density. The regular grid is frequently over a two-dimensional space but can be three-dimensional, and even four-dimensional if sampling over time is also included. *See also* image processing.

digital logic A methodology for dealing with expressions and *state tables containing discrete (usually two-state) variables: in this sense the term is synonymous with *Boolean algebra (*see also* multivalued logic). The term is also applied to the hardware – components and circuits – in which such expressions and tables are implemented. *See also* digital design, logic circuit, combinational circuit, sequential circuit, q-ary logic.

digital signal A waveform or signal whose voltage at any particular time will be at any one of a group of discrete levels, generally two; a two-level signal is sometimes called a *binary digital signal* or *binary signal*. In binary logic circuits, in which only two discrete voltage levels are used, one level will correspond to logic 1 (true), usually the high level, and the other will correspond to logic 0 (false).

digital signal processing (DSP) The branch of *signal processing that uses digital systems to operate on signals. The advantages of digital over analog signal processing are that memory is more easily employed (so that time may be rerun in different speeds and directions) and that a wider range of arithmetic operations and algorithmic complexity is possible; the main advantage, however, is that the possible precision is arbitrarily high. The main disadvantage is that in some instances digital techniques are slower than analog techniques. Many specialized digital devices have been developed that retain the advantages but nevertheless operate at high speed, at the cost of flexibility.

digital sorting *Another name for* radix sorting.

digital system Any system handling digital (discrete) *signals. *See* discrete and continuous systems.

digital-to-analog converter *See* D/A converter.

digital video Video output based on digital rather than analog signals. *See also* codec.

digital video interactive *See* DVI.

digitization The process of quantizing a *signal and representing it in digital form. *See also* quantization, discrete and continuous systems, digitizer, A/D converter.

digitizer 1. A device that produces a digital representation of an object. Digitizers use various technologies – optics, acoustics, magnetostriction, electromagnetics, resistance, capacitance, etc. – to calculate the position of the stylus or *puck that is used to input the data values. A digitizer can be two- or three-dimensional. A common application is to capture information related to schematic line drawings.

2. *Another name for* quantizer, but generally

implying that the output is encoded into *binary numbers.

digraph *Short for* directed graph. *See* graph.

Dijkstra's algorithm A method, developed by E. W. Dijkstra in 1959, to find the *shortest path from a specified *vertex in a *weighted graph to all other vertices in the graph.

DIL *Acronym for* dual in-line. *See* DIP, DIL switch.

DIL switch A device similar in form to a *DIP, but instead of an integrated circuit the package contains a row of small switches making or breaking the circuit between opposite pairs of legs. DIL switches are commonly used for setting the default state of printers, terminals, etc.

dimension (dimensionality) of an *array. The number of subscripts or indexes needed to locate any element in the array.

diminished radix complement *Another name for* radix-minus-one complement.

diminishing increment sort *Another name for* Shell's method.

diode An electronic device, generally of semiconductor material, that has two terminals and is capable of allowing current flow in one direction only. The terminals are called the *anode* and *cathode*. The diode presents a very low (high) impedance when a *forward bias (*reverse bias) is applied.

diode-transistor logic *See* DTL.

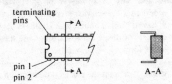

DIP

DIP 1. *Short for* dual in-line package. An *integrated circuit encapsulated in a rectangular plastic or ceramic package with a row of metal legs down each of the long sides (*see* diagram). The legs are terminating pins. The number of terminations and hence the package size is a function of the number of external connections to the chip. The legs can

either be soldered into holes in a *printed circuit board or inserted into a *chip socket.
2. *Abbrev. for* document image processing.

direct-access storage device (DASD) One of a class of storage devices in which physical *records are *addressable and can therefore be accessed in any order: a sequential search is not required. For all practical purposes direct-access storage is synonymous with disk storage.

direct addressing The "normal" mode of addressing in which the address specified in the instruction is the *absolute address to be used. *See also* addressing schemes.

direct-coupled machines A system in which two (or more) machines are connected by a high-speed link in order to perform the total workload. Typically a small machine, the *master*, deals with file editing, job submission, and all scheduling. Larger jobs that would take too long to process on this small machine are passed to a larger machine, the *slave*, for processing, the results being returned to the user via the small machine. *See also* master-slave machine.

direct data entry (DDE) *See* data entry.

direct digital control (DDC) Control of a process by a digital computer, the information being supplied to the process as (appropriately timed) sequences of digits. *See* numerical control.

directed graph (digraph) *See* graph.

directed set A subset X of a *partially ordered set S, such that every finite subset of X has an *upper bound in X itself. As a special case of this, a *chain* is a countable subset of the form

$$x_0 \subseteq x_1 \subseteq x_2 \subseteq \ldots$$

where $\subseteq$ denotes the partial ordering on S.

directed tree *See* tree.

direction keys *See* arrow keys.

directive *Another name for* pseudoinstruction.

direct memory access (DMA) A method whereby I/O processes can obtain access to the CPU's memory while a program is running. This is accomplished by permitting the I/O controller or channel that has been previously instructed to move a block of data to

or from the memory to temporarily take control of the memory for (usually) one *memory cycle by specifying the memory address, thus allowing a single word (or group of words if the memory is so organized) to be read or written. The method is therefore also referred to as *cycle stealing*. The timing requirement is normally that of the slower external device and is prompted by the ability of that device to receive or provide desired data, hence the alternative synonym *data break*.

directory A means of locating data items, usually files. A directory can be regarded as establishing a set of links between named data items and their locations in a *direct-access storage device. In many systems the directories are highly structured; their organization reflects the relationships between various categories of file. For example, the directory may allow one user to have other subordinate users, and permit controlled access by these subordinate users to their own and others' files.

A directory may contain the names of files and of other directories. For instance, if directory x contained directory y, which contained file z, then it would be necessary to include x, y, and z in any reference to the file. *See also* access path.

directory tree A directory hierarchy. The *root directory* forms the top level in the hierarchy and is not contained by any other directory. A directory within another directory is known as a *subdirectory.

direct product (product group) of two *groups G and H with group *operations ρ and τ respectively. The group consisting of the elements in the *Cartesian product of G and H and on which there is a *dyadic operation $\circ$ defined as follows:

$$(g_1, h_1) \circ (g_2, h_2) = (g_1 \rho g_2, h_1 \tau h_2)$$

The identity of this group is then just (e_G, e_H), where e_G and e_H are the identities of groups G and H respectively. The inverse of (g, h) is then (g^{-1}, h^{-1}).

These concepts can be generalized to deal with the direct product of any finite number of groups on which there are specified group operations.

Dirichlet region *See* Voronoi diagram.

disable 1. To make a device inactive.
2. To suppress the action of an interrupt.

disarm To put a device into a state that is still serviceable but requires a preparatory action before it can be used.

disassembler A program that attempts to translate machine code back into assembly language as an aid to debugging. A simple disassembler operates on one instruction at a time, translating the operation code to the appropriate mnemonic, displaying register references and addressing modes in the symbolic form used in the assembly language, and converting addresses into hexadecimal or symbols. More ambitious disassemblers try to show the structure of the program by replacing branch destinations with alphanumeric symbols, and placing the corresponding symbol as a label in the appropriate position in the program.

disc *UK spelling of* disk, sometimes preferred in UK computer literature.

disconnected graph *See* connected graph.

discourse understanding The subproblem of natural-language processing of determining the meaning of a text or dialogue. Discourse understanding is a specialization of *natural-language understanding in that it particularly addresses the problem of the meaning of utterances in the context of the whole text or dialogue, and with particular reference to how the discourse unfolds. In contrast, mainstream natural-language understanding typically takes no account of pragmatic setting and analyzes utterances in isolation from the text or dialogue in which they occur.

discrete and continuous systems Systems by which *signals are recorded, communicated, or displayed may represent the data in discrete form (e.g. as integers) or in continuous form (as "real" numbers). An important classification results from the choice of discrete or continuous representation of the amplitude, and of discrete or continuous representation of the time at which the amplitude occurred. *Analog computers employ physical quantities that are approximations

to continuous representations. Discrete representations of both time and amplitude are required by *digital computers.

The question of whether the signal (or its source) is intrinsically discrete or intrinsically continuous is unresolvable: any experiment to determine this would require infinite *bandwidth (or infinite time) and infinite *signal-to-noise ratio, and so would be impossible in practice. All that is in question is whether a discrete or continuous representation is more convenient, or useful, or appealing.

Signals that appear intuitively to be continuous-time or continuous-amplitude, but for which a discrete-time or discrete-amplitude representation is preferred, are said to have been *time-quantized* or *amplitude-quantized*. Time quantization is either adequate or inadequate according to *Nyquist's criterion. Time-quantized signals are said to be *sampled*, and the systems that handle them are called *sampled-data systems*. Amplitude quantization worsens the signal-to-noise ratio, an effect describable as the introduction of *quantization noise.

Time and amplitude must both be quantized for processing by digital computers (or by other digital devices), which operate at finite speeds on finite amounts of data held to finite precisions. The same physical constraints operate, although in a different way, to limit the extent to which analog computers (or other analog devices) can approximate to the continuous representation of signals.

See also quantization.

discrete channel A communication *channel whose input and output each have an alphabet of distinct letters, or, in the case of a physical channel, whose input and output are *signals that are discrete in time and amplitude (*see* discrete and continuous systems). The size of the alphabet, or the number of amplitude levels, is usually finite.

The *discrete memoryless channel (DMC)* has the property that its treatment of a symbol input at a certain time does not depend on the symbols input, or its treatment of them, at any earlier time.

The *discrete channel with memory (DCM)*

has the property that its action depends on its inputs at a number of earlier times.

See also Shannon's model, channel coding theorem.

discrete cosine transform (DCT) A mathematical operation that analyzes an arbitrary waveform into a summation of cosine functions:

$$C(u) = \sqrt{(2/N)} \sum_{x=0}^{N-1} f(x)\cos[(2x+1)u\pi]/2N$$

where the waveform $f(x)$ is approximated by N samples at $x = 0,1,...N-1$.

Discrete cosine transforms find application in image-compression techniques, for example in *JPEG.

discrete event simulation *See* simulation.

discrete Fourier transform (DFT) *See* Fourier transform.

discrete mathematics A branch of mathematics dealing with finite sets and calculations (rather than infinite processes such as taking limits and convergence or differentiation of *continuous functions). Its boundaries are not precise but its study includes parts of logic, computer science, statistics, and operations research. Some important problems that may be regarded as part of discrete mathematics are finite sets (*see* set), *algorithms, graph theory, *formal language theory and some topics in abstract algebra.

discrete process control *See* process control.

discrete signal *See* discrete and continuous systems.

discrete source A source of information whose output has an alphabet of distinct letters or, in the case of a physical source, whose output is a *signal that is discrete in time and amplitude (*see* discrete and continuous systems). The size of the alphabet, or the number of amplitude levels, is usually finite, although for mathematical analysis it may conveniently be regarded as potentially infinite.

The *discrete memoryless source (DMS)* has the property that its output at a certain time does not depend on its output at any earlier time.

The *discrete source with memory (DSM)*

has the property that its output at a certain time may depend on its outputs at a number of earlier times: if this number is finite, the source is said to be of *finite order*, otherwise it is of *infinite order*. DSMs are usually modeled by means of *Markov chains; they are then called *Markov sources*.

An *ergodic source* has the property that its output at any time has the same statistical properties as its output at any other time. Memoryless sources are, trivially, always ergodic; a source with memory is ergodic only if it is modeled by an ergodic Markov chain.

See also information theory, Shannon's model, source coding theorem.

discrete structure A *set of discrete elements on which certain operations are defined. Discrete implies noncontinuous and therefore discrete sets include *finite and *countable sets but not uncountable sets such as the real numbers. The term discrete structure covers many of the concepts of modern algebra, including integer arithmetic, *monoids, *semigroups, *groups, *graphs, *lattices, *semirings, *rings, *fields, and *subsets of these.

discrete system *See* discrete and continuous systems.

discretionary access control (DAC) A form of *access control in which subjects may themselves create and alter *access rights to objects, limited by any overriding constraints imposed by system administrators. *Compare* mandatory access control.

discretization The process of replacing a problem defined on a continuum, say an interval [0,1], by an approximating problem on a finite set of points, say nh,

$$n = 0,1,2,...,N,$$
$$\text{where } h = 1/N$$

Examples arise in many branches of numerical analysis, principally ordinary and partial differential equations where the *finite-difference method and the finite-element method are common forms of discretization. For the ordinary differential equation

$$y' = f(x,y),$$
$$0 \leq x \leq 1, y(0) = y_0,$$

a simple discretization is given by *Euler's method*:

$$(1/h)(y_{n+1} - y_n) = f(x_n, y_n)$$

where

$$x_n = hn, n = 0,1,\ldots,N,$$
$$h = 1/N$$

and y_n denotes the approximation to the true solution $y(x)$ at the point x_n. *See also* discretization error.

discretization error The error in a numerical method that has been constructed by the discretization of a "continuous" problem. The term is widely used in the context of solving *differential equations. A distinction must be made between global and local errors.

For example, in Euler's method (*see* discretization) the global error, or *global discretization error*, is the error in the discrete solution to the problem, specifically

$$y_n - y(x_n)$$

The *local discretization error* is the amount by which the continuous solution fails to satisfy the discrete formula:

$$(1/h)(y(x_{n+1}) - y(x_n)) - f(x_n, y(x_n))$$

Speaking generally, estimates of local errors are used in choosing the grid spacing h hence providing a means of indirectly controlling the global error.

discriminant analysis *See* multivariate analysis.

disjoint A term applied to two sets that have no element in common, i.e. such that the *intersection of the sets results in the *empty set. A number of sets are said to be *mutually disjoint* if each pair is disjoint.

disjunction A logical expression of the form

$$a_1 \vee a_2 \vee \ldots \vee a_n$$

where $\vee$ is the *OR operation. A particular disjunction of interest is the *disjunctive normal form* of a Boolean expression involving n variables, $x_1, x_2, \ldots, x_n$. Each a_i is then of the form

$$(y_1 \wedge y_2 \wedge \ldots y_n)$$

where $\wedge$ is the *AND operation and each y_i is equal to x_i or the complement of x_i. Reducing expressions to disjunctive normal form provides a ready method of determining the *equivalence of two Boolean expressions. *See also* propositional calculus. *Compare* conjunction.

disjunctive normal form *See* disjunction.

disk An item of storage medium in the form of a circular plate. These devices are at present (1996) principally *magnetic disks, in which the information is stored via *magnetic encoding. *See also* optical disk, magneto-optic storage.

disk array A disk subsystem comprising a collection of disk drives together with *array management software* that controls the drives so that they are seen by the host operating software as one or more *virtual disk drives. The array management software may reside in the host system or in the disk subsystem, in which case it is better described as firmware. A disk that is under the control of array management software is known as a *member disk. *See also* RAID.

disk cache An instance of *cache memory used to store recently read sections of disk file on the grounds that they may well be required again shortly, and to store items required to be written to disk until a convenient time. The former technique is safe, but the latter is more sensitive to power or systems failures and other unexpected events and can be disabled. The technique is used because the RAM of cache memory is much faster to access than disk storage.

disk cartridge An *exchangeable disk store, now obsolete, that took the form of an assembly containing a single rigid *magnetic disk permanently housed within a protective plastic cover. It was introduced by IBM in 1964. The cartridge, according to its type, could be loaded vertically onto its drive (*top-loading*), or horizontally from the front (*front-loading*). Either way the cartridge hub, to which the disk was clamped, centered onto the drive spindle and was magnetically clamped. The cover contained apertures to allow fixing of the cartridge to the drive, and a door that the drive opened to allow insertion of the magnetic heads. Once loaded, the disk could rotate clear of the covers. Disk cartridges had storage capacities up to 50 megabytes, depending on track density, bit density, and disk size.

Similar cartridges are used for *optical

disks, with capacities from a few hundred megabytes to several gigabytes. In some cases the disk is extracted mechanically from the cartridge for use, rather than rotated within it.

disk drive (disk unit) A device with *read/write heads and associated electronics that can store and retrieve data from one or more rapidly rotating *magnetic disks. The disks may be *hard disks or *floppy disks. The term can also be applied to devices operating with *optical disks.

In a magnetic disk drive the data is recorded on one or both sides of a disk in a set of concentric tracks, which are usually subdivided into *sectors. The read/write heads of the disk drive are mounted on arms that can be moved, by means of an *actuator, to position the heads accurately over the required track. As the disk rotates, the sectors on that track are made accessible. Storage locations can be accessed directly and in any order; typical *seek times are in the range 8–20 milliseconds while the *latency may be 8 milliseconds. The data is encoded according to a particular *disk format. *See also* access time, fixed disk drive, floppy-disk drive, disk array, RAID.

diskette, diskette drive *Other names for* floppy disk, floppy-disk drive.

disk format The *format of information recorded on magnetic (or optical) disk, allowing a system to recognize, control, and verify the data. There are two levels at which formats are defined.

(a) The way in which the data stream is divided into separately addressable portions, called *sectors, with *address marks and data marks to differentiate between the different types of information within the sector, and with a *cyclic redundancy check or *error-correcting code also provided.

(b) The way in which the binary information is encoded as a pattern of magnetic flux reversals.

Since recordings on disks are made as a serial bit stream on a single track at a time, special provision has to be made to allow the read electronics to acquire and maintain bit and byte synchronization. Bit synchroniza-

tion is achieved when the read electronics can provide a data clock (known as the *read clock*) of the correct phase so that the data can be encoded. All modern *fixed disk drives make use of a *phase-locked loop (PLL)* to generate the read clock from the data stream; currently the most common encoding scheme is RLL (see below). Very early floppy disk drives did not need a PLL because the encoding scheme used was FM (see below), which is self-clocking. Byte synchronization is achieved with the aid of address marks or data marks, as appropriate.

The common methods of encoding are as follows.

Run-length limited encoding (RLL) is a form of *NRZ (nonreturn to zero) recording in which groups of bits are mapped into larger groups before recording. A frequently used method known as 2–7 (at least 2 zeros between ones and no more than 7 zeros between ones) uses the "n to 2n" mapping table shown in the diagram. The restriction of 2 zeros between ones allows increased packing density and reduced intersymbol interference of the magnetic pattern, and that of no more than 7 zeros between ones eases the design of the phase-locked loop.

possible data sequences			*code sequence*
10			0100
11			1000
01 →	010		100100
	011		001000
00 →	000		000100
	001 →	0010	00100100
		0011	00001000

RLL, mapping table of the 2–7 method

Other similar codes are *GCR (group code recording)*, which breaks the data stream into 4-bit groups and maps these into 5-bit groups, *EIR (error-indicating recording)*, a form of 4 to 6 mapping that uses only the groups with odd parity, i.e. 3 or 5 ones, and *3PM (three-phase modulation)*, which has a minimum sequence of 2 zeros and a maximum of 11 zeros.

Frequency modulation (FM; F2F) is a form of self-clocking recording. The beginning of each bit cell is marked by a clock pulse recorded as a change in the direction of the magnetic flux. If the cell is to represent a binary 1 a second pulse or transition is written at the center of the cell, otherwise there is no further change until the start of the next cell. If the frequency of the clock is F then a stream of 1s will result in a frequency of $2F$ (hence F2F recording). In this form of recording the minimum separation between transitions is half of one cell and the maximum is one cell.

In *modified frequency modulation (MFM)* a binary 1 is always represented by a transition at the center of a bit cell but there is not always a transition at the boundary of the cell. A transition is written at the start of a bit cell only if it is to represent a binary 0 and does not follow a binary 1. Thus the minimum separation between transitions is one cell and the maximum is two cells. For the same spacing of flux transitions the MFM method allows twice as many bits to be encoded in a unit distance; it is thus sometimes referred to as a *double-density recording*.

Modified modified frequency modulation (M^2FM) is a modified form of MFM that deletes flux transitions between two 0s if they are followed by a 1.

Optical disk formats are broadly similar to those of magnetic disk, except that the tracks usually take the form of a continuous spiral and the path of this is often determined by a groove pressed into the disk surface during manufacture (*see also* CD-ROM format standards).

See also formatter.

disk pack One form of *exchangeable disk store, now obsolete, that consisted of an assembly of identical 14″ diameter rigid *magnetic disks mounted coaxially and equally spaced. A similar nonrecording protective disk was fitted above the top recording disk with another one below the bottom recording disk. The whole assembly was rigidly clamped together, and was designed for dynamic stability at high rotation on a *disk drive. The whole pack, when not mounted on the drive, was contained within sealed plastic covers, in two parts, which helped to ensure that the pack was protected from damage, dust, and contamination. The bottom cover was removed before mounting the pack on the drive; the top cover could only be removed when the pack had been mounted.

Storage capacities ranged from 30 to 300 megabytes, over the range of track densities up to 400 tracks per inch, recording densities up to 6000 bits per inch, and pack sizes of 5 to 12 disks. Disk packs were introduced by IBM in 1963, and most types are subjects of international standards.

disk stack *See* fixed disk drive.

disk striping *See* RAID, stripe disk.

disk unit *Another name for* disk drive.

dispatcher *Another name for* low-level scheduler. *See* scheduler.

dispersion *See* measures of variation.

displacement mapping A method of approximating a bumpy surface by offsetting the base surface by the appropriate bump height and then rendering the surface. It gives a more realistic rendering than *bump mapping but is more expensive to perform.

display 1. A device that can be attached to a computer in order to present transient images – textual or pictorial – on its screen (*see* text mode, graphics mode). The most widely used display device is the *cathode-ray tube with color specified by RGB signals. Although domestic TV receivers have been used as computer-driven displays, it is usual to have specially designed units: for prolonged use by one operator it is necessary to optimize the screen characteristics and provide a sharper and more stable image to avoid unnecessary fatigue.

Other display technologies used, in particular for portable systems, are *flat-panel displays. These include *LCDs (liquid-crystal displays), *plasma panels, and *electroluminescent displays.

2. A method of presenting graphical or pictorial images. *See* raster-scan display, vector display.

3. To make information visible in a temporary form.

display adapter Hardware that can be fitted to a personal computer to enable it to drive an enhanced display. The enhancement may be for graphics or for an enhanced resolution and/or larger text display.

display processor A specialized *I/O processor used to mediate between a file of information that is to be displayed and a display device. It reformats the information as required and provides the information in accordance with the timing requirements of the display system.

distributed array processor *See* array processor.

distributed artificial intelligence (DAI) An approach to *artificial intelligence in which processing takes place not in a single algorithm but is distributed across a number of *agents, possibly many. Each agent is autonomous, with its own actions and *belief space, and the behavior of the whole system, which may or may not solve a particular problem, is characterized by its emergent properties.

distributed computing environment *See* DCE.

distributed database A *database in which the data is contained within a number of separate subsystems, usually in different physical locations. If the constituent subsystems are essentially similar, the system is said to be *homogeneous*, otherwise it is said to be *heterogeneous*. Distributed database systems may vary very considerably. At one extreme is the type where the complete system was conceived, designed, and implemented as a single entity; such systems exist within large commercial organizations and are usually homogeneous. At the other extreme is the case where a number of existing systems, originally planned as isolated systems, continue in their normal operation but in addition are loosely linked to provide a larger distributed system; in this instance the system is often heterogeneous.

Distributed database systems are currently an active topic for database research and development, largely because of the availability of national and international communication facilities.

distributed file system A system in which a

number of users, using different processors, have the possibility of shared access to one another's *files. *Compare* distributed database.

distributed problem solving An approach whereby a problem is decomposed into many smaller subproblems that are then distributed to different processing systems.

distributed processing The organization of processing to be carried out on a *distributed system. Each *process is free to process local data and make local decisions. The processes exchange information with each other over a data communication network to process data or to read decisions that affect multiple processes. *See also* open distributed processing, client/server.

distributed queue dual bus *See* DQDB.

distributed system Any system in which a number of independent interconnected computers can cooperate. *See* distributed processing, client/server.

distribution *See* frequency distribution, probability distributions.

distribution counting sort A sorting algorithm that stores, for each sortkey, the number of records with the given sortkey (thus anticipating that keys might not be unique). With this information it is possible to place the records correctly into a sorted file. The algorithm is useful when the keys fall into a small range and many of them are equal.

distributive lattice A *lattice L, with meet and join operations $\land$ and $\lor$ respectively, in which the two *distributive laws hold for all elements in L. Since these laws are self-duals, the principle of *duality continues to hold for distributive lattices.

distributive laws The two self-dual laws
$$x \land (y \lor z) = (x \land y) \lor (x \land z)$$
$$x \lor (y \land z) = (x \lor y) \land (x \lor z)$$
that are satisfied by all elements $x, y,$ and z in a *Boolean algebra possessing the two operations $\land$ and $\lor$. In the first law the operation $\land$ is said to be distributive over the operation $\lor$, and vice versa for the second law.

dithered color Softened boundaries between different colors, produced by adding noise to a picture. *See* dithering.

dithering Reducing the effect of sharp edges in a picture when intensities jump from one discrete value to another. A small random intensity called *dither noise* is added to the picture intensities at each point. *Ordered dithering* uses intensities in a matrix that is laid down on the picture in a periodic manner.

dither noise *See* dithering.

diverse programming (n-version programming) The implementation to a common specification of two (or more) different versions of a program, usually using two completely different teams of programmers. The purpose is to create versions of the program that are unlikely to have the same faults. On comparison of the two programs, identification of any differences can point to errors that occurred in interpreting the specification, errors in design, and errors during implementation.

    The use of diverse programming inevitably leads to an increase in the development cost of a software system, but this is compensated by an increase in confidence in the quality of the software and often leads to a lower cost in validation, verification, and testing.

divide and conquer sorting A sorting algorithm that is similar to *radix sorting but works from the most significant digit of the sortkey down to the least significant.

divided difference *See* interpolation.

divider *See* counter.

DLL *Abbrev. for* dynamic link library. A file of procedures residing on disk that is available to an executing program so that relevant procedures can be read into memory and executed at run time. The advantage is that the executables are smaller, the link libraries can be shared, and, providing the interface remains unchanged, can be updated without recompiling the application. Although extra time is spent in disk input/output, *disk caching and faster disk subsystems make this a valuable technique. *See also* overlay.

DMA *Abbrev. for* direct memory access.

DME *Trademark, acronym for* direct machine environment. A system offered by ICL as a

means of using the microcode capabilities of their 2900 range of machines to allow users to run ICL 1900 series software, including the GEORGE operating system. Originally offered as an interim product for users migrating from 1900 to 2900 systems, DME is sufficiently attractive to be used as a main operating environment.

DML *Abbrev. for* data manipulation language. *See* database language.

DNS *Abbrev. for* domain name server.

docking station At its simplest, a *VDU display and keyboard together with a box containing a power supply into which slides a *laptop or other small portable computer. This obviates the necessity of having both a *desktop and a laptop. The laptop slides into the docking station and effectively becomes a desktop. More complex docking stations can contain extra disk storage, sockets for *add-in cards, network connections, and other enhancements.

document A piece of text considered to be a single item and usually stored as a *file. The document might be a letter, a report, a chapter, etc. It will usually have a unique name, and may have other attributes attached to it, such as a brief description of what it contains and who composed it.

documentation All material that serves primarily to describe a system and make it more readily understandable, rather than to contribute in some way to the actual operation of the system. Documentation is frequently classified according to purpose; thus for a given system there may be requirements documents, design documents, and so on. In contrast to documentation oriented toward development and maintenance of the system, user documentation describes those aspects of the system that are of interest to end-users.

document description language A language for describing the structure and contents of a document, for example Interpress (Xerox) and DDL (Imagen). *See also* SPDL.

document image processing (DIP) The management of documents throughout their life cycle from creation to death. It includes the capture of documents as *digital images, typically by means of *document scanners, and the storage, indexing, retrieval, processing, transmission, and printing of these documents. *Optical disks are often used for archival storage. With the advances in portable computers, portable DIP is now feasible. DIP systems can also be used on networks, allowing several users to access the document files.

document processing The machine processing (reading, sorting, etc.) of documents that are generally readable both by people and machines, e.g. bank checks, vouchers from credit card transactions, and accounts from public utilities. In addition to the printed information for human interpretation, there is also some encoding that is machine-readable and may be in an *OCR or *MICR font.

document reader A machine for reading documents that are encoded in a way that is readable by person and machine. *See also* document processing.

document scanner A device that can input the optical image of a document page. It may be combined with internal or host resident processing of the input to manipulate the image or recognize text and output strings of character codes. Scanners can be hand-held where very small quantities are concerned and cost is more significant than accuracy; however, surprisingly good results can be achieved. *Flatbed and *drum scanners are available where higher throughput or resolution is required.

document sorter A device that can read information encoded on documents and place them into separate stacks related to that code. Bank checks are processed in this way. *See also* document processing.

do loop A counting loop in a program, in which a section of code is obeyed repeatedly with a counter taking successive values. Thus in Fortran,

$$\text{DO } 10 \text{ I} = 1,100$$
$$\langle\text{statements}\rangle$$
$$10 \quad \text{CONTINUE}$$

causes the $\langle$statements$\rangle$ to be obeyed 100 times. The current value of the counter variable is often used within the loop, especially

to index an array. There are many syntactic variants: in Pascal and Algol-related languages the same basic construct appears as the *for loop*, e.g.

```
for i := 1 to 100 do
    begin
        ⟨statements⟩
    end
```

This kind of loop is a constituent of almost all programming languages (except APL, which has array operations defined as operators in the language).

See also do-while loop.

DOL system *See* L-system.

domain 1. In general, a sphere of control, influence, or concern.

2. *See* function, relation, category. *See also* range.

3. of a network. Part of a larger network. A domain is usually defined in terms of some property, such as that part of the network that is under the jurisdiction of a single management body (a *management domain*), or where all the network addresses are assigned by a single controlling authority (a *naming domain*). *See also* domain name server.

4. In the *relational model, a set of possible values from which the actual values in any column of a table (relation) must be drawn.

5. In *denotational semantics, a structured set of mathematical entities in which meanings for programming constructs can be found. The idea first arose in the work of Dana Scott, who with Christopher Strachey pioneered this mathematical approach to programming language semantics. The approach focuses on *fixed-point theorems. Scott required domains to be *complete lattices, but this has been simplified through a great deal of mathematical research. There are now many kinds of domains, but a commonly used one is the *Scott–Ershov domain*, which is a consistently complete algebraic cpo (complete *partial ordering). For such mathematical structures a fine theory of constructing new domains from old and solving fixed-point equations has been developed. The *domain theory* has many applications in finding semantics for programming and specification languages, and approximating data types. Mathematically the theory is closely linked to topology and algebra.

6. *See* protection domain.

domain knowledge That knowledge which is specific to an application, as distinguished from general strategic or control knowledge that is independent of the details of any particular application. For example, data about the flight routes covered by a particular airline is domain knowledge, unlike search algorithms that might be used to locate the cheapest entry.

domain modeling The modeling of a part, or domain, of the external world with which a class of systems (possibly an individual system) will interact. The domain, which is often called the *application domain* or *problem domain*, contains the entities that are referred to by the information processed in a class of systems. A domain may include, for instance, natural phenomena, human artifacts, organizational functions, and information structures. Examples of domains are air traffic control, currency dealing, telecommunication switching, and supermarkets.

The purpose of a domain model is to enhance understanding of the structure and behavior of the domain, and of the requirements for systems that are to be embedded in it; a model could be said to provide the basic semantics for a class of systems. Domain modeling may have two benefits: (a) many individual systems may be tailored or instantiated from a single model; (b) the model may be more stable and longer lasting than individual systems. The more that either of those benefits can be obtained, the greater is the potential return on investment in the model. Achieving them, however, may mean that a domain model must be shared among a number of developers, and contributed to by a number of users; that may be difficult in the face of commercial competitive pressures.

domain name server (DNS) A system that provides mappings between the human-oriented names of users or services in a network, and the machine-oriented network addresses of the named entity. The term is used primarily within the Internet, although other networks have similar facilities. The mapping is usually hierarchical, with the hierarchy reflected in the human-oriented names. In general terms the boundaries of a *domain will coincide with some form of natural boundary within the network environment, such as a country, a community of users within a country, or the users on a site. *See also* FQDN.

domain theory *See* domain.

dominator A vertex x_i on a graph G is a dominator of vertex x_j, relative to vertex x_k, if every path from x_j to x_k traverses x_i. This is used in flow analysis for code optimization.

dongle A hardware device provided by a supplier of proprietary software and attached to an input/output port on the system. When interrogated by the software, the dongle returns a unique validation code, thus ensuring that illegal copies of the software are not run on other unlicensed systems.

do-nothing instruction *Another name for* no-op instruction.

don't care *Informal* A condition in a logic network in which the output is independent of the state of a set of given inputs.

dope vector A vector of data used to assist in accessing the elements in an *array. The dope vector contains

(a) the address of a fixed element in the array – this may be the first element present or the element that has all subscripts equated to zero;

(b) the number of subscripts associated with the array, i.e. its dimensionality;

(c) the *stride* associated with each subscript position, i.e. the number of stored elements that must be skipped over when a subscript's value is changed by 1.

The position in memory of an element is found by taking the inner product of the strides with the differences between the actual subscript values and those that correspond to the fixed element referred to in (a), and adding to this the address of the fixed element.

DORIS A proprietary method developed by British Aerospace from both *MASCOT and *CORE. It provides full system life-cycle coverage for both software and hardware development.

DOS 1. *Short for* MS-DOS.

2. *Acronym for* disk operating system. The original DOS (*trademark*) written by IBM for the series-700 computers was one of the first major operating systems to be offered by a mainframe manufacturer. It was introduced shortly after IBM's still more primitive system, *OS. DOS gave users the ability to construct files on disks that held images of punched cards and that could serve as the input to programs; similarly output ultimately destined for printers was *spooled into temporary disk files. The user was responsible for much of the management of these files, and had to contend with details of their physical location on disk and with their creation and disposal.

Because most operating systems are now based on the use of disk storage, the suffix -DOS forms the final part of the name of many of them.

dot diffusion A type of digital *halftone.

dot matrix printer A printer that creates each character from an array of dots that are usually formed by transferring ink by mechanical impact. It may be a *serial printer, printing a character at a time, or a *line printer.

The serial printer has a print head containing typically 9, 18, or 24 electromagnetically operated styluses. In a *wire printer* the styluses are steel or tungsten wires that are constrained by a guide at the printing tip. The styluses may also be short rods rigidly attached to a pivoting armature or spring fingers. The head is mounted on a carriage that is moved along guides so that it travels parallel to the paper and the position of the line to be printed. The styluses are selectively operated to build up alphanumeric characters and other shapes from a matrix of small dots. Alphanumeric characters of data-processing quality are built up on a matrix of 7 or 9 dots high by 4 or 5 dots wide. These usually have voids and scalloped edges, which can however be removed by making repeated passes of the head along the same line but printing the dots in a slightly different place on each

pass: the dots can thus be made to overlap in both horizontal and vertical lines. More recent designs of printers have 18 or 24 styluses and can produce characters that more closely resemble ordinary typewritten quality. The generally available speed range is 100–400 characters per second (cps) for print of data-processing quality, and up to 100 cps for a higher-quality character.

A widely adopted design for dot matrix line printers is to have a row of spring fingers that span the line to be printed. Such printers operate at 200–900 lines per minute.

Some dot matrix printers include the ability to print in seven colors using a multicolor ribbon. Ribbonless printers in which the ink is fed directly to the styluses have been demonstrated.

double buffering 1. A form of *buffering in which two buffers are used. On output the program can be filling one buffer while the device empties the other; the buffers then exchange roles. A similar technique is used for input.

2. In computer graphics, switching between two (or more) *frame buffers to allow picture composition to be performed simultaneously with display.

double click *See* click.

double complement of a *set S. The *complement of the set S', where S' itself is just the complement of S; the double complement of S is thus S itself. In logic double complement implies *double negation* of an element x, say, i.e. x itself.

double-density recording *Another name for* modified frequency modulation. *See* disk format.

double-length arithmetic *See* double precision.

double negation *See* double complement.

double precision The use of double the usual number of bits to represent a number. Arithmetic performed on double-precision numbers is called *double-precision* (or *double-length*) *arithmetic*. For floating-point numbers, most computers use the same number of bits for the exponent in single-length and double-length forms. Consequently, if the length of a single-precision number is l bits, p of which are used for the mantissa, then the mantissa of a double-precision number occupies $(p + l)$ of the $2l$ bits. Occasionally, *multiple precision*, i.e. more than double precision, may be available. Some computers implement double precision in hardware; higher precision, for example quadruple precision, is almost always achieved by software.

doubly linked list (two-way linked list; symmetric list) A *linked list where each item contains links to both its predecessor and its successor. This makes it possible to traverse the list in either direction. The flexibility given by double linking must be offset against the overhead of the storage and the setting and resetting of the extra links involved when items are inserted or removed.

do-while loop A form of programming loop in which the condition for termination (continuation) is computed each time around the loop. There are several variants on this basic idea. For example, Pascal has

    while ⟨condition⟩ do
        begin
            ⟨statements⟩
        end

and also

    repeat
        ⟨statements⟩
    until ⟨condition⟩

The first is a *while loop* and the second is a *repeat-until* loop. Apart from the obvious difference that the first specifies a continuation condition while the second specifies a termination condition, there is a more significant difference. The while loop is a *zero-trip* loop, i.e. the body will not be executed at all if the condition is false the first time around. In contrast, the body of a repeat-until loop must be obeyed at least once.

Similar constructs are found in most languages, though there are many syntactic variations. *See also* do loop.

down *Informal* Denoting a system that is unavailable. It is either switched off or is switched on and being repaired.

downline The direction from a central or controlling *node to a remote node in a hierarchical network, or (sometimes) the direction

away from the current node without respect to hierarchical ordering. The word is often used as a verb: to downline or to *downline load*, i.e. to send data from a central node to a remote end-user's node in a network. The remote node may not have the facilities to store the data permanently, in which case the downline load would be necessary each time the remote node is restarted. When the remote node does have permanent storage facilities, downline loading may be used to supply newer versions of data to the remote node. *Compare* upline.

download To load *downline, i.e. to send data from a central node in a network to a remote end-user's node.

down operation *Another name for* P operation. *See* semaphore.

downsizing *Informal* Moving away from mainframe-based computer organization toward a distributed environment such as a network of workstations.

downtime The percentage of time that a computer system is not available for use.

DP *Abbrev. for* data processing.

DPCM *Abbrev. for* differential PCM. *See* pulse code modulation.

dpi *Abbrev. for* dots per inch.

DQDB *Abbrev. for* distributed queue dual bus. A form of network originally designed for use with optical fibers in metropolitan area networks. The system is based on two unidirectional buses, usually referred to as the *A-bus* and *B-bus*, that pass in opposite directions through a number of nodes. Traffic on these buses is processed in *cells, each holding 53 bytes, with a 5 byte header and a 48 byte payload. This cell size is chosen to allow seamless interworking with *ATM-based networks.

The head end of the A-bus and the tail end of the B-bus are collocated in a single node, and the tail end of the A-bus and the head end of the B-bus are again collocated in a node. Each head end transmits a stream of cells, which it either uses for its own transmissions and marks as being full, or marks as free; at the tail end the incoming cells are discarded. Any node can use one of the buses to pass packets to a node downstream of the sending node, and the receiving node can similarly use the other bus for the return traffic; thus each bus carries traffic in only one direction, but any two nodes have a full duplex connection. If there is a failure of either a node or a bus, the nodes immediately adjacent to the failure will reconfigure so as to take on the roles of the head and tail ends for the appropriate buses. At start-up, or after a failure and reconfiguration, nodes can identify which bus to use for which addresses by examining the source addresses of incoming packets on each bus.

As each cell passes through each node, the node has the opportunity to convert a single bit within the cell to a request for access to the bus. Each node also maintains counters of requests for access to the bus, and of free cells, and the nodes are thus able to cooperate to implement what is in effect a first come first served queue for access to the two buses.

drag *See* click.

DRAM *Abbrev. for* dynamic RAM. *See* dynamic memory, RAM.

draughts-playing programs *See* checkers-playing programs.

DRAW *Abbrev. for* direct read after write. In optical or magnetic data storage, a writing technique in which each bit of data is read immediately after it is written. This enables an erroneous sector to be recognized before the next sector starts to be written and errors can be managed accordingly, generally by flagging the defective sector or block and repeating the same data in the next sector. Nearly all magnetic tape drives, and many optical disk drives, use this technique. *See also* DRDW.

The term is sometimes erroneously used in an optical-storage context simply to imply that written information is immediately ready for reading, without an intermediate processing operation such as would be required for photographic recording.

DRCS *Abbrev. for* dynamically redefinable character set.

DRDW *Abbrev. for* direct read during write. In optical data storage, a writing technique in which each signal element is check-read as it is written, by sensing the light reflected from the medium. It serves the same purpose as *DRAW. In magnetic tape storage, the term is sometimes used to mean the same as DRAW.

drive *Short for* disk drive or tape drive, magnetic or optical.

driver 1. A routine within an operating system that handles the individual peripheral units on the computer system. Of necessity a driver routine is required to deal with the intimate details of the construction of each unit and of its real-time behavior. Consequently at least some of the driver will often need to be written in a machine-oriented programming language.
2. An electronic circuit, often available in the form of a logic gate, that is capable of providing large currents or voltages to other circuits connected to the driver's output. These devices are often used to place signals onto bus lines, hence the term *bus driver*.

drop-down menu *Another name for* pull-down menu.

drop-in In magnetic recording technology (disk and tape), the presence among the signals read from the device of one or more bits that had not been deliberately written there. This is the result of a fault condition, often imperfect erasure of data previously on the medium, and will generally be a problem only in interrecord gaps (elsewhere it will be dealt with by the same means provided for *drop-out): magnetic tape and disk systems normally have means of identifying and coping with this problem.

drop-on-demand inkjet printer *See* inkjet printer.

drop-out In magnetic recording technology (disk and tape), the loss of one or a sequence of bits due to a fault condition, most frequently a flaw in the recording medium. Magnetic tape and disk systems employ some form of redundancy to detect and frequently correct the resulting data errors.

drum plotter *See* plotter.

drum printer (*UK name:* **barrel printer**) A type of *solid-font *line printer, first marketed in 1955 but now becoming obsolete. The font is etched or engraved on the outer surface of a cylinder – known as the *drum* (or *barrel*) – that extends across the full width of the line to be printed. This was the first type of computer printer to use the "hit-on-the-fly" principle, used on *chain printers and train printers and current band printers, and it was a significant change from the mechanically intensive printers that preceded it.

drum scanner A form of *document scanner where the original document to be scanned is wrapped around a drum and then scanned by moving the detector head longitudinally as the drum is rotated. Drum scanners are used where the highest resolution is required, as in typesetting applications.

dry run Execution of a program in a manner analogous to a *production run, but for purposes of checking that the program behaves correctly rather than for producing useful results. The results of execution are compared with expected results; any discrepancies indicate an error of some sort that must be investigated before the program is put into production usage.

DS *Abbrev. for* double sided. Describing a *floppy disk in which both sides are used for storing data.

DSM *Abbrev. for* digital storage medium.

DSP *Abbrev. for* digital signal processing.

DSPACE *See* complexity classes.

DSS *Abbrev. for* decision support system. *See* management information system.

DTE *Abbrev. for* data terminal equipment. The side of an interface that represents the user of the data communication services in a standard such as RS232C or X25. DTEs are usually computers or computer terminals. *Compare* DCE.

DTIME *See* complexity classes.

DTL *Abbrev. for* diode–transistor logic. An early form of *logic family, normally produced in integrated-circuit form, whose principal switching components consist of diodes and transistors.

DTP *Abbrev. for* desktop publishing.

D-type flip-flop *See* D flip-flop.

dual *See* duality.

dual attach *See* fiber distributed data interface.

dual in-line package *See* DIP.

duality The property exhibited by the laws and rules of *set algebra, the *propositional calculus, and *Boolean algebra that each law or rule has a *dual* law or rule, constructed by the simultaneous replacement of each occurrence of 0 by 1, 1 by 0, ∨ by ∧, and ∧ by ∨. Such a pair of laws or rules is then said to be *self-dual*. Thus *de Morgan's laws, for example, are self-dual.

If a law or rule contains the *partial ordering ≤ inherent in any lattice, then in obtaining duals this should be replaced by ≥ and vice versa; thus inequalities should be reversed.

dual port memory A memory that is capable of receiving two concurrent access requests. Depending upon the internal memory organization, responses may or may not be simultaneous. Close-coupled *multiprocessor systems use these memories.

dual processor A *multiprocessor system with two central processors. Use of this term sometimes implies a two-processor system in which one processor is redundant so that the total system has a very high level of reliability.

dummy instruction (dummy) An item of data in the form of an *instruction that is inserted in the *instruction stream but is not intended to be executed. *See also* no-op instruction.

dump 1. In a system handling large numbers of users' files stored on magnetic disks, one of the periodic records of the state of the disks that are made on some form of offline storage device. This protects against failures either in hardware or software that can lead to the *corruption of stored information. In the event of a system error that causes information to be lost, the most recently copied version of the information can be reinstated from the dump.

On a large multiuser system, the total volume of stored information means that it may not be practicable to dump all the information on every occasion. In these cases an *incremental dump* can be taken, containing only those files that are marked as having been altered since the last dump; this reduces the total amount of information to be copied during the dump, allowing dumps to be made more frequently.

2. A printed version of the contents of system memory taken when a system crash has occurred. In principle it is possible to determine the immediate cause of a system crash by studying the dump and determining the reason for any inconsistencies in its contents. In practice this may be difficult even with the assistance of dump analysis software.

3. To take a dump (defs. 1 or 2).

dump check A copy of the contents of all the workspace associated with a job or *process. If the job or process subsequently fails, it can be restarted at the point at which the dump check was taken. Note that the status of peripheral devices allocated to the job or process must be considered as constituting part of its workspace.

dump point *See* checkpoint.

duplex (full duplex) Involving or denoting a connection between two endpoints, either physical or logical, over which data may travel in both directions simultaneously. *See also* half duplex, simplex, return channel.

duty cycle For pulsed or square-wave signals, the ratio of pulse duration to pulse spacing, often expressed as a percentage. A square wave signal normally has a 50% duty cycle, i.e. pulse duration is equal to the time between pulses.

DVI *Trademark; abbrev. for* digital video interactive. A variant of the *CD-ROM read-only optical disk format intended for the recording of images, including animated sequences. The technology encompasses motion video (with companion audio), audio, video stills, and text. A DVI end-user system includes special-purpose video, audio, and CD-ROM interface boards. *See also* CD-ROM format standards.

dyadic Having two operands.

dyadic operation (binary operation) defined on a set S. A function from the

domain $S \times S$ into S itself. Many of the everyday arithmetic and algebraic operations are dyadic, e.g. the addition of two integers, the union of two sets, and the conjunction of two Boolean expressions. Although basically functions, dyadic operations are usually represented using an infix notation, as in

$$3 + 4, U \cup V, P \wedge Q$$

A symbol, such as $\circ$, can be used to represent a generalized dyadic operation.

When the set is finite, *Cayley tables and sometimes *truth tables are used to define the meaning of the operation.

Dyck language A concept used in *formal language theory. Let Σ be the alphabet

$$\{a_1, \ldots, a_n, b_1, \ldots, b_n\}$$

The Dyck language over Σ is the set of all strings that can be reduced to the empty string Λ by "cancellations" of the form

$$a_i b_i \rightarrow \Lambda$$

For example,

$$\Sigma = \{(,)\}$$

gives the Dyck language of all balanced parenthesis strings. An important theorem characterizes the *context-free languages as those representable as the homomorphic image (*see* homomorphism) of the intersection of a Dyck language and a *regular language.

dye-polymer media A class of optical recording media in which the sensitive layer consists of dye particles dispersed in a binder. Both *rewritable and *write-once recording are possible. Dye-polymer media are potentially cheaper than those using other materials (such as *magneto–optic storage media), but have taken longer to develop. One of the first successful applications of dye-polymer media is in *CD-THOR disks.

dynamic Capable of changing or of being changed. With reference to operating systems, the implication is that the system is capable of changing while it continues to run. As an example, the total amount of memory available may be defined by the contents of a word within the operating system. If this word can be altered without stopping the system and reloading a fresh copy of the operating system, then it is possible to alter dynamically the total amount of memory on the system.

With reference to programming, the adjective is applied to operations that take place while a program is running, as compared with those that take place during the compilation phase. For example, dynamic arrays are allocated space while the program is running.

Compare static.

dynamic allocation An allocation that is made dynamically, i.e. while the system is running, rather than statically at the time of first initiating the system.

dynamically redefinable character set (DRCS) 1. A feature of some printer controllers that allows the character set in use to be changed via commands in the data stream. The character sets invoked may be resident in the printer or may be downloaded via the interface.
2. A feature of many display terminals whereby the font may be redefined via the interface, allowing nonstandard character sets (e.g. Greek or Cyrillic) or special type fonts to be displayed. A hard copy of the display screen requires a compatible printer.

dynamic data structure A data structure whose organizational characteristics may change during its lifetime. The adaptability afforded by such structures, e.g. linked lists, is often at the expense of decreased efficiency in accessing elements of the structure. Two main features distinguish dynamic structures from *static data structures. Firstly, it is no longer possible to infer all structural information from a *header; each data element will have to contain information relating it logically to other elements of the structure. Secondly, using a single block of contiguous storage is often not appropriate, and hence it is necessary to provide some storage management scheme at run-time.

dynamic link library *See* DLL.

dynamic logic *See* modal logic.

dynamic memory A form of *volatile semiconductor memory in which stored information is degraded with time. The most common example is dynamic *RAM (usually abbreviated to DRAM) where the logic state to be entered in each cell is stored as a voltage on the small capacitance associated with the gate of the MOS output transistor for the cell. The voltage decays away with time because of leakage currents in the cell, and so it must be *refreshed (i.e. recharged) periodically by external circuitry.

dynamic programming The mathematical theory and planning of multistage decision processes; the term was introduced by Richard Bellman in 1957. It may be regarded as a branch of *mathematical programming concerned with *optimization of problems formulated as a sequence of decisions. Applications are very varied, including engineering problems and company planning.

dynamic testing *See* testing. *Compare* static analysis.

E

EAPROM *Acronym for* electrically alterable programmable read-only memory. A form of *PROM in which the contents of selected memory locations can be changed by applying suitable electric signals, as in the case of *EAROM.

EARN *Acronym for* European Academic and Research Network. Originally established in the mid-1980s, EARN was initially a European copy of the IBM-sponsored *Bitnet system and used the same software running only on IBM 370 architecture systems. As with Bitnet, the software was subsequently ported onto other hardware, especially onto Digital Equipment's VAX systems, and the functionality was expanded from the original message switching system that used large-scale systems as the message switches to one using separate front-end systems.

EAROM *Acronym for* electrically alterable read-only memory. A form of semiconductor memory in which it is possible to change the contents of selected memory locations by applying suitable electric signals. Normally these changes are infrequent.

EBCDIC *Acronym for* extended binary coded

decimal interchange code. An 8-bit *character encoding scheme used primarily on IBM machines. *See also* character set.

EBNF *Abbrev. for* extended BNF.

EBONE The European *backbone network, a cooperative venture between the *PTTs, the European academic and research community, and the European Commission.

ECB *Abbrev. for* Electronic Codebook. *See* Data Encryption Standard.

ECBS *Abbrev. for* engineering of computer-based systems.

echo 1. The reflection of transmitted data back to its source (or, as a verb, to reflect transmitted data back to its source). For example, characters typed on the keyboard of a data terminal (connected to a computer) will not appear on the display of the terminal unless they are echoed. The echoing process may be done locally by the terminal itself, by a modem, or by an intervening communication processor. Echoing may also be done by the computer to which the terminal is attached. If the terminal itself echoes the characters, it is often said to be in *half-duplex mode*, although the term *local-echo mode* would be more accurate. In full-duplex character-at-a-time transmission, echoing is generally done at the computer, thus permitting certain application programs, such as editors, to determine whether or not incoming characters should be echoed. Half-duplex and/or line-at-a-time transmission generally implies local echoing.

2. A phenomenon in voice circuits (e.g. telephone circuits) that upsets the operation of *modems. Most modems therefore incorporate *echo suppression*.

echo check A way of establishing the accuracy achieved during the transfer of data over a data link, computer network, etc. When the data is received it is stored and also transmitted back to its point of origin in the transmission loop where it can be compared with the original data.

The term is also applied to other circumstances in which a transmitted signal directly causes a return signal. For example, in some line printers the sharp rise in the current

waveform of an electromagnet drive pulse, which occurs when the armature impacts, is sometimes used to verify that the intended event has occurred.

echoing 1. The immediate notification to the operator of the current value of an input device. *See also* acknowledgment, prompt, feedback.

2. The process of reflecting data back to source. *See* echo.

echo suppression *See* echo.

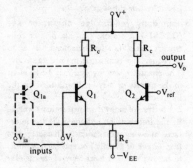

Two-input ECL OR gate

ECL *Abbrev. for* emitter-coupled logic. A high-speed *logic family available in the form of integrated circuits based on *bipolar transistors. The fast switching speeds are achieved by means of a design that avoids driving the transistors into saturation.

The basic circuit element is based on a difference amplifier, as shown in the diagram (ignoring dashed lines). In this symmetrical circuit the combined emitter current flowing through the resistor R_e is substantially constant. If the voltage V_i is equal to V_{ref} then each transistor, Q_1 and Q_2, conducts by the same amount and the output is at V_{ref}. If V_i is increased above V_{ref} by more than about 0.1 volts, Q_1 will be turned on while Q_2 turns off. As a result V_o increases to V^+. Similarly if V_i is decreased below V_{ref} by more than about 0.1 volts, V_o will decrease to some value largely determined by V_{EE}, R_e, and R_c.

By placing transistors in parallel with Q_1, as shown by the dashed lines, an ECL *OR gate is produced. Additional buffering is required on the gate output to provide the correct voltage swings for subsequent gate inputs.

ECL provides the highest speed of any silicon-based logic family but its power dissipation is high and the output voltage swing is small.

ECMA European Computer Manufacturers Association, founded in 1961 and based in Geneva. "European" is to be taken as operating in Europe rather than European owned. The aims of ECMA are "to promote, in the general interest and in collaboration with national and international organizations, all ways and means destined to facilitate and standardize the utilization of data processing systems." Examples of its work are the *standardization of *PL/I and *PCTE.

edge 1. A connection between two vertices of a *graph.

2. *See* edge detector.

edge board A *circuit board that is a modular part of a larger circuit. The term *edge card* is often used synonymously but is sometimes considered smaller than an edge board. Connections between this module and other modules are made through a printed-circuit pattern on the edge of the board that mates with an *edge connector. The edge connector is normally located on a *backplane or *motherboard, which contains wiring that ties all modules together.

edge card *See* edge board.

edge connector Part of a *printed circuit board where a number of the metallic conducting tracks meet the edge of the board, at right angles, to form the male half of a plug and socket. The tracks are broadened, thickened, and usually gold-plated to provide good electrical contact. A single edge connector may have a hundred or more individual connections, half on each side of the board. The female half of the connector is a multiway socket whose sprung metal contacts can mate with the corresponding pads on the PCB. Connections to various points on the circuit board may then be made indirectly via the socket. *See also* backplane.

edge detector In *gray-level *image pro-

cessing, images of typical scenes contain large areas of gradual intensity change, called *segments, bounded by narrow regions of very rapid intensity change, called *edges*. An edge detector is a procedure or rule that locates a series of points, arranged roughly in a line, where rapid intensity changes have occurred. A set of edges can then be used by other operators, such as *line finders, to build up the outline of object features. Many different forms of edge detectors have been developed in image processing, including the *Laplacian operator.

edge-triggered flip-flop *See* flip-flop.

EDI *Abbrev. for* electronic data interchange.

EDIF *See* EDIFACT.

EDIFACT An international standard, ISO 9735: Electronic Data Interchange For Administration, Commerce, and Transport, giving the application-level syntax rules for messages between companies concerning orders and services. It superseded *EDIF* (electronic data interchange format), the interim standard format for messages about company orders and purchases. *See also* electronic data interchange.

Edison A programming language for designing reliable real-time programs for multiprocessor systems. Edison is *block-structured and includes modules, concurrent statements, and when statements.

edit To create, modify, or add to a *document. Editing operations include delete, insert, move, copy, search, replace, include another file, justify, and paginate. *See also* word processing.

editor *See* link editor, text editor.

Edmonds' algorithm A method of finding the maximum branching of a *weighted directed *graph, due to J. Edmonds (1965).

EDP *Abbrev. for* electronic data processing. *See* data processing.

EDS 1. Electronic Data Systems. The second largest computer services company in the world in terms of revenue (1993 figures), specializing in *facilities management and systems integration. It was founded by Ross Perot, independent candidate in the US presidential election in 1992, and is now owned by General Motors. It is ranked number nine in terms of revenue in the list of the world's top IT suppliers (1993 figures).

2. *Abbrev. for* exchangeable disk store.

EDSAC *Acronym for* Electronic Delay Storage Automatic Calculator. A machine designed in 1946 by M. V. Wilkes of Cambridge University, UK, inspired by the stored-program concept being taught in the US by von Neumann and others. The design was notable for using acoustic *delay lines for memory. EDSAC began operations in May 1949, becoming the first complete operational stored-program computer. *See also* Manchester Mark I.

edutainment *Multimedia software providing both education and entertainment.

EDVAC *Acronym for* Electronic Discrete Variable Automatic Computer. An early stored-program electronic digital computer, originally commissioned from the University of Pennsylvania's Moore School by the US Army in 1944 while the *ENIAC was still under construction, but not operational until 1952. In 1945 John von Neumann prepared a proposal for the EDVAC that described the logical design of a computer with a "stored program", where the instructions to the machine would be stored in substantially the same fashion as the data. Although there is some disagreement as to whether von Neumann or the team of Mauchly and Eckert originated the stored-program concept, this was its first written documentation. Regardless of its origin, the stored-program model that formed the basis of the EDVAC design motivated all subsequent machine designs.

EEPROM *Acronym for* electrically erasable programmable read-only memory. A form of *EPROM in which the entire contents can be erased by subjecting the device to suitable electric signals, as in the case of *EEROM.

EEROM *Acronym for* electrically erasable read-only memory. A form of semiconductor memory in which the entire contents can be erased by subjecting the device to suitable electric signals. After erasing, the device can be reprogrammed. This procedure may be repeated hundreds of times without damaging the device.

effective address An *absolute address that is either a direct address or has been computed by one of the *addressing schemes such as augmenting, relative addressing, or indexing.

effective computability Let

$$N = \{0,1,...\}$$
$$N^k = N \times ... \times N$$
(with k factors)

A *partial function

$$f : N^k \to N$$

is effectively computable if there is an *effective procedure* or algorithm that correctly calculates f. An effective procedure is one that meets the following specifications. Firstly, the procedure must consist of a finite set of "simple" instructions and there must be no ambiguity concerning the order in which the instructions are to be carried out. Secondly, if the procedure is given a k-tuple x in the domain of f, then after a finite number of steps, the calculation must terminate and output $f(x)$; if the procedure is given a k-tuple not in the domain of f it must not output a value. *See also* Church–Turing thesis.

effective enumeration *See* enumeration.

effective procedure *See* effective computability.

EFT *Abbrev. for* electronic funds transfer.

EFTPOS *Abbrev. for* electronic funds transfer at point of sale. *See* point-of-sale system.

EFTS *Abbrev. for* electronic funds transfer system.

EGA *Abbrev. for* enhanced graphics adapter. An obsolete color *graphics adapter that could provide eight modes of display including the two *CGA modes. The EGA was developed by IBM and became available on a wide range of other computers.

egoless programming An approach to software development based on consensus within a small team. The aim is to produce software that is the product of the team rather than of one or a few individuals. The motivation is to avoid personal identification with output, promote group identification, and make it easier for the team to conduct an objective evaluation of the programs produced.

EIA Electronics Industries Association, a US legislation-oriented information, education, and lobbying group made up of manufacturers of electronic equipment.

Eiffel An *object-oriented programming language.

eigenfunctions *See* eigenvalue problems.

eigenvalue problems Problems that arise frequently in engineering and science and fall into two main classes. The standard (matrix) eigenvalue problem is to determine real or complex numbers,

$$\lambda_1, \lambda_2, ... \lambda_n \ (eigenvalues)$$

and corresponding nonzero vectors,

$$x_1, x_2, ..., x_n \ (eigenvectors)$$

that satisfy the equation

$$Ax = \lambda x$$

where A is a given real or complex $n \times n$ matrix.

By analogy the continuous eigenvalue problem is to determine similar eigenvalues and corresponding nonzero functions (*eigenfunctions*) that satisfy the equation

$$Hf(x) = \lambda f(x)$$

where H is a given operator on functions f. A simple example arising from a vibrating-string problem is

$$y''(x) = \lambda y(x),$$
$$y(0) = 0, y(1) = 0$$

where values of the parameter λ (eigenvalues) are required that yield nontrivial eigenfunctions $y(x)$ (i.e. $y(x) \neq 0$). *Finite-difference methods applied to such problems generally lead to matrix eigenvalue problems.

eigenvectors *See* eigenvalue problems.

EIR *Abbrev. for* error-indicating recording. *See* disk format.

EISA *Acronym for* extended Industry Standard Architecture. A *bus structure for microcomputers with Intel 32-bit microprocessors, based on and compatible with that used by IBM in their AT series ISA (*see* Industry Standard Architecture). EISA was developed by manufacturers other than IBM as an alternative to IBM's *MCA (micro channel architecture), which is not compatible with earlier systems.

elapsed time The actual time between two

events, measured by a "clock on the wall". *Compare* CPU time.

electrographic printer A term that embraces *electrostatic, *electrosensitive, and *electrophotographic printers.

electroluminescent display A type of *flat-panel display that uses the property of *electroluminescence*, whereby a phosphor will emit photons of radiation when placed in an electric field. The phosphor, usually one emitting yellow light, is incorporated in a thin coating on the screen; an additional coating of blue phosphor can produce full color. Electroluminescent screens are used in some large screen displays, such as airport announcement boards. Use of this technology in portable computers is at present limited to providing back lighting for *LCDs.

electromagnetic beam deflection *See* beam deflection.

electromagnetic compatibility *See* EMC.

electronic (as opposed to *electric*). Originally, concerned with the movement of electrons in free space, i.e. in vacuum tubes (UK: valves). Then, by extension, concerned with the movement of charges in semiconductors. Now, by extension, concerned with the representation, storage, and transmission of information by electrical means. That is now what distinguishes electronic engineering from electrical engineering, the latter dealing with energy rather than with information.

electronic blackboard *See* whiteboard.

electronic data interchange (EDI) A generic term covering various standards that describe the format, content, and structure of data to be exchanged between computer systems. It is usually used to describe standards at the application level of the OSI *seven-layer reference model.

electronic data processing (EDP) *See* data processing.

electronic filing A computer-based system for the storage, cataloguing, and retrieval of documents. It is central to the success of a comprehensive *office automation system in that it provides the basic object management required to create, manipulate, and delete "office objects", which may be letters, complex reports, charts, graphs, or any other information that may be stored in a computer system.

A comprehensive electronic filing system should give a high degree of security for the objects entrusted to it, both against computer failure and against unauthorized access, together with flexible methods of organizing these objects. It should also provide shared access to community items while preserving privacy for confidential items.

Objects in an electronic filing system will generally be stored on magnetic disk or tape; some systems use microfilm techniques for bulk storage of items. Current systems generally allow the cataloguing of "paper objects" that cannot be copied onto the computer system. This allows an easier transition to the computer-based system from an environment that previously relied on paper filing techniques.

electronic funds transfer system (EFTS)
Generally, the use of computers in effecting payments between individuals and/or organizations. In some cases the term is used to refer to advanced future systems in which debits and credits are made simultaneously with the transactions that give rise to them. In other cases its use covers all computer-based funds transfer systems, including *ATMs (automated teller machines), *EFT-POS and debit cards, EFT-EDI (*electronic data interchange) systems, and the US automated clearing house (ACH) network. There are several major worldwide EFT networks, including the *SWIFT* (Society for Worldwide Interbank Financial Transmission) network.

Full-scale EFTS cause particular anxiety to those who are concerned about the freedom and privacy of the individual in the information society, since they would enable very accurate profiles to be obtained of people's activities.

electronic mail (e-mail or email) Messages sent between users of computer systems, the computer systems being used to hold and transport messages. Sender and receiver(s) need not be online at the same time, or even on the same continent, to communicate.

Electronic mail is an important component of an office automation system.

The originator of a message creates a specially formatted message file by running a mail-sending program. The message may often be entered and modified using the general-purpose editor of the user's choice. When the message is complete, it is posted to a message transport system, which takes responsibility for delivering the message. This may involve passing the message through a *store-and-forward relay system when the sender and receiver are not connected to the same computer. At some later time the message is delivered into the recipient's incoming "mailbox". The recipient runs a program that retrieves incoming messages, allowing items to be filed, listed, forwarded, replied to, etc. Frequently a single user-interface program is used to send and receive messages both locally and worldwide.

Originally electronic mail was performed by using standard text hardcopy or CRT terminals. Newer systems support the composition and delivery of *multimedia mail*, which can combine text, graphics, voice, fax, and other forms of information in a single message. Other functions often performed by an electronic mail system include verification of a user's identity, expansion of named mailing lists into lists of recipients, and the location of a user on the basis of partial information (directory services).

The CCITT electronic-mail standard is X400.

electronic organizer A pocket-sized computer with a smaller than standard keyboard and an *LCD screen, designed to fulfill the function of a paper-based personal organizer. It normally has a less sophisticated operating system than a *laptop or *desktop computer, but has efficient scheduling, alarms, note-taking and address-book functions and will allow the transfer of information between itself and larger machines.

electronic point-of-sale system *See* EPOS, point-of-sale system.

electronic publishing Publication of information through electronic media as opposed to paper, so that it can be accessed by computer. Books, journals, etc., can be distributed on *CD-ROM for use on a personal computer, and the network distribution of electronic publications is becoming increasingly important. In both cases, the information is not just text and graphics but may also include video, animated graphics, and audio (*see* multimedia). *See also* desktop publishing, hypertext.

The law of *copyright gives authors and/or publishers control over the use of their work, and applies both to paper and electronic media. Computers make the copying of information very easy, and if a computer is connected to a network then publications can be copied to multiple sites. Practical approaches to providing protection against copyright infringement are under investigation.

electrophotographic printer Any printer in which the required image is written by a beam of light onto a photoconductive drum or band that has a uniform electric charge over its surface. The action of the light beam produces a charge pattern on the photoconductor, which is then developed by applying particles of pigment that are attracted to the image but are repelled by the background. The image is then transferred to paper by pressing the paper against the drum or band and applying an electric field. The toner is fixed to the paper by heat and/or pressure or by passing through a solvent vapor bath.

This type of printer can yield very good print quality, forming its image as a fine matrix of dots. It can thus readily produce graphics and a wide variety of typestyles. The best-known example is the *laser printer.

electrosensitive printer An obsolete type of printer that produced the required image by passing an electric current into the surface of specially prepared paper. The most common form used paper with one surface coated first with a layer of carbon black and then with a fine coat of aluminum to give it a white appearance. The writing was done by a row of styluses that could be separately energized to pass sufficient electric current into the surface to vaporize the aluminum locally and expose the black undersurface.

electrostatic beam deflection *See* beam deflection.

electrostatic printer A type of printer (no longer in widespread use) in which the required image is first written as a pattern of electrostatic charge, and is then made visible by bringing the pattern into contact with particles of pigment that carry a charge of opposite polarity. The pigment is only attracted to the charge pattern and is subsequently fused or bonded to the paper.

In some designs the charge pattern is applied by styluses directly to paper that has been specially treated. An alternative approach is to apply the pattern to a metal drum with a suitable coating such as aluminum oxide. The pattern is made visible by washing the paper or drum with a colloidal suspension of charged particles of pigment. The image on a drum is transferred to plain paper by pressure and the application of an electric field. The particles of pigment are very fine and thus penetrate the fibers of the paper and form a permanent image. The charge can also be applied to the drum by the controlled projection of ions.

In some literature the term is used to refer to all printers in which an electrostatic image is formed as one of the steps in the process, including *electrophotographic printers.

electrostatic storage device An obsolete storage device in which the data was stored as a charge pattern within a *cathode-ray tube and could be read by a scanning beam of electrons. The data was not usually visible. One of the early designs was the *Williams-tube store*, developed by F. C. Williams of the University of Manchester, UK; it was one of the earliest forms of random-access memory. Electrostatic storage was used on a number of first-generation computers (Ferranti Mark I, Whirlwind, IBM 701, IAS). It gave a significant reduction in storage cost compared to the mercury *delay line memory, but the information had to be frequently regenerated (rewritten) and was lost when power was removed. It was displaced in processor designs in the mid-1950s by *core stores.

More advanced electrostatic devices have been developed but these did not reach the market.

electrothermal printer A type of *thermal printer in which a thermoplastic ink is transferred from a ribbon to the base medium (usually paper or transparent film) by localized heating. The heating occurs as current is passed from discrete electrical contacts on the print head through a resistive layer in the ribbon to a common return layer. Compared with *thermal transfer printers, the print quality is less dependent on the surface finish of the receiving medium but the complexity of the ribbon makes the cost of usage higher. Improvements in thermal transfer printers have made electrothermal technology less attractive.

element 1. of a set. *Another name for* member. **2.** *See* logic element.

ELSE rule The last (usually rightmost) rule of an incomplete *decision table, i.e. a table that does not include all possible combinations of conditions. The ELSE rule defines the step set for all actions not satisfying the explicit rules of the decision table. A table with an ELSE rule is complete since all possible combinations are taken into consideration.

EMACS An extensible portable display editor that is distributed freely as part of *GNU. A derivative, Micro EMACS, runs on IBM PCs and compatible machines. EMACS is particularly popular with programmers since its programmable interface allows it to be customized to suit individual preferences.

e-mail (or email) *Short for* electronic mail.

EMAS *Acronym for* Edinburgh multiaccess system. An operating system that was originally developed at the University of Edinburgh and is intended to support large numbers of interactive terminals. It was one of the earliest systems to be implemented almost entirely in a high-level language. A special implementation language, IMP, was devised for this purpose.

embedded computer Any computer used as a component in a device whose prime function is not that of a computer. One example is a weapons-guidance system. Another is a computer-controlled blood analyzer that uses a minicomputer or microcomputer to control various tests that are run on blood in order to produce an integrated printout of all test results. Many domestic electronic products now contain embedded computers.

embedded servo *See* actuator.

embedding A method of including information from one application in another. For instance a graph from a spreadsheet, the source, could be embedded in a word-processor document, the destination. Embedding is different from *copying in that the application that created the embedded information can be started up from within the destination application if any modification is required. Embedding is also different from linking, where no information is copied into the destination, only the whereabouts of the source and what application created it. *See also* object linking and embedding.

EMC *Abbrev. for* electromagnetic compatibility. The property of equipment to work satisfactorily in an environment with other equipment. All pieces of electric equipment emanate electromagnetic (EM) radiation and are in turn susceptible to it. EMC measurements aim to characterize this property and conformance with legally enforced standards is mandatory.

EMI *Abbrev. for* electromagnetic interference. Disturbance to a signal involving any form of electromagnetic (EM) radiation. *See also* EMC.

emittance texture A pattern of light arising from light emitting from a surface such as a stained glass window.

emitter-coupled logic *See* ECL.

:-)	smiling
:-(	sad or frowning
:-[	sour
!-)	winking
:-D	laughing

Emoticons

emoticon (contraction of emotion + icon) A combination of punctuation marks, and sometimes other characters, first used in *electronic mail and intended to convey the mood of the writer; emoticons are also called *smileys*, regardless of mood. E-mail messages are largely restricted to the *ASCII character set, which precludes the use of text attributes such as bold, italic, or underline but does have a full set of punctuation marks. These are typically used to make faces sideways on the line (see table).

empty list (null list) *See* list.

empty medium A *data medium that does not contain variable data but may have a frame of reference or preformatting. *Compare* virgin medium.

empty set (null set; void set) A *set with no elements. It is usually denoted by φ.

empty string (null string) A string whose *length is zero. It is commonly denoted by ε or Λ. The possibility of strings being empty is a notorious source of bugs in programs.

EMS memory *See* expanded memory.

emulation The exact execution on a given computer of a program written for a different computer, accepting the identical data and producing the identical results. Emulation is thus the imitation of all or part of one computer system by another system. It may be achieved by software, microprogram, or hardware. A particular emulation could be used as a replacement for all or part of the system being emulated, and furthermore could be an improved version. For example, a new computer may emulate an obsolete one so that programs written for the old one will run without modification. *See also* simulation, compatibility.

emulator Any system, especially a program or microprogram, that permits the process of *emulation to be carried out.

enable To selectively activate a device or function. When a number of devices are connected in parallel, selective operation can be achieved by an enabling action – such as a signal on a discrete line or a pattern of signals on the common line or lines – that will set only the desired device into a state in which it can receive further signals. *Compare* inhibit.

enable pulse A pulse that must be present to allow other signals to be effective in certain electronic logic circuits. Although the term is now used to describe an electronic logic function it was originally used in an analogous way in connection with *core stores, where the coincidence of two pulses was required to change the state of a core: one of the pulses was the write pulse and could be common to a number of cores; an enable pulse was simultaneously applied to a particular core and thus enabled the write pulse to change the state of that core.

encapsulation 1. *See* object, information hiding.
2. *See* internetworking.

encoder 1. The means by which an encoding process is effected (*see* code). It may be implemented in hardware or software, the process being algorithmic in nature.
2. A logic circuit, usually an integrated circuit, that generates a unique *n*-bit binary word, indicating which of its 2^n input lines is active, i.e. at logic 1. A *keyboard encoder*, for example, may be required to generate a unique binary code indicating which key on the keyboard has been pressed.
   If two or more of the device inputs can be active simultaneously then a *priority encoder* is required, which usually encodes only the highest-order data input.

encoding 1. The transformation of a message into an encoded form. *See* code.
2. The representation of symbols in some alphabet by symbols or strings of symbols in some other alphabet. A common example is *binary encoding.

encryption The processing of a message by a sender in order to render it unintelligible to other than authorized recipients. *See also* cryptography.

end-around-carry A type of carry that is required when a *radix-minus-one complement representation of integers is used and two integers so represented are summed. If a carry is generated at the most significant end of the two numbers, then this carry must be added to the digit at the least significant end of the result to give the radix-minus-one complement representation of the sum.

end-around shift *Another name for* circular shift. *See* shift.

endomorphism A *homomorphism from an *algebra to itself.

endorder traversal *Another name for* post-order traversal.

end-to-end control Control acting between two applications that are communicating across one or more networks. Data traversing a network must be protected against a number of possible forms of error. An individual unit of data may be corrupted, lost completely, or delivered more than once; successive units of data may be delivered in the wrong order. The sender may attempt to transmit data more quickly than the receiver can receive it, or some part of the route can actually carry it. Within the network, the transmitter and receiver at the two ends of an individual link will cooperate to control some of these errors, and this is known as *point-to-point control*. However, it may also be necessary to require the applications at each end of the overall connection to cooperate in protecting against other forms of error, and this is end-to-end control.

end-to-end encryption The transfer of an encrypted message across a system without intermediate stages of decryption and re-encryption. *Compare* link encryption.

energizer A hardware or software mechanism that is used as an aid in testing the behavior of a subsystem. The intention is that the energizer should drive the subsystem in a way that simulates its actual application, and should at the same time analyze the responses from the subsystem in order to detect any erroneous behavior.

engineering of computer-based systems (ECBS) A narrower form of *systems engineering that addresses only those systems which are computer-based. This is a very important subset of systems engineering, but is still very much wider than *software engineering. It encourages a holistic view of a system, its environment, and its components. Often the components of computer-based systems are also (lower-level) computer-based systems. ECBS pays great attention to addressing nonfunctional properties of a proposed design, and the need for give-and-take between different design options prior to committing to an implementation. Give-and-take is seen as a crucial aspect of such developments because it is here that competing requirements and conflicts (especially commercial versus technical risk) can be addressed.

enhanced small-device interface *See* ESDI.

ENIAC *Acronym for* Electronic Numerical Integrator and Calculator. The first general-purpose electronic calculator, designed and built by John W. Mauchly and J. Presper Eckert Jr. at the University of Pennsylvania's Moore School during the period 1943–46. Originally designed for the production of ballistic tables for the second world war, the machine was not completed until after the war ended. It was widely used for scientific computation until the early 1950s. *See also* UNIVAC.

enterprise modeling A form of *domain modeling where the domain is all or part of a single enterprise, plus relevant parts of the environment(s) in which the enterprise does business.

enterprise server 1. A *server intended to provide service to an entire organization rather than to a selected subset of the organization. It is most likely to be the system maintaining a corporate database, where there are high levels of interaction between the separate entries in the database, and between the separate uses made of the database by the individual members of the organization. The enterprise server may be a server in a *client/server environment. **2.** *Informal name for* mainframe.

entity In programming, any item, such as a data item or statement, that can be named or denoted in a program.

entity-relationship-attribute diagram, model *See* ERA diagram, ERA model.

entropy A measure of the amount of information that is output by a source, or throughput by a channel, or received by an observer (per symbol or per second). Following Shannon (1948) and later writers, the entropy of a *discrete memoryless source with alphabet $A = \{a_i\}$ of size n, and output X at time t is

$$H(X) = \sum_{i=0}^{n-1} p(x_i) \log_b(1/p(x_i))$$

where

$$p(x_i) = \text{Prob }\{X_t = a_i\}$$

The logarithmic base b is chosen to give a convenient scale factor. Usually,

$b = 2$

$b = e = 2.718\,28\ldots$

or

$b = 10$

Entropy is then measured in *bits*, in *natural units* or *nats*, or in *Hartleys*, respectively. When the source has memory, account has to be taken of the dependence between successive symbols output by the source.

The term arises by analogy with entropy in thermodynamics, where the defining expression has the same form but with a physical scale factor k (Boltzmann constant) and with the sign changed. The word *negentropy* is therefore sometimes used for the measure of information, as is *uncertainty* or simply "information".

entry point (entry) The instruction to which control is transferred when a subroutine is called.

entry time The time at which a *process is started or restarted by the process scheduler.

enumeration A list of items in order. Thus the items are organized in such a way that they can be counted, and for each nonnegative integer i within an appropriate range there is a unique item associated with it. An enumeration may be finite or infinite; when an infinite set is involved, the infinite set must be *countable. An enumeration is said to be *effective* if there is an *algorithm for producing the enumeration.

Enumeration is used to define *data types in languages of the Pascal and Jovial families. It also plays a significant role in *combinatorics where one might typically talk of an enumeration of *permutations or *combinations, of *binary trees, of *graphs, of *groups, etc.

enumeration type A *data type comprising values that are explicitly defined by the programmer.

environment (software environment) The set of facilities, such as operating system, windows management, database, etc., that is available to a program when it is being executed by a processor.

environment mapping The process of reflecting the surrounding environment in a shiny object. A simplified *ray-tracing algorithm is used to model the environment: only the reflected ray is traced and the process is terminated at a depth of two (i.e. after two intersections).

EOB *Abbrev. for* end of block.

EOD *Abbrev. for* end of data. A code that is written into a serially accessed memory, such as a magnetic tape file, immediately after the last data record. It thus indicates the starting point for new records. When these are added, the original EOD code is erased and a new one written at the end of the added data.

EOF *Abbrev. for* end of file.

EOJ *Abbrev. for* end of job.

EOR *Abbrev. for* end of record.

EOT 1. *Abbrev. for* end of transmission. A character sequence on a data link indicating that the current transmitter has nothing further to send. Active stations on the data link return to their idle state and wait for a new series of messages.
2. *Abbrev. for* end of tape.

EOT marker *Short for* end of tape marker. A feature of a *magnetic tape by which the tape transport senses on the tape the end of the volume into which data can be or has been recorded. It is complementary to the *BOT marker, and is similarly defined by the standard pertaining to the type of tape.

epimorphism A *homomorphism that, when viewed as a *function, is a *surjection.

epistemology The study of knowledge: a branch of philosophy important in *artificial intelligence for theoretical investigations of belief and knowledge representation.

EPLD *Abbrev. for* erasable programmable logic device. A *PLD in which the programming is erasable (*see* programmable device).

epoch The time interval between successive elements of a discrete-time signal, or between the discrete-time samples of a continuous-time signal (*see* discrete and continuous systems). Usually, for a given signal, the epochs are of a fixed size.

EPOS 1. *Acronym for* electronic point of sale, usually used with other words, as in EPOS terminal, EPOS system. *See* point-of-sale system.

2. A first-generation *IPSE developed in Germany and used widely for real-time systems development. EPOS provides an integrated set of tools for requirements expression, data structure and design, code generation, documentation, and project planning and control.

EPPT *Abbrev. for* European printer performance test. A standardized test for establishing the throughput of office printers. The familiar ratings of characters per second, lines per minute, etc., cannot be relied upon to give a true indication of the throughput achievable in a real application. A set of benchmark tests agreed by a group of European printer manufacturers define standard letter, spreadsheet, and graphic printouts and the way in which the task is timed. These tests were standardized as ECMA 132 and have since been superseded by ISO 10561.

EPROM *Acronym for* erasable programmable read-only memory. A type of *PROM that is capable of being programmed a number of times by the user. The contents of EPROMs are generally erased (i.e. reset to their non-programmed state, usually logic 1) by exposure to hard ultraviolet radiation. The EPROM may then be reprogrammed, i.e. selected elements set to logic 0, using a *PROM programmer. *See also* EEPROM.

equation An expression that asserts the equality of two *terms. To be precise, an equation has the following form. Let Σ be a *signature and let $t_1(X_1,\ldots,X_n)$ and $t_2(X_1,\ldots,X_n)$ be two terms over Σ involving the variables $X_1,\ldots,X_n$. Then

$$t_1(X_1,\ldots,X_n) = t_2(X_1,\ldots,X_n)$$

is an equation.

Equations are a natural means of expressing possible relationships between the functions in a signature. In fact, the equations can be used to specify or define the functions uniquely using initial algebra semantics (*see* equational specification).

Most systems in science and engineering are described mathematically using equations. Two stages are involved: a mathematical model of the system is made using sets and functions; some functions are known and others are to be found. Equations are postulated to define the unknown functions in terms of one another and the known functions. Research has shown that the same process is possible for computing systems. Indeed, theoretically it is known that any computing system, or any physical system that can be faithfully modeled using digital computation, can be characterized by small sets of equations. *See also* computable algebra.

equational logic *See* Birkhoff's completeness theorem.

equational specification A set of *equations that specifies a computing system or abstract data type. More precisely, the system or data type is modeled by an *algebra, and this algebra is defined by the equations using *initial-algebra semantics.

signature	*arithmetic with square;*
sort	*nat;*
constant	$0: \rightarrow nat$
operations	$succ: nat \rightarrow nat$
	$add: nat \times nat \rightarrow nat$
	$mult: nat \times nat \rightarrow nat$
	$sq: nat \rightarrow nat$
end	

equations	$add(x, 0) = x$
	$add(x, succ(y)) = succ(add(x, y))$
	$mult(x, 0) = 0$
	$mult(x, succ(y)) = add(mult(x, y), x)$
	$sq(x) = mult(x, x)$
end	

Fig. *a* Equational specification of an algebra of natural numbers

signature	*square algebra;*
sort	*nat;*
constant	$0: \rightarrow nat$
operations	$succ: nat \rightarrow nat$
	$sq: nat \rightarrow nat$
end	

Fig. *b* Subsignature used in reduct

Let A be an algebra of signature Σ. Then A is said to have an equational specification (Σ, E), under initial-algebra semantics, if E is a set of equations over Σ such that the initial algebra $T(\Sigma, E)$ is isomorphic with A. For example, the algebra

$$A = (\{0,1,2,\ldots\}; 0, n+1, n+m, n.m, n^2)$$

of natural numbers is specified by means of (Σ, E) shown in Fig. a.

An *equational specification with hidden functions and sorts* is an equational specification in which extra or hidden functions and sorts of data are allowed in order to construct equations. Inventing and adding functions, and even data types, to specify a computation or to a model a system is an obvious and natural technique. Consider the algebra

$$B = (\{0,1,2,\ldots\}; 0, n+1, n^2)$$

of numbers with signature Σ^{SQ} shown in Fig. b. The algebra B is a *reduct of the algebra A of numbers given above, i.e.

$$A|_\Sigma{}^{SQ} = B,$$

and B can be specified by specifying A using the equational specification (Σ, E) given above. If A is isomorphic with the initial algebra $T(\Sigma, E)$, then the reduct

$$T(\Sigma, E)|_\Sigma{}^{SQ}$$

is isomorphic with the algebra B. Thus (Σ, E) is an equational specification of B with two hidden functions, namely addition and multiplication.

The square algebra B cannot be given a finite equational specification without using hidden functions; thus the technique is essential. It is known that any computable algebra can be given an equational specification using as little as six hidden functions and four equations, and initial-algebra semantics.

The general definition is as follows. An algebra A of signature Σ is said to have an equational specification (Σ_0, E_0) with hidden functions and sorts, under initial-algebra semantics, if $\Sigma \subseteq \Sigma_0$, and E_0 is a set of equations over Σ_0 such that the reduct

$$T(\Sigma_0, E_0)|_\Sigma$$

of the initial algebra $T(\Sigma_0, E_0)$ with respect to Σ is isomorphic with A.

See also computable algebra.

equational term rewriting system *See* term rewriting system.

equipotent *See* cardinality.

equivalence 1. The logical connective combining two statements or formulas P and Q in such a way that the outcome is true if both P and Q are true or if both are false, as shown in the table. P and Q are said to be *equivalent*. The connective can be read as "if and only if" or "iff", and is usually denoted by one of the following symbols:

$$\equiv \;\leftrightarrow\; \longleftrightarrow\; \Leftrightarrow$$

See also exclusive-NOR gate, propositional calculus.

2. A relationship between objects that are operationally or structurally indistinguishable, e.g. in *combinational circuits, *graphs, or *grammars. Equivalence is less strong than identity or equality but much more useful in practice. *See also* machine equivalence.

P	F	F	T	T
Q	F	T	F	T
$P \equiv Q$	T	F	F	T

Truth table for equivalence

equivalence class A *subset of a set S (on which an *equivalence relation is defined) that consists of all the elements of S that are equivalent to each other, and to no other elements of S. An equivalence relation provides a partitioning (*see* covering) of a set into a number of mutually *disjoint equivalence classes.

The relationship "has the same surname as" defined on the set of people produces an equivalence class consisting of all those with Jones as surname, another consisting of those with Smith as surname, and so on.

equivalence gate *See* exclusive-NOR gate.

equivalence relation A *relation that is *transitive, *symmetric, and *reflexive. The concept is a convenient generalization or abstraction of equality. It covers most notions of equals, equivalence, and similarity as defined between triangles, algorithms, Boolean expressions, algebraic structures, statements, etc. *See also* equivalence class, partial ordering.

equivalent binary digits For a given source alphabet, S, the number of equivalent binary digits is the minimum number of bits that need to be taken in a *block code to give at least as many codewords as there are symbols in S.

equivalent trees *Similar trees with the same data at corresponding nodes.

ERA diagram *Short for* entity-relationship-attribute diagram. A diagrammatic notation for describing and documenting an *ERA model. Entities are shown as boxes in the ERA diagram and have an entity name; usually names are required to be unique. Attributes are generally shown as annotations of the entity boxes. Relationships are shown as lines between entity boxes. Markings on the line indicate the name(s) of the relationship, cardinality of the relationship (one to one, one to many, or many to many), and whether the relationship is optional or mandatory. Many *software tools for editing diagrams can handle ERA diagrams.

ERA model *Short for* entity-relationship-attribute model. A model of a set of data items and relationships between them in terms of the *entities, relationships, and *attributes involved.

Entities have attributes and have relationships with other entities. They have an entity name; usually names are required to be unique. Entities are often implemented as a record comprising a number of fields.

Attributes are usually represented in a *data dictionary and describe the characteristic features of the entity. Each attribute is named; usually names of attributes are required to be unique. Attributes are often implemented as fields with values.

Each relationship has two names (a forward and a reverse name); usually relationship names are required to be unique. There can be more than one relationship between a pair of entities.

See also ERA diagram.

erasable programmable logic device *See* EPLD.

erasable PROM *See* EPROM. *See also* programmable device.

erase head *See* magnetic tape.

eraser An item of electronic equipment that can carry out the erasure process for an *EPROM. It often consists of an enclosed source of ultraviolet radiation, close to which the EPROM may be placed, and a timer.

erasure channel A communication *channel in which the effect of *noise is to cause the *decoder sometimes to be presented with an "error" symbol to decode. The decoder may then act in the knowledge that in such symbol positions the symbol actually transmitted is unknown: it is thus in a better position than when presented with an incorrect symbol but not the knowledge that it is incorrect (other than can be deduced by using an *error-detecting or *error-correcting code).

ergodic source *See* discrete source.

ergonomics The study of the interaction of people and the equipment with which they work. In computing, ergonomics is applied mainly to the field of *workstation technology.

error 1. The difference between a computed, observed, or measured value or condition and the true, specified, or theoretically correct value or condition.
2. An incorrect result resulting from some *failure in the hardware of a system.
3. An incorrect step, process, or data definition in for example a program. *See also* semantic error, syntax error.

error analysis A term that when applied to *numerical analysis refers to the mathematical analysis that describes the various aspects of error behavior in numerical methods (or algorithms). *Convergence* of an algorithm is a fundamental requirement. Most algorithms result in the construction of a sequence of approximations. If this sequence tends more and more closely to the true solution of the problem, the algorithm is convergent. How fast the algorithm converges is important for its efficiency; some insight is provided by the *order of the method. Since most algorithms are terminated before convergence is reached, the size of the error after a finite number of steps must be estimated. How big the error is at most can be determined from an *error bound*. This must be reasonably "sharp", i.e. it must not grossly overestimate the error. How big the error is approximately is referred to as an *error estimate* and is usually determined from an asymptotic formula. Such estimates are widely used in step-by-step methods for *ordinary differential equations; here the stepsize, h, must be small enough for the estimate to be accurate.

In *numerical linear algebra *backward error analysis* has proved very successful in analyzing errors. In this approach it is shown that the numerical solution satisfies exactly a perturbed form of the original problem. Bounds for the perturbations are determined and these can be inserted into standard results, thus producing a bound for the error in the numerical solution. The approach can be applied to other areas.

error bound *See* error analysis.

error burst *Another name for* burst error.

error control (error management, error handling) The employment, in a computer system or in a communication system, of *error-detecting and/or *error-correcting codes with the intention of removing the effects of error and/or recording the prevalence of error in the system. The effects of errors may be removed by correcting them in all but a negligible proportion of cases. Error control aims to cope with errors owing to *noise or to equipment malfunction – in which case it overlaps with fault tolerance (*see* fault-tolerant system) – but not usually with the effects of errors in the design of hardware or software.

Error control is expensive: the balance between the cost and the benefit (measured by the degree of protection) has to be weighed within the technological and financial context of the system being designed. *See also* error recovery.

error-correcting code A *code that is designed for *channel coding, i.e. for encoding information so that a decoder can correct, with a high probability of success, any errors caused in the signal by an intervening noisy channel.

Error-correcting codes may be *block codes or *convolutional codes, and in either case are employed in a *forward error-correction system. The most common error-correcting block codes are the *Hamming codes, *Bose-Chaudhuri-Hocquenghem (BCH) codes, *Reed-Solomon (RS) codes, *simplex codes, and the *Golay (23, 12) code.

Since errors may be corrected by detecting them and requesting retransmission, the process of error correction is sometimes taken to include *backward error-correction systems and, hence, *error-detecting codes.

See also Shannon's model, coding theory, coding bounds.

error correction *See* error recovery, error-correcting code.

error-detecting code A *code that is designed for *channel coding, i.e. for encoding information so that a decoder can detect, with a high probability of success, whether an intervening channel has caused an error in the signal.

Error-detecting codes are usually *block codes, and are generally employed in a *backward error-correction system. The most common error-detecting codes are the *cyclic redundancy checks, of which the simple parity check is a technologically important case.

See also error-correcting code, Shannon's model, coding theory, coding bounds, Hamming distance.

error detection The detection of errors in data handled by a peripheral device or communication link; it is often associated with *error recovery and *error correction. Data to be stored or transmitted can be coded in a way that allows most errors to be detected. The simplest *error-detecting code is the addition of a parity bit to each byte of data, but more powerful codes are often used which operate on larger units such as a sector or block. Some devices also check for marginal conditions, such as low signal amplitude, which are associated with data errors. In storage peripherals, errors may be detected at the time data is written (as in *DRDW and *DRAW), as a separate operation after writing (*verification), or during a read operation at some later time. Error detection does not normally involve a bit-by-bit comparison with the original data even if this is still held in a buffer or in host memory. *See also* error control.

error diagnostics Information that is presented following the detection of some error condition and is mainly intended to assist in identifying the cause of the error.

As an example, consider the compilation and subsequent execution of some program. *Syntactic errors* in the program, i.e. failure of the program to conform to the defined *syntax of the programming language, would normally be detected at compilation time, and the compiler would then generally produce error diagnostics to indicate both the location and the kind of error (unrecognized statement, undeclared identifier, etc.). At execution time certain kinds of *semantic errors* may be detected, i.e. improper behavior of a program that conforms to the defined syntax of the language (such as attempted division by zero). In this case the error diagnostics may be produced by some run-time system. *See also* error routine.

error estimate *See* error analysis.

error handling *Another term for* error control.

error-indicating recording (EIR) *See* disk format.

error management *Another name for* error control.

error message *See* error routine.

error propagation A term that refers to the way in which, at a given stage of a calculation, part of the error arises out of the error at a previous stage. This is independent of the further *roundoff errors inevitably introduced between the two stages. Unfavorable error propagation can seriously affect the results of a calculation.

The investigation of error propagation in simple arithmetical operations is used as the basis for the detailed analysis of more extensive calculations. The way in which uncertainties in the data propagate into the final results of a calculation can be assessed in practice by repeating the calculation with slightly perturbed data.

error rate 1. of a communication channel. The frequency with which errors or noise are introduced into the channel. Error rate may be measured in terms of erroneous bits received per bits transmitted. For example, one or two errors per 100 000 bits might be a typical rate for a narrowband point-to-point line. The distribution of errors is usually nonuniform: errors tend to come in bursts (*see* burst error). Thus the error rate of a channel may be specified in terms of percentage of error-free seconds. Frequently an error rate is expressed as a negative power of ten: an error rate of one bit per 100 000 would be expressed as an error rate of 10^{-5}.

Another method of presenting error rate is to consider the errors as the result of adding the data signal to an underlying error signal. The extent of error can then be expressed as the *entropy of the error signal, or, in the case of physical signals, as the ratio of the strengths of the two signals – the *signal-to-noise ratio – expressed in decibels.

2. of a data storage subsystem. A measurement of the proportion of errors occurring in data transfers to or from the storage medium. It is usually expressed in terms of the average number of bytes or bits of data transferred per error, e.g. 1 error per 10^9 bytes, although it can also be useful to express the rate as the average time between errors for typical usage of the subsystem, e.g. 1 undetected error in 6 weeks at 10% duty cycle.

The error rates most frequently specified relate to the following.

A *transient (or recoverable) read error* occurs during reading and can be recovered by the error recovery procedure prescribed for the storage subsystem (*see* error recovery). A typical figure for magnetic tape is 1 in 10^9 bytes. Where the recording format provides sufficient redundancy to allow some error to be recovered *on-the-fly*, i.e. without re-reading the data, it is necessary to define also the *raw error rate*, which is the rate that would be perceived if on-the-fly error recovery was not applied.

A *permanent (or irrecoverable) read error* cannot be recovered by the prescribed error recovery procedure. A typical figure is 1 in 10^{11} bytes.

A *transient (or recoverable) write error* occurs during writing and can be recovered by the error recovery procedure prescribed.

It is desirable, though not easy, to distinguish two components of this error rate: errors attributable firstly to flaws in the media and secondly to failings of the device (one reason for the difficulty is that these tend to interact). A typical figure for magnetic tape, excluding media errors, is 1 in 10^8 bytes.

A *permanent (or irrecoverable) write error* cannot be recovered by the prescribed procedure. Again it is necessary to distinguish between media flaws and device errors: rather than give a figure for the latter it is usual to regard each occurrence as a fault to be accounted for in the failure rate of the device (*see* hardware reliability).

An *undetected error* is an error that is not detected by the storage subsystem, presumably because of some inadequacy in the error check facilities defined by the format or in their implementation, or because of errors occurring outside the ambit of these facilities (*see* data integrity). A typical figure is 1 in 10^{13} bytes: a higher figure may well be achieved but is difficult to demonstrate.

Note that error rates depend on the *error recovery procedure used; specified figures are therefore valid only in the conditions defined or assumed in the specification.

error recovery 1. The ability of a compiler to resume parsing of a program after encountering a syntax error.

2. Any process whereby it is possible to recover the data from a data unit (such as a sector or block) that has been shown by an *error detection procedure to contain one or more errors. There are two approaches: *retry* and *error correction*. Retry involves rereading the data unit from the storage medium or retransmitting it over the communication link; this may be repeated more than once. Error correction depends on the data coding being sufficiently redundant to allow errors to be recovered by logical manipulation of the data without rereading it (*see* error-correcting code). In each case, recovery may need intervention by the host software or may be carried out automatically by the device. Where recovery is automatic, the host is able to monitor the number of errors that are recovered.

When the error is detected during writing or verification, the faulty data unit may be corrected or replaced (*see* write error recovery); in a device with powerful error correction, such as an optical disk drive, this is not always necessary.

error routine Any routine within a program that is entered as a result of some error condition having been detected. The actions taken by such a routine will be dependent upon the reliability requirements that the program is expected to meet and upon the strategy for error analysis and recovery. A typical error routine might simply produce an *error message* (i.e. a message that reports the occurrence of an error) or it might attempt to diagnose the cause of the error or attempt to recover so that normal operation can continue.

error seeding *See* seeding.

escape character A character that changes the meaning of a character or characters immediately following. It is like a temporary *shift character. The *ASCII characters ESC and DLE are used in this way. Graphic characters (*see* character set) are also used as escape characters in particular contexts.

escape sequence An *escape character with the associated following characters, used for controlling a peripheral device. *See also* control sequence.

ESD *Abbrev. for* electrostatic discharge. A mechanism that affects the reliability and often brings about the failure of active electronic components, such as insulated-gate FETs (MOSFETs).

ESDI *Abbrev. for* enhanced small-device interface. A scheme for connecting hard disks to microcomputers with a serial transfer rate of 10–25 MHz. It allows a disk controller to communicate with the disk drive through standard cables and connectors using standard control and data signals. ESDI has been largely superseded by *IDE and *SCSI device attachment standards.

ESF coating A transparent conducting layer deposited on the surface of a *cathode–ray tube (CRT) that allows the surface charge to leak away, thus reducing the ESF (electrostatic field) to negligible values. The high accelerating voltage (14–25 kilovolts) of CRTs can produce an electrostatic charge on the surface. This is analogous to the charge produced by friction with highly insulating materials. It is claimed by some experts that this can be harmful to users. There is currently no consensus as to the levels or exposure limits that should be enforced.

ESPITI *See* ESSI.

ESPRIT *Acronym for* European Strategic Programme for Research in Information Technology. There have been three ESPRIT programs: ESPRIT I, 1984–87; ESPRIT II, 1987–91; ESPRIT III, 1991–94. They were funded by the European Community, and formed major components of the Community's successive R&D *Framework Programmes* (I, II, and III respectively). To qualify for support under ESPRIT, a project had to involve precompetitive collaboration between at least two industrial organizations in different countries of the European Community; research organizations could additionally be involved. Funding was normally on the basis of 50% of total project costs for industrial partners and 100% of marginal costs for academic partners. Research has been undertaken under headings such as microelectronics, peripherals and interfaces, systems and software engineering, knowledge engineering, advanced and high-performance architectures, business and home systems, and computer-integrated manufacturing.

Under *Framework IV*, 1995–99, the ESPRIT label has been dropped; the program now goes under the name *RTD Programme in Information Technologies* (RTD is short for Research and Technological Development). The balance of emphasis has moved away somewhat from the production of new research results toward the exploitation of existing results.

See also ESSI.

ESSI *Acronym for* European Systems and Software Initiative. A program of technology transfer and software process improvement within *ESPRIT III. As distinct from the main body of ESPRIT, which supported R&D projects, ESSI had the goal of improv-ing software development practice in industry and business. The ESSI pilot phase (1993–96) supported 93 Application Experiments (process improvement activities), nine Dissemination Actions, and a training program (*ESPITI*: European Software Process Improvement Training Initiative). The Framework IV Programme, 1995–99 (*see* ESPRIT), includes a continuation of ESSI under the name *Software Best Practice*.

ETB A *control character used to mark the end of a transmission block. *See also* ETX/ACK.

Ether *See* Ethernet.

Ethernet A very widely used *local area network system. Ethernet uses *broadcast *packets that are transmitted over a purely passive medium, usually referred to as the *Ether*. In practice the Ether usually takes the form of a *coaxial cable (*see also* thick wire), but the system can also use *twisted pairs and *optical fiber. The system operates at a nominal speed of 10 megabits per second (Mbps), and implements the two lower layers of the ISO/OSI *seven-layer reference model. A fast Ethernet system, operating at 100 Mbps, is also available. Ethernet was originally developed in 1976 at Xerox PARC, operating at 4 Mbps. Later it was offered as a standard jointly sponsored by Digital Equipment, Intel, and Xerox. The formal definition of the Ethernet standard is available as ISO 802.3.

Each system on the network, usually a computer, connects to the Ether by means of a *station*, each station having a unique 48-bit address. All packets contain the address of the sending station and the address of the receiving station. When a packet is transmitted it is broadcast to all the stations. Each station will receive all packets, but will only pass packets addressed to that station to the system connected to it. A packet can be marked as a "broadcast" to be accepted by all the systems connected to the Ether.

Ethernet stations use a protocol known as CSMA/CD – Carrier Sense Multi-Access/Collision Detection – to insert a packet onto the Ether. (CSMA/CD is also the formal name for Ethernet.) When a station wishes to transmit a packet, it monitors the Ether for the presence of signals from other stations. If no signal is present then the station starts to transmit, and continuously compares the signal on the Ether with the data it is transmitting. Any difference indicates that another station has also started to transmit a packet, and that there is a *collision* between the two packets. This can occur because the distance separating the two transmitting stations is such that, although both stations had started to transmit during the period when the other was monitoring the Ether, the outgoing signal had not yet reached the other station. Both stations immediately cease transmission, wait for different times, and then retry the transmission. This system has the advantage that the mechanism for gaining access to the Ether is fully distributed and self-starting. Its main drawbacks are the unpredictability of the time needed to gain access, and the fact that the effective bandwidth actually diminishes under heavy loads as the probability of a collision increases. The limits to the length of the Ether cable are determined by the need to reduce the probability of a collision to an acceptable level, achieved by reducing the maximum time needed for a signal to traverse the Ether.

The physical size of the Ethernet can be increased by the use of repeaters, which simply amplify the signals, and by *bridges and *routers, which store and retransmit a complete packet.

Ethernet card An *add-in card that allows a computer system to exchange data with an *Ethernet network. Most cards can handle some alternative connection methods, for instance multipin *AUI, coaxial *thin wire, and unshielded *twisted pair, as well as providing buffering between the Ethernet and the memory of the computer.

ETX/ACK A method of terminating a series of transmissions relating to a single complete transaction using *control characters. The sending device transmits an 'ETX' (end-of-text) control character when a transaction is completed, and the receiving device acknowledges the satisfactory receipt of the ETX with an 'ACK' (*see* acknowledgment).

Termination of transmissions in this way should not be confused with the *flow control necessary to regulate traffic during the transmission process.

Euclidean norm (two-norm) *See* approximation theory.

Euclid's algorithm An algorithm for finding the greatest common divisor of two integers, m and n. If $m > n$ divide m by n and let r be the remainder. If $r = 0$ then n is the answer; otherwise apply the same algorithm to the integers n and r.

Eudora An electronic-mail system originally developed for Apple Macintosh systems but subsequently implemented on a number of other hardware platforms.

Euler cycle (Euler path) A *path in a directed *graph that includes each edge in the graph precisely once; thus it represents a complete traversal of the arcs of the graph. The concept is named for Leonhard Euler who introduced it around 1736 to solve the *Königsberg bridges problem. He showed that for a graph to possess an Euler cycle it should be *connected and each vertex should have the same number of edges entering it as leaving it.

Euler operators Operations on objects that satisfy *Euler's formula in order to transform the object into a new object that also satisfies Euler's formula. Adding an edge that divides an existing face is an example of an Euler operator; one edge and one face is added in this way, which preserves Euler's formula unchanged.

Euler's formula A formula that states necessary but not sufficient conditions for an object to be a *simple polyhedron*. An object with V vertices, E edges, and F faces satisfies the formula

$$\chi = V - E + F$$

where χ is called the *Euler characteristic* of the surface in which the object is embedded. For a plane *connected graph, the formula takes the form

$$V - E + F = 1$$

For a simple polyhedron in Euclidean 3-space, the formula has the form

$$V - E + F = 2$$

A simple polyhedron is any polyhedron that can be continuously deformed into a sphere, assuming that its faces are treated like sheets of rubber. All faces are bounded by a single ring of edges: there are no holes in the faces; each edge joins exactly two faces and is terminated by a vertex at each end. At least three edges meet at each vertex.

Euler's method *See* discretization.

EuLisp A modern dialect of *LISP developed in Europe as a candidate for international standardization.

EUREKA A European program of development in a wide range of technologies including *information technology (IT). The projects are collaborative with at least two different companies from different countries participating in a project. Some funding is provided by the national funding agencies. It is not limited to European Union countries. EUREKA is oriented nearer to marketplace development than *ESPRIT.

Euronet A collaborative network that links together a number of the academic and research *packet switching networks in Europe.

evaluation function A procedure that uses *domain knowledge to determine a perceived value of a situation during a *search process. It must be custom designed and implemented for each application. Evaluation functions have conflicting requirements as they must produce a relevant and accurate "figure of merit" (which may be expensive to compute) but are used a great many times during a search (and so must be very fast and efficient. Frequently this conflict is handled by using *heuristics in the evaluation process.

even parity A property that holds when a group of binary values contains an even number of 1s. *See* parity.

event-driven A way of describing behavior in which distinct events are identified, and each event is linked to a defined sequence of actions taken whenever the event occurs.

event input Asynchronous input that adds input events to an input queue. The applica-

tion can remove events from the queue as and when it desires.

event tree analysis A systematic approach to reasoning about the consequences of some initial event, and whose purpose is to identify *hazards in a *system. It uses diagrams in the form of trees.

evolutionary programming A branch of *artificial intelligence that, by analogy with the phenomena of evolution in nature, attempts to develop software through processes of natural selection and reproduction.

Excel *Trademark* A widely used *spreadsheet from Microsoft.

exception An event occurring during execution of a program that makes continuation impossible or undesirable. Examples include division by zero, arithmetic overflow, array reference with index out of bounds, fault condition on a peripheral, and external interrupt. Many programming languages respond to an exception by aborting execution, but some (e.g. Ada) allow the programmer to provide a piece of code – called an *exception handler* – that is automatically invoked when the exception occurs. This can take appropriate remedial action, then either resume execution of the program (at the point where the exception occurred or elsewhere) or terminate the program in a controlled manner.

exception handling Mechanisms in a programming language for dealing with *exceptions. Many languages make no such provision; among those that do are Ada, C++, Modula 3, and PL/I.

excess-3 code An 8421 *code for which the weighted sum of the four bits in each codeword is three greater than the decimal digit represented by that codeword. For example, 9 is represented by 1100, the weighted sum of which is

$$8\times1 + 4\times1 + 2\times0 + 1\times0 = 12$$

excess factor *Another name for* bias. *See* floating-point notation.

excess-n notation (excess notation) *See* floating-point notation.

exchangeable disk store (EDS) An obsolete storage medium consisting of a magnetic *disk pack or *disk cartridge that could be removed from its host system for library storage, and be replaced by another EDS of the same type. The store could be fitted to another host system having the same type of drive and means of recording and reading data. *Compare* fixed disk drive.

exchange selection *Another name for* bubble sort.

A1 A2 ⟩⟩⟩⟩— B

inputs	A1	0	0	1	1
	A2	0	1	0	1
output	B	1	0	0	1

Two-input EXNOR gate, circuit symbol and truth table

exclusive-NOR gate (EXNOR gate) An electronic *logic gate whose output is logic 0 (false) only when any one of its inputs is logic 1 (true) and all the others are logic 0, otherwise the output is logic 1. It implements the logical operation of *equivalence and has the same *truth table. It is thus also known as an *equivalence gate*. Like the *exclusive-OR gate it can be used as a simple digital *comparator. The diagram shows the circuit symbol and truth table of a two-input gate.

exclusive-OR gate (EXOR gate) An electronic *logic gate whose output is logic 1 (true) only when any one of its inputs is logic 1 and all the others are logic 0 (false),

A1 A2 ⟩⟩⟩⟩— B

inputs	A1	0	0	1	1
	A2	0	1	0	1
output	B	0	1	1	0

Two-input EXOR gate, circuit symbol and truth table

P		F	F	T	T
Q		F	T	F	T
P XOR Q		F	T	T	F

Truth table for exclusive-OR operation

otherwise the output is logic 0. It therefore implements the logical *exclusive-OR operation and has the same *truth table; it is thus sometimes known as a *nonequivalence gate*. Like the *exclusive-NOR gate it can be used as a simple digital *comparator. The diagram shows the circuit symbol and truth table for a two-input gate.

exclusive-OR operation The logical *connective combining two statements, truth values, or formulas P and Q in such a way that the outcome is true if either P or Q (but not both P and Q) is true, as shown in the table. Since the outcome is true precisely when the operands are different, it is sometimes referred to as the *nonequivalence operation*. It can be represented in a variety of ways, the more common methods being XOR, xor, and ∨. *See also* OR operation.

executables Files that when loaded into memory can be executed directly.

execute To carry out an instruction or program. This includes interpreting machine instructions, performing subroutines, and applying functions to sets of parameters.

execute phase The time during a program run in which the target program is actually being executed.

execute step The step in instruction execution that performs the operation(s) of the instruction and the associated memory references. *See* control unit.

execution states The various states in which a computer system may be operating; these states have differing degrees of ability or privilege attached to them. There may be two or more states. In the simplest case there is a *supervisor state* (or *executive state*) and a *user state*. With more than two execution states at different levels, differing degrees of privilege may be granted. These states can represent some of the used resources in an access matrix. *See* access control.

execution time *See* run time.

executive program An early name for a *supervisor. In current terminology an executive is not strictly speaking a program since the latter is usually taken to refer to one or more processes that are collaborating in order to achieve results on behalf of a single user. By contrast an executive is responsible for the supervision of many disjoint processes, which do not cooperate in any way.

executive state (supervisor state) *See* execution states.

exerciser A device or program used to test a subsystem by thoroughly and repetitively performing each of its designed functions and monitoring the results. An example is a floppy-disk exerciser.

exhaustive search A mechanical search algorithm that systematically examines all the nodes in a search tree, an example being a *breadth-first search. Although usually very simple to program and requiring no *domain knowledge, in most cases the *combinatorial explosion will prohibit the use of exhaustive search.

existential quantifier *See* quantifier.

exit point (exit) The point at which control leaves a subroutine.

EXNOR gate *Short for* exclusive-NOR gate.

EXOR gate *Short for* exclusive-OR gate.

expanded memory (EMS memory) A way of accessing IBM-PC-type memory above 1 Mbyte by mapping it one 16-Kbyte page at a time into dedicated areas of RAM (called page frames) in the upper memory region lying between 640 Kbyte and 1 Mbyte. Originally developed in conjunction by Lotus, Intel, and Microsoft, the EMS method of increasing the amount of memory accessible to this type of machine has been largely superseded by *extended memory (XMS).

expansion of an algebra. An *algebra formed by adding some new operations, and possibly new carriers, to another algebra.

expansion card *Another name for* add-in card.

expansion slot The connectors and physical supports into which an *add-in card is inserted. The number and type of expansion slots is an important characteristic in distinguishing different types of computer. In general, the more expansion slots, the more upgradable is a computer. Most expansion slots connect to one of the many kinds of

*bus or sometimes into a proprietary *backplane or *motherboard.

expectation *See* measures of location.

experimental design A system of allocating treatments to experimental units so that the effects of the treatments may be estimated by *statistical methods. The basic principles of experimental design are *replication*, i.e. the application of the same treatment to several units, *randomization*, which ensures that each unit has the same probability of receiving any given treatment, and *blocking*, i.e. grouping of similar units, each one to receive a different treatment. *Factorial designs* are used to allow different types of treatment, or *factors*, to be tested simultaneously. *Analysis of variance is used to assess the significance of the treatment effects. *See also* missing observations, fractional replication.

expert systems Computer programs built for commercial application using the programming techniques of *artificial intelligence, especially those techniques developed for problem solving. Expert systems have been built for a variety of purposes including medical diagnosis, electronic fault finding, mineral prospecting, and computer-system configuration. *See also* knowledge base, inference engine.

explicit address *Another name for* absolute address.

exploratory data analysis (EDA) A term invented by J. W. Tukey to denote techniques for looking at numerical data with a view to discerning pattern. Exploratory data analysis is open-ended and makes few prior assumptions about the nature of any pattern that may be found. Graphical techniques are freely used. It can be contrasted with model-fitting techniques, which make highly specific prior assumptions. *Statistical methods contain aspects of both these processes.

exponent *See* floating-point notation.

exponentially bounded algorithm *See* complexity measure.

exponential waveform A nonrepetitive waveform that rises or falls exponentially from some initial value at some initial time, according to the law

$$y(t) = e^{at}$$

For $a>0$ the waveform rises without bound with increasing time t; for $a<0$ the waveform decays to zero. One way in which logic signals can become corrupted as they travel through a system is for their switching edges to become exponentials.

exponentiation The *operation of raising to a power. Repeated multiplication of a quantity x by itself n times is written as x^n. When x is nonzero the value of x^0 is normally assumed to be 1.

Alternatively x^n can be defined inductively (*see* induction) in the following way:

$$x^0 = 1$$
$$x^n = x \times x^{n-1} \text{ for } n > 0$$

The concept of exponentiation can be extended to include exponents that are negative, fractional, or variable or are complex numbers. Exponentiation is an operation that is supplied in some form in most common programming languages (the significant exception being Pascal). It is also a fundamental part of the *floating-point notation for real numbers.

export list In modular languages such as *Modula 2, a list of the names declared inside a module that are accessible to other modules.

expression A component of a programming language that defines the computation of a value, e.g.

$$(-b+sqrt(b*b-4*a*c))/(2*a)$$

expression of requirements A statement of the requirements that some envisaged computer system (or program) is expected to meet. In order to define these requirements adequately, it is normally necessary for the expression of requirements to address not just the envisaged system but also the environment in which that system is to operate.

A good expression of requirements should be one of the earliest products of any system-development project, and for a project of significant size it is of crucial importance, not least because errors introduced at the requirements stage tend to be the most expensive to correct. Since it is the first rea-

sonably complete description of any given system, its production presents several significant problems. In particular it may be necessary to obtain information from many individuals, none of whom have a full understanding of all aspects of the envisaged system. There may therefore be a need to resolve several confused, incomplete, and inconsistent views in order to produce a single coherent whole.

The expression of requirements is a primary vehicle for communication between the procurers of a system and its developers. Since it is unreasonable to expect potential users of a system to understand software-oriented expressions of requirements, it is useful to distinguish between *user requirements* and *system* or *software requirements*. User requirements are stated briefly in natural language using the jargon of the problem domain and primarily defining the nature of the problem to be solved by the computer-based system. This description should be free from any solution bias. System or software requirements represent the first step toward a solution to the problem and should be based on an abstract model but omitting any detailed design or implementation bias.

extended addressing Any of several methods that permit access to memory with *address space larger than the address space normally accessible in an instruction. *See also* extended memory, addressing schemes.

extended BNF (EBNF) A notation for defining the *syntax of a programming language based on *BNF (Backus normal form). EBNF overcomes the main disadvantages of BNF, which are that repetition has to be expressed by a recursive definition and that options and alternatives require auxiliary definitions, by incorporating a notation to specify repetition and alternation. For example, compare the BNF definitions shown in Fig. 1 with the equivalent EBNF definitions in Fig. 2. EBNF uses {...} to denote repetition, | to denote alternatives, (...) to group constituents, and [...] to denote options. Another significant difference is in the way literals are distinguished from syntactic categories. In BNF, literals are plain and syntactic categories are enclosed in angle brackets; in EBNF, syntactic categories are plain and literals are enclosed in quotation marks. This allows EBNF to define its own syntax.

⟨digit string⟩ ::= ⟨digit⟩ | ⟨digit⟩⟨digit string⟩
⟨sign⟩ ::= + | −
⟨unsigned number⟩ ::= ⟨digit string⟩ |
                      ⟨digit string⟩.
⟨number⟩ ::= ⟨unsigned number⟩ |
             ⟨sign⟩⟨unsigned number⟩

Fig. 1 BNF notation

digit-string = digit {digit}
unsigned-number = digit-string[.]
number = unsigned-number|
         ("+" | "−") unsigned-number

Fig. 2 Extended BNF notation

extended memory (XMS memory) A way of accessing IBM-PC-type memory above 1 Mbyte, used by Intel 80286 processors and above. These processors can address the high memory directly, but the XMS protocol allows a number of programs to share this resource without destructive interactions. XMS memory was developed by Lotus, Intel, Microsoft, and AST.

extended precision *Double precision or more than double precision.

extensibility The capability of a programming language to accept definitions of new constructs.

extensible addressing See addressing.

extensible language A programming language having the property of *extensibility.

extension of a source. In coding theory, the process of encoding several symbols at a time, or the results thereof. If the symbols of a *q-ary information source are taken r at a time, and the words of length r are treated (e.g. encoded) as if they were themselves symbols of an alphabet of size q', then this compound source is called the rth *extension* of the original source. See also source coding theorem.

extension field See polynomial.

external device A device that is subsidiary or peripheral to a computer system, usually a terminal or other remote device. In some I/O instructions the designation of an external device is made by specifying a (usually binary) number that distinguishes that device from all others. This number is often called the *external device address* although, strictly speaking, it is not an address in the true sense. See also address space.

external fragmentation A form of *fragmentation that arises when memory is allocated in units of arbitrary size. When a large amount of memory is released, part of it may be used to meet a subsequent request, leaving an unused part that is too small to meet any further requests.

external interrupt An interrupt that is initiated by a device that is not part of the processor. Peripherals and communication connections are sources of external interrupts.

external node *Another name for* leaf node.

external path length of a tree. The sum of the lengths of all paths from the root to an external (i.e. a leaf) node.

external schema of a database. *Another name for* user view.

external sorting See sorting.

external storage Any type of storage device that is connected to and controlled by a computer but is not integrated within it. Generally the devices are peripheral units such as disk drives or tape transports. An external storage device may be shared by more than one computer.

extrapolation The estimation of the value of a function (given other values of the function) at a point beyond the interval in which the data lies. One possible approach is to use the value of an *interpolation polynomial at this point. An important case arises when the data consists of approximations to the solution of a problem, for different values of a parameter controlling the magnitude of the acceptable error in the method used. A more powerful method can be constructed by extrapolating to the limiting case of the parameter, where the error is zero, using theoretical results giving the dependence of the error on the parameter. This is called *Richardson extrapolation* (or the *deferred approach to the limit*).

extrapolation method A *numerical method for the solution of a problem based on repeated *extrapolation, to produce increasingly more accurate results, from a sequence of basic approximations utilizing different values of a parameter, such as the stepsize (*see* finite-difference method).

Important examples are the *Romberg method for *numerical integration and *Gragg's extrapolation method for the solution of *ordinary differential equations based on the *midpoint rule. An essential requirement for such methods are theoretical results establishing the existence of an expansion for the error in (usually even) powers of the parameter, for sufficiently smooth problems.

extrinsic semiconductor *See* semiconductor.

F

facet Any of the planar elements into which curved surfaces are broken for *rendering.

facial animation *See* computer animation.

facilities management The arrangement under which a specialist company takes over complete responsibility for running the information-processing systems of a user company.

facsimile Systems that provide electronic transmission of ordinary documents, incuding drawings, photographs, and maps. The original document is scanned at the sending station, converted into an analog or digital representation, and sent over a communication channel to the receiving station, which constructs a duplicate image on paper; this image is referred to as a *facsimile*. Early facsimile systems were exclusively analog, but new systems have been designed that use digital techniques for data encoding and transmission. Commercial facsimile services are known as *fax*.

factorable code An *error-correcting code that can be considered as the result of several coding stages, the output of each being encoded by the next. The constituent codes are the factors of the original compound code. *See* concatenated coding systems.

factor analysis *See* multivariate analysis.

factorial designs *See* experimental design.

FADEC *Abbrev. for* fully authorized digital engine control. A system in avionics for direct computer control of the engine (with safety implications).

Fagan inspection *See* code inspection.

fail-safe Denoting or relating to a computer system that does not make an error in spite of the occurrence of a single fault. *See also* fault-tolerant system.

fail-soft Denoting or relating to a computer system that can continue to provide a reduced level of service in spite of the occurrence of a single fault. The system is then said to be in a state of *graceful degradation*. *See also* fault-tolerant system.

failure An event or condition in which an entire computer system or some part of it is unable to perform one or more prescribed functions. The failure may be due to a random process causing the hardware to cease to function, in which case hardware *maintenance is required. Failure may also be due to a systematic cause such as an unrevealed or uncorrected *fault* in hardware or software. The fault may be due to an *error*, i.e. a mistake, occurring during (for example) design, specification, or operation. Each fault built into the hardware or software may be later revealed through a variety of processes such as *review, *static analysis, *testing, or failure during operation of the computer. The result of revealing the fault at any time is a failure event for the hardware or software. Whether the failure is significant depends on the consequences and the timing.

There is thus a relationship between failure, fault, and error. Note however that the terms are sometimes used synonymously. *See also* fault-tolerant system.

failure modes, effects, and criticality analysis (FMECA) A systematic and disciplined approach to the task of measuring the relative criticality of the different components in a *safety-critical or *safety-related system. The purpose is to identify components whose design may merit special attention.

failure rate The number of *failures of a specified category in a given period, in a given number of computer runs, or in some other given unit of measure. The failure rate of a system or component varies during its lifetime, at first decreasing as problems are detected and repaired and finally increasing due to deterioration. Between these two periods the rate usually remains steady.

failure recovery A procedure that allows for restart of a failed system in a way that either eliminates or minimizes the amount of incorrect system results. This usually requires the program that was running to have used a *checkpoint procedure.

fairness See fair surface design.

fair surface design The requirement that the shape between specific sections of a design must be consistent with the overall smoothness or *fairness* of the shape. For example, a timber ship requires the planking not to have hollows and bumps between the ribs. See also lofting.

fallback The *restarting of a process at a *checkpoint after correction of a fault. See also failure recovery.

false position method (Latin: **regula falsi**) An *iterative method for finding a root of the *nonlinear equation $f(x) = 0$. It employs the same formula as the *secant method, but retains at each stage the two most recent estimates that bracket the root in order to guarantee convergence. Modifications to this general strategy are required to avoid one end-point remaining fixed and slow convergence. The resulting methods are both fast and reliable.

fan-in 1. The number of input lines (normally fixed) to a logic gate or logic device.
2. The number of software modules that call this module.

Fano coding (Shannon–Fano coding) See source coding.

Fano decoding The decoding of a *convolutional code by Fano's algorithm.

fan-out 1. The maximum number of devices that can be safely driven by the output from a logic gate or logic device (which have only a limited ability to drive other devices from their output terminals). If the fan-out is exceeded the voltage levels corresponding to a logic 1 and a logic 0 become more similar and errors are more likely.
2. The number of software modules that are called by this module.

FAQ *Acronym for* frequently asked question, with the overtone that the answer is well known. One response to a FAQ is an RTM (read the manual).

farm An arrangement in which several computers cooperate concurrently in the solution of a problem. One of the computers will act as a *scheduler while the remainder act as workers. Each worker has the same copy of the *code and is able to accept a task from the scheduler, carry out the process, then return the result. A farm could comprise a network of *transputers or other similar microprocessors.

FAST *Acronym for* Federation Against Software Theft. A body set up by the UK software industry to promote the effective and legal use of software, and to take action against those who breach copyright law by making unlicensed copies of proprietary software.

fast Ethernet A new standard version of *Ethernet that operates at 100 Mbps. It uses essentially the same formal structures and broadcast technology as the internationally standardized 10 Mbps Ethernet but operates at a ten times higher bit rate.

fast Fourier transform (FFT) An algorithm that computes the discrete *Fourier transform accurately and efficiently on digital computers. FFT techniques have wide applicability in linear systems, optics, probability theory, quantum physics, antennas, and signal analysis.

father of a node. *Another name for* parent, now rarely used.

father file See file recovery.

fault *See* failure.

fault detection Determination, normally by detection of a failure in a *check, that a fault (error) has occurred in a logic circuit, arithmetic circuit, or an information transfer.

fault diagnosis The task of determining where in a (repairable) computer system a fault has occurred and what the logical nature of that fault is.

fault-tolerant system A computer system that is capable of providing either full functionality (*fail-safe) or reduced functionality (*fail-soft) after a failure has occurred. Fault tolerance is usually provided through a combination of redundant system elements and error detection and correction procedures.

fault tree analysis A systematic and disciplined approach to the analysis of events or situations, and whose purpose is to identify *hazards that may compromise *safety. It uses diagrams in the form of trees.

fax 1. A *facsimile transmission service.
2. A document sent by fax.
3. To send or communicate by fax.

fax card An *add-in card that allows a computer to be connected to a phone line and to transmit or receive fax messages. The card and its associated software allow anything that can be displayed on the screen to be converted into a fax image and transmitted, just like a fax machine. Incoming faxes are treated initially as graphic images, and if they contain text that is to be edited or incorporated into a word processor document for instance, then they must be subject to an *optical character recognition (OCR) process.

FCC Federal Communications Commission, the US regulatory commission for public communications. Its jurisdiction includes land line, cable, radio, and satellite communications.

FDDI *Abbrev. for* fiber distributed data interface.

F distribution An important *probability distribution used to test the significance of estimated mean squares in an *analysis of variance and in *regression analysis. Theoretically the F distribution is the distribution of the ratio of two independent random variables S_1/f_1 and S_2/f_2, where S_1 has the *chi-squared distribution on f_1 *degrees of freedom and S_2 has the chi-squared distribution on f_2 degrees of freedom. Tables of critical values of the F distribution for ranges of f_1 and f_2 are widely available, but direct computation requires lengthy algorithms to compute the incomplete beta function.

FDM *Abbrev. for* frequency division multiplexing.

feasibility study A study carried out prior to a development project in order to establish whether the proposed system is feasible and can serve a useful purpose. Feasibility studies can be purely paper exercises or can involve the construction of experimental or prototype systems. Often a feasibility study will not address the entire scope of the proposed system, but will concentrate on specific areas where the feasibility is regarded as questionable or the potential risk is greatest.

feature detection The processing of raw data to assess the presence of a given property. Examples are seen in *image processing, the early stages of *pattern recognition, and some *neural networks. Features often detected in images include edges, lines, contours, regions, and object fragments.

feature modeling The modeling of complex objects using functionally significant entities such as holes and slots rather than using low-level geometric entities.

feed 1. A device for moving media to a position at which the data can be read or printed.
2. To cause data or media to be entered into a system or peripheral.

feedback Response to operator input that indicates that the input has been understood and the desired action accomplished. *See also* acknowledgment, prompt, echoing.

feedback queue A form of scheduling mechanism often used in multiaccess systems. Individual *processes are allocated a *quantum of time on the processor. A process once started is allowed to run until it has exhausted its quantum, until it initiates a transfer on a peripheral device, or until an interrupt generated by some other process occurs. If the quantum is exhausted, the process is assigned a longer quantum and rejoins the queue. If the process initiates a transfer, its quantum remains unaltered and it rejoins the queue. If an externally generated interrupt occurs, the interrupt is serviced. Servicing the interrupt may free some other process already in the queue, in which case that process may be preferentially restarted.

feedback register (feedback shift register) A *shift register, generally consisting of several cells, in which the first cell has its input supplied by a combinational logic function of the parallel outputs of several cells and of a possible external input. An important case is the *linear feedback register* in which *linear logic is employed for the feedback function.

The linear feedback register has the effect of deconvolving the external serial input with the sequence of combinational coefficients (*see* convolution). If the external input is regarded as a *polynomial in which powers of the indeterminate denote succession in time, and if the combinational coefficients are regarded likewise as a second polynomial, then the linear feedback register has the effect of dividing the former polynomial by the latter. When used in coding or in digital signal processing, feedback shift registers may be binary or *q-ary and may be implemented in hardware or software.

When there is no external serial input, the linear feedback register can be used on its own to generate *m-sequences or, with parallel loading of the shift register with a source word, as an *encoder for *simplex codes; either of these applications requires that the feedback logic coefficients represent a *polynomial that is primitive. *See also* Good–de Bruijn diagram.

feed-forward (shift) register A *shift register, generally consisting of a number of cells, several parallel outputs of which are combined in a combinational logic function. An important case is the *linear feed-forward register* in which *linear logic is employed for the feed-forward function.

The linear feed-forward register has the effect of convolving the serial input to the register with the sequence of combinational coefficients (*see* convolution). If the input is regarded as a *polynomial in which powers of the indeterminate denote succession in time, and if the combinational coefficients are regarded likewise as a second polynomial, then the linear feed-forward register has the effect of multiplying these polynomials.

When used in coding or in digital signal processing, feed-forward registers may be binary or q-ary, and may be implemented in hardware or software.

Feistel cipher A type of *binary cipher designed in the 1970s by Horst Feistel (of IBM). It is a repetitive *mixed cipher. The existence of its *inverse (for the purpose of *decryption) is assured by the careful use of the *exclusive-OR operation within its algorithm. Two important implementations are the *Data Encryption Standard (DES) and its precursor Lucifer.

Ferranti Mark I The world's first commercially available computer, built by the electrical engineering firm Ferranti Ltd., based in Manchester, UK, and delivered in 1951 as a production version of the University of Manchester's *Manchester Mark I. Ferranti's link with the university was established in 1948. The Mark I was followed into production by the Mark I Star (1953), Pegasus I and II (1956, 1959), and *Atlas (1963).

ferrite A sintered ferromagnetic material plus ceramic that combines the high magnetic permeability of the former with the high electric resistance of the latter. This means that ferrite can be used for magnetic cores in high-frequency and high-speed switching circuits in which iron losses are a problem. *See also* core store.

ferroelectric display A type of *flat-panel technology that is bistable, allowing images to be retained even after power has been removed. Images can be retained for at least six years.

FET *Abbrev. for* field-effect transistor.

fetch-execute cycle (instruction cycle) The two steps of obtaining and executing an instruction. *See* control unit.

fetch protect Restriction of the memory

reading privilege in a particular memory segment. *See* memory protection.

FFT *Abbrev. for* fast Fourier transform.

FiberChannel A network system designed primarily to support the connection of peripheral units to mainframes, or enterprise servers, within a single computer room or small building. The system was brought about largely by IBM but other suppliers have adopted the product. FiberChannel originally used low-cost optical *multimode fibers, but versions for *monomode fiber and *coaxial cable are also specified. It uses a packet structure with the minimum of overheads, allowing a high proportion of the available data rate to be devoted to users' data. It was originally specified for operation at 100 Mbps but is intended to scale to speeds that increase in powers of two up to a rate of 1.6 Gbps. FiberChannel has inevitably been brought into service to provide private backbone services within a LAN, but its deliberately restricted packet format means it may not be suitable for WAN applications.

fiber distributed data interface (FDDI) A high-speed network system designed to operate over distances of tens of kilometers. The system uses a pair of *optical fibers to carry a single signal path. Two such pairs may be used to interconnect nodes so as to form a ring (so-called *dual attach*), or a single pair of fibers may be used to connect a spur extension to a node on the ring that acts as a wiring concentrator (so-called *single attach*). The ring is normally treated as a primary ring carrying live traffic, and a secondary ring used for fault identification. If a node or an optical path fails, the system will reconfigure by "wrapping" the ring in order to isolate the faulty node or path, and to use the secondary ring as the return path for packets.

The FDDI system operates at a nominal 100 Mbps of data, using the pair of fibers to encode four bits of original data onto five bits of self-clocking signals, and with an actual bit rate of 140 Mbps. Access to the ring uses a modified version of a *token ring protocol, in which more than one token can be present on the ring at any one time. In principle FDDI allows up to 500 nodes to connect to a single ring and this can give a long latency between a node wishing to transmit and the arrival of a token allowing it to do so. To control this, a node wishing to acquire the token will defer to requests for the token from nodes with a higher priority. The system actually uses two separate sets of priorities – one for synchronous traffic, for which each node is guaranteed an agreed data rate, and one for asynchronous traffic, where a node can use any spare capacity not taken up by other nodes.

Although its original design was directed at metropolitan area network (MAN) services, FDDI is used in LAN services, especially as a *backbone between *routers or to connect a specific *server with very heavy traffic requirement to the backbone.

fiber optics A means of transmitting analog or digital information using light signals over an *optical fiber*. An optical fiber is a thin transparent filament made either of glass or, for short distances, special plastics; the diameter of the fiber ranges downward from 125 micrometers, with a number of preferred sizes now being adopted as standard. The information is carried as a light signal, typically in the infrared with a wavelength of about 1200 to 1550 nanometers, and generated by an electrical-to-optical *transducer, usually a switchable semiconductor laser. Light of wavelength 1200 nm has a frequency of 250 000 gigahertz (GHz), and is in principle capable of transmitting at bit rates of the order of 100 000 Gbps. The highest bit rates achieved in the laboratory are of the order of 1000 Gbps, and the highest rates in normal use are of the order of a few hundred Mbps, the limits being set by the speeds at which the semiconductor lasers and the optical-to-electrical transducers can operate.

A variety of methods are used to reduce the loss of the optical signal and hence increase signaling distance. The material of which the fiber is made is very pure, and by varying the refractive index of the material across the fiber it is possible to cause light rays at less than a certain angle to the axis of the fiber to be totally internally reflected back into the fiber. This reflection may take place at a discrete boundary between glasses of different refractive index (*stepped index fiber*), or may take place in a region of gradually varying refractive index (*graded index fiber*). If the fiber is made very thin, with a diameter of the order of the wavelength of the light, the light rays can only propagate along the fiber (*monomode fiber*). On a very long path, it is necessary to install amplifiers to regenerate the signal – by converting it from an optical to an electrical form, amplifying the electrical signal, and then reconverting it to an optical signal. Some amplifier designs exploit the nonlinear optical properties of certain glasses to allow direct amplification of the optical signal using a locally powered second laser as the power source.

Fibonacci search A searching algorithm that uses Fibonacci numbers in a way that is analogous to the use of powers of 2 in the *binary search. *See* Fibonacci series.

Fibonacci series A sequence of numbers in which each number is the sum of the two preceding numbers, e.g.

$$0,1,1,2,3,5,8,\ldots$$

The *Fibonacci numbers* F_n are formally defined to be

$$F_0 = 0, F_1 = 1,$$
$$F_{n+2} = F_{n+1} + F_n, \ n \geq 0$$

Any positive number m can be represented uniquely as a sum of Fibonacci numbers, where the greatest F_n in the expansion does not exceed m and where no two of the F_n are adjacent numbers in the Fibonacci series.

fiche *Short for* microfiche. *See* COM.

field 1. (data field) An item of data consisting of a number of characters, bytes, words, or codes that are treated together, e.g. to form a number, a name, or an address. A number of fields make a *record and the fields may be fixed in length or variable. The term came into use with punched card systems and a field size was defined in terms of a number of columns. **2.** Normally a way of designating a portion of a *word that has a specific significance or function within that word, e.g. an address field in an instruction word or a character field within a data word. **3.** In mathematics, a commutative *ring containing more than one element and in which every nonzero element has an *inverse with respect to the multiplication operation.

Apart from their obvious relationship to arithmetic involving numbers of various kinds, fields play a very important role in discussion about the analysis of *algorithms. Results in this area mention the number of operations of a particular kind, and these operations are usually related to addition and multiplication of elements of some field.

field bus A standardized interface, using serial communications, that is widely employed to interconnect systems used in industrial automation.

field-effect transistor (FET) A semiconductor device having three terminals: *source*, *gate*, and *drain*. Current flow in a narrow conduction *channel* between drain and source is controlled by the voltage applied between gate and source, which can deplete the conduction channel of charge carriers. If the source and drain regions are composed of n-type semiconductor the conduction channel is n-type; these devices are called *n-channel* devices. Devices with p-type source, drain, and channel are called *p-channel* devices. In contrast to *bipolar transistors, FETs are *unipolar devices*; the current flow is electrons (in n-channel devices) or holes (in p-channel devices).

In the *junction FET* the channel is a composite part of the structure. In the *MOSFET the gate is insulated from the source and drain regions and the channel forms when the gate voltage is applied. Unlike the bipolar transistor both types of FET require virtually no input current to the gate except a pulse to charge or discharge the gate capacitance. Junction FETs have relatively slow *switching speeds compared with MOSFETs and bipolar transistors, and are therefore not used in logic circuits.

field-programmable devices *See* programmable devices, PLA.

FIFO (or fifo) *Acronym for* first in first out. *FIFO list* is another name for *queue.

fifth generation The types of computer currently under development in a number of countries, especially Japan, and predicted as becoming available in the 1990s. The features are conjectural at present but point toward "intelligent" machines, which may have massively parallel processing, widespread use of intelligent knowledge-based systems, and natural language interfaces. Progress has not been as fast as originally planned although some significant advances have been made.

file Information held on *backing store (i.e. usually on magnetic disk or magnetic tape) in order (a) to enable it to persist beyond the time of execution of a single job and/or (b) to overcome space limitations in main memory. Files may hold data, programs, documents, pictures, or any other information. They are referred to by *file name. Files with a very brief existence (i.e. in case (b) above, or where they simply carry information between one job and the next in sequence) are called *work files*. *See also* master file, data file.

file activity Any storage or retrieval activity performed on a *file. In some systems a record is kept of file activity and the information is used to optimize the use of available *backing store. For example, a file for which the activity has fallen below a certain level may be moved offline.

file descriptor Information that describes a file, giving details such as its *file name, generation number, date of last access, expiry date, and the structure of the records it contains. It is normally stored as a header record at the front of the file, held on magnetic tape or on disk.

file directory *See* directory.

file editing *See* file updating.

file extension *See* file name.

file format The way in which the information in a *file is encoded. There are many proprietary formats – nearly every application has its own, often changing with new versions – as well as standard file formats such as *RTF or strings of *ASCII characters. In some systems, such as Apple Macintosh, the information about file format and originating application is part of the file, but in other systems it is up to the user to know what the format is, although there are more or less strict file-naming conventions. The multiplicity of file formats is a continuing problem for both software developers and users.

file integrity *See* database integrity.

file locking A method of ensuring that if one *process is altering the contents of a *file, other processes cannot access the file until the updating activity has been successfully completed. The actual operation of the file-locking mechanism will normally form a part of the operating-system services that allow access to files, and the lock is applied to the file in its entirety. *See also* record locking, semaphore.

file maintenance Software processes concerned with maintaining *file integrity and file efficiency, usually of *data files. It is concerned with the internal organization of files (unlike *file management, which is not). It is not concerned with changing values within a file (unlike *file updating, which is), although the term is sometimes misused to include such activity.

file management Software processes concerned with the overall management of *files, for example their allocation to space in *backing store, control over access, writing *backup copies, and maintaining *directories. Basic file management is normally performed by *operating systems, though this may be supplemented by *file management systems. *See also* file maintenance.

file management system A software system that provides facilities for *file management (often specifically of *data files) at a level above that offered by *operating systems (but in the case of data files below that offered by *database management systems).

file manager A program for organizing a set of files.

file mark *See* tape mark.

file name An identifying character string used to refer to a *file. The name can be generated by software or created by the user. It usually gives some hint as to the contents of the file. Different operating systems have different rules and conventions for file-name construction. Often the rules allow (or require) the final section of the name (the *file extension*) to be separated by a period (full stop) and used to indicate the type of file. Sometimes upper and lower case letters are not distinguished. The maximum length of the name is often strictly enforced. Usually all letters and digits are allowable and some special characters.

file organization The structure of a file (especially a data file), defined in terms of its components and how they are mapped onto backing store. Any given file organization supports one or more file *access methods. Organization is thus closely related to but conceptually distinct from access methods. The distinction is similar to that between *data structures and the procedures and functions that operate on them (indeed a file organization is a large-scale data structure), or to that between a logical schema of a database and the facilities in a data manipulation language (*see* database language). There is no very useful or commonly accepted taxonomy of methods of file organization: most attempts confuse organization with access methods (which are easier to classify).

file protection The protection of files from the mistaken or unauthorized storage or retrieval of information (or, in the case of program files, from mistaken or unauthorized execution). Protection may be (a) physical, concerned with the security of the media on which files are held, and implemented by operating procedures, or (b) logical, concerned with the security of the contents of files, and implemented by software.

file recovery The process of restoring *file integrity once a file has been found to be incorrect. There are two main classes of method. In a *transaction processing system, in which a *master file is updated incrementally, the method is based on *backup copies and *recovery logs. In a *batch processing system, in which a master file is updated by being completely rewritten, the last version of the master file serves as the backup, and the transaction file serves as the recovery log. (The last version of the master file is then referred to as the *father* or *parent*, the version before that as the *grandfather* or *grandparent*, and so on.)

file server A *server specifically designed to support the storing of data, usually but not necessarily in a networked environment. The file server will be equipped with long-term storage, typically magnetic disks, with a means of making *backup copies of files, typically high-capacity magnetic tape drives, and with high-bandwidth connections to the network. The system software will often be designed so that end-users need not be aware of the fact that their files are not held locally on their own workstation, but are held on the file server. In some systems the use of a file will cause it to be automatically copied onto the user's workstation, while in others the file will remain on the file server as the user works on the file. Some systems allow the user to specify where the file will be held while it is active.

file transfer The act or process of transferring a file from one computer system to another, usually but not necessarily across a network. The problems associated with a file transfer between two identical computer systems are minimal, but they increase when the systems use different hardware and run under different operating systems. *See also* file transfer protocol.

file transfer protocol (FTP) A *protocol used to allow a file to be transferred across a network from one computer system to another. The protocol must manage both the physical act of transferring the data across the network, and the differences in the way in which a file is represented in the sending and receiving systems.

file updating Changing values in one or more records of a file, especially a data file, without changing the organization or semantics of the file. File updating may be done in one of two ways. The first, common in *data processing, is when the updating process is carried out separately from the entry of amendments and "invisibly" from any human operator. The second is when records are displayed on an interactive device, and an operator can then amend a record while able to see it: this method is sometimes also called *file editing*.

fill area primitive A computer-graphics output primitive that specifies a closed curve to be filled with a solid color, a hatching, or a pattern.

fill character *Another name for* ignore character.

filling *See* area filling.

filter 1. A program that processes a sequential stream of text, carrying out some simple transformation, e.g. condensing multiple spaces to single spaces, counting words, etc. In the *UNIX system powerful effects can be created by connecting a series of filters in a *pipeline*, where each filter takes as its input the output produced by its predecessor.
2. A simple electric circuit or some more complicated device used in the process of *filtering.

filtering 1. The processing of a *signal (by a simple electric circuit or by some more complicated device) in such a way that the behavior of the signal is affected in either the *time domain* or in a *transform domain*.

In time-domain filtering each element of the original signal is replaced by a sequence of elements, proportional in amplitude to the original signal but spaced in time; the sum (assuming linear fitering) of these sequences forms the new signal. In transform-domain filtering the elements of the original signal are not those of its amplitude but rather of its components under, for example, *Fourier analysis or *Walsh analysis; they are then spaced not in time but in *frequency or *sequency respectively. Many other transforms are also used.

Filtering, both in the time domain and in various transform domains, is of great importance in *multiplexing. A simple but very common example of filtering in the frequency (Fourier) domain is the use of resonant circuits to effect *low-pass, *band-pass, *high-pass, and *band-stop functions; these are much used, e.g. in *data transmission lines and *modems.
2. A technique for *anti-aliasing. Aliasing occurs in an image when the sampling rate is not high enough to capture the changes in the image. Filtering applied to a scene spreads the influence of a pixel across the scene. Thus every object makes some contribution to each of the final-image pixel intensities. The value of the pixel in the antialiased image is computed as the weighted sum of its immediate neighbors with the weight inversely related to distance.

3. *See* masking.

filtering bridge *See* bridge.

find 1. One of the basic actions performed on *sets that, when applied in the form

$$find(el)$$

produces the set of which *el* is currently a member; if *el* is in no set or in more than one set the effect of the operation is undefined. *See also* operations on sets.
2. In word processing, *another name for* search.

find and change *Another term for* search and replace.

finger *Informal* A utility program designed to find publicly available information about a named user or service.

finite automaton *See* finite-state automaton.

finite-difference method A widely applicable *discretization method for the solution of *ordinary and *partial differential equations. In this approach all derivatives are replaced by approximations that involve solution values only, so in general the differential equation is reduced to a system of *nonlinear equations or *linear algebraic equations. For example, in the problem

$$y'' + by' + cy = d \quad 0 \le x \le 1,$$
$$y(0) = \alpha, y(1) = \beta,$$

where b, c, d, α, and β are given constants, the interval $[0,1]$ is first divided into equal subintervals of length h; h is called the *step-size* (or *mesh* or *grid size*). This gives the *mesh points* (or *grid points*) x_n,

$$x_n = nh,$$
$$n = 0,1,\ldots,N+1,$$
$$h = 1/(N+1)$$

At interior mesh points the derivatives are now replaced by finite-difference approximations, e.g.

$$y'(x_n) \approx (\tfrac{1}{2}h)[y(x_{n+1}) - y(x_{n-1})]$$
$$y''(x_n) \approx (1/h^2)[y(x_{n+1}) - 2y(x_n) + y(x_{n-1})]$$

When combined with the boundary conditions these approximations result in a system of equations for approximations to $y(x_n)$, $n = 1, 2,\ldots, N$. Nonlinear differential equations yield a system of nonlinear equations.

finite-element analysis *See* finite-element method.

finite-element method A widely applicable approach to solving *ordinary and particularly *partial differential equations and similar problems. The approach embraces several variants, principally *Galerkin's method* and the *Rayleigh–Ritz method*. The basic idea, however, is the same and involves approximating the solution of the problem by a linear combination:

$$u(x) = \sum_{j=1}^{n} c_j \phi_j(x)$$

The functions $\phi_1, \phi_2, \ldots, \phi_n$ are always chosen to be simple and are called *trial functions*. The success of the method is due in part to choosing these functions to be low-degree *splines. This in turn generally leads to a system of equations for the coefficients c_1, $c_2, \ldots, c_n$ that involves the treatment of *sparse matrices, i.e. matrices in which a large proportion of the elements are zero; very efficient software can then be used.

In Galerkin's method the criterion for choosing the coefficients is that the amount by which $u(x)$ fails to satisfy the equation is in a certain sense small. The Rayleigh–Ritz method is a *variational method. The finite-element method can in general be regarded as a process in which a solution in an infinite-dimensional space is replaced by an approximation that lies in a finite-dimensional subspace. The whole process is referred to as *finite-element analysis*.

finite field (Galois field) A (mathematical) *field with a finite number of elements. The number of elements must be of the form p^k where p is some prime number and k is a positive integer. Results concerning finite fields are of particular relevance in the areas of error detection and error correction.

finite-length arithmetic (fixed-length arithmetic) The approximation to real arithmetic in a computer. The term arises since the precision to which *real numbers can be represented as floating-point numbers in a computer is limited by the length of the mantissa. *See* floating-point notation.

finite-model theory A branch of the study of computational *complexity in which *complexity classes are characterized by definitions that use logical languages applied to finite structures. Connections between resource bounds and formal definitions constitute a research area with great potential.

finite sequence (list) *See* sequence.

finite set A *set with a finite number of elements.

finite-state automaton (FSA; finite-state machine) A simple kind of *automaton. The input string is read once from left to right, looking at each symbol in turn. At any time the FSA is in one of finitely many internal *states*; the state changes after each input symbol is read. The new state depends on the symbol just read and on the current state. An FSA is therefore determined by a function f

$$f: I \times Q \rightarrow Q$$

where I is the set of possible input symbols, Q is the set of states, and $I \times Q$ is the *Cartesian product of I and Q. Q must be finite.

	1	2	3	4
a:	2	2	2	4
b:	1	3	1	4
c:	1	1	4	4

Equivalent transition table and diagram of an FSA

The function f is called a *state-transition function*. It is commonly represented either by a table or by a directed *graph, known respectively as a *state-transition table* and a *state-transition diagram*. The figure shows two equivalent representations in which

$$I = \{a,b,c\},$$
$$Q = \{1,2,3,4\}$$

In this example,

$$f(a,1) = 2,$$
$$f(c,4) = 4, \text{ etc.}$$

f extends to strings in the obvious manner: in the example,

$$f(bc,2) = 4,$$
$$f(aaa,3) = 1, \text{ etc.}$$

Let Q be divided into *accepting states* and

rejecting states, and let q_0 be some member of Q (referred to as the *start state*). The *language recognized* by the FSA is the set of all w such that

$$f(w, q_0)$$

is an accepting state, i.e. the set of all strings that take the start state to an accepting state. For example, in the FSA shown in the figure let q_0 be 1 and let 4 be the only accepting state; the language recognized is then the set of all strings over $\{a,b,c\}$ that somewhere contain *abc* as a substring. A language recognized by an FSA is known as a *regular language.

A generalization is to allow more than one state to which the FSA can move, for a given input symbol and current state. This gives a *nondeterministic FSA*. The input string is then accepted if there is some sequence of choices of moves leading to an accepting state. Such a machine can always be converted to a deterministic one recognizing the same language.

See also sequential machine, minimal machine.

FIPS *Acronym for* Federal Information Processing Standards. Standards that the US government uses in its procurement efforts and that are adopted (rarely created) and maintained by the US National Institute of Standards and Technology, NIST (formerly the National Bureau of Standards).

Fire codes A family of *polynomial *block codes designed to correct *burst errors.

firewall A system designed to control the passage of information from one network into a second network. Typically a firewall will be used as a means of reducing the risk of unwanted access to sensitive systems, where one carefully regulated network contains the sensitive systems and is connected to a larger less-regulated network. A firewall can be effective if access to the firewall itself is carefully regulated.

firing rule *See* Petri net.

firmware System software that is held in read-only memory (*ROM).

FIRST *Acronym for* Forum of Incident and Response Teams. An international group bringing together those working on the provision of protection against computer misuse. *See also* computer emergency response team.

first-class type in the design of a programming language. A *type whose *objects can take part in the full range of operations available within the language (such as declaration of constants and variables of the type in question, assignment of values, employment as fields of records and as elements of arrays, occurrence as parameters and return values of functions). The objects of a first-class type are *first-class objects*. For example, functions are first-class in Algol 68 but not in Algol 60, Pascal or Ada.

first fit A method of selecting a contiguous area of memory that is to be allocated for a segment. The *free-space list is scanned in order of starting address, and the allocation made from the first free area whose size exceeds that of the request. Despite its apparent simplicity this algorithm has a number of desirable properties in terms of performance.

first generation of computers. The series of calculating and computing machines whose designs were started between 1940 (approximately) and 1955. These machines are characterized by electronic tube (valve) circuitry, and delay line, rotating, or electrostatic (Williams tube) memory. The majority of them embodied the stored program concept. For the most part, first-generation machines used as input/output punched paper tape, punched card, magnetic wire, magnetic tape, and printers. Despite these seeming handicaps, impressive computations in weather forecasting, atomic energy calculations, and similar scientific applications were routinely performed on them.

Important first-generation development machines include the *Manchester Mark I, *EDSAC, *EDVAC, *SEAC, *Whirlwind, *IAS, and *ENIAC while the earliest commercially available computers include the *Ferranti Mark I, *UNIVAC I, and *LEO I.

first in first out *See* FIFO.

first normal form *See* normal forms.

first-order logic *Another name for* predicate calculus.

first-order term *See* term.

fixed-base system *Another name for* fixed-radix system. *See* number system.

fixed disk drive A *disk drive in which the storage medium is permanently attached within the device. The drive may contain more than one disk – the so-called *disk stack*. Current data-processing systems use fixed disk storage rather than demountable storage. Early fixed disk drives used disks with a diameter of 36 inches. The size, in inches, has progressively decreased in the sequence 14, 10.5, 9, 8, 5.25, 3.5, 2.5, 1.8, 1.3. Not all manufacturers used all of these sizes but currently 3.5 inch disk drives are used throughout the industry, with capacities up to 8 gigabytes. Portable PCs currently use 2.5 inch disk drives with capacities up to 1 gigabyte.

fixed head of a disk drive. A read/write head that cannot be moved relative to the center of the disk. A large number of these heads are usually incorporated into an assembly so that there is a "head per track", and such drives may be referred to by this expression. The advantage of a fixed head is that the average *access time is reduced to the time for half a revolution since there is no track seek time required. Some drives have both fixed and moveable heads but these are now (1995) largely obsolete.

fixed-length arithmetic *Another name for* finite-length arithmetic.

fixed-length code A *code in which a fixed number of source symbols are encoded into a fixed number of output symbols. It is usually a *block code. (The term fixed-length is used in contrast to *variable-length, whereas block code can be contrasted with *convolutional code.)

fixed point *See* fixed-point theorem.

fixed-point notation A representation of real numbers in which the position of the *radix point is fixed. The position of the point determines the absolute precision of the representation. If the point is fixed at the right-hand end of the number then all of the fixed-point numbers are integers. Due to a number of difficulties, fixed-point arithmetic is rarely used in a modern computer for calculations involving real numbers.

fixed-point theorem A theorem concerning the existence and nature of fixed points used to give solutions to equations. A *fixed point* of a *function f

$$f : X \to X$$

is an element x such that $f(x) = x$. A *least fixed point* is one that, among all the fixed points of f, is lowest in some *partial ordering that has been imposed on the elements of X. Specifically, if $\leq$ is a partial ordering of X then x is a least fixed point if for fixed point y we have $x \leq y$.

The most often-cited form of fixed-point theorem to do with computing is due originally to S. C. Kleene, and originated in *recursive function theory. It states that, subject to certain assumptions, notably that f is continuous, f has a least fixed point, x_f, which moreover can be characterized as the limit of a sequence $x_0, x_1, x_2, \ldots$ of approximations. This abstract fact is of great relevance to the semantics of programming languages, in particular in specifying the precise meaning of constructs like *iteration, *recursion, and recursive types using *equations.

fixed-radix system (fixed-base system) *See* number system.

fixed word length computer A computer in which data is constrained to lie within words that are all of the same length. By extension the term is sometimes used to imply that all instructions also fit within one word. *Compare* variable word length computer.

flag A *variable whose value indicates the attainment of some designated state or condition by an item of equipment or a program. The flag is subsequently used as a basis for conditional branching and similar decision processes. *See also* sentinel.

flame *Informal* **1.** An angry or abusive e-mail message from one user to another.
2. A flood of e-mail messages from a large group of users to one specific user, who is judged to have offended against some standard of decent behavior. The individual messages may each be angry or abusive, but in some cases the actual messages may have no

real purpose other than to overload the recipient's system, typically by sending as a mail message the entire contents of some very large data set such as the text of all the help files on a system.

flat addressing *See* addressing.

flatbed plotter *See* plotter.

flatbed scanner A *scanner in which the sheet to be scanned is placed flat onto the bed of the device. Such scanners may handle a single sheet at a time or may be provided with a document feeder.

flat file model *Another name for* relational model.

flat pack A type of *integrated-circuit package that can be mounted on the top surface of a printed circuit board and involves no penetrating pins. This can result in a higher component packing density.

flat-panel display (flat screen) A type of *display device where the depth is much less than a conventional *cathode-ray tube for the same image size. Various flat-panel technologies, including *LCDs and *plasma panels, are competing to produce reliable high-resolution color displays, both large and small.

flat screen *See* flat-panel display.

flexible array An *array whose lower and/or upper bounds are not fixed and may vary according to the values assigned to it. *See also* string.

flexible disk cartridge In international standards, the formal name for a *floppy disk.

flexible manufacturing system *See* FMS.

flicker A perceived rapid periodic change of a displayed image. This is mainly a problem with cathode-ray tube displays. Flicker is perceived by users when the refresh frequency is below the *CFF. It is claimed to induce headaches and eyestrain with prolonged usage. *See also* interlacing.

flip-flop (bistable) An electronic circuit element that is capable of exhibiting either of two stable states and of switching between these states in a reproducible manner. When used in *logic circuits the two states are

made to correspond to logic 1 and logic 0. Flip-flops are therefore one-bit memory elements and are frequently used in digital circuits.

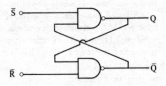

$\bar{S}$	$\bar{R}$	Q	$\bar{Q}$
1	1	no change	
1	0	0	1
0	1	1	0
0	0	1	1
		(disallowed)	

RS flip-flop, logic diagram and truth table

The simplest form is the *RS flip-flop*; an implementation using *NAND gates is shown in the diagram together with the flip-flop's truth table. A logic 1 on one of the two inputs either sets the Q output to logic 1 or resets Q to logic 0. Output $\bar{Q}$ is the logical complement of Q. When $\bar{R}$ and $\bar{S}$ are both logic 1 (which is equivalent to R and S both logic 0), Q does not change state. The situation of both $\bar{R}$ and $\bar{S}$ at logic 0 is ambiguous and is avoided in more complex flip-flop implementations (*see* JK flip-flop). The outputs of this (and other) flip-flops are not just functions of the inputs but depend on both inputs and outputs. The device is thus a simple *sequential circuit.

Extra logic gating may be included in the RS device, and in more complex flip-flops, to allow a clock signal to be input to the flip-flop, so producing a *clocked flip-flop* (*see* clock). The Q output will not then change state until an active edge of the clock pulse occurs (*edge-triggered device*) or a complete clock cycle has occurred (*pulse-triggered device*). Provision may also be made to set up a given output regardless of the state of the inputs.

Various forms of flip-flop are available to perform specific functions; these include

*JK, *D, *T, and *master-slave flip-flops. Flip-flops are important as memory devices in digital counters. The RS flip-flop is often considered to be the *universal flip-flop* since it forms the basic building block for more sophisticated implementations. JK, master-slave, and D flip-flops are all available in the standard TTL and CMOS series of integrated-circuit components.

float An operator or function that converts a number in *fixed-point notation into an equivalent *floating-point form.

floating-point accelerator (FPA) A device to improve the overall performance of a computer by removing the burden of performing floating-point arithmetic from the central processor.

floating-point notation A representation of real numbers that enables both very small and very large numbers to be conveniently expressed. A floating-point number has the general form

$$\pm m \times R^e$$

where m is called the *mantissa*, R is the *radix (or base) of the number system, and e is the *exponent*.

The following format is typical of the floating-point representation used in computers. The first bit is a *sign bit*, denoting the sign of the mantissa. This is followed by a fixed number of bits representing the exponent, which is in turn followed by another fixed number of bits representing the magnitude of the mantissa. The exponent is often represented using *excess-n notation*, whereby a number, called the *characteristic* (or *biased exponent*), is stored instead of the exponent itself. To derive the characteristic for a floating-point number from its exponent, the *bias* (or *excess factor*) n is added to the exponent. For example, for an 8-bit characteristic, exponents in the range -128 to $+127$ are represented in excess-128 notation by characteristics in the range 0 to 255.

A nonzero floating-point number is *normalized* if the leading digit in its mantissa is nonzero.

floating-point operation The addition, subtraction, multiplication, or division of two floating-point operands to produce a floating-point result. There is an international standard (IEEE standard 754: 1985) that is designed to ensure the reproducibility of floating-point operations. *See also* floating-point notation, flops.

flood-fill The act or process of filling an area with a specific color by starting from a specified interior point (sometimes called the *seed*) and recursively changing the colors of neighboring points that lie within the boundary.

floor If x is a real number, then floor(x), also written as $\lfloor x \rfloor$, is the largest integer less than or equal to x.

flop 1. A unit of computational cost associated with matrix and vector operations. The term is widely used in algorithms for *numerical linear algebra. A flop is approximately the amount of work required to compute, for example in Fortran, an expression of the form

$$S = S + A(I,J) * X(J)$$

i.e. a floating point multiplication and a floating point addition, along with the effort involved in subscripting. Thus for example, Gaussian elimination for a system of *order n requires a number of flops of order n^3 (*see* linear algebraic equations). As computer design and architecture change, this unit of cost may well undergo modification.

2. *Short for* floating-point operation. *See also* flops.

floppy disk (diskette) A flexible *magnetic disk consisting of a circular polyester substrate (with a central hole) coated with magnetic oxide and permanently enclosed within a stiff jacket, the inside of which is lined with a cleaning material. The jacket has a radial slot on each side through which the read heads (or head and support pad in the case of a single-sided floppy disk) can contact the disk. As with other magnetic disks, data is recorded in concentric tracks in the magnetic coating; the tracks are divided into *sectors. Developing technology has enabled recording density and track density to be raised, thus increasing total storage capacity. A small *index hole* in the jacket and disk is provided so that a photosensor may be used to generate an index pulse once per revolution. An aperture, the *write protect notch*, on one edge of the jacket can be blocked to prevent the drive from writing to the disk.

The most common size of floppy disk is 3½ inches, the 5¼ inch disk now (1995) falling into disuse. The jacket of the former is of hard plastic with a metal shutter protecting the read-write slot, while the latter has a flexible jacket and is protected by a paper envelope when not in use. Both kinds of disks come in normal and high-density qualities, and the high-density forms currently (1995) hold 1.44 or 2.88 megabytes (3½″) or 1.2 megabytes (5¼″).

floppy-disk drive (diskette drive) A device that accepts flexible magnetic disks, i.e. *floppy disks, and reads or writes magnetic patterns that correspond to the data to be retrieved or stored. The data is encoded in one of the appropriate *disk formats. The floppy disk is put into the mechanism through a slot that is normally covered by a hinged flap or door. The mechanism automatically locates and clamps the disk and rotates it at a speed of 300 rpm. The *read/write heads contact the disk through apertures in its cover.

The floppy-disk drive was first introduced by IBM as a diagnostic software load device but it is now used extensively as a data storage device on small computing systems. *See also* disk drive.

flops (or **FLOPS**) *Acronym for* floating-point operations per second. A commonly used measure of *computer power for very powerful computers (*supercomputers, *vector-processing computers) and *array processors. The rating of a computer, which in very powerful machines is measured in tens of Gflops (i.e. tens of billions of flops), must be qualified by a statement of the precision to which the operations are carried out.

floptical disk A hybrid optical and magnetic disk. The data is written and read by a magnetic head in the usual way, but head tracking is controlled by an optical servo track and head. This gives more precise tracking than the conventional magnetic servo track, so data tracks can be packed more closely. The disk capacity is considerably more than that of a conventional floppy disk.

flowchart A low-level graphical representation of the structure of a program, with emphasis on control flow and the primitive actions performed by the program rather than on the data structures employed by the program. It consists of a set of *boxes* of various shapes, interconnected by a set of directed *arcs*. The arcs indicate flow of control while the various box shapes indicate different kinds of action or decision. Within the boxes any notation can be employed to describe the action or decision; typical notations are *pseudolanguage and natural language.

Flowcharts have been used extensively for many years but are now rather unpopular. For one reason they tend to obscure the structure of programs that follow the tenets of structured coding (*see* structured programming) and, more important, they ignore the topic of data structuring.

flow control Procedures used to limit the rate at which data is transmitted to the rate at which it can be received. There are two major classes of flow control: *end-to-end* and *hop-by-hop*. End-to-end flow control limits the amount of data according to the capacity of the final destination to absorb it, without regard to the path through the network taken by the data (which may vary from message to message). Hop-by-hop flow control limits the amount of data sent according to the capacity of each individual node and/or link on the path through the network. In this latter case, the path is usually constant for the lifetime of the connection between sender and receiver. *See also* window (def. 3), acknowledgment.

Floyd method A method for proving the partial correctness of a program (*see* program correctness proof). Certain points in the program are designated as *cut-points*, and to each cut-point is attached an *inductive assertion*. The inductive assertions are chosen so that, whenever a cut-point is reached, the program is in a "correct state", i.e. one that satisfies the inductive assertion attached to that point. To establish this, it is necessary to consider each "minimal path", i.e. each path leading from a cut-point directly to a cut-point, and to show that, provided the program is already in a correct state, it will still be in one after following that path.

fluid logic A means of implementing logic functions, not by the normal use of electronic circuitry but by the flow of incompressible fluids (liquids) or gases through tubing containing intersections and constrictions. The logic gates so formed are useful in situations in which high electromagnetic interference prevents the use of electronic components. If the working medium is a gas, the term *pneumatic logic* is often used.

Flynn's classification *See* concurrency.

FM or **f.m.** *Abbrev. for* frequency modulation. *See* modulation.

FMECA *Abbrev. for* failure modes, effects, and criticality analysis.

FMS *Abbrev. for* flexible manufacturing system. The term *computer-integrated manufacturing (CIM) is now preferred.

FMV *Abbrev. for* full-motion video.

FOCUS *Acronym for* Focus on Computing in the United States. *See* AFIPS.

folding 1. An important method in *program transformation, introduced by Burstall and Darlington. Many simple mathematical techniques for processing the *equations and formulas of algebra and logic have important consequences when applied to programs. Folding is an example. It concerns programs that are expressed as collections of equations forming *recursive function definitions (programs written in a *functional language are often essentially in that form). The idea is to derive new equations, and in doing so one of the characteristic steps is to replace an instance of a right-hand side of an existing equation by the corresponding instance of the left-hand side (*folding*) or vice versa (*unfolding*). The resulting new equations form a new program equivalent to the original one. Programs derived in this way can often display significantly different efficiency conditions from the original programs.
2. A simple method of *hashing a key, in which the key is subdivided into several parts that are added together to give an address. The *folding ratio* is the ratio of the sizes of the

domain of this hashing function to the size of its range.

Times NR MT	The Quick Brown Fox
Arial	The Quick Brown Fox
Arial, bold italic	***The Quick Brown Fox***
GillSans, italic	*The Quick Brown Fox*
DomCasual	The Quick Brown Fox
Script MT	*The Quick Brown Fox*
Courier	The Quick Brown Fox

Commonly used fonts

font In computing, a set of letters, numbers, punctuation marks, and symbols of a given size and design that may be displayed or printed. Different designs are shown in the table. Most fonts are subject to copyright restrictions. The font size, i.e. the height of the printed letters and other characters, is specified in units called *points*, where 1 point equals 0.0138 inches in the US and UK.

Displayed or printed text can be enhanced using various features, including the following:

bold, *italic*, underline, shadow

A font may be of fixed size when the shape is described by an array of *pixels. Such fonts are commonly found in text terminals and printers where they occupy very little space and require no processing or manipulation of the data. Fixed fonts provide the fastest printing and display but cannot satisfactorily be increased or reduced in size, i.e. scaled. With a *scalable font* the character and symbol shapes are stored as a set of vectors and instructions. Because the data is described mathematically, it is possible to display and print such fonts to any desired size. The most common scalable-font systems are True Type and Adobe Types 1 and 3.

A font usually has *proportional spacing*, where each character and symbol is allotted a horizontal space commensurate with its width (as in the print you are now reading). In *monospace fonts*, such as Courier, each character or symbol is allocated the same width. *See also* kerning.

font cartridge A small device that can be

plugged into a printer and contains font-symbol definitions, usually in ROM. Many printers provide for the fitting of a font cartridge (or several) as a cost-effective way of enhancing the font repertoire. The user can buy and install only those fonts required. Cartridge fonts are being gradually replaced by scalable *fonts that are downloaded from the host computer. This offers greater choice, but use of fonts built into a printer or a font cartridge gives improved printing speed.

footprint The area of front panel, desk, or floor space occupied by a device: thus if a CD-ROM drive is described as having a 5¼″ floppy footprint it will fit the same shape and size of panel opening as a standard 5¼″ floppy-disk drive.

foreground processing Processing that supports interaction in a system that supports both interactive and batch operations. *See also* background processing.

foreign key If, in designing a database using the *relational model, the key attribute of one relation is included as a nonkey attribute in some other relation then it is said to be a foreign key in that relation and similarly if the key is compound. *See* referential integrity.

forest A directed *graph that is a collection of *trees. If the root is removed from a tree together with the arcs emanating from that root, the resulting collection of subtrees forms a forest.

for loop *See* do loop.

form 1. A page of printer media. It may be a single sheet or a multipart set, i.e. a number of sheets interleaved with carbon paper or coated so that a single impact will produce similar marks on all sheets. The sheets are frequently joined to form a continuous web, with sprocket holes at the edges to allow automatic feeding through printers. The paper may be preprinted with headings, fixed information, and lines or boxes. Paper used for general-purpose listing is often preprinted with closely spaced groups of lines – a *stave* – to aid visual alignment.
2. The data structure within a computer system representing the final result to be printed or displayed.

formal language 1. A language with explicit and precise rules for its syntax and semantics. Examples include programming languages and also logics such as *predicate calculus. Thus formal languages contrast with natural languages such as English whose rules, evolving as they do with use, fall short of being either a complete or a precise definition of the syntax, much less the semantics, of the language.
2. A finite or infinite set of *strings, considered in isolation from any possible meaning the strings or the symbols in them may have. If A is any set, an *A-language* (or *language over A*) is any set of A-words (*see* word). A is referred to as the *alphabet* of such a language.

formal language theory The study of *formal languages in the sense of sets of strings. A major branch of formal language theory concerns finite descriptions of infinite languages. Such a representation takes the form of an abstract device for generating or recognizing any string of the language (*see* grammar, L-system, automaton). This branch of the subject has applications to the *syntax of programming languages (as distinct from their *semantics, which require quite different mathematical tools). Thus the set of all legal Pascal programs can be thought of as a formal language over the alphabet of Pascal tokens (*see* lexical analyzer). Grammars provide the basis for describing syntax, while automata underly the design of parsers for it. On the other hand it was the desire to formalize natural languages that led to the initiation of the subject in 1956 by Noam Chomsky.

Automata also provide an abstract model for computation itself, thus linking formal language theory with the study of *computability and *complexity. Other issues in formal language theory include decidability of properties of languages, *closure properties of language classes, and characterizations of language classes (*see* Dyck language). An example of a long-standing open question is the decidability of equivalence for deterministic *push-down automata.

The subject has been extended beyond the study of strings to include the study of sets of trees, graphs, and infinite strings, resulting in many more applications.

formal logic The study of the analysis of propositions and of proofs, paying attention only to abstract symbols and form and paying no attention whatsoever to the meaning of the abstractions. *See also* symbolic logic.

formal parameter *See* parameter.

formal specification 1. A *specification written and approved in accordance with established standards.

2. A *specification written in a formal notation, such as *VDM or *Z.

formal system An *interpretation of a *formal language.

formant A natural resonant frequency of the vocal tract whose frequency values are independent of the source location. *See* copy synthesis.

format 1. The defined structure of the pattern of information that is to be processed, recorded on magnetic or optical media, displayed on a screen, or printed on a page.

2. To put data into a predetermined structure or divide a storage medium, such as a disk into sectors, so that it is ready to receive data.

See disk format, tape format, printer format, CD-ROM format standards, file format, instruction format.

formatter 1. of a storage subsystem. The logic assembly that determines the *format of data recorded on magnetic or optical media, and forms part of a device controller. *See also* disk format, tape format.

2. **(text formatter)** A program that accepts text with embedded formatting instructions and produces a new version of the document with the specified margins, justification, pagination, etc.

3. A program that checks the surface of a magnetic disk or tape by writing and then reading a set pattern to every point on the medium. Any unusable or damaged portions will be marked as such to avoid their use for data storage; alternative portions may be assigned in their place. New media must be formatted before use; the re-formatting of

used media has the effect of totally erasing all the data stored thereon, although specialized recovery techniques can sometimes save information after accidental re-formatting.

form factor 1. The shape of a piece of equipment expressed either in height, width, and depth or in terms of a standard item such as a 5¼ inch disk drive or a 19 inch rack.

2. The fraction of radiation diffusely emitted from one surface that is received by another. Form factors are used in *radiosity calculations and are strictly geometric quantities whose values depend only on the shape and relative location of the surfaces in the scene. Form factors are independent of view and hence do not have to be recomputed for a change of view.

form feed (FF) A format command for printers and displays signaling the requirement that the data that follows should be printed or displayed on the next sheet or form. In printers with continuous stationery this causes the paper to be thrown to the start of the next page. In printers with cut-sheet feeders it causes the current sheet to be ejected and printing to continue on the next sheet.

form letter A letter that is to be sent to a number of different destinations with only minor differences in each copy, such as the date, address, salutation, and perhaps items in the body of the letter. The letter is stored as a *word-processor document. Each of the points where variable information occurs is marked by a *place holder*, and before printing the place holders are replaced by the specific information. If a number of letters are to be produced at once, then the variable information can be stored as a list of names, addresses, and other information. If only one letter at a time is produced, then the place holders can be replaced directly from the keyboard. *See also* mailmerge.

form overlay The predetermined patterns of printed lines, logos, and fixed information that may be produced by a computer printer in addition to the variable information. Many nonimpact printers and some impact matrix printers can print the form overlay concurrently with the variable data.

form stop A sensor on a printer that generates

a signal to indicate that there is insufficient paper to allow printing to continue.

FORTH A programming language formerly much in vogue among users of microcomputers. FORTH operands are held on a *stack, and programs take the form of strings in *reverse Polish notation. A vital feature of FORTH is that a symbol (a WORD) can be associated with any program string, and such a user-defined word can then be used in expressions on equal terms with the system words (operators). This makes FORTH a flexible *extensible language in which it is possible to define a customized language for, say, the control of a scientific instrument. The FORTH system is very compact; the interpreter and the dictionary containing the system-defined words can be fitted into 8K bytes. FORTH is now little used, but the same principles are found in *PostScript.

Fortran (or **FORTRAN**) *Acronym for* formula translation. A programming language widely used for scientific computation. The first version, Fortran I, was issued by IBM in 1956, to be succeeded by Fortran II in 1958. This in turn was succeeded by Fortran IV, also known as Fortran 66 when it was standardized by ANSI. This became the workhorse of the scientific world until it was replaced by Fortran 77. This version retained the flavor of the original Fortran but introduced some more modern concepts as a gesture towards *structured programming. The latest version, Fortran 90, appeared after long and acrimonious discussion, and incorporates a large number of new capabilities. It incorporates most of the concepts and facilities of modern languages, though not always expressed in the most elegant manner.

Fortran programs use a notation strongly reminiscent of algebra (hence formula translation), and it is thus fairly easy for the scientist to specify a computation. Fortran II introduced the important idea of independent compilation of subroutines, making it possible to establish libraries of scientific subroutines. The efficient code produced by the early Fortran compilers did much to ensure the acceptance of high-level languages as a normal mode of use of computers.

forward bias The d.c. voltage required to maintain current flow in a *bipolar transistor or *diode or to enhance current flow in a *field-effect transistor. For example, a silicon diode will conduct current only if its anode is at a positive voltage compared to its cathode; it is then said to be *forward biased*. This voltage will be approximately 0.6 volts. *Compare* reverse bias.

forward chaining (data-driven processing) A control procedure used in problem solving and *rule-based systems. When a data item matches the antecedent part of a rule, then the conditions for that rule have been satisfied and the consequent part of the rule is executed. The process then repeats, usually through some form of conflict-resolution mechanism to prevent the same rules firing continuously. *Compare* backward chaining.

forward error correction (forward error protection) Error correction that is accomplished by appending redundant data to actual data so that certain kinds of errors can be both detected and corrected. This differs from many error correction methods used in communications in that there is no request to resend the data (e.g. from a memory); there is thus no reverse message, hence the word forward. The nature of the redundancy is a function of the expected type of error. *See also* backward error correction, error-correcting code.

forward error recovery A mechanism that prepares a system for possible future errors by recording information to be used in the event of a detected error.

forward pruning A technique for reducing the number of *nodes to be examined at each level in a search process. An *evaluation function can be used to prune unpromising nodes or a mechanical method might be used, such as *beam search* – expand only n nodes at each level.

Fourier analysis The analysis of an arbitrary waveform into its constituent sinusoids (of different frequencies and amplitudes). *See* Fourier transform. *See also* orthonormal basis.

Fourier descriptors A method used in object

recognition and *image processing to represent the boundary shape of a *segment in an image. The first few terms in a *Fourier series provide the basis of a *descriptor. This type of object descriptor is useful for recognition tasks because it can be designed to be independent of scaling, translation, or rotation.

Fourier series The infinite trigonometric series

$$\tfrac{1}{2}a_0 + \sum_{n=1}^{\infty} (a_n \cos nx + b_n \sin nx)$$

By suitable choice of the coefficients a_i and b_i, the series can be made equal to any function of x defined on the interval $(-\pi, \pi)$. If f is such a function, the *Fourier coefficients* are given by the formulas

$$a_n = (1/\pi) \int_{-\pi}^{\pi} f(x) \cos nx \, dx$$
$$(n = 0,1,2,\ldots)$$
$$b_n = (1/\pi) \int_{-\pi}^{\pi} f(x) \sin nx \, dx$$
$$(n = 1,2,\ldots)$$

Fourier transform A mathematical operation that analyzes an arbitrary waveform into its constituent sinusoids (of different frequencies and amplitudes). This relationship is stated as

$$S(f) = \int_{-\infty}^{\infty} s(t) \exp(-2\pi i f t) \, dt$$

where $s(t)$ is the waveform to be decomposed into a sum of sinusoids, $S(f)$ is the Fourier transform of $s(t)$, and $i = \sqrt{-1}$. An analogous formula gives $s(t)$ in terms of $S(f)$, but with a normalizing factor, $1/2\pi$. Sometimes, for symmetry, the normalizing factor is split between the two relations.

The Fourier transform pair, $s(t)$ and $S(f)$, has to be modified before it is amenable to computation on a digital computer. This modified pair, called the *discrete Fourier transform (DFT)* must approximate as closely as possible the continuous Fourier transform. The continuous time function is approximated by N samples at time intervals T:

$$g(kT), \quad k = 0,1,\ldots n-1$$

The continuous Fourier transform is also approximated by N samples at frequency intervals $1/NT$:

$$G(n/NT), \quad n = 0,1,\ldots N-1$$

Since the N values of time and frequency are related by the continuous Fourier transform, then a discrete relationship can be derived:

$$G(n/NT) = \sum_{k=0}^{N-1} g(kt) \exp(-2\pi i n k / N)$$

four Russians algorithm *Another name for* Kronrod's algorithm.

fourth generation of computers. A designation covering machines that were designed after 1970 (approximately), i.e. the current generation. Conceptually the most important criterion that can be used to separate them from the *third generation is that they have been designed to work efficiently with the current generation of high-level languages – *fourth-generation languages – and are intended to be easier to program by their end-user. From a hardware point of view they are characterized by being constructed largely from *integrated circuits and have multi-megabyte fast RAM fabricated in MOS technology. These volatile memories are intimately connected to high-speed disk units so that on power failure or switch-off data in MOS memory is retained by automatic transfer to the disks. On switch-on commonly the system is started up from a bootstrap ROM, which loads the operating system and resident software back into the MOS memory as required.

fourth-generation language (4GL) A term used in the data processing community for a high-level language that is designed to allow users who are not trained programmers to develop applications, in particular for querying databases and generating reports. 4GLs are usually nonprocedural languages in which the user describes what is wanted in terms of application, not the computer. The processor takes the user's description and either interprets it directly or generates a program (in a database query language or Cobol) that will perform the desired operation. For this reason the latter are sometimes called *application generators*.

FP A notation for functional programming proposed by J. W. Backus in 1978. Backus propounded a general functional style of programming, and developed an *algebra of functional programs. FP has not been developed as a practical programming language, but has enriched the conception of functional programming.

FPA 1. *Abbrev. for* floating-point accelerator.
2. *Abbrev. for* function point analysis.

FPGA *Abbrev. for* field-programmable gate array. A *PGA that may be programmed by the user, i.e. on the customer's premises. *See also* programmed logic.

FPLA *Abbrev. for* field-programmable logic array. *See* PLA.

FQDN *Abbrev. for* fully qualified domain name. The full name of an organization as registered with a *domain name server.

fractal A set whose Hausdorff-Besicovitch dimension strictly exceeds its topological dimension. Intuitively, a fractal is a set which at all magnifications reveals a set that is exactly the same (self-similar). Such sets can be generated by the repeated application of some collection of maps. The term is generally associated with Benoit Mandelbrot and appeared in the literature in the late 1970s. Many naturally occurring objects, such as trees, coastlines, and clouds, are considered to have fractal properties, hence their interest to computer graphics.

fractal image compression A *lossy image compression technique based on splitting an image into parts that can each be represented by *fractals. The representation of an image by a fractal consists of finding an image transformation that, when applied iteratively to any initial image at the decoder, produces a sequence of images that converges to a fractal approximation of the original. Essentially the encoding of the image is then an encoding of the transformation for each part of the image parts, and a description of the decomposition into parts. Fractal compression is computationally intensive. It has the ability to render images that appear lossless at one extreme and on the other hand the compressed images can be very small in size while still producing recognizable images.

fraction (fractional number) A number that admits of a *countable set of parts of a whole, i.e. a *rational number or a number represented in *floating-point notation.

fractional-level zooming Zooming in on an image at a rate that requires interpolation between the known values of the image at specific points.

fractional part 1. The part of a number to the right of the radix point.
2. *Another name for* mantissa. *See* floating-point notation.

fractional replication An important technique in *experimental design for reducing the number of treatment combinations tested, allowing more factors to be included in the experiment without increasing the number of observations. For example, seven factors at two levels each may be tested on a balanced set of 32 combinations without loss of important information, compared with the full set of 128 combinations.

fragmentation The creation of many small areas of memory, which may arise as a side effect when memory is allocated to and then released by processes. When a process requests a memory allocation, it is assigned the use of a contiguous area, often part of a larger area none of which is currently assigned to any process. The fragments of unallocated memory thus generated can in time become so small that they are not capable of meeting the requests of any process, and they then lie idle. *Defragmentation is a process that, by consolidating memory which is in use, creates larger contiguous areas of unused memory, of a size that allows them to be allocated to meet requests by processes. *See also* external fragmentation, internal fragmentation.

frame 1. The total amount of information presented on a display at any one time.
2. A single message or packet on a data link using a *data link control protocol such as HDLC, ADCCP, etc. The frame is the unit of error detection, retransmission, etc. A special pattern of bits – a flag – marks the beginning and ending of the frame. In the HDLC protocol, a flag is the 8-bit sequence

01111110

that when followed by any sequence of bits other than another flag denotes the beginning of a frame of data; the flag is maintained as a unique synchronizing sequence of bits since the rules of the protocol require that a 0 is automatically inserted by the sending equipment whenever it detects the presence of five 1s in the input data stream.

3. In general, a complete or self-identifying message in a data communication system.

4. A section of a recording on magnetic tape that comprises a single bit in each track.

5. *See* frames.

frame buffer An area of memory used to store information related to the pixels of a display. A frame buffer for a color display has a set of *planes* each defining one bit of the color information of each point. Typically a color display will have a frame buffer with up to 24 planes, 8 each for defining red, green, and blue values (*see* RGB color model).

frame grabber An input device, such as a video camera with associated hardware, that allows a *frame of a display to be captured. *See also* image capture.

frameless rendering Randomizing the order in which pixels in a scene are updated to give an impression of continuous movement and *motion blur without the computational cost.

frame relay A form of network transmission in which *packets from different lower-speed sources are encapsulated together to form a very large *frame, up to several hundred bytes in length, which is then transported as a unit on a single higher-speed bearer. The frame will usually have a fixed length, and more or less fixed internal structure. The fixed size and relatively simple internal structure of the frames means that the switching activity can be implemented with a considerable degree of hardware assistance, while the larger frame size reduces the ratio of overheads to useful payload. In particular it is possible to allow packets to enter or leave the frame relay system using an assembly of standardized products.

frames A *knowledge representation formalism. A frame is a list of named slots. Each slot can hold a fact, a pointer to a slot in another frame, a rule for deriving the value of the slot, or a procedure for calculating the value. Frames can be used to represent all the knowledge about a particular object or event. They are often arranged in hierarchies in

which frames representing particular entities inherit their slot values from ancestor frames representing generic entities. *See also* object-oriented programming.

Framework Programmes, I–IV *See* ESPRIT.

FranzLisp A dialect of *LISP, now superseded by *Common LISP.

Fredholm integral equation *See* integral equation.

freedom of information A catch phrase that has several meanings:

1. a lack of censorship – a state where there is no restriction on the recording of information or on the use of that information;

2. deregulation of the communications media – the removal of restrictions on the use of broadcasting frequencies and communication cables;

3. fair use of *copyright material – the right to impart news and information in western society;

4. the rights an American citizen has under the Freedom of Information Act to study almost any records concerning a government department;

5. technological transfer to third world countries – the rights of underprivileged people to high-technology information free of charge.

In this last case the difficulties in associating the concept of property to information, and the way in which the imparting of information leads to the creation of yet more information, are supporting arguments in favor of free or low-cost technological transfer.

free list *Another name for* available list.

free monoid A particular kind of *monoid, usually involving *strings. Note first that *concatenation is an *associative operation and also that, if Λ is the *empty string, then

$$\Lambda w = w = w\Lambda$$

for all strings w, i.e. Λ is an identity element. Hence, for any alphabet A (*see* formal language), the set of all A-words forms a monoid under concatenation. Furthermore this monoid has the algebraic property of "freeness", which here means that, given any other monoid M and a function f from A to M, there is precisely one way of extending f to a monoid *homomorphism from A^* to M.

There are other free monoids, but they are all *isomorphic to monoids of strings under concatenation. Hence the latter are representative of the free monoids and the phrase is often taken to refer to them specifically. *See also* initial algebra.

free occurrence *See* free variable.

free semigroup A *free monoid, but without the *identity element. *See also* semigroup.

Free Software Foundation (FSF) A US organization that aims to make high-quality software freely available for everyone.

free-space list A list of unoccupied areas of memory in main or backing store. It is a special case of an *available list.

free text retrieval *Another name for* full text retrieval.

free variable In an expression, a variable whose value must be known in order for the whole expression to be evaluated. The idea depends on distinguishing different ways in which variables can occur in expressions; it arises in connection with all variable-binding operators, such as the logical *quantifiers and function symbols. It can also be seen as a formalization of the idea of *global and *local variables in programs.

For example, in the following *lambda expression,

$$\lambda f . g(f(\lambda x . x),x,y),$$

the variable x occurs three times. The first occurrence, since it immediately follows a λ, introduces a new "binding" of x, and is therefore called a *binding occurrence*. The second occurrence of x falls inside the "scope" of this binding and is therefore called a *bound occurrence*. The third x is not within the scope of any such binding and is therefore called a *free occurrence*. Equally, the variable f has a binding occurrence and a bound occurrence, while g and y just have one free occurrence each. Since only x, y, and g have free occurrences, they are referred to as the free variables of the expression. The value of the whole expression then depends on what values are given to these free occurrences.

Note that freeness depends on the expression under consideration; thus, although f does not occur free in the whole expression above, it does so in the subexpression

$$g(f(\lambda x . x),x,y).$$

freeware Unlicensed software that may be used and distributed without payment.

freeze-frame A single *frame of video information that may be "grabbed" for observation or capture.

frequency The number of complete cycles of a periodically variable quantity, such as a pulse or wave, that occurs in unit time. It is measured in hertz.

frequency distribution A table of the number of occurrences of each of a set of classified observations. The occurrences might arise from the throw of dice, the measurement of a man's height in a particular range of values, or the number of reported cases of a disease in different groups of people classified by their age, sex, or other category.

It is usual practice to choose a fairly small number of categories so that the *relative frequencies within categories are not too small. If no definite upper or lower limits are known, all values above (or below) a certain value are grouped into a single category known as the *upper (or lower) tail*.

Frequency distributions may be summarized by computing *statistics such as the mean (or other *measures of location) and the standard deviation (or other *measures of variation), and sometimes measures of asymmetry or skewness and of compactness (i.e. the proportion of the sample in the center and in the tails).

The term frequency distribution is applied to observed data in a sample. In contrast, *probability distributions are theoretical formulas for the *probability of observing each event. Fitting probability distributions to observed frequency distributions is a fundamental *statistical method of data analysis.

frequency divider An electronic device that is capable of dividing the frequency of a given digital input pulse train by a fixed integer value, n. It often consists of an n-stage *counter, the output frequency at the nth stage of counting being an nth submultiple of the input frequency.

frequency division multiplexing (FDM) A form of *multiplexing in which the *bandwidth of the transmission medium is divided into logical channels over which multiple messages can be simultaneously transmitted. FDM is commonly used worldwide to combine multiple voice-grade telephone signals: 4000 hertz (Hz) is allocated for each channel, 3000 Hz per signal plus a 500 Hz *guard band* (unused frequency band) on either side of the signal. Each signal starts at DC, but the different signals are raised to different frequencies so that the signals do not overlap. Despite the guard bands, strong signal spikes at the edges of a channel can overlap into the next channel, causing noise interference.

See also broadband networking, time division multiplexing.

frequency function *See* probability distributions.

frequency modulation (FM, f.m.) *See* modulation. *See also* disk format.

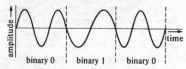

Frequency shift keying, 2 states

frequency shift keying (FSK) A method for representing digital data with analog signals by using a change in the frequency of the carrier to represent information. It is thus a type of *modulation. FSK with two frequencies, corresponding to the digital values 0 and 1 (*see* diagram) is the primary method used by low-speed *modems. *See also* digital data transmission.

Fresnel factor A factor that describes how light is reflected from each smooth microfacet within a rough surface, as a function of incidence angle and wavelength. This is used in the *Cook–Torrance model.

friction drive *See* platten.

front-end processor An *I/O processor that is used to format and/or process input data. The term is sometimes used to refer to a *communication processor. *Compare* back-end processor.

FSA *Abbrev. for* finite-state automaton.

FSF *Abbrev. for* Free Software Foundation.

FSK *Abbrev. for* frequency shift keying.

FST *Abbrev. for* flatter squarer tube. A cathode-ray tube (CRT) in which the radius of curvature is large and the corner radii small, making the screen surface appear nearly planar. Earlier CRTs were more rounded.

FTAM *Acronym for* File Transfer, Access, and Management. An ISO *protocol that deals with the handling of files in a networked environment. As well as allowing the transfer of files between different operating system environments, the protocol also caters for the situation in which two systems linked via a network wish to allow a *process on one system to access and manipulate parts of a file on the other system. This greater functionality entails a much more complex negotiation phase at the start of the access or manipulation than is needed for the simple transfer of a complete file from one system to the other.

FTFL code *Short for* fixed-to-fixed-length code. *Another name for* fixed-length code, block code.

FTP *Abbrev. for* file transfer protocol.

FTVL code *Short for* fixed-to-variable-length code. *Another name for* variable-length code.

Fujitsu A Japanese manufacturing conglomerate. It was a prime investor in the Amdahl Corporation in its formative stages, and owns *ICL. It is best known as a manufacturer of IBM-compatible mainframes but is active in all areas of the industry. Fujitsu is second only to IBM in worldwide IT revenue (1993 figures).

full adder *See* adder.

full backup A *backup of a set of specified files, often the entire contents of a disk, regardless of when they were last modified. A *differential backup* is a backup of a set of specified files, often a disk's entire contents, that includes only those files modified since the last full backup. A restore operation would involve the full backup plus the differential backup. An *incremental backup* is a backup of a set of specified files, often a disk's entire contents, that incudes only those files modified since the last incremental backup. In the latter case a restore operation would involve the last full backup plus all the subsequent incremental backups.

full custom A technique used for the design of *integrated circuits that involves the manipulation of circuit designs at the semiconductor device level. If the device is based on silicon technology for instance, the designer will be concerned with the definition and characterization of silicon structures that will form the elementary components of the IC. The geometric shapes of these components are laid out with a polygon editor on a CAD (*computer-aided design) system. The shapes thus produced may be combined with others from a standard cell library to form the overall geometric design of the IC. Electric characteristics appropriate for the semiconductor materials that will be used to fabricate the IC are then associated with this geometric definition so that electric simulation of the behavior of the IC can be carried out. The geometric definition forms the basis of the masks that will be used for fabrication of the device by a process of photolithography. *See also* semicustom.

full duplex *Another name for* duplex.

full-motion video (FMV) The real-time display of full-screen motion video. The large data rates involved and the need to decompress images in real time means that it is difficult to achieve.

full subtractor *See* subtractor.

full text retrieval (free text retrieval) A form of *information retrieval in which the full text of a document is stored, and retrieval is achieved by searching for occurrences of a given string in the text. This technique can be compared with the alternative of retrieving information by matching one of a set of predetermined keywords.

full tree A tree of *degree m and *depth k in which every node at depth less than k has m children and thus, in particular, all leaf nodes are at depth k.

function 1. from one set X to another set Y. A *relation R defined on the *Cartesian product $x \times y$ in which for each element x in X there is precisely one element y in Y with the property that (x,y) is a member of R. It is then customary to talk about a function f, say, and to write

$$f : X \to Y$$

The unique association between elements x and y is denoted by

$$y = f(x) \text{ or } y = fx$$

X is called the *domain* of f, Y the *codomain* of f. Further, y is the *value* of f at the point x or the *image* of x under f. We say that f is a *mapping* or *transformation* between sets X and Y or that f maps X into Y, and that f maps x into y. When the domain X is the Cartesian product of n sets then f is a function of n variables. Otherwise it is a function of one variable.

Examples of functions are readily obtained from the mathematical equivalents of standard functions and operations typically supplied in programming languages. The usual trigonometric functions *sin*, *cos*, and *tan* are functions of one variable. The rule for converting from characters into their integer codes or equivalents is a function.

Functions are often represented pictorially as *graphs.

See also bijection, injection, surjection, operation, homomorphism.

2. A *program unit that given values for input parameters computes a value. Examples include the standard functions such as $sin(x)$, $cos(x)$, $exp(x)$; in addition most languages permit user-defined functions. A function is a "black box" that can be used without any knowledge or understanding of the detail of its internal working. In some languages a function may have *side effects.

functional cohesion *See* cohesion.

functional dependency *See* normal forms.

functional design A design method in which the system is seen from the functional viewpoint. The design concentrates on isolating high-level functions that can then be decomposed into and synthesized from lower-level functions. Development proceeds as a series of *stepwise refinements of functionality. *Compare* data-driven design.

functional languages (applicative languages) A class of programming languages whose programs compute *functions. In practice, the class of functional languages are a subclass of the *declarative languages, and are based on *lambda calculus or *recursion equations. Typically a program in a functional language consists of an unordered set of equations that characterize functions and their values. Functions are specified by use of recursion, other functions, and values. Values are characterized as functions applied to other values. Ultimately the set of equations that is the program must characterize all functions and values in terms of the primitive functions and values provided by the language. The values characterized by the equations include the values computed by executing the program.

functional partitioning A technique of system or program decomposition in which the primary criterion is that each identified module should contain only elements that all contribute to the achievement of a single goal. Thus each module should perform a single function in the broad sense of an identified job of work (the definition of which is both subjective and dependent upon the level of consideration). The technique is often associated with a general approach, termed *structured design*, that was developed by IBM in the early 1970s.

functional specification *See* module specification.

functional testing *See* performance testing.

functional unit Any major component of a computing system, e.g. CPU, main memory, backing store unit, peripheral device.

function key A key on a *keyboard that initiates an operation or inputs a code that will subsequently initiate an operation.

function point analysis A method derived originally by Albrecht at IBM to estimate the relative complexity and work content of developing a software system. The requirements of a software system are analyzed for five categories: inputs, outputs, files, interfaces, and enquiries. Each of these is then classified into parts that are simple, average, or complex. The results are represented as counts in a matrix with a total of 15 cells;

each raw count is weighted by multiplying it by standard factors, and the unadjusted function point count, U, is then obtained by summing each cell-weighted value.

The processing complexity for the software is estimated for each of 14 general characteristics that cover the type of product, and how it is to be used and installed. For each characteristic a value is selected to represent its scale of influence. The 14 values are summed to give the processing complexity adjustment, PC, which will range from 0 to 70. The PC is used to calculate the adjusted function point score from its unadjusted score U. A measure of the work involved in developing the software is then obtained from a formula that allows for further score adjustments where necessary.

functor A *function that maps one *category into another. In computing terms a special functor represents mappings between mathematical concepts, such as *sets and *functions, and their implementation in a programming language; this is often called the *representation functor*. The idea generalizes to include mappings between different *abstract machines.

fusible link (fuse link) A physical link providing electric continuity across an individual cell in the memory array of a *PROM. With this link intact the cell, when interrogated, will display a known *logic state. During programming this link can be destroyed, forcing the cell to take on the complementary logic state; this process is irreversible.

Fusible links are used in a similar manner in field-programmable logic arrays (*see* PLA).

FutureBus *Trademark* An asynchronous backplane bus specified in the IEEE-896 standard for processor system interconnection. It features multiplexed 32-bit data and address lines and uses a *handshaking protocol to allow communication between devices of differing response times. Multiple bus mastership is supported and up to 20 devices can be connected.

fuzzy control The application of *fuzzy logic to continuous *process-control problems. As an alternative to classical mathematical control techniques, a rule-based controller can be built using rules like 'if the temperature is fairly high, then slightly reduce the flow'. The adjectives are converted into fuzzy variables, which are used in a fuzzy-logic algorithm to produce the control outputs. Such rules are captured from expert human controllers by *knowledge acquisition techniques. Some fuzzy controllers have reported performance at least as good as human operators.

fuzzy logic (fuzzy theory) A branch of logic designed specifically for representing knowledge and human reasoning in such a way that it is amenable to processing by computer. Thus fuzzy logic is applicable to *expert systems, *knowledge engineering, and *artificial intelligence.

The more traditional propositional and predicate logics do not allow for degrees of imprecision, indicated by words or phrases such as fairly, very, quite possibly. Instead of truth values such as true and false it is possible to introduce a multivalued logic consisting of, for example, the values true, not true, very true, not very true, more or less true, not very false, very false, not false, and false. Alternatively an interval such as [0,1] can be introduced and the degree of truth can be represented by some real number in this range. Predicates are then functions that map not into {true, false} but into these more general domains.

Fuzzy logic is concerned with the study of *sets and *predicates of this kind. There emerge such concepts as *fuzzy sets*, *fuzzy relationships*, and *fuzzy quantifiers*.

G

G *Symbol for* giga-, as in GHz (gigahertz) and Gbyte (gigabyte). *See* giga-.

Galerkin's method *See* finite-element method.

gallium arsenide (GaAs) devices Semiconductor integrated-circuit devices that are implemented using gallium arsenide as the intrinsic *semiconductor material in preference to, say, silicon. Gallium arsenide has certain advantages over other semiconductor materials, in particular in high-speed applications and in the fabrication of optical and optically coupled devices such as light-emitting diodes and optoisolators.

Galois field *Another name for* finite field (named for the French mathematician Évariste Galois).

games console *See* computer games.

game theory A mathematical theory of decision-making by participants with conflicting interests in a competitive situation, originated by Emile Borel in 1921 and rigorously established by John von Neumann in 1928. The theory attempts to gain insights into economic situations by isolating these aspects, which occur in their simplest form in games of strategy.

In a two-player game, as defined by the theory, each participant has a choice of plays for which there are several possible outcomes, gains or losses, depending on the opponent's choice. An optimum strategy states the relative frequency with which a player's choices should be used, so as to maximize his average gain (or minimize his average loss). The problem of determining the optimum strategy can be formulated as a problem in *linear programming. Generalizations to *n*-person games are included in the theory.

game tree A *tree investigated during a *tree search process performed during computer game playing. *See also* computer chess.

Gane–Sarson An early method of *structured systems analysis.

Gantt chart A form of diagram that depicts the duration of (usually) development activities as horizontal bars extending from their planned starting date to their estimated completion date. The diagram can thus be used to gain a visual impression of a development plan.

gap theorem A theorem in complexity theory that, like the *speedup theorem, can be expressed in terms of abstract complexity measures (*see* Blum's axioms) but will be more understandable in the context of time:

given any *total *recursive function

$$g(n) \geq n$$

there exists a total recursive function $S(n)$ such that

$$\text{DTIME}(S(n)) = \text{DTIME}(g(.S(n)))$$

(*see* complexity classes). In other words there is a "gap" between time bounds $S(n)$ and $g(S(n))$ within which the minimal space complexity of no language lies.

This has the following counter-intuitive consequence: given two universal models of computation, say a Turing machine that makes one move per century and the other a random-access machine capable of performing a million arithmetic operations per second, then there is a total recursive function $S(n)$ such that any language recognizable in time $S(n)$ on one machine is also recognizable within time $S(n)$ on the other.

garbage Information in a memory that is no longer valid or wanted. It is usually the result of *memory compaction operations. The removal of this superfluous information from the memory is known as *garbage collection* and is usually associated with memory compaction.

garbage collection *See* garbage.

gate *See* logic gate.

gate array A form of *programmable device in which the component *logic gates can be interconnected in an arbitrary manner during manufacture to give a *combinational or *sequential circuit of considerable *height.

gateway A device that interconnects two *networks, and whose presence is usually visible to network users (as distinct from a *bridge, whose presence is generally not visible). A gateway may be required to deal with one or more of the following differences between networks it connects:

(a) change of addressing *domain – where the networks have addressing domains managed by separate groups, a gateway may be used to handle address transformations for messages traversing the gateway;

(b) control of charging – where the networks have different approaches to charging (e.g. a local area network that imposes no charges

connecting to a wide area network that charges on a per-packet basis), a gateway may be used to handle user authorization and usage accounting;

(c) change of protocol – where the networks use different protocols, a gateway may be used to carry out necessary protocol conversion (if practicable) or to intercept attempts by a user on one network to use functions not available on the other and to supply suitable responses.

The terms bridge, gateway, and *relay are among those whose meanings vary between different communities of users at a given time, and within a given community of users at different times.

gather write The function of writing to memory a block of data comprising items of data that have been retrieved directly from scattered memory locations and/or registers.

Gaussian distribution *Another name for* normal distribution.

Gaussian elimination *See* linear algebraic equations.

Gaussian noise *Noise whose distribution of amplitude over time is *Gaussian.

Gaussian quadrature *See* numerical integration.

GB (or **Gb**) *Symbols for* gigabyte. *See* giga-, byte.

Gbps *Abbrev. for* gigabits per second, i.e. usually 10^9 bits per second. *See* giga-, bps.

GBS method The Gragg–Burlisch–Stoer *extrapolation method based on theoretical results obtained by Gragg, implemented by Burlisch and Stoer. *See* Gragg's extrapolation method.

Gbyte *Abbrev. for* gigabyte. *See* giga-, byte.

GCD *Abbrev. for* greatest common divisor.

GCR *Abbrev. for* group code recording. *See* disk format, tape format.

GDI *Abbrev. for* graphical device interface.

generalized additive models Statistical models introduced by T. Hastie and R. Tibshirani and used for smoothing data with sums of components of linear or nonlinear curves. The models are more general than *generalized linear models.

generalized Church–Turing thesis *See* abstract computability theory.

generalized linear model (GLM) In regression analysis, one of a wide class of model in which the fitted value is a *transformation of a *linear predictor* and the *frequency distribution is not necessarily the *normal distribution. Apart from the standard linear regression model (*see* regression analysis), the most important cases are (a) for integer counts, the logarithmic transformation and the *Poisson distribution, and (b) for proportions, the logistic transformation and the *binomial distribution.

GLMs may be used in regression analysis where inspection of *residuals indicates that the distribution is other than the normal distribution, and may also be used to analyze *contingency tables.

The analysis uses the method of maximum *likelihood, solved by iterative use of *weighted least squares estimation.

generalized sequential machine *See* sequential machine. *See also* gsm mapping.

general-purpose computer (GP computer; GP) A computer that can be used for any function for which it can be conveniently programmed.

general-purpose interface bus (GPIB) *See* IEEE.

general recursive function *See* recursive function.

generating polynomial *See* polynomial.

generations of computers. An informal system of classifying computer systems as advances have been made in electronic technology and, latterly, in software. Since the design of digital computers has been a continuous process for the past five decades – by a wide variety of people in different countries, faced with different problems – it is difficult and not very profitable to try and establish where 'generations' start and finish. *See* first generation, second generation, third generation, fourth generation, fifth generation.

generative grammar A set of formal rules that projects a finite set of sentences upon the potentially infinite set of sentences that constitute the language as a whole; the term was originally introduced by Noam Chomsky (1957). Among models of generative grammar that have been investigated are finite-state, *phrase-structure, and *transformational grammars.

generator 1. A program that accepts the definition of an operation that is to be accomplished, and automatically constructs a program for the purpose. The earliest example of this kind of program was the *sort generator*, which took a specification of the file format and the sorted order required, and produced a sorting program. This was followed by *report generators*, which constructed programs to print reports from files containing information in a specified format. The best-known program of this kind is *RPG II. *See also* application generator.

2. An element g of a *group G with the property that the various powers

$$g^0, g^1, g^2, \ldots$$

ultimately include all the elements of G. Such a group is said to be a *cyclic group*; it is also an abelian *group. Generators can also be defined for *monoids in a similar way.

The set of generators S of a group G is a subset of G having the property that every element of G can be expressed as a combination of elements of S. *See also* group graph.

generator matrix *See* linear code, convolutional code.

generic A term used in *Ada to denote a *subprogram or *package that can be parameterized with *parameters that can be types and subprograms as well as values and variables. A generic package or subprogram provides a template from which a particular *instantiation can be produced by providing the appropriate parameters.

generic compaction *See* probabilistic compaction.

genetic algorithm A technique in *artificial intelligence that uses the ideas of genetic mutation, recombination, and survival of the fittest. A large population of potential solutions is maintained from which pairs are cross-matched to produce new members.

The best examples in the population are used to breed the next generation.

geodesic *See* reachability.

geodesic curves Curves that are the shortest distance between two points.

geographic(al) information system (GIS; geomatics (in Canada), **geomatique** (Francophone)) An *information system for providing users with information about objects and features in their geographical contexts. A GIS allows users to display and analyze geographical relationships, and to investigate the effects of changes to the locations or characteristics of objects and features that are represented. The objects may be physical or administrative. Typical GIS applications are in Land Registry/Land Information Systems (LIS), in mapmaking, in land and resource management (e.g. by local authorities and utilities such as gas supply and distribution), and in market research, demographic studies, and environmental work.

A GIS typically consists of a special *database management system (normally *relational or *object-oriented) that recognizes locational relationships, with closely integrated graphical input and output facilities, together with user facilities for manipulation and analysis of the objects and features in the database. The locational characteristics of objects and features may be recorded in vector form, i.e. in the form of coordinates in the real world (latitude and longitude, or some other grid system); alternatively the geographical region covered may be represented in raster form, i.e. as a regular (quasi-rectangular) pattern of cells in which objects are stored. Some systems provide integration of both forms of representation.

The objects in a GIS may represent points such as an individual mountain peak, lines such as a road or river, polygons such as a forest or the boundary of an administrative area, or continua such as elevation or climate. (Continua are commonly represented in a raster rather than a vector GIS.) The spatial data for a GIS may come from a variety of surveying techniques, including remote sensing imagery and global positioning sys-

tems, or from a postal address by *geocoding* (using existing data about the area covered by each zip code or postcode).

The database language includes facilities for locational queries (such as "how many hospitals are there in Hampshire?") and locational responses (such as "where are the vineyards in California"), as well as statistical analyses.

geometric modeler A software system providing facilities for describing the geometry of objects, typically solids and surfaces.

gesture A type of input to a computer where the meaning depends on the time-related positions input from the device. For example, using a *dataglove the user might beckon with a finger to indicate a zoom in on the display.

Gflops (GFLOPS, gigaflops) A billion floating-point operations per second. *See* flops.

GIF *Acronym for* graphics image format. An *image file format developed by Compu-Serve Inc. It is designed for efficient online transmission of color raster images. GIF is widely used on the *World Wide Web for incorporating images into Web pages.

giga- (symbol: G) A prefix indicating a multiple of one billion, 10^9, as in gigahertz and gigavolt. When the binary number system is used in a structure or process (as in semiconductor RAM or ROM) the prefix then indicates a multiple of 2^{30}, i.e.

$$1\,073\,741\,824,$$

as in gigabyte and gigabit. The context usually clarifies which meaning is intended, although, being quite close numerically, the meanings are often considered more or less equivalent.

GIGO *Acronym for* garbage in garbage out, signifying that a program working on incorrect data produces incorrect results.

Gilbert–Varshamov bound The theorem that the maximum possible number, N, of codewords in a *binary *linear *block code is bounded by

$$N \geqslant 2^n \bigg/ \sum_{r=0}^{d-1} \binom{n}{r}$$

where the *code length is n digits, and the

codewords are at a minimum *Hamming distance *d*. *See also* coding bounds, Hamming bound.

GINO–F *Acronym for* graphical input output. A package of Fortran subroutines for computer graphics. The GINO–F subroutines define a "language" for the production of graphics, including three-dimensional objects viewed in various projections. GINO–F attempts to separate the abstract description of the display from the device-dependent features of a particular device, and thus gives a degree of device independence. GINO–F was a de facto graphics standard for many years, especially in the UK, but is now little used having been superseded by *GKS and *PHIGS.

GIS *Abbrev. for* geographic(al) information system.

GKS *Abbrev. for* graphical kernel system. A set of graphical functions used by applications programmers with the names and functions defined in ISO 7942 (first edition, published in 1985). The language bindings (the way the functions can be invoked from standard programming languages) are defined in ISO/IEC 8651. GKS is divided into a number of levels with increasing functionality in either input or output. The lowest level (0a) is simple support for two-dimensional graphical output. The highest level (2c) handles complex input requests and simultaneous output to multiple workstations. A three-dimensional version, *GKS-3D, has also been defined by ISO. A major revision of GKS was completed and published in 1994 (second edition) and is generally called *GKS-94.

GKS-3D The ISO 8805 standard, Graphical Kernel System for Three Dimensions. A set of graphical functions for viewing three-dimensional objects on a two-dimensional display. *See also* GKS.

GKS-94 An updated version of the *GKS standard that provides a richer set of graphical output primitives, enhances the input model, and provides more sophisticated storage facilities by means of a picture part store. The levels of GKS have been removed.

4GL *Abbrev. for* fourth-generation language.

glass-box testing (white-box testing) A style of *testing that considers the inputs, the outputs, and the relationships specified between them, together with knowledge of the internal structure or processing, in order to derive test inputs that will demonstrate that the required outputs occur. Usually the term is applied to software. *Compare* black-box testing.

glass teletype A simple *VDU, now obsolete, that emulated the properties of a *teletypewriter. These devices evolved into today's terminals, offering many additional emulations and features.

glitch An intermittent transient fault that occurs when two communicating *asynchronous processes fail to complete their hardware interface *protocol. It is usually caused by a *flip-flop in a metastable state.

global A term used to define the *scope of an entity: global entities are accessible from all parts of a program. By contrast, *local entities are accessible only in the program module within which they are defined.

global discretization error *See* discretization error.

global illumination An illumination model in which all objects are considered as potential sources of illumination for all other objects in the scene.

global optimization *See* optimization (in programming).

glossy reflection The calculated reflection from a surface that takes account of how glossy it is. *See also* specular reflection.

glyph A recognizable abstract graphic symbol that is independent of any specific design. Thus a letter A is a glyph although its precise form will depend on the *font chosen.

GNU 1. A portable UNIX-compatible software system that is freely distributed. Although copyright, it is licensed for use, modification, and subsequent distribution under the same terms. GNU is a self-referential acronym for GNU's Not UNIX. **2.** The project of developing this software.

goal-directed processing *Another name for* backward chaining.

Gödel numbering of a formal system. A one-to-one mapping (i.e. an *injection) of the symbols, formulas, and finite sequences of formulas of the formal system onto some subset of the natural numbers. The mapping must be such that there is an algorithm that, for any symbol, formula, or finite sequence of formulas, identifies the corresponding natural number; this is the *Gödel number* of that object. There must also be an algorithm that, given any natural number, indicates whether it is the Gödel number of the object; if it is, the algorithm must identify the object.

Conferring Gödel numberings has the effect of permitting statements about elements in the nonnumeric system to be transformed into statements about natural numbers. Conversely, since much is known about natural numbers, it becomes possible to prove assertions about aspects of nonnumeric systems. The mapping was first used by the German mathematician Kurt Gödel.

Gödel's incompleteness theorems Two fundamental theorems in mathematical logic, proved by Kurt Gödel in 1931. The first concerns the formalization of basic arithmetic. Gödel showed that, in any logical system powerful enough to express arithmetical operations, there must exist sentences that are neither provable nor refutable in the logical system. In consequence there exist statements about arithmetic that, while true, cannot be proved in the logical system. The second theorem states that no logical system can be powerful enough to provide a proof of its own consistency. These discoveries marked a turning-point in our understanding of formal reasoning. For example, they forced the abandonment of "Hilbert's program", i.e. of the search for a provably consistent and complete formal basis for the whole of mathematics itself.

Equally significant are the proof methods that Gödel used. One device was to encode logical formulas as numbers (*see* Gödel numbering), so that manipulations of formulas could be "programmed" as numerical computations. (This early exercise in numerical data representation and programming also marked the beginning of *recursive function theory.) The other device was to use this numerical encoding to produce a formula that in effect asserts its own unprovability. The idea is seen in statements such as "this sentence is false", the Cretan liar paradox, and Russell's paradox. Gödel's construction however is formal: the reference to "this sentence" is handled by the numerical encoding, without any need for vague English words. A relationship exists with the paradoxical *combinator, while a similar approach can be used to show the undecidability of the *halting problem as well as many results in *complexity theory, where Gödel numbering is applied to *Turing machines rather than logical formulas.

Gödel is also responsible for a *completeness theorem.

Golay codes A family of *perfect *linear *error-correcting *block codes, of which the most important is the binary (23,12) Golay code. There is also a ternary (11,6) Golay code. Golay codes can be arranged to be *cyclic.

golden section search A *binary search algorithm, but instead of taking the middle element of the next section a proportion is taken that, on average, speeds up the convergence.

Good–de Bruijn diagram (Good–de Bruijn graph) A directed *graph illustrating the possible succession of states of a *shift register. Each possible state of the shift register (indicated by its contents) is represented by a node in the graph; from each node a set of arcs lead to all its possible immediate successors. (Succession involves one clocking of the shift register, with some serial input.) If there are n cells in a *q-ary shift register, there will be q^n nodes, each with q arcs leading from it, and thus q^{n+1} arcs altogether.

When the serial input is some function of the current state, the behavior of the shift register is described by a Good–de Bruijn graph with some arcs deleted: such subgraphs are used in the study of *feedback registers.

goodness-of-fit test A statistical *significance test of the hypothesis that a sample *frequency distribution is adequately explained by fitting a particular model.

When data are counts of numbers of occurrences, the test uses the *chi-squared distribution. Testing goodness of fit of continuous observations is less easy, requiring understanding of *analysis of variance, and is only possible when some observations are replicated.

gopher A software utility that is used on a workstation connected to a network, and acts on behalf of the user in carrying out routine tasks of collecting information from services attached to the network. The term is used especially in connection with a set of utilities (*Gopher*) freely available to users of the *Internet. Gopher presents the user with a hierarchy of nodes, each of which is either a menu (a directory of material accessible at this point), a search node (a set of documents that can be searched using keywords), or a leaf node (a document containing text or other forms of material that the workstation can display). Gopher does not provide embedded links to other documents as found in the *World Wide Web, and is therefore rather less flexible. This in turn means that Gopher is simpler to implement. *See also* WAIS.

Goppa codes A family of *linear *error-correcting *block codes. The most important classes of Goppa codes are the *Reed–Solomon codes and the binary *Golay (23,12) code. Goppa codes are not in general *cyclic.

GOSIP *Acronym for* government open systems interconnection profile. A set of functional standards based predominantly on ISO OSI standards and intended to form the basis for the procurement of computer systems to be purchased by the UK government.

GOTO statement A program statement that causes a *jump; it is thus a jump instruction in a high-level language. It causes the normal flow of control to be broken by designating an explicit successor statement, usually identified by a label, e.g.

> GOTO 99
> ⟨statements⟩
> 99: ...

Modern programming practice deprecates the use of GOTO since its use makes programs more difficult to follow, the flow of control being less visibly explicit. GOTO is, however, sometimes unavoidable, particularly in error situations where it is necessary to abort execution of a number of nested loops or procedures, when the language does not provide for exceptions.

Gouraud shading An approach to shading a planar *facet of a surface that uses linear interpolation of intensities calculated at the vertices of the facet.

GP *Short for* general purpose, general-purpose computer.

GPIB *Abbrev. for* general-purpose interface bus. *See* IEEE.

graceful degradation *See* fail-soft.

graded index fiber *See* fiber optics.

Gragg's extrapolation method (GBS method) An *extrapolation method for the solution of *ordinary differential equations based on the *midpoint rule. For stiff problems a similar scheme can be based on the implicit midpoint rule:
$$y_{n+1} = y_n + hf(x_n + \tfrac{1}{2}h, (y_n + y_{n+1})/2)$$
where h is the stepsize.

grammar One of the principal ways of specifying an infinite *formal language by finite means. A grammar consists of a set of rules (called *productions* or *rewrite rules*) that may be used to derive one string from another by substring replacement. The strings of the specified language are obtained by repeated application of these rules, starting from some initial string. A grammar however has the additional feature that the alphabet is divided into a set T of *terminal symbols* and a set N of *nonterminal symbols* (or variables). While productions may be composed arbitrarily of terminals and nonterminals, the specified language contains strings of terminals only.

A grammar G can therefore be defined as comprising two sets of symbols T and N, a *semi-Thue system over the union $T \cup N$, and a distinguished member S of N. The *language generated by* G is the set of all strings over T that can be derived from S by a sequence of substring replacements (*see* semi-Thue system); S is known as the *start symbol* or *sentence symbol*. As an example, let

T be $\{b,c\}$, N be $\{S,A\}$ and let the productions be

(1) $S \to SA$
(2) $S \to A$
(3) $A \to bc$

Then, for instance, starting from S we can derive $bcbcbc$ via the following sequence (among others):

SA	by production 1
SAA	by production 1
AAA	by production 2
$bcAA$	by production 3
$bcbcA$	by production 3
$bcbcbc$	by production 3

The language generated is

$$\{bc, bcbc, bcbcbc, \ldots\}$$

These are the only strings of bs and cs in $\{b,c\}^*$ derivable from the start symbol S by the three production rules. A string such as $SAbcA$, which is derivable from S but still contains nonterminals, is referred to as a *sentential form*.

This is the most general form of grammar. Typically however some restriction is placed on the form that productions may take (*see* regular grammar, context-free grammar, context-sensitive grammar). The syntax of programming languages is usually specified by context-free grammars; the example given above is context-free, although the language can be specified by a regular grammar.

A slightly different way of generating a language is by means of an *L-system (or Lindenmeyer system). A different approach altogether is to define a machine that tests any string for membership of the language, i.e. an *automaton.

grandfather file (grandparent file) *See* file recovery.

granularity A measure of the size of the *segments into which memory is divided for purposes of either *memory protection or *virtual-memory management.

graph 1. A nonempty but finite set of *vertices* (or *nodes*) together with a set of *edges* that join pairs of distinct vertices. If an edge e joins vertices v_1 and v_2, then v_1 and v_2 are said to be *incident* with e and the vertices are said to be *adjacent*; e is the unordered pair (v_1,v_2).

A graph is usually depicted in a pictorial form in which the vertices appear as dots or other shapes, perhaps labeled for identification purposes, and the edges are shown as lines joining the appropriate points. If direction is added to each edge of a graph, a *directed graph* or *digraph* is obtained. The edges then form a finite set of *ordered pairs of distinct vertices, and are often called *arcs*. In the pictorial representation, arrows can be placed on each edge. With no direction specified, the graph is said to be *undirected*.

Although helpful visually these representations are not suitable for manipulation by computer. More useful representations use an *incidence matrix or an *adjacency matrix.

Graphs are used in a wide variety of ways in computing: the vertices will usually represent objects of some kind and the edges will represent connections of a physical or logical nature between the vertices. So graphs can be used to model in a mathematical fashion such diverse items as a computer and all its attached peripherals, a network of computers, *parse trees, logical dependencies between *subroutines or nonterminals in a *grammar, *VLSI diagrams, and related items in *databases. *Trees and *lists are special kinds of graphs.

Certain variations exist in the definition of a graph. There is some dispute about whether one edge can join a vertex to itself, whether empty sets are involved, whether an infinite number of vertices and edges are permitted, and so on.

See also connected graph, network, weighted graph.

2. of a function f. The set of all *ordered pairs (x,y) with the property that $y = f(x)$. Often such a graph is represented by a curve.

graphical device interface (GDI) The interface between a graphics system and a device. The *CGI is an ISO standard interface. The *X Windows protocol and *PostScript are de facto GDI standards. Use of standard device interfaces allows the same program to generate output for a range of devices without the need to change the program.

graphical kernel system *See* GKS.

graphical user interface (GUI) An interface between a user and a computer system that makes use of input devices other than the keyboard and presentation techniques other than alphanumeric characters. Typical GUIs involve the use of *windows, *icons, *menus, and *pointing devices. The windows can contain control objects such as *slider bar, *radio buttons, *check boxes, and *pick lists, as well as textual or graphical information. The objects forming the interface display have attributes such as the ability to be resized, moved around the display, shrunk down to an icon, or given different colors. Perhaps the best-known GUIs are those used on Microsoft *Windows PCs and Apple Macintosh computers, although there are several others in common use.

graphic characters *See* character set.

graphics *See* computer graphics.

graphics accelerator Additional hardware used in a graphics display to perform basic operations faster. At the lowest level this might be line-drawing hardware. For more sophisticated devices, *clipping, *rendering, and effects such as fog can be realized by graphics accelerators. Use of such hardware gives the opportunity for more complex images to be displayed in real time.

graphics adapter (or adaptor) A printed circuit board that can be added to a personal computer to enable it to drive a particular type of graphics display. It therefore determines the maximum graphics capability of the system. The most widely used graphics adapters are for IBM and IBM-compatible systems and include *VGA and *SVGA.

graphics image format *See* GIF.

graphics mode A way of displaying images on a computer screen or other graphics device such that the basic unit is the *pixel. The *resolution and complexity of the image depends on how many pixels there are in total, and how many bits are assigned to each pixel. The more bits per pixel, the more different colors or shades of gray. A single graphics device can operate in a number of different graphics modes with different resolutions and color selections. A common

mode for a *desktop PC would be 1024 by 768 pixels with 256 different colors – chosen from a much larger number – available for each pixel. *See also* text mode, computer graphics.

graphics primitive A basic nondivisible graphical element for input or output within a computer-graphics system. Typical output primitives are *polyline, *polymarker, and *fill area. *Clipping of an output primitive cannot be guaranteed to produce another output primitive. Output primitives have *attributes such as line style and pattern associated with them. Typical input primitives are *locator, *choice, and *valuator. Input primitives often have a style of *echoing associated with them.

graphics program A computer program where the main output is provided by a graphical display.

graphics tablet *Another name for* data tablet.

graphics workstation *See* workstation.

graph plotter *See* plotter.

graph rewrite system A set of rules, usually in the form of equations, that describe computations that may be carried out on *graphs; these take the form of changes that may be made to graphs (either finite or infinite).

gravity field An imaginary field placed around certain positions on a graphical display to aid user input. For example, when inputting a line drawing, existing end points of lines may have gravity fields associated with them that attract the *locator input device. As the device approaches the point it will therefore snap onto the point with the gravity field. A gravity field greatly assists the input of a connected set of lines for the operator, who only needs to get close to the desired position rather than identifying it precisely.

Gray Book A publication by the National Computer Security Center (*NCSC) that deals with the security aspects of subsystems intended to form secure parts of an overall secure system.

Gray code A binary (n, n) *block code having the following properties:

　　(a) there are 2^n codewords, each of length n bits;

　　(b) successive codewords differ by the complementation of a single bit, i.e. the *Hamming distance between them is unity.

A Gray code can be conveniently represented by its *transition sequence*, i.e. the ordered list of bit positions that change when moving from one codeword to the next. The *Good-de Bruijn graph of a Gray code forms a *Hamiltonian cycle. Gray codes are used in encoding the positions of shafts, wheels, etc., in order to avoid the problems that would arise when several digits were supposed to change at the same time.

gray importer A term used to describe a company that buys products retail in one country (typically the USA) and sells them in another (typically the UK), relying for its profit and its competitiveness on the different pricing policies in operation in the two countries. Thus, if a printer manufacturer sells a printer at US$500 retail in the USA, then it may well be priced at £500 (perhaps $800, depending on the current exchange rate) in the UK, if bought through an official importer. It is the difference between these prices that is exploited by the gray importer.

gray-level array An array of numbers, each of which represents the level of brightness in the corresponding area of a visual scene. The gray-level array might represent the output of a television camera or similar device.

gray-level image The image corresponding to a *gray-level array.

gray-scale A scale of variations in the *luminance value of "white" light from black to white. Shades of gray are defined as gray-scale graduations that differ by $\sqrt{2}$.

greatest common divisor (GCD) of two integers m and n. The largest integer, d, that exactly divides both m and n. If $d = 1$ then m and n are said to be *relatively prime*. For example, the GCD of 18 and 24 is 6; 21 and 25 are relatively prime.

greatest lower bound *See* lower bound.

greedy method An algorithm that, with a certain goal in mind, will attempt at every stage to do whatever it can, whenever it can, to get nearer to that goal immediately. In other words the method surrenders a possible longer-term advantage in favor of an immediate move toward the objective.

Green Book 1. The *coloured book defining the virtual terminal protocol used within the UK academic community.
2. *See* CD-ROM format standards.

Greibach normal form A restricted type of *context-free grammar, namely one in which all productions have the form
$$A \rightarrow bC_1 \ldots C_n$$
i.e. each right-hand side consists of a terminal followed by (zero or more) nonterminals. Any context-free language is generated by such a grammar, except that derivation of the empty string, Λ, requires the additional production
$$S \rightarrow \Lambda$$
One significance of this form is that it makes clear the existence of an equivalent *pushdown automaton: on reading b the PDA can pop A from the stack and push $C_1 \ldots C_n$.

Grey Book The *coloured book defining the electronic mail protocol used within the UK academic community. *See also* Gray Book.

grid *See* mesh.

Grosch's law The best known of many attempts to provide a measure of computer performance in terms of price, originally formulated by H. R. J. Grosch in 1953 as:
$$\text{performance} = \text{constant} \times \text{price}^2$$
Reliance on this law, which was approximately true at the time, led to the concept of "economy of scale", i.e. that large computers were less expensive per operation than small computers. Since that time other values of the exponent have been suggested: a good case can be made for the value 1 rather than 2. Current (LSI) technology has almost completely invalidated Grosch's law.

ground term (closed term) *See* term.

group A *set G on which there is defined a *dyadic operation $\circ$ (mapping $G \times G$ into G) that satisfies the following properties:

　　(a) $\circ$ is *associative;

(b) ∘ has an identity, i.e. there is a unique element e in G with the property that

$$x \circ e = e \circ x = x$$

for all x in G; e is called the *identity* of the group;

(c) *inverses* exist in G, i.e. for each x in G there is an inverse, denoted by x^{-1}, with the property that

$$x \circ x^{-1} = x^{-1} \circ x = e$$

These are the *group axioms*.

Certain kinds of groups are of particular interest. If the dyadic operation ∘ is *commutative, the group is said to be a *commutative group* or an *abelian group* (named for the Norwegian mathematician Niels Abel).

If there is only a finite number of elements n in the group, the group is said to be *finite*; n is then the *order* of the group. Finite groups can be represented or depicted by means of a *Cayley table.

If the group has a *generator then it is said to be *cyclic*; a cyclic group must be abelian.

The group is a very important *algebraic structure that underlies many other algebraic structures such as *rings and *fields. There are direct applications of groups in the study of symmetry, in the study of transformations and in particular *permutations, and also in error detecting and error correcting as well as in the design of fast adders.

Groups were originally introduced for solving an algebraic problem. By group theory it can be shown that algorithmic methods of a particular kind cannot exist for finding the roots of a general polynomial of degree greater than four. *See also* semigroup.

group code *Another name for* linear code.

group code recording (GCR) *See* disk format, tape format.

group graph A directed *graph that represents a finite *group; the vertices of the graph represent elements of the group and the edges represent *generators of the group. If edge E (representing generator g) joins vertices V and V' (representing group elements v and v' respectively) then

$$v \circ g = v'$$

where ∘ is the group operation. Each vertex of the group graph will have outdegree (*see*

degree) equal to the number of generators of the group.

group mark A notation within a record that indicates the start or finish of a group of related fields. In the case of repeated fields, the group mark often indicates the number of repetitions of such fields.

groupware Software that supports the cooperation of a group of people, usually working in a distributed environment.

Grzegorczyk hierarchy *See* hierarchy of functions.

gsm mapping *Short for* generalized sequential machine mapping. A function that is the response function of a generalized *sequential machine, and therefore generalizes the notion of *sequential function. Without constraining the machine to have a finite state-set, generalized sequentiality is equivalent to the following property of *initial subwords preservation*:

for all u,v in I^*, $f(uv)$ has the form $f(u)w$ for some w in O^*, where I^* and O^* are the sets of all input and output strings.

GUI *Abbrev. for* graphical user interface.

gulp *Rare* Several, usually two, *bytes.

hacker 1. A person who attempts to breach the *security of a computer system by access from a remote point, especially by guessing or otherwise obtaining a *password. The motive may be merely personal satisfaction, for example by endeavoring to access a system in another country, but it may occasionally have a sinister intent.

2. Originally, a person who had an instinctive knowledge enabling him or her to develop software apparently by trial and error.

hacking Unauthorized access to computer material. *See also* hacker, Computer Misuse Act 1990.

Hadamard codes *See* Hadamard matrices.

Hadamard matrices A family of matrices, a

Hadamard matrix H of order m being an $m \times m$ matrix, all of whose elements are either +1 or –1, and such that

$$H H^T = \lambda I$$

where H^T is the *transpose of H, I is the *identity matrix, and λ is a scalar quantity. They are usually written in "normalized" form, i.e. the rows and columns have been signed so that the top row and left column consist of +1 elements only. Hadamard matrices exist only for order $m = 1, 2,$ or $4r$ for some r. It is known that they exist for all orders $m = 2^s$. It is conjectured, but not known that they exist for all orders $m = 4r$.

The rows of any Hadamard matrix form an *orthonormal basis, from which property follows many of their applications in the theory of *codes, *digital signal processing, and statistical *sampling. When the order $m = 2^t$, they are called *Sylvester matrices*.

A Sylvester matrix has an equivalent matrix whose rows form a set of m-point *Walsh functions or, in a different arrangement, Paley functions. Various *linear *Hadamard codes* can be derived from a normalized Sylvester matrix in which +1 has been replaced by 0, and –1 by 1.

half adder *See* adder.

half duplex Involving or denoting a connection between two endpoints, either physical or logical, over which data may travel in both directions, but not both simultaneously. An important parameter of a half-duplex connection is the *turnaround time*, i.e. the time it takes to reverse the roles of sender and receiver. *See also* duplex, simplex.

half-height factor The physical dimensions of a piece of equipment with a *form factor such that two of them stacked on top of one another occupy the same space as a standard item such as a 5¼ inch disk drive.

halfplane The set of points to the left or right of a given line on a plane. A line divides a plane into two halfplanes.

half subtractor *See* subtractor.

halfsurface The set of points to the left or right of a given plane. A plane divides three-dimensional space into two halfsurfaces.

halftone A digital process used to create the effect of shading with a wide range of gray values or colors when only two-level pixel values or a much limited range of values is available. By varying the ratio of black to white pixels in each small area of the screen, the eye sees a continuous intensity at normal viewing distance due to the limited resolving power of the eye. (The printing industry uses dots of ink whose size or density varies.)

half word A unit of storage comprising half the number of bits in a computer's *word.

halt (or HALT) A program instruction that stops execution of the program. Originally a halt instruction actually halted the processor (hence the name), but now it more often causes a *trap into the operating system so that the operating system can take over control and, for example, start another program.

halting problem A *decision problem that was discovered and investigated by Alan Turing in 1936. Suppose M is a *Turing machine and let x be an input to M. If we start the machine running two things might happen: after a finite number of steps the machine might stop, or it might run on forever. Is there any way to test, given M and x, which of these two situations will occur? This is the halting problem. In fact there is no algorithm or effective procedure that, given any Turing machine and its input, will decide whether or not the calculation ever terminates.

Assuming the Church–Turing thesis, the halting problem is algorithmically unsolvable or undecidable. It is one example of many unsolvable problems in mathematics and computer science. It has profound practical implications: if it were solvable it would be possible to write a program tester that, given (say) any Pascal program and its input, would print "yes" if the program terminated after a finite number of steps and "no" if it did not. For any programming language that can define the *recursive functions, no such termination program exists.

Hamiltonian cycle (Hamilton cycle) A *cycle of a *graph in the course of which each vertex of the graph is visited once and once only.

Hamming bound (sphere-packing bound)

The theorem that the number, N, of codewords in a *binary *linear code is bounded by

$$N \le 2^n / \sum_{r=0}^{e} \binom{n}{r}$$

where the *code length is n digits, and the code is capable of correcting e errors. *See also* coding bounds, Gilbert–Varshamov bound.

Hamming codes A family of *binary *linear *perfect *error-correcting *block codes. They are capable of correcting any single error occurring in the block. Considered as (n, k) block codes, Hamming codes have

$$n = 2^m - 1, \quad k = n - m$$

where m characterizes the particular code. Where multiple-error-correcting abilities are required, Hamming codes may be generalized into *Bose-Chaudhuri-Hocquenghem (BCH) codes. The code was discovered by R. W. Hamming in 1950.

Hamming distance (Hamming metric) In the theory of *block codes intended for error detection or error correction, the Hamming distance $d(u, v)$ between two words u and v, of the same length, is equal to the number of symbol places in which the words differ from one another. If u and v are of finite length n then their Hamming distance is finite since

$$d(u, v) \le n$$

It can be called a distance since it is nonnegative, nil-reflexive, symmetric, and triangular:

$$0 \le d(u, v)$$
$$d(u, v) = 0 \quad \text{iff} \quad u = v$$
$$d(u, v) = d(v, u)$$
$$d(u, w) \le d(u, v) + d(v, w)$$

The Hamming distance is important in the theory of *error-correcting codes and *error-detecting codes: if, in a block code, the codewords are at a *minimum Hamming distance d* from one another, then

(a) if d is even, the code can detect $d - 1$ symbols in error and correct $\frac{1}{2}d - 1$ symbols in error;

(b) if d is odd, the code can detect $d - 1$ symbols in error and correct $\frac{1}{2}(d - 1)$ symbols in error.

See also Hamming space, perfect codes, coding theory, coding bounds, Hamming bound.

Hamming metric *Another name for* Hamming distance.

Hamming radius *See* Hamming space.

Hamming space In coding theory, a mathematical space in which words of some given length may be situated, the separation of points in the space being measured by the *Hamming distance. The dimensionality of the space is equal to the number of digits in the words; the coordinate in each dimension is given by each successive digit in the words.

The *Hamming sphere* is the set of all words in Hamming space whose Hamming distance from some given word (the "center") does not exceed some given value (the *Hamming radius*).

Hamming sphere *See* Hamming space.

Hamming weight In coding theory, the number of nonzero digits in a word. It is numerically identical with the *Hamming distance between the word in question and the *zero word.

handle A means of uniquely identifying an object, or a property of an object. In programming, a handle is a *pointer to a pointer to a variable. This level of indirection can simplify the passing of references to the variable between parts of the program. In a graphical environment, a handle is a marker associated with an image. One very common form is as a small square in the border of a *window: different handles may be used to *drag the window, so changing its position, to reshape the window, so changing its aspect ratio, or to rescale the window, so changing the size of its contents. *See also* bottom-up parsing.

handshake (or handshaking) An exchange of signals that establishes communications between two or more devices. The handshake synchronizes the devices and allows data to be transferred successfully. The signals have various meanings, including

"I am waiting to transmit."
"I am ready to receive."
"I am not ready to receive."
"I am switched on."
"The data is available."
"Data has been read successfully."

See also asynchronous interface.

hands off *See* hands on.

hands on A mode of operation of a system in which an operator is in control. The operator literally has hands on a keyboard and other switches to control the processes to be carried out by the system. The dependence on the capability of the operator to run a medium-size or large computer has been reduced by the introduction of supervisor programs or operating systems.

When no operator intervention is required the mode of operation can be described as *hands off*.

hang-up 1. A state in which a program has come to an unexpected halt, e.g. because it is trying to read data from a device that is not connected to the processor.
2. In the context of time-sharing systems, the signal received by the program when a remote terminal breaks its connection ("hangs up the telephone").

Hanoi *See* Towers of Hanoi.

hard copy A printed or otherwise permanent copy of data from a processing system.

hard disk 1. A *magnetic disk consisting of a rigid aluminum substrate coated or plated – usually on both sides – with a magnetic material. Hard disk is used as a generic term and includes the magnetic disks used in *Winchester technology. *Compare* floppy disk, optical disk.
2. A disk permanently mounted in its drive; in certain circumstances disk plus drive may be demountable.

hard return In word processing, the action prompted by the "Enter" or *carriage return key and used, for example, to mark the end of a paragraph; it causes a new line to be started at that point in the text. Other new lines will be inserted where necessary throughout the paragraph by the word-processing program to avoid text exceeding the right-hand margin; these are *soft returns*, and will normally be moved around automatically as the text is modified.

hard-sectored disk *See* sector.

hardware The physical portion of a computer system, including the electrical/electronic components (e.g. devices and circuits), electromechanical components (e.g. a disk drive), and mechanical (e.g. cabinet) components. *Compare* software.

hardware character generation A technique whereby a device such as a *VDU, printer, or plotter will, on receipt of certain codes, display characters of a style and size determined by the device's internal circuitry. The computer driving the peripheral specifies only which character is to be displayed; it has no control over the individual *pixels that make up the character.

hardware circuitry *See* logic circuit.

hardware description An unambiguous method of describing the interconnection and behavior of the electrical and electronic subset of the computer hardware. There are a number of computer hardware description languages (*see* CHDL).

hardware maintenance *See* maintenance.

hardware reliability A statement of the ability of hardware to perform its functions for some period of time. It is usually expressed as MTBF (mean time between failures).

hardware security The use of hardware, e.g. *bounds registers or *locks and keys, to assist in providing computer security.

hardwired Denoting circuits that are permanently interconnected to perform a specific function, as distinct from circuits addressed by software in a program and therefore capable of performing a variety of functions.

Harvard Mark I The name given at Harvard University to the Automatic Sequence Controlled Calculator (ASCC), an electromechanical computer based on the ideas of Harvard's Howard H. Aiken. This machine, which performed calculations using rotating shafts, gears, and cams, following a sequence of instructions on paper tape, was started in 1937; it was financed by IBM, built in collaboration with IBM engineers at their laboratories in Massachusetts, and became operational at Harvard in 1944. It was donated by IBM to Harvard later that year. The Mark I was used by the US navy for ballistics and ship design. Aiken's Harvard Mark II, based on electrical relays, was operational in Sept. 1948.

hash function *See* hashing algorithm, hashing.

hashing A technique that is used for organizing tables to permit rapid *searching or *table lookup, and is particularly useful for tables to which items are added in an unpredictable manner, e.g. the symbol table of a compiler. Each item to be placed in the table has a unique *key*. To place it in the *hash table* a *hash function* is used, which maps the keys onto a set of integers (the *hash values*) that range over the table size. The function is chosen to distribute the keys fairly evenly over the table (*see* hashing algorithm); since it is not a unique mapping, two different keys may map onto the same integer.

In the simplest version of the technique, the hash value identifies a primary position in the table; if this is already occupied, successive positions are examined until a free one is found (treating the table as circular). The item with its key is inserted in the table at this position. To locate an item in the table a similar algorithm is used. The hash value of the key is computed and the table entry at this position is examined. If the key matches the required key, the item has been located; if not, successive table positions are examined until either an entry with a matching key is found or an empty position is found. In the latter case it can be concluded that the key does not exist in the table, since the insertion procedure would have placed it in this empty position. For the technique to work, there must be rather more table positions than there are entries to be accommodated. Provided that the table is not more than 60% full, an item can on average be located in a hash table by examining at most two table positions.

More sophisticated techniques can be used to deal with the problem of *collisions*, which occur when the position indicated by the hash value is already occupied; this improves even further the performance of the table lookup. Table lookup and insertion of new items can be interleaved, but if items are deleted from the table the space they occupied cannot normally be reused.

hashing algorithm An algorithm that, for a given key k, yields a function $f(k)$; this in turn yields the starting point for a *hash search* for the key k. The function f is called the *hash function*. A typical hash function is the remainder modulo p, where p is a prime,

$$f(k) \equiv k \pmod{p}$$

where k is interpreted as an integer. Another hash function uses a constant A and defines $f(k)$ as the leading bits of the least significant half of the product Ak. *See also* hashing.

hash P complete *See* counting problem.

hash search *See* hashing algorithm.

hash table *See* hashing.

hash total A number produced by adding together (or otherwise combining) corresponding fields over all the records of a file, when such a total does not have any external meaning but is used solely to verify the records in the file. The hash total is amended whenever a change occurs to the relevant field; the file is verified by recomputing the hash total, and any corruption to the values in the field will be shown by a discrepancy between the stored total and the recomputed total. *See also* control record.

hash value *See* hashing.

Hatley–Pirbhai A particular variant of *structured systems analysis developed by Derek Hatley and Imtiaz Pirbhai for use in real-time systems development. In addition to the techniques used in structured systems analysis, Hatley–Pirbhai introduces the concept of control bars in dataflow diagrams described by state-transition diagrams.

Hayes command set A set of modem control commands originated by the Hayes Corp. but now supported by virtually all modem suppliers. The commands all start with the character group AT followed by specific characters for controlling all aspects of the set-up and data flow through a modem. Such modems are said to be *Hayes-compatible* or *Hayes modems*.

Hayes-compatible, Hayes modem *See* Hayes command set.

hazard 1. A situation or event whose realization has the potential for damage to human life, society, the economy, or the environment. *See also* hazard and operability study.

2. A potential or actual malfunction of a *logic circuit during change(s) of state of input variables. Hazards result from the non-ideal behavior of actual switching elements, e.g. noninstantaneous operation, turn-on time different from turn-off time.

In the UK the word hazard is sometimes used as the equivalent of *race condition.

hazard and operability study (HAZOP) A systematic investigation covering all stages of the life cycle, whose purpose is to identify all possible situations that could lead to hazards (which have been previously identified) in a particular system, taking into account the environment in which it must operate. Usually the study involves the investigation of previous disasters or similar situations, using these to indicate areas of particular attention.

HAZOP *Acronym for* hazard and operability study.

HCI *Abbrev. for* human–computer interface (or interaction).

HD *Abbrev. for* high density, in floppy–disk recording.

HDD *Abbrev. for* hard disk drive. *See* disk drive.

HDLC *Abbrev. for* high-level data link control. A *data link control protocol developed by ISO in response to IBM's *SDLC protocol, which is a subset of HDLC. CCITT defined a different subset of HDLC (*see* LAP) as the second (data link) layer of the X25 protocol.

HDTV *Abbrev. for* high-definition television system. A new television format that produces images of similar quality to 35 mm film. The screen size will normally be on 56 inch tubes or larger, with at least 1100 scan lines. Several different formats are currently under development.

head 1. The part of a peripheral mechanism that is in contact with the medium or very close to it and that is directly responsible for writing data or patterns onto the medium or for reading or erasing them. The word is most frequently used of a *magnetic head* in a *disk drive or tape transport (*see* magnetic tape), an *optical head* in an optical storage device, or a *print head* in a *serial printer. *See also* read/write head.

2. (headend) One end of a transmission medi-um. The head has some form of control over the contents of the medium and of access to it. *See also* DQDN, broadband coaxial system.

3. (header) The part of a *cell or *packet that contains routing and control information used to control the passage of the cell or packet across a *packet switching network. *See also* frame relay, cell relay.

4. The first item in a *list.

head crash The accidental and disastrous contact of a *read/write head with the surface of a hard disk as it rotates in a *disk drive. Normally the head flies just above the surface. The disk has to be thrown away after a head crash as the head is much larger than the track spacing and the contact destroys the track so affected – and any data stored in that track and adjacent tracks. A head crash is often caused by the head passing over a dust grain on the surface. Particles of surface material produced by the contact cause other tracks to be destroyed.

The possibility of a head crash is reduced by keeping the disk clean and at a constant temperature and humidity. Disks are copied at regular intervals so that in the event of a crash a duplicate is available. *Fixed disk drives have greatly reduced the probability of a head crash because they are sealed (except for a "breather" filter) and have an internal filter through which the air inside the drive circulates.

headend *See* head.

header Some coded information that precedes a more general collection of data and gives details about it.

The header of a data-structure representation is logically distinct from the data elements themselves and may serve several purposes:

(a) to hold global information about the whole structure, e.g. list length, array index bounds;

(b) to represent an empty structure;

(c) to provide links into the structure, e.g. pointers to first and last nodes in a list;

(d) to represent the entire structure in any other data structures of which it may be a part.

In networking, the header (or head) of a cell or packet is the part that holds routing and control information used to control the passage of the cell or packet across a network.

head-mounted display (HMD) A headset with two stereoscopic images that give the person wearing the device a three-dimensional view of a virtual scene.

head-per-track drive *See* fixed head.

heap 1. An area of storage used for the allocation of data structures where the order of releasing the allocated data structure is indeterminate. *Compare* stack.

2. A *complete binary tree in which the value at each node is at least as large as the values at its children (if they exist).

heapsort A sorting algorithm developed by Williams and Floyd in 1964 and employing the ideas of *tree selection. It is more efficient for larger numbers of records but on average is inferior to *quicksort. However, the worst possible distribution of keys does not cause the efficiency of heapsort to deteriorate too much. The worst case for quicksort can then be worse. Some of the ideas of heapsort are relevant to *priority queue applications.

height 1. of a node in a tree. The length of a longest path from the node to a *leaf node.

2. of a tree. The maximum height of any node in a tree. The height of a given tree will have the same numerical value as the *depth of that tree.

height-balanced *See* balanced, AVL tree.

helical scan A method of using magnetic tape, derived from video recording, in which the tape is wrapped in a helical path around a rotating drum so that one or more heads embedded in the drum record diagonal tracks on the tape. The tape is moved slowly so that a separate track is recorded at each pass of a head.

Helical scan allows data to be recorded at a very high density and hence at very low storage cost. When first introduced (using standard video cartridges) the error rates were too high for general use. More recently powerful error-correcting codes have been introduced, and in this form the method is suitable for backing up hard disks and for short-term archiving (long-term stability has yet to be proved). The *digital audio tape (DAT) cartridge is popular for this purpose; larger cartridges with capacities of tens of gigabytes are also in use.

help desk A location where queries by phone, e-mail, fax, personal callers, etc., are dealt with by human staff, usually assisted by computer software. Large commercial help desks operate almost entirely by phone, while smaller help desks internal to organizations may have predominantly personal callers. There are a number of models of help desk: *unskilled*, where all queries are passed on, *skilled*, where up to 90% of the queries are answered at the desk, and *expert*, where all queries are expected to be answered at the desk. Which model is used depends on how broad or specialized are the topics covered by the desk, and what staff are available.

Help-desk software is used to keep track of help-desk queries. The software will allow the details of the problem to be entered, and its progress to be monitored as it is passed from the desk to one or more specialists. It will also help to ensure that all problems are eventually answered, and that the details of the solution are stored to assist in the solution of future problems.

help system The part of an interactive system responsible for providing the user with information about the workings of the program on request. Help can be obtained in a number of ways: by typing the word "help", by pressing a particular *function key on the keyboard, or by using a mouse or other pointing device to select a "help" item from a menu. Help can be hierarchical, where each topic has subtopics that can be explored down to an arbitrary number of levels, or context-sensitive, where the information provided is appropriate to the part of the program currently being used. Some help systems can be browsed through like a manual. A particular system may combine any or all of these methods. A good help system is a crucial feature of any nontrivial program.

hemi cube A half-cube that defines the half-space above the surface of interest used as a projection surface.

He model An illumination model that includes directional diffuse and ideal specular terms to account for surface reflection plus an ideal diffuse component to accommodate subsurface scattering (*see* diffuse reflection, specular reflection).

Hermite interpolation *See* interpolation.

hertz (symbol: Hz) The SI unit of *frequency. A periodic phenomenon has a frequency of one hertz if each cycle of the phenomenon repeats itself in a period of one second. A *megahertz* (MHz) is one million (10^6) hertz.

heuristic A "rule of thumb", based on *domain knowledge from a particular application, that gives guidance in the solution of a problem. Unlike algorithms, heuristics cannot have proven performance bounds owing to their open-ended dependence on specific application knowledge; an example is 'if the sky is cloudy then carry an umbrella.' Heuristics may thus be very valuable most of the time but their results or performance cannot be guaranteed.

heuristic search A search process that uses *domain knowledge in *heuristic rules or procedures to direct the progress of a search algorithm. It has the effect of pruning the search space and is used in applications where a *combinatorial explosion means that an *exhaustive search is not possible.

Hewlett–Packard A manufacturer of electronic instruments, calculators, data-gathering equipment, medical equipment, and high-performance workstations, based in California. It is noted as the first manufacturer of a hand-held calculator. It is a major developer of software for use in its own products and has exploited this fact by marketing development tools for its own workstations. In terms of revenue, it is the fourth largest IT company in the world (1993 figures).

hex *Short for* hexadecimal.

hexadecimal notation The representation of numbers in the positional number system with base 16. The sixteen hexadecimal digits are usually represented by 0–9, A–F. Any hex number can be simply converted into its binary equivalent, and any binary number into its shorter hex equivalent.

hex pad A *keypad with 16 keys that are labeled 0–9, A–F so that they correspond to *hexadecimal notation.

hidden-line/hidden-surface removal (HLHSR) Removal of those parts of a scene that are obscured by objects nearer to the viewer. There is a whole range of methods for doing this operation. The *Z-buffer is often used to hold depth information concerning objects. *See* hidden-line removal, hidden-surface removal.

hidden-line removal An algorithm used in computer graphics to determine which lines should not be visible when a three-dimensional surface is displayed.

hidden-surface removal The process of eliminating the representation of surfaces in three-dimensional graphics that would be obscured by opaque foreground surfaces if photographed by a hypothetical camera.

hierarchical addressing *See* addressing.

hierarchical B-splines A sequence of *B-splines where the next in the sequence has a defined relationship to the previous one; it may, for example, be twice as fine. Hierarchical B-splines are used in adapting functions to local detail (*see also* wavelets).

hierarchical class structure *See* object-oriented programming.

hierarchical cluster analysis *See* cluster analysis.

hierarchical communication system 1. A physical organization of communications facilities, each higher level covering a wider or more general area of operation than the next lower level. As an example, a large bank might have a *local area network within each branch, connecting the teller stations. Several branches might be linked to a data *concentrator, connected to regional concentrators, which in turn link to the bank's main data processing center.
2. A logical organization of communication facilities, in which the lowest levels deal with the physical network while higher levels deal with the communication between specific applications. *See also* protocol.

hierarchical database system A *database management system that implements the *hierarchical data model. The best-known hierarchical DBMS is *IMS.

hierarchical data model A *data model based on one–many relationships between aggregations of fixed numbers of data items, such an aggregation being termed a *segment*. A database record type comprises a number of segment types, arranged in a hierarchy, commencing with the root segment type; below the root segment type there is zero, one, or more segment types at the first level, with a similar structure below each of these first-level types at the second level, and so on. Thus each segment type except the root is dependent on a segment type at the immediately higher level. A database record instance comprises a single instance of the root segment type and zero, one, or more instances of each of its types at the first level. Corresponding to each of these first-level instances, there will be zero, one, or more instances of each of the appropriate second-level types, and so on. Only the root segment can have an independent existence.

IMS, an important database management system supplied by IBM, is based on and implements this data model.

hierarchical encoding A method of image coding that represents an image using a sequence of *frames of information. The first frame is followed by frames that code the differences between the source data and the reconstructed data from the previous frames for that image. Hierarchical encoding is one of the options in the *JPEG standard.

hierarchical memory structure *See* memory hierarchy.

hierarchical radiosity *Radiosity specifications where a coarse level of detail is used to model the interaction between distant objects and a fine level of detail for near objects (*see also* wavelets).

hierarchy A set of entities that are partially ordered; the word is frequently misused. *See* partial ordering.

hierarchy of functions A sequence of sets of functions F_0, F_1, F_2,... with the property that

$$F_0 \subseteq F_1 \subseteq F_2 \subseteq \ ...$$

(*see* subset). Typically the functions in F_0 will include certain initial functions; the sets of functions F_1, F_2,... are normally defined by combining initial functions in some way.

Hierarchies of *primitive recursive functions can be defined by letting F_i represent those functions that can be computed by programs containing at most i loops nested one within the other. Then

$$F_i \subseteq F_{i+1}$$

for all integers $i > 0$. The *union of all these sets includes all the primitive recursive functions and only those functions. Consequently the hierarchy is often called a *subrecursive hierarchy*. This same hierarchy can be expressed in a slightly different form, so resulting in the *Grzegorczyk hierarchy*.

In an attempt to circumvent problems caused by *recursion, Bertrand Russell invented a *theory of types*, which essentially imposed a hierarchy on the set of functions; functions at one level could be defined only in terms of functions at lower levels.

The study of hierarchies of functions dates from work of David Hilbert around 1926 on the foundations of mathematics. More recent interest stems from their applicability to computational *complexity.

higher-order term *See* term.

high-level design (architectural design) *See* program decomposition, program design, system design.

high-level language A variety of programming language in which the *control and *data structures reflect the requirements of the problem rather than the facilities actually provided by the hardware. A high-level language is translated into *machine code by a *compiler.

high-level scheduler *See* scheduler.

highlight 1. The portion of light from a surface that is due to *specular reflection and transmission.
2. *See* highlighting.

highlighting A way of making a portion of a document stand out. The actual effect used can normally be defined by the user, but usually a *default technique is available such as boldface type, reverse video, or contrasting color.

high-order language *Another name for* high-level language, used only by the US Department of Defense.

high-pass filter A *filtering device that permits only those components in the *Fourier transform domain whose frequencies lie above some critical value to pass through with little attenuation, all other components being highly attenuated.

High Sierra standard A standard defining the format of data files recorded on CD-ROM, now superseded by ISO 9660. The name derives from the place where the steering committee first met. *See* CD-ROM format standards.

highway *Another (UK) name for* bus.

hill climbing A fast but sometimes unreliable *optimization method. When searching for the minimum/maximum value of a function a random step is taken; if the value improves it replaces the current value, then another random step is taken. This method is fast and relatively easy to program but does not allow *backtracking and therefore can become trapped on local minima/maxima in the search space.

A *heuristic variation uses an *evaluation function to examine and select the best successor from the current position. This produces a faster ascent through the problem space.

hi res *Short for* high resolution (often not very high *resolution but rather better than the lowest resolution).

histogram A chart showing the *relative frequencies with which a measurable quantity takes values in a set of contiguous intervals. The chart consists of rectangles whose areas are proportional to the relative frequencies and whose widths are proportional to the class intervals. It can be used to picture a *frequency distribution.

hit rate 1. The fraction of references to one level of the *memory hierarchy that must otherwise be fulfilled in the less accessible

levels within the hierarchy. Thus for a *cache memory the hit rate is the fraction of references that do not result in access to main memory. For a *page the hit rate is the fraction of references that do not result in a page turn.

2. The proportion of records or blocks on a file that are retrieved or updated in a batch run or in a given period of time.

HLHSR *Abbrev. for* hidden-line/hidden-surface removal.

HLS color model A *color model that defines colors by the three parameters *hue (H), lightness (L), and *saturation (S). It was introduced by Tektronix Inc. Hue lies on a circle, saturation increases from center to edge of this circle, lightness goes from black to white. This model uses the same hue plane as the *HSV model, but it replaces value (V) by an extended lightness axis so that the maximum *color gamut is at L=0.5 and decreases in each direction towards white (L=1) and black (L=0). The HLS color model is represented by a double hexagonal cone, with white at the top apex and black at the bottom.

HMD *Abbrev. for* head-mounted display.

HMI *Abbrev.* for human-machine interface. *See* human-computer interface.

HMOS A name applied by Intel Corp. to high-speed MOS technology, usually NMOS although it can be used in CMOS. HMOS implies both a short channel between source and drain, and also design (layout) rules that deal with minimum feature size of less than two micrometers.

Hoare logic A formalism for partial correctness proofs (*see* program correctness proof). Sentences have the form

$$\{p\} \ S \ \{q\}$$

where p and q are assertions and S is a program. The meaning of such a sentence is that, starting from a state in which p is true, if S terminates it will result in a state in which q is true; p is a *precondition and q is a *postcondition for S. A Hoare logic for a particular programming language comprises a system of axioms and rules for deducing such sentences from other simpler ones. By repeated use of these rules it is possible ultimately to derive facts about an entire program, starting from facts about its smallest constituents. Like the *Floyd method however, the approach requires judicious choice of loop *invariants. As another application, Hoare logics can be taken as *axiomatic semantics for programming languages. The theory of Hoare logic is determined by the assertion language for writing the pre- and postconditions (such as predicate logic) and the programming language (such as **while** programs). Many remarkable insights into program correctness have been obtained from the mathematical study of Hoare logic.

HOL A system for specifying, designing, and verifying the design of digital systems; it was devised at Cambridge University, UK. The HOL system includes a theorem prover, an editor, and consistency checkers. The HOL specification language has basic types that handle n-bit digital numbers, the natural numbers, and the Boolean values true/false. More complex types can be built by binding together the basic types. A library of functions and list operators is used to perform transformations on variables.

hold time The length of time for which a signal must be held constant on a *bus, following the instant when all devices using the signal have nominally responded to its presence.

Hollerith code A code for relating alphanumeric characters to holes in a punched card. It was devised by Herman Hollerith in 1888 and enabled the letters of the alphabet and the digits 0–9 to be encoded by a combination of punchings in 12 rows of a card.

holographic memory A storage device that records binary information in the form of holograms, which are produced (as interference patterns) on photographic or photochromic media by means of laser beams, and are read by means of low-power laser beams. The advantage of a hologram is the way in which the image is dispersed over the recording surface so that dust or scratches do not totally obscure data though they may reduce the contrast. Several projects have attempted to apply this technology but none have been commercially successful.

holographic scanner A type of *scanner in which a beam of light (usually from a laser) is deflected by a rotating hologram so that it scans a plane in a multitude of directions. Some of the light reflected from an object on or close to the plane is returned via the hologram and brought to focus on a sensor. The most widely known use is for reading *bar codes at retail checkouts.

home page The first page (loosely the first screen) of information that is retrieved when the use of a URL on the *World Wide Web leads to a new *server. The home page typically contains introductory information about the facility that has been accessed, together with links to the actual details of services or information.

homogeneous coordinates A coordinate system that algebraically treats all points in the projective plane (both Euclidean and ideal) equally. For example, the standard homogeneous coordinates $[p_1, p_2, p_3]$ of a point P in the projective plane are of the form $[x, y, 1]$ if P is a point in the Euclidean plane $z=1$ whose Cartesian coordinates are $(x, y, 1)$, or are of the form $[a, b, 0]$ if P is the ideal point – the point at infinity – associated to all lines in the Euclidean plane $z=1$ with direction numbers $a, b, 0$. Homogeneous coordinates are so called because they treat Euclidean and ideal points in the same way.

Homogeneous coordinates are widely used in computer graphics because they enable affine and projective transformations to be described as matrix manipulations in a coherent way.

homomorphic image of a formal language. *See* homomorphism.

homomorphism A structure-preserving mapping between *algebras. A homomorphism allows the modeling, simulation, or representation of the structure of one algebra within another, possibly in a limited form. Let A and B be algebras and h a function from A to B. Suppose that A contains an n-ary operation f_A, while B contains a corresponding operation f_B. If h is a homomorphism it must satisfy

$$h(f_A(a_1, \ldots, a_k)) = f_B(h(a_1), \ldots, h(a_k))$$

for all elements $a_1,...,a_k$ of A and every "corresponding" pair of operations of A and B.

The idea that f_A and f_B are "corresponding" operations is made precise by saying that A and B are algebras over the same *signature Σ, while f is an operation symbol in Σ with which A and B associate the operations f_A and f_B respectively. A homomorphism from A to B is any function h from A to B that satisfies the condition given above for each f in Σ. As applications of this idea, the semantic functions involved in *denotational semantics can be viewed as homomorphisms from algebras of syntax to algebras of semantic objects. Usually, to define a semantic function by induction on terms is to define a homomorphism on a term algebra. In several important cases, compilers can be designed as homomorphisms between two algebras of programs.

Special cases of this general definition occur when A and B belong to one of the familiar classes of algebraic structures. For example, let A and B be *monoids, with *binary operations $\circ_A$ and $\circ_B$ and *identity elements e_A and e_B. Then, rewriting the general condition above, a homomorphism from A to B satisfies

$$h(x \circ_A y) = h(x) \circ_B h(y)$$
$$h(e_A) = e_B$$

A further specialization from *formal language theory arises with monoids of *words, where the binary operation is *concatenation and the nullary operation is the empty word. Let S and T be alphabets, and let h be a function from S to T^*, i.e. a function that gives a T-word for each symbol in S. Then h can be extended to S-words, by concatenating its values on individual symbols:

$$h(s_1,...,s_n) = h(s_1),...,h(s_n)$$

This extension of h gives a monoid homomorphism from S^* to T^*. Such an h is said to be Λ-free if it gives a nonempty T-word for each symbol in S.

h can be further extended to a mapping on languages, giving, for any subset L of S^*, its homomorphic image $h(L)$:

$$h(L) = \{h(w) \mid w \in L\}$$

Similarly the inverse homomorphic image of $L \subseteq T^*$ is

$$h^{-1}(L) = \{w \mid h(w) \in L\}$$

These language-mappings are also homomorphisms, between the monoids of languages over S and over T, the binary operation being concatenation of languages.

HOOD *Acronym for* hierarchical object-oriented design. HOOD was developed specifically for the European Space Agency and very closely follows the structure of the *Ada programming language. It provides diagram notations to depict nested *packages and tasks; it also provides specification of these items in terms of procedures, functions, variables, types, etc. It indicates how higher-level *objects are decomposed into lower-level objects and also how the interface of the high-level object is mapped to the interface(s) of lower-level objects.

hook into *Informal* To make a connection to a network, or to a specific device or service on a network.

hop *See* store-and-forward. *See also* flow control.

HOPE A *functional language, one of the first such languages to be widely used.

horizon effect In computer game playing or other search processes, a large search tree has to be explored. It is usual to set a maximum depth limit (D) beyond which it is considered uneconomic to search further. The horizon effect refers to the fact that interesting results will always exist beyond any depth D and therefore in any given search will not be discovered. Variable *evaluation functions and dynamic search-depth controls have been used in attempts to deal with this problem.

horizontal check *See* cyclic redundancy check.

horizontal microinstruction *See* microprogramming.

horizontal recording *See* magnetic encoding.

Horn clause In the clausal form of logic, an expression of the form

A if B_1 and B_2 and ... and B_n

This should be contrasted with the general form of clause

A_1 or A_2 or ... or A_m
if
B_1 and B_2 and ... and B_n

where $A_1 \ldots A_m$ are the alternative conclusions and $B_1 \ldots B_n$ are the joint conditions. A Horn clause is a special case of this general form in that it contains at most one conclusion.

Horn clauses were first investigated by the logician Alfred Horn. The majority of formalisms employed in computer programming bear greater resemblance to Horn clauses than to the more general form. The logic programming language *Prolog is based upon the Horn clause subset of logic.

Horner's method An algorithm for evaluating a *polynomial by adding brackets in such a way that no powers greater than one need be evaluated. This reduces the number of evaluations. The polynomial, in effect, ends up in the following form:

$$p(x) = [\ldots((anx + a(n-1))x + a(n-2))x \ldots a]x + a0$$

host computer (host) 1. A computer that is attached to a *network and provides services other than simply acting as a *store-and-forward processor or communication switch. Host computers range in size from small microcomputers to large time-sharing or batch mainframes. Many networks have a hierarchical structure, with a *communication subnetwork providing *packet-switching services for host computers to support time-sharing, remote job entry, etc. A host computer at one level of a hierarchy may function as a packet or message switch at another. 2. A computer used to develop software for execution on another computer, known as the *target computer*. 3. A computer used to emulate another computer, known as the *target computer*. *See also* emulation.

host language *See* database language.

hot key 1. A key or combination of keys on a computer keyboard that has been programmed to cause an immediate change in the operating environment, such as the execution of a *pop-up program. 2. To use such a key.

hot link 1. A technique for ensuring that when one object is embedded in another, the latest version of the embedded object is always seen (*see* embedding). This is achieved by using a reference to the embedded object rather than a copy of it. For instance if part of a spreadsheet were embedded in a word-processor document, a hot link would ensure that if the spreadsheet were updated, the changes would also appear in the document. *See also* object linking and embedding. 2. A word or phrase in a *hypertext document that when selected using a mouse or cursor keys causes information relevant to the word or phrase to be displayed. If this were a hypertext dictionary, selecting "*hypertext" above would cause the appropriate definition to be displayed. The hot link is usually *highlighted in some way.

housekeeping Actions performed within a program or system in order to maintain internal orderliness rather than to address the externally imposed requirements. For example, the housekeeping of a program often includes *memory management.

HPF *Abbrev. for* highest priority first. Where several *processes are free to proceed, the *scheduler will initiate the process that has been assigned the highest priority.

HP-PA *Trademark; abbrev. for* Hewlett–Packard precision architecture. *See* RISC.

HSI *Abbrev. for* human-system interface. *See* human-computer interface.

HSV color model A *color model that defines colors by the three parameters *hue (H), *saturation (S), and value (V). The HSV color model is an inverted hexagonal cone with black at the apex (V=0) and white at the center (V=1) of the hexagonal base. The three primary (red, green, blue) and three secondary (cyan, magenta, yellow) hues are located at the vertices of the hexagon. *See also* HLS color model.

HTML *Abbrev. for* hypertext mark-up language.

HTTP *Abbrev. for* hypertext transport protocol. An application-level protocol with the lightness and speed necessary for distributed collaborative hypermedia information systems. It is generic, stateless, and object-oriented, with typing and negotiation of data representation, allowing systems to be built independently of the data being transferred. By extension of its request methods (commands), it can be used for many tasks, such as name servers and distributed object-management systems. HTTP has been in use by the *World Wide Web since 1990.

hub In general, a unit that operates in some sense as the center of a star configuration. In the case of a network, a hub acts as a local concentrator that allows a number of devices, connected to the hub in a star configuration, to connect to a network with an arbitrary configuration. In the special case of an *Ethernet network, a hub may refer to a device that provides connection for a number of end-user devices, each using a dedicated *twisted-pair (*CAT-3 or CAT-5 cables) local connection, to an Ethernet segment running on either a coaxial cable (*thick or thin Ethernet) or an optical fiber.

hub polling *See* polling.

hue The perceived main wavelength of light defining a color. White, gray, and black may be considered as colors but not hues.

Huffman encoding A (usually) *binary encoding of the elements of a finite set, A,

$$A = \{a_1, a_2, \ldots, a_n\}$$

where each element a_i in A has an assumed probability p_i of occurring in a message. The binary encoding satisfies the *prefix property and is such that messages will have a minimum expected length. Thus an element a_i with a high probability of occurring in a message is encoded as a short binary string while an element with a low probability of occurring is encoded with a longer string. *See also* source coding.

human-computer interface (HCI) The means of communication between a human user and a computer system, referring in particular to the use of input/output devices with supporting software. Devices of increasing sophistication are becoming available to mediate the human-computer interaction. These include graphics devices, touch-sensitive devices, and voice-input devices. They have to be configured in a way that will facilitate an efficient and desirable interaction between a person and the computer. *Artificial intelligence techniques of knowledge representation may be used to model

the user of a computer system, and so offer the opportunity to give personalized advice on its use. The design of the machine interface may incorporate *expert-system techniques to offer powerful *knowledge-based computing to the user.

HCI is a branch of the science of ergonomics, and is concerned especially with the relationship between workstations and their operators. The aim is to develop acceptable standards for such aspects as display resolution, use of color, and navigation around an application.

The terms *human-system interface* (HSI), *human-machine interface* (HMI), and *man-machine interface* (MMI) are all used as synonyms.

hybrid computer A computer (system) that contains both a digital and an analog computer. The digital computer usually serves as the controller and provides logical operations; the analog computer normally serves as a solver of differential equations.

hybrid integrated circuit A complete electronic circuit that is fabricated on an insulating substrate using a variety of device technologies. The substrate acts as a carrier for the circuit and also has the interconnecting tracks between devices printed on it by multilayer techniques (*see* multilayer device). Individual devices, which comprise chip diodes, transistors, integrated circuits, and thick-film resistors and capacitors and which form the circuit function, are attached to the substrate and are connected together using the previously defined interconnecting tracks.

HyperCard *Trademark* A software system originally developed for the Apple Macintosh family of computers and based on the concept of *stacks. It uses the *wimp interface to switch between, select from, and structure *objects on screen and in the underlying database, and to pass messages between objects. New data can be entered into objects, for example a diary. A new application can be constructed by manipulating objects on screen: there is no need to program in the conventional sense, although a *scripting language, *HyperTalk*, is provided. Hyper-

Card has been used to implement *hypertext-style systems and facilitates the authoring of multimedia applications.

hypercube In its simplest form, a four-dimensional cube, which can be considered as two three-dimensional cubes connected at equivalent corners. Connecting the corners of four-dimensional cubes gives a five-dimensional hypercube. In general, an $(n+1)$-dimensional hypercube can be generated by connecting the corners of n-dimensional hypercubes, and has twice as many corners as the n-dimensional hypercube.

Several *multiprocessing systems have an architecture based on the hypercube, where processors replace corners and communication links replace edges. In an n-dimensional hypercube network, no processor is more than n links from any other processor; doubling the number of processors by using an $(n+1)$-dimensional network means information has to travel over only one additional connection. However, as the number of processors increases, the number of connections each one must make has also to be increased.

hyperedge *See* hypergraph.

hypergraph A generalization of the concept of a *graph in which each edge is associated not with the normal two vertices but with an ordered set of n vertices; such an edge is known as a *hyperedge* and n is the *type* of that edge. The hyperedges thus relate an arbitrary number of vertices in a given subset of the graph.

hypermedia An extension of *hypertext to include multimedia, i.e. graphics, video, and audio as well as textual material.

hypertext A generic term covering a number of techniques used to create and view multi-dimensional documents, which may be entered at many points and which may be browsed in any order by interactively choosing words or key phrases as search parameters for the next text image to be viewed (*see* hot link). Generally a *wimp style interface is used and tools are provided to help structure the text, create indexes of the text of a document, and to cross-reference between

documents. The technique is related to full-text database systems.

The concept can be explained by example. A novel can be considered to be a document in a single dimension, normally read from start to finish sequentially. An encyclopedia is an example of a multidimensional document that is read in small parts only, and the part to be read is selected from and the encyclopedia entered via an index. Information relevant to a word or phrase in the encyclopedia entry can be displayed by means of a hot link. For the encyclopedia the order of reading is often controlled by an association of ideas by the reader.

Hypertext systems provide facilities for windowing viewed text, selecting next view by mouse/keyboard marking of text fragments, searching the text database or indexes, and displaying the new text. *See also* hypermedia.

hypertext mark-up language (HTML) A strictly defined method of presenting textual material intended for use in the *World Wide Web. In addition to the normal features of a *mark-up language allowing control of page layout and character format, HTML makes provision for the inclusion of active links; these hold a *URL, and can act as pointers to other HTML documents located either on the same server or elsewhere in the World Wide Web.

hypertext transfer protocol *See* HTTP.

I

i386, i486 *Trademarks. See* Intel.

IA5 *Abbrev. for* International Alphabet, Number 5. An internationally agreed alphabet, specified by *CCITT. It consists of a subset of *ISO-7 in which characters that are "for national use" are either specified or not used at all.

IAB *Abbrev. for* Internet architecture board. A volunteer body responsible primarily for the development and approval of technical standards for use on the *Internet.

IAL *Acronym for* international algorithmic language, the original name for the language later called Algol 58 and now obsolete. *See* Algol. *See also* JOVIAL.

IAS *Abbrev. for* immediate access store.

IAS computer The model for a class of computing machines designed by John von Neumann. The IAS (Institute for Advanced Study) machine was started at Princeton in 1946 and was completed in 1951. This machine used *electrostatic storage devices – cathode-ray tubes – as the main memory. Such tubes, called Williams tubes, could each store 1024 bits. Other computers modeled after the IAS computer included ORACLE, JOHNNIAC, ILLIAC I, MANIAC, and IBM 701.

IBG *Abbrev. for* interblock gap. *See* tape format.

IBM International Business Machines Corporation. IBM was incorporated in 1911, in the USA, as the Computing Tabulating Recording Company as a result of the merger of three companies, one of which had been Hermann Hollerith's Tabulating Company, formed in 1896. It adopted its present name in 1924.

IBM occupied a dominating position in the computer industry from the mid-1950s to the 1980s. It was the largest computer manufacturer in the world, by any measure, and produced a wide range of processors, peripherals, software, and associated products, as well as related services. It operated all over the world. It owed its dominance primarily to its marketing strength. The architecture of its 360 range of computers, introduced in the early 1960s, became a de facto standard for mainframes.

The incorporation of the microprocessor into desktop computers of sufficient power to run useful business applications, changed the emphasis from low volumes of mainframe computers, IBM's traditional strength, to very large numbers of smaller systems. It was IBM's version of the personal computer, the IBM PC, that set the standard, but paradoxically it was during the 1980s that IBM gradually lost its dominance. The very success of the PC series led competitors to introduce compatible machines as IBM had put the PC architecture in the *public domain. These *IBM-compatible machines sold at generally lower prices. In addition the growth of independent software producers meant that customers were no longer constrained to buy from IBM. IBM's subsequent ranges of personal computers, including the PS/2 series, have not achieved the same success.

IBM continues to produce mainframes and powerful RISC systems so that it is still the largest IT supplier in the world in terms of revenue (1993 figures), but its influence over the market has dramatically decreased.

IBM-compatible A computer functionally identical to an IBM PC and able to accept all hardware and software intended for it. This was an important concept in the early 1980s when the IBM PC was emerging from among a number of other contenders as the one to copy. As IBM's share of the market declined, the term became *PC-compatible*. Currently (1995) the proliferation of *buses and the ability of the PC operating systems to operate on *microprocessors other than those used by the original IBM PC has made the concept less straightforward.

IBM system 360 IBM's *third generation computer family that used essentially the same architecture to span a wide range of performance and price objectives. The common architecture permitted upward mobility of users to larger versions of the same machine when their workload grew. Programs written for a smaller version of the 360 would run unchanged on the larger machines. Many of the principles embodied in the 360 operating systems are still to be found in contemporary IBM mainframes.

IC *Abbrev. for* integrated circuit.

I²C *Abbrev. for* inter-integrated circuit. A component-level interconnection bus that involves only two wires, a clock and a bidirectional serial data line. Components equipped with this interface include an integrated protocol to simplify system construction.

ICL International Computers Ltd. As ICT, International Computers and Tabulators

Ltd., ICL was one of a considerable number of British computer companies active in the late 1950s and the 1960s. The computer manufacturing interests of Ferranti and Elliott Brothers were taken over by ICT in the 1960s, at which point the name ICL was adopted; at the same time, the computing interests of English Electric, *Leo Computers, and Marconi were merged into a single company, which was also taken over by ICL, in the 1970s. In 1984, ICL itself became a wholly owned subsidiary of the UK company, Standard Telephones and Cable Ltd (STC). It ceased to be a UK company in the early 1990s, when it was taken over by the Japanese company, *Fujitsu. It is number 20 in the list of top IT companies in the world in terms of revenue (1993 figures).

icon A small picture used in place of another entity. *Window managers often use icons to represent devices, wastebaskets, etc. Some window systems use icons to represent another view of a window.

ICON A programming language developed as a successor to *SNOBOL. ICON is a general-purpose programming language in the style of Pascal, but includes many features for processing strings of characters and other non-numerical data. ICON's main use is in research in humanities computing, and in teaching computing to students of the humanities.

ICR *Abbrev. for* intelligent character recognition. A system of *OCR (optical character recognition) in which the meaning is assigned after reference to things other than merely the printed shape. Basic OCR systems rely on matching the scanned shape with a set of templates held within a store or on processing the image to extract features, such as lines and loops, and then searching for a match. Both approaches need good-quality printing to achieve usable recognition rates. In desktop publishing applications it is possible to use context to assist the recognition process. The resident dictionary or spelling checker can be used and provision may also be made for the unrecognized shape to be displayed so that the operator can assign a meaning that is then stored for future reference.

IDE 1. *Abbrev. for* interactive development environment. A suite of programs for program or application development with a common *user interface, often a *graphical user interface, and including *software tools for code writing and editing, compilation, execution, and debugging with an easy and consistent way of moving between the various functions.
2. *Abbrev. for* integrated device electronics. A method of interfacing hard disk drives to PCs using the *ISA bus originally developed for the IBM PC AT in 1986. It is a system-level interface in that it makes no assumptions about the disk hardware but accepts a stream of formatted data.

IDEF A nonproprietary form of *SADT developed by the US Air Force.

idempotent law The law satisfied by any *dyadic operation ∘ for which
$$x \circ x = x$$
for all elements x in the domain of ∘. *Union and *intersection of sets satisfy these laws. In a *Boolean algebra both of the dyadic operations are idempotent.

identification 1. The process of determining the identity of a user or a using process; it is necessary for *access control. Identification is usually accomplished by *authentication.
2. The process of determining how a control parameter influences a system.

identifier A string of characters used to identify (or *name) some element of a program. The kind of element that may be named depends on the programming language; it may be a variable, a data structure, a procedure, a statement, a higher-level unit, or the program itself.

identity burst *See* tape format.

identity element of a *set S on which some *dyadic operation ∘ is defined. An element e with the property that
$$a \circ e = e \circ a = a$$
for all elements a in S. It can be shown that e is unique. In normal arithmetic, 0 and 1 are the identity elements associated with addition and multiplication respectively. In a

*Boolean algebra, 0 and 1 are the identities associated with the OR and the AND operations respectively.

identity function A *function

$$I : S \rightarrow S$$

with the property that

$$I(s) = s \text{ for all } s \text{ in } S$$

Such a function leaves every element in its domain unaltered. Identity functions are needed for such purposes as the definition of *inverses of functions.

identity matrix (unit matrix) A *diagonal matrix, symbol I, with each diagonal element equal to one.

idle time *See* available time.

IDMS A database management system based on the *CODASYL network model.

IDP *Abbrev. for* integrated data processing. *See* data processing.

IEC International Electrotechnical Commission, an international body concerned with the standardization of electrical and electronic components.

IEEE Institute of Electrical and Electronics Engineers, formed in 1963 by the merger of the IRE (Institute of Radio Engineers) and the AIEE (American Institute of Electrical Engineers), and representing electrical and electronics engineers throughout the world. The IEEE Computer Society (IEEE-CS) is one of several special-interest groups.

The IEEE is an accredited organization for writing US national standards, in telecommunications and computing (*see* ANSI). For example, *IEEE-488* is an 8-bit parallel bus system standard for interfacing between programmable instrumentation and a central control system; initially promoted by Hewlett-Packard as *HP-IB*, it is also known as *GPIB* (*general-purpose interface bus*). *IEEE-802* is concerned with various aspects of local area networks.

if and only if statement A well-formed formula of the form

$$A \equiv B$$

where A and B are also appropriate well-formed formulas. *See* biconditional, propositional calculus.

IFE *Abbrev. for* intelligent front end.

iff *Short for* if and only if.

IFIP International Federation for Information Processing, founded in 1959 under the auspices of UNESCO and coming into official existence in 1960. It is a multinational federation of professional/technical societies, or groups of such societies, concerned with information processing. Each member country has only one such society or group as a full member. IFIP aims to "promote information science and technology, advance international cooperation in the field of information processing, stimulate research, development, and application of information processing, further dissemination and exchange of information on information processing, and encourage education in information processing."

IFS *Abbrev. for* iterated function system.

if then else statement The most basic conditional construct in a programming language, allowing selection between two alternatives, dependent on the truth or falsity of a given condition. Most languages also provide an *if … then* construct to allow conditional execution of a single statement or group of statements. Primitive languages, such as Basic in its original form, restrict the facility to a conditional transfer of control, e.g.

"IF A = 0 THEN 330"

which is reminiscent of the conditional jump provided in the order code of every CPU. *See also* conditional.

IGBT *Abbrev. for* insulated-gate *bipolar transistor, usually applied in the computerized control of high-power systems such as traction motors.

IGES *Acronym for* initial graphics exchange specification. An *ANSI standard developed in 1980 for exchanging product data between applications. This standard is being replaced by *STEP.

ignore character (fill character) A character used in transmission to fill an otherwise empty position and whose value is thus ignored.

IH *Abbrev. for* interrupt handler.

IIF *Abbrev. for* Image Interchange Facility, a

part of the *IPI standard.

I²L *Abbrev. for* integrated injection logic. A bipolar integrated-circuit technology that allows extremely high component densities on a chip. It is used for complex LSI functions such as microprocessors and is simpler to fabricate than either TTL or MOS. It also has lower power requirements and reasonably good switching speeds.

ill-conditioned *See* condition number.

illegal character Any character not in the *character set of a given machine or not allowed by a given programming language or protocol.

illegal instruction An instruction that has an invalid *operation code. It is sometimes deliberately inserted in an instruction stream when debugging in order to have a program halt, or interrupt, at a particular point.

ILLIAC IV An *array processor that was designed by Daniel Slotnick and used a 16-by-16 array of processing units (PUs), each interconnected to its four nearest neighbors. The array of PUs was regulated by a single processor that controlled the flow of instructions to the PUs. The ILLIAC IV was sponsored by ARPA and built by Burroughs Corporation. It became operable at the Ames Research Center of NASA in the early 1970s, and was finally dismantled in 1981.

illumination The distribution of light falling on a surface. *See* local illumination, global illumination.

image 1. A copy in memory of data that exists elsewhere.
2. *See* digital image.
3. *See* function.

image capture (image acquisition) The process of obtaining a digital image from a vision sensor, such as a camera. Usually this entails a hardware interface known as a frame grabber, which captures single frames of video, converts the analogue values to digital, and feeds the result into the computer memory. The conversion process is often accompanied with *image compression.

image compression The reduction of the number of bits used to define an image.

Many techniques are available. For example, run-length encoding allows a set of pixels having the same color to be specified by the color and number of pixels with that color in a sequence. Other techniques include *fractal image compression and *wavelet image compression. Compression can produce an approximation of the image, in which case it is not possible to decompress the image and retrieve the original form. *See also* lossy compression, lossless compression, discrete cosine transform.

image display The process of displaying an image on a *display.

image file format A format for defining an image. Examples are *TIFF, *IIF, and *GIF.

image grabber *See* video scanner.

Image Interchange Facility (IIF) A part of the *IPI standard.

image management system (IMS) A management system for handling digital images. An example is Starlink, used in astronomy.

image processing (picture processing) Processing of the information contained in a *digital image. Image processing operations include contrast distortion, expansion of a specified range of brightness, bright outlining of objects, correction of over- or underexposure of portions of the image, recognition (and perhaps counting) of predefined objects, and comparison of one image with another. The last two of these operations are examples of *pattern recognition. Some of the more advanced operations make use of the concepts of *artificial intelligence. The development of image processing has been prompted by applications such as satellite and unmanned spaceprobe observations, undersea exploration, medical physics, and industrial robotics.

Image Processing and Interchange *See* IPI.

image tearing The appearance of jerking between discrete image positions. It occurs in displays with only a single *frame buffer. *See also* double buffering.

image understanding Advanced *image processing in which *artificial-intelligence techniques are used to interpret images by locating, characterizing, and recognizing objects and other features in the scene.

image warping A continuous transformation of an image on a plane. It is used to compensate for errors in the device that performed the initial sensing of the information.

immediate access store (IAS) A memory device in which the access time for any location is independent of the previous access and is usually of the same order as the cycle time of the processor. Such devices are normally only used for main memory.

immediate addressing A method used to refer to data (often small constants or similar) that is located in an address field of an instruction. Strictly this is not a method of generating an address at all; it does provide a reference to the desired data in a way that is both compact and requires less memory reference time.

immunization A technique of generic *virus detection in which, by ensuring that the checksum of its code remains unchanged, a program itself verifies that it has not been infected by a virus.

IMP *Acronym for* interface message processor. One of the switching computers that together formed the *backbone network for the *ARPANET.

impact printer Any device that makes use of mechanical impact to print characters onto paper. Typewriters come within this definition but the term is not usually applied to machines that are only operated through a keyboard. A character may be formed by impacting an inked ribbon against the paper with an engraved type character, or it may be built up from a number of dots printed by the impacts of separate styluses. *See* solid-font printer, dot-matrix printer.

imperative languages A class of programming languages. With an imperative language a program explicitly states how the desired result is to be produced but does not explicitly define what properties the result is expected to exhibit – the result is defined only implicitly as whatever is obtained by following the specified procedure (*compare* declarative languages).

The procedure for producing the desired result takes the form of a sequence of operations, and thus with imperative languages the notions of flow of control and ordering of statements are inherent. Such a language is typically characterized by the presence of the *assignment statement, which, being destructive (the assigned value replaces the previous value of the variable), also depends on the notion of ordering. Imperative languages are closely associated with the von Neumann model of computation, and the majority of widely used languages – including Cobol, Fortran, and Pascal – are imperative.

implementation The activity of proceeding from a given design of a system to a working version (known also as an *implementation*) of that system, or the specific way in which some part of a system is made to fulfill its function. For example, a control unit may be implemented by random logic or by microprogramming; a multiplier may be implemented by successive additions and shifts or by a table lookup. Another example occurs in computer families, where different implementations may differ in the type of circuit elements used or in the actual parallelism (as opposed to logical parallelism) of the ALU.

With software, use of the term normally implies that all major design decisions have been made so that the implementation activity could be relatively straightforward. For many systems a number of important characteristics may not become bound until the implementation activity; examples include the programming language in which the system is written, the type of computer employed, the actual hardware configuration, or the operating system used. With such systems there may be a number of distinct implementation activities in order to provide several versions of the system, e.g. written in different languages or operating on different hardware.

implicant A *product term that covers at least one of the *standard sum of product terms in a *Boolean function, but will introduce no new (unwanted) standard sum of product terms.

A *prime implicant* is an implicant that includes a *standard product of a function that is not otherwise included.

implicit surface A surface defined by those points that satisfy

$$f(x,y,z) = c$$

for some constant c. If f happens to be an algebraic function then this is an *algebraic surface. If a surface is defined implicitly, there is an easy test of whether a point (x,y,z) lies on the surface or is inside or outside the surface.

implied addressing (inherent addressing) A type of *addressing scheme, the term referring to the fact that in many instruction formats the location of one or more operands is implied in the instruction name and is specified in the instruction description. An implied address is usually that of one of the machine registers. *See also* accumulator.

import list In modular languages such as *Modula-2, a list of the names used inside a module that are declared in other modules.

imprecision Humans have expert abilities to reason with vague information; they seem to use approximations, abstractions, and qualitative data very effectively, in place of precise numeric information. This has been explored in *artificial intelligence with reasoning systems that employ approximate models and vague values. In order to implement these ideas, techniques such as *fuzzy logic and *qualitative reasoning have been developed.

impulse noise *Noise of large amplitude and some statistical irregularity, affecting an analog channel severely but (relatively) infrequently. In contrast, *white noise affects it (relatively) unseverely but continuously. Impulse noise affecting an analog channel carrying a binary signal usually causes *burst errors.

IMS 1. *Trademark* A well-established *database management system supplied by IBM. It is based on and implements the *hierarchical data model, but has gained additional non-hierarchical features as a result of practical needs. DL/1 is the data manipulation language of IMS.

2. *Abbrev. for* image management system.

inactive Not running (pertaining to the state of a process).

incidence matrix A representation of a *graph G employing a *matrix in which there is a row for each vertex v of G. The entries on this row are just the vertices that are joined by an edge to v.

inclusive-OR gate *Another name for* OR gate.

inclusive-OR operation *Another name for* OR operation, making explicit the difference between this and the *exclusive-OR operation.

incomplete knowledge-based system *See* completeness.

incompleteness theorems *See* Gödel's incompleteness theorems.

inconsistent If a *knowledge base uses default assumptions or stores tentative conclusions then, as a result of *inference, it may produce new facts that conflict with existing facts; it is then said to be inconsistent. This can occur in *nonmonotonic reasoning and systems that use *inheritance and must be either avoided or handled by special treatment if the integrity of the system is to be maintained. *See* default rules.

increment To increase the contents of a *register or *counter by one.

incremental backup *See* full backup.

incremental compaction (incremental compression) *See* statistical compaction.

incremental compiler A compiler that can compile partial programs, and can compile additional statements for a program without recompiling the whole program. Incremental compilers were at one time in vogue for interactive programming, but interactive language systems nowadays are almost always implemented in an interpretive manner.

incremental dump *See* dump.

incremental learning *See* machine learning.

incremental plotter A device that can draw graphs and other line images when fed with digital data. The plotter forms the image by moving a pen or the paper or both in a succession of increments. The increments are typically 200 per inch for drum plotters and can be 500 per inch for flatbed plotters. *See also* plotter.

indegree *See* degree.

indeterminate system A logic system whose *logic states are unpredictable.

index A list of values of some particular data item contained in a record, enabling it to be retrieved more rapidly than by simple serial search. For example, a *subscript is a value, usually integral, that selects a particular element of an array. The B+ tree (*see* B–tree) is an efficient form of multilevel index. *See also* indexed file.

indexed addressing (indexing) A method of generating an *effective address that modifies the specified address given in the instruction by the contents of a specified *index register. The modification is usually that of addition of the contents of the index register to the specified address. The automatic modification of index–register contents results in an orderly progression of effective addresses being generated on successive executions of the instruction containing the reference to the index register. This progression is terminated when the index register reaches a value that has been specified in an index-register handling instruction.

indexed file A data file in which records can be accessed by means of an *index. If the same field is used both in the index and for sequencing the records in the file, the index is called a *primary index* (and the file is called an *indexed sequential file*). Otherwise the index is called a *secondary index* (*see* inverted file).

indexed sequential file A file combining properties of *random-access files and *sequential files. *See* indexed file, ISAM.

index register A register that can be specified by instructions that use *indexed addressing. An index register is usually controlled by one or more instructions with the ability to increment or decrement the register by a fixed amount, to test the register for equality with a specified value (often zero), and to jump to a specified location when equality is

achieved. It may be part of the *processor status word.

indicator 1. A bit or bit configuration that may be inspected to determine a status or condition. Examples are an *overflow bit, a device status, any portion of the *program status word. *See also* qualifier register.
2. A visual, sometimes aural, indication of the occurrence of a specific status or condition, e.g. system running (halted), undefined instruction.

indirect addressing A method of addressing in which the contents of the address specified in the instruction (which may itself be an *effective address) are themselves an address to be used to provide the desired memory reference. Two memory references are thus needed to obtain the data.

One use of indirect addressing is to supply a way of circumventing short address field limitations since the first memory reference provides a full word of address size. Another use is as a pointer to a table. Since an operand is not available at the usual time in the fetch-execute cycle, completion of that cycle must be deferred until the operand is finally available. Indirect addressing is thus sometimes referred to as *deferred addressing*.

individual attributes *Attributes of a graphical output primitive specified by a global variable that is attached to the primitive. Each output device is required to render the primitive as close to the specified value as possible.

induction 1. A method of logical inference in which a general but not necessarily true conclusion is drawn from a set of particular instances. In *machine learning, for example, the term induction is used to describe an approach to machine learning in which generalized structures or statements are inferred from particular examples.
2. A process for proving mathematical statements involving members of an ordered set (possibly infinite). There are various formulations of the principle of induction. For example, by the *principle of finite induction*, to prove a statement $P(i)$ is true for all integers $i \geq i_0$, it suffices to prove that

(a) $P(i_0)$ is true;

(b) for all $k \geq i_0$, the assumption that $P(k)$ is true (the *induction hypothesis*) implies the truth of $P(k+1)$.

(a) is called the *basis* of the proof, (b) is the *induction step*.

Generalizations are possible. Other forms of induction permit the induction step to assume the truth of $P(k)$ and also that of

$$P(k-1), P(k-2), ..., P(k-i)$$

for suitable i. Statements of several variables can also be considered. *See also* structural induction.

industrial robotics The branch of *robotics concerned with industrial and manufacturing applications. Industrial robots usually take the form of a manipulator arm equipped with an end effector and various sensors. Most commercial industrial robots have very limited sensory capabilities and follow fixed but reprogrammable sequences of operation. Many different programming languages have been adapted or developed for these robots. Current research and development is focused on tasks such as automatic assembly, automatic planning, visual guidance, and error recovery.

Industry Standard Architecture The *architecture developed by IBM for its PC AT (advanced technology) series and opened up for use by other manufacturers. Renamed *ISA* it became the de facto architecture for personal computers for many years. *See also* EISA, MCA, local bus architecture.

inequality A *binary relation that typically expresses the relative magnitude of two quantities, usually numbers though more generally elements of a partially ordered set (*see* partial ordering).

The inequalities defined on the integers usually include

    < (less than)
    ≤ (less than or equal to)
    > (greater than)
    ≥ (greater than or equal to)
    ≠ (not equal to)

A similar set of inequalities is usually defined on the *real numbers; such inequalities can produce errors when used in programming languages because of the inherent inaccura-

cies in the way real numbers are usually represented.

The term inequality is often applied to any comparison involving algebraic expressions and using the above symbols. A special case is the *triangle inequality*:

$$|a + b| \leq |a| + |b|$$

where $|\ |$ denotes the absolute value function.

inference A rule or process that derives a new fact from a given set of facts. There are three main methods: *deduction, *abduction, and *induction. Examples of these styles of inference can be seen in *theorem proving, *expert systems, and *machine learning, respectively.

inference engine Within the context of *expert systems, the part of the expert system program that operates on the *knowledge base and produces inferences. If the knowledge base is regarded as a program then the inference engine is the interpreter. The expressions in the knowledge representation language are its inputs, and its outputs constitute an interpretation of this input with respect to stored knowledge. The interpreter may be logic-based in that it operates within a certain logic formalism, for instance first-order *predicate calculus.

infinite resolution The ability to zoom in on an image at any level and still have an appropriate level of *resolution of the image.

infix notation A form of notation in which operators appear between their operands, as in

$$(a + b) * c$$

Infix notation requires the use of brackets to specify order of evaluation, unlike prefix and postfix notation, i.e. *Polish notation and *reverse Polish notation respectively.

influence In *regression analysis, the effect on estimates of *parameters of varying the value of a particular observation. Observations that have greatest influence are also called *leverage* points. Influence functions help to warn of possible over-reliance on too few data values, and also provide a method of allocating new data observations most effectively.

infobahn *Informal* Any form of high-speed computer network, especially the *Internet.

informatics A word that first appeared in Russian (informatika) in 1966 with the following definition (OED): the scientific discipline that investigates the structure and properties (not specific content) of scientific information, as well as the regularities of scientific information activity, its theory, history, methodology, and organization. It has since acquired a less specialized meaning and a wide usage in German (Informatik) and French (l'informatique): broadly, the study and practice of computer science, information technology, and information processing. Its use in English falls within that range of meaning, but the word is rarely used.

information Generally, information is whatever is capable of causing a human mind to change its opinion about the current state of the real world. Formally, and especially in science and engineering, information is whatever contributes to a reduction in the uncertainty of the state of a system; in this case, uncertainty is usually expressed in an objectively measurable form. Commonly, this is done by means of Shannon's *entropy. Nevertheless, this formula for uncertainty involves probabilities, and these may well have to be subjective. If that is so, the formal measurement must be qualified as depending on subjective probabilities, and "uncertainty" must be replaced by "opinion, or personal estimate, of uncertainty".

Information must be distinguished from any medium that is capable of carrying it. A physical medium (such as a magnetic disk) may carry a logical medium (data, such as binary or text symbols). The information content of any physical objects, or logical data, cannot be measured or discussed until it is known what range of possibilities existed before and after they were received. The information lies in the reduction in uncertainty resulting from the receipt of the objects or the data, and not in the size or complexity of the objects or data themselves. Questions of the form, function, and semantic import of data are only relevant to information inasmuch as they contribute to the

reduction of uncertainty. If an identical memorandum is received twice, it does not convey twice the information that its first occurrence conveyed: the second occurrence conveys no information at all, unless, by prior agreement, the number of occurrences is itself to be regarded as significant.

Information has ramifications in security, politics, culture, and the economy, as well as in science and engineering. The extent to which information is used as an economic commodity is one of the defining characteristics of the "post-industrial" society, hence the phrase "the information society".

information destination *See* Shannon's model.

information engineering The engineering approach applied to *information systems. The term shows considerable variation in scope. At its broadest, it refers to the engineering discipline covering a spectrum from *software engineering and *systems engineering to device-level electronics. At its most limited (but perhaps best known), it is the name of a specific proprietary method for the development of organizational information systems, primarily associated with James Martin; this method begins with *enterprise modeling and carries through to the generation of program code, and a number of software toolsets are available for its support.

information hiding A principle, used when developing an overall *program structure, that each component of a program should *encapsulate* or hide a single design decision. The principle was first expounded by David Parnas, who advocated an approach to program development in which a list is prepared of design decisions that are particularly difficult or likely to change; individual components, known as *modules*, are then defined so that each encapsulates one such decision. The interface to each module is defined in such a way as to reveal as little as possible about its inner workings.

This approach leads to modules that are readily understood and can be developed independently. More important, it also leads to programs that are easy to change, with many desired changes requiring modification of only the inner workings of a single module.

information management system A term sometimes used synonymously with *database management system (DBMS) although normally used in a more general sense. The term has no widely accepted definition and thus can be applied to any system of software that facilitates the storage, organization, and retrieval of information within a computer system, without the implication that it need have all the essential characteristics of a DBMS. The information held may include sound fragments, images, and video sequences in addition to the usual textual and numerical information. These newer forms of computer-held information are sometimes argued as being a defining characteristic of the term, notwithstanding that DBMS are developing to provide for such forms of information.

information processing The derivation of "information objects" from other "information objects" by the execution of algorithms: the essential activity of computers.

The term has related meanings outside the computing field. It is used in psychology, for instance, and may also be used to refer to clerical operations.

information retrieval Strictly, the activity of retrieving previously stored information. The term is sometimes used to mean *information storage and retrieval (as in information retrieval application).

information science The branch of knowledge concerned with the storage, organization, retrieval, processing, and dissemination of information. The term was coined in the aftermath of the spread of computers and the corresponding revolution in information-handling techniques. Information science therefore inevitably pays substantial attention to, but is not confined to, what can be achieved with computers.

information sciences A cluster of separate but related branches of knowledge, including *computer science, *information systems, and library science.

information source *See* Shannon's model.

information storage and retrieval (ISR) The linked activities of storing and retrieving information, and the strategies and techniques for doing so. The activities are linked because the means of retrieving information are dependent on the means by which it was stored. The storage strategy must be designed for the most efficient retrieval, consistent with the characteristics of the information and the time and cost that can be tolerated.

information structure *Another name for* data structure.

information superhighway *Informal* Any form of high-speed computer network, especially the *Internet. *See also* National Information Infrastructure.

information system A computer-based system with the defining characteristic that it provides information to users in one or more organizations. Information systems are thus distinguished from, for example, real-time control systems, message-switching systems, software engineering environments, or personal computing systems.

The term could have a very much wider meaning than that suggested, considering the range of meaning of the words *information and *system. It could, for instance, be broadened to include all computer-based systems, or further broadened to include many non-computer-based systems. Thus, within the domain of computer-based systems, the more specific term *organizational information system* is sometimes used.

Information systems include *data processing applications, *office automation applications, and many *expert system applications. When their primary purpose is to supply information to management, they are commonly called *management information systems.

The following are among the more important characteristics of information systems, and make their design and construction particularly difficult.

(a) Their environment is complex, not fully definable, and not easily modeled.

(b) They have a complex interface with

their environment, comprising multiple inputs and outputs.

(c) The functional relationships between inputs and outputs are structurally, if not algorithmically, complex.

(d) They usually include large and complex databases (or, in future, knowledge bases).

(e) Their "host" organizations are usually highly dependent on their continuing availability over very long periods, often with great urgency attending their initial provision or subsequent modification.

See also information systems.

information systems (IS) The branch of knowledge concerning the purpose, design, uses, and effects of information systems in organizations. IS is an interdisciplinary study, drawing chiefly from *computer science on the technical side and from business/management studies on the organizational side; it may also, however, embrace aspects of economics, psychology and sociology, statistics, and operations research.

information technology (IT) Any form of technology, i.e. any equipment or technique, used by people to handle *information. Mankind has handled information for thousands of years; early technologies included the abacus and printing. The last four decades or so have seen an amazingly rapid development of information technology, spearheaded by the computer; more recently, cheap microelectronics have permitted the diffusion of this technology into almost all aspects of daily life and an almost inextricable cross-fertilizing and intermingling of its various branches. The term information technology was coined, probably in the late 1970s, to refer to this nexus of modern technology, electronic-based, for handling information. It incorporates the whole of computing and telecommunication technology, together with major parts of consumer electronics and broadcasting. Its applications are industrial, commercial, administrative, educational, medical, scientific, professional, and domestic.

The advanced nations have all realized that developing competence in information technology is important, expensive, and difficult; large-scale information technology systems are now economically feasible and there are national programs of research and education to stimulate development. The fundamental capabilities that are usually recognized to be essential comprise VLSI circuit design and production facilities, and a common infrastructure for the storage and transmission of digital information (including digitized voice and image as well as conventional data and text). Major research problems include improved systems and software technology, advanced programming techniques (especially in *knowledge-based systems), and improved *human-computer interfaces.

information theory The study of information by mathematical methods. Informally, information can be considered as the extent to which a message conveys what was previously unknown, and so is new or surprising. Mathematically, the rate at which information is conveyed from a source is identified with the *entropy of the source (per second or per symbol). Although information theory is sometimes restricted to the entropy formulation of sources and channels, it may include coding theory, in which case the term is used synonymously with *communication theory.

INFORMIX *Trademark. See* database management system.

infrared interface An interface where communication is achieved by transmission of infrared radiation instead of the conventional electrical signal connection. Such interfaces may be used for purposes of electrical isolation.

INGRES *Trademark* A relational *database management system marketed by Computer Associates (CA).

inherent addressing *Another name for* implied addressing.

inherently ambiguous language A context-free language that has no nonambiguous grammar (*see* ambiguous grammar). An example is the set

$$\{a^i b^j c^k \mid i = j \text{ or } j = k\}$$

inheritance In a hierarchy of *objects an object generally has a parent object (superclass) at the next higher level in the hierarchy and one or more child objects (subclass) at the next lower level. Each object can have various *attributes associated with it. The attributes can be local to that object, or can be inherited from the parent object. Attributes can be further inherited by child objects (often without limit on the number of inheritances). In addition an object can be an instance of a more general object (not a parent object) with which it shares variables and also inherits its attributes.

Inheritance is thus a means by which characteristics of objects can be replicated and instantiated in other objects. Inheritance is both static by *abstract data type and dynamic by *instantiation and value. *Inheritance rules* define what can be inherited and *inheritance links* define the parent and child of inheritance attributes.

See also object-oriented programming.

inhibit To prevent the occurrence of an event, e.g. to use a logic gate to inhibit another signal. *Compare* enable.

initial algebra An *algebra A, from some class of algebras C, such that for every algebra B in C there is a unique *homomorphism from A to B. Such an algebra is said to be initial in the class C or, more precisely, initial in the *category that has all the algebras in C as its objects and all the homomorphisms between them as its *morphisms. Depending on the choice of C, there may or may not exist initial algebras; however if any do exist they will all be isomorphic to each other. If C is the class $Alg(\Sigma, E)$ of all Σ-algebras satisfying a set E of *equations or *conditional equations, then C has an initial algebra. If the set E is recursive enumerable then the initial algebra is *semicomputable*.

Initial algebras have importance for the *semantics of programming languages, *abstract data types, and *algebraic specifications. Of particular significance is the fact that, in the class of all Σ-algebras for a given *signature Σ, an initial algebra is given by the *terms or *trees over Σ; this is often called the *term algebra* for Σ.

initialization The act of assigning initial values to variables before the start of a computa-

tion. Some programming languages provide a facility for specifying initial values when a variable is first declared.

initial-value problem *See* ordinary differential equations, partial differential equations.

injection (one-to-one function) A *function with the property that distinct elements in its domain are mapped onto distinct elements in the codomain. Formally,
$$f: X \to Y$$
is an injection if
$$f(x_1) = f(x_2) \text{ implies } x_1 = x_2$$
A common use of injections is to map or include elements of some smaller set, such as the set of integers, into a larger set, such as the set of real numbers.

inkjet printer An output device that creates characters and graphics by firing a stream of ink drops at a surface from one or more banks of tiny nozzles. The rapid displacement required to eject the drops from the nozzles may be achieved by surface boiling of the ink using tiny electric heating elements behind each nozzle, or by mechanical pressure using piezoelectric crystals behind the nozzles. The technology has developed to the extent that such printers can (on suitable media) offer comparable resolution and quality to the *laser printer but at a much lower cost. Inkjet technology is also suitable for color printing, nozzles being fed with three or four different color inks (*see* CMY, CMYK color models). Inkjet printers can also act as *plotters.

There are three main types of inkjet device. In the *continuous inkjet printer* a continuous stream of electrically charged ink drops are fired toward the surface. The desired image is created by deflecting unwanted drops into a gutter. The *drop-on-demand inkjet printer* fires ink only at the points of the surface necessary to create the desired image. The *phase-change inkjet printer* uses solid ink that is heated so that it leaves the nozzle as a liquid but returns to the solid state as it reaches the image surface; a major advantage is that it does not need special paper for good results as other inkjet devices do.

in-line function A short function whose code

is inserted by the compiler at the point of call, thereby avoiding the overhead of a normal function call.

inner code *See* concatenated coding system.

inoculation A technique for virus prevention in which a *vaccine*, the *signature (but not the harmful code) of a virus, is deliberately added to a program. This is effective only against those specific viruses that are programmed to avoid reinfecting code by detecting the presence of their own signature.

inorder traversal *Another name for* symmetric order traversal.

input 1. The process of entering data into a processing system or a peripheral device, or the data that is entered.

2. A signal that is applied to an electrical circuit, such as a logic circuit.

3. To enter data or apply a signal.

input area The area of main memory that is currently allocated to hold incoming data. The processing system will usually retrieve data from the input area and transfer it to a working area or register before it is processed. The result of the processing may be written to an *output area. Subroutines are usually organized so as to replenish the input area from a source such as an input peripheral or communication line and clear the output area by transfer to backing store.

input device Any device that transfers data, programs, or signals into a processor system. Such devices provide the human-computer interface, the *keyboard being the most common example. Early computers also used punched paper tape and cards but these are now obsolete. Current devices include *pointing devices, *data collection terminals, *speech recognition units, magnetic *card readers, and *document scanners. *See also* logical input device.

input-limited process A process whose speed of execution is limited by the rate at which input data is available or obtained.

input/output (I/O) The passing of information into or out of the central processing unit of a computer system, or the part of the system primarily dedicated to this activity. An important function of most I/O equipment

is the translation between the host processor's signals and the sounds, actions, or symbols that are understood or generated by people. In some cases it may be translation between two types of machine-readable signals, as when a *bar-code scanner reads the data-encoded package and translates it into an ASCII code. *See also* I/O.

inquiry station A terminal from which information can be retrieved from a *database. Generally the terminal has a display and a keyboard, but there may also be ancillary devices such as a *badge reader. The user makes the inquiry via the keyboard either in the form of a question in plain text or by indicating a selection from a menu on the display. The display will show a series of possible selections that successively narrow the field of search. An inquiry station may also update information as the result of an action arising from an inquiry. An airline booking terminal is an example of an inquiry station. *See also* interrogation.

inscribe To encode a document by printing information that is readable by both a person and a machine.

insert 1. One of the basic actions performed on *sets that, when applied in the form

$$insert(el, S)$$

adds the element *el* to the set *S*. If *el* is already in *S* the operation has no effect on the membership of *S*. *See also* operations on sets.

2. One of the basic actions performed on *lists, that places a new element into a list, not necessarily at one end or the other.

install 1. To take software from the distribution files, which can be on floppy disks, CD-ROM, tapes, or on a remote networked computer, and place it in its permanent location from where it will be executed. The installation process is not just a straight copy as it involves unpacking compressed files, configuring the software to suit its environment, and perhaps allowing the installer to choose how much of the software to install. A typical installation program will offer choices of minimum, custom, or full installations.

2. To fit new hardware features to a computer.

instance *See* instantiation, unification. *See also* object-oriented programming.

instantaneously decodable *See* prefix codes.

instantiation 1. The creation of a particular instance of an object class, generic unit, or template.

2. The application of a parameterized abstract data type to a particular set of parameters.

instruction The description of an operation that is to be performed by a computer. It consists of a statement of an operation to be performed and some method of specifying the operands (or their locations) and the disposition of the result of the operation. Instructions are often divided into classes such as *arithmetic instructions, *program control instructions, *logic instructions, and *I/O instructions. They may or may not be of fixed length. The set of operations available in a particular computer is known as its *operation code or order code. *See also* instruction format.

instruction counter (program counter) A counting *register that normally increments in each instruction cycle to obtain the program sequence (i.e. the sequence of instructions) from the memory locations. This counter will have its contents changed by branch instructions to obtain the next instruction from the branch target. The instruction counter forms part of the *processor status word; this enables subsequent restarting of an interrupted program.

instruction cycle *Another name for* fetch-execute cycle. *See* control unit.

instruction format An instruction is normally made up of a combination of an *operation code and some way of specifying an *operand, most commonly by its location or *address in memory though *nonmemory reference instructions can exist. Some operation codes deal with more than one operand; the locations of these operands may be specified using any of the many *addressing schemes.

Classically, the number of address references has been used to specify something about the architecture of a particular computer. In some instruction formats and machine architectures, the number of operand references may be fixed; in others

the number is variable. In the former case descriptions of formats include *one-address, two-address, three-address,* and (now rarely) *four-address.* An example (symbolically) of a one-address instruction is

   add x   i.e.

     add contents of address x
     to contents of accumulator;
     sum remains in accumulator.

An example of a three-address instruction is

   add x,y,z   i.e.

     add contents of address x
     to contents of address y;
     sum is placed in location z.

In some cases the last address is the address of the next instruction to be executed. The ability to specify this address was important when rotating (drum) main memories were prominent. Thus a two-address instruction such as

   add x,y   i.e.

     add contents of address x
     to contents of address y;
     sum is placed at address y,

may become

   add x,y,z   i.e.

     add contents of address x
     to contents of address y;
     sum is placed at address y;
     next instruction is taken
     from address z.

The latter may be called either a three-address instruction or a *two-plus-one-address* instruction. In a similar way the term *one-plus-one address* instruction represents a one-address instruction together with the address where the next instruction is to be found. In these two cases the instructions do not come from sequential addresses; an instruction counter, if present, is bypassed.

The figure shows three examples of possible/typical instruction formats.

In early computers instruction formats were forced into a fixed word size, that of the computer. An instruction format consisted of two fields: one containing the operation code and the other containing the address(es). As additional features of address modification became available, it was necessary to add special bit positions in the instruction word to specify functions such as *indirect address-

operation code	address
5	13

Simple one-address instruction

operation code	select partial word	destination register	index register	index register increment / indirect addressing		address
6	4	4	4	1	1	16

Complex one-address instruction

operation code	register containing one operand	index register	base address register	address (as modified by index and base) of second operand
8	4	4	4	12

Complex two-address instruction using registers and memory

Instruction formats

ing, use of *index registers, use of base registers in *relative addressing, etc. Still other bits were sometimes used to allow for reference to parts of a data word; this was usually as fractions of the word, as character positions, more recently as byte positions.

As *registers became common, distinct operation codes were used to refer to register locations; these could be specified in many fewer bits than normal addresses, and variable-length instruction formats were developed. *See also* stack processing, zero-address instruction.

instruction register *See* control unit.

instruction repertoire *Another name for* instruction set.

instruction sequencing The order in which the instructions in a program are carried out. Normally the sequence proceeds in a linear fashion through the program, and the address of the instructions is obtained from the program counter in the *control unit. This sequence is interrupted when a *branch instruction is executed; at such a time the address of the branch instruction is inserted into the program counter and the process continues.

instruction set (instruction repertoire) The totality of *instructions that a computer

is capable of performing. The list of all the *operation codes and the permitted *addressing schemes pertinent to each.

instruction stream The sequence of *instructions from memory to the control unit.

instrument To add code to software, or devices to hardware, in order to monitor (and sometimes control) operation of a system or component while under test or analysis. The code or devices so used are called *instrumentation*. Instrumenting code may, for example, write to a report file the before and after values of a variable together with a source reference to the code each time the variable is referenced. Some software environments provide tools to automatically add (and remove) the instrumentation and to analyze report files or screen-directed output.

integer A whole number, as opposed to a *rational or *real number. The concept of *integer type is used for computer representation of a finite subset of the integers.

integer programming *See* mathematical programming.

integer type (type integer) A *data type comprising only integer (whole number) values, lying between specified maximum and minimum values; legal operations include integer arithmetic operations such as addition, subtraction, and multiplication.

integral domain *See* ring.

integral equation Any equation for an unknown function $f(x)$, $a \le x \le b$, involving integrals of the function. An equation of the form

$$f(x) = \int_a^x K(x,y)f(y)\,\mathrm{d}y + g(x)$$

is a *Volterra equation* of the second kind. The analogous equation with constant limits

$$f(x) = \int_a^b K(x,y)f(y)\,\mathrm{d}y + g(x)$$

is a *Fredholm equation* of the second kind. If the required function only appears under the integral sign it is a Volterra or Fredholm equation of the first kind; these are more difficult to treat both theoretically and numerically. The Volterra equation can be regarded as a particular case of the Fredholm equation where

$$K(x,y) = 0 \text{ for } y > x$$

Fredholm equations of the second kind occur commonly in boundary-value problems in mathematical physics. Numerical techniques proceed by replacing the integral with a rule for *numerical integration, leading to a set of *linear algebraic equations determining approximations to $f(x)$ at a set of points in $a \le x \le b$.

integrated circuit (IC) An implementation of a particular electronic-circuit function in which all the individual devices required to realize the function are fabricated on a single *chip of semiconductor, usually silicon. The individual devices normally consist of semiconductor diodes and transistors.

In *MOS integrated circuits* the active devices are *MOSFETs, which operate at low currents and high frequencies. A very large number of MOSFETs can be packed together on one silicon chip, i.e. MOS circuits have a high packing density. They also consume very little power. The development of MOS technology has allowed extremely complex functions to be performed on a single chip.

In *bipolar integrated circuits* the components are *bipolar transistors and other devices that are fabricated using the p-n junction properties of semiconductors. Compared with MOS circuits, bipolar circuits have higher operating speeds but have the disadvantages of high power consumption and low packing density. They are also less simple to fabricate than MOS circuits.

The improvement in the fabrication technology of integrated circuits has made possible the construction of a huge number of components on a single chip. These may be combined on the chip to make a wide variety of digital and analog circuits. The complexity of a digital circuit produced on a single chip is usually described in terms of the number of *transistors involved, or sometimes the number of *logic gates. This leads to the following differentiation:

VLSI	very large-scale integration;
LSI	large-scale integration;
MSI	medium-scale integration;
SSI	small-scale integration.

Digital integrated circuits are often represented by their logic function rather than their electronic function in order to ease their understanding. *See also* hybrid integrated circuit.

integrated data processing (IDP) *See* data processing.

integrated device electronics *See* IDE.

integrated office system (IOS) A program for use on a personal computer or small multiuser business computer that combines some of the functions otherwise performed by a series of single-purpose programs. A typical mix of functions in an integrated office system might be *spreadsheet, *word processor, *database management system, and graphics. The results of the various sections can usually be merged to form a final document containing pictorial, tabular, and textual material.

integrated project support environment *See* IPSE, PSE (def. 2).

integrated services digital network *See* ISDN.

integrated systems factory *See* ISF.

integration testing *See* testing.

integrity 1. Resistance to alteration by system errors. A user who files data expects that the contents of the files will not be changed by system errors in either hardware or software. Since such errors inevitably will occur from time to time, the prudent system manager maintains a system of protective *dumps, organized in such a way that there always exists a valid copy of a recent version of every file on the system. For this to be possible, the manager must run system utilities that operate at such a level of privilege that they bypass the normal checks present to maintain the *privacy and *security of users' files. The dump utilities must be able to read the users' files in order to make copies, and must have write access to the users' files in order to reinstate a recent version of a file lost or corrupted by system error. Thus the system for maintaining the integrity of a user's files automatically constitutes a security *vulnerability and represents a weakening of the system for maintaining privacy.

2. (safety integrity) The probability of a system always performing at some level of *safety.

Integrity level A measure of the safety *integrity in a given system, expressed variously as a number (e.g. 1, 2, 3, or 4) or using a descriptor (such as high or low) with these being well defined in particular situations.

integro-differential equation Any equation for an unknown function involving integrals and derivatives of the function. Many different types can arise and there is no straightforward classification. The initial-value problem (*see* ordinary differential equations) given by

$$f'(x) = F\left(x, f(x), \int_a^x K(x,y)f(y)\,dy\right)$$
$$f(a) = f_0$$

also contains features common to Volterra integral equations (*see* integral equation). Boundary-value problems and equations involving partial derivatives also occur in practice.

Intel A US corporation that is a leading manufacturer of *integrated circuits (chips), particularly noted for its important range of *microprocessor chips. The current range is shown in the table. The *Pentium* processor, Intel's most highly integrated semiconductor device, together with the previous generations – the *Intel486* and *Intel386* processors – run most current operating systems and support leading graphical user interfaces. In the Intel486 and Intel386 range, the standard

Trademarked name	Intel486SX i486SX	Intel486DX i486DX	Intel486SL i486SL	Intel486DX2 i486DX2 Intel486DX4 i486DX4	Pentium
previous name	80486SX	80486DX	80486SL	80486DX	
internal bus width (bits)	32	32	32	32	32
external bus width (bits)	32	32	32	32	64
clock frequencies (MHz)	16, 20, 25, 33	25, 33, 50	25, 33	50, 66 (DX2) 75, 100 (DX4)	60, 66, 100, 133
math coprocessor	Intel487SX i487SX	built-in	built-in	built-in	built-in

Current range of Intel microprocessor chips (June 1995)

DX suffix is replaced by SX to denote a lower-performance CPU without a built-in mathematics *coprocessor, while the SL suffix is for a variant with low power consumption for mobile computers. The DX2 and DX4 ranges have doubled and tripled internal clock speeds respectively. The clock rates indicated (June 1995) are undergoing frequent upward modification.

All Intel486 and Intel386 processors are informally known by the numbers alone, and all used to have an 80 prefix. For instance, 386, 80386, Intel386 (*trademark*), and i386 (*trademark*) are synonymous. Preceding the 80386 range were the 80286, the 8086, and the 8088. Processors from the 8086 to the i486SX have optional math coprocessors distinguished by having a 7 in their number instead of a 6; hence the i387, i487.

Intel was the first manufacturer of microprocessors with the 4004 and 8008 chip sets. The original IBM PC and its successors and clones all used Intel processors or copies of them. In addition to its processor chips, Intel also sells system products, including both board-level products and the Paragon range of supercomputers. It is ranked number 41 in terms of revenue in the list of the world's top IT suppliers (1993 figures).

Intel386, Intel387 *Trademarks. See* Intel.

Intel486, Intel487 *Trademarks. See* Intel.

intellectual property A term that is increasingly difficult to define. It combines the traditional core of rights covered by patent, trademark, and copyright law coupled with more recent additions such as the protection of registered designs, design right, plant-breeders' rights, semiconductor topography rights, performing rights, and lending rights. A working definition is that it is the species of legally enforceable right associated with intangible aspects of physical items.

intelligent character recognition *See* ICR.

intelligent copier A *digital copier in which image manipulation, scaling, merging, reversing, etc., can be performed before printing.

intelligent front end (IFE) A program designed to improve the accessibility of an existing program or computer system. IFEs are useful where complex and highly sophisticated software already exists. The expertise to use this software may take considerable time to acquire; the purpose of an IFE is to alleviate this. The IFE may contain knowledge about the domain of the software (e.g. mathematics or finite element modeling) and also expert knowledge about how best to use the software to solve problems in that domain. IFEs have been built for a wide range of programs (e.g. statistics, finite element modeling, and ecology) and are potentially important in widening the availability of existing software.

intelligent network A rather general term used to describe a computer network, especially one with the ability to continue operation in the event of failure of some of the network components.

intelligent terminal A device with some processing capability, by means of which information may be transferred to and from a larger processing system. The device is often a combination of a display and keyboard with at least one built-in microprocessor to provide facilities such as editing and prompts for the operator. Modern application terminals for banking, retail, and industrial data collection are other examples of intelligent terminals.

intensity A nontechnical synonym for both *luminance and brightness. Luminance is the measured light intensity reflected or emitted by a surface in a given direction per unit of apparent area. Brightness is a psycho-physiological attribute of visual perception in which a source appears to emit or reflect more or less light.

interaction The term used when an operator interacts with a computer by means of a set of input devices to achieve a desired effect. *See also* acknowledgment, prompt, echoing, feedback.

interactive The word used to describe a system or a mode of working in which there is a response to operator instructions as they are input. The instructions may be presented via an input device such as a keyboard or mouse, and the effect is observable sufficiently rapidly that the operator can work almost continuously. This mode of working is thus sometimes referred to as *conversational mode*. An interactive system for multiple users will achieve the effect by time sharing. *See also* multiaccess system.

interactive development environment *See* IDE.

interactive graphics A computer graphics system that allows the operator or user to interact with the graphical information presented on the display using one or more of a number of input devices, some of which are aimed at delivering positions relevant to the information being displayed. Almost all computer workstations and personal computer systems are now able to be used interactively.

interblock gap (IBG) *See* tape format.

interface 1. A common boundary between two systems, devices, or programs.
2. The signal connection and associated control circuits that are used to connect devices. *See also* standard interface.
3. Specification of the communication between two program units. For example, if a procedure does not refer to nonlocal variables, its interface is defined by the parameter list. Careful definition of interfaces makes it possible to use a program unit without knowledge of its internal working, and is vital to the design of a system that is to be implemented by a team of programmers. The concept is an important feature of *Ada; in Ada a *package is defined in two parts, the interface and the body. The interface specifies exactly what identifiers are visible outside the package, and is sufficient to permit separate compilation of program units that use the package. Similar facilities are found in *Modula 2 and *Turbo Pascal.
4. To provide an interface.
5. To interact.

interior node *Another name for* nonterminal node.

interior path length of a tree. The sum of the lengths of all paths from the root to an interior (i.e. a nonterminal) node.

interlacing A method of displaying a video image by tracing out alternate *scan-lines in successive fields. (A field is a single complete scanning of the screen.) When alternate lines have been traced out, the scanning spot flies back to the top of the screen to trace out the remaining lines in the spaces between those of the first descent. This allows a lower refresh rate (and lower bandwidth requirements for lower frame rate) to produce an image that appears flicker-free.

interleaving A technique for achieving *multiprogramming in a relatively simple system without a supervisor program. Each of the programs that are to be run concurrently are broken down into segments that are then linked up into a single program. The function of each segment and the order of linking is arranged so that maximum use is made of processor time. A segment that initiates a transfer to a peripheral, i.e. a relatively slow task not requiring processor activity, is linked to a segment of some other program for which processor activity is required. A multiplexer channel interface will interleave transfers from several slow peripherals.

interlock A hardware or software method of coordinating and/or synchronizing multiple processes in a computer. Such a method can be used, for example, in the situation in which a certain process should not begin until another process is completed. A common interlock method uses *flags to do this. Another typical situation is one in which requests for some service, e.g. memory access, arrive simultaneously. A hardware interlock procedure will force the requests to become sequential, usually according to a predefined rule.

intermediate storage Any part or type of storage that is used for holding information between steps in its processing.

internal fragmentation A form of *fragmentation that arises when allocations of memory are made only in multiples of a subunit. A request of arbitrary size must be met by rounding up to the next highest multiple of the subunit, leaving a small amount of memory that is allocated but not in use. Internal fragmentation is reduced by reducing the size of the subunit; such a reduction increases *external fragmentation.

internal schema of a database. *Another name for* storage schema.

internal sorting *See* sorting.

Internet (Net) The global informal network that now links a very substantial fraction of the world's computer networks. The Internet is an extraordinary development that stems from the original *ARPANET, which was initiated in North America in 1969. In broad terms the Internet does not offer services to end-users, but serves primarily to interconnect other networks on which end-user services are located. It provides basic services for *file transfer, *electronic mail, and remote login, and high-level services including the *World Wide Web and the *MBONE.

The Internet is global, with connections to nearly every country in the world; the qualification "nearly" is present in part because the number of countries connected continues to increase, and in part because the Internet is deliberately nonpolitical and tends to deal with nongovernmental levels within a country. The Internet is informal, with a minimal level of governing bodies and with an emphasis in these bodies on technical rather than on administration or revenue generation. To date (Spring 1995) the major users of the Internet have been the academic and research communities, but it is inevitable that this situation will change rapidly in the next few years with the growth in commercial interest in the exploitation of the Internet. In addition the flow of data across borders is a highly complex legal matter, involving the *copyright and *data protection legislation of the countries involved.

internet protocol A *protocol that allows traffic to pass between networks. The most widely used is *IP, the Internet Protocol. *See also* internetworking.

internetworking Connecting several computer *networks together to form a single higher-level network, as occurs in the *Internet. There are two basic approaches: *encapsulation* and *translation*. The junctions between networks are called *gateways, and their functions depend on which internetworking approach is taken.

When encapsulation is used, a new protocol layer (or layers) is defined; this provides uniform semantics for services such as *datagram packet switching, *electronic mail, etc. When a message is entered into the internetwork, it is wrapped (encapsulated) in a network-specific protocol (local network datagram headers, or *virtual circuits). The encapsulated packet is sent over the network to a gateway, which removes the old network-specific encapsulation, adds a new set of network headers, and sends the packet out on another network. Eventually the message reaches its destination, where it is consumed.

When protocol translation is used, messages are sent on a local network using the protocols and conventions of that network. A gateway receives the message and transforms it into the appropriate message on another network; this may involve interpreting the message at multiple protocol levels.

The encapsulation approach provides a uniform set of semantics across all networks, while the translation approach results in unanticipated problems due to subtle differences between protocols. The encapsulation approach generally requires that new software be written for all hosts on all networks, while the translation approach requires new software only in the gateways. *See also* IP.

interoperability The ability of systems to exchange and make use of information in a straightforward and useful way; this is enhanced by the use of standards in communication and data format.

interpolation A simple means of approximating a function $f(x)$ in which the approximation, say $p(x)$, is constructed by requiring that

$$p(x_i) = f(x_i), i = 0,1,2,\ldots,n$$

Here $f(x_i)$ are given values $p(x_i)$ that fit exactly at the distinct points x_i (*compare* smoothing). The value of f can be approximated by $p(x)$ for $x \neq x_i$. In practice p is often a polynomial, linear and quadratic polynomials providing the simplest examples. In addition the idea can be extended to include matching of $p'(x_i)$ with $f'(x_i)$; this is *Hermite interpolation*. The process is also widely used in the construction of many numerical methods, for example in *numerical integration and *ordinary differential equations. The interpolating polynomial can be represented in many equivalent forms. For example, when the x_i are equally spaced, the forward and backward difference forms (*see* difference equation) are convenient. More commonly, nonequally spaced x_i give rise to the *divided difference* form, which incorporates successive differences

$$(f(x_{i+1}) - f(x_i))/(x_{i+1} - x_i),$$
$$i = 0,1,2,\ldots,n-1$$

These are the first divided differences; second divided differences are obtained by a similar differencing process and so on for higher order differences.

interpretation The process of attaching meanings to the expressions of a *formal language – or the meanings so attached. Without interpretation, expressions are purely formal entities, neutral with respect to meaning; this neutrality allows one to separate syntactic from semantic concerns, and to consider different interpretations for one formal language. The following are examples: *propositional logic interpretations attach *Boolean values to primitive symbols; *predicate logic interpretations involve *relations or *functions over some underlying *set; *algebras similarly attach sets and functions to the symbols of a *signature. Interpretations are made in the semantics of programming languages. An interpretation can give completely arbitrary meanings to primitive symbols. By contrast, a *model* must also satisfy certain logical sentences.

interpreter A language processor that analyzes a line of code and then carries out the specified actions, rather than producing a machine-code translation to be executed later.

interpretive language A programming language that is designed for or suited to interpretive implementation. It is typically a language that is designed to be used in an interactive manner during program development or prototyping; examples include *Basic and *REXX.

interprocess communication (IPC) In general any communication between processes, or more specifically a collection of rules and conventions that govern the passing of information between processes, especially in a *client/server environment.

interquartile range *See* measures of variation.

interrogation The sending of a signal that will initiate a response. A system may interrogate a peripheral to see if it requires a data transfer. The response is normally a status byte. When a number of devices are interrogated in a sequence the process is called *polling. Interrogation terminals are more generally called *inquiry stations.

interrupt A signal to a processor indicating that an *asynchronous event has occurred. The current sequence of instructions is temporarily suspended (interrupted), and a sequence appropriate to the interruption is started in its place. Interrupts can be broadly classified as being associated with one of the following.

(a) Events occurring on peripheral devices. A processor having initiated a transfer on a peripheral device on behalf of one process may start some other process. When the transfer terminates, the peripheral device will cause an interrupt. *See also* interrupt I/O.

(b) Voluntary events within processes. A process wishing to use the services of the operating system may use a specific type of interrupt, a *supervisor call (SVC)*, as a means of notifying the *supervisor.

(c) Involuntary events within processes. A process that attempts an undefined or prohibited action will cause an interrupt that will notify the supervisor.

(d) Action by operators. An operator wishing to communicate with the supervisor may cause an interrupt.

(e) Timer interrupts. Many systems incorporate a timer that causes interrupts at fixed intervals of time as a means of guaranteeing that the supervisor will be entered periodically.

See also interrupt handler.

interrupt-driven Denoting a *process that is restarted by the occurrence of an *interrupt. When a process initiates an auxiliary action to be carried out by some other process (for example, when a *device driver starts the hardware action that will output data to a disk drive), the initiating process may need to suspend its own activities until such time as the auxiliary action runs to completion. The initiating process may do this by running a *loop of instructions that repeatedly tests whether the auxiliary action has been completed, then loops back to repeat the test if the action is not yet complete. No other process can run during this time, which is clearly wasteful. In an interrupt-driven process some other process is allowed to run, and the device responsible for the auxiliary action is able to signal with an interrupt that it has completed its work. The operating system will detect the occurrence of an interrupt, determine which process is now free to proceed, and schedule that process to be restarted. *See also* polling.

interrupt handler (IH) A section of code to which control is transferred when a processor is interrupted. The interrupt handler then decides on what action should be taken. For instance, a *first level interrupt handler (FLIH)* is the part of an operating system that provides the initial communication between a program or a device and the operating system. When an interrupt occurs, the current state of the system is stored and the appropriate FLIH is executed: it leaves a message for the operating system and then returns, restoring the system to its original state and allowing the original task to continue as though nothing had happened. The operating system will periodically check for new messages and perform the appropriate actions.

interrupt I/O A way of controlling input/output activity in which a peripheral or terminal that needs to make or receive a data transfer sends a signal that causes a program interrupt to be set. At a time appropriate to the priority level of the I/O interrupt, relative to the total interrupt system, the processor enters an *interrupt service routine (ISR)*. The function of the routine will depend upon the system of interrupt levels and priorities that is implemented in the processor.

In a single-level single-priority system there is only a single I/O interrupt – the logical OR of all the connected I/O devices. The associated interrupt service routine polls the peripherals to find the one with the interrupt status set.

In a multilevel single-priority system there is a single interrupt signal line and a number of device identification lines. When a peripheral raises the common interrupt line it also sets its unique code on the identification lines. This system is more expensive to implement but speeds the response.

In a single-level multiple-priority system the interrupt lines of the devices are logically connected to a single processor interrupt in such a way that an interrupt from a high-priority device masks that of lower-priority devices. The processor polls the devices, in priority order, to identify the interrupting device.

A multilevel multiple-priority system has both the property of masking interrupts according to priority and of immediate identification via identification lines.

interrupt mask A means of selectively suppressing interrupts when they occur so that they can be acted upon at a later time. *See also* masking.

interrupt priority An allocated order of importance to program interrupts. Generally a system can only respond to one interrupt at a time but the rate of occurrence can be higher than the rate of servicing. The system control may arrange *interrupt masks to suppress some types of interrupt if a more important interrupt has just occurred.

interrupt service routine (ISR) *See* interrupt I/O.

interrupt vector *See* vectored interrupts.

intersection 1. of sets. The set that results from combining elements common to two sets S and T, say, usually expressed as

$$S \cap T$$

$\cap$ is regarded as an *operation on sets, the *intersection operation*, which is *commutative and *associative. Symbolically

$$S \cap T = \{x \mid x \in S \text{ and } x \in T\}$$

When two sets S and T intersect in the empty set, the sets are *disjoint. Since the intersection operation is associative, it can be extended to deal with the intersection of several sets.

2. of two graphs, G_1 and G_2. The graph that has as vertices those vertices common to G_1 and G_2 and as edges those edges common to G_1 and G_2.

intersegment linking The links between the *segments of a (large) program. Where segments are separately compiled it is necessary to provide a mechanism for transferring control out of one segment and into another, usually by introducing a specific type of labeled statement that identifies the point at which a segment can be entered, and whose value can be made accessible to other segments when the program is link-edited.

interval analysis A general method for analyzing the approximation errors that arise through doing imprecise floating-point arithmetic on digital computers.

interval timer A digital circuit that is used to determine the time interval between an initial trigger pulse and subsequent *logic states that appear after a predetermined delay.

intrinsic semiconductor (i-type semiconductor) *See* semiconductor.

invariant A property that remains TRUE across some transformation or mapping. In the context of *program correctness proofs, an invariant is an assertion that is associated with some program element and remains TRUE despite execution of some part of that element. For example, a *loop invariant* is an assertion that is attached at some point inside a program loop, and is TRUE whenever the attachment point is reached on each iteration around the loop. Similarly a *module invariant* is associated with a given module, and each operation provided by the module assumes that the invariant is TRUE whenever the operation is invoked and leaves the invariant TRUE upon completion.

Note that invariants cannot accurately be described as TRUE AT ALL TIMES since individual operations may destroy and subsequently restore the invariant condition. However the invariant is always TRUE between such operations, and therefore provides a static characterization by which the element can be analyzed and understood.

inverse 1. (converse) of a binary *relation R. A derived relation R^{-1} such that

$$\text{whenever } x\,R\,y$$
$$\text{then } y\,R^{-1}\,x$$

where x and y are arbitrary elements of the set to which R applies. The inverse of "greater than" defined on integers is "less than".

The inverse of a function
$$f : X \to Y$$
(if it exists) is another function, f^{-1}, such that
$$f^{-1} : Y \to X$$
and
$$f(x) = y \text{ implies } f^{-1}(y) = x$$
It is not necessary that a function has an inverse function.

Since for each monadic function f a relation R can be introduced such that
$$R = \{(x,y) \mid f(x) = y\}$$
then the inverse relation can be defined as
$$R^{-1} = \{(y,x) \mid f(x) = y\}$$
and this always exists. When f^{-1} exists (i.e. R^{-1} is itself a function) f is said to be *invertible* and f^{-1} is the *inverse* (or *converse*) *function*. Then, for all x,
$$f^{-1}(f(x)) = x$$

To illustrate, if f is a function that maps each wife to her husband and g maps each husband to his wife, then f and g are inverses of one another.

2. *See* group.

3. of a *conditional $P \to Q$. The statement $Q \to P$.

inverse homomorphic image *See* homomorphism.

inverse matrix For a given $n \times n$ matrix of numbers, A, if there is an $n \times n$ matrix B for which
$$AB = BA = I$$
where I denotes the *identity matrix, then B is the inverse matrix of A and A is said to be *invertible* with B. If it exists, B is unique and is denoted by A^{-1}.

inverse power method An *iterative method used to calculate *eigenvalues other than the dominant (largest in value) eigenvalue. *See also* power method.

inverse video *Another term for* reverse video.

inverted file A *data file in which one or more secondary indexes are used (*see* indexed file). For each indexed field, the file is said to be inverted with respect to that field. If secondary indexes exist to all possible fields, the file is said to be *fully inverted*.

input A	0	1
output B	1	0

Inverter circuit symbol and truth table

inverter (negator) An electronic *logic gate that inverts the signal it receives so that a logic 1 (true) is converted to logic 0 (false) and vice versa. It therefore implements the logical *NOT operation. The diagram shows the circuit symbol and *truth table.

invertible matrix *See* inverse matrix.

involution operation Any *monadic operation f that satisfies the law
$$f(f(a)) = a$$
for all a in the domain of f. The law is known as the *involution law*. It is satisfied by the elements of a *Boolean algebra where the monadic function is the process of taking a complement. Taking complements of sets and negation in its different forms also satisfy the law, as does the principle of *duality as it applies in Boolean algebras.

I/O *Abbrev. for* input/output.

I/O buffering The process of temporarily storing data that is passing between a processor and a peripheral. The usual purpose is to smooth out the difference in rates at which the two devices can handle data.

I/O bus A *bus, or signal route, to which a number of input and output devices can be connected in parallel.

I/O channel *See* channel.

I/O control Either the hardware that controls the transfer of data between main memory and peripheral devices, or the part of the system software that in turn controls that hardware.

I/O device Any unit of a system that is the

entry and/or exit point for information. Such devices are the link between the system and its environment. *See also* input device, output device.

I/O file A file used to hold information immediately after input from or immediately before output to an *I/O device.

I/O instruction One of a class of *instructions that describes the operations concerned with input and output.

I/O-limited Denoting a process that is either *input-limited, *output-limited, or both.

I/O mapping A technique used primarily in microprocessing whereby peripheral devices are interfaced to a processor whose architecture supports input and output instructions. An I/O mapped device is assigned one or more of the processor's I/O port addresses, and data and status information are transferred between the processor and the peripheral device using the processor's input and output instructions.

ionographic printer A type of *electrostatic printer in which the required electrostatically charged image is formed by the controlled projection of ions. Once expected to provide a lower cost than laser printers, ionographic printers are not now widely used.

IOP *Abbrev. for* I/O processor.

I/O port *See* port.

I/O processor (IOP) A specialized computer that permits autonomous handling of data between I/O devices and a central computer or the central memory of the computer. It can be a programmable computer in its own right; in earlier forms, as a *wired-program computer, it was called a *channel controller*. *See also* direct memory access.

I/O register A *register, perhaps one of several, used during the process of exchanging data between I/O devices and the main computer. An I/O register often has the ability to compose smaller units, such as bytes or characters, into units of machine-word size, or to perform the reverse decomposition.

I/O supervisor A more specific term than *I/O control, referring almost invariably to the appropriate software within the operating system.

I/O switching A means of selecting one out of several alternative hardware routes to a particular peripheral device, with consequent benefits either in system throughput or reliability.

IP *Abbrev. for* Internet Protocol. The basic protocol used to allow the *Internet to exchange data with a network attached to the Internet. *See also* TCP/IP.

IPC *Abbrev. for* interprocess communication.

IPI *Abbrev. for* Image Processing and Interchange. A multipart ISO/IEC standard (12087) that provides a model for the representation and manipulation of images in a digital form. Part 1 is a Common Architecture. Part 2 is the Programmer's Imaging Kernel System (IPI-PIKS), which defines processing operations on images. Part 3 is the Image Interchange Facility (IPI-IIF) for interchanging images; the IIF provides functionality for the storage and transfer of images, which can incorporate a wide variety of image structures and compression techniques.

IPL 1. *Abbrev. for* initial program load. In the context of IBM mainframes, the action of loading the operating system software into a "cold" machine.

2. *Abbrev. for* information processing language. In the early days of research into artificial intelligence the need for special-purpose languages capable of manipulating *dynamic data structures was recognized. IPL-I to IPL-V were a series of *list-processing languages developed to meet this need. They have long been obsolete.

IPO *Abbrev. for* input-process-output. A method for representing system designs in terms of system functions and relations between system functions. The method provides a simple diagram notation. Each IPO diagram has a name describing the function to be performed, usually some reference number, and a substructure of three rectangular boxes, one each for the input, process, and output for the named function. Relationships between IPO diagrams are shown as a functional hierarchy with unnamed links between boxes named and/or referenced.

IPSE *Acronym for* integrated *project support environment. Within the *Alvey Programme of IT research and development in the UK, three generations of IPSE were described.

First-generation IPSEs were characterized as comprising a set of *tools to support programming activities throughout the *software life cycle and a set of management tools to support project, configuration, and quality management activities across all life-cycle activities. These tools stored all project information as files within a filestore. However there was a low degree of integration, interaction, and exchange of information between the various tools. There was also limited flexibility in the choice of tools and methods available within the IPSE.

Second-generation IPSEs are characterized as having an *object management system (OMS) usually based on a *relational database. Through the OMS the tools could exchange information and cooperate in providing coverage of the various activities taking place within and across life-cycle phases. Second-generation IPSEs also had a common user interface to the tools, but not necessarily a public tool interface (*PTI).

Third-generation IPSEs are characterized by in-built support from *knowledge bases and *expert systems to guide the user in the choice of tools and methodology for software development and management.

Further concepts included an *IPSE framework* that provided the basic user support of an OMS, a user interface, and the ability to add user-selected methods and tools. IPSE frameworks would be configurable to create the specific environment required by a user for the user's application domain. To enable tool integration, IPSE frameworks used a PTI that specified the interfaces to the OMS and the user interface.

IRQ *Abbrev. for* interrupt request. *See* interrupt, interrupt I/O.

irradiance The light (strictly the radiant flux) arriving at a point of a surface.

irradiance gradient The rate of change of light arriving at a point on a surface.

irrecoverable error of peripheral storage. *See* error rate.

irreducible polynomial *See* polynomial.

irreflexive relation A *relation R defined on a set S and having the property that $x R x$ does not hold for any x in the set S. Examples are "is son of", defined on the set of people, and "less than", defined on the integers. *Compare* reflexive relation.

irreversible encryption A cryptographic process that transforms data deterministically to a form from which the original data cannot be recovered, even by those who have full knowledge of the method of encryption. The process may be used to protect stored *passwords in a system where the password offered is first encrypted before it is matched against the stored encrypted password. Illegal access to the stored password therefore does not permit access to the system.

IS *Abbrev. for* information systems.

ISA *See* Industry Standard Architecture.

ISAM *Acronym for* indexed sequential access method. An *access method for data files, supporting both *sequential access and indexed access (*see* indexed file). *Cobol contains facilities for defining files to be accessed in this way, and the access method is implemented by an ISAM utility package. *See also* VSAM.

ISDN *Abbrev. for* integrated services digital network. ISDN has been developed, primarily by the *PTTs, as a vehicle for the provision of a single service that carries all forms of digitally encoded traffic on a common platform. ISDN is in principle capable of carrying speech, data, and video traffic, and currently (Spring 1995) offers a range of data rates – from 64 Kbps up to 1.536 Mbps (in North America) or 1.920 Mbps (in Europe); these data rates will certainly increase with time. In general, ISDN services are presented as multiple 64 Kbps services rather than as a single higher-speed service. The service is engineered so that, for the lower data rates, existing speech-quality *local loops can be used from customers' premises to an exchange supporting ISDN access. For higher speeds it is necessary to install higher-grade *bearers, typically an optical fiber. The main service offering is for *virtual circuits with fast call set up and clear down; the tariff structure is based on a standing charge plus a usage charge based on aggregated call duration. The presence of a call-duration component means that beyond a certain point users will find it more effective to use a permanent leased connection to a standard digital bearer.

Basic-rate ISDN (B/ISDN) is an internationally standardized service that provides digital access at 64 Kbps, referred to as a *B-channel*, and can carry one channel of digitized speech, or data. A *D-channel* operates at 16 Kbps and is intended primarily for data. A typical local loop can operate at 144 Kbps, and can support two B-channels and a D-channel.

Primary-rate ISDN (P/ISDN) is an internationally standardized service that provides digital access at 1.536 Mbps (1.920 Mbps in Europe), usually presented as 23 B-channels and one D-channel (30 B-channels and one D-channel in Europe). In addition some operators are now providing so-called *N/ISDN*, which offers multiple B-channels with several options on the number of channels in the range 1–30.

Broadband ISDN is offered in a variety of formats in different countries, with total bandwidths as high as those offering the service feel able to operate, up to tens or hundreds of Mbps.

ISF *Abbrev. for* integrated systems factory. A third-generation *IPSE.

ISO International Organization for Standardization, the body responsible for all international data-processing standards, and many others. It was founded in 1946 and its members comprise national standards bodies in over 70 countries. It is of interest in the area of information processing in that it establishes the standard link protocols, coding standards, machine-readable media-interchange standards, etc., that are required to make it possible for data to be communicated electronically between equipment of various manufacturers and from various countries.

ISO-7 An internationally agreed character code (ISO 646-1973), using 7 bits for each character. The code includes certain positions designated for national use, to allow different countries to include special characters for letters with diacritical marks, or currency symbols, etc. The US version is *ASCII, which is commonly used in computing.

isolation Any technique aimed at separation of the parts of a system or its database in order to enhance computer security.

isoline A line consisting of all points with an associated value that is the same.

isolux curves Curves of constant *irradiance over a surface.

isomorphism A *homomorphism that, when viewed as a function, is a *bijection. If

$$\phi : G \to H$$

is an isomorphism then the *algebras G and H are said to be *isomorphic* and so exhibit the same algebraic properties. *Isomorphic trees* are *trees that are isomorphic as directed graphs.

ISO/OSI reference model A general architecture proposed by the International Standards Organization for communication systems, allowing open systems interconnection. *See* seven-layer reference model.

isosurface A surface consisting of all points with an associated value that is the same.

ISP *Abbrev. for* instruction set processor. A programming language for the algorithmic description of instruction sets and architectures. It was developed in conjunction with *PMS and is an effective *register transfer language to describe computer architectures and thus to enable their *simulation.

ISR 1. *Abbrev. for* interrupt service routine. *See* interrupt I/O.
2. *Abbrev. for* information storage and retrieval.

IT *Abbrev. for* information technology.

iterated function system (IFS) A large class of deterministic *fractals that may be partitioned into tiles. Such fractals are called *tiling structures*. An IFS is a representation scheme for tiling structures that makes an explicit mapping from the tiling structure into its tiles.

iterated map A *function

$$f : X \to X$$

from which is defined the iteration

$$x, f(x), f(f(x)), f(f(f(x))), \ldots$$

for any element x in set X. Thus a new function

$$F : X \times N \to X$$

is created by

$$F(x,t) = f^t(x)$$

where N is the set of natural numbers. The construct that makes F from f is, under certain circumstances, equivalent with the construct of *primitive recursion. Iterated maps are used to model the dynamical behavior of computers (for example, by iterating a next state function) and physical systems (for example, a neurone firing), and to generate fractals.

iteration 1. The repetition of a numerical or nonnumerical process where the results from one or more stages are used to form the input to the next. Generally the recycling of the process continues until some preset bound is achieved, or the process result is constantly repeated. This is one of the key ideas used in the design of *numerical methods (*see also* iterative methods).

An iterative process is *m-stage* if the new value is derived from m previous values; it is *m-stage, sequential* if the new value depends upon the last m values, i.e.

$$x^{k+1} = G_k(x^k, x^{k-1}, \ldots, x^{k-m+1})$$

The iteration is *stationary* if the function G_k is independent of k, i.e. the new value is calculated from the old values using the same formula. For example,

$$x^{k+1} = \frac{1}{2}(x^k + a/x^k)$$

is a stationary, one-stage iteration (used for evaluating the square root of a); this is a particular application of *Newton's method. The *secant method is a stationary two-stage sequential iteration. *False position is an example of a nonsequential iteration.

2. of a formal language. *See* Kleene star.

iterative deepening A technique used to enhance *depth-first search. The search tree is first processed to a maximum depth of two, and then the whole process is repeated to a depth of three, then again to four, and so on to the maximum depth n. Surprisingly, this costs little more than a single search to depth n (due to the exponential growth rate of the *branching fact the solution. *See also* combinatorial explosion.

iterative improvement A technique that approaches a solution by progressive approximation, using the kth approximate solution to find the $(k+1)$th approximate solution (*see also* iteration). Examples of methods that rely on iterative improvement are the Jacobi method and Gauss–Seidel method, used in *numerical analysis.

iterative methods *Numerical methods that are based on or utilize the idea of *iteration. Such methods are widely used in the solution of many different types of problem, ranging from linear and nonlinear *optimization to discretized systems of *partial differential equations. Starting from an initial estimate x_0 of the solution x^*, the methods generate a sequence of approximations $x_0, x_1, x_2, \dots$ The main objectives are to design methods that will converge from poor initial estimates and also converge rapidly in the vicinity of x^*. Different ideas may be employed in these two phases. *Newton's method, together with its variants, is of fundamental importance for all types of *nonlinear equations.

For the linear system $Ax = b$ where A is large and perhaps sparse (*see* sparse matrix), or has some other special structure, an important class of iterative methods is obtained by "splitting" A into the form $A = M - N$. The splitting is such that systems of the form $Mz = d$ are "easy" to solve, e.g. M could be lower triangular. The iteration then takes the form

$$Mx_{k+1} = Nx_k + d, k = 0,1,2,\dots,$$

where x_0 is an approximation to the solution. Convergence for any x_0 is guaranteed if all the eigenvalues (*see* eigenvalue problems) of $M^{-1}N$ have modulus less than one. The objective is to choose splittings for which each step is efficient and the convergence is rapid.

In *partial differential equations, linear systems arise for which the method of *successive over-relaxation* is particularly suitable. This is given by

$$(D + \omega L)x_{k+1} = \{(1 - \omega)D - \omega U\}x_k + \omega b,$$

where $A = D + L + U$, D consists of the diagonal elements of A, and L,U are respectively the strictly lower and upper triangular parts. The scalar ω is a free parameter and is chosen to try to maximize the rate of convergence. For special problems in partial differential equations, optimal values of ω can be computed. More recently the sucessive over-relaxation method is an important technique in the *multigrid method.

ITron *See* Tron.

J

jackknife A statistical technique in which, given a data set with n observations, the analysis is recalculated n times omitting each observation in turn (removed with a "jackknife"). The *mean and *variance of the estimated *parameters in the model may be compared with those obtained from the full set. The method is related to statistical *bootstrap estimation.

Jackson method *See* JSD, JSP.

JANET *Acronym for* Joint Academic Network. The UK network that links all Universities and Research Council sites. It was formed by amalgamating a number of separate networks, and formally constituted as a single system in 1984. The name was at one time used for some other networks, all of which have ceased to operate, and is now used solely for the UK Academic Network that is operated by *UKERNA*, the UK Education and Research Network Association. *See also* SuperJANET.

Java A language for *object-oriented programming on the Internet, especially applicable to the *World Wide Web; it was developed from 1990 at Sun Microsystems by P. Naughton. The output produced by a Java compiler is not executable code but an intermediate representation, known as *bytecode*, that is designed to translate directly into *native machine code for high performance. Bytecode can thus be interpreted on any computer on which the Java *run-time system is installed, allowing cross-platform portability (*see* platform, portable). Allegedly, full security is provided as no Java program can break out of this run-time environment or access unprotected system resources. Java is optimized for small networked applications that are dynamically downloaded across the Internet. These small programs, known as *applets*, can react to user input.

JCL *Abbrev. for* job-control language.

jitter The variations in the arrival time of a supposedly synchronous signal. Jitter may be caused by the fact that the original source of the signals has variations from its ideal periodic time, or by variations in the transit time from the signal source to the point at which the arrival times are actually observed, caused either by variations in the pathlength or in the speed at which the signal travels. In practice it is likely that all three effects contribute, and jitter is nearly always present.

J	K	Q	$\overline{Q}$
0	0	Q_n	$\overline{Q}_n$
0	1	0	1
1	0	1	0
1	1	$\overline{Q}_n$	Q_n

JK flip-flop, truth table and symbol

JK flip-flop A clocked flip-flop that has two inputs, J and K, and two outputs Q and $\overline{Q}$. The truth table for this device is shown in the diagram, along with the circuit symbol. Q_n represents the state of the Q output prior to the current active transition of the clock. The ambiguous condition of J and K both being true, logic 1, causes the device to "toggle", i.e. change to the complementary logic state, on active transitions of the clock signal. The JK flip-flop (together with the D flip-flop) is the most useful type of flip-flop and is available as a standard integrated-circuit package. *See also* flip-flop.

job A set of programs and the data to be manipulated by these programs. The word also means the execution of the set of programs. In its simplest form a job may consist of loading a binary program and then executing this program using supplied data. In more complex forms whole series of steps may be taken, certain of which may be contingent on the outcome of earlier steps. The complete description of a job is written in a *job-control language.

job-control language (JCL; command language) A language used to write the sequence of commands that will control the running of a job. In a normal programming language the objects manipulated and the operations applicable to these objects correspond to variables within the original problem. In a JCL the objects manipulated are such things as complete programs, or the input and output streams for these programs. Most JCLs incorporate features to control the sequence in which actions will be performed, including some form of conditional statement.

job mix The set of jobs actually being executed within a multiprogramming system at any one time. *See* scheduler.

job scheduling Selecting jobs for execution. *See* scheduler.

job step A single identifiable execution of a program on its data within a job. A typical job step will load a program module and execute it with appropriate data from files, producing output in files suitable for passing on to the next job step. Each job step will also produce an indication as to whether or not its outcome was successful.

job stream A sequence of jobs awaiting processing.

Johnson counter A type of digital counter characterized by a unique sequence of states. The sequence has the effect of "filling up" the counter with 1s from left to right, and then "filling up" with 0s again.

Josephson junction A junction between two metals that exhibits controllable electron tunneling properties at cryogenic temperatures. First reported by Brian Josephson in 1962, it is a superconducting device that can act as an extremely fast electronic switch with very low power dissipation. *See* Josephson technology.

Josephson technology A computing technology based on *superconductivity and electron tunneling between metals. These effects usually occur at extremely low temperatures, obtained by immersing the whole system in liquid helium or liquid nitrogen. Logic circuits and nonvolatile memories can be made out of the technology, which has the potential for ultrafast switching speeds and very low power dissipation (*see* Josephson junction). This combination of properties offers the potential of extremely fast computers that can be realized within minimum linear dimensions and that do not have the heat-transfer problems of VLSI silicon devices. As switching speeds become measured in picoseconds, system linear dimensions must be reduced accordingly. (One nanosecond is the order of 10 cm on a transmission line.)

journal tape The record produced in an *audit trail. It was once usually a magnetic tape.

JOVIAL *Acronym for* Jules' own version of international algorithmic language. A programming language designed by Jules Schwarz of System Development Corporation for military command-and-control systems. It was based on the international algorithmic language (IAL), otherwise known as *Algol 58, suitably extended for its purpose. JOVIAL was implemented on a number of military computers, and is still in use for military projects in the US.

joystick A device for generating signals that can cause the cursor or some other symbol to be moved rapidly about on a display screen. It is a shaft, several cm in height, that is vertically mounted in a base and can be pulled or pushed by the fingers in any arbitrary direction. The normal mode of operation is to tilt the joystick from its upright position to produce the corresponding direction of cursor motion; in some cases it may respond to finger pressure in the desired direction of cursor motion.

JPEG 1. *Acronym for* Joint Photographic Expert Group, the committee – a joint CCITT and ISO/IEC group – that works on the storage and transmission of still images and developed the ISO 10918 standard (see below). **2.** The ISO 10918 standard, Digital Compression and Coding of Continuous Still Images, developed by JPEG for *image compression of single digital images. The goal was to develop a general-purpose compression standard to meet the needs of almost all *continuous-tone still-image applications, reducing either the bandwidth needed to transmit the image or the amount of memory needed to store it.

In its simplest mode of operation, JPEG can be thought of as compressing an image broken into 8 by 8 blocks of pixels. Each 8 by 8 block is processed by a pipeline of processes: *discrete cosine transform to produce a representation of the sample as a collection of DCT coefficients, which are then quantized and entropy encoded (Huffman or arithmetic coding options exist). Decoding is the reverse of this process.

In addition, JPEG defines a *lossless compression mode based on a simple predictive method. There is also a *hierarchical encoding mode of operation that provides a pyramidal encoding at multiple resolutions, each differing by a factor of two in the horizontal direction, vertical direction, or both, from its adjacent encoding.

JPEG also makes provision for representing multiple-component images (color, spectral bands or channels), where each component consists of a rectangular array of samples.

See also MPEG.

JSD *Abbrev. for* Jackson system development. A proprietary structured method for the analysis and design of data processing and real-time systems, originally devised by Michael Jackson in 1983. JSD is fully integrated with *JSP (Jackson structured programming). The JSD notation covers entity structures (similar to *SSADM entity life histories), and network diagrams connecting entity and process structures. Rules assist the designer to iteratively structure and sequence the design and to transform and trace requirements into the software design.

JSP *Abbrev. for* Jackson structured programming. A proprietary brand of *structured programming, developed by the British consultant Michael Jackson specifically for use in *data processing. He observed that the inputs and outputs of programs could be defined in terms of particular data structures, which are mostly static and easier to define than programs. He then proposed that programs should be constructed by a systematic method based on data structure diagrams.

Two main problems arise. First, it may not be possible to combine the separate data structure diagrams involved in a program because of what are called *structure clashes*; this is solved by a form of program decomposition called *inversion*. Second, error handling is not accommodated by the simple method, and gives rise to a technique called *backtracking*, which is programmed by using *assertions together with the notation posit/quit/admit.

JSP is used in conjunction with Cobol and PL/I. Translators exist to convert from textual equivalents of Jackson data-structure diagrams into the required target language. It is claimed that the same code will always be produced from a given data specification.

JTMP *Abbrev. for* Job Transfer and Manipulation Protocol. *See* Red Book.

jukebox *Informal name for* optical disk library.

jump 1. A departure from the normal sequential execution of program instructions. The departure is achieved during execution by means of a *jump instruction*. (Jump instruction is usually regarded as synonomous with *branch instruction.) A jump may be *conditional or *unconditional. *See also* GOTO statement.

2. (transfer) To undergo such a departure.

jump instruction (branch instruction) *See* jump.

junction The area of contact between two *semiconductor materials having different electric properties, or between a semiconductor and a metal. Junctions play a fundamental role in semiconductor devices. The most frequently used is the *p-n junction*, which is formed between n-type and p-type *semiconductors. A p-n junction has rectifying properties as a result of the potential barrier built up across the junction by the diffusion of electrons from the n-type to the p-type material.

justify 1. To achieve uniform vertical edges to pages or columns of material printed or displayed on a screen. Information can be aligned along the left or right margin or centered between the margins. In the latter case, the space between words and/or letters is increased until the line fills the distance between the margins.
2. To move the bit pattern stored in a register so that either the least or most significant bit is at the appropriate end of the register.

K

K (or k) *See* kilo–.

KADS *See* knowledge acquisition.

Kamarkar's method *See* linear programming.

Karnaugh map (Veitch diagram) A graphical means for representing *Boolean expressions so that the manner in which they can be simplified or minimized is made apparent. It may be regarded as a pictorial representation of a *truth table or as an extension of the *Venn diagram. The method was proposed by E. W. Veitch and modified slightly by M. Karnaugh. The Karnaugh maps for expressions involving one, two, three, and four variables are shown in the diagram. When $n = 2$, for instance, the 00 square represents the term $a'b'$ (where $'$ denotes negation), the 11 square represents ab, and so on.

Terms that differ in precisely one variable can be combined. Such terms will appear as adjacent squares on a Karnaugh map and so can readily be identified. For example, the terms abc and abc' can be combined since

$$abc \vee abc' = ab$$

These two terms should each occupy one square on the $n = 3$ map and appear side by side, i.e. share a common edge. However, so too should the $a'b'c$ and the $ab'c$ squares. This complication can be overcome by stipulating that the two edges marked with dashes should be identified or joined together, i.e. the Karnaugh map for $n = 3$ should be drawn on one side of a ring of paper. When $n = 4$ the situation is even more complex: the two edges marked with dashes are identified, as are the dotted edges. The map can then be viewed as drawn on the outside of a torus.

Karnaugh maps are useful for expressions of perhaps up to six variables. When $n > 6$, the maps become unwieldy and too complex. Alternative methods of simplification, such as the Quine–McCluskey algorithm, are then preferable.

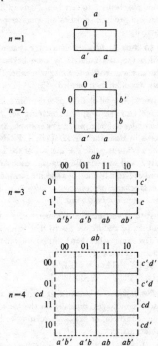

Karnaugh maps

kB (or **KB, Kb**) *Symbols for* kilobyte. *See* kilo-, byte.

Kbps *Abbrev. for* kilobits per second, i.e. usually 1000 bits per second. *See* kilo-, bps.

KBS *Abbrev. for* knowledge-based system.

Kbyte *Abbrev. for* kilobyte. *See* kilo-, byte.

K-complexity *See* Kolmogorov complexity.

k-connectivity *See* connectivity, connectedness.

KDC *Abbrev. for* key distribution center (in *data security).

KDD *Abbrev. for* knowledge discovery in databases. *See* data mining.

Kermit A widely used set of utility programs that allows a computer to support terminal access across a network, and to carry out file transfers. The Kermit package, which is freely available, requires a suitably configured computer – typically an IBM-compatible personal computer or an Apple Macintosh with a network card or modem attachment.

kernel The lowest layer into which a large operating system is subdivided, each layer dealing with some aspect of the system hardware. The kernel is responsible for allocating hardware resources to the processes that make up the operating system and to the programs running under the operating system. Formal verification of the kernel is usually necessary for systems professing high *integrity or *security. *See* security kernel.

Nucleus is a near-synonym for kernel and tends to be used where the effects are achieved by a mixture of normal programming and microcoding. The microprogram is written in such a way as to complement the functions achieved by the normal code, with a gain in running speed.

kernel field *Another name for* base field. *See* polynomial.

kerning In printing, the adjustment of the spacing between adjacent characters, using the natural slope in the letters, in order to improve the text appearance. Kerning is used in the more advanced desktop publishing applications and is of particular value when using italic fonts, as shown in the diagram.

Kerning

Kerning

Letters that are kerned (top) and unkerned (bottom)

key 1. A value used to identify a member of a set. Usually the elements of the set are records (*n*-tuples), in which one of the fields holds the key. Variations allow multiple key fields or any field to be used as a key.
2. A value used to establish authority to access particular information. *See* locks and keys.
3. A value used as a basis for encryption. *See* cryptography.
4. *See* keyboard.

keyboard An array of keys that may be captioned buttons or marked areas on a plane, each of which can cause a discrete signal or action when pressed with a finger. In current systems the operation of the key is detected and turned into a coded electrical signal; in the past mechanical coupling was used to allow depression of keys to directly punch a pattern of holes in a punch card or paper tape, or to print a character.

Computer keyboards consist of the standard typewriter layout – the QWERTY keyboard – plus some additional keys. These can include a *control key*, *function keys*, *arrow keys*, and a *numeric keypad*. The control key operates in the same way as a shift key but allows noncharacter information to be sent to the computer; the function keys send not one but a whole sequence of characters to the computer at a time, and can often be programmed by the user to send commonly used sequences; the *arrow keys are used, for example, to move the screen cursor to a new position; the numeric *keypad duplicates the normal typewriter number keys and speeds up the entry of numerical data.

keyboard encoder *See* encoder.

key frame Any of the main representations of a scene between which intermediate frames are interpolated to produce the sequence of frames necessary for an animation.

keypad A limited but compact form of keyboard, sometimes hand-held, with a small number, often 12 or 16, of captioned buttons or pressure-sensitive areas on a plane. It is used in conjunction with data collection equipment or as a means of entering limited information such as a personal identification number (PIN).

keypunch A *card punch controlled from a keyboard.

key sorting A form of *address table sorting in which the sortkey is placed with the addresses.

key to disk An obsolete data entry system in which the data entered by a number of keyboard operators was accumulated on a magnetic disk. The data was often then verified. The small computer routing the data from the operator to the correct file on the disk could also be used to carry out *data validation and produce statistics on operator productivity.

key to tape An obsolete data entry system in which the data entered by each keyboard operator was written to a magnetic tape. The data was often then verified.

keyword A symbol in a programming language that has a special meaning for the *compiler or *interpreter. For example, keywords in Basic include IF, THEN, PRINT. The keywords guide the analysis of the language, and in a simple language each keyword causes activation of a specific routine in the language processor. *See also* keyword parameter, reserved word.

keyword parameter A parameter of a subroutine, procedure, or macro that is identified by name rather than by its position in the parameter list, e.g.
   SORT(INPUT = FILE A,
   OUTPUT = SYSPRINT)

kill file *Informal* A system that identifies and discards messages, typically on the basis of who sent them, or keywords relating to the subject matter.

kilo- A prefix indicating a multiple of 10^3 (1000), as in kilogram and kilowatt; the symbol for kilo- should then be k (not K), as in kg and kW. When the binary number system is used in a structure or process (as in semiconductor RAM or ROM), kilo- then indicates a multiple of 2^{10} (1024), as in kilobyte and kilobit; the symbols k and K are both commonly used, as in kB or KB (symbols for kilobyte). The context usually clarifies which meaning of kilo- is intended, although being numerically close the meanings are often considered more or less equivalent.

Kilostream *Trademark* British Telecom's lower-speed digital leased-circuit service. Kilostream circuits are available as a fully digital service, operating at 2.4, 4.8, 9.6, 19.2, 48, and 64 Kbps. There is also a service called *Kilostream N*, which offers speeds in preset multiples of 64 Kbps up to 1.024 Mbps. Kilostream is also available as an international service. *See also* Megastream.

Klatt synthesizer A speech synthesizer written by Dennis Klatt at MIT. It is used in a variety of hardware products, for example DecTalk(c) from Digital and TextAssist(c) from Creative Labs. The code runs on *digital signal processing (DSP) hardware. A version of the code has been placed in the public domain. *See also* speech synthesis.

Kleene closure *Another name for* Kleene star.

Kleene-plus *See* Kleene star.

Kleene star (star closure; Kleene closure; iteration) An operation on *formal languages that gives for any language L the language L^*, defined by

$$\{\Lambda\} \cup L \cup LL \cup LLL \cup \ldots$$

where Λ is the empty word. Thus a *word w is in L^* if and only if it has the form

$$w_1 w_2 \ldots w_n$$

with each w_i in L, i.e. is a *concatenation of words in L.

The *Kleene-plus* (L^+) of L, is defined by

$$L \cup LL \cup LLL \cup \ldots$$

Thus L^+ comprises the nonempty strings of L^*.

Kleene's theorem 1. on *regular expressions. A theorem in *formal language theory proposed by S. C. Kleene and stating that a language is definable by a regular expression if and only if it is recognized by a *finite-state automaton. A regular expression equivalent to a finite-state automaton can be found by solving a set of simultaneous linear equations (*see* linear grammar, Arden's rule). Regular expressions were first used to characterize the power of certain *neural networks.

2. on fixed points. *See* fixed-point theorem.

k lookahead *See* LR parsing, LL parsing.

kludge *Informal* An inelegant but effective mechanism (software and/or hardware).

KMP algorithm *Short for* Knuth–Morris–Pratt algorithm.

knapsack problem A common example of an integer programming problem: a knapsack has volume V and there are an unlimited number of each of N different items. For $i = 1, \ldots, N$ one unit of item i has known volume V_i and known value m_i. Integer numbers of the various items may be put into the knapsack and the objective is to pack as much value as possible into the knapsack without exceeding the total volume V.

knot 1. An intersection of arcs in a *graph that is not a *planar graph. Where the arcs represent linear code sequences in a program, and the nodes represent branch points in the program, then the presence and frequency of knots is a measure of the *complexity of the program (*see* control-flow graph).

2. *See* spline.

knowledge Information that can be expressed as a set of facts and is known to an *agent or program. Knowledge can be distinguished from *information or *data by its embodiment in an agent; for example, an agent might receive information that increases its knowledge.

knowledge acquisition A range of techniques that are used to obtain *domain knowledge about an application for the purpose of constructing an *expert system. Knowledge acquisition covers all forms of knowledge and any methods by which they may be obtained. Various aids have been developed, such as *KADS*, a major system that consists of both a methodology and a set of tools. *Knowledge elicitation* is a subfield of knowledge acquisition concerned with systematic procedures for gleaning knowledge from human experts. Many tools are borrowed from psychology; for example, repertory grids are used to help draw out discriminations between classes of data items.

knowledge base A collection of *knowledge, usually relevant to a particular application domain, that has been formalized in an appropriate scheme to support reasoning processes. *Rule-based formalisms are often used but there are other methods of *knowledge representation. Knowledge bases are different from *databases in that (a) they not only store data but facilitate modification, revision, and other forms of internal manipulation of the knowledge, (b) they are also able to handle knowledge that is incomplete (*see* completeness), *inconsistent, and *uncertain, and (c) they may use imperative as well as declarative forms of knowledge.

knowledge-based system (KBS) A computer system that uses a *knowledge base to support reasoning processes in order to solve an application problem. *Expert systems are examples, but knowledge-based systems can take many other forms and can be found in many areas of *artificial intelligence.

knowledge discovery in databases (KDD) *See* data mining.

knowledge elicitation *See* knowledge acquisition.

knowledge engineering The branch of artificial intelligence that is concerned with building *expert systems.

knowledge engineering toolkits Large software packages that provide a range of facilities for the construction of and experimentation with different *knowledge-based systems. A range of *knowledge representation devices and different *inference engines are usually included. Using a knowledge engineering toolkit, elaborate systems of more sophistication and power than conventional *expert systems can be built, but considerable initial learning is required to master the facilities.

knowledge representation The datastructure techniques and organizing notations that are used in *artificial intelligence. These include *semantic networks, *frames, *logic, *production rules, and *conceptual graphs.

Knuth–Bendix algorithm A partial algorithm for turning a finite *term rewriting system (e.g. derived from a set of equations) into an equivalent complete set of rewrite rules. The algorithm, however, does not always return an input. The process is relevant to the implementation of specification languages, such as OBJ, that allow *equational specifications to be written and executed symbolically.

Knuth–Morris–Pratt algorithm (KMP algorithm) A method of finding patterns, developed by D. E. Knuth, J. H. Morris and V. R. Pratt. It can be used for example to find a certain pattern within a list of letters: the first letter in the list is stored in an array and subsequent letters added until the pattern is no longer followed or is completed; on failure the next letter is chosen and so on.

Kolmogorov complexity (K-complexity) A theory of computational *complexity based on the amount of information contained within entities. It was developed by the Russian mathematician Andrei Kolmogorov.

Königsberg bridges problem A problem solved by Euler in about 1736 for the inhabitants of Königsberg (now Kaliningrad). Two islands in a river are connected to each other by one bridge and to the banks by six other bridges; one island has two bridges from the left bank and two from the right bank while the other island has one bridge from the left bank and one from the right bank. The problem is whether or not it is possible to follow a circular walk starting and finishing at the same river bank and crossing each bridge precisely once. *See* Euler cycle.

Kraft's inequality When an instantaneously decodable code is to be formed from an alphabet of q letters, with the ith codeword being λ_i letters in length, Kraft's inequality

$$\sum_{i=1}^{n} q^{-\lambda_i} \leq 1$$

is a necessary and sufficient condition for such a code to be constructable with n codewords. In a code with no codewords remaining for allocation, the equality sign operates. *See also* prefix codes.

kriging A statistical technique for interpolating between points in space, developed originally in the mining industry for locating profitable minerals. The analysis involves modeling the relationship between deviations from the trend at neighboring points in space in order to find the best predictor at any point that was not sampled. The *covariance function may depend both on distance and on orientation.

Kronrod's algorithm (four Russians algorithm) A method of Boolean matrix multiplication developed by M. A. Kronrod. It saves computational time and storage space by doing computations in a strict order.

Kruskal's algorithm A method of finding the minimum-cost *spanning tree of a weighted undirected *graph, proposed by J. B. Kruskal Jnr (1956).

L

label 1. (tape label; volume label) A record at the very start of a magnetic tape, holding the identity and other characteristic information about the tape. Labels are written by the utility program, and checked at run time by the operating system to ensure that the specified tape is the one that has been loaded. A tape label only holds information about the physical tape, which remains constant irrespective of the file(s) held on the tape. Labels are thus distinct from file *headers, which precede every file on a tape.

Magnetic and optical disks normally have similar labels, though there is no commonly accepted term for them.

2. (statement label) A numeric or alphanumeric identifier associated with a line or statement in a program and used in other parts of the program to refer to that statement.

lambda calculus (λ-calculus) A formalism for representing functions and ways of combining functions, invented around 1930 by the logician Alonzo Church. The following are examples of λ-expressions:

$\lambda x.x$ denotes the *identity function*, which simply returns its argument;

$\lambda x.c$ denotes the *constant function*, which always returns the constant c regardless of its argument;

$\lambda x.f(f(x))$ denotes the composition of the

function f with itself, i.e. the function that, for any argument x, returns $f(f(x))$.

Much of the power of the notation derives from the ability to represent higher-order functions. For example,

$$\lambda f.\lambda x.f(f(x))$$

denotes the (higher-order) function that, when applied to a function f, returns the function obtained by composing f with itself.

As well as a notation, the λ-calculus comprises rules for *reducing* λ-expressions to equivalent ones. The most important is the rule of β-*reduction*, by which an expression of the form

$$(\lambda x.e_1)(e_2)$$

reduces to e_1 with all *free occurrences of x replaced by e_2. For example,

$$(\lambda x.f(\lambda x.x,x))(a)$$

reduces to

$$f(\lambda x.x,a)$$

As a second example, involving a functional variable, the expression

$$(\lambda f.f(a))(\lambda x.g)(x,b))$$

reduces to

$$(\lambda x.g(x,b))(a)$$

and hence to

$$g(a,b)$$

In theoretical terms, the formalism of λ-calculus can be shown to be equivalent in expressive power to that of *Turing machines. It has a special role in the study of programming languages: one can point to its influence on the design of functional languages such as J. McCarthy's LISP; to P. Landin's reduction of Algol 60 to λ-calculus, and to D. Scott's construction of a set-theory meaning for the full unrestricted λ-calculus – a construction that ushered in the theory of *domains in the *denotational semantics of programming languages.

lambda expression (λ-expression) An expression in the *lambda calculus.

Lambert's law The law stating that *diffusely reflected and transmitted light is scattered in all radiated directions with equal intensity and that this intensity is proportional to three values: the intensity of the incident light, the reflectance of the surface, and the cosine of the angle between the surface normal and the direction of the incident light. In computer graphics the law is particularly useful for diffuse surfaces such as chalk.

LAN *Acronym for* local area network.

language *See* programming language, specification language, formal language.

language concatenation *See* concatenation.

language construct A syntactic structure or set of structures in a language to express a particular class of operations. The term is often used as a synonym for *control structure.

LAP *Acronym for* link access protocol. The second-layer (data link layer) protocol that is a subset of *HDLC and is used in *X25-based networks in setting up channels between *DTE and *DCE. An alternative protocol, *LAP-B*, developed after LAP, allows the DTE/DCE interface to operate in "balanced mode".

Laplacian operator A high-pass filter that is used in *image processing to detect edges in an intensity-gradient image (*see* edge detector). Mathematically, the operator is based on the two-dimensional sum of the second derivatives of the image convolved with a Gaussian curve. The second derivatives detect rapid intensity changes and the Gaussian smooths out the effects of noise. The operator shows an interesting correspondence with biological detectors.

laptop computer A personal computer that can be simply carried around by one person and used in transit from internal battery power. Laptops typically have all the features of a *desktop model but have a flat display screen, either a *plasma panel or an *LCD display, that folds over the keyboard when not in use. They are constructed from components chosen for their lightness, small size, and low power consumption. These tend to make laptops more expensive than their desktop equivalents. *See also* notebook, palmtop computer.

large-scale integration *See* LSI, integrated circuit.

laser A light source with special properties (principally spectral purity, narrow output beam, and ease of modulation) that make it particularly useful in optical storage devices

and some kinds of printer, and also in *fiber optics communication systems.

laserdisk Colloquially, an *optical disk; more specifically, a particular form of read-only optical disk using analog rather than digital technology.

laser printer An *electrophotographic printer in which a laser is used as the light source; the laser beam is modulated to produce the image. The term is also often used to refer to *page printers of this type that use *LEDs or *LCDs as the active element. This type of printer is now very widely used as an office printer, frequently shared among a number of users. Most laser printers use single sheets of paper or transparent media and provide media-handling facilities; some can handle more than 15 pages per minute. Laser printers produce a very high standard of print. The higher-end range of laser printers offers resolutions of greater than 600 dots per inch. Prices have now fallen to a level where the cheaper models are affordable even on single workstations. Color laser printers are available but involve complex hence costly technology.

last in first out *See* LIFO.

latch An electronic device that can store temporarily a single bit of data. It can be considered as an extension of a simple *flip-flop. The storage is controlled by a *clock signal, a given transition of which fixes the contents of the latch at the current value of its input. The contents will remain fixed until the next transition of the clock.

latency The time taken for the start of a given sector of data on a storage disk to reach the read/write head. The time is measured from the instant that the head settles at the track within which the sector lies. The average latency is the time for half a revolution of the disk. *See also* seek time, access time.

LaTeX A macro package built on top of *TeX. LaTeX implements a form of descriptive markup system, in which the user specifies the function of each piece of text (heading, paragraph, footnote, etc.) but not its printed appearance. The actual layout is defined in a collection of style files, thus ensuring uniformity of appearance and conformity to house style. LaTeX hides much of the complication of TeX from the user, and is widely used in the academic community as a way of producing typeset research papers and reports.

Latin alphabet One of several *character sets based on the letters used for writing Latin. (In contrast with Latin, these alphabets distinguish I from J, and U from V.) They, along with sets in Cyrillic, Arabic, Greek, and Hebrew, are included in ISO 8859: Information Processing – 8-bit single-byte coded graphic character sets. Each Latin alphabet contains the *ASCII character set, and includes additional characters with diacritical marks for various languages. Table 1 (overleaf) shows the code table for Latin alphabet No. 1, which covers Danish, Dutch, English, Faroese, Finnish, French, German, Icelandic, Irish, Italian, Norwegian, Portuguese, Spanish, and Swedish; Table 2 (overleaf) shows the distribution of languages within Latin alphabets Nos. 1–5.

lattice An *algebraic structure, such as a *Boolean algebra, in which there are two *dyadic operations that are both *commutative and *associative and satisfy the *absorption and *idempotent laws. The two dyadic operators, denoted by $\wedge$ and $\vee$, are called the *meet* and the *join* respectively.

An alternative but equivalent view of a lattice is as a set L on which there is a *partial ordering defined. Further, every pair of elements has both a greatest *lower bound and a least *upper bound. The least upper bound of $\{x, y\}$ can be denoted by $x \vee y$ and is referred to as the *join* of x and y. The greatest lower bound can be denoted by $x \wedge y$ and is called the *meet* of x and y. It can then be shown that these operations satisfy the properties mentioned in the earlier definition, since a partial ordering $\leq$ can be introduced by defining

$$a \leq b \text{ iff } a \vee b = a$$

Lattices in the form of Boolean algebras play a very important role in much of the theory and mathematical ideas underlying computer science. Lattices are also basic to much of the approximation theory underlying the ideas of *denotational semantics.

layer in *open systems interconnection (OSI). *See* seven-layer reference model.

lazy evaluation An execution mechanism in which an object is evaluated only at the time when, and to the extent that, it is needed. This allows programs to manipulate objects, such as lengthy or infinite lists, whose evaluation would otherwise be needlessly time-consuming or indeed fail to terminate at all. An illustration is the problem of comparing two *trees, t_1 and t_2, to test whether the *leaves of t_1, read from left to right, form the same list as the leaves of t_2. The simplest solution is first to construct the two leaf-lists and then to compare them element by element. Lazy evaluation allows this program to interleave the construction of the two leaf-lists and then test for equality. The program can then terminate as soon as the lists are found to differ, without having unnecessarily constructed both lists in toto. *See also* strictness.

LBA *Abbrev. for* linear-bounded automaton.

LCA *Abbrev. for* logic cell array. A form of *PAL in which the programming information is held in a SIPO (serial in, parallel out) *shift register, so that the mode of operation of the device can be read into it when the system of which it is a part is started up. The contents of the register, and therefore the mode of operation of the LCA, remain unchanged while the system is running.

LCC *Abbrev. for* leadless chip carrier.

LCD *Abbrev. for* liquid-crystal display. A *flat-panel display that is incorporated in most portable computers, where it can produce a monochrome or color image. LCDs are also used in other digital instruments. Early LCDs suffered from poor contrast between light and dark combined with narrow viewing angles. Several different forms of construction now offer improved viewing characteristics.

LCD technology is based on *liquid crystals*. These are common organic compounds that, between specific temperature limits, change their crystal structure to allow them to flow like a liquid. *Supertwisted nematic displays* use rod-shaped (nematic) crystals. The crystals are organized between two transparent polar-

	00	01	02	03	04	05	06	07	08	09	10	11	12	13	14	15
00			SP	0	@	P	`	p			NBSP	°	À	Ð	à	ð
01			!	1	A	Q	a	q			¡	±	Á	Ñ	á	ñ
02			"	2	B	R	b	r			¢	²	Â	Ò	â	ò
03			#	3	C	S	c	s			£	³	Ã	Ó	ã	ó
04			$	4	D	T	d	t			¤	´	Ä	Ô	ä	ô
05			%	5	E	U	e	u			¥	µ	Å	Õ	å	õ
06			&	6	F	V	f	v			¦	¶	Æ	Ö	æ	ö
07			'	7	G	W	g	w			§	·	Ç	×	ç	÷
08			(	8	H	X	h	x			¨	¸	È	Ø	è	ø
09			)	9	I	Y	i	y			©	¹	É	Ù	é	ù
10			*	:	J	Z	j	z			ª	º	Ê	Ú	ê	ú
11			+	;	K	[	k	{			«	»	Ë	Û	ë	û
12			,	<	L	\	l	|			¬	¼	Ì	Ü	ì	ü
13			-	=	M	]	m	}			SHY	½	Í	Ý	í	ý
14			.	>	N	^	n	~			®	¾	Î	Þ	î	þ
15			/	?	O	_	o				-	¿	Ï	ß	ï	ÿ

Table 1   Latin alphabet No. 1

Africaans:	3	French:	1, 5	Norwegian:	1, 4, 5
Albanian:	2	German:	1, 2, 3, 4, 5	Polish:	2
Catalan:	3	Greenlandic:	4	Portuguese:	1, 5
Czech:	2	Hungarian:	2	Rumanian:	2
Danish:	1, 4, 5	Icelandic:	1	Serbocroatian:	2
Dutch:	1, 3, 5	Irish:	1, 5	Slovak:	2
English:	1, 2, 3, 4, 5	Italian:	1, 3, 5	Slovene:	2
Esperanto:	3	Lappish:	4	Spanish:	1, 3, 5
Estonian:	4	Latvian:	4	Swedish:	1, 4, 5
Faroese:	1	Lithuanian:	4	Turkish:	3, 5
Finnish:	1, 4, 5	Maltese:	3		

Table 2   Languages in Latin alphabets Nos. 1–5

ized layers with 90° between the directions of polarization. The crystals form a spiral between the two layers so that light can be rotated and passed through the material unchanged. When an electric field is applied, the orientation of the crystals is disturbed thus stopping the light passing. Controlling the electric field applied to each pixel results in an image. It is possible to switch modes up to 120 hertz. In consequence, by shuttering white light through colored dye filters it is possible to turn a monochrome display into a color one. The same shuttering system can be used to generate stereo images.

Supertwisted nematic displays may be *passive-matrix LCDs*, containing no active (switching) electronic components. A much higher performance, especially for color displays, is obtained from *active-matrix LCDs*. In this construction, a diode using thin-film transistor (TFT) technology is added to each *pixel to ensure no sneak currents cause neighboring pixels to be partially illuminated.

LCDs are expensive when compared to CRT displays of similar resolution. They also have a much lower power consumption than CRT displays but since they do not emit light they must rely on external ambient illumination or be provided with back lighting.

LCM *Abbrev. for* least common multiple.

LCSAJ *Abbrev. for* linear code sequence and jump. A section of program code that will always be executed in sequence and followed by a particular sequence. *See also* control-flow graph.

LDU decomposition *See* LU decomposition.

leader A blank section of a tape, preceding recorded information, that is needed for threading the tape into a reading device.

leading edge of a pulse. *See* pulse.

leadless chip carrier (LCC) A form of *integrated circuit packaging where connections to the device are not made by means of pins extending beneath the device (as for instance in *DIPs), but instead by means of studs arranged around the package's periphery. This means that the device can be inserted into a socket mounted on a PCB or mounted directly.

leaf *Short for* leaf node.

leaf node (terminal node; tip node; external node) Any node of a tree with no descendants and hence of *degree zero.

learning *See* machine learning.

leased line A dedicated telephone/data line that is leased from the *PTT and is permanently connected between two points.

least common multiple (LCM) of two integers m and n. The smallest integer p such that m divides p exactly and n divides p exactly. For example, the LCM of 9 and 6 is 18.

least fixed point *See* fixed-point theorem.

least significant character In a *string where the position of a character determines its significance, the character at the end of least significance. Such a string is normally written with the least significant position on the right. For example, the *least significant digit (LSD)* and the *least significant bit (LSB)* contribute the smallest quantity to the value of a digital or binary number.

least squares approximation *See* approximation theory.

least squares, method of A method of estimating *parameters in a model by minimizing the sum of squares of differences between observed and theoretical values of a variable. If

$$y_i, i = 1,\ldots,n,$$

is a sample of n observations, and μ_i is a set of theoretical values corresponding to a set of unknown parameters, θ, and a set of known associated observations, x_i, then the criterion to be minimized with respect to variations in θ is the sum of squares,

$$\Sigma(y_i - \mu_i)^2$$

The values of θ at which the minimum occurs are known as *least squares estimates*.

The method of *weighted least squares* is used when each observation is associated with a weight, w_i (*see* measures of location), and the criterion to be minimized is

$$\Sigma w_i(y_i - \mu_i)^2$$

See also likelihood, regression analysis.

least upper bound *See* upper bound.

LED display A device used in some instruments to display numerical and alphabetical characters. It consists of an array of *light-emitting diodes*, LEDs, which are semiconductor diodes that emit light when a *forward bias is applied. LEDs are small, cheap, and have relatively low current and voltage requirements and long life. Their power consumption is, however, significantly higher than that of *LCDs. In an LED display these diodes are arranged in such a way that by selectively illuminating individual ones in the array, simple characters are formed on the display. Seven diodes suffice to display the digits and some letters.

Single LEDs are used almost universally where single on/off indicators are needed. They may be red, green, or yellow but blue is not yet widely available.

Lee distance (Lee metric) In the theory of *block codes intended for error detection or error correction, a distance measure analogous to the *Hamming distance but modeling more accurately a *linear *q-ary channel, such as the phase-modulated carrier used in *modems. When $q = 2$ or $q = 3$, the Lee and Hamming distances are the same.

left-linear grammar *See* linear grammar.

left shift *See* shift.

left subtree *See* binary tree.

left-to-right precedence A simple form of *precedence hierarchy, used in APL, in which operators are taken in the order in which they appear in the expression. Each operator takes everything to the right as its right operand, thus

$$a * b + c$$

evaluates as

$$a * (b + c)$$

Note that, paradoxically, left-to-right precedence actually causes operators to be applied in right-to-left sequence.

legacy applications Applications that are still in use though written using languages that are no longer current.

legacy networks Networks that use earlier technologies, and that almost any organization using networks for more than a year or so will have in operation. The major problem facing those with one or possibly several legacy networks is in trying to decide whether to design a new network so as to interwork with the legacy network, or to replace the legacy network at the same time as installing the new network. The interworking option will increase the complexity of the new network and tend to reduce its functionality. The replacement option will increase the overall cost of the new network.

legged robots Mobile robot systems that locomote by means of legs rather than wheels. This includes multilegged systems similar to insects with six or eight legs, systems with two legs (bipeds), and even one leg, as in the hopping machines developed at MIT. Such research produces results on dynamics, mobility, and active balance. *See also* mobile robotics.

Lempel–Ziv compaction A *data compaction method that uses a *VTVL or *VTFL code. It uses *statistical compaction, and is particularly suited to adaptive implementation.

Lempel–Ziv–Welch (LZW) compaction An improved form of *Lempel–Ziv *data compaction. It is provided, for example, as a standard tool in the *UNIX operating system. Typically, it achieves compaction ratios approaching 2 for English text, more than 2 for tabulated data text and for source programs, and about 1.5 for binary object programs. Binary data in *floating-point notation is almost incompressible owing to the near-random nature of the *mantissas.

length 1. of a sequence. The *cardinality of the domain of the *sequence. Thus the sequence

$$a_1, a_2, \ldots, a_n$$

has length n.
2. of a string. The upper bound of the *string, hence the number of elements in the string.
3. of a vector. The number of elements in the *vector.

length-increasing grammar *See* context-sensitive grammar.

LEO A line of computers, and a company, of historic importance in the British computing industry. J. Lyons & Co (a large firm in the catering industry) initiated in 1947 a project to build a computer to mechanize clerical functions in their own offices. (This decision was almost simultaneous with a similar decision in the US by Eckert and Mauchly, which led to *UNIVAC 1.) The project was led by T. R. Thompson, a mathematician, and J. Pinkerton, an electrical engineer. The machine they built, LEO (Lyons Electronic Office), was fully operational at the end of 1953.

In 1954, Leo Computers Limited was founded. The company traded until 1963, when it was merged with the computing division of English Electric. During that time it marketed the LEO III, an extremely advanced commercial machine for its time. *See also* ICL.

letter (in formal language theory) *See* word.

letter distribution *See* Parikh's theorem.

letter-equivalent languages *See* Parikh's theorem.

level of a node in a tree. A numerical value equal to one greater than the *depth of the same node. The level of the root node is thus one; the level of any other node is one greater than that of its parent. In some texts, the term level is used as a synonym for depth.

leverage point *See* influence.

LEX A lexical analyzer generator for the *UNIX system. LEX automatically generates a *lexical analyzer, given the syntactic rules describing the *tokens of a language. It is usually used in conjunction with the compiler generator *YACC.

lexical analyzer (scanner) The part of a *compiler that breaks up the input into meaningful units, e.g. names, constants, reserved words, operators. The lexical analyzer will also remove redundant characters, e.g. spaces, and may deal with character-set mappings, e.g. replacing upper-case letters by the equivalent lower-case letters. The units recognized by the lexical analyzer are called *tokens*, and are output in some conveniently coded form for subsequent processing by the compiler.

lexicographic order The order of words in a dictionary, given the order of letters in the alphabet. In general, let a set S be *well-

ordered by relation $<$, and for $n > 0$ let T be a set of n-tuples

$$(x_1, x_2, \ldots, x_n)$$

of elements x_j in S. Then the ordering relation $<$ over such n-tuples can be defined so that

$$(x_1, \ldots, x_n) < (y_1, \ldots, y_n)$$

iff $x_1 < y_1$ or there is some k, $1 \le k \le n$, for which

$$x_i = y_i \text{ for } 1 \le i < k$$
$$x_k < y_k$$

The set T is in lexicographic order if the n-tuples are sorted with respect to this relation. The concept can be extended to strings whose lengths may be different. The order would then be that in which words are placed in a dictionary.

lexicographic sort Any sorting algorithm for putting n-tuples into *lexicographic order.

Liang–Barsky clipping A graphics algorithm for *clipping a line with respect to a rectangular boundary based on a parametric representation of the line and finding the points where the line enters the region and leaves the region.

library *See* program library, link library, DLL, optical disk library, tape library.

life cycle *See* software life cycle, system life cycle.

LIFO or **lifo** *Acronym for* last in first out. *LIFO list* is another name for *stack. A stack implemented in hardware is sometimes referred to as a *lifo*.

light-emitting diode (LED) *See* LED display.

lighting model (shading model) A model of the interaction of light with a scene. *See also* illumination, rendering, ray tracing, radiosity.

light intensity *See* intensity.

light pen A penlike input device that is used with a *cathode-ray tube display to point at items on the screen or to draw new items or modify existing ones. The light pen has a photosensor at the tip that responds to the peak illumination that occurs when the CRT scanning spot passes its point of focus. The display system correlates the timing of the pulse from the photosensor with the item being displayed to determine the position of the light pen.

The light pen is used to draw items with the aid of a tracking cross. As the light pen is moved across the screen, the part of the tracking cross sensed changes thus allowing the direction of movement of the light pen to be ascertained. The tracking cross can be redrawn to locate it at the expected new center of the light pen's position and thus appears to follow the light pen.

likelihood The *probability that an observation belongs to a *probability distribution with *parameters θ, considered as a function of the parameters rather than of the observation.

The method of *maximum likelihood*, originated by R. A. Fisher, estimates *parameters in statistical models by maximizing the likelihood of observing the data with respect to the parameters of the model. The values taken by the parameters at the maximum are known as *maximum likelihood estimates*. This method is computationally equivalent to the method of *least squares when the distribution of the observations about their theoretical means is the *normal distribution.

limited license A license granted to a customer that limits the use that is made of a computer program. Under *copyright law, limited licenses restrict customers from legally being entitled to use several copies of individual programs at the same time or use copies on anything except a particular computer.

Linda A particular model for *distributed processing in which the *processes communicate by inserting, examining, and deleting objects in a common *bag. It is architecture-independent.

Lindenmeyer system *See* L-system.

linear algebraic equations (simultaneous equations) A problem in *numerical linear algebra that requires the solution of n equations in the unknowns $x_1, x_2, ..., x_n$ of the form

$$Ax = b$$

where A is a square $n \times n$ matrix. The solution obtained by computing the inverse matrix and forming $A^{-1}b$ is less accurate and

requires more arithmetical operations than elimination methods. In *Gaussian elimination* multiples of successive equations are added to all succeeding ones to eliminate the unknowns $x_1, x_2, ..., x_{n-1}$ in turn. Properly used, with row interchanges to avoid large multiples, this leads to a solution that satisfies exactly a system close to the one given, relative to the machine precision. The accuracy of the solution, which can be cheaply estimated, depends on the *condition number of the problem.

Many other methods are used to deal with matrices of special form. Very large systems where the matrix A has predominantly zero entries occur in the solution of *partial differential equations. Elimination methods tend to fill in the zeros causing storage problems and *iterative methods are often preferred for such problems.

linear array *Another name for* one-dimensional array, i.e. for a *vector. *See also* array.

linear-bounded automaton (LBA) A *Turing machine M such that the number of tape cells visited by M is bounded by some linear function of the length of the input string. Of equivalent power is the smaller class of Turing machines that visit only the cells bearing the input string. The *context-sensitive languages are precisely those recognized by such Turing machines.

linear channel A transmission channel in which the information *signal and the *noise signal combine additively to form the output signal. In a *q-ary linear channel, with a finite number, q, of amplitudes, the signals add modulo-q; in the binary case ($q = 2$), this has the same effect as an *exclusive-OR operation between the signals.

linear codes In coding theory, codes whose encoding and decoding operations may be expressed in terms of linear operations. The term is usually applied to certain *error-correcting codes in which the encoding operation involves a *generator matrix* and the decoding operation involves a *parity-check matrix*. Linear codes are, therefore, also called *parity-check codes*. A particular linear code forms a commutative *group that has the zero codeword as its identity.

In the case of linear (n, k) *block codes, the generator matrix is $k \times n$ and the parity-check matrix is $(n - k) \times n$; the elements of both matrices are elements of the base field (this being $\{0, 1\}$ for *binary codes). *See also* convolutional code.

linear grammar A *grammar in which each production contains at most one nonterminal in its right-hand side. Such a grammar is *right-linear* if a nonterminal can only occur as the rightmost symbol, i.e. if each production has one of the forms

$$A \rightarrow w$$
$$A \rightarrow wB$$

where A and B are nonterminals and w is a string of terminals. A *left-linear grammar* can be similarly defined:

$$A \rightarrow w$$
$$A \rightarrow Bw$$

The right- and left-linear grammars generate precisely the *regular languages.

The word linear relates to an analogy with ordinary algebra. For example, a right-linear grammar such as

$$S \rightarrow aS \,|\, abT \,|\, abcT \,|\, abcd$$
$$T \rightarrow S \,|\, cS \,|\, bcT \,|\, abc \,|\, abcd$$

corresponds to the simultaneous linear equations

$$X = \{a\}X \cup \{ab,abc\}\, Y \cup \{abcd\}$$
$$Y = \{\Lambda,c\}X \cup \{bc\}\, Y \cup \{abc,abcd\}$$

where X and Y are sets of strings and Λ is the empty string. *Union and *concatenation play roles analogous to addition and multiplication. The smallest solution to the equations gives the language generated by the grammar. *See* Arden's rule.

linear independence A fundamental concept in mathematics. Let

$$x_1, x_2, \ldots, x_n$$

be m-component vectors. These vectors are linearly independent if for some scalars $\alpha_1, \alpha_2, \ldots, \alpha_n$,

$$\sum_{i=1}^{n} \alpha_i x_i = 0$$

implies

$$\alpha_1 = \alpha_2 = \ldots = \alpha_n = 0$$

Otherwise the vectors are said to be *linearly dependent*, i.e. at least one of the vectors can be written as a linear combination of the others. The importance of a linearly independent set of vectors is that, providing there are enough of them, any arbitrary vector can be represented uniquely in terms of them.

A similar concept applies to functions $f_1(x), f_2(x), \ldots, f_n(x)$ defined on an interval $[a,b]$, which are linearly independent if for some scalars $\alpha_1, \alpha_2, \ldots, \alpha_n$, the condition,

$$\sum_{i=1}^{n} \alpha_i f_i(x) = 0$$

for all x in $[a,b]$, implies

$$\alpha_1 = \alpha_2 = \ldots = \alpha_n = 0$$

linear list *See* list.

linear logic A system of *combinational and possibly *sequential circuits in which the combinational component comprises *exclusive-OR gates only. This is sometimes referred to as *strongly linear logic* in order to distinguish it from *weakly linear logic* in which *inverters are permitted.

In nonbinary (q-valued) systems, the EXOR gates are generalized to modulo-q adders and subtractors.

linearly dependent *See* linear independence.

linear multistep methods An important class of methods for the numerical solution of *ordinary differential equations. For the initial-value problem

$$y' = f(x,y), \, y(x_0) = y_0$$

the general form of the k-step method is

$$\sum_{i=0}^{k} \alpha_i y_{n+i} = h \sum_{i=0}^{k} \beta_i f_{n+i}$$

where $f_r = f(x_r, y_r)$ and h is the stepsize, $h = x_r - x_{r-1}$. The formula is said to be *explicit* if $\beta_k = 0$ and *implicit* otherwise.

The most important and widely used formulas of this type are the *Adams formulas* and the *backward differentiation formulas* (*BDF*). These formulas are derived from *interpolation polynomials to previously computed values of $f(x,y)$ or $y(x)$ respectively. They form the basis for some of the best modern software, in which the stepsize and the step number k are chosen automatically. The BDF codes, intended for stiff equations (*see* ordinary differential equations), have been particularly successful in relation to other methods used for the same class of problems.

Linear multistep methods are more efficient than *Runge-Kutta methods when evaluations of $f(x,y)$ are sufficiently expensive. The ease with which the step number k can be varied automatically permits the design of codes that can be efficient over a wide range of requested accuracies.

linear predictor *See* generalized linear model.

linear programming A technique in *optimization, pioneered by George B. Dantzig, that is widely used in economic, military, and business-management decisions. It deals with the problem of finding nonnegative values of the variables $x_1, x_2, ..., x_n$ that satisfy the constraints

$$a_{i1}x_1 + a_{i2}x_2 + ... + a_{in}x_n = b_i,$$
$$i = 1, 2, ..., m$$

and minimize the linear form

$$c_1x_1 + c_2x_2 + ... + c_nx_n$$

Maximizing problems and problems with inequality constraints or unrestricted variables can be converted to this form. An optimum solution (if any exist) is known to be a *basic feasible solution*, which is one that satisfies the constraints and has at most m positive x_i values.

Computationally such problems are solved by the *simplex method*, an algorithm that terminates after a finite number of steps. It starts at a basic feasible solution and moves through the set of such solutions in such a manner that the value of the linear form is nonincreasing. Very large problems occur in practice involving *sparse matrices. Recent work has shown that iterative infinite algorithms are sometimes faster, notably *Kamarkar's method*.

linear recurrence A relationship that defines the next term in a sequence in the form of sums and differences of multiples of earlier terms in the sequence. For example,

$$a_{r+1} = 2a_r + 1$$
$$b_{r+1} + 2b_r - b_{r-1} = 0$$

See also recurrence.

linear regression model *See* regression analysis.

linear structure (totally ordered structure) A collection of items ordered by a single property so that each item, except possibly for the first or last, has a unique "predecessor" and a unique "successor". It is the most commonly used structure and

appears under a variety of names depending on storage representation and its intended use. Linked representations are normally called *lists while sequential representations are called *arrays.

line feed (LF) 1. A format command for printers and displays, signaling the requirement that the data that follows should be printed or displayed one line pitch below the preceding data. In impact printers it invokes the physical movement required to move the paper at right angles to the print line by a distance equal to the previously specified pitch between printed lines. In nonimpact page printers it invokes an analogous action in the stored image that is subsequently transferred to the paper in a continuous movement. 2. A format command that with some operating systems is used to terminate a line of input and an implicit CR (carriage return) actioned so that the next input is displayed/printed at the start of the next line.

line finder An *image-processing procedure that detects abrupt changes in intensity in *gray-level images. Line finders may look for the boundaries of *segments, or for bars (with two edges), or other linear structure. They may operate on the raw data or they may take the output after processing with *edge detectors.

line printer A computer output device that produces a line of print per cycle of its operation. The number of character positions in a line generally ranges from 80 to 160, and lines are printed at rates from 150 to 3000 lines per minute. A complete line of information has to be assembled in a buffer memory within the machine before it can start printing. When a line of print has been completed a paper-feed system moves the paper so that the position for the next line of print is opposite the printing mechanism.

The paper to be printed is usually supplied as a continuous web of up to 2000 forms divided by perforations. To ensure positive control of the forms, the margins are punched with holes that engage on the tractors of the printer's paper-feed system. *See also* band printer.

line protocol A formally specified set of possible bit sequences that will guarantee that two ends of a communication link will be able to pass information between them in an understandable way. A number of standards have been devised for the implementation of such protocols.

line switching The most common form of concentration (*see* concentrator), used to connect *n* transmitting devices to *m* receiving devices, where *n* is much greater than *m*. Buffering of data is done by the input devices of the line-switching system if the transmission medium is busy.

link 1. To join together two or more separately compiled program modules, usually with additional library modules, to form an executable program. *See also* link editor.

2. (linkage) A part of a program, possibly a single instruction or address, that passes control and *parameters between separate portions of the program. The instruction, address, etc., *links* the separate portions.

3. (pointer) A character or group of characters that indicates the storage of an item of data. Thus when a field of an item A in a data structure contains the address of another item B, i.e. of its first word in memory, it contains a link to B. Two items are *linked* when one has a link to the other. An important case is the link left pointing into the calling code by the *call of a subroutine, i.e. the value of the *program counter at the point of call. *See also* linked list.

4. A word or phrase in a *hypertext document that when selected in some way leads the user to another part of the document or a different document.

5. (line) A path for communication that may be physical (as in a circuit) or either physical or logical (as in a channel). *See also* data link.

link access protocol *See* LAP.

linkage *Another name for* link (def. 2).

linkage editor *Another name for* link editor.

link editor (linkage editor, linker) A utility program that combines several separately compiled modules into one, resolving internal references between them. When a program is assembled or compiled, an intermediate form is produced into which it is

necessary to incorporate library material containing the implementation of standard routines and procedures, and to add any other modules that may have been supplied by the user, possibly in other high-level languages. The final stages of *binding references within the original program to storable address forms appropriate to the hardware is performed by the link editor. *See also* link loader, loader.

linked list (chained list) A *list representation in which items are not necessarily sequential in storage. Access is made possible by the use in every item of a *link that contains the address of the next item in the list. The last item in the list has a special *null link* to indicate that there are no more items in the list. *See also* doubly linked list, singly linked list.

link encryption The transfer of an encrypted message across a system where the message is decrypted and reencrypted after each stage of its journey. Typically, link encryption is used in a switched communication network where the message is decrypted at each switching node to read the routing information prior to reencryption and onward transmission via the appropriate switch outlet. *Compare* end-to-end encryption.

link layer of network protocol function. *See* seven-layer reference model.

link library A library of functions some of which are *linked into the compiled code of a program in order to produce the executable version. The linking process is performed once only, permanently embedding copies of the required library functions in the executable. *Compare* DLL.

link loader A utility program that combines all the separately compiled modules of a program into a form suitable for execution. *See also* link editor, loader.

link testing *Testing of a group of modules to ensure that the modules operate correctly in combination. It is normally performed after the individual modules have been tested in isolation and prior to the integration testing that is performed for the complete system.

liquid-crystal display *See* LCD.

LISP *Acronym for* list processing. A programming language designed for the manipulation of nonnumeric data. The basic data structure is a *list whose elements are either atomic symbols or lists. An unusual feature of LISP is that programs are also expressed as lists, i.e. the programs and the data they manipulate have an identical structure. Pure LISP is a *functional language, having no assignment operator. The original LISP 1.5 developed into two distinct dialects, *FranzLisp* and *MACLisp*, but these have been combined to form *Common LISP. LISP is the language used for much *artificial intelligence research. *See also* EuLisp.

list A finite ordered *sequence of items $(x_1, x_2, \ldots x_n)$, where $n \geq 0$. If $n = 0$, the list has no elements and is called the *null list* (or *empty list*). If $n > 0$, the list has at least one element, x_1, which is called the *head* of the list (*see also* header). The list consisting of the remaining items is called the *tail* of the original list. The tail of the null list is the null list, as is the tail of a list containing only one element.

The items in a list can be arbitrary in nature, unless stated otherwise. In particular it is possible for an item to be another list, in which case it is known as a *sublist*. For example, let L be the list

$$(A, B, (C, D), E)$$

then the third item of L is the list (C,D), which is a sublist of L. If a list has one or more sublists it is called a *list structure*. If it has no sublists it is a *linear list*. The two basic representation forms for lists are sequentially allocated lists and *linked lists, the latter being more flexible.

listing *Short for* program listing.

list insertion sort *See* list sorting.

list processing A programming technique for dealing with data structures that consist of similar items linked by pointers (*see* linked list).

list sorting A form of sorting that utilizes a link field in each record. The *links are manipulated so that each link points to the following record in the sorted file to form a straight linear *list. An insertion sort that utilizes link fields is a *list insertion sort*.

list structure *See* list.

literal A word or symbol in a program that stands for itself rather than as a name for something else, i.e. an object whose value is determined by its denotation. Numbers are literals; if other symbols are used as literals it is necessary to use some form of quoting mechanism to distinguish them from variables.

literate programming A style of programming introduced by D. E. Knuth in which the code is split up into fragments, each accompanied by a paragraph or paragraphs of explanatory text. The fragments are presented in the order most appropriate for explanation, rather than the order dictated by the rules of the programming language. A utility called *tangle* is used to rearrange the code fragments into the right order for compilation. Knuth's system, called *WEB*, was developed for Pascal programs, but versions for C have also been produced.

little-endian Denoting an addressing organization whereby the section of a memory address that selects a byte within a word is interpreted so that the largest numerical byte address (e.g. 11) is located at the least significant end of the addressed word. *See also* big-endian.

liveness A property of a system that it will eventually do something good. Possible causes of loss of liveness include *deadly embrace and *starvation. *Compare* safety.

LL parsing The most powerful *top-down parsing technique that proceeds without backtracking, LL standing for *L*eft-to-right *L*eftmost derivation sequence. In general an LL parser uses a k-symbol lookahead, where k is an integer ≥ 1, to effect parsing decisions. For most practical purposes, however, k is taken to be 1.

An LL parser may be implemented as a *pushdown automaton or by the method of recursive descent (*see* top-down parsing). In the former method a stack is used to store that portion of a leftmost *derivation sequence that has not been matched against the input string. Initially the start symbol of the grammar is pushed onto an empty stack. Subsequently, if the top element of the stack is a terminal symbol it is matched against the next symbol in the input string. If they are the same then the stack symbol is popped and the input marker advanced, otherwise there is an error in the input string. If the top stack symbol is a nonterminal A, say, it is removed from the stack and replaced by the right-hand side symbols of a production with left-hand side A. The right-hand side symbols are pushed onto the stack in right-to-left order. Thus if the production is

$$A \to XYZ$$

the first symbol to be stacked is Z, then Y, and finally X. The choice of a production is made by consulting a parsing table that contains an entry for each combination of non-terminal symbol and k-symbol lookahead. Parsing is successfully completed when the input is exhausted and the stack is empty.

A grammar that can be parsed using this technique is said to be an *LL(k) grammar*. Not all grammars are LL(k); in particular any grammar that uses left recursion is not LL(k) for any value of k.

load and go A method of operation, now obsolete, in which program loading together with a possible compiling or assembling is followed immediately by the program's execution phase.

load and store A method of operation, now obsolete, in which program loading together with a possible compiling or assembling is concluded by storage of the object code.

loader A utility program that sets up an executable program in main memory ready for execution. This is the final stage of the compiling/assembly process. *See also* link editor, link loader.

local A term applied to entities that are accessible only in a restricted part of a program, typically in a procedure or function body. By contrast, *nonlocal* entities are accessible in a wider scope and *global entities are accessible throughout a program. The use of local entities can help to resolve naming conflicts, and may lead to a more efficient use of memory.

local area network (LAN) A *network that in general is operated as a subsidiary activity by a single organization for its own exclusive use, the typical LAN having an overall size of a few kilometers or less. Normally the organization is located on a single site, or a small number of nearby sites, and the LAN constitutes a single management and naming *domain. LANs generally provide high-speed (100 Kbps to 100 Mbps) data communication services to directly connected computers. *Gateways are used to connect local networks to each other, or to longer-distance communication networks. Due to limited distance, controlled environments, and (usually) homogeneous implementation, local networks have very low error rates and can utilize simplified data communication protocols. *See also* metropolitan area network, wide area network.

local bus A bus used for the connection of digital system components such as processors, memories, and disk controllers to form a computer entity. Its use may be restricted to the connection of devices within the immediate locality of the processor and it may be implemented as a *backplane. *See also* VME bus, local area network.

local bus architecture A processor architecture based on a *local bus interconnection of basic computer system components. The use of a standardized local bus facilitates the rapid design of application-specific digital systems using off-the-shelf processor, memory, and other system components.

local device A device, such as a hard disk or printer, attached directly to the user's computer rather than at some other point on the network, in which case they are *remote devices.

local discretization error *See* discretization error.

local-echo mode *See* echo.

local error A measure of the accuracy over one step of a method for the numerical solution of *ordinary differential equations. This is a useful concept in the practical implementation of numerical methods. If the step is described by the general formula

$$y_{n+1} = y_n + h\phi(x_n, y_{n-1}, \ldots, y_{n-k}; h)$$
$$x_{n+1} = x_n + h$$

then the local error is defined to be

$$y_{n+1} - z(x_{n+1})$$

where $z(x)$ is the exact solution of the differential equation through the previous computed point, i.e. it satisfies $z(x_n) = y_n$.

An estimate of the local error is normally obtained by using two different formulas on each step (*see* predictor-corrector methods). This estimate is kept below a user-specified tolerance, if necessary by rejecting steps and repeating with a reduced stepsize h. With further modifications this leads to efficient and reliable variable stepsize programs.

The local error is related to the local truncation error (*see* discretization error), which is defined in terms of the exact solution of the original problem rather than the current computed values used here.

local illumination An illumination model in which the illumination of a surface depends solely on its own characteristics and those of the light sources.

localization The action of tailoring a generic software product, such as an application package, by setting local parameters or configuration data.

local loop The (twisted pair) connection from a switching exchange to the subscriber terminal.

local optimization (peephole optimization) *See* optimization (in programming).

location (storage location, memory location) Any place in computer memory in which an item of data – usually a word or byte – can be stored in binary form. Each location can be identified by an *address, allowing items of data to be stored there or retrieved from there. The terms location and address are thus used interchangeably.

location operator An operator in a programming language that yields the address of its operand.

locator A type of input to a graphics system that defines a position, possibly with other information. *See also* logical input device.

lock 1. (lock primitive) An indivisible operation that allows a *process to ensure that it alone has access to a particular resource. On a single-processor system the indivisible nature of the operation can be guaranteed by turning off interrupts during the action,

ensuring that no process switch can occur. On a multiprocessing system it is essential to have available a *test-and-set instruction that, in a single uninterruptible sequence, can test whether a register's contents are zero, and if they are will make the contents nonzero. The same effect can be achieved by an exchange instruction. *See also* unlock, semaphore.

2. *See* locks and keys.

lockout A mechanism for arranging controlled access to a shared resource. *See* lock, semaphore.

locks and keys A system of *memory protection in which segments of memory are assigned identification numbers (the locks) and authorized users are provided the numbers (the keys) by the operating system. This provision is done by a privileged process in some location, such as a *program status word, not accessible to the user.

lofting Constructing a number of longitudinal curves to blend a set of previously defined cross-sections in order to represent a surface (*see* blend). The term originates from the days of manual ship design: traditionally these curves were drawn full size; the drawings were too large to handle and lay out conveniently in the drawing office and were therefore stored and dealt with in large attics, called lofts.

logarithmic search algorithm *Another name for* binary search algorithm.

log file A file that is used to record transactions against a database as they occur and is distinct from the database itself. Update transactions must be recorded to provide for database recovery, the information written to the log file usually also including before and after images of the database records (or pages) changed. Information on query-only transactions may also be recorded. The log file will be used to create a *recovery log, to provide an *audit trail, and by database administration for performance monitoring and improvement.

The recording of information on a log file is known as *logging*.

logic 1. A knowledge representation and reasoning formalism originally developed by mathematicians to formalize mathematical reasoning. In mathematical logic the investigation involves mathematical methods taken from algebra or the theory of algorithms. The two most common systems are *propositional calculus and *predicate calculus.

Logic has been widely adopted within artificial intelligence, for example as an alternative to *production rules in expert systems and for representing the meaning of natural language statements (*see* natural-language understanding). Many alternative logics have been developed in artificial intelligence to represent the vagueness and uncertainty of common sense (as opposed to mathematical knowledge) and to represent the tentative nature of *common-sense reasoning; these include *nonmonotonic reasoning and uncertain reasoning (*see* uncertainty).

2. *See* digital logic, computer logic.

logical 1. Involving or used in logic.
2. Conceptual or virtual, or involving conceptual entities, as opposed to physical or actual.

logical cohesion *See* cohesion.

logical connective *See* connective.

logical encoding The representation of symbols in a source alphabet by strings of logical values. It is hence equivalent to binary encoding.

logical expression *Another name for* Boolean expression.

logical formulas A representation of meaning or knowledge. *See* logic, resolution.

logical input device An abstraction of one or more physical devices that delivers logical input values to an application. Graphics standards divide the primitive input devices into the logical classes *locator, *stroke, *valuator, *choice, *pick, and *string.

logical operator, logical operation *See* logic operation.

logical record *See* record.

logical schema (conceptual schema) The encoding of the *data model of a database in the relevant *database language. It is sometimes simply referred to as the *schema* of a database. *See also* storage schema, user view.

logical shift *See* shift.

logical type 1. (Boolean type) A *data type comprising the logical values *true* and *false*, with legal operations restricted to *logic operations.
2. Loosely, an *abstract data type.

logical value (Boolean value) Either of the two values *true* and *false* that indicate a truth value. Although a single bit is the most obvious computer storage structure that can be applied to logical data, larger units of store, such as a byte, are frequently used in practice since they can be addressed distinctly.

logic analyzer An electronic instrument that monitors the *logic states of digital systems and stores the results for subsequent display. The storage of data is initiated in the analyzer by the recognition of preset "trigger states" as these arise in the system under test. *Synchronous* analyzers sample data at intervals determined entirely by the external system. *Asynchronous* analyzers sample at intervals determined internally by the analyzer. The essence of a logic analyzer is that it copes with many (often 8, 16, or 32) channels in parallel, and that the data recorded can be read back from memory at will, either in binary or after *decoding in some way, often by means of a *disassembler.

logic bomb Code introduced into a program to have an undesirable effect following the occurrence of some later event. For example, a logic bomb may be programmed to destroy valuable data should the programmer's name ever be deleted from the firm's payroll file.

logic card A printed circuit board that is of a standard size and carries a number of digital logic devices in a circuit arrangement capable of fulfilling a specific function. The board will, in general, also carry a standard connector by means of which power and ground connections are provided and control and data signals may be transferred to and from a standard *bus.

logic cell array *See* LCA.

logic circuit An electric circuit concerned with logic systems. The term *logic device* is often used synonymously. A logic circuit is required to produce specified binary outputs as a result of specified binary inputs. This may be accomplished by using *logic gates, producing what is called *hardware circuitry*. Alternatively the inputs may be associated with the address lines of a *ROM and the outputs with the data lines of a ROM; this is called *firmware circuitry*.

Hardware circuitry constructed from integrated-circuit packages on circuit boards requires two types of wiring. The first type carries the logic information between gates. The second type provides the power for the individual chips. The process of locating the power paths so that they do not interfere with the logic paths is called *power routing*.

Logic circuitry may be mathematically analyzed using *Boolean (or switching) algebra. In this representation the binary 1 is associated with the *identity element and the logic 0 is associated with the null element, i.e. zero.

See also combinational circuit, sequential circuit, digital logic, multivalued logic.

logic design *Another name for* digital design.

logic device *See* logic circuit.

logic diagram A diagram that displays graphically, by interconnection of *logic symbols, the digital design of a *logic circuit or system.

logic element A small part of a digital *logic circuit, typically a *logic gate. Logic elements can be represented by *operators in symbolic logic.

logic family A range of electronic devices that is made by the same manufacturing technique and provides a number of logic functions. The range includes *logic gates, *flip-flops, and *counters. Families in common use are *ECL and *TTL, which are based on *bipolar transistors, and the *NMOS and *CMOS families, which are based on *MOSFETs.

Logic families vary as regards *switching speed, *propagation delay, and power dissipation, although developments in the fabrication technology of the different families often improve these characteristics. A member of a logic family whose output changes state typically within a few nanoseconds (10^{-9} seconds) is considered a high-speed logic device. These devices are also characterized by short propagation delays, also in the order of a few nanoseconds. A particular family is characterized by its *delay-power product, a figure of merit that is frequently quoted in catalogues. *See also* logic circuit.

logic function *Another name for* Boolean function.

logic gate A device, usually but not exclusively electronic, that implements an elementary logic function; examples include *AND, *OR, *NAND, and *NOR gates, and *inverters. There are typically between two and eight inputs and one or two outputs. In order to represent the two *logic states, true and false, in electronic logic gates, the input and output signals are held at either of two different voltage levels; a high voltage level usually represents true (logic 1) and a low level false (logic 0).

Each type of logic gate has a *logic symbol that conveys its logic function but does not indicate the electronic circuitry involved. The use of these symbols in circuit diagrams simplifies the understanding of a complex logic circuit and means that technological advances in electronics need not be taken into account.

Logic gates based on *fluid logic have been successfully used as have *optical switches used as logic gates. *See also* logic circuit, digital logic, multivalued logic.

logic instruction An instruction that performs one of the class of *logic operations on one or more specified operands. These operations may apply to a single variable, as in complementation, or more generally are defined on two variables. *See also* Boolean algebra.

logic languages *See* logic programming languages.

logic level 1. In a *combinational circuit, the maximum number of logic gates between any input and any output. The logic level represents a measure of delay time through such a circuit.

2. Either of the two voltage levels used in a binary *logic gate. *See also* multivalued logic.

logic operation An operation on *logical values, producing a Boolean result (*see also* Boolean algebra). The operations may be *monadic or *dyadic, and are denoted by symbols known as *operators*. In general there are 16 logic operations over one or two operands; they include *AND, *OR, *NOT, *NAND, *NOR, *exclusive-OR, and *equivalence.

Logic operations involving more than two operands can always be expressed in terms of operations involving one or two operands. Those involving two operands can be expressed in terms of other operations involving one or two operands.

*Logic circuits are fabricated for the implementation of logic operations on their input signals. The inputs may be words (or bytes), and the logic operation is applied to each bit in accordance with Boolean algebra.

logic operator *See* logic operation.

logic probe An item of electronic test equipment that is capable of displaying the logic state – true (logic 1), false (logic 0), or undefined – of a digital signal applied to its input probe. It is generally used to check the operation of individual devices within a digital logic circuit.

logic programming languages (logic languages) A class of programming languages, and a subclass of the *declarative languages, that is based on the use of logical formulas. The interpreter is usually some version of *resolution, or another logical inference process. The ideal is that the programmer has only to make a series of true assertions about the problem and the interpreter will find a way to run these as a program to solve the problem. In practice, it is still necessary for the programmer to give regard to the procedural interpretation of these logical assertions. The most widely used realization of these ideals is the *Prolog programming language.

Logic programming languages are important because of their declarative nature, their potential power and flexibility, and their suitability for execution on highly parallel architectures.

logic state The logical sense, true or false, of a given binary signal. A binary signal is a *digital signal that has only two valid values. In physical terms the logical sense of a binary signal is determined by the voltage level or current value of the signal, and this in turn is determined by the device technology. In *TTL circuits, for example, a true state is represented by a logic 1, approximately equal to +5 volts on a signal line; logic 0 is approximately 0 volts. Voltage levels between 0 and +5 volts are considered undefined.

Since only two logic states, logic 1 and logic 0, are possible, the techniques of *Boolean algebra may be used to analyze digital circuits involving binary signals. The term *positive logic* is applied to circuits where logic 1 is assigned to the higher voltage level; in *negative logic* circuits a logic 1 is indicated by the lower voltage level. *See also* multi-valued logic.

logic symbols A set of graphical symbols that express the function of individual *logic gates in a *logic diagram. The most common symbols are those for the simple Boolean functions and for flip-flops, as shown in the diagram overleaf.

login (logon) The process by which a user identifies herself or himself to a system. The terms are also used as verbs: log in, log on, or *sign on*. A system with many registered users will require each user to log in, and to produce some form of *authentication (such as a password) before allowing the user access to system resources. The login activity will also open an *accounting file for the session.

logistic function A ratio of sums of exponentials widely used in statistical analysis. The logistic function lies in the range (0,1), and its inverse, known as the *logit* of a proportion, is the logarithm of the odds-ratio (*see* odds).

logit *See* logistic function.

LOGO A programming language developed for use in teaching young children. LOGO is a simple but powerful language: it incorporates the concept of *procedures, and helps children to think algorithmically. The original version of LOGO incorporated *turtle graphics.

logoff (logout) The process by which a user terminates a session. The terms are also used

Combinational logic symbols
AND function

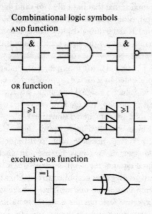

OR function

exclusive-OR function

Indicator symbols
negation indicator

polarity indicator

Flip-flops

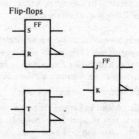

Commonly used logic symbols

as verbs: log off, log out, or *sign off*. By logging off, the user ensures that all the system resources that have been used during the session are accounted for, and any temporary files created during the session are deleted.

logon 1. (or **log on**) *See* login.

2. A unit of information, equal to the product of one unit of *bandwidth by one unit of time, in Denis Gabor's physical theory of communication. In contrast, Shannon's mathematical theory of communication uses the concept of *entropy.

logout (or **log out**) *See* logoff.

longitudinal redundancy check (LRC) *See* cyclic redundancy check.

lookahead *Short for* carry lookahead.

lookahead unit A unit forming part of an instruction unit pipeline in computers such as *Stretch.

lookup table *See* table lookup.

loop 1. A sequence of instructions that is repeated until a prescribed condition, such as agreement with a data element or completion of a count, is satisfied. *See also* do loop.

2. A configuration of a *local area network

that consists of nodes connected serially in a ring topology. *See* ring network.

3. (local loop) The (twisted pair) connection from a switching exchange to the subscriber terminal.

loop invariant *See* invariant.

lossless coding Coding in which no *information whatsoever is lost during the *encoding (or *decoding) process. Generally, *encryption and *decryption are lossless, as is *channel coding. Strictly, *data compaction is lossless, while *data compression is not, but the latter term is often used for the former. The decoding of (i.e. recovery from) compression and compaction are lossless. But the decoding of a signal received from a *channel is usually lossy (strictly not lossless) by design, since the *noise at least must be lost: the message entering the channel will usually have been prepared so as to permit this loss by the use of an *error-correcting code.

lossless compression Any method of *compression that allows the original data to be recovered from the compressed data. *See also* lossless coding.

lossy coding Any form of coding in which *information is or may be lost. *See* lossless coding.

lossy compression *Compression of data that approximates the original data so that it is not possible for it to be recovered identically. However a good approximation should always be possible. *See also* lossless coding.

Lotus 1-2-3 *Trademark* A *spreadsheet program from Lotus Development Corp. for personal computers. It also provides simple statistical and database facilities and graph drawing of pie charts, bar charts, and line graphs.

lower bound 1. of a set S on which the *partial ordering $<$ is defined. An element l with the property that $l < s$ for all s in S. Also l is a *greatest lower bound* if, for any other lower bound h, $h < l$.

Since numerical computing demands the truncation of infinite arithmetic to finite arithmetic, the computation of greatest lower bounds of real numbers, indeed of any limit, can only be achieved to a machine tolerance, usually defined to be machine precision: the smallest epsilon eps, such that
$$1.0 + \text{eps} > 1.0$$
in computer arithmetic. *See also* upper bound.

2. of a matrix or vector. *See* array.

low-level language A variety of programming language in which the control and data structures directly reflect the underlying machine architecture.

low-level scheduler (dispatcher) *See* scheduler.

low-pass filter A *filtering device that permits only those components in the *Fourier transform domain whose frequencies lie below some critical value to pass through with little attenuation, all other components being highly attenuated.

lpm *Abbrev. for* lines per minute, one of the terms used to describe the rate of output of line printers.

LPT port The name of a parallel printer port on an IBM PC or compatible. There can be up to three of these ports, called LPT1, LPT2, and LPT3. They are *Centronics interfaces and while designed with printers in mind can be used for other devices such as tape backup systems or network connections.

LQ *Abbrev. for* letter quality. Printed output indistinguishable from that produced by a good electric typewriter. *See also* NLQ.

LRC *Abbrev. for* longitudinal redundancy check. *See* cyclic redundancy check.

LRM *Abbrev. for* language reference manual. The reference manual for the *Ada language is commonly known as "the LRM".

LR parsing A *bottom-up parsing technique, LR standing for *L*eft-to-right *R*ightmost derivation sequence. Originally developed by D. E. Knuth, it is the most powerful left-to-right, no backtracking parsing method for *context-free grammars.

An LR parser consists of a pushdown stack, a parsing table, and a driving routine. The driving routine is the same for all grammars. The stack is manipulated by the driving routine using the information contained in the top stack element and the next k symbols in the input stream (called the k *lookahead*); k is an integer ≥ 0, but for most practical purposes $k = 1$. The stack consists of a string
$$s_0 X_0 s_1 X_1 \ldots s_n X_n s_{n+1}$$
where each X_i is a symbol of the input grammar and each s_i is called a *state*.

The parsing table is indexed by pairs (s, a) where s is a state and a is the lookahead. Each entry in the table has two parts: (a) an action, which may be shift, reduce p (for some production p), accept, or error, and (b) a state, called the *goto state*. When the action is shift, the next input symbol and goto state are pushed onto the stack (in that order). When the action is reduce p the top $2l$ elements of the stack will spell the right-hand side of p but with goto states interspersed, where l is the length of this right-hand side. These $2l$ elements are popped from the stack and replaced by the left-hand side of p and the new goto state. This operation corresponds to adding a new node to the *parse tree for the input string. The accept action is only encountered when the start symbol S is the only symbol on the stack (i.e. the stack contains $s_0 S s_1$ for some states s_0 and s_1) and the lookahead is the end-of-input symbol. It signifies that parsing has been successfully completed. On the other hand an error entry in the parse table indicates an error in the input string.

A grammar that can be parsed by an LR parser using k-symbol lookahead is called an *LR(k) grammar*. The power of the LR parsing method comes from the fact that the LR(1) grammars properly include other grammar types like precedence grammars and LL(1) grammars (*see* LL parsing). This and its efficiency make it a popular choice of parsing method in *compiler-compilers. If a grammar is not LR(1) this will be evidenced as multiply defined entries in the parsing tables called *shift-reduce conflicts* or *reduce-reduce conflicts*.

Many different parsing tables may be constructed for one grammar, each differing in the number of states it defines. The so-called *canonical LR table* tends to be too long for practical purposes and it is commonly replaced by an *SLR* (simple LR) or *LALR* (lookahead LR) table. A grammar that is LR(1) may not however be SLR(1) or LALR(1).

LSD, LSB *Abbrevs. for* least significant digit, least significant bit. *See* least significant character.

LSI *Abbrev. for* large-scale integration, i.e. integrated-circuit fabrication technology that allows a very large number of components (at least 10 000 transistors) to be integrated on a single chip. *See* integrated circuit, VLSI.

L-system (Lindenmeyer system) A way of generating infinite sets of strings. L-systems are similar to *grammars with the crucial difference that, whereas for grammars each step of derivation rewrites a single occurrence of a nonterminal, in an L-system all nonterminals are rewritten simultaneously. An L-system is therefore also known as a kind of *parallel rewriting system*. L-systems were first defined in 1968 by A. Lindenmeyer as a way of formalizing ways in which biological systems develop. They now form an important part of *formal language theory.

The subject has given rise to a large num-

ber of different classes of L-systems. The simplest are the *DOL systems*, in which all symbols are nonterminals and each has a single production. For example, with productions

$$A \rightarrow AB$$
$$B \rightarrow A$$

one derives starting from A the sequence

A AB ABA ABAAB ABAABABA ...

This is called the *sequence* of the DOL-system, while the set of strings in the sequence is called the *language*. The *growth-function* gives the length of the ith string in the sequence; in the example this is the Fibonacci function.

Note that the productions define a *homomorphism from $\{A,B\}^*$ to itself. A DOL-system consists therefore of an alphabet Σ, a homomorphism h on Σ^*, and an initial Σ-word w. The sequence is then

$$w \ h(w) \ h(h(w)) \ ...$$

The letter D in DOL stands for deterministic, i.e. each symbol has just one production. An *OL-system* can have many productions for each symbol, and is thus a *substitution rather than a homomorphism. Other classes are similarly indicated by the presence of various letters in the name: T means many homomorphisms (or many substitutions); E means that some symbols are terminals; P means that no symbol can be rewritten to the empty string; an integer n in place of O means context-sensitivity – the rewriting of each symbol is dependent on the n symbols immediately to the left of it in the string.

LU decomposition A method used in *numerical linear algebra in order to solve a set of linear equations,

$$Ax = b$$

where A is a square matrix and b is a column vector. In this method, a lower *triangular matrix L and an upper triangular matrix U are sought such that

$$LU = A$$

For definiteness, the diagonal elements of L may be taken to be 1. The elements of successive rows of U and L may easily be calculated from the defining equations.

Once L and U have been determined, so that

$$LUx = b,$$

the equation

$$Ly = b$$

is solved by *forward substitution*. Thereafter the equation

$$Ux = y$$

is solved for x by *backward substitution*. x is then the solution to the original problem.

A variant of the method, the method of *LDU decomposition*, seeks lower and upper triangular matrices with unit diagonal and a diagonal matrix D, such that

$$A = LDU$$

If the matrix A is *symmetric and positive definite, there is an advantage in finding a lower triangular matrix L such that

$$A = L L^{T}$$

(*see* transpose). This method is known as *Cholesky decomposition*; the diagonal elements of L are not, in general, unity.

luminance A measure of the light intensity reflected or emitted by a surface in a given direction per unit of apparent area. The unit of measurement is the candela per square meter.

lurker *Informal* Someone who uses a bulletin board or Usenet service but does not submit any material.

LZW *Abbrev. for* Lempel–Ziv–Welch (compaction).

M

M *Symbol for* mega-, as in MHz, Mbyte, Mbps. *See* mega-.

Mac *Short for* Macintosh. *See* Apple Computer Inc.

MAC 1. A project at Massachusetts Institute of Technology to introduce the first practical *multiaccess system. The name is an acronym derived from machine-aided cognition (expressing the broad project objective) and multiple-access computer (describing its major tool). The system incorporated not only a new approach to operating systems, but also introduced novel forms of highly interactive compilers and of terminals. *See also* MULTICS.

2. *Abbrev. for* mandatory access control.

3. *See* MAC layer.

Mach bands Illusory light and dark bands that are seen at the transitions between uniformly illuminated regions of uniform density. Mach bands arise because the human visual system is good at recognizing edges and thus enhances the intensity change between the regions so that the lighter side appears lighter and the darker side appears darker. This is a particular problem with shading algorithms, such as *Gouraud shading, which cause a change in intensity to appear at the edge of an object between two polygons. *Phong shading reduces Mach banding.

machine Usually, a real or imagined computer (*see also* virtual machine, abstract machine, Turing machine), which may or may not be sequential and deterministic. In formal language theory it may imply a *sequential machine.

machine address *Another name for* absolute address, now deprecated.

machine code The *operation code of a particular machine, and hence, by association, code specific to a particular machine.

machine equivalence The property describing two usually abstract machines that can simulate one another. Machines M_1 and M_2 are said to be equivalent if M_1 can simulate M_2 and M_2 can simulate M_1. Given precise definitions of the machines, precise definitions of simulation can be formulated. *See* machine simulation.

machine-independent A term applied to software that is not dependent on the properties of a particular machine, and can therefore be used on any machine. Such software is also described as *portable*.

machine intelligence *Another name for* artificial intelligence.

machine language Strictly, the written representation of machine code. The term is also used as a synonym for machine code.

machine learning A branch of *artificial intelligence concerned with the construction of programs that learn from experience. Learning may take many forms, ranging from learning from examples and learning by analogy to autonomous learning of concepts and learning by discovery.

Incremental learning involves continuous improvement as new data arrives while *one-shot* or *batch learning* distinguishes a training phase from the application phase. *Supervised learning* occurs when the training input has been explicitly labeled with the classes to be learned.

Most learning methods aim to demonstrate generalization whereby the system develops efficient and effective representations that encompass large chunks of closely related data.

machine simulation The process whereby one machine M_1 can be made to simulate or behave like a second machine M_2. There are a number of ways of formalizing simulation for each class of machines. For example, let there be *functions g and h that perform encoding and decoding roles respectively:

$$g : M_1 \to M_2, \quad h : M_2 \to M_1$$

g encodes information for machine M_1 and produces corresponding information for machine M_2; h is the *inverse function. Machine M_2 is said to simulate machine M_1 if it is possible to specify a translation algorithm such that, when given a program P_1 for M_1, it produces a corresponding program P_2 for M_2; further, the effect of P_1 on M_1 should be equivalent to the effect of

applying function g
then executing P_2 on M_2
then applying function h.

In symbols,

$$P_1 = h\, P_2\, g$$

An equally useful formulation has functions

$$g : M_1 \to M_2, h : M_1 \to M_2$$

and the simulation criterion

$$h\, P_1 = P_2\, g$$

Machine simulation of this kind is generally discussed for idealized abstract machines, such as *Turing machines, and for formal models of microprocessors. It provides a useful approach to defining the correctness of implementations. *See also* machine equivalence.

machine translation The use of computers in translating from one natural language to another. This was originally a branch of *artificial intelligence research, but commercial translation systems are now used regularly in professional translation bureaus. Fully automatic translation is not achievable but human post-editing can give acceptable results.

machine word *See* word.

Macintosh (Mac) Any of a range of *personal computers from *Apple Computer Inc.

MAC layer *Short for* media access control layer. One or more layers in a *protocol stack that deal(s) with the issues of allowing a transmitter, wishing to send information, to gain access to the actual transmission medium. In particular the MAC layer is usually responsible for the resolution of *contention for access to the transmission medium.

MACLisp A dialect of *LISP, now superseded by *Common LISP.

macro *Short for* macroinstruction. An instruction in a programming language (almost always but not necessarily *assembly language) that is replaced by a sequence of instructions prior to assembly or compiling. A *macroassembler* permits the user to define macros, specifying the macroinstruction form, its arguments, and a replacement text (otherwise called the *body* of the macro), and then allows macroinstructions to be interspersed among the assembly code. On encountering a macro the assembler replaces it by the macro body, substituting the parameters provided in the places marked in the macro body. The macro thus provides a mechanism for inserting a particular body of text at various places in a program (and is thus the same thing as an open *subroutine, though this nomenclature is obsolete).

A *macroprocessor* provides similar facilities, though not in combination with an assembler. It accepts macro definitions and then reads arbitrary text in which *macro calls* (i.e. instances of a macro name) can occur. Text is copied to the output until a macro name is encountered: when this happens the arguments (parameters) are found and the macro call is replaced by the macro body in the output stream, with appropriate substitution of the parameters.

macroassembler *See* macro.

macrogenerator *Another name for* macroprocessor. *See* macro.

macroinstruction *See* macro.

macroprocessor (macrogenerator) *See* macro.

magnetic bubble memory A type of digital memory in which data is represented by magnetic bubbles that are made to move through a stationary planar medium by applying suitable magnetic fields; the bubbles are tiny circular areas (stable magnetic domains) in which the medium is magnetized in the reverse direction to the rest of the medium. Bubble memory thus differs from magnetic tape and disk stores, in which the medium moves and the data bits are stationary with respect to it.

Bubble memory consumes little power, has a large functional *packing density, is normally nonvolatile, and is resistant to cosmic rays and similar particles. Having no moving parts it is more rugged than disk memory. Bubble memory has found limited application where these properties are of value. However the initial promise of the technology (pioneered by Bell Telephone Laboratories) has not been realized in full since manufacturing costs have proved higher than expected.

magnetic card A data medium consisting of a card that is partly or completely coated on one side with ferromagnetic film on which data can be encoded and read (*see* card reader). The credit card is one example, the encoding being restricted to a single *magnetic stripe* that can contain three tracks. Other sizes of card have been used as interchangeable media in data-processing and word-processing applications, one example being the IBM magnetic card. In the late 1960s a number of mass storage devices were designed in which large magnetic cards were filed and retrieved automatically. These were superseded by *automated tape libraries and *magnetic disk stores.

magnetic cell A *memory element in which two different states of its magnetic flux pattern are used to represent binary values. The element may be a ferromagnetic core, part of a perforated ferromagnetic plane, or the intersection of two coated wires, and it can store a single bit of information.

magnetic disk A rotatable storage medium usually in the form of a circular aluminum plate coated on both sides with magnetic material, followed by some form of lubricating layer(s). The magnetic coating on early disks was a ferric oxide in a binder. Current disks have a thin metallic film, such as cobalt/nickel or cobalt/chrome, which is created by vacuum deposition (i.e. sputtering). The lubricating layer is a coat of carbon a few angstroms thick, sometimes followed by a proprietary lubricant. Metallic coatings have advantages in being homogeneous, having a better hysteresis loop shape, and allowing storage densities 10 times that achievable with conventional ferric oxide coatings. Flexible magnetic disks (i.e. *floppy disks) with oxide coating provide low-cost lightweight media that can be handled in a normal office environment.

Data is stored on and retrieved from magnetic disks by means of a *disk drive. *See also* access time, fixed disk drive, Winchester technology, memory hierarchy.

magnetic drum The earliest form of rotating magnetic storage device, used in some of the first computers at a time when random-access store was volatile, bulky, and expensive. The drum therefore formed the main memory of some of these machines, the random-access stores being used only as registers. Although random-access store developed rapidly it was still relatively expensive and the drum was retained as a local backing store on some computers. Magnetic disk, when introduced, took over a large part of the backing store function. Drums remained in use however on certain systems that required faster access than was generally provided by disk, but today they are obsolete apart from a few special applications.

A magnetic drum consists of a cylinder whose curved surface is coated with a suitable recording medium, either metal or iron oxide. On the *head-per-track drum* the drum rotates past a number of fixed read/write heads, one for each track of recorded information. On the *moving-head drum* the drum rotates past a single head or small group of heads that can be moved axially to access any track. The latter was rapidly superseded by disk stores but the head-per-track drum survived: track selection requires only electronic switching between heads rather than movement of the head so that such drums have much shorter access times than disk stores.

magnetic encoding The method by which binary data is recorded on magnetic media. In *horizontal recording* on magnetic disks, tapes, and cards, magnetic domains in the media are aligned along the direction of the applied magnetic field with either north or south pole leading: each domain is a tiny bounded region in which the magnetic moments of the component atoms are aligned, and it therefore behaves like a magnet. The domains are arranged end to end along a track, which may be either a concentric ring on a disk or run the length of a tape or card. There may not be a one-to-one relationship between the binary information of the data and the orientation of the magnetic domains. *See* disk format, tape format.

In 1975 Shun-ichi Iwasaki published his work on *vertical recording* methods. The magnetic domains are oriented through the thickness of the magnetic film and have either a north or a south pole at the exposed surface. The magnetic material is usually a vacuum-deposited film of metal such as an alloy or combination of cobalt and chromium over a layer of permalloy. Linear densities as high as 200 000 bits per inch have been demonstrated. Vertical recording can thus yield an increase of at least 25 times and possibly 100 times the bit density achievable by current horizontal recording techniques.

magnetic head *See* head.

magnetic-ink character recognition *See* MICR.

magnetic media The various types of media, including *magnetic disk and *magnetic tape, on which data recording is effected by writing a magnetic pattern onto the magnetizable surface of the medium. The term distinguishes these types of media from others that use different recording techniques, e.g. optical disks and paper tape.

magnetic stripe *See* magnetic card.

magnetic tape An information storage medium consisting of a magnetic coating on a flexible backing in tape form. Data is recorded by *magnetic encoding of tracks on the coating according to a particular *tape format.

Magnetic tape is wound on *reels* (or *spools*). These may be used on their own, as *open-reel tape*, or they may be contained in some sort of *magnetic tape cartridge for protection and ease of handling. Early computers used open-reel tape, and this is still sometimes used on large computer systems although it has been widely superseded by cartridge tape. On smaller systems, if tape is used at all it is normally cartridge tape.

Magnetic tape is used in a *tape transport* (also called a *tape drive*, *tape deck*, *tape unit*, or *MTU*), a device that moves the tape over one or more magnetic *heads. An electrical signal is applied to the *write head* to record data as a magnetic pattern on the tape; as the recorded tape passes over the *read head* it generates an electrical signal from which the stored data can be reconstructed. The two heads may be combined into a single *read/write head*. There may also be a separate *erase head* to erase the magnetic pattern remaining from previous use of the tape.

Most magnetic-tape formats have several separate data tracks running the length of the tape. These may be recorded simultaneously, in which case, for example, a byte of data may be recorded with one bit in each track (*parallel recording*); alternatively, tracks may be recorded one at a time (*serial recording*) with the byte written serially along one track. For parallel recording and some serial recording, there is a separate head (or set of read and write heads) for each track, assembled into a single multitrack head unit; other mechanisms have a single track head that is moved across the width of the tape to record separate tracks. A third method is *helical-scan recording where the heads are mounted in a rotating drum around which the tape is wrapped on the skew, as in a video recorder, so that tracks run diagonally across the tape.

Where write and read heads are close together, the magnetic signals may be read back and checked for correctness as soon as they are written; this is called a *read-while-write check*.

Standard open-reel tape is ½ inch wide and carries nine data tracks, recorded in parallel; the most widely used reel is 10.5 inches in diameter holding 2400 feet of tape, and such a *volume* holds up to 140 megabytes of data depending on the tape format. 1200 or 600 foot tapes, on smaller reels, are sometimes used. Other formats are employed for special purposes. Tape cartridges are much more variable in size and capacity because there are so many different formats; volume capacity varies from a few megabytes to tens of gigabytes.

Magnetic tape has been used for offline data storage, backup, archiving, data interchange, and software distribution, and in the early days (before disk storage was available) also as online backing store. For many of these purposes it has been superseded by magnetic or optical disk or by online communications. For example, although tape is a *nonvolatile medium, it tends to deteriorate in long-term storage and so needs regular attention (typically an annual rewinding and inspection) as well as a controlled environment. It is therefore being superseded for archival purposes by optical disk. Magnetic tape is still extensively used for backup; for this purpose, interchange standards are of minor importance, so proprietary cartridge-tape formats are widely used.

magnetic tape cartridge (tape cartridge)
A casing containing one or more reels carrying a length of *magnetic tape, so arranged that it can be loaded on a suitable tape transport for access without the tape being handled by the operator. There are many forms of tape cartridge, some containing both the file reel on which the tape is wound and the

take-up reel, and some the file reel only. The term is also used to describe a file reel without a separate casing but with some other provision, such as a special leader to protect the tape and avoid the need for the operator to touch it.

The best-known forms of tape cartridge are as follows.

(a) The *autoload cartridge*, introduced by IBM and consisting essentially of a collar clamped around the periphery of a standard 10½″ reel of ½″ wide magnetic tape. Its purpose is to facilitate *autothreading of tape on suitably equipped tape transports. The reel can be removed from the cartridge for use on other transports.

(b) The *DC300 cartridge*, introduced by 3M and consisting of a metal and plastic casing containing two small reels of ¼″ wide magnetic tape. Variants of this cartridge carry 300, 450, or 600 feet of tape in similar housings; the latter two are the *DC450* and *DC600 cartridges*. *DC1000* and *DC2000 cartridges* are similar but smaller. All these cartridges are used mainly on small computers in an office environment.

(c) The *digital cassette*, based on the standard audio cassette developed by Philips and made to similar dimensions though with more precision.

(d) Various designs of cartridge containing a relatively short length of wide tape on a single reel, used in *automated tape libraries.

(e) Cartridges consisting of a few hundred feet of ½″ wide tape on a single reel permanently mounted in an outer casing, with a coupling attached to the outer end of the tape to allow the end to be drawn out and mechanically loaded into the tape path of a suitable cartridge tape drive. The most widely used design is the *3480 cartridge*, introduced by IBM in 1984 for its 3480 cartridge tape drive and since adopted by other manufacturers.

(f) Cartridges consisting of small (typically 3″ or 4″ diameter) reels of ½″ tape without an outer casing, but with a tough protective leader slightly wider than the tape so that it gives full protection when wound onto the reel.

magnetic tape unit (MTU) *Another name for* tape transport. *See* magnetic tape.

magnetographic printer A type of printer in which the required image is first written on a band or drum of magnetic recording material as a pattern of closely spaced magnetic poles. The image is then developed by brushing it with a pigment that is also ferromagnetic and thermoplastic. The image is transferred and bonded to paper by applying pressure and/or heat.

magneto-optic (M-O) storage A storage method, used in rewritable optical disk drives, that combines magnetic and optical recording techniques. The disk is coated with film that initially is uniformly magnetized. A laser beam is used to demagnetize a small spot on the film by heating it above a critical temperature (the Curie point or compensation point), and a local magnetic field determines the direction in which the spot is magnetized when it cools. To read the information, the disk is scanned by polarized light from a low-power laser. The plane of polarization of the light reflected from a magnetized surface is rotated according to the direction of the magnetic field – the Kerr effect. This rotation, though small, can be detected and the original binary signal can be reproduced. In early M-O disk drives data had to be erased separately (usually during the previous revolution of the disk) before it could be rewritten, but direct rewriting is now possible.

The M-O technique achieves recording densities similar to those of other optical stores and much higher than has been achieved by magnetic recording. M-O media compete with *dye-polymer media in the rewritable disk field. Dye-polymer media are in principle cheaper to make and need a simpler drive, but successful M-O media were produced some years before comparable dye-polymer media.

magnetostrictive tablet A type of *data tablet that consists of an array of wires that will propagate strain waves at the speed of sound. As the device can be controlled by signals moving at the speed of light, the difference in arrival times can be used to define a position.

mag tape *Short for* magnetic tape.

mail *See* electronic mail.

mailmerge A technique whereby a list of names and addresses can be merged with a *form letter to produce a set of personalized letters to a number of people, known as a *mailshot*. The same list can also be used to produce address labels. The technique is quite general and can be used wherever a list of items is to be printed or displayed in a number of different ways.

mailshot *See* mailmerge.

mainframe 1. Generally, the combination of central processor and primary memory of a computer system. The term excludes the I/O, backing store, etc., and is sometimes used synonymously with central processor. **2.** Any large computer system.

main memory (main store; main storage; RAM; primary memory) The storage that is closely associated with the processor of a computer system and from which the program instruction and data can be directly retrieved and to which the resulting data is written prior to transfer to *backing store or *output device. In modern machines this is *semiconductor memory but in earlier machines *core stores and *delay lines were used.

The majority of storage activity generated by a processor in the execution of a program is directed at the main memory. In a modern processor, however, there is usually a further small high-speed memory interposed between the processor and main memory that holds recently accessed main-memory data for rapid reaccess. This small high-speed memory is known as a *cache. The main memory is normally used in conjunction with a backing store with a much larger capacity. *See also* memory hierarchy.

main program The section of a program that is entered first and from which program units and procedures are called. It is the outermost block of a block-structured program.

main store, main storage *Other names for* main memory.

maintenance 1. (hardware maintenance) The performance of *preventive or *remedial maintenance on hardware in order to anticipate the onset of incipient faults or to correct a *failure due to a hardware fault.

2. *See* software maintenance.

majority element (majority gate) A logic element with an odd number of inputs, and whose output agrees with the majority of the inputs. *See also* threshold element.

make A utility program – developed initially to run under UNIX – that can interpret a *build script* (provided as an input file) containing instructions defining how, for example, to build a program from a set of source text files. The instructions can indicate the tools (such as language compilers, link editors, etc.) to be used to transform the text to intermediate forms, and then to convert these intermediate forms into an executable binary. An important feature of make is its ability to rebuild a program after some of its components have been changed. When operating in this mode, make will interpret the interdependency information inherent in the build script and use this to carry out the minimum set of operations. Thus, for example, if a source language module (or any of the definition files upon which it depends) has not been changed, then it will not recompile the module. Make was designed to work closely with *sccs.

malfunction The occurrence of a fault, usually a hardware fault.

MAN *Acronym for* metropolitan area network.

managed data network service (MDNS) A network service in which the contractor provides not only the basic *bearer mechanisms between access points, but also a range of management activities, typically those ensuring that the end-user will receive an agreed level of service measured in terms of availability, recovery from breakdowns, traffic levels, response times, and so on. Much of the necessary equipment and services can meet the needs of a number of different clients that are based in the same or in overlapping geographical areas, so reducing the total cost of the contractor's operation. The advantage to the user of an MDNS is that the responsibility of providing standby facilities and trained maintenance are delegated to the provider of the MDNS, which should offset the user's loss of flexibility.

managed device A device, especially an active component in a network, that is capable of receiving instructions and fresh information from elsewhere on the network, and of returning responses to queries from elsewhere on the network. For this to be possible the device must itself be an addressable entity on the network. *See also* SNMP.

management information system (MIS) An *information system whose prime purpose is to supply information to management. The early concept of an MIS, commonplace in the 1960s and early 1970s, was that systems analysts would determine the information requirements of individual managers in an organization, and would design systems to supply that information routinely and/or on demand.

Decision support systems (DSS) form a newer class of MIS, giving managers much greater independence in their use of computer-based information. They depend on the union of office information systems (including personal computing facilities for managers, operated by themselves) with more conventional database and data-processing systems. They assume that managers will be able to build and access their own personal databases, as well as accessing the corporate databases, and that they will be able to formulate their own access enquiries without depending on specialist intermediaries.

manager A program for organizing a resource such as a set of files (a *file manager*), the windows of a graphical user interface (a *windows manager*), a database (a *database management system), or the allocation of RAM (a *memory manager*; *see* memory management).

Manchester Mark I The world's first operational stored-program computer, running its first program in June 1948. It was designed by T. Kilburn and F. C. Williams at the University of Manchester, UK, commencing in 1946. Several improvements were added and the first realistic problem to be solved by the machine was achieved in April 1949, shortly before *EDSAC began operations. It became the world's first commercially available computer when marketed by Ferranti Ltd in 1951 as the Ferranti Mark I. The effectiveness of the machine was due to its use of *electrostatic (Williams tube) storage.

mandatory access control (MAC) A form of secure *access control in which the *access rights to objects are set by system administrators and cannot be made more permissive by other users. *Compare* discretionary access control.

man-machine interface (MMI) *Another term for* human-computer interface.

Mann Whitney U-test *See* nonparametric techniques.

mantissa (fractional part) *See* floating-point notation.

many-sorted algebra *See* algebra.

many-sorted predicate calculus (many-sorted first-order logic) *See* predicate calculus.

many-sorted signature *See* signature.

map 1. (mapping) *See* function.
2. *See* memory map.
3. *See* bitmap, pixmap.
4. *See* Karnaugh map.

MAP *Acronym for* Manufacturing Automation Protocol. A set of *protocols originally devised by a group of US manufacturers of mechanical engineering products. This original group has been expanded to include other parties, and the protocols have become ISO OSI (*open systems interconnection) standards. The protocols are intended to facilitate the exchange of data relevant to mechanical-engineering design and manufacture. They cover not only the problems of process control and assembly within a single manufacturing plant, but also the exchange of design and manufacturing data between a main contractor and his subcontractors. *See also* TOP, STEP.

MAPI *Trademark; acronym for* messaging application program interface. A system from Microsoft that is designed to facilitate the handling of e-mail messages from within some other application, such as a word processor or spreadsheet.

map method A procedure for minimizing Boolean functions using a *Karnaugh map.

mapping 1. (map) *See* function.
2. *See* memory mapping, I/O mapping.

marching cubes An algorithm that creates a triangle representation of an *isosurface from a volumetric dataset. The basis of this algorithm is a sequential *tessellation of the boundary *voxels by small triangles. The algorithm was originally presented by Lorensen and Cline. A refinement, called *marching tetrahedra*, deals with some of the ambiguous cases not covered by marching cubes.

marching tetrahedra *See* marching cubes.

marginal check (marginal test) *See* preventive maintenance.

mark 1. One of the binary signaling states on serial communication lines of terminals; the other state is called *space*. Mark often corresponds to a negative voltage, space to a positive voltage.
2. A line drawn on specially formatted cards or forms that are used with *mark sensing or *mark reading equipment.
3. *See* tape mark.

marker on a magnetic tape. *See* BOT marker, EOT marker.

Markov chain A sequence of discrete random variables such that each member of the sequence is probabilistically dependent only on its predecessor. An *ergodic* Markov chain has the property that its value at any time has the same statistical properties as its value at any other time.

Markov source A *Markov chain, whose random variables are regarded as *internal states*, together with a mapping from these internal states to the symbols of some *external alphabet*. The mapping need not be a *bijection. A Markov source is ergodic if and only if its underlying Markov chain is ergodic. *See also* discrete source.

mark reading (mark scanning) *See* OMR.

mark sensing A method for data input in which electrically conductive marks, usually made with a soft graphite pencil on a preformatted card or form, are electrically sensed. This method has been displaced by the more reliable method of *OMR (i.e. optical mark reading) in which the marks are detected photoelectrically.

mark-space ratio See pulse train.

mark-up language A notation for defining the structure and formatting of a document by using ordinary characters embedded in the text. This system of tags identifies the logical components of the document and relates them to a syntactic definition of the document structure. See also SGML, hypertext mark-up language.

marriage problem In a certain community every boy knows exactly *k* girls and every girl knows exactly *k* boys. The problem is to show that every boy can marry a girl he knows and vice versa. This problem is a case of showing that any *bipartite graph whose *vertices all have the same nonzero number of edges incident to it has a *perfect matching.

MASCOT Acronym for modular approach to software construction operation and test. A method for designing and building software, aimed at real-time embedded systems and originally devised by Ken Jackson and Hugo Simpson at the Royal Signals and Radar Establishment, UK.

MASCOT comprises a design method, a diagrammatic and textual notation, and a model environment supporting the building, testing, and execution of systems. It may be applied to both single processor and distributed multiprocessor systems.

The design method is based upon identifying the dataflow through the system, and the data accumulation within the system. The design consists of concurrent active components (*activities*) and passive components (*intercommunication data areas*, of which *pools* and *channels* are special cases), possibly arranged hierarchically.

The notation provides for describing software components and the interfaces between them, together with a set of rules for assembling and testing them. It shows the network of intercommunicating processes, possibly in a hierarchy. In general, there is equivalence between the components of the design and the modules of the implementation.

MASCOT was devised to be language-independent. The original tools to support MASCOT were for use with *CORAL; tools are now available for use with *Pascal and *Ada. MASCOT is compatible with the *CORE requirements method and is an integral part of *DORIS.

masking 1. (filtering) A logical operation carried out on a byte, word, or field of data in order to modify or identify a part of it. A bit pattern – the same length as the item to be masked – is generated and stored in a register as a *mask*. By use of the appropriate operation, e.g. subtract, logical AND, logical OR, the mask can be used to suppress bits in the data, or set them to zero, etc. The process is used for purposes such as identifying the presence of high-priority bits in a status byte or resetting interrupts.

2. The use of a chemical shield, the *mask*, to determine the pattern of interconnects in an integrated circuit. Read-only memories (*ROMs) and programmable logic arrays (*PLAs) are customized for their particular applications by the masking process, unless they are field-programmable. See programmable devices.

mask-programmable device See programmable devices, ROM.

massively parallel See MPP, connectionism.

mass storage An online backing store system capable of storing larger quantities of data (sometimes an order of magnitude more) than conventional backing store. The quoted capacity of mass storage has increased with advances in technology: in the early 1960s a megabyte of storage came in this category; the term currently applies to devices that can store several hundred gigabytes of data.

master See master-slave system, bus arbitration.

master file A *data file that persists over time and is subject to *file updating and *query processing. A master file is thus distinct, for instance, from a *transaction file, an *I/O file, or a *work file.

mastering of a CD-ROM disk. See master tape.

master record A record on a *master file.

master-slave flip-flop A type of clocked
*flip-flop consisting of master and slave ele-
ments that are clocked on complementary
transitions of the clock signal. Data is only
transferred from the master to the slave, and
hence to the output, after the master-device
outputs have stabilized. This eliminates the
possibility of ambiguous outputs, which can
occur in single-element flip-flops as a result
of *propagation delays of the individual logic
gates driving the flip-flops.

master-slave system A system that has more
than one processor and in which one of the
processors is designated as being the *master*
and all other processors are *slaves*. The master processor is capable of actions that the
slaves cannot perform, usually in connection
with resource scheduling and the initiation of
peripheral transfers. This approach means
that the problems of *synchronization are
greatly reduced, since only the master
processor can be active in what might otherwise be *critical regions. It has the drawbacks of introducing an artificial asymmetry
between processors, and of causing delays
when processes that might be able to proceed
are in fact delayed since the only available
processors do not have the necessary privileges.

master tape 1. In data processing, a magnetic
tape volume that is used without any change
to its contents. It is usually protected by a
*write ring, or some equivalent mechanical
device, by which the operator can protect the
tape from being erased or over-written even
though this is commanded by the host.
2. A tape used in the preparation of a *CD-
ROM disk. It contains all the information to
be placed on the disk, in a format defined by
the disk manufacturer. A *master disk* is prepared from this tape (by *mastering*), and many
final disks can then be copied by a pressing
process.

matching of a graph. *See* perfect matching.

mathematical programming A wide field of
study that deals with the theory, applications,
and computational methods for *optimization problems. An abstract formulation of
such problems is to maximize a function f

(known as an *objective function*) over a constraint set S, i.e.

$$\text{maximize} f(x), x \in S \subseteq R^n,$$

where R^n denotes the space of real n-
component vectors x,

$$x = (x_1, x_2, \ldots, x_n)^T$$

and f is a real-valued function defined on S.
If S consists only of vectors whose elements
are integers, then the problem is one of
integer programming. *Linear programming
treats the case of f as a linear function with S
defined by linear equations and/or constraints. Nonlinear objective functions with
or without constraints (defined by systems of
*nonlinear equations) give rise to problems
generally referred to as optimization problems.

Mathematical-programming problems
arise in engineering, business, and the physical and social sciences.

matrix A two-dimensional *array. In computing, matrices are usually considered to be
special cases of n-dimensional arrays,
expressed as arrays with two indices. The
notation for arrays is determined by the programming language. The two dimensions of
a matrix are known as its *rows* and *columns*; a
matrix with m rows and n columns is said to
be an $m \times n$ matrix.

In mathematics (and in this dictionary),
the conventional notation is to use a capital
letter to denote a matrix in its entirety, and
the corresponding lower-case letter, indexed
by a pair of subscripts, to denote an element
in the matrix. Thus the i,jth element of a
matrix A is denoted by a_{ij}, where i is the row
number and j the column number.

A deficient two-dimensional array, in
which one of the dimensions has only one
index value (and is consequently elided), is a
special kind of matrix known either as a *row
vector* (with the column elided) or *column vector* (with the row elided). The distinction
between row and column shows that the two
dimensions are still significant.

matrix inversion A numerical method by
which the *inverse matrix of a given matrix is
produced.

matrix multiplication The multiplication of
two matrices A and B according to the rule

$$c_{ij} = \sum_{k=1}^{n} a_{ik} b_{kj}$$

matrix norm *See* approximation theory.

matrix printer A printer that forms the character or shape to be printed from an array of dots. The dots can be formed on paper by a stylus impacting an inked ribbon, by separate drops of ink ejected from a nozzle, or by one of the other nonimpact technologies in which dots are formed by changing the color of the media by heating (thermal printer) or by ink adhering to an electric charge or magnetic pole pattern (electrographic and magnetographic printers).

A significant advantage of matrix printers over *solid-font printers is the ability to accommodate a very large repertoire of character shapes and styles and also to print the ideograms of oriental languages and script characters of Arabic. Diagrams and pictures can also be reproduced. When the term is used in reference to a single type of printer it generally means an *impact printer or *dot matrix printer.

matrix-updating methods *See* optimization.

maximize In a *graphical user interface, to cause a *window to expand to its maximum size, usually filling the entire screen. The action is achieved by clicking on the maximize button or selecting "maximize" from a window control menu. The maximum size and the behavior of items within the window (do they get enlarged too or is more seen of them?) are determined by the window definition.

maximum-length sequence *See* m-sequence.

maximum-likelihood decoding A strategy for decoding an *error-correcting code: it chooses the *codeword conditional upon whose occurrence the probability of the word actually received is greatest. *Compare* minimum-error decoding.

maximum likelihood, method of *See* likelihood.

max sort A *sorting algorithm in which the largest key in the unsorted section of the file is successively placed at the end of the file, which becomes the sorted section of the file.

maxterm (standard sum term) A sum (OR) of n Boolean variables, uncomplemented or complemented but not repeated, in a Boolean function of n variables. With n variables, 2^n different maxterms are possible. The complement of any maxterm is a *minterm. *See also* standard product of sums.

MB (or Mb) *Symbols for* megabyte. *See* mega-, byte.

MBONE A *multicast *backbone service that allows the transmission of messages to one or more destinations. It supports multimedia applications such as videoconferencing. MBONE is used for the *Internet. It employs a class D Internet address (*see* TCP/IP) to route a packet to one or more LANs, and then relies on the facilities within these LANs to route the packet to the required destinations.

Mbps *Abbrev. for* megabits per second, usually 10^6 (one million) bits per second. *See* mega-, bps.

Mbyte *Abbrev. for* megabyte. *See* mega-, byte.

MCA *Trademark; abbrev. for* micro channel architecture. An IBM *bus structure for personal computers that was introduced in 1987 with the IBM PS/2, models 50 and above, and is the successor to the structures used in the IBM PCs. It was made necessary by the requirements of 32-bit microprocessors. *See also* EISA.

MCAV *Abbrev. for* modified constant angular velocity. A modification of *CAV in which the rotation rate of the disk is constant but the clock rate and data transfer rate are varied in proportion to the radius of the track being accessed, thus obtaining the high data density of *CLV without the long access time that usually goes with it. In practice the tracks are usually grouped into 4 to 8 bands; clock and data rates vary between bands but not within a band.

MCGA *Abbrev. for* multicolor graphics array. An extension of the *CGA, now obsolete. Unlike the CGA it was analog in composition.

MCLV *Abbrev. for* modified constant linear velocity. A modification of *CLV in which the data tracks on an optical disk are grouped in a number of bands; the same angular velocity is used while accessing all the tracks within a band, but a different velocity is used for each band. It is thus a compromise between CLV and *CAV.

MDNS *Abbrev. for* managed data network service.

MDR *Abbrev. for* memory data register.

Mealy machine *See* sequential machine.

mean *See* measures of location.

mean deviation *See* measures of variation.

means/ends analysis A technique used in *artificial intelligence for forming plans to achieve goals. A plan consists of a sequence of actions. The sequence is put together by comparing the goals that each action achieves (the means) with the goals and action preconditions that must be achieved (the ends).

measure 1. A quantity ascertained or ascertainable by measurement.

2. A number assigned to a property of an entity according to well-defined rules, so as to describe or represent that property objectively.

3. A number or other *symbol assigned to a specific property by means of observation.

measurement of appearance The family of measurements necessary to characterize the color and surface finish of an object.

measures of location Quantities that represent the average or typical value of a *random variable (*compare* measures of variation). They are either properties of a *probability distribution or computed *statistics of a sample. Three important measures are the *mean*, *median*, and *mode*.

The *mean* of a sample of n observations, denoted by $\bar{x}$, is

$$\sum_i x_i/n$$

The mean of a probability distribution, denoted by μ, is

$$\sum x.p(x)$$

for a discrete distribution and

$$\int x.f(x)\, dx$$

for a continuous distribution; it is also called the *expectation* of x, denoted by $E(x)$.

A *weighted mean* is used when members of a sample are known with different reliability.

To each observation x_i corresponds a *weight* w_i, and now $\bar{x}$ is

$$\sum (w_i.x_i)/\sum w_i$$

If each observation is the mean of w observations, the formulas for the weighted and unweighted means agree.

The *median* is the value of x exceeded by exactly half the sample or distribution. The median of a distribution is the value for which the cumulative distribution function, $F(x)$, equals 0.5 (*see* probability distributions).

The *mode* is the most commonly occurring value. For distributions in which the frequency function, $f(x)$, has one or more local maxima, each maximum is called a mode.

These measures may be illustrated on the following sample of eight values of x:

$$1,1,1,2,3,3,5,7$$

The mean is 2.875, the median is 2.5, and the mode is 1.

measures of variation Quantities that express the amount of variation in a *random variable (*compare* measures of location). Variation is sometimes described as *spread* or *dispersion* to distinguish it from systematic trends or differences. Measures of variation are either properties of a *probability distribution or sample estimates of them.

The *range* of a sample is the difference between the largest and smallest value. The *interquartile range* is potentially more useful. If the sample is ranked in ascending order of magnitude two values of x may be found, the first of which is exceeded by 75% of the sample, the second by 25%; their difference is the interquartile range. An analogous definition applies to a probability distribution.

The *variance* is the expectation (or mean) of the square of the difference between a *random variable and its mean; it is of fundamental importance in statistical analysis. The variance of a continuous distribution with mean μ is

$$\int (x - \mu)^2 f(x)\, dx$$

and is denoted by σ^2. The variance of a discrete distribution is

$$\sum (x - \mu)^2.p(x)$$

and is also denoted by σ^2. The sample variance of a sample of n observations with mean $\overline{x}$ is

$$\Sigma (x_i - \overline{x})^2 / (n - 1)$$

and is denoted by s^2. The value $(n - 1)$ corrects for *bias.

The *standard deviation* is the square root of the variance, denoted by σ (for a distribution) or s (for a sample). The standard deviation has the same units of measurement as the mean, and for a *normal distribution about 5% of the distribution lies beyond about two standard deviations each side of the mean. The standard deviation of the distribution of an estimated quantity is termed the *standard error*.

The *mean deviation* is the mean of the absolute deviations of the random variable from the mean.

mechanical verifier A system that provides automated assistance to the production of a *program correctness proof. Typically such a system consists of two distinct parts: a *verification condition generator* and a *theorem prover*. The former is responsible for generating the theorems that must be proven in order to demonstrate that *preconditions and *postconditions are consistent with the semantics of the statements to which they relate. The theorem prover is then responsible for proving these verification conditions.

Different mechanical verifiers vary considerably in their capabilities. A relatively simple verifier might require that assertions giving all relevant information are attached between every pair of successive statements (simple or compound), and would present any nontrivial verification conditions to the user for manual proof; this approach is sometimes called an *assertion checker*. A more sophisticated mechanical verifier requires only major assertions to be attached prior to verification (perhaps only the input assertion and output assertion) and is able to generate its own intermediate assertions as necessary. Further, the theorem prover is capable of proving complex verification conditions, perhaps presenting only the occasional lemma to the user for confirmation.

mechatronics An engineering discipline that attempts to integrate technologies from

mechanical engineering, electronics, and computer software and hardware in order to design and create flexible "smart" machines. Mechatronics is closely related to *robotics, but covers relatively less complex systems such as intelligent door locks, cameras, photocopiers, and washing machines.

median *See* measures of location.

medium (plural: **media**) *See* data medium.

meet operator *See* lattice.

mega- (symbol: M) A prefix indicating a multiple of one million (10^6), as in megahertz and megawatt. When the binary number system is used in a structure or process (as in semiconductor RAM or ROM), the prefix then indicates a multiple of 2^{20}, i.e. 1 048 576, as in megabyte or megabit. The context usually clarifies which meaning is intended, although being numerically close the meanings are often considered more or less equivalent.

Megastream *Trademark* British Telecom's higher-speed digital leased-circuit service. Megastream circuits (or more correctly *virtual circuits) are available as a fully digital service, operating at 2.048 and 8.192 Mbps. International Megastream is offered at speeds between 1.536 and 2.048 Mbps. *See also* Kilostream.

member (element) of a *set S. An object x that is in S, usually denoted by $x \in S$. One of the basic actions that can be performed on sets is asking whether or not an object is in a set. *See also* operations on sets.

member disk A disk that is under the control of array management software (*see* disk array). Disk drives may be array members for part of the time and be used as conventional disk drives otherwise. *See also* RAID.

memory A device or medium that can retain information for subsequent retrieval. The term is synonymous with *storage* and *store*, although it is most frequently used for referring to the internal storage of a computer that can be directly addressed by operating instructions. *See* main memory, cache, semiconductor memory, memory hierarchy, memory management.

memory card An *add-in card containing memory chips either directly mounted on the card or arranged in *SIMMS that plug into sockets on the card.

memory compaction (block compaction) Any of several methods used to relocate information blocks in main memory in order to maximize the available free space in the memory. *See also* storage allocation.

memory cycle 1. The complete sequence of events for a unit of memory to go from a quiescent state through a read and/or write phase and back to a quiescent state.
2. The minimum length of time that is required between successive accesses (read or write) to a memory. *See also* cycle.

memory data register (MDR) A *register used for holding information (either program words or data words) that is in the process of being transferred from the memory to the central processor, or vice versa.

memory dump A representation, which can be read by a person, of the contents at some time of some part of the main memory of a computer system. A variety of representation formats might be employed, but typically these would all be relatively low-level – e.g. purely numeric or assembler-code format. A memory dump is normally taken for *postmortem purposes.

memory element A device that stores one item of information: if it has q stable states it is said to be *q-ary, and if $q = 2$ it is said to be binary. It is usually implemented electronically, sometimes with the assistance of the magnetic, optical, or acoustic properties of a storage medium. In practice, most memory elements are binary. In fast computer circuitry, the *flip-flop is the most common type of memory element.

Memory elements are employed specifically in computer memories and generally in *sequential circuits. A memory element is any smallest part of such a system that possesses more than one stable state. For example, a binary *shift register contains four flip-flops and has 16 states, but each of its four memory elements has only two states; a similar ternary shift register would have 81 states, but would still consist of four memory elements, each having three states.

memory fill An aid to program debugging in which every location in the memory is filled with a predetermined character before being overwritten by the incoming program.

memory guard A form of hardware *interlock used in some systems to control access to memory that is currently involved in a peripheral transfer. At the time of initiating the transfer the channel sets an indication that the buffer area is associated with the transfer; this indication is cleared by the channel on completion of the transfer. Any attempt to access the buffer area (other than by the channel) will suspend the process attempting to access the buffer until the transfer has been completed.

memory hierarchy For physically different kinds of *memory there are significant differences in the time to read or write the contents of a particular *location in memory, the amount of information that is read or written on a given occasion, the total volume of information that can be stored, and the unit costs of storing a given amount of information. To optimize its use and to achieve greater efficiency and economy, memory is organized in a hierarchy with the highest performance and in general the most expensive devices at the top, and with progressively lower performance and less costly devices in succeeding layers. The contents of a typical memory hierarchy, and the way in which data moves between adjacent layers, might be organized as follows.

1. **Register** – A single word held in each *register of the *processor; typically a word contains 4 bytes. This is sometimes not thought of as part of the hierarchy.

2. **Cache** – Groups of words within the *cache; typically a single group in the cache will hold 64 words (say 256 bytes), and there will be, say, 1024 such groups, giving a total cache of 256 Kbytes. Single words pass between the cache and registers within the processor. All transfers into and out of the cache are controlled entirely by hardware.

3. **Main memory** – Words within the main (*random-access) memory. On a very high performance system, groups of words corresponding to a group within the cache are

Unit	System class	Realized as	Access time †	Cost of unit, $	Capacity	Cost/bit ‡	Notes
processor register	E, M W, D, L	ECL flip-flops MOS flip-flops	0.1 ns 2 ns	10 0.1	64 bits 16 bits	15 c 1 c	(1)
cache	E, M W, D, L	MOS flip-flops MOS inverters	1 ns 5 ns	10K 100	256 Kbytes 32 Kbytes	0.5 c 40 mc	(2)
main memory	E, M W, D, L	MOS inverters MOS inverters	20 ns 20 ns	100K 400	512 Mbytes 8 Mbytes	2 mc 0.5 mc	(3)
swapping device	E All	MOS inverters hard disk	1 ms 20 ms	50K 1K	2 Gbytes 500 Mbytes	0.3 μc 0.03 μc	(4)
disk	All	hard disk floppy disk: online offline	20 ms 50 ms minutes	1K 100 1	500 Mbytes 2 Mbytes 2 Mbytes ·	0.03 μc 0.6 μc 6 nc	(5)
magnetic tape	E, M All	reel to reel: online offline video cassette: online offline	 100 s minutes 100 s minutes	 10K 10 1K 10	 100 Mbytes 100 Mbytes 4 Gbytes 4 Gbytes	 1 mc 1 μc 3 nc 0.03 nc	 (5) (5)
library	All	CD-ROM: online offline	 1s minutes	 200 20	 600 Mbytes 600 Mbytes	 4 μc 0.4 μc	 (5)

†   Units are minutes or seconds (s), milliseconds (ms), microseconds (μs) and nanoseconds (ns); access times are given as an average figure.

‡   Units are cents (c) and the subdivisions millicents (mc), microcents (μc) and nanocents (nc).

Memory hierarchy

transferred between the cache and the main memory in a single cycle of main memory. On lower-performance systems the size of the group of words in the cache is larger than the width of the memory bus, and the transfer takes the form of a sequence of memory cycles. The algorithm that controls this movement is implemented entirely in hardware. Main memory sizes are very variable – from as little as 1 Mbyte on a small system up to several Gbytes on a high-performance system.

4. Online backing store – Blocks of words held on permanently connected *backing store. There may be two somewhat distinct forms of activity here:

(a) **swapping device** – pages (of say 4 Kbytes) or segments (up to many Mbytes) of memory held on a *swapping device are transferred as complete units between their backing-store home and a page frame or segment area in main memory, under the control of an algorithm implemented by the software of the operating system but with hardware assistance to indicate when pages or segments are to be moved;

(b) **backing store** – complete files, or clearly identifiable subsections of large files, are moved between the backing-store device and the main memory in response to explicit actions by the programmer, usually by a supervisor call to the operating system.

5. Demountable storage – Complete files, backed up onto removable disks or magnetic tape within the file store system and the archiving system. Complete files are transferred in either direction. The creation of backup copies and the reinstatement of a backed-up file may be automatic, or may require direct intervention by the end user. For larger systems the backup medium is typically a modified form of a video or audio cassette system, possibly mounted in some form of computer-controlled cassette-handling robot system. Smaller systems may use a cassette system or floppy disks.

6. Read-only library – Complete files, and collections of associated files relating to a single application, held on read-only devices such as *CD-ROM, or on a device with some form of write-protection control. Complete

sets of files are read into the system from the read-only device, but for obvious reasons there are never any transfers from the system to the device.

The table indicates the typical access times, capacities, and unit costs for memory in each of these broad categories. Five main categories of system are considered:

E   enterprise servers
M   mid-range servers
W   workstations
D   desktop personal computers
L   laptop and fully portable personal computers

It is emphasized that this division is rather arbitrary, with no clear boundaries between systems. The capacity and performance of all systems continually increases, and there are many anomalies in the systems available in the marketplace, especially in the workstation, desktop, and laptop systems. The figures quoted are typical mid-range figures for performance, capacity, and costs (as at Spring 1995) and are clearly intended to be purely indicative of trends. With these caveats, the overall picture is reasonably consistent.

The following notes relate to the table:

(1) In practice the registers on most current systems are part of a single chip, and it is difficult to identify accurately the cost of any single register.

(2) On smaller systems the cache may be integrated with the processor proper, and again it is difficult to identify accurately the cost of any single register.

(3) All systems use the same basic device for the actual storage. The higher unit costs on the larger systems arise from the inclusion of error-detection and error-recovery circuitry, and a wide data path between the memory and the cache.

(4) The swapping device on large systems may take the form of semiconductor memory or high-performance disks, or a mix of the two.

(5) The access time for any offline device is quoted as "minutes". There are specific exceptions for offline tapes or cassettes held in some form of automated handler, where access time will typically be in the order of tens of seconds at worst. There is a similar

exception for systems that handle multiple CD-ROMs. The unit cost for an online device includes the cost of the transport as well as the recording medium; for an offline device the cost quoted is purely for the recording medium.

memory management Control of the *memory hierarchy of a system as a whole, or control of allocation at a fixed level within the memory hierarchy. In the former case information stored within the system is shuttled between one realization of memory and another, the objective being to maintain maximum *hit rate in each form of memory. This movement may be controlled by

(a) voluntary user action, e.g. copying a file from disk to memory in order to edit it;

(b) system software, e.g. transfer of a page between swapping device and memory when a page fault occurs;

(c) system hardware, e.g. movement of a set of words from memory to cache when a word within the set is accessed.

At a given level of the hierarchy the operating system will control what fraction of that level is to be allocated to each process. This can clearly only occur where control is by system software, and refers most particularly to the allocation of memory to a process, or to the allocation of space on the swapping device. Movement between disk and magnetic tape is often separately treated as archiving. *See also* storage protection.

memory map A schematic presentation of the use to which memory is being put, often presented as a byproduct during the compilation of a program. The memory map may be useful in the diagnosis of faults in the compiled program, especially when used in association with a *memory dump.

memory mapping A technique for managing peripheral devices, used on many microprocessor systems and on some smaller miniprocessor systems. The control registers of the peripheral device appear to the processor as words in memory whose contents can be written and read using the normal store and fetch operations.

memory protection Any of many methods for controlling access to or use of memory.

This control may be to prevent inadvertent user interference, to provide for system security, or both.

A mechanism for controlling the types of access permitted to an area of memory is known as a *memory protect*. In virtual memory systems it may be possible to assign certain areas as being capable of designated modes of access; for example, an area that is known to contain only the code of shared subroutines may be designated as having "execute only" access, and can only be read during the instruction–fetch phase of executing an instruction. The permitted mode of access may differ for different processes. Definition of memory areas may use *bounds registers; fixed memory areas may be controlled by *locks and keys; individual words may be controlled by *tags.

A violation of the memory protection system usually leads via an *interrupt to a forced process termination.

memory reference instruction An *instruction that has one or more of its operand addresses referring to a location in memory, as opposed to one of the CPU registers or some other way of specifying an operand location.

memory-resident program A program that once loaded into memory stays there and can be accessed or reactivated whenever necessary without having to load another copy from disk. *See* TSR, device driver.

memory-to-memory instruction An instruction that transfers information from a memory and returns it to a memory. The information may be modified during the transfer (e.g. incremented); the information may or may not be returned to the same location. The term is also used to refer to an instruction that transfers information between levels of a *memory hierarchy. Transfers may be word by word or block transfers.

menu A list of options that may be displayed either vertically or horizontally on a screen and from which one or more items may be selected using an input device. (The input technique itself is also called a menu.) If a mouse or other *pointing device is available, then the *cursor may be moved to the desired item and a selection made by clicking a mouse button or its equivalent. Alternatively the cursor may be moved by means of the arrow keys on the keyboard. Each item in the menu may have a unique number or letter to identify it, or the first or some other character unique to the item may be emphasized in some way. In this case the selection may be made by pressing the appropriate key on the keyboard. *See also* pull-down menu, pop-up menu, tear-off menu.

menu bar In either a text- or graphics-based user interface, a row, usually horizontal, of words or abbreviations that when activated by a pointing device or a sequence of key depressions cause some appropriate action. This may involve the display of *menus.

menu bypass A technique whereby expert users of a *menu-driven program may avoid the rather slow and cumbersome process of stepping through a number of menus. This usually involves pre-empting the menus by typing in the selections before they appear.

menu-driven program A program that obtains input from a user by displaying a list of options – the *menu – from which the user indicates his/her choice. Systems running menu-driven programs are commonplace, ranging from microprocessor controlled washing machines to bank cash dispensers. In the case of the cash dispenser, single keys are pressed to indicate the type of transaction (whether a receipt is wanted with cash or a statement of the bank balance is required) and with many, a single key is pressed to indicate the amount of money required.

Menu-driven systems are advantageous in two ways: firstly, because input is via single key strokes, the system is less prone to user error; secondly, because only a limited range of characters are "allowed", the way in which the input is to be entered is unambiguous. This contributes toward making the system more user-friendly.

mergeable heap Any data structure representing a set of ordered elements that can support the insertion and deletion of elements as well as the set operation of union

and the calculation of the minimum elements in a set. *See also* operations on sets.

merge exchange sort *Another name for* Batcher's parallel method.

merge sort *See* merging.

merging Combining multiple sets of data to produce only one set, usually in an ordered sequence. This approach is usually employed in external *sorting, where the data is kept on backing store. The *polyphase merge sort is an example of a merging method.

mesh (grid) The result of subdividing a region in time and/or space into smaller subregions. A rectangular region in the x,y-plane can thus be divided into smaller rectangles by lines parallel to the x- and y-axes. The points of intersection of the lines are called the *mesh* (or *grid*) *points*. A *discretization method replaces *differential equations defined in a region by a finite set of equations, which define approximations to the exact solution at the mesh points. The *finite-difference and *finite-element methods are important methods of this general type. *See also* adaptive meshing.

mesh interconnection 1. (crossbar switch) A form of network connection in which each possible transmitter can establish a direct connection to each possible receiver.
2. A set of network connections in which there is more than one route between any two nodes on the network, thus giving resilience against the failure of any single link between any pair of nodes.

message 1. The unit of information transferred by a *message switching system. Messages may be of any length, from a few bits to a complete file, and no part of a message is released to its final recipient until all of the message has been received at the network node adjacent to the destination.
2. *Another name (deprecated) for* packet. The distinction between packet and message is valuable, since it refers to whether or not a partial transmission of a complete document can occur; a *packet switching system may allow this whereas a *message switching system may not.

3. *See* Shannon's model (of a communication system).

4. A specially formatted document sent in an *electronic mail system.

5. *See* object, object-oriented programming.

message passing A way of designing a software system that involves concurrent processes sending data encapsulated as messages to each other. The advantage of the approach is that it provides a low level of coupling between the concurrent processes such that the messages can be passed either directly within a single processor or indirectly using a *LAN or *WAN communications medium.

In some forms of message passing the recipient is named specifically by the sender; in other forms the recipient is not defined by the sender but by the way in which the network of concurrent processes is defined. The latter scheme provides a very good basis for reusing the concurrent processes, because they are independent of each other. *UNIX processes use this form of communication; the processes are independent and the connectivity is defined (at a higher level) by defining "pipes" that convey messages generated by one process to one other process. A similar scheme is provided by *MASCOT. Most *object-oriented design methods include some form of message passing, especially to transmit events from one object to another. In these approaches the recipient is usually defined explicitly, which thereby increases the coupling between the objects.

message queueing The process of storing a message in a node of a *message switching network until sufficient resources are available for the message to be forwarded to the next node along the path to its destination.

message store A system that can hold *electronic-mail messages for a user whose normal means of dealing with incoming e-mail is not currently active. Most implementations of e-mail expect the system to which the mail is addressed to respond to the receipt of the incoming message; if the system to which the mail is addressed is not active (for example a workstation that has been switched off overnight), the absence of

any response may lead to the sending system assuming that the mail is incorrectly addressed. In this situation, the user may elect to have mail delivered to a message store, which will normally be operating at all times. Any e-mail that is delivered can be collected later when the user queries the message store from his or her workstation.

message switching A data-switching strategy that requires no physical path to exist between sender and receiver before communication can take place. Message switching passes *messages via relays, called *switching offices*, in a *store-and-forward network. Each switching office receives a message, checks it for errors, and retransmits it to the next switching office on the route to the destination. Because of the large buffers and variable delays of message switching, most computer networks use *packet switching or *circuit switching techniques for their underlying network components, and add message switching functions (such as *electronic mail and *file transfer protocol) at higher levels.

message switching network A network in which data is moved as complete messages of arbitrary length, rather than being subdivided into packets, which contain a variable amount of data but with a fixed upper limit on length, or as cells, which contain a fixed amount of data.

meta-assembler A program that accepts the syntactic and semantic description of an assembly language, and generates an *assembler for that language. *Compare* compiler-compiler.

metaballs A representation used in computer graphics to efficiently model *soft objects*, i.e. objects that can be deformed.

metafile A mechanism for storing and transmitting graphical information in a device-independent way. *See* CGM.

METAFONT A system for designing digital typefaces, designed to complement the *TeX typesetting system. The designer specifies character shapes in terms of curves called *splines*, and the system then generates bitmap images for use in printing.

metalanguage A language used to specify some or all aspects of a programming language. *BNF and *SGML are examples.

methodology 1. In general, a coherent set of methods used in carrying out some complex activity. The word is most frequently used in terms such as *programming methodology* or *(system) design methodology*. In the UK the word *method* is usually preferred for this meaning.
2. (especially in the UK) The science or study of method.

methods In object-oriented programming, the procedures of an *object.

metric 1. A number representing the degree to which software, or an entity related to software, possesses some notional property, as observed or perceived by an individual or group.
2. *Informal name for* measure.
3. A specific type of *mapping in which the codomain is a number, and the triangle *inequality applies.

metropolitan area network (MAN) A network intermediate between a *local area network (LAN) and a *wide area network (WAN); the term was originally used to refer to a network serving a single town or district. There are no formal rules to determine whether a given network should be classified as a LAN, MAN, or WAN, and the differences lie as much in their style of organization as in their technology or geographical or physical size.

A MAN may either be operated as a joint activity by a number of separate organizations, which may set up a jointly owned enterprise to operate the MAN, or it may be operated by a company that specializes in the operation of networks and acts as a managing agent on behalf of the organizations that require the MAN. The MAN interconnects the LANs of the organizations that operate the MAN, but may also provide immediate connection to the MAN for organizations that do not operate their own internal LAN.

Mflops (MFLOPS, megaflops) A million floating-point operations per second. *See* flops.

MFM *Abbrev. for* modified frequency modulation. *See* disk format.

M²FM *Abbrev. for* modified modified frequency modulation. *See* disk format.

MHS *Abbrev. for* message handling system. A form of *electronic mail service.

MICR *Abbrev. for* magnetic-ink character recognition. A process in which data, printed in ink containing ferromagnetic particles, is read by magnetic read heads. The shape of the characters resembles those of normal typescript but each generates a unique signal as it is scanned by the read head. The most common application is for encoding numbers on bank checks.

There are two standardized fonts: the E13B and CMC7. The E13B font is very rectangular in appearance and some parts of the vertical limbs may be thickened to accentuate the difference in the generated wave form. This font is widely used in the US and the UK. The CMC7 font has the character shape sliced into seven vertical strips with the six intervening spaces either wide or narrow. Each of the numerical symbols and the four special symbols is coded with a combination of two wide and four narrow spaces.

micro 1. (symbol: μ) A prefix to a unit, indicating a submultiple of one millionth, 10^{-6}, of that unit, as in microsecond.
2. *Short for* microcomputer.

microcircuit An *integrated circuit, generally one performing a very complex function. An example is a *microprocessor comprised of ALU, control circuits, registers, program counter, and some memory, all within a single integrated circuit.

microcode A sequence of *microinstructions, i.e. the program code in a microprogrammed *control unit. *See* microprogramming.

microcomputer 1. A computer system that utilizes a *microprocessor as its central control and arithmetic element. The *personal computer is one form. The power and price of a microcomputer is determined partly by the speed and power of the processor and partly by the characteristics of other components of the system, i.e. the memory, the disk units, the display, the keyboard, the flexibility of the hardware, and the operating system and other software.

Memory sizes range from a few megabytes up to tens of megabytes and the access speed can also vary considerably. The capacity of floppy disk drives varies over a much smaller range, starting at less than 0.5 Mbyte but usually not extending as far as 3 Mbytes. Hard disk capacities lie in the hundreds of Mbytes for personal computers but up to several gigabytes for *file servers and other more powerful systems; *optical disks extend this range. Microcomputer *displays range from domestic TV receivers to high-definition color monitors based on a CRT technology in advance of current TV standards. Other kinds of display include flat LCD and plasma screens used on *laptops, *notebooks, and other portable models. There are many keyboard designs, and the number and arrangement of keys is not a guide to quality, rather the physical construction and action. The flexibility of the hardware can be measured by the number and type of enhancements available. These might include extra memory, more disk drives, *coprocessors, *pointing devices, communications interfaces, and the ability to participate in networks. The *operating system can be characterized by its use of memory, how much can be accessed and how well it is done, how many tasks can be run concurrently, and how it appears to the user.

2. A single integrated circuit containing all the logic elements needed for a complete computer system.

microcontroller 1. A microprocessor designed specifically for use in device control, communication control, or process-control applications. A typical microcontroller chip might have a relatively short word length, a rich set of bit-manipulation instructions, and lack certain arithmetic and string operations found on general-purpose microprocessors. **2.** A microprocessor-based device or system designed for control applications.

microfiche, microfilm *See* COM.

microinstruction One instruction in a microprogram that specifies some of the detailed control steps needed to perform an *instruction. *See* microprogramming.

micronet A near-obsolete term for a local area network, occasionally reappearing usually in connection with microprocessor applications.

micropipeline An asynchronous processing pipeline (*see* pipeline processing). It is a self-timed FIFO buffer that may include computational elements between its stages.

microprocessor A semiconductor chip, or chip set, that implements the *central processor of a computer. Microprocessors consist of, at a minimum, an *ALU and a *control unit. They are characterized by speed, word length (internal and external), *architecture, and *instruction set, which may be either fixed or microprogrammed. It is the combination of these characteristics and not just the *cycle time that determines the performance of a microprocessor.

Most microprocessors have a fixed instruction set. Microprogrammed processors have a control store containing the microcode or firmware that defines the processor's instruction set; such processors may either be implemented on a single chip or constructed from *bit-slice elements. *RISC microprocessors are designed to execute a small number of simple instructions extremely fast.

The processor's architecture determines what register, stack, addressing, and I/O facilities are available, as well as defining the processor's primitive data types. The data types, which are the fundamental entities that can be manipulated by the instruction set, have included bit, nibble (4 bits), byte (8 bits), word (16 bits), and double words (32 bits). Note that a word is usually defined as the number of bits in the processor's internal data bus rather than always being 16 bits. Instructions generally include arithmetic, logical, flow-of-control, and data movement (between stacks, registers, memory, and I/O ports). With some microprocessors, *coprocessors can be added to the system in order to extend the range of data types and instructions supported, e.g. floating-point numbers and the set of arithmetic operations defined on them.

The first microprocessor, the four-chip set Intel 4004, appeared in 1971 accompanied by considerable debate about its utility and marketability. It was the outcome of an idea proposed by Ted Hoff of *Intel Corp. for a calculator that could implement a simple set of instructions in hardware but permitted complex sequences of them to be stored in a read-only memory (ROM). The result of his proposal was a design for a four-chip set consisting of a CPU, *ROM, *RAM, and a *shift-register chip, the chip design proceeding in 1970 under the direction of Federico Faggin, later the founder of Zilog, Inc. The Intel 4004 had a 4-bit data bus, could address 4.5 Kbytes of memory, and had 45 instructions. Its 8-bit counterpart, the Intel 8008, was introduced in 1974 and its improved derivative, the Zilog Z80, in 1976. By this time there were over 50 microprocessors on the market.

The next generation of microprocessors included the Zilog Z8000, Motorola 68000, Intel 8086, National 16000, as well as the older Texas Instruments 9900 and Digital Equipment Corporation LSI-11. All of these chips use a 16-bit-wide external data bus. Higher performance microprocessors that use 32-bit external data buses include the Intel386, Intel486, Motorola 68030, and Digital's VAX 78032 and 78132 (processor and FPA). Processors using a 64-bit external bus are now available, an example being Intel's Pentium processor. RISC microprocessor chips with a 64-bit architecture include the *PowerPC and *Alpha AXP.

microprogramming A method of accomplishing the *control unit function by describing the steps in that function as a sequence of register-transfer level operations that are much more elementary than *instructions. In this method of designing and building a control unit, an additional memory, commonly called a *microprogram store*, contains a sequence of *microinstructions*. A number of microinstructions will be required to carry out an ordinary machine instruction, thus the microprogram store

should be faster – have a shorter *cycle time – than the normal fast memory.

Microinstructions are usually classified as either *horizontal* or *vertical*. In a horizontal microinstruction most of the bit positions have a one-to-one correspondence with specific control functions. Horizontal microinstructions provide explicit control of functions at particular points within the CPU. For example, a particular bit in the microinstruction would call for a specific register to be cleared at a specific clock time. A vertical microinstruction generally contains highly coded fields describing elementary operations to be performed by certain elements of the control unit and *ALU, and the sources and destinations of information passing between these units. In such a microinstruction, a field, say of three bits, might be decoded to indicate which of eight registers is to be one source of an operation to be performed in an ALU. Other fields would define the operation and any other necessary sources. Horizontal microinstructions will in general contain more bits, or be wider, hence the word horizontal. Vertical microinstructions, although containing fewer bits, require more decoding.

Some microprogrammed control units go through two levels of microprogramming. The first level consists of addresses of horizontal microinstructions. The second level is the used or useful subset of all horizontal microinstructions. This provides for more efficient use of a horizontal microprogram memory at the expense of two memory references per microinstruction execution. In this form of microprogramming the first memory has been called the microprogram store and the second memory has been called the *nanostore*.

The control units of most CISC processors are microprogrammed. This permits a more orderly and flexible approach to control unit design and permits changes in a control unit by changing the memory contents. Most microprogram stores are made with *ROM. These memories are generally faster and are potentially less prone to errors. Other microprogram stores, usually called *writeable control stores (WCS)*, are made with *RAM.

These provide greater ease of change of control unit function; in some cases users are permitted or encouraged to "build" specialized instructions. Some microprogrammed control units have a mixture of ROM and RAM microprogram stores. These permit special microprograms to be loaded for maintenance and diagnostic purposes.

Manufacturers of supercomputers have not in general employed microprogramming because they have been prepared to accept the higher complexity of *hardwired control for the sake of ultimate performance. The simpler designs of current RISC processors have also opted for hardwired techniques to optimize instruction-execution rates of their simple instruction sets.

microprogram store (control memory) The memory that contains a microprogram. It may be fixed (ROM) or alterable (writeable control store). *See* microprogramming.

microrelief A technique used in optical recording. The surface of the medium is impressed with a very fine pattern that scatters light. When a spot on the surface is heated by a laser beam, the material flows to leave a smooth reflective surface. The technique is sometimes called *moth-eye* recording because the pattern resembles that of the cornea of a moth's eye.

microsequence A sequence of *microinstructions, i.e. a microprogram or a portion thereof. *See* microprogramming.

Microsoft The *wunderkind* of the software industry: the largest independent software producer in the world, founded by Bill Gates in 1982. Microsoft produces, among other products, *MS-DOS, *Windows, *Word, *Excel, *Access, *Visual Basic, and *Visual C++. As a software producer it is second only to IBM in terms of revenue and is ranked as number 19 by revenue in the list of the world's top IT companies (1993 figures).

middleware 1. (firmware) Products that in some sense occupy a position between hardware and software. It is usually system software held in *ROM. In particular where microcoded systems are used, the actual microcode is sometimes spoken of as middleware.

2. Software that occupies a position between the *operating system and *applications programs, particularly in a distributed system.

MIDI *Acronym for* musical instrument digital interface. The means whereby an electronic musical instrument can communicate with other MIDI instruments and computers. Many *sound cards provide MIDI input and output facilities.

midi-tower A computer system box (*see* desktop) that is small enough to stand on a desk usually alongside the monitor. The dimensions are such that height > depth > width. Peripherals such as floppy or CD-ROM disk drives or backup tape streamers are usually mounted horizontally in the front surface one above the other. *See also* tower.

midpoint rule The explicit rule

$$y_{n+2} = y_n + 2h f(x_{n+1}, y_{n+1})$$

for the solution of ordinary differential equations (h is the stepsize). It is an example of a *linear multistep method, important for its use as the basis of *Gragg's extrapolation method.

migration path The series of steps undertaken to allow an organization to move away from its current position. The term is frequently used in connection with the introduction of new aspects of an IT service, where it is essential both to maintain an existing service, to introduce a new service, and to allow the old and the new services at least to coexist and possibly to interwork. *See* legacy network.

millennium bug Any software problem arising as the date changes to 1 Jan 2000 when previous dates in the software have been abbreviated (e.g. 88 rather than 1988). Problems will occur, for instance, with comparisons or calculations of time intervals and chronological sorting.

milli- (symbol: m) A prefix to a unit, indicating a submultiple of one thousandth, 10^{-3}, of that unit, as in millisecond.

MIMD processor *Short for* multiple instruction (stream), multiple data (stream) processor. *See* concurrency.

MIME *Acronym for* multipurpose Internet

messaging extensions. A system designed to support the encoding of information other than straightforward text, such as digitized audio or video signals, so as to allow the signals to be transferred as the contents of e-mail messages.

min *Abbrev. for* minimum. **1.** One of the basic actions performed on a set on whose elements a *total ordering $\leq$ is defined; when applied in the form *min*(S) it produces the smallest element of the set S with respect to $\leq$.

2. A *monadic operation applied to a language L and defined in such a way that *min*(L) is the set of strings in L that have no proper *prefixes that are also in L.

minicomputer (mini) Originally, a computer that physically went within a single equipment cabinet, i.e. on the order of a few cubic feet. Compared with larger computers, minicomputers were cheaper and slower, with smaller memory and usually shorter word length. The word minicomputer is no longer used very specifically. It predates the term *microcomputer and the boundary between these two classes of device is unclear.

minimal algebra An *algebra generated by elements named as constants in its *signature. Every element of the algebra can be constructed by finitely many applications of the basic operations to the constants. The simplest example is the algebra

$$(\{0, 1, 2, \ldots\} \mid 0, n+1)$$

wherein all natural numbers can be constructed by applying the *successor function $n+1$ to the constant 0 sufficiently many times.

minimal machine An abstract machine possessing no redundant states. To any *finite-state automaton or *sequential machine there corresponds a unique (up to isomorphism) minimal machine that recognizes the same language (in the case of finite automata) or has the same response function (in the case of sequential machines). This is true for infinite as well as finite state-sets.

There are two ways in which a state q may be "redundant": it is either "inaccessible" in that there is no input string that takes the start-state to q, or else it is equivalent to

another state q' in that the subsequent behavior of the machine is the same whether it is in state q or q'. In a minimal machine all inaccessible states have been dropped and all equivalent states have been merged. There is a simple algorithm that will give the minimized version of any machine. *See also* Myhill equivalence, Nerode equivalence.

minimax A basic algorithm in *artificial intelligence, in particular when constructing programs to play games such as chess. A *tree of possible moves, alternating with possible opponent's moves, is constructed to some depth. Evaluation of the positions at the leaves is then passed back up the tree, choosing always the minimum evaluation for the opponent and the maximum for the program itself. *See also* computer chess.

minimax procedure A procedure usually used in *approximation theory in order to find an approximating function, often a polynomial, that has the smallest maximum error on a given interval.

minimization 1. The process of manipulating a logical expression and thereby transforming it into a simpler but equivalent expression with the same truth table. In practice this commonly means reducing the number of *logic gates, gate inputs, or *logic levels in a *combinational circuit that realizes the logical expression. Minimization methods include use of *Karnaugh maps and algebraic manipulation (often computer-aided).

2. The process of converting a *finite-state machine to an equivalent *minimal machine.

3. In the study of *effective computability, the process of defining a new function by searching for values of a given function using the *minimization operator* or *μ-operator*. The functions involved are usually over the *natural numbers. Let g be a function of $n+1$ variables. Then, for any given values of $x_1, \ldots, x_n$, the expression

$$\mu y \cdot g(x_1, \ldots, x_n, y)$$

is evaluated by searching for the smallest value of y for which

$$g(x_1, \ldots, x_n, y) = 0$$

This can be done by letting y run through all natural numbers, in increasing order, until a suitable y is found, whereupon that value of y

is returned as the value of the μ-expression. If no suitable y exists the μ-expression is undefined. Also it may happen that before a suitable y is found a value of y is encountered for which

$$g(x_1,...,x_n,y)$$

is itself undefined; in this case again the μ-expression is undefined.

This construct is used to define a function f of n variables from the function g of $n+1$ variables:

$$f(x_1,...,x_n) = \mu y \cdot g(x_1,...,x_n,y)$$

Because of the possibility of the μ-expression being undefined, f is a *partial function. The process of searching for values, and the use of minimization, are essential factors that allow the formalism of *recursive functions to define all the computable functions.
4. *See* optimization.

minimization operator (μ-operator) *See* minimization.

minimize In a *graphical user interface, to cause a *window to contract down to an *icon, normally close to one edge of the screen. The action is achieved by clicking on the minimize button or selecting "minimize" from a window control menu.

minimum-access code A form of programming for early computers with magnetic-drum storage. It was also known as *optimum programming*. In programs for this kind of machine, each instruction specified the address of its successor, and it was desirable to place instructions in addresses so chosen that they were available under the reading heads when required. Since the execution time of instruction varied, it was necessary to work out how far the drum would rotate during execution of an instruction: this then determined the optimum position of its successor. Since this address might already be occupied, obtaining an optimal (or nearly optimal) distribution of instructions on the drum was extremely difficult.

The most widely used machine of this kind was the IBM 650; the success of the machine was largely due to the SOAP assembler, which produced near-optimal code positioning without any special effort on the part of the programmer.

minimum-cost spanning tree *See* spanning tree.

minimum-error decoding A strategy for decoding an *error-correcting code: it chooses the *codeword most likely to have been transmitted, given the word actually received. This is by contrast with *maximum-likelihood decoding, but the two strategies become identical when all the codewords are equally probable.

minterm (standard product term) A product (AND) of n Boolean variables, uncomplemented or complemented but not repeated, in a Boolean function of n variables. With n variables, 2^n different minterms are possible. The complement of any minterm is a *maxterm. *See also* standard sum of products.

mipmap A pyramidal structure used in mapping two-dimensional textures; mip stands for *multum in parvo* – Latin: many things in a small place. The use of mipmaps – *mipmapping* – enhances bilinear interpolation (which may be used to smoothly translate and magnify the texture) with interpolation between prefiltered versions of the map (which may be used to compress many pixels into a small place).

A mipmap is indexed by three coordinates: U, V, and D. U and V are spatial coordinates of the map and D is used to index and interpolate between different levels of the pyramid. A mipmap is organized as a two-dimensional array, where successively filtered and down-sampled versions of each color component of the image are instanced above and to the left of the originals, in a series of smaller and smaller images, each half the linear dimension (a quarter of the number of samples) of its parent. With this memory organization, addressing the maps is possible with binary scaling, which is inexpensive. When a target pixel is covered by a collection of source pixels, the mipmap pixels corresponding most closely to this collection are used to give a filtered value. Linear interpolation between levels of filtering (levels in the pyramid) is used to further smooth the values.

mips *Abbrev. for* million instructions per second. A measure of processing speed.

MIRANDA A functional programming language, similar to *ML.

mirror disk Part of a *mirror set* in which two or more disk drives contain identical images of user data. A mirror set provides a very reliable single *virtual disk drive whose capacity is equal to that of its smallest *member disk. *See also* RAID, stripe disk.

mirroring *See* RAID.

mirror set *See* mirror disk.

MIS *Abbrev. for* management information system.

MISD processor *Short for* multiple instruction (stream), single data (stream) processor. *See* concurrency.

missing observations Values unavoidably absent from a set of structured data, as in an *experimental design. Algorithms exist to estimate values to be substituted for those that are missing, to allow the analysis to be completed.

mixed alphabet An *alphabet that has been subjected to a *permutation for incorporation in an *encryption algorithm, usually to effect a substitution (*see* substitution cipher).

mixed-base system *See* number system.

mixed cipher A cipher that incorporates both *transposition and *substitution operations, often repeating these alternately. Mixed ciphers are usually *block ciphers. The *Data Encryption Standard is a mixed cipher.

mixed logic A *digital design that includes both *positive and *negative logic.

mixed-radix system *See* number system.

ML A *functional language developed at Edinburgh University in the late 1970s to support a formal proof system (Logic for Computable Functions), which was later developed into a general-purpose functional programming language. *See also* standard ML.

MMI *Abbrev. for* man-machine interface. *See* human-computer interface.

MNP *Abbrev. for* microcomputer networking protocol. *See* protocol.

M-O *Abbrev. for* magneto-optic. *See* magneto-optic storage.

MOB *Acronym for* movable object block. *Another term for* sprite.

mobile computing Generally, any application in which the computing system used is not assigned a specific location. In some cases the movement of the system is an essential element of the application; for example the system may be mounted in a vehicle, or may be used by someone whose work demands visits to different locations with no on-site computing facilities. In other cases it is the end-user who may move from place to place, each equipped with computing facilities, and along the way the user is able to use any network-connected workstation that will automatically reconfigure itself so as to reconstruct the environment he or she was last using on some other workstation. This requires the user to carry a machine-readable identification.

mobile robotics The branch of *robotics concerned with movable robot systems that are able to locomote within an environment or terrain. Mobile robotics and robots are mainly used in research on navigation and exploration, with applications for *autonomous guided vehicles. Recent research in *behavior-based systems has used *legged robots as mechanical analogues of insects and simple animals.

MOD A file format used to store Amiga Module music files. This format stores the sampled digital sounds as well as the patterns and performance data. Programs that create and play these files are commonly called *trackers*. There is currently a large number of variants to cope with 16-bit sampled sound, 32 channels, and *wave-table synthesis sound cards.

modal dialogue *See* dialogue management.

modal logic Any logical system that allows the use of *modal operators* designed to explore modes of truth. The two most common operators are "necessity" and "possibility", usually written as □ and ◇, where □F expresses "F is necessarily true" and ◇F that "F is possibly true". The objective of modal logic is to pin down meanings and laws of reasoning for these modes of truth. Modal logic has been developed in philosophy and is now the basis of advanced technologies in computer science.

For a modal operator α, the value of a formula αF in an *interpretation I depends on the values of F in a whole class of interpretations related to I, rather than on the value of F in just I itself as is the case in a nonmodal logic. Thus □F is true in an interpretation (or *world*) w if F is true in all worlds w' related to (or *accessible from*) w, while ◇F is true in w if F is true in at least one such w'. In discussing the semantics of modal logic, therefore, one considers *frames* of the form (W,R), where W is a set of worlds and R is an *accessibility relation* on W. Each world attaches a value to all the primitive symbols in the language.

In *dynamic logic* the modal operators correspond to programs, and the worlds correspond to states of execution. Then the formula αF is true in a particular state s if F is true in all states reachable from s by running the program α. Dynamic logic is similar to *Hoare logic in the fact that its formulas involve both programming and logical constructs.

In *temporal logics the modal operators deal with interpretations that might depend on the time: formulas express "F is sometimes true" or "F is always true". Other modal operators express notions of belief, desirability, and obligation. All these ideas are of great relevance in reasoning about programs and systems. Hence recent years have seen extensive use of modal logics in *program verification and *formal specification, especially for concurrent programs and systems.

mode 1. A term used in many contexts concerning the operation and use of a computer system. For example: conversational mode refers to interactive computer use; interpretive mode refers to a way of executing a language; there are addressing modes in instruction descriptions.

2. *See* measures of location.

model A simplified representation of something (the *referent*). The representation may be physical or abstract, and may be restricted to certain properties of the referent. In computing, models are usually abstract and are typically represented in a diagramming notation, such as *dataflow diagrams (in *functional design), *ERA diagrams (for a *data model), or *state-transition diagrams (for a model of behavior); in the case of the *relational model the referent is the target system while in the *waterfall model, *V-model, and *spiral model the referent is the development process. In computer graphics, models are used to create realistic images of objects and their attributes (*see* color model, lighting model, reflectance model).

model-based reasoning An approach in *artificial intelligence that relies on the use of a model as the basis of its inferencing abilities rather than empirical information. A model is a principled representation of a problem domain that has predictive and explicative features. An example is seen in diagnosis applications where model-based reasoning offers an alternative to methods based on *probabilistic reasoning.

model-based specification A form of specification, usually *software specification, that is developed by creating a mathematical model of that system. Typically the mathematical model is expressed in terms of objects and operations, and these are defined using such mathematical concepts as *sets, *relations, and *functions.

modeless dialogue *See* dialogue management.

modeling The act of creating a *model of something for a particular purpose, such as to describe it, understand it, or derive some properties. The process involves deciding which simplifications, idealizations, or abstractions to make, what kinds of representations to adopt, and how to express the selected properties of the referent. The context of a prospective system may be modeled as part of the *systems analysis. A program or software-based system may be modeled to produce an abstract design or for nonfunctional properties such as performance.

modeling clip A clip defined at the modeling stage of constructing objects to be viewed. *See also* clipping.

model numbers In the language Ada, the set of values of a variable that are guaranteed to be exactly represented for the requested accuracy of the variable. The implementation will typically use a greater accuracy which has a larger range than that requested. Consequently the implemented accuracy will usually be higher, and other values will also be exactly represented. Associated with each implemented value will be a *model interval*, which defines the degree of uncertainty in the value. If a value is a model number then the model interval is zero; if a value is not a model number then the model interval is defined by the two model numbers surrounding the value.

modem *Short for* modulator and demodulator. A device that can convert a digital bit stream into an analog signal suitable for transmission over some analog communication channel (*modulation), and can convert incoming analog signals back into digital signals (*demodulation). Modems are used to connect digital devices across analog transmission lines. Most modems are designed to match specific national or international standards so that data communication equipment from one manufacturer can talk to that of another.

Modems can be packaged in many ways: as *add-in cards or *PCMCIA cards allowing personal computers to communicate over ordinary phone lines, as small external units, or as rack-mounted sets for large applications requiring many simultaneous connections.

modifier bits Usually a small subset of bits (i.e. bit locations) in an instruction, used to provide some additional specification of the way in which the operation code and/or operand addresses are to be used or interpreted. *See* instruction format.

mod-n counter (modulo-n counter) *See* counter.

Modula A programming language developed from *Pascal as a research exercise to demonstrate that operating systems can be written entirely in a high-level language. It is now superseded by the languages *Modula 2 and *Modula 3.

Modula 2 A high-level programming lan-

guage designed by Wirth (the designer of Pascal) as the programming language for the Lilith personal computer system. Modula 2 is a derivative of *Pascal. Its name derives from the fact that a program is made up of *modules* – collections of procedures and data objects that exist independently of other modules and have a controlled interface with other modules (*compare* package (as used in Ada)). Modula 2 also provides facilities for describing parallel computations together with their interaction and synchronization. It is now available on most popular computers.

Modula 3 A programming language based on *Modula 2 and incorporating many new features, including *objects and classes, *exception handling, *garbage collection, lightweight processes (*threads*), and the isolation of unsafe features.

modular arithmetic (residue arithmetic) Arithmetic based on the concept of the *congruence relation defined on the integers and used in computing to circumvent the problem of performing arithmetic on very large numbers.

Let $m_1, m_2, \ldots, m_k$ be integers, no two of which have a common factor greater than one. Given a large positive integer n it is possible to compute the remainders or residues $r_1, r_2, \ldots, r_k$ such that

$$n \equiv r_1 \pmod{m_1}$$
$$n \equiv r_2 \pmod{m_2}$$
$$\ldots$$
$$n \equiv r_k \pmod{m_k}$$

Provided n is less than

$$m_1 \times m_2 \times \ldots \times m_k$$

n can be represented by

$$(r_1, r_2, \ldots, r_k)$$

This can be regarded as an internal representation of n. Addition, subtraction, and multiplication of two large numbers then involves the addition, subtraction, and multiplication of corresponding pairs, e.g.

$$(r_1, \ldots, r_k) + (s_1, \ldots, s_k) =$$
$$(r_1 + s_1, \ldots, r_k + s_k)$$

Determining the sign of an integer or comparing relative magnitudes are less straightforward.

modular counter *See* cascadable counter.

modular programming A style of programming in which the complete program is decomposed into a set of components, termed *modules, each of which is of manageable size, has a well-defined purpose, and has a well-defined interface for use by other modules. Since the only alternative – that of completely monolithic programs – is untenable, the point is not whether programs should be modular but rather what criteria should be employed for their decomposition into modules. This was raised by David Parnas, who proposed that one major criterion should be that of *information hiding. Prior to this, decomposition had typically been performed on an ad-hoc basis, or sometimes on the basis of "stages" of the overall processing to be carried out by the program, and only minor benefits had been gained. More recently there has been great emphasis on decomposition based on the use of *abstract data types and on the use of *objects or object orientation; such a decomposition can remain consistent with the principles of information hiding.

modulation The process of varying one signal, called the *carrier*, according to the pattern provided by another signal. The carrier is usually an analog signal selected to match the characteristics of a particular transmission system. Modulation signals and techniques may be combined to produce composite signals carrying many independent channels of information (*see* multiplexing).

The primary types of modulation are as follows:

(a) *Amplitude modulation (AM)* – the strength or amplitude of the carrier signal is varied. This form of modulation is not often directly used in computer communication.

(b) *Frequency modulation (FM)* – the frequency of the carrier is varied. This technique is often used by *modems. *See also* frequency shift keying.

(c) *Phase modulation (PM)* – the phase of the carrier wave is varied. This technique is often used together with amplitude modulation in high-speed modems. *See also* phase shift keying.

(d) *Pulse code modulation (PCM)* – an analog signal is encoded as a series of pulses

in a digital data stream. This technique is used by *codecs.

The term shift keying, as in frequency shift keying, denotes specialized modulation techniques in which the modulating signal is digital rather than analog.

modulator A device that translates a digital signal into an analog signal: the modulator uses the digital signal as a pattern that determines the wave shape that the analog signal will have. A *demodulator performs the reverse transformation to recover the original digital signal. *See also* modulation, modem.

module 1. A programming or specification construct that defines a software component. Often a module is a unit of software that provides users with some data types and operations on those data types, and can be separately compiled. The module has an interface in the form of a heading that specifies the data types and operations the module provides its users. Mathematically, the syntax of the interface is a *signature and the semantics of a module is a class of *algebras of that signature. In some programming languages that provide modules, they are called by other names such as package, cluster, or object. The concept developed as a programming construct to support *information hiding and *abstract data types. The theory of program construction based on modules is a promising, but difficult, area of research. 2. A component of a hardware system that can be subdivided. ·

module coding review *See* review, code inspection.

module design review *See* review.

module invariant *See* invariant.

module specification A precise statement of the effects that a software module is required to achieve. It can be employed both by the implementer of the module, since it gives a definitive statement of the requirements that are imposed on the module, and by users of the module, since it gives a precise statement of what the module provides. A good module specification makes no commitment as to how the module's effects are achieved.

A variety of techniques have been developed for module specification. A *functional specification* identifies the operations that the module makes available and provides an individual specification for each operation, typically in the form of an input-output specification describing the mapping that the operation provides from a set of input values to a set of output values. In the typical case where a module has local data, a simple functional specification will need to refer to this local data when specifying each individual operation. This tends to obscure the specification, and also violates the principle that a specification should state what a module does but not how this is done.

The state machine model technique developed by Parnas treats the module as a *finite-state machine and distinguishes operations that can observe the state of the machine from those that can alter the state of the machine. The specification is given by indicating the effect of each operation that can change the state on the result of each operation than can observe the state. This technique therefore avoids the need to refer to the module's local data.

The same applies to the technique of *algebraic specification, largely due to Guttag and Horning. With this technique, which is tailored to the specification of *abstract data type modules, the specification is given in two parts – a syntactic specification and a set of equations. The syntactic specification states the names, domains, and ranges of the operations provided by the module. Each equation specifies the net effect of some sequence of operations (or perhaps a single operation), and the complete set of equations must be sufficient to specify the effects of all operations under all conditions.

Because of the need for precision, module specifications are best given in some formal *specification language*. A variety of such languages have been developed, many drawing heavily on first-order *predicate calculus. Specific examples include the SPECIAL language of the HDM system, which adopts the finite-state machine approach, and the language used by the AFFIRM system, which employs algebraic specification techniques.

module testing (unit testing) *See* testing.

modulo-*n* check *Another name for* checksum.

modulo operation An arithmetic operation in which the result is the remainder after one integer is divided by another. Hence

$$i \text{ modulo } j \text{ or } i \text{ mod } j$$

is the remainder of the division of integer i by integer j. The exact definition of the operation, when the integers may be negative, is not defined. *See also* modular arithmetic.

MOHLL *Acronym for* machine-oriented high-level language. A programming language with the control structures of the typical high-level language (if-then, while-do, etc.), whose data types and structures map onto the underlying machine architecture. Thus such a language will allow variables of type bit, byte, word, etc. These languages, also known simply as *machine-oriented languages*, provide an alternative to assembly language for systems programming at the hardware-interface level. Well-known examples are *Babbage and *PL/360. MOHLLs are now largely replaced by the language *C. *Compare* problem-oriented language.

monadic Having one operand.

monadic operation (unary operation) defined on a set S. A *function from the domain S into S itself. The *identity function is a monadic operation. Other examples are the operations of *negation in arithmetic or logic and of taking *complements in set theory or in *Boolean algebra. Although basically functions, monadic operations are frequently represented using a special notation, e.g. $\neg A$ or A' or $\bar{A}$. When the set S is finite, a *truth table can be used to define the meaning of the operation.

monalphabetic *See* substitution cipher.

monic polynomial *See* polynomial.

monitor 1. A device that is used for checking the progress and operation of a system. A display and keyboard may be used in the roles of both a control console and a monitor. Display screens without keyboards may be used as remote monitors to allow the status of the system to be observed from remote locations.

2. *Another name for* supervisor, or even a complete operating system.

3. A programming construct devised by Hoare to allow controlled sharing of resources by otherwise asynchronous processes, and involving the provision of controlled passing of variables between the processes.

monochrome display A display where the picture consists solely of a single color (with variations of shade in some models: *see* grayscale). Monochrome displays may have white, amber, or green screens. The choice of screen color depends on users' preferences, with strong claims being made by the advocates of each color. Monochrome displays are found in terminals and monitors using CRT or LCD technology. In display technology, much higher resolution can be achieved by monochrome than is possible in color displays and for a given performance monochrome displays cost much less than a similar color product.

monoid A *semigroup that possesses an *identity element, *e*. If *S* is a semigroup on which there is defined a *dyadic operation ∘, then

$$x \circ e = e \circ x = x$$

for all elements *x* in *S*. Monoids play an important role in various areas of computing, especially in the study of *formal languages and *parsing.

monomode Describing or involving the form of electromagnetic signal that is carried by a waveguide with a cross section that is small, or of the same order of size, compared with the wavelength of the electromagnetic wave. The wave will only propagate purely along the axis of the waveguide, with very little degradation apart from a possible loss of amplitude. This is especially valuable for systems using digital signals, which in general rely on the preservation of sharp edges in the signals. *See also* fiber optics, multimode.

monomorphism A *homomorphism that, when viewed as a function, is an *injection.

monostable (one-shot) A digital circuit that has only one stable output state. It is constructed in such a way that it may be triggered by an externally generated signal to produce a single pulse. The time duration of the pulse is specified by the choice of external components, usually a capacitor.

monotonic 1. Assuming that appropriate *ordering relations exist on the domain *A* and codomain *B* of the function *f* : *A* → *B*, then *f* is said to be monotonic if for all *a* in *A* and *b* in *B* for which *a* ≤ *b* then *f*(*a*) ≤ *f*(*b*).
2. *See* weakening.

Monte Carlo methods Numerical methods in which randomly generated numbers play a part in the calculations. A probabilistic model is constructed, corresponding to the mathematical or physical problem, and random samples are taken within the model. By taking more samples, a more accurate estimate of the result is obtained. Such methods are used for example on problems in particle physics, evaluation of multiple integrals, traffic problems, and large-scale operational problems generally. *See also* stochastic process.

MOO *Acronym for* multiuser object oriented. A system that has been developed from the early text-based multiuser adventure games, and offers a purely text-based environment allowing multiple users to establish *virtual circuits and interact with other users and with end-user systems.

Moore machine *See* sequential machine.

morphing *Derived from* metamorphosis. Changing the shape of an object to produce unusual effects. Morphing is often used in computer graphics to change one object into another.

morphism *See* category.

Mosaic A utility that allows a user at a networked workstation to access information on the *World Wide Web. *See also* Cello.

MOSFET (MOS transistor) *Acronym for* metal oxide semiconductor field-effect transistor. A type of *field-effect transistor that has an insulating layer of oxide, usually silicon dioxide, separating the gate from the drain-source conduction channel in the semiconductor. In an *NMOS* the channel is formed between n-type source and drain by negative charge carriers (i.e. electrons). In a *PMOS* the channel is formed between p-type source and drain by positive charge carriers (i.e. holes).

MOSFETs require no gate input current, other than a pulse to charge or discharge their input capacitance. They can operate at higher switching speeds and lower currents than *bipolar transistors. However, *integrated circuits fabricated in MOS technology often operate at slower speeds than their bipolar counterparts because of the space allocated to each transistor.

MOS integrated circuit *See* integrated circuit.

MOS transistor *Another name for* MOSFET.

most significant character The character in the most significant position in a number, word, signal, etc. Common examples are the *most significant digit (MSD)* and the *most significant bit (MSB)*, which contribute the greatest quantity to the value of a digital or binary number.

mother *Another name for* parent, rarely used.

motherboard A *printed circuit board into which other boards can be plugged. In some microcomputer systems the motherboard carries all the major functional elements, e.g. the processor and some of the memory; the function can be enhanced by additional boards that perform specific activities such as memory extension or disk control and that communicate to the motherboard via sockets onto a standard bus. *See also* backplane.

moth-eye *See* microrelief.

motion blur The artifact by which fast-moving objects appear blurred. Each frame in a conventional film is an average sample taken over about half the time it takes to record the frame. In consequence, fast-moving images appear blurred. Temporal *aliasing is more severe in the case of computer-generated images where the image is likely to be defined at a specific point in time. In computer animation, the created images are often deliberately blurred to achieve a similar effect to the conventional camera and enhance the simulation of motion.

motion prediction Prediction of the motion in subparts of an image in order to improve activities such as *compression.

Motorola A US corporation originally devoted to the production of car radios and other forms of mobile entertainment and communication. In the late 1950s it entered the semiconductor field and is now a major US producer of *VLSI chips. Its 68000 series of high-performance processors is widely used in workstations. Although generally regarded as a better design than the equivalent *Intel processor chips, it has not achieved the same sales volumes.

mouse A *pointing device that is moved by hand around a flat surface: the movements in the x- and y-directions on the surface are communicated to a computer and cause corresponding movements of the cursor on the display. The mouse's movements are sensed by the rotation of a ball in its base. The ball is restrained within a socket so that less than half of its surface is exposed, and supported on bearings so that it is free to rotate. The mouse has one or more buttons to indicate to the computer that the cursor has reached a desired position. It is normally connected by cable to the computer; a "tail-less" mouse communicates by means of infrared or optical rather than electrical signals.

movement file *Another name for* transaction file.

moving-average methods *See* time series.

MPC *Abbrev. for* multimedia personal computer. A minimum specification for a PC-compatible computer configuration that makes the PC suitable for use with *multimedia CD-ROM disks. The specification defines the type of processor and screen, the amount of memory and disk capacity, and the relevant peripherals (*CD-ROM drive, *sound card, and loudspeakers) together with supporting software. Currently there are two versions of the specification: MPC1, the original form, and MPC2, which calls for a higher standard of equipment including a double-speed CD-ROM drive. Most multimedia disks are described as *MPC compatible*, and this usually refers to MPC2.

MPEG 1. *Acronym for* Moving Picture Experts Group, the committee – a joint CCITT and ISO/IEC group – that works on the storage and transmission of moving images, especially video images, and developed the ISO 11172 standard (see below).

2. The ISO/IEC 11172 standard, Compression of Moving Images with Audio and Timing Data. It is designed to reduce the amount of information needed to describe a video sequence, so reducing either the bandwidth required to transmit the sequence or the amount of memory needed to store it. The MPEG-1 standard is for digital storage media such as CD-ROM; the MPEG-2 standard is for high-quality video transmission such as digital broadcasting.

The MPEG video-compression algorithm relies on two basic techniques: block-based motion compensation for the reduction of temporal redundancy (effectively recognizing the similarity between adjacent frames in the video) and DCT (*discrete cosine transform) compression for the reduction of spatial redundancy (*see* JPEG).

MPP *Abbrev. for* massively parallel processor. A high-performance computer system providing a new approach to supercomputing but with very specialized programming requirements.

MPR The Swedish National Board for Measurement and Testing. MPR2 is often wrongly quoted as the Swedish standard for emissions from *VDUs. The relevant recommendations from this body are MPR 1990:8 Swedac Test methods for visual displays and MPR 1990:10 User's Handbook for evaluating visual display units. The latest versions of these carry the additional title *TCO 92 and recommend tighter limits.

MPU *Abbrev. for* microprocessor unit, the primary control and arithmetic element of a microcomputer system. *See* microprocessor.

MSD, MSB *Abbrevs. for* most significant digit, most significant bit. *See* most significant character.

MS-DOS *Trademark, abbrev. for* Microsoft disk operating system. An operating system written by Microsoft to be marketed with the early release of the IBM Personal Computer. The prefix MS is used to help distinguish the product from the large number of similarly titled DOS products. When IBM first announced the IBM PC, the company intended that it would run under CP/M, a popular proprietary operating system then available on other hardware platforms. In the event, Microsoft offered IBM their own product, which was to some extent a modified version of CP/M and was to be known as MS-DOS. The rest is history.

In common with other versions of DOS, MS-DOS has limited functionality, offering a *command-line interface, management of peripheral devices, management of files, and no multitasking. The initial hardware restriction of the IBM PC to a total of 640 Kbytes of memory is embedded in MS-DOS. Despite these limitations, there is little doubt that a larger number of computers run a version of MS-DOS than any other operating system.

m-sequence A periodic sequence of symbols generated by a linear *feedback shift register whose feedback coefficients form a primitive *polynomial. A *q-ary register (with q prime) whose generating polynomial is of degree n will have period $q^n - 1$, provided that the initial state is nonzero, and its contents will proceed through all the nonzero q-ary n-tuples. The termwise modulo-q sum of two m-sequences is another m-sequence: the m-sequences (of a given generating polynomial), together with the zero sequence, form a *group.

The term is short for maximum-length sequence. It is so called because the generating shift register only has q^n states, and so such a register (with arbitrary feedback logic) cannot generate a sequence whose period exceeds q^n. But with linear logic the zero state must stand in a loop of its own (*see* Good–de Bruijn diagram) and so the period of a linear feedback register cannot exceed $q^n - 1$. This period, which can be achieved when and only when the polynomial is primitive, is therefore the maximum that can be achieved.

m-sequences have many useful properties. They are employed as *pseudorandom sequences, *error-correcting codes (as they stand, or shortened, or extended), and in determining the time response of linear channels (*see* convolution). *See also* simplex codes.

MSI *Abbrev. for* medium-scale integration, i.e.

integration in the range of 100 to 10 000 transistors on a single chip. *See* integrated circuit.

MSR *Abbrev. for* magnetic stripe reader. A device for reading the data from the magnetic stripe on the back of credit cards and similar cards. *See also* magnetic card.

MS Windows *See* Windows.

MTA *Abbrev. for* message transfer agent. An entity that takes an e-mail message created by the sender's *user agent, and delivers it to the receiver's user agent. If delivery is not possible because the receiver's user agent is not active (for example because it runs on a personal computer that is currently disconnected from the network or is not powered on), the message will be placed in the *message store to await collection by the receiver's user agent when it becomes active.

MTBF *Abbrev. for* mean time between failures. A figure of merit for system reliability.

MTBI *Abbrev. for* mean time between incidents. A measure of reliability similar to *MTBF but sometimes distinguished from it by the exclusion of failures that can be rectified without engineer attention.

MTS *Acronym for* Michigan terminal system. An operating system that was developed at the University of Michigan in the late 1960s, and was specifically intended to offer interactive computing to large numbers of users, each carrying out relatively straightforward tasks.

MTTR *Abbrev. for* mean time to repair. *See* repair time.

MTU *Abbrev. for* magnetic tape unit. *See* magnetic tape.

mu-law (μ-law) encoding *See* pulse code modulation.

multiaccess system A system allowing several users to make apparently simultaneous use of the computer. Each user has a terminal, typically a keyboard plus VDU display, and is connected via a multiplexer or front-end processor to the main system. As individual users type their commands, the system will multiprogram among the several users of the system, each command being processed as it is received. *See also* time sharing.

multiaddress *Short for* multiple-address.

Multibus *Trademark* A flexible bus structure designed by Intel Corp. that was used in many commercial microprocessor systems. Multibus is capable of supporting both 8- and 16-bit processors and 20-bit addresses, allowing up to one megabyte of physical address space. It supports master-slave and multi-master configurations, with *handshaking to permit devices of different speeds to communicate. Up to 16 masters can share Multibus resources.

multicasting A transmission system in which messages are directed to a particular group of nodes on a network. It is thus intermediate between a transmission directed to a single address and one directed to all the addresses on a network (*see* broadcasting).

multicore cable *See* cable.

MULTICS *Trademark* A *multiaccess operating system designed in project *MAC to provide a MULTiplexed Information and Computing Service. The MULTICS system made extensive use of "rings" of hardware protection of access to memory in order to achieve management of a very large virtual memory. Users operating on files move their entire file into memory in order to operate on it. The MULTICS system was implemented on specially commissioned hardware constructed by General Electric, and the entire project was later taken over by Honeywell Computer Systems.

multidimensional array An *array of *dimension greater than one.

multidimensional spreadsheet A *spreadsheet having more than two dimensions. The basic spreadsheet is a table of rows and columns, and so is regarded as two-dimensional. A third dimension can be pictured as a stack of tables, or pages of a workbook. Mathematically there is no difficulty in having as many dimensions as required, but the visual representation on a flat display screen gets rather difficult after the third dimension.

multidrop line A single communication line

that connects multiple stations – terminals or computers. Typically, one station will use *polling to coordinate access to the line and prevent collisions (multiple stations transmitting at once). A control protocol such as *SDLC is used. *See also* multipoint connection. *Compare* point-to-point line.

multigrid methods A broad class of methods for the numerical solution of certain classes of *partial differential equations. In its simplest form, after a suitable *finite-difference replacement of the problem, a system of *linear algebraic equations is obtained, perhaps involving thousands of unknowns. These equations are solved iteratively by a process that involves the solution of smaller linear systems arising from a sequence of coarser meshes (*see* finite-difference method). The method of successive over-relaxation has an important role in the solution of these subsystems. *See* iterative methods.

multilevel memory A memory system containing at least two memory subsystems with different capacity and access-time attributes. *See* memory hierarchy.

multilevel security A *security processing mode where users with differing security clearances have correspondingly limited access to a database holding objects of different classifications. Output material may carry *trusted *security labels.

multilinked Having a *link to several distinct data structures. For example, a *sparse matrix is frequently held so that each element belongs to two separate linear lists corresponding to a row list and a column list. A multilinked structure is sometimes called a *multiple chain*.

multimedia The combined use of digitized information representing text, sound, and still or video images, or the media so used. The term can refer to any interactive system and any data storage medium, but is widely applied to data stored on *CD-ROM and accessed by a personal computer: the dialogue with the user makes use of the various media in an integrated way. The PC must be equipped with a CD-ROM drive; it usually also has a *sound card and a pair of loudspeakers, since the audio capability of an ordinary PC is very limited. The *MPC specification defines these and other technical requirements. A multimedia PC may in addition have a *MIDI interface, which allows the connection of more sophisticated sound equipment and electronic musical instruments.

multimedia mail *See* electronic mail.

multimode Describing or involving the form of electromagnetic signal that is carried by a waveguide with a cross section that is large compared with the wavelength of the electromagnetic wave. The wave can propagate in directions at an angle to the axis of the waveguide, undergoing a series of internal reflections along its length. This causes a gradual degradation of the signal. *See also* fiber optics, monomode.

multimode counter *See* counter.

multipart stationery *See* stationery.

multiple-address machine A computer whose *instruction format specifies (for at least some instructions) more than one operand address.

multiple assignment A form of *assignment statement in which the same value is given to two or more variables. For example, in Algol,

$$a := b := c := 0$$

sets a, b, c to zero.

multiple chain *See* multilinked.

multiple inheritance *See* object.

multiple instruction, multiple data (MIMD) *See* concurrency.

multiple precision (multiprecision) *See* double precision.

multiple-range tests *Significance tests for differences between means of several samples. The significance levels are adjusted to take account of the fact that more than one comparison is being made.

multiple regression model *See* regression analysis.

multiple-valued logic *See* multivalued logic.

multiplexed bus A type of bus structure in which the number of signal lines comprising the bus is less than the number of bits of data, address, or control information being transferred between elements of the system. For example, a multiplexed address bus might use 8 signal lines to transmit 16 bits of address information. The information is transferred sequentially, i.e. time-domain multiplexed, with additional control lines being used for sequencing the transfer.

multiplexer 1. A device that merges information from multiple input channels to a single output channel. *See* multiplexing.

2. A *combinational circuit that converts from 1 of m inputs to n outputs, where $m \leq 2^n$. *See also* data selector/multiplexer.

multiplexer channel *See* channel.

multiplexing The process of combining multiple messages simultaneously on the same physical or logical transmission medium. There are two main types: *time division multiplexing (TDM) and *frequency division multiplexing (FDM). In TDM a device is allocated specific time slots in which to use the transmission medium. FDM divides the transmission medium into channels of smaller *bandwidth to which the user has exclusive rights. FDM and TDM can be combined to provide devices with time slots of logical channels.

multiplier A specific part of an *ALU that is used to perform the operation of multiplication. It is not always explicitly present in an ALU; for example, a multiplication can be accomplished by a sequence of additions and shifts under the direction of the *control unit.

multiply connected Denoting a node in a communication network that has links, circuits, or channels to more than one of its neighbors. If one link fails, the node may still communicate using the remaining links.

multipoint connection A connection of a number of terminals in parallel, analogous to a *multidrop connection. Sometimes the terms are used as synonyms, although multidrop strictly implies that the connections are all served from a common connection point (node), whereas multipoint implies that connections are made through a series of (analog) bridging connections where some or all of the terminals are served by different common

carrier offices interconnected by communication trunks.

multipoint line A data communication link that connects more than two *nodes. Individual nodes are identified by unique addresses. A *data link control protocol is used to determine which node has the right to transmit on the line, and which node(s) should be receiving.

multiport memory A memory that provides more than one access *port to separate processors. The mechanism may be a *bus. It is used as a method of interconnecting computers. *See also* shared memory, central processor.

multiprecision (multiple precision) *See* double precision.

multiprocessing system (multiprocessor; multiunit processor) A system in which more than one processor may be active at any one time. While the processors are actively executing separate processes they run completely asynchronously. However it is essential to provide synchronization between the processors when they access critical system resources or critical regions of system code. A multiprocessing system is also a *multiprogramming system. *See also* concurrency.

multiprocessor *Another name for* multiprocessing system.

multiprogramming system A system in which several individual programs may be active. Each active program implies a running *process, so there may be several processes, but only one process runs at any one time on any particular processor. It is perfectly feasible to run a multiprogramming system containing only one processor; a *multiprocessing system, containing several processors, will also be a multiprogramming system.

multiresolution image An image where the *resolution varies depending on the complexity of the scene at each point of the image.

multisession compatible *See* CD-ROM format standards.

multiset *Another name for* bag.

multitape Turing machine A *Turing machine that has a finite number of tapes, each tape having a tape head that can move independently. Such machines have the same computational power as single-tape Turing machines. Consider a multitape Turing machine M. If for no input word of length n does M scan more than $L(n)$ cells on any tape then M is said to be an $L(n)$ *tape-bounded Turing machine*. If for no input word of length n does M make more than $T(n)$ moves before halting then M is said to be a $T(n)$ *time-bounded Turing machine*.

multitasking The concurrent execution of a number of tasks, i.e. of a number of jobs or processes. *See* parallel processing.

multithreading A form of code that uses more than one *process or processor, possibly of different types, and that may on occasions have more than one process or processor active at the same time. *See also* single threading, threading.

multiunit processor *Another name for* multiprocessing system.

multiuser system A system that is (apparently) serving more than one user simultaneously, i.e. a *multiprogramming or *multiprocessing system.

multivalued logic (nonbinary logic) Digital logic for use in *logic circuits that are designed to handle more than two levels (voltages, etc.). In q-valued logic there are q levels and each *memory element (flip-flops, etc.) can exist in q different states. The classification of logic circuits into *combinational and *sequential circuits applies to multivalued logic exactly as it does to binary logic.

There is much interest currently in *ternary logic* ($q = 3$) and, to a somewhat lesser extent, in *quaternary logic* ($q = 4$). Such logics promise reduced numbers of logic gates, memory elements, and – perhaps most significantly – interconnections. Ternary logic is simple to implement in *CMOS technology, and is likely to become important in the design of *VLSI circuits. Its increased logical richness is shown by the fact that there are 16 possible two-input binary gates, but 19 683 such ternary gates (ignoring degeneracies in both cases).

multivariate analysis The study of multiple measurements on a sample. It embraces many techniques related to a range of different problems.

*Cluster analysis seeks to define homogeneous classes within the sample on the basis of the measured variables. *Discriminant analysis* is a technique for deciding whether an individual should be assigned to a particular predefined class on the basis of the measured variables. *Principle component analysis* and *factor analysis* aim to reduce the number of variables in the study to a few (say two or three) that express most of the variation within a sample.

Multivariate *probability distributions define probabilities for sets of random variables.

multivibrator An electronic oscillator that consists of two resistor-capacitor amplifier stages that interact in such a way that the amplifier's outputs are complementary and exhibit two stable mutually exclusive states, i.e. fully on and fully off. The circuit can be made to oscillate continuously, producing a square wave (astable mode), produce single pulses (monostable mode), or change state on application of an external trigger (bistable mode). *See also* flip-flop.

multiway search tree of degree n. A generalization of a *binary search tree to a tree of degree n where each node in the ordered tree has $m \leq n$ children and contains $(m-1)$ ordered key values, called subkeys. For some given search key, if the key is less than the first subkey then the first subtree (if it exists) is searched for the key; if the key lies between the ith and $(i + 1)$th subkey, where

$$i = 1, 2, \ldots, m-2$$

then the $(i + 1)$th subtree (if it exists) is searched; if the key is greater than the last subkey then the mth subtree (if it exists) is searched. *See also* B-tree.

Munsell color model A *color model based on perceptual principles, proposed by the American artist Albert Munsell in 1905. It is based on the dimensions of *hue (H), value (V), and chroma (C), the visual characteristics of color in paint rather than light.

mu operator (μ-operator, minimization operator) *See* minimization.

mutual exclusion A relationship between processes such that each has some part (the *critical section) that must not be executed while the critical section of another is being executed. There is thus exclusion of one process by another. In certain regions of an operating system, for example those dealing with the allocation of nonsharable resources, it is imperative to ensure that only one process is executing the relevant code at any one time. This can be guaranteed by the use of *semaphores: at entry to the critical region of code a semaphore is set; this inhibits entry to the code by any other process until the semaphore is reset as the last action by the process that first entered the critical region.

Myhill equivalence An *equivalence relation arising in *formal language theory. If L is a language over alphabet Σ (*see* word) then its Myhill equivalence is the relation $=_M$ on Σ^* defined as follows:

$$u =_M u'$$

if, for all w_1, w_2 in Σ^*,

$$w_1 u w_2 \in L \quad \text{iff} \quad w_1 u' w_2 \in L$$

Similarly (and more generally), if f is a function from Σ^* to any set, its Myhill equivalence is defined by:

$$u =_M u'$$

if, for all w_1, w_2 in Σ^*,

$$f(w_1 u w_2) = f(w_1 u' w_2)$$

See also Nerode equivalence.

An important fact is that L is *regular iff the equivalence relation $=_M$ is of finite index (i.e. there are finitely many *equivalence classes). Indeed, L is regular iff it is a union of classes of any equivalence relation of finite index. In addition $=_M$ is a *congruence on Σ^*, i.e.

$$u =_M u' \text{ and } v =_M v' \text{ implies}$$
$$uv =_M u'v'$$

The equivalence classes therefore can be *concatenated consistently and form a *semigroup. This is in fact the semigroup of the *minimal machine for L (or f).

N

naive physics A model of simple physics of the word as experienced by people in their everyday lives. An area of research in *artificial intelligence, naive physics is an important component of *common-sense reasoning and is closely linked to *qualitative reasoning.

NAK The "negative acknowledge" control character. *See* acknowledgment.

name A notation for indicating an entity in a program or system. (The word can also be used as a verb.) The kinds of entity that can be named depend on the context, and include variables, data objects, functions, types, and procedures (in programming languages), nodes, stations, and processes (in a data communication network), files, directories, devices (in operating systems), etc. The name denotes the entity, independently of its physical location or address. Names are used for long-term stability (e.g. when specifying a node in a computer program) or for their ease of use by humans (who recognize the name more readily than an address). Names are converted to addresses by a process of *name lookup*.

In many languages and systems, a name must be a simple identifier, usually a textual string. In more advanced languages, a name may be composed from several elementary components according to the rules of the language.

name lookup *See* name.

nameset An identification attribute (in the form of a set of names) associated with a graphical output primitive in standards such as *GKS-94 and *PHIGS. The attribute is used to filter or select groups of primitives for manipulation or display.

namespace The names of the variables accessible at a particular point in the text of a program. *See* block-structured languages.

NAND gate An electronic *logic gate whose output is logic 0 (false) only when all (two or more) inputs are logic 1 (true), otherwise it is logic 1. It thus implements the logical *NAND operation and has the same *truth table. The diagram shows the usual circuit symbol of a two–input gate (which implies by the small circle that it is equivalent to an *AND gate whose output has been inverted) and the associated truth table.

inputs	A1	0	0	1	1
	A2	0	1	0	1
output B		1	1	1	0

Two-input NAND gate, circuit symbol and truth table

P	F	F	T	T
Q	F	T	F	T
$P\|Q$	T	T	T	F

Truth table for NAND operation

NAND operation The logical *connective combining two statements, truth values, or formulas P and Q in such a way that the outcome is true only if either P or Q or both is false (*see* table). The NAND operation may be represented by the *Sheffer stroke*, $|$, or by Δ. $P \mid Q$ is just the negation of $P \wedge Q$, hence the name (*see* AND operation).

The NAND operation is of particular significance to computer designers since any Boolean expression can be realized by an expression using only the NAND operation. In practical terms, circuits can be built using only *NAND gates.

nano- (symbol: n) A prefix to a unit, indicating a submultiple of one billionth, 10^{-9}, of that unit, as in nanosecond.

nanostore *See* microprogramming.

narrow A term a is said to narrow to a term b using a substitution s (which replaces a variable v by expression e) provided a is obtained from b by replacing an instance of e in b by v.

narrowband *See* bandwidth.

Nassi–Shneiderman chart (NS chart) A kind of diagram (devised 1973–74) for representing the sequence of execution in a program. The diagram takes the form of a rectangle divided mainly into smaller rectangles with the sequence of execution going from top to bottom of the diagram. There are various standard constructs, including NS sequence structures, NS repetition structures, and NS selection structures.

National Information Infrastructure A term much used by politicians to refer to the totality of network services used within a country to carry its information, especially the extended services advocated by US Vice President Gore.

native code *See* native software.

native software Software specifically written, compiled, or assembled to run on a particular system. *Native code* uses all the individual features of the target system with no regard for generality or portability.

natural binary-coded decimal (NBCD) *See* binary-coded decimal.

natural-language understanding The processing of utterances in human language (natural language as opposed to programming language) in order to extract meaning and respond appropriately. The main natural language studied has been written English, although there has also been work on other languages and on speech (*see* speech understanding). The processing requires both syntactic knowledge about the language concerned and semantic knowledge of the relationship between the utterance and what it means, usually in a *knowledge base containing an internal representation of the world. Grammatical and semantic rules are used to analyze the utterance into *logical formulas or *semantic networks, where the meaning representation can be used by a reasoning system. *See also* discourse understanding.

natural number (natural) A number that can count the members of a *set. In effect, the natural numbers are the nonnegative *integers, i.e. the set $\{0,1,2,...\}$.

NBCD *Abbrev. for* natural binary-coded decimal. *See* binary-coded decimal.

NCP *Abbrev. for* network control protocol. A

transport layer protocol that was designed for the *ARPANET. The DARPA internetworking project developed the TCP protocol to replace NCP. *See also* TCP/IP.

NCR *See* AT&T.

NCSC National Computer Security Center, a US agency active in formulating bases for the classification and evaluation of secure systems. For an establishment working in such a topic the Center has a remarkably open approach to the publication of material.

NDC *Abbrev. for* normalized device coordinates. A coordinate system, usually in the range 0 to 1 in each dimension, that acts as a generic device-coordinate system used within a graphics system such as *GKS. *See also* device coordinates.

NEC Corporation A Japanese electronics company that produces a wide range of computer products and is number three in the list of the world's largest IT companies by revenue (1993 figures).

negation 1. In arithmetic, the operation of changing the sign of a nonzero arithmetic quantity; the negation of zero is zero. Negation is usually denoted by the minus sign.
2. In logic, the application of the *NOT operation on a statement, truth value, or formula.

negation as failure A rule of *inference that assumes a fact is false when all possible proofs of the fact being true have failed. This is exactly equivalent to negation when the *closed-world assumption holds – if some information is not contained within the system as a truth, then it is assumed false. Negation as failure is an important feature of the language *Prolog.

negative acknowledgment *See* acknowledgment. *See also* backward error correction.

negative display A display where data is presented as light symbols on a dark background. The light characters are often green, white, or amber according to the user's preference. Many display terminals allow the user to select either this mode (generally called *normal*) or *positive display (generally called *reverse*).

negative logic 1. A logic system in which the normal meanings of the binary signal levels are interchanged, e.g. high voltage equals logic 0, low voltage equals logic 1.
2. (complementary logic) A logic system in which all the Boolean variables and Boolean functions behave as though they were complements.
Compare positive logic.

negator *Another name for* inverter.

negentropy *See* entropy.

nerd *Derogatory slang* Someone who spends excessive time using a computer, often with unreasonable enthusiasm. (The term is also used more generally.)

Nerode equivalence An *equivalence relation, $=_N$, arising in *formal language theory. It is defined analogously to the *Myhill equivalence by the weaker properties:

for a language L over Σ,
$$u =_N u'$$
if, for all w in Σ^*,
$$uw \in L \quad \text{iff} \quad u'w \in L$$
and for a function f,
$$u =_N u'$$
if, for all w in Σ^*,
$$f(uw) = f(u'w)$$

Although coarser than the Myhill equivalence, it is finite only if the latter is. Unlike the latter, it gives only a right congruence:
$$u =_N u' \quad \text{implies} \quad uv =_N u'v$$
and thus does not give rise to a *semigroup. The number of *equivalence classes is the number of states in the *minimal machine for L.

nested blocks, nested scopes *See* block-structured languages.

nesting A feature of language design in which constructs can be embedded within instances of themselves, e.g. nested loops:

```
while b1 do
begin
    while b2 do
    begin
        ...
    end;
end;
```

Nesting of blocks in *block-structured languages provides an elegant, though not entirely practicable, control over the scope of *identifiers, since identifiers are local to the innermost level of nesting at which they are declared.

nesting store *Another name for* stack, implemented in hardware. *See* stack processing.

Net *Short for* Internet.

netgod *Derogatory slang* Someone who knows, or more often thinks he knows, all there is to be known about networking. Note the emphasis on gender – most netgods are male – and on knowledge rather than understanding.

netiquette *Informal* (contraction of network etiquette) The guidelines that constitute good behavior on a network, especially the Internet, and that, like all forms of etiquette, tend to be determined by a self-appointed group. A breach of netiquette, such as *spamming, may attract a *flame as a response. Netiquette should not be confused with the behavior formalized in an *acceptable use policy, contractual commitments, or the results of properly enacted legislation.

Netnews *Another name for* Usenet.

netpolice *Derogatory slang* Those who take on the role of enforcing their own views as to correct behavior on a network.

Netware *Trademark* A network-based system from Novell Corp. for use on assemblies of IBM PCs. (The name *Novell* is sometimes applied to the Netware product.) The Netware system functions essentially by allowing some of the disk drives within a PC to be replaced by a network connection to a file server, and by similarly allowing some of the standard peripheral devices such as printers to be replaced by a network connection to a print server. Although this may lead to some lowering of overall performance, there are corresponding gains in operational flexibility. The system allows a user to move freely between PCs in different locations on the network, while still retaining access to his or her files, and also releases the individual user from the need to take protective dumps, which can be centrally managed.

network 1. In communications, a rather loosely defined term applied to a system that consists of terminals, *nodes, and interconnection media that can include lines or trunks, satellites, microwave, medium- and long-wave radio, etc. In general, a network is a collection of resources used to establish and switch communication paths between its terminals. A given network may be classified as a *local area network, a *metropolitan area network, or a *wide area network, the differences lying as much in their style of organization as in their technology or geographical or physical size. *See also* network architecture, packet switching, message switching, network delay.

2. In electronic circuitry, an interconnection of various electrical elements. A *passive network* contains no active (amplifying or switching) elements such as transistors; a *linear network* is a passive network that contains no nonlinear elements such as diodes.

3. (net) In mathematics, a *connected directed *graph that contains no cycles. Interconnections involving objects such as telephones, logic gates, or computers could be represented using a connected but not necessarily directed graph.

network architecture The design and implementation of a communication network with respect to its communication disciplines and its interconnection topology. Network architecture deals explicitly with the encoding of information, its transmission, *error detection, *error correction, and *flow control, techniques for *addressing subscribers on the network, analysis of network performance under abnormal or degraded conditions (such as missing communication lines or improperly functioning switching nodes), etc. Examples of generalized network architectures are OSI (*open systems interconnection, an architecture propounded by the ISO) and SNA (systems network architecture, proposed and supported by IBM).

Interconnection topology is also considered a part of network architecture. There are three generic forms of topology: *star*, *ring*, and *bus*. Star topology consists of a single hub node with various terminal nodes connected to the hub; terminal nodes do not interconnect directly. By treating one terminal node as the hub of another star, a *treelike* topology is obtained. In ring topology all nodes are on a ring and communication is generally in one direction around the ring; some ring architectures use two rings, with communication in opposite directions. Various techniques (including time division multiplexing, token passing, and ring stretching) are used to control who is allowed to transmit onto the ring. Bus topology is noncyclic, with all nodes connected; traffic consequently travels in both directions, and some kind of arbitration is needed to determine which terminal can use the bus at any one time; Ethernet is an example. Hybrids that mix star and ring topologies have been employed.

A special area of network architecture is involved with the necessary disciplines required of some of the newer network architectures (*see* ring network, token ring, Ethernet).

network delay Broadly speaking, the time needed for a signal to traverse a network. The extent of the delay caused by the network may be effectively constant, but in most cases it is variable. If the variable delay can be guaranteed not to exceed some predetermined value, then the network has a *bounded delay. In other cases the delay is not bounded but can grow without limit, although with a decreasing probability of a longer delay.

In a *circuit switching network the only significant delay arises from the finite speed with which the signals propagate along the transmission medium. For electrical signals on a conducting wire, electromagnetic waves in free space, or light signals in an optical fiber, this speed is of the same order as the speed of light, 300 000 km per second, and the network delay in a circuit-switched system is of the order of 3–5 microseconds per km. There may also be delays arising from the finite time needed by amplifiers or repeaters to pass a signal from their input to output; these delays are again in the order of microseconds. The delay in a signal crossing the Atlantic (5000 km) is of the order of 25 milliseconds, and for a signal routed via a geostationary satellite (total round trip of 80 000 km) it is of the order of 400 milliseconds.

In a *packet switching network the situation is more complex. The time needed to traverse the network is normally measured as the period between the sender indicating that the transmission is to start, and the delivery of the last bit of the packet to the destination. This time is the sum of times needed to traverse each sector of the network, and contains a number of different contributions. If the data source is not capable of generating a network packet directly, it will need to be connected to a *PAD that will assemble the data into packets; devices that can generate their own packets will not require a PAD. It may well be that although a PAD is not present as a separate component, it is still there conceptually, where for example a (human) user is using a PC or workstation to connect to a remote system. Once packets have been generated, each packet will move between successive pairs of network nodes until it reaches the destination. Each sector has contributions from

(a) the transit time along the medium connecting the two nodes;

(b) the time needed to disassemble the outgoing packet into its component bits at the transmitting node (necessarily identical with the time needed to reassemble the incoming packet at the receiving node);

(c) the time needed by the switching process within the receiving node to determine the route the outgoing packet is to follow, and carry out the switching.

The first of these is essentially similar to the transit time in a circuit-switched network, and has a similar value of say 3–5 microseconds per km. The second is essentially equal to the packet size multiplied by the inter-bit time on the transmission line. The third is a function of the organization of the switching nodes, of their processing speeds, and of the extent to which the switching must be delayed until the information needed to allow switching to start is determined by the internal structure of the packet. The use of *cell relay systems, in which switching can start before the entire packet has been received, allows this time to be reduced.

A heavily loaded system will have queues (lines) of packets in each node, leading to a further complication. The queue may either be of outgoing packets awaiting the attention of the switching process to determine on which onward connection they should be transmitted, or of packets that have been rerouted to an onward connection that is already active, requiring the packet to wait until those ahead of it have been transmitted.

In networks using only terrestrial links, the total network delay is typically dominated by packet assembly times, (b) above. This is not the case where satellite links are used, especially where geostationary satellites are involved.

network fax A fax system in which the digital information that comprises the fax message is transmitted across a data network, rather than across a speech network using modems. The system may well be embedded as a feature in a more general-purpose environment such as a word-processing system.

Network File Service (NFS) A set of protocols that run over an *Ethernet network and offer support for *file transfer and access, and for *paging. The system was originally developed by *Sun to allow the use of workstations without disks: it provides the ability for one workstation, without disks, to use another workstation, with disks, to supply both a file store and paging support. The system is now offered by other suppliers and has become a de facto standard for work of this kind.

network front end An auxiliary processor or system attached to another, usually larger, computer specifically to connect that computer to a network. The goals of a network front end are to improve overall performance by doing network-related tasks that would be expensive on the main computer, and to convert the standard interfaces and protocols used by the external network into a form better suited to the local system's internal operation (and vice versa). A network front end may also be used to multiplex a single network interface among several computers, in which case the network front end may be considered a *gateway or *bridge.

network interconnection *See* internetworking, Internet.

network layer of protocol function. *See* seven-layer reference model.

network management The activity of managing a (computer) network. Networks, especially data networks, are complex and contain independently operating units, often from a number of different suppliers, as well as using services provided by other agencies such as *PTTs for some parts of the network. In order for the network to be run reliably, for faults to be identified, isolated, and repaired, and for the network as a whole to be developed in a controlled manner, it is necessary to have a management activity operating at several levels:

(a) routine collection of data on traffic;

(b) routine collection of data on failures of connections and of network nodes;

(c) ability to query the status of network nodes in order to assist in fault location;

(d) ability to control the status of network nodes, including resetting, restarting, and reloading with software;

(e) ability to withdraw network nodes from service, and to reconfigure routing information.

Ideally, the manager would like to be able to perform all these activities from a workstation connected to the network. For this to be done, the nodes must themselves be treated as addressable objects on the network, and there must be a protocol that allows suitably authorized and qualified personnel to carry out both the routine activities (a) and (b) above, and to take corrective action in the event of a failure. There is a suitable protocol, *SNMP (simple network management protocol), and nearly all suppliers now market products that can process SNMP queries and commands.

network topology *See* network architecture.

network virtual terminal (NVT) *See* TELNET. *See also* virtual terminal.

neural computer A computer system based on a *neural network.

neural network (or **net)** A form of computation inspired by the structure and function of the brain. One version of this is as follows. The topology is a *weighted directed graph. *Nodes in the graph can be on or off. Time is discrete. At each time instant all the on nodes send an impulse along their outgoing arcs to their neighbor nodes. All nodes sum their incoming impulses, weighted according to the arc. All the nodes at which this sum exceeds a threshold turn on at the next time instant; all the others turn off. Computation proceeds by setting some input nodes, waiting for the network to reach a steady state, and then reading some output nodes. Nodes can be trained, using examples, to recognize certain patterns, for instance to classify objects by features. *See also* connectionism, back propagation, perceptron.

neuron A node in a *neural network.

News *Short for* Netnews.

newsgroup *See* Usenet.

Newton–Cotes rules *See* numerical integration.

Newton's method An iterative technique for solving one or more *nonlinear equations. For the single equation

$$f(x) = 0$$

the iteration is

$$x_{n+1} = x_n - f(x_n)/f'(x_n),$$
$$n = 0,1,2,\ldots$$

where x_0 is an approximation to the solution. For the system

$$f(x) = 0,$$
$$f = (f_1, f_2, \ldots, f_n)^{\mathrm{T}},$$
$$x = (x_1, x_2, \ldots, x_n)^{\mathrm{T}},$$

the iteration takes the mathematical form

$$x_{n+1} = x_n - \mathcal{J}(x_n)^{-1} f(x_n),$$
$$n = 0,1,2,\ldots$$

where $\mathcal{J}(x)$ is the $n \times n$ matrix whose i,jth element is

$$\partial f_i(x)/\partial x_j$$

In practice each iteration is carried out by solving a system of linear equations. Subject to appropriate conditions the iteration converges quadratically (ultimately an approximate squaring of the error occurs). The disadvantage of the method is that a constant recalculation of $\mathcal{J}$ may be too time-consuming and so the method is most often used in a modified form, e.g. with approximate derivatives. Since Newton's method is derived by a linearization of $f(x)$, it is capable of generalization to other kinds of nonlinear problems, e.g. boundary-value problems (*see* ordinary differential equations).

NFS *See* Network File Service.

nibble *Rare* Half a byte, i.e. generally four bits.

NIFTP *Abbrev. for* network independent file transfer protocol. The *file transfer protocol defined by the *Blue Book and used within the UK academic community.

nine's complement *See* radix-minus-one complement.

N/ISDN *See* ISDN.

NLQ *Abbrev. for* near letter quality. Printed output somewhat inferior to that produced by a good electric typewriter but acceptable for most purposes. *See also* LQ.

NMOS A type of *MOSFET.

no-address instruction An instruction that does not require the designation of an operand address, e.g. "complement the accumulator". *See also* implied addressing, zero-address instruction, stack processing.

node 1. A point in a computer *network where communication lines, such as telephone lines, electric cables, or optical fibers, are interconnected. The device used to make the connection(s) may be a simple electric *interface – as used in a *local area network. In more complex longer-distance networks a computer is required.

Node computers vary in their functional capabilities but their basic use is to switch incoming information to the necessary output line so that the information ultimately reaches its specified destination. The information may be transmitted as a whole or may be split into segments (*see* packet switching, message switching). When the information reaches its final destination, the node computer at this point will send it through to the recipient(s).

Nodes can also be called *stations*, and in many X25 networks the switching nodes are known as *exchanges*.

2. A substructure of a hierarchical data structure that cannot be further decomposed, e.g. a vertex in a *graph or *tree.

Noetherian *See* abstract reduction system.

noise Any signal that occurs in an electronic or communication system and is considered extraneous to the desired signal being propagated. Noise can be introduced, for example, by external disturbances and may be deleterious in a given system since it can produce spurious signals, i.e. errors.

The *noise immunity* is a measure of the magnitude of external disturbances that a digital circuit can tolerate without producing errors. Logic values are represented electronically by two different voltage levels. Any noise introduced into logic circuitry by external disturbances is added (or subtracted) from the real digital logic signal. The *noise margin* is the maximum noise voltage that can be added or subtracted from the logic signal before a threshold voltage for a logic state is passed. *See also* impulse noise, white noise, Gaussian noise.

noise immunity *See* noise.

noiseless coding In communication theory, the use of a code to improve the efficiency of a *communication system in which *noise is absent or negligible. Noiseless coding is thus generally the same as *source coding. Note that the process of coding is itself usually noiseless: there is no need for encoders or decoders to introduce noise, so the term noiseless coding is not used to imply the absence of such noise.

noise margin *See* noise.

noise sequence *See* pseudonoise sequence.

noise source *See* Shannon's model.

noisy mode A method of operation that is sometimes used when normalizing a floating-point number. If the mantissa is shifted m bits to the left during normalization, then in noisy mode the digits generated to fill the m rightmost bits in the normalized mantissa are not necessarily zeros.

nonbinary logic *Another name for* multivalued logic.

nondestructive read The process of reading a memory device in such a manner that the contents of the memory are not altered. The reading of most integrated-circuit devices is nondestructive.

nondeterminism A mode of computation in which, at certain points, there is a choice of ways to proceed: the computation may be thought of as choosing arbitrarily between them, or as splitting into separate copies and pursuing all choices simultaneously. The precise form of nondeterminism depends on the particular model of *computation.

For example, a nondeterministic *Turing machine will have a choice of moves to make for a given internal state and tape symbol being read. After a choice has been made, other choice-points will be encountered. There is therefore a *tree whose paths are all possible different computations, and whose *nonterminal nodes represent choice-points. If, for example, the algorithm performs some kind of "search", then the search succeeds if at least one sequence of choices (path through the tree) is successful.

Nondeterministic constructs in programming languages can offer a choice of control, e.g.

$$\text{do } S_1 \text{ or } S_2 \text{ od}$$

or a choice of data, e.g.

$$y := ? \text{ and } y := x.R(x);$$

These latter select a value for y randomly and such that it satisfies test R. Many algorithms are expressed most conveniently using such constructs; nondeterminism also arises naturally in connection with *interleaving and *concurrency.

Nondeterminism is important in the field of *complexity: it is believed that a nondeterministic Turing machine is capable of performing in "reasonable time" computations that could not be so performed by any deterministic Turing machine (*see* P=NP question).

nonequivalence gate *Another name for* exclusive-OR gate.

nonequivalence operation *Another name for* exclusive-OR operation.

nonerasable programmable device *See* programmable device.

nonfunctional requirements *See* software requirements specification.

nonhierarchical cluster analysis *See* cluster analysis.

nonimpact printer A printer in which the image is formed without use of mechanical impact. *Inkjet, *thermal, and *electrographic printers are examples of this type.

nonlinear equations In general, a problem that requires the determination of values of the unknowns $x_1, x_2, ..., x_n$ for which

$$f_i(x_1, x_2, ..., x_n) = 0,$$
$$i = 1, 2, ..., n$$

where $f_1, f_2, ..., f_n$ are given algebraic functions of n variables, i.e. they do not involve derivatives or integrals. This in both theory and practice is a very difficult problem. Such systems of equations arise in many areas, e.g. in numerical methods for nonlinear *ordinary and *partial differential equations. When $n = 1$ the single equation can be solved by a variety of effective techniques (all involving *iteration); the case of *polynomial equations can give rise to complex solutions. For systems of equations, *Newton's method and principally its many variants are widely used. For cases of extreme difficulty where, for example, only poor starting approximations are available, methods based on the idea of *continuation can be of value.

nonlinear regression model *See* regression analysis.

nonlocal entity *See* local.

nonmemory reference instruction An instruction that can be carried out without having to obtain an operand from, or return a result to, memory. Immediate instructions and some branch instructions are examples. *See also* zero-address instruction.

nonmonotonic reasoning A form of reasoning in which the acquisition of new knowledge can cause earlier conclusions to be withdrawn, so that the body of inferred knowledge does not grow monotonically (i.e. does not increase consistently) with the body of received knowledge. Various systems of nonmonotonic reasoning have been developed, among which are nonmonotonic logic, circumscription, default reasoning, autoepistemic logic, and negation as failure.

nonparametric techniques *Statistical methods that make no assumptions about the precise form of the *frequency distribution from which the data are sampled. They are mainly of use for hypothesis testing using the information in the rank order within each sample. For example, the *Mann Whitney U-test* may be used to test whether two samples are drawn from the same distribution, and the *rank correlation coefficient* may be used to test whether two variables are independent.

These methods can be contrasted with *parametric techniques*, which require specific models with *parameters to be estimated.

nonpreemptive allocation An allocation that does not preempt a resource from a process to which it is already allocated. *Compare* preemptive allocation.

nonprocedural language *Another name for* declarative language.

nonreturn to zero *See* NRZ.

nonsingular matrix A square matrix, A, of numbers whose *determinant is nonzero. A is nonsingular if and only if it is invertible (*see* inverse matrix).

nonstop processing The use of multiple computers in a redundant configuration to provide high *availability of computing service and tolerance to failures of service in a single computer.

nonterminal (nonterminal symbol) *See* grammar.

nonterminal node (interior node) of a tree. Any node that is not a terminal node (i.e. a leaf node) and hence has one or more children.

nonvolatile memory A type of memory whose contents are not lost when power to the memory is removed. *ROM and *PROM are examples. *Compare* volatile memory.

non von Neumann architecture Any computer architecture in which the underlying model of computation is different from what has come to be called the standard von Neumann model (*see* von Neumann machine). A non von Neumann machine may thus be without the concept of sequential flow of control (i.e. without any register corresponding to a "program counter" that indicates the current point that has been reached in execution of a program) and/or without the concept of a variable (i.e. without "named" storage locations in which a value may be stored and subsequently referenced or changed).

Examples of non von Neumann machines

are the *dataflow machines and the *reduction machines. In both of these cases there is a high degree of parallelism, and instead of variables there are immutable bindings between names and constant values.

Note that the term non von Neumann is usually reserved for machines that represent a radical departure from the von Neumann model, and is therefore not normally applied to multiprocessor or multicomputer architectures, which effectively offer a set of cooperating von Neumann machines.

no-op instruction (pass instruction; do-nothing instruction) An instruction that causes no action to take place in the computer except for consumption of time and instruction storage space. There are several uses for this instruction including time adjustment of a program, filling out program space in a system where instruction boundaries do not always coincide with word boundaries, and replacement of unwanted instructions without having to recompute all other program addresses.

inputs	A1	0	0	1	1
	A2	0	1	0	1
output	B	1	0	0	0

Two-input NOR gate, circuit symbol and truth table

NOR gate An electronic *logic gate whose output is logic 1 (true) only when all (two or more) inputs are logic 0 (false), otherwise it is logic 0. It thus implements the logical *NOR operation and has the same truth table. The diagram shows the usual circuit symbol of a two-input gate (which implies by the small circle that it is an inclusive *OR gate whose output has been inverted) and the associated truth table. *See also* exclusive-NOR gate.

norm *See* approximation theory.

normal distribution (Gaussian distribution) An important *probability distribution for data in the form of continuous measurements. The frequency function is given by

$$(2\pi\sigma^2)^{-\frac{1}{2}} \exp[-\frac{1}{2}(x - \mu)^2/\sigma^2]$$

The distribution is symmetric about the mean, μ, and its variance is σ^2. The range of x is infinite $(-\infty, \infty)$. Many sampling distributions tend to the normal form as the sample size tends to infinity.

normal forms 1. A term applied to a relation (table) in a relational database. A table is said to be in *first normal form* if it conforms to the constraint of the *relational model that each entry is an elementary data item. In defining further normal forms the concept of *functional dependency* is used. This concept is quite distinct from that of *function since it requires the context of relation for its definition. A functional dependency thus exists only within a particular relation.

Given two attributes A and B of a relation, then B is functionally dependent on A if whenever any two tuples (rows) of the relation have the same value for A, they will necessarily also have the same value for B. Notationally this is written $A \rightarrow B$, often colloquially expressed as "A determines B". This definition is readily generalized to the case where A and B are arbitrary subsets of attributes, which is the definition used in the theoretical development. A logical consequence of the definition is that if the values of a particular attribute in a relation are necessarily all distinct (e.g. if it is a key) then all other attributes of the relation are functionally dependent on it, and similarly for a set of attributes (e.g. a compound key).

A relation is in *second normal form* if it has a single attribute that can serve as a key or, if having a compound key, all other attributes are functionally dependent on the whole of the key and not just part of it. A relation is in *third normal form* if it contains no functional dependencies among its nonkey attributes. The concepts of second and third normal form are widely understood and used in practical database design, the functional dependencies usually being a reflection within the tables of real-world functions that exist in the application domain.

Further normal forms, less used in practice, are Boyce–Codd, fourth and fifth. Fourth normal form also uses the concept of multivalued dependency and fifth normal form that of join dependency.

2. *See* abstract reduction system.

normalized coordinates *See* NDC, NPC.

normal plots Graphical plots of ranked *residuals against percentage points of a *normal distribution to test the assumption of normality in a statistical analysis. If the plotted points do not lie roughly on a straight line the analysis may have to be changed, for example by *transformation of the data.

normal subgroup *See* coset.

P	F	F	T	T
Q	F	T	F	T
$P \downarrow Q$	T	F	F	F

Truth table for NOR operation

NOR operation The logical *connective combining two statements, truth values, or formulas P and Q in such a way that the result is true only if both P and Q are false (*see* table). The NOR operation is the dual of the *NAND operation (*see* duality). It may be represented by the *Pierce arrow*, $\downarrow$, or by ∇. $P \downarrow Q$ is just the negation of $P \vee Q$, hence the name (*see* OR operation).

The NOR operation is of particular significance to computer designers since any Boolean expression can be expressed using the NOR operation alone. In practical terms, circuits can be built using only *NOR gates.

NOS *Acronym for* network operating system.

notch filter *See* band-stop filter.

notebook A computer about the size of a piece of A4 paper (about 20 by 30 cm) and a few cm thick with a hinge along the long side. When opened up, a full-sized keyboard and monochrome or color LCD screen are revealed. Notebooks can have all the processing power and features of *desktop computers, but at a somewhat higher price as the special low power consumption processor and the small lightweight components are currently more expensive. To increase their flexibility the pointing device is often a *trackerball embedded in the keyboard rather than a mouse, which requires a hard flat surface to operate successfully. *See also* subnotebook, palmtop computer.

not-equivalence gate *Another name for* exclusive-OR gate.

NOT gate *Another name for* inverter.

NOT operation A logical *connective with just one operand. When applied to a statement, truth value, or formula P, the outcome is false if P is true, and vice versa, i.e. it produces a negation. It can be denoted in a variety of ways, e.g.

$$\text{not } P, \neg P, \sim P, P', \overline{P}$$

Novell Inc. A US-based developer and supplier of local area network software, a field in which it has a dominating position through its *Netware product. In 1994 Novell acquired Borland's spreadsheet Quattro Pro and the word-processing system WordPerfect from WordPerfect Corp. It is ranked number 54 in terms of revenue in the list of the world's top IT suppliers (1993 figures).

NP, NP-complete *See* P=NP question.

NPC *Abbrev. for* normalized projection coordinates. A viewing transformation that maps a world-coordinate position into one in NPC space. *See also* world coordinates.

npn *See* bipolar transistor.

NREN *Acronym for* national research and education network. The term was first used by Vice President Gore when announcing plans for the network intended to link all publicly funded research and education centers in the US.

NRZ *Abbrev. for* nonreturn to zero. A way of encoding binary signals that aims to achieve the highest possible data transfer rate for a given signal frequency. The name is derived from the principle of operation, i.e. the signal line does not return to zero – make any transition – between a succession of 1 bits. The method was first used for communications signaling in which there was always a 1 bit at the start of a character and thus there was a predictable and acceptable short interval over which the sending and receiving devices had to maintain synchronism independently.

Many variants of the basic principle have been derived to overcome synchronization problems that occur at high speeds and long bit streams. *See also* disk format, tape format.

NS chart *See* Nassi–Shneiderman chart.

NSPACE, NTIME *See* complexity classes.

n-tuple An ordered set with an unspecified but finite number (n) of elements. *See* ordered pair, Cartesian product.

n-type semiconductor *See* semiconductor.

nucleus *See* kernel.

nullary operation *See* operation.

null character A special character in a *character set, denoting nothing, and usually (as in ASCII and EBCDIC) represented by zero.

nullity of a graph. *See* connected graph.

null link *See* linked list.

null list (empty list) *See* list.

null matrix (zero matrix) A square matrix, all the elements of which are zeros.

null set *Another name for* empty set.

null string *Another name for* empty string.

number cruncher *Informal name for* supercomputer.

number system Although early number systems were not positional, all of the number systems most commonly used today are *positional systems*: the value of a number in such a system is determined not just by the digits in the number but also by the position in the number of each of the digits. If a positional system has a *fixed radix* (or *fixed base*) R then each digit a_i in any number

$$a_n a_{n-1} \ldots a_0$$

is an integer in the range 0 to $(R - 1)$ and the number is interpreted as

$$a_n R^n + a_{n-1} R^{n-1} + \ldots + a_1 R^1 + a_0 R^0$$

Since this is a polynomial in R, such numbers are sometimes called *polynomial numbers*. The decimal and binary systems are both fixed-radix systems, with a radix of 10 and 2, respectively.

Fractional values can also be represented in a fixed-radix system. Thus,

$$.a_1 a_2 \ldots a_n$$

is interpreted as

$$a_1 R^{-1} + a_2 R^{-2} + \ldots + a_n R^{-n}$$

In a *mixed-radix* (or *mixed-base*) *system*, the digit a_i in any number

$$a_n a_{n-1} \ldots a_0$$

lies in the range 0 to R_i, where R_i is not the same for every i. The number is then interpreted as

$$(\ldots((a_n R_{n-1}) + a_{n-1})R_{n-2} + \ldots + a_1)R_0 + a_0$$

For example, 122 days 17 hours 35 minutes 22 seconds is equal to

$$(((((1 \times 10) + 2)10 + 2)24 + 17)60 + 35)60 + 22 \text{ seconds}$$

numerical analysis A branch of mathematics/computer science dealing with the study of *algorithms for the numerical solution of problems formulated and studied in other branches of mathematics. Numerical analysis now plays a central role in engineering and in the quantitative parts of pure and applied science. The tasks of numerical analysis include the development of fast and reliable *numerical methods together with the provision of a suitable *error analysis. The algorithms are developed as computer programs, taking full account of machine architectures such as parallelism.

numerical code A code whose target alphabet contains only digits and/or strings of digits, e.g. a binary code.

numerical control The application of digital computer techniques to the control of a manufacturing process. The concept has been applied primarily to various kinds of machine tools such as milling machines, metal-cutting lathes, welding machines, and some specialized machines. The machines are controlled by numerical specification of parameters such as position, where the numbers are usually calculated beforehand (offline) by a computer and recorded on a medium such as punched paper tape. If the computer is directly connected for online control, the technique is called *computer numerical control (CNC)*. *See also* computer-aided manufacturing, computer-integrated manufacturing.

numerical differentiation The problem of approximating the derivative of a function using values of the function. An obvious approach is to use the derivative of an *interpolation polynomial. Such estimates involve differences of function values, and loss of potential accuracy occurs, due to *cancellation, if the data values are at points too close together.

numerical integration (quadrature) The problem of finding the numerical value for a definite integral. The underlying approximation behind most methods is the replacement of a function $f(x)$ by an *interpolation polynomial, based on a set of points $x_1, x_2, \ldots, x_n$. This leads to integration rules of the form
$$\int_b^a w(x)f(x)\mathrm{d}x \approx w_1 f(x_1) + w_2 f(x_2) + \ldots + w_n f(x_n)$$
in which the w_i are called *weights*.

The standard problem has a,b finite and $w(x) \equiv 1$. For this case the rules with equally spaced points x_i are called *Newton–Cotes rules*. Well-known examples are the *trapezium rule and *Simpson's rule. Most program libraries implement the more powerful *Gaussian rules* in which the points x_i are chosen to maximize the *degree of precision. This is achieved by choosing the x_i as the zeros of the Legendre polynomials that are *orthogonal polynomials with respect to $w(x) \equiv 1$ on the interval $[-1, 1]$. Another important idea is the *extrapolation method due to Romberg, based on the trapezium rule.

For infinite range problems Gaussian rules can also be defined in terms of suitable orthogonal polynomials. A useful case is where
$$w(x) = e^{-x}, a = 0, b = \infty$$
where the appropriate orthogonal polynomials determining the x_i are the Laguerre polynomials.

In practice the interval of integration is subdivided and the chosen rule applied to each subinterval, together with a companion rule to provide an error estimate (*see* error analysis). By then subdividing the interval where the error is largest, a greater concentration of effort is placed where the integrand is most difficult. This is known as *adaptive quadrature*. Such nonuniform distribution of effort, adapted to the particular problem, is essential for the efficient solution of all practical problems.

Multiple integrals over a large number of dimensions may be treated by *Monte Carlo methods, involving the use of randomly generated evaluation points.

numerical linear algebra A fundamentally important subject that deals with the theory and practice of processes in linear algebra. Principally these involve the central problems of the solution of *linear algebraic equations
$$Ax = b$$
and the *eigenvalue problem in which eigenvalues λ_k and the eigenvectors x_k are sought where
$$Ax_k = \lambda_k x_k$$

Numerical linear algebra forms the basis of much scientific computing. Both of these problems have many variants, determined by the properties of the matrix A. For example, a related problem is the solution of overdetermined systems where A has more rows than columns. Here there are good reasons for computing x to minimize the norm
$$\|Ax - b\|_2$$
(*see* approximation theory).

A major activity is the computing of certain linear transformations in the form of matrices, which brings about some simplification of the given problem. Most widely used are orthogonal matrices Q, for which
$$Q^T Q = I$$
(*see* identity matrix, transpose). An important feature of large-scale scientific computing is where the associated matrices are sparse, i.e. where a high proportion of the elements are zero (*see* sparse matrix). This is exploited in the algorithms for their solution.

There is now available high-quality software for an enormous variety of linear algebra processes.

numerical methods Methods designed for the constructive solution of mathematical problems requiring particular numerical results, usually on a computer. A numerical method is a complete and unambiguous set of procedures for the solution of a problem, together with computable error estimates (*see* error analysis). The study and implementation of such methods is the province of *numerical analysis.

numerical stability *See* stability.

numlock A key controlling the mode of the numeric pad on a keyboard whereby the keys produce numeric codes. An alternative mode allows the keys to be used for cursor control.

NURBS *Acronym for* nonuniform rational B-splines. The ratio of two nonuniform *B-spline curves.

n-version programming *Another name for* diverse programming.

Nyquist interval The time interval between successive samples of a continuous-time band-limited signal that is being sampled at the Nyquist rate. *See* Nyquist's criterion.

Nyquist rate *See* Nyquist's criterion.

Nyquist sampling The process of *sampling a continuous-time band-limited channel at, or possibly more frequently than, the Nyquist rate. *See* Nyquist's criterion.

Nyquist's criterion The statement that when a continuous-time *band-limited channel is to be sampled, the *sampling process may or may not cause information to be lost according to whether the sampling rate, ν, is less than, greater than, or equal to twice the *bandwidth, W.

If $\nu = 2W$, sampling is said to occur at the *Nyquist rate*.

If $\nu < 2W$, *sub-Nyquist sampling* is said to take place, and some information will be lost; this may be quite acceptable in certain cases.

If $\nu > 2W$, *super-Nyquist sampling* occurs; it cannot cause any more information to be extracted than sampling at the Nyquist rate.

Super-Nyquist sampling (at somewhat over the Nyquist rate) is, however, commonly employed to allow a margin of safety since there may be some doubt about the actual value of the bandwidth. There is no harm in it, if it is convenient, but the samples taken at a super-Nyquist rate will not be independent of one another.

See also discrete and continuous systems.

Nyström methods A class of *Runge–Kutta methods directly applicable to second-order equations of the form

$$y'' = f(x, y, y'), \quad a \le x \le b,$$
$$y(a) = y_0, \quad y'(a) = y_0'$$

without requiring a reduction to first-order systems (*see* ordinary differential equations). *Extrapolation methods and *linear multi-step methods of this direct type have also

been developed. Such methods can be particularly advantageous for equations of the type $y'' = f(x, y)$, where y' does not appear explicitly.

OBERON A programming language developed as a successor to *Modula 2.

OBJ An executable *specification language.

object A term loosely used to describe an identifiable component of a software system or design, now more commonly applied to a component that is in some sense self-contained, having an identifiable boundary. In *object-oriented design, objects are the basic components from which the model of the system to be implemented is constructed.

In *object-oriented programming, the term has a more precise definition. An object is an instance of a component comprising data structures and procedures (called *methods*) for manipulating the structures. These methods are activated by *messages* sent to the object, and the interior structure of the object is entirely hidden from any other object (a property called *encapsulation*). Objects are derived from a template, and the collection of objects that are instances of a particular template are said to form a *class*. A particularly important feature is *inheritance*, which allows new classes to be defined in terms of existing classes, inheriting some or all of the properties of an existing class. Some systems implement *multiple inheritance*, which allows a class to inherit properties from more than one parent class.

See also object-oriented architecture, object-oriented language.

object code The output of a *compiler.

object language The language in which the output of a *compiler or *assembler is expressed.

object linking and embedding (OLE) A set of techniques for incorporating an *object from one application in another. An embedded object has no permanent connection with its parent application, but when activated the parent application is launched. For instance an embedded picture in a word processor, when activated, might cause the paint program to appear with the picture loaded ready to be modified or viewed. When an object is linked into a target application the parent application can be active, and any changes made by the parent application are immediately displayed in the embedded object (*see* hot link). OLE techniques all differ from a simple copy, where the object has no further connection with the parent application and becomes part of the target.

object management system (OMS) That part of an *IPSE which is concerned with maintaining information about the system under development. The OMS may be based on a relational database management system, and includes relationships between elements such as derivation and configurations.

object-oriented architecture An architecture in which everything (processes, files, I/O operations, etc.) is represented as an *object. Objects are *data structures in memory that may be manipulated by the total system (hardware and software); they provide a high-level description that allows for a high-level user interface. Objects have descriptors that are referred to variously as *names*, *pointers*, and *labels*. These descriptors also provide information as to the type of object and a description of capabilities that apply to the particular object. Object-oriented architecture systems can thus be considered as an extension or generalization of *capability architecture systems, and have the same ability to provide a basis for protection and computer security.

Examples of object-oriented architecture systems are the IBM System 38, the Intel iAPX 432, and the Carnegie-Mellon experimental C.mmp/Hydra.

object-oriented database A term not well defined but applied to software products that provide *persistence for applications written in *object-oriented languages with features such as rollback and recovery. Thus ONTOS provides persistence for C++ and GemStone

for a variant of Smalltalk-80. There is no generally accepted object-oriented *data model on which products can be based as with the *relational model, although various proposals have been and are being made. It remains unclear whether all the concepts of object-oriented programming are relevant in the database context.

object-oriented design (OOD) A software development technique in which the system is seen as a collection of *objects that communicate with other objects by passing *messages*. Design is targeted toward defining the kinds of objects, the *methods* (i.e. procedures of objects), and the messages passed. OOD is based on the principle of *information hiding. *See also* message passing.

object-oriented language (OOL) A programming language used in *object-oriented programming. In such a system the concept of procedure and data, which is embodied in conventional programming systems, is replaced by the concepts of *objects and messages: an object is a package of information and a description of its manipulation, and a message is a specification of one of an object's manipulations. Unlike a procedure, which describes how manipulations should be carried out, a message merely specifies what the sender wants done, and the receiver determines exactly what will happen. *See also* Smalltalk, C++.

object-oriented programming (OOP) A programming technique that combines *data abstraction, *inheritance, and dynamic type binding. The central feature is the *object, which comprises a data structure definition and its defined procedures in a single structure. Objects are instances of a class, each instance having its own private instance variables. The class definition defines the properties of the objects in a class. Hierarchical class structures are possible in which objects in a class inherit the properties of the parent class in addition to properties explicitly defined for the class. This facilitates sharing of code, since users can inherit objects from system collections of code.

The procedures of an object (often called *methods*) are activated by *messages* sent to the object by another object. Thus in an object-oriented programming system the basic control structure is *message passing. The programmer identifies the real-world objects of the problem and the processing requirements of those objects, encapsulating these in class definitions, and the communications between objects. The program is then essentially a simulation of the real world in which objects pass messages to other objects to initiate actions.

The most complete realization of an object-oriented programming system is *Smalltalk; the concepts also appear in combination with conventional languages, for example *C++ and *CLOS.

object program Like object code, the output of a *compiler. The object program is the translation into *object language of the *source program.

object-space octree An *octree used to model an object in *world coordinates.

occam *Trademark* A programming language devised specifically for use with *transputer based systems. occam facilitates the writing of parallel programs for execution on one or more transputers, and is intended to be the normal way of programming transputers. The current version is occam 2.

occam programs are built up from *processes*, which may be executed sequentially or in parallel: the simplest process is a sequence of actions (assignment, input, or output). Input and output take place through *channels* that link processes, and *synchronization of parallel processes is achieved by causing a process that requests input to halt until some other process generates an output on the specified channel.

It is straightforward to write complex parallel programs in occam: the user does not need to be aware of the number of transputers actually executing his/her program, since processes are distributed over available transputers in a transparent manner by the underlying system.

OCR *Abbrev. for* optical character recognition. A process in which a machine scans, recognizes, and encodes information printed or typed in alphanumeric characters. The first devices, marketed around 1955, could only recognize a limited repertoire of characters that had to be produced in a font that was optimized for machine recognition but was still recognizable by people. By the mid-1970s OCR A font and OCR B font were the dominant fonts and were close to a normal letter-press appearance. Modern OCR equipment can read most typed or printed documents and high recognition rates are achieved (*see* ICR). OCR A and B fonts are still used for applications requiring high accuracy and in cases when context cannot aid recognition. In some instances printed information intended for *MICR (magnetic-ink character recognition) is read by optical recognition techniques, as with some check readers associated with bank teller terminals.

Input devices and software that can recognize handwritten characters are becoming available. The accuracy of such systems is not yet sufficient for them to be widely adopted.

octal notation The representation of numbers in the positional number system with radix 8. The octal digits are denoted by 0–7. Any octal number may be simply converted into its binary equivalent, and any binary number into its shorter octal equivalent.

octant *See* octree.

octet Eight contiguous bits; an eight bit byte. The term is used instead of byte to prevent confusion in cases where the term has pre-existing hardware associations, as in machines with 7-bit bytes, 9-bit bytes, 12-bit bytes.

octree A representation of space and solid objects used in *computer graphics and *spatial reasoning; it is a *tree structure. The space around the origin point is divided up into eight *octants*. Each octant is marked occupied or free according to whether there is any object occupying that location in the environment to be represented. Each occupied octant is then divided again into eight subspaces and the process continues recursively until sufficient resolution has been achieved. The representation is efficient where large volumes of space are unoccupied, and the level of detail required is in proportion to the spatial complexity of the object structure. The two-dimensional version is called a *quadtree.

ODA *Abbrev. for* open document architecture. Originally called office document architecture, it was renamed when it was taken up by ISO (ISO 8613) as part of the set of standards aimed at enabling easy interchange of information between computer systems. *See also* SPDL.

odd-even check *Another name for* parity check.

odd-even rule A rule for determining whether a point is inside a polygon boundary by counting the intersections that a line from the point to infinity makes with the boundary. If the number is odd, the point is inside the boundary.

odd-even transposition sort A refinement of the *bubble sort in which adjacent pairs, starting with an odd position, are sorted then adjacent pairs, starting with an even position, are sorted. The two phases alternate until sorting is completed.

odd parity A property that holds when a group of binary values contains an odd number of 1s. *See* parity.

odds The ratio of the *probability that an event occurs to the probability that it does not occur. The ratio of two odds, known as the *odds-ratio*, is used especially in the comparison and modeling of conditional probabilities.

ODP *Abbrev. for* open distributed processing.

OEM *Abbrev. for* original equipment manufacturer. A *systems house or *systems integrator that purchases large quantities of equipment from a supplier for use in the systems it produces and, for this reason, enjoys a special relationship with the supplier; it may, for example, receive early information about new or upgraded products as well as substantial discounts. Because the meaning of the term is rather ambiguous, it is sometimes misused to mean the supplier rather than the systems house. The term was widely used during the 1980s.

OFB *Abbrev. for* Output Feedback. *See* Data Encryption Standard.

office automation The application of computers to office tasks. This may involve the use of *electronic filing systems, *word processing systems, *computer graphics systems, *electronic mail, *desktop publishing, *decision support systems, *database management systems, and *teleconferencing or *videoconferencing systems.

office software product (office suite) A collection of items of software from a single supplier that is useful in an office environment and is sold as a single item. The components typically include a selection from a word processor, spreadsheet, presentation graphics package, meeting scheduler and appointment manager, and perhaps a database system as an optional extra. There are significant cost savings over buying the items separately or making a selection from different suppliers, and there may be compatibility advantages. *Compare* integrated office system.

offline (or off-line) Of peripheral devices or files: not .connected to the system or not usable. A device may be physically connected but offline if the system has been instructed not to use it.

OLE *Acronym for* object linking and embedding.

Olivetti An Italian company, based in Ivrea and originally well known for manufacturing office machinery, particularly typewriters. It first started to develop computers in the 1960s but sold its computer interests to General Electric in 1968, by whom they were subsequently sold to Honeywell. It re-entered the market with a range of small machines in the late 1970s and is now an important supplier of office systems; it is number 14 in terms of revenue in the list of the world's top IT suppliers (1993 figures).

OMR *Abbrev. for* optical mark reading. A method for data input in which marks made on preformatted documents are sensed by photoelectric means. The marks are interpreted as either characters or values according to their position on the form. This provides an efficient type of data input in applications in which there are relatively few answers to a limited number of questions. No further data preparation activity or machines are required since the reader can be connected directly to the system. Special readers are available to handle large documents. OMR documents are printed on paper, and information to the user as to where the marks should be put and what significance they will have is usually printed in a color that will not be detected by the photoelectric sensors. Machine-readable timing marks are preprinted along the edge of the document.

OMS *Abbrev. for* object management system.

OMT *Abbrev. for* Object Modeling Technique. An object-oriented method developed by Jim Rumbaugh.

one-address instruction *See* instruction format.

one-level store The original term used for what is now called *virtual memory. The term arose from the fact that although the memory in use was found on units at different levels within the *memory hierarchy, the user saw all his memory at a single level of accessibility.

one-pass program A program that requires only one linear forward scan of its input data.

one-plus-one address instruction *See* instruction format.

one's complement *See* radix-minus-one complement.

one-shot *Another name for* monostable.

one-to-one function *Another name for* injection.

one-to-one onto function *Another name for* bijection.

one-way filter A type of access controller that restricts the flow of information in a distributed system having parts of differing security clearance. The filter allows a part with high clearance to read from a part of lower clearance but prevents the converse operation.

one-way linked list *Another name for* singly linked list.

online (or **on-line**) **1.** Connected to the system and usable. *See also* offline.

2. In automaton theory, describing an automaton that, having read the first k symbols of the input string, has already produced the first k symbols of the output string. The concept of being online is analogous to the initial subwords-preserving property of *gsm-mappings.

O notation, o notation *See* order.

on-the-fly error recovery *See* error rate.

onto function *Another name for* surjection.

OOD *Abbrev. for* object-oriented design.

OOL *Abbrev. for* object-oriented language.

OOP *Abbrev. for* object-oriented programming.

op-amp *Short for* operational amplifier.

op code *Short for* operation code.

open To instruct an application that a particular file is required for reading, writing, or both. When a file is opened, its name is passed to the operating system, which locates it and checks that it exists and is available – creating it if necessary – before giving to the application status information and the location of the first record. Once a file has been opened for writing it is normally unavailable to other applications until it has been *closed (*but see* record locking).

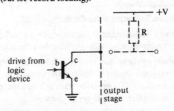

Open-collector device

open-collector device A particular implementation of an electronic logic device in which the output of the device is formed by the open-circuit collector termination of the output transistor (*see* diagram). The device's output is thus active-low and a *pull-up resistor is required to establish the active-high state. These devices are used to drive loads with high supply voltages or to implement *wired-logic buses.

open distributed processing (ODP) An *open system of *distributed processing. In a distributed processing system the various cooperating *processes that jointly make up the total activity may run on separate processing systems linked only by communications channels. In an open distributed system the components are physically separated and are linked by communications channels that use *open systems standards for their interfaces and protocols, and the intercommunication between the processes is again in accordance with a (different) set of open systems standards. It is clear that there is still a long way to go before open distributed processing will be a commercial reality.

Open-GL *Trademark* A computer-graphics system with similar functionality to *PHIGS. It is available on a number of computer systems.

open-reel tape *See* magnetic tape.

open shop A method of running a computing facility such that the design, development, writing, and testing of computer programs is carried out by the problem originator and not by specialist computing staff. *Open shop operation* is the operation of a computing system by the writer or user of a program and not by specialist computer operators. *Compare* closed shop.

Open Software Foundation *See* OSF.

open subroutine *Obsolete name for* in-line *subroutine, usually provided by a *macro.

open system Any system in which the components conform to nonproprietary standards rather than to the standards of a specific supplier of hardware or software.

open systems interconnection (OSI) A concept whereby communications-oriented computer equipment with different *protocols can be interconnected by means of a data network. The principal methods being developed are those of the major computer vendors and of the International Standards Organization (ISO). The term open systems interconnection is specifically related to the efforts of the ISO and its *seven-layer reference model.

open term *See* term.

operand 1. A quantity upon which a mathematical or logical operation is performed.
2. The parts of a machine instruction that specify the objects upon which the operation

is to be performed. For instance, in the instruction

ADD A,B

A and B are the operands and could be *registers in the central processor, or actual values, or *addresses of values, or even addresses of addresses of values.

operating system (OS) The set of software products that jointly controls the system resources and the processes using these resources on a computer system. Major products include *MS-DOS and *UNIX, and the large mainframe operating systems used in commercial applications.

operation 1. A *function from S^m (*see* Cartesian product) into S itself, where S is some set specific to the function. Such a function is usually referred to as an m-ary or m-adic operation over S, m being some *natural number, sometimes referred to as the *arity of the operation. The most common operations are the *dyadic (or binary) operations that map $S \times S$ into S and the *monadic (or unary) operations that map S into S. The case where the arity is zero gives the so-called *nullary* operations, which correspond simply to elements of S. There is also a more general kind of operation that involves more than one set. For example, in a *finite-state automaton the next state depends on the current input symbol and the current state, and is thus given by a dyadic operation from $I \times Q$ into Q, where I is the set of input symbols and Q the set of states. *See also* logic operation, arithmetic operation, operations on sets.
2. *Another name for* instruction (in a computer), as designated by an *operation code.
3. In a programming language. Whatever is carried out by an *operator (def. 2), or, more generally, anything that can take place within a program: a *declaration, an *assignment, a *selection, a *loop, the call of a *function, and so on.

operational amplifier (op-amp) A very high gain voltage amplifier having a differential input, i.e. its output voltage is proportional to (and very much greater than) the voltage difference between its two inputs. Operational amplifiers usually have feedback circuits of resistors and/or capacitors connected between their output and inputs. These circuits make op-amps operate as voltage amplifiers with a gain precisely defined by the values of the resistors, or else enable them to perform mathematical operations, such as integration, or signal-conditioning functions, such as filtering.

operational research *See* operations research.

operational semantics An approach to the *semantics of programming languages that uses the concept of an "abstract machine" that has a state and some primitive instructions or rules that cause the states to change. The machine is defined by specifying how the components of the state are changed by each of the instructions or rules. Computations are sequences of state transitions. The abstract machine is not meant to be a model of any realistic machine or machine language; it is meant to be simple enough so that the language can be unambiguously defined by simple rules for state transitions. The semantic description of a programming language specifies a translation into this operational model. Examples of this approach include the Vienna Definition Language used to define PL/I, which was the first method for defining the semantics of a programming language.

operation code (op code; order code)
1. The portion of the *instruction that specifies the operation to be performed by the instruction. *See also* instruction format.
2. The set of such portions available for a particular computer, and defining the repertoire of operations it can perform.

operation register The part of the *control-unit instruction register that contains the *operation code.

operations on sets The simple *operations that can be performed on sets are those of *union, *intersection, and *complement, and possibly *set difference. Using these it is possible to create new sets from existing sets. Certain other actions that have to be performed on sets are sometimes considered as operations, although they do not conform to the strict definition of the word. These

include the actions *find, *insert, *delete, *split, and *min.

operations research (operational research; OR) The study of some human operation or set of operations by quantitative means. It is usually conducted with the aid of computer modeling; models may be hypothesized and fitted to experimental data, or experimental data may be analyzed to derive a model. Once a model is available, the effects of changes in the operations under study can be developed and predicted in a quantitative way.

operation table *Another name for* Cayley table.

operator 1. A person responsible for the immediate supervision of the hardware of a computer system.
2. A function that can be applied to one or more operands so as to yield a result. It is (usually) a symbol representing an operation to be carried out, as opposed to a *variable, which represents a data value. *See also* arithmetic operator, logic operation, relational operator, precedence.

optical card A form of *optical storage in which the medium is in credit-card form, intended for uses similar to those of a magnetic-stripe card but with much higher capacity (several megabytes).

optical character recognition *See* OCR.

optical computing Computing based on the use of logic elements, in the form of *optical switches, that employ light beams as logic signals instead of the voltage or current levels of conventional electronic logic elements. These optical switches may use light beams exclusively or a combination of electronic and optical signals, depending on the application.

optical disk A type of *optical storage in which the medium is in the form of a disk that is rotated to give one dimension of access while the light beam is scanned radially to give a second dimension. In nearly all cases the disk is exchangeable. This is easily arranged because there is a substantial clearance, typically 1 mm, between the surface of the disk and the nearest component of the optical system. The optical system is heavy and expensive compared to the corresponding components of a magnetic disk drive, so most optical drives are designed to access a single recording surface: if the disk has recording surfaces on both sides it is removed from the drive and reversed to give access to the second surface. (This is done automatically when the drive forms part of an *optical disk library.) A few drives can access both sides of the disk. Multiple disk packs are not used.

Rewritable, write-once, and read-only media have been developed for optical disk drives: *multifunction* drives can read two or all three of these media types. Disk sizes range from 350 mm downward with 300 mm and 130 or 120 mm the most widely accepted, although smaller sizes are becoming popular. The only widely used format for read-only disks is *CD-ROM.

The first optical disk drives suitable for data storage (with a read error rate after correction better than 1 in 10^{12} bits) appeared on the market at the end of 1984: these all used *write-once media on large-diameter disks (350 mm to 200 mm). Read-only disks, particularly CD-ROM, appeared about the same time. Rewritable disks became practicable several years later because of difficulty in developing reliable media, but have now replaced write-once disks for many purposes. Optical disks are very robust, need no special environmental control, and have an almost unlimited life.

Optical disks have higher capacity than magnetic disks of similar cost, but their performance is lower than that of hard magnetic disks although higher than that of floppy disks. They are therefore rarely used as the working store of a computer, but are suitable for archival storage, backup, and data distribution and exchange. They are widely used for storage of *bitmapped images, such as scanned documents, because of their low cost per bit. Such images have natural redundancy so a poorer error rate is acceptable; in the early days of optical storage, optical disks without error correction (giving a read error rate of about 1 in 10^5) were used for storing scanned documents written in Japanese

Kanji characters, but nowadays a high level of error correction is used in nearly all cases so that the disks and drives are adaptable to all purposes. An exception is the format used for sound and video (but not text or digital data) on CD-ROM, where a higher error rate is acceptable as this material is naturally redundant.

See also optical disk library.

optical disk library (jukebox (*informal*)) A peripheral device in which many optical disks (usually in cartridges) are stored in slots in a storage rack. The device contains one or more *optical disk drives; any disk can be taken from its slot and loaded into a drive by a *picker mechanism*, at the command of the host computer. The picker can also return a disk to its slot, turn a disk over (since most drives can only read one side), and move a disk to or from a *drawer* where it can be reached by the operator. Standard disks and cartridges are used.

optical fiber A thin transparent fiber used to carry optical signals, typically in the infrared with a wavelength of 1200–1550 nanometers. Optical fibers require special units to convert electric signals to light energy at the transmitting end, and to convert light energy to electric signals at the receiving end. Equipment is also needed to handle whatever lower-level *protocols are to be used across the optical fiber. A variety of methods are used to reduce the loss of the optical signal. *See* fiber optics.

optical flow An image in which the color of a pixel represents the motion occurring at that location in the image. An optical flow field is the instantaneous velocity vector field for an image of a moving environment. From operations on local velocity contours it is possible to deduce the movements of objects in the image and the general relative movement of the observer. *See also* active vision.

optical font A printing font or style of character specially designed to be accurately read by reading machines and by people. The most widely used are OCR A and OCR B and they are defined in internationally recognized standards. Although reading machines are available that can process a wide variety of fonts, provided that they are clearly printed, lower-cost machines and lower error rates can be achieved if the specialized optical fonts are used. *See also* OCR.

optical mark reading *See* OMR.

optical media *See* optical storage.

optical storage The storage or retrieval, or both, of data or images by optical means. Numerous methods have been explored, including holography, but current techniques depend on the use of a semiconductor laser and optical system to generate a very small spot of light (typically one micrometer in diameter) focused on a thin layer of a suitable medium to access each information element in turn. The principal configurations used are *optical disk, *optical card, and *optical tape.

When writing data or images, the beam power is sufficient (typically 10 milliwatts) to heat the illuminated area of the medium so as to change its optical characteristics, reversibly or irreversibly. (In the case of *magneto-optic recording, a magnetic field is also applied to control the state taken by the element of the medium as it cools.) When reading, the beam power is reduced to the point where it does not produce any change in the state of the medium, and the light reflected (or in some cases transmitted) by each element is detected and its intensity or polarization is observed to decide whether it represents a 1 or 0 bit.

Optical storage is capable of higher areal storage densities than have been achieved by magnetic media, and does not require the close medium-to-head spacing of magnetic storage. The medium is rugged, since the sensitive layer is beneath a clear protective layer; the light beam is out of focus at the surface of this and thus reasonably insensitive to dust or scratches. There is thus the potential of low-cost storage on rugged readily interchangeable volumes. On the other hand the optical components are relatively expensive and bulky, and the flaw density in the medium (relative to the element size) is higher than in magnetic storage thus requiring elaborate error correction techniques for most applications.

Three classes of media can conveniently be distinguished: *rewritable*, where recorded data can be erased and rewritten as in magnetic storage; *write-once* (or *WORM*), where information once written cannot be erased; *read-only*, where the information is impressed on the medium during manufacture and cannot subsequently be changed. Some technologies allow two of these classes to be combined on the same media volume.

Write-once media offer permanent storage once recorded and so are an attractive alternative to magnetic tape for archival storage. Read-only media are a very cheap means of distributing large amounts of data, such as images, or software in machine-readable form (*see* CD-ROM). Rewritable media compete more directly with magnetic storage, but are becoming popular for backup and for the storage of *bitmapped images, which tend to need very large files.

optical switch A device whose optical transmission properties (e.g. refractive index and polarizing properties) can be varied by an externally applied field or by some other external influence. Electric, magnetic, and surface acoustic wave techniques are all used for this purpose. By these means, light may be deflected away from a detector, thus switching the beam. LCD shutters are also used. The light that is processed in this way often originates in a laser source. Optical switches can be used, for example, as logic elements (*see* optical computing).

optical tape An optical medium in tape form. It is handled by a mechanism similar to a *magnetic tape drive, but written and read by similar methods to those used in *optical disk drives. Capacity per volume is very high but the mechanism is expensive. It is not widely used.

optimal binary search tree A *binary search tree constructed to be of maximum expected efficiency for a given *probability distribution of search data.

optimization The process of finding the best solution to some problem, where "best" accords to prestated criteria. The word is used in a number of contexts.

1. In mathematics the word is generally used

to describe the theory and practice of maximizing, or minimizing, a function (known as an *objective function*) of several variables that may be subject to a set of constraints. The special case of a linear objective function is the subject of *linear programming. The case of nonlinear objective functions, with or without constraints, is treated in a quite well-developed field. The unconstrained optimization problem (usually expressed as *minimization*) is:

$$\text{minimize } f(x)$$

where $f(x)$ is the given objective function of n real variables,

$$x = (x_1, x_2, \ldots, x_n)^T$$

A necessary condition for a minimum is that

$$\partial f / \partial x_i = 0, \, i = 1, 2, \ldots, n$$

which is a system of *nonlinear equations. *Newton's method can be applied, but in practice this technique has been extensively modified to improve computational efficiency. *Matrix-updating methods* are a broad class of methods that involve a sophisticated means of computing approximations to the matrices required in Newton's method.

For constrained problems, x must also satisfy a system (possibly nonlinear) of equations or inequalities. Some of the ideas and methods for unconstrained problems can be suitably modified to handle the constraints. A successful technique is *sequential quadratic programming.

Optimization problems are widespread in control theory, chemical engineering, and many other fields.

2. In programming the word is usually applied to part of the code-generation phase of a *compiler, denoting production of object code that is in some sense optimal, i.e. making best use of the resources provided by the target machine, or at least using these resources in a manner that is not blatantly wasteful. Programs can be space-efficient in the sense of occupying minimal storage, or time-efficient in the sense of executing in the minimum time.

Compiler optimization is usually directed toward generating time-efficient programs, and takes three forms. *Global optimization* seeks to reorder the sequencing of a program so as to eliminate redundant computations

(moving invariant operations outside loop bodies, coalescing loops, etc.). *Register optimization* adjusts the allocation of machine registers to variables and intermediate quantities in such a way as to minimize the number of occasions on which a register has to be stored and later reloaded. *Local (peephole) optimization* seeks to adapt the code to exploit particular features of the machine architecture and to remove local mishandling such as loading a register with a value that it already contains.

optimum programming *Another name for* minimum-access code.

optional product *See* consensus.

optoelectronics An increasingly important technology concerned with the generation, processing, and detection of optical signals that represent electric quantities. Major areas for application of this technology include communications, where digital or analog information can be transmitted over optical fibers (*see* fiber optics), and where two unconnected electric circuits may exchange signals by means of an optical link yet remain electrically isolated; these latter devices are called *optoisolators*. The technology is also being used to implement logical gating functions employing *optical switches, the advantages being high speeds of operation (*see* optical computing).

Optical signals may be generated from electric signals using *transducers such as switchable semiconductor lasers. Detection of optical signals is often achieved using *phototransistors*, i.e. *bipolar transistors whose base drive is made dependent on incident light. *See also* optical storage.

optoisolator *See* optoelectronics.

OR 1. *Abbrev. for* operations research.
2. *See* OR gate, OR operation.

Oracle A US corporation whose principal product is the DBMS *ORACLE. Software sales and maintenance account for the bulk of the company's sales but it is also a significant provider of services. Oracle is ranked number 46 in terms of revenue in the list of the world's top IT suppliers (1993 figures).

ORACLE *Trademark* A *relational database

management system developed and supplied by Oracle Corporation. It runs on a wide range of platforms, from mainframes to workstations, and a suite of application development tools is available.

Orange Book 1. The *coloured book that defines a network service running over a *Cambridge Ring.
2. A publication by the National Computer Security Center (*NCSC) concerned with *security evaluation.
3. The proprietary standard defining the CD-R format, or the publication setting it out. *See* CD-ROM format standards.

order 1. A means of indicating the way a function varies in magnitude as its argument tends to some limits, usually zero or infinity. More precisely if there is some constant K such that

$$|f(x)| \leq K \, \phi(x)$$

for all $x \geq x_1$, then we say that $f(x)$ is order $\phi(x)$ as x tends to infinity, and we write

$$f(x) = O(\phi(x))$$

For example,

$$100x^2 + 100x + 2 = O(x^2)$$
$$\text{as } x \to \infty$$

If

$$\lim_{x \to a} f(x) \, / \, g(x) = 0$$

then we write

$$f(x) = o(g(x))$$

For example,

$$x = o(x^2) \quad \text{as } x \to \infty$$

Both these notations are statements about maximum magnitude and do not exclude f from being of smaller magnitude. For example,

$$x = O(x^2)$$

is perfectly valid, but equally

$$x = O(x)$$

If

$$\lim_{x \to a} f(x) \, / \, g(x) = \text{const. } k \neq 0$$

then we write

$$f(x) \approx k \, g(x) \quad \text{as } x \to a$$

For example,

$$10x^2 + x + 1 \approx 10x^2$$
$$\text{as } x \to \infty$$

The term order and the O notation is used in numerical analysis, particularly in *discretization methods. In *ordinary differen-

tial equations, if h denotes the stepsize, then a method (or formula) has order p (a positive integer) if the global *discretization error is $O(h^p)$. This means that as the step size h is decreased, the error goes to zero at least as rapidly as h^p. Similar considerations apply to *partial differential equations. High-accuracy formulas (order up to 12 or 13) are sometimes used in methods for ordinary differential equations. For reasons of computational cost and stability, low-order formulas tend to be used in methods for partial differential equations.

The term is also used to refer to the speed of convergence of iteration schemes, for example *Newton's method for computing the zero of a function $f(x)$. Subject to appropriate conditions, Newton's method converges quadratically (or has order of convergence 2), i.e. an approximate squaring of the error is obtained in each iteration.
2. *Another name for* operation code.

order code *Another name for* operation code.

ordered pair A pair of objects in a given fixed order, usually represented by

$$(x, y) \text{ or } \langle x, y \rangle$$

for objects x and y. Two ordered pairs are said to be equal if and only if the first elements of each pair are equal and the second elements are equal. Typical situations in which ordered pairs are used include discussion of points in the Cartesian plane or complex numbers.

The idea can be extended to cover ordered triples, such as

$$(x_1, x_2, x_3)$$

and indeed ordered n-tuples, such as

$$(x_1, x_2, \dots x_n)$$

ordered set 1. A sequence of objects in a given fixed order. An *ordered pair is an example.
2. *Another name for* partially ordered set. *See* partial ordering.

ordered tree *See* tree.

ordering relation A relation that is *reflexive, *antisymmetric, and *transitive. The relation "less than or equal to" on integers is an ordering relation. *See also* partial ordering. *Compare* equivalence relation.

order of precedence *See* precedence.

ORDER REGISTER

order register *Another name for* instruction register. *See* control unit.

order statistics A branch of statistics that uses not the numerical value of an observation but its ranking relative to other observations. The *r*th *order statistic* of a sample of *n* observations is simply the *r*th smallest variate value in the sample. Examples of statistical tests for ordering include: the median test, the sign test, Cochran's test, the Wald-Wolfowitz "runs test", the Mann-Whitney test, the Wilcoxen test, the Kruskal-Wallis test, and the Friedman test.

ordinary differential equations *Differential equations that involve one independent variable, which in practice may be a space or time variable. Except in simple cases the solution cannot be determined analytically and approximation methods are used.

Numerical methods are mainly developed for equations involving first derivatives only, written in the form

$$y' = f(x, y), \quad a \leq x \leq b,$$

where *y* and *f* are *s*-component vectors with component functions

$$y_i(x),$$
$$f_i(x, y_1(x), y_2(x), \ldots, y_s(x))$$

Equations involving higher derivatives can be equivalently written in this form by introducing intermediate functions for the higher derivatives. Alternatively direct methods may be derived for such problems (*see* Nyström methods).

In general, *s* conditions must be imposed to determine a particular solution. If the values $y(a) = y_0$ are specified, it is an *initial-value problem*. These problems can be solved directly using step-by-step methods, such as *Runge-Kutta methods, *linear multistep methods, or *extrapolation methods, which determine approximations at a set of points in [*a*,*b*]. The problem is a *boundary-value problem* if the *s* conditions are given in terms of the component functions at *a* and *b*. In general, such problems require iterative methods, such as the *shooting method. However, if *f* is linear in *y*, *finite-difference methods can be advantageous. Excellent software has been developed for both types of problem.

An area of particular interest in many applications is the solution of *stiff equations*. A stiff system possesses solutions that decay very rapidly over an interval that is short relative to the range of integration, and the solution required varies slowly over most of the range. To allow large steps in the slowly varying phases, it is necessary to use special methods, such as the implicit *trapezoidal rule*:

$$x_{n+1} = x_n + h$$
$$y_{n+1} = y_n + \tfrac{1}{2}h(f(x_{n+1}, y_{n+1}) + f(x_n, y_n))$$

At each step a system of equations has to be solved for y_{n+1}, using very often a modification of *Newton's method. More straightforward explicit methods rapidly lead to catastrophic error growth unless the stepsize *h* is prohibitively small. These problems are still the subject of very active research interest.

organizational information system *See* information system.

inputs	A1	0	0	1	1
	A2	0	1	0	1
output B		0	1	1	1

Two-input OR gate, circuit symbol and truth table

OR gate An electronic *logic gate whose output is logic 0 (false) only when all (two or more) inputs are logic 0, otherwise it is logic 1 (true). It therefore implements the logical *OR operation and has the same *truth table. The diagram shows the usual circuit symbol and the truth table for a two-input gate. The device is more correctly called an *inclusive-OR gate* since the condition of both inputs true generates a true output. *See also* exclusive-OR gate.

original equipment manufacturer *See* OEM.

OROM *Abbrev. for* optical read-only memory. *See* optical storage.

OR operation (inclusive-OR operation) The logical *connective combining two statements, truth values, or formulas *P* and *Q* in such a way that the outcome is true if either P or Q or if both P and Q is true (*see* table). The latter outcome distinguishes the OR from the *exclusive-OR operation. The OR operation is usually denoted by $\vee$ and occasionally by $+$. It is one of the dyadic operations of *Boolean algebra and is both *commutative and *associative.

One way of implementing the OR operation (e.g. in LISP) is to test P first, and then evaluate Q only if P is false. The resulting operation is noncommutative; in some languages there is a distinct notation for this.

When it is implemented as a basic *machine code instruction, OR usually operates on pairs of bytes or pairs of words. In these cases the OR operation defined above is normally applied to pairs of corresponding bits.

P	F	F	T	T
Q	F	T	F	T
$P \vee Q$	F	T	T	T

Truth table for OR operation

orthogonal analysis, orthogonal basis *See* orthonormal basis.

orthogonal equations *See* orthogonal term rewriting system.

orthogonal functions Let

$$f_1(x), f_2(x), \ldots, f_n(x)$$

be a set of functions defined on the interval (a,b); also let $w(x)$ be a given positive function (a *weight function*) on (a,b). The functions $f_i(x)$,

$$i = 1,2,\ldots,n$$

are said to be orthogonal with respect to the interval (a,b) and weight function $w(x)$, if

$$\int_a^b w(x) f_i(x) f_j(x) \, dx = 0,$$

$$i \neq j, \ i,j = 1,2,\ldots,n$$

If, for $i = j$,

$$\int_b^a w(x) f_i^2(x) \, dx = 1,$$

$$i = 1,2,\ldots,n$$

then the functions are said to be *orthonormal*.

A similar property is defined when (a,b) is replaced by the set of points

$$x_1, x_2, \ldots, x_N$$

and the integral is replaced by a sum,

$$\sum_{k=1}^{N} w(x_k) f_i(x_k) f_j(x_k) = 0,$$

$$i \neq j$$

Orthogonal functions play an important part in the approximation of functions and data.

orthogonal list A two-dimensional orthogonal list has list cells that are linked symmetrically to both left and right horizontal neighbors and up and down to vertical neighbors. This idea can be generalized to higher dimensions and suggests an efficient representation for *sparse matrices.

orthogonal matrix A matrix Q is orthogonal if $Q^T Q = I$, where I is the *identity matrix and Q^T denotes the *transpose of Q.

orthogonal memory *See* associative memory.

orthogonal term rewriting system There are several useful conditions on the set E of *equations defining a *term rewriting system that lead to a well-behaved reduction system $\rightarrow_E$. A commonly used condition is *orthogonality*. If a set E of equations is orthogonal then its term rewriting system $\rightarrow_E$ is *Church–Rosser. A set of equations is orthogonal if it is left-linear and nonoverlapping:

the set E of equations is *left-linear* if for all $t = t' \in E$, each variable that appears in t does so only once;

the set E of equations is *nonoverlapping* if

(a) for any pair of different equations $t = t'$, $r = r' \in E$, the terms t and r do not overlap in the following sense – there exist closed substitutions τ, ρ of t, r such that $\rho(r)$ is a subterm of $\tau(t)$ and the outermost function symbol of $\rho(r)$ occurs as part of t,

(b) for any rule $t = t' \in E$, t does not overlap with itself in the following sense – there exist closed substitutions τ, ρ of t such that $\tau(t)$ is a proper subterm of $\rho(t)$ and the outermost function symbol of $\tau(t)$ occurs as a part of t.

orthonormal analysis *See* orthonormal basis.

orthonormal basis The set of orthonormal functions employed in calculating the terms of a transform of the kind exemplified by the *Fourier transform and the Walsh transform (*see* Walsh analysis): the orthonormal basis of the Fourier transform consists of the imaginary exponential functions, and that of the Walsh transform consists of the *Walsh functions.

In order to calculate the terms of a transform effectively, the basis functions must be *orthogonal but need not also be normal (orthonormal). Such a non-normalized basis is called an *orthogonal basis*. The calculation of the transform terms is correspondingly called *orthonormal analysis* or *orthogonal analysis*. Such analysis is only possible if there are sufficient functions in the set to form a basis: such a set is called a *complete set of functions*.

orthonormal functions *See* orthogonal functions.

OS *Abbrev. for* operating system. The abbreviation was used as the name for a specific operating system (OS/360) introduced by IBM, but is now used generically.

OS/2 *Trademark* An operating system produced in the late 1980s by IBM and Microsoft for microcomputers with Intel 80286 and 80386 processors, specifically the IBM PS/2 range. OS/2 allows *multitasking and programs larger than the MS-DOS 640 kilobyte limit. It has a *graphical user interface. Although OS/2 was all but eclipsed by *Windows, a new version, OS/2 Warp, was released by IBM in 1994 and has revived its popularity.

oscillation sort A method of *sorting in which *sortkeys are alternately distributed onto tapes and merged so that much of the sorting takes place before the input has been completely examined. The tapes are read both forward and backward.

oscillator An electronic circuit that switches back and forth between states. The astable *multivibrator is an example.

oscilloscope An item of electronic test equipment that can display a wide variety of waveforms of electric signals. It does this effectively by "plotting" the amplitude variations of the signal with time on a display device, normally a *cathode-ray tube. The electron beam of the CRT is deflected horizontally so that the display is scanned linearly in a preset time period. Vertical beam deflections, derived from the input signal, are then superimposed on the display, the horizontal and vertical deflections being synchronized by means of trigger circuits. *See also* storage oscilloscope.

OSF Open Software Foundation, an IT industry organization founded in 1988 to promote public standards for *UNIX. Founder members included *IBM, *Digital Equipment Corp., *Hewlett-Packard, *Microsoft, and Nixdorf (now Siemens Nixdorf).

OSF/Motif *Trademark* A graphical user interface available under license from *OSF, based on Microsoft Presentation Manager, Hewlett-Packard New Wave, and the DEC Windowing Toolkit implementation of *X Windows.

OSI *Abbrev. for* open systems interconnection.

OSI reference model *See* seven-layer reference model.

outdegree *See* degree.

outer code *See* concatenated coding system.

outlier *See* residual.

output 1. The result of data-processing activity when it is presented external to the system, or the process of presenting the data externally. The output from a computer can be in a form for use by people, e.g. printed or displayed, or it may be ready for input to another system or process, when it may be encoded magnetically or optically on a tape or disk. 2. A signal that is obtained from an electrical circuit, such as a logic circuit. 3. To produce a result or signal.

output area The area of main memory that is allocated for storage of data prior to transfer to an output device. *See also* input area.

output device Any device that converts the electrical signals representing information within a computer into a form that can exist or be sensed outside the computer. Printers and visual displays are the most common type of output device for interfacing to people, but voice is becoming increasingly available (*see* audio response unit). Devices such as magnetic tape transports are really types of intermediate or backing store but are sometimes referred to as output devices.

output-limited process A process whose speed of execution is limited by the rate at which output data can be accepted.

overflow The condition that arises when the result of an arithmetic operation exceeds the size of the location allotted for receipt of that result, or the amount by which the result exceeds the allotted number.

overlap A form of parallelism in which events that are not mutually dependent take place concurrently in order to increase computer performance, e.g. fetching a second instruction while a first instuction is being executed. When there is overlap between portions of arithmetic operations (i.e. when the portions are *overlapped*), the process is usually called *pipelining.

overlay A section of code that is loaded into memory during the execution of a program, overwriting what was previously there. The loading of an overlay is under the explicit control of the programmer, and should not be confused with *paging. In general several overlays are loaded into the same area of memory, "overlaying" the code already residing in that part of memory. Overlays can be thought of as a form of voluntary memory management.

overwrite To destroy information in a memory location by writing in new information.

own coding The practice of providing (and filling) place holders in a general-purpose software package where pieces of ordinary program can be inserted. It should be noted that there is loss of security when this practice is adopted.

P

P *See* P=NP question.

pack To store compactly in order to reduce the amount of memory required to hold the same data. There are several ways of doing

this, for example by storing several bytes in one word or by replacing multiple occurrences of a character or word by a triplet consisting of

(a) a special code indicating the start of a triplet;

(b) a single instance of the replicated character or word;

(c) a count of the number of times the character or word occurs.

package 1. *See* application package.

2. In *Ada, a self-contained collection of entities (data objects and procedures) that are available for other parts of a program to use. A package consists of two parts that can be separately compiled: its *specification* and its *body*. The specification provides the public information about the entities that the package makes available, in the form of declarations of constants, variables, and data types, and procedure headers. It may also contain a private part giving further information about types and constants that is needed by the compiler but not by a programmer using the package. The package body contains the procedure bodies for the procedures that form part of the package, together with local variables and types that these procedures may need. The separation of specification and body means that the implementation of the procedures is hidden from the users, thus a package is a realization of an *abstract data type.

Similar features are found in other languages, particularly Modula 2: here the term *module* is used in preference to package. In Modula 2 a module comprises a *definition part* and an *implementation part*, corresponding to the specification and body of the Ada package. The main difference is that the definition part of a module contains declarations of all the objects required by the module, together with an *export list* specifying which objects are visible outside the module.

packed decimal An economical method of storing decimal digits represented as binary-coded decimals (BCD), using only four bits per digit. Thus two decimal digits may be stored in one *byte. This is only slightly less compact than storing a number in binary, and avoids decimal-to-binary conversion. *See also* character encoding.

packet A group of bits of fixed maximum size and well-defined format that is switched and transmitted as a composite whole through a *packet switching network. Any message that exceeds the maximum size is partitioned and carried as several packets.

Typically each packet contains addressing information defining the source and the destination of the packet, control information defining the type of data carried in the packet, and some form of checksum to verify that the packet has been correctly received. In many systems the packet may hold several hundred bytes and the internal structure can vary from one packet to the next. *See also* cell, frame.

packet assembler/disassembler *See* PAD.

packet radio A transmission method that makes use of radio broadcast signals carrying *packets of data. There is no assurance that only a single transmitter is active at a time, so it is necessary to have a convention for the action to be taken when packets "collide". Logically, packet radio is essentially equivalent to bus architecture networks that are used in some local *network architectures.

packet switching A technique by which communication resources are allocated dynamically to multiple communicating entities. Messages between entities are partitioned into segments with a fixed maximum size. The segments, or *packets*, are passed through a *store-and-forward switching network until they reach their destination (or are discovered to be undeliverable). The packets are reassembled, if necessary, into complete messages when they reach their destination. Packet switching, as it applies to electronic communication, was first proven feasible by the development of the *ARPANET in 1969.

A *packet switching network* may provide a variety of levels of service, depending upon the sophistication of the underlying communication technology and the requirements of the network's customers. The simplest packet switching networks provide only *datagram service, which is unordered unreliable delivery of packets. Other networks may provide only reliable individually flow-controlled *virtual circuits. The decision between datagrams, virtual circuits, or other modes of operation can be made independently for the internal operation of a packet switching network, and the interface that it presents to its customers. *See also* cell, frame.

packet switching network *See* packet switching.

Packet SwitchStream *Trademark* British Telecom's public X25-based *packet switching service.

packing density 1. (functional packing density) A measure of the number of electronic devices per unit area contained on one *integrated circuit.

2. (recording density) A measure of the amount of information in a given dimension of a storage medium.

PAD *Acronym for* packet assembler/disassembler. A translating computer that provides access for asynchronous character-at-a-time terminals to a synchronous *packet switching network.

padding A filler used to extend a string or record to some prescribed length. *See also* block.

page The unit of interchange between memory and swapping device involved in a *paging system. The number of words or bytes in a page is usually fixed for a given system and is almost invariably an exact power of 2. The term *page frame* is used as an alternative name for page, but is more particularly used to apply to the copy of a page that is held on the swapping device.

page break An indication in a document stored on disk or displayed on a screen that when the document is printed, a new page will be started at that point. The page break can be inserted by the user, or generated automatically by the software.

page description language (PDL) A protocol for defining a page of text, including images and graphics. *PostScript is a PDL. *See also* SPDL.

page frame *See* page.

page printer A type of printer that prints a

complete page of output in one cycle. It is generally a *nonimpact printer, such as a *laser or *inkjet printer, in which the printing process requires continuous movement of the paper. The information for one page of output is usually accumulated within a buffer in the printer before the printing process is started. *Compare* line printer, serial printer.

page table A table within a computer that contains a mapping between logical page addresses and physical page addresses. In many systems the table is supported in a fast-acting memory area. *See* paging.

paging A method of managing *virtual memory. The logical address is subdivided into two fields: the low-order bits indicate a word or byte within a *page and the high-order bits indicate a particular page. Active pages are held in main memory and a page that is not active may be transferred out to the *swapping device. An *associative memory indicates the physical location within memory of those pages that are present. For pages that are not in memory the associative memory will contain a pointer to the backing-store home for that particular page. When reference occurs to a page, an interrupt is generated if the page is not in main memory and the operating system will transfer the relevant page from the swapping device into main memory.

paging drum One form of *swapping device used to hold the images of *pages no longer held in main memory in a *paging virtual management system. Paging drums typically are designed to have a relatively small capacity, low latency, and very high transfer rate.

painter's algorithm An algorithm for displaying three-dimensional scenes where the objects are rendered from the furthest to the nearest in much the same way as artists paint oil paintings. If objects intersect, they are broken into smaller parts so that no object can be both in front of and behind another.

paint program A computer-graphics system that defines pictures as though paint was being applied to a canvas. Various standard shapes are usually available plus the ability to draw freehand with various brushes and fill in areas with a range of patterns.

PAL *Abbrev. for* programmable array logic. A form of *PLA in whose *sum of products the products (*AND operations) are programmable, but the sums (*OR operations) are either fixed, or programmable only to a limited extent. In the latter case, any product terms that can take part in a programmable sum are called *shareable P terms*.

palette The choice of colors or shades available to a computer program. The size of the palette may vary from two (as in monochrome with no intervening graduations) to many millions. The colors in the palette are normally chosen from a much larger number, such as a choice of 256 chosen from 4096; the numbers are usually powers of 2.

palmtop computer A very small computer that can be hand-held and carried in the pocket. Palmtops feature a small *LCD screen and a compressed keyboard. Most models offer personal organizer, diary, address list, and calculator. Some models are programmable and can support file transfer to larger host computers. A palmtop is smaller than a *subnotebook.

paper slew (*UK name*: **paper throw**) A rapid and continuous movement of the paper in a line or serial printer such that the space of several line pitches occurs without printing. In high-performance line printers the slew rate may be 75 inches per second (190 cm/s).

paper tape An obsolete but once widely used data medium in the form of a continuous tape of paper with uniform width and thickness and specified physical attributes; other materials included laminates of paper and polyester. Data was encoded by punching patterns of holes on the tape. Generally a data character was punched as a coded set of holes across the tape at standard pitch. One-inch wide tape could accommodate characters of up to 8 bits. In addition to the data *tracks* running along the length of the tape, a full track of smaller-diameter sprocket or feed holes became an essential feature for synchronization. The data and feed holes were later sensed optically, thus the optical characteristics of the material became part of the specification. The tape was normally wound onto a core of standardized dimensions.

Punched paper tape was in use for data communication purposes (telex) prior to its use for computer input/output. It has also been used for programmed control of industrial equipment, and the preprogrammed control of continuous paper through computer printers.

paper tape I/O An obsolete but once widely used means of entering data into and extracting it out of a processor system using punched *paper tape as the medium. Paper tape I/O was adopted for many of the early computers: *tape punches* and *tape readers* were already in use for telex and were lower in cost than punched card equipment.

Early tape readers operated at about 10 characters per second (cps) by moving the tape in discrete steps, and sensed the holes by pressing a row of pins against the tape. The next generation of machines moved the tape continuously and sensed the holes via star-shaped wheels that rotated only when the points engaged a punched hole. Photoelectric sensing allowed speeds of up to 1500 cps to be achieved by 1975. There have been higher-speed readers but they were not able to stop within a character pitch. Tape punches as fast as 300 cps have been available but 110 cps was the more usual speed for volume output.

paper throw *UK name for* paper slew.

paper white display A *positive display where the background is white and the characters dark.

PAR *Acronym for* positive acknowledgment and retransmission. *See* backward error correction.

paradigm A model or example of the environment and methodology in which systems and software are developed and operated. For one operational paradigm there could be several alternative development paradigms. Examples are functional programming, logic programming, semantic data modeling, algebraic computing, numerical computing, object-oriented design, prototyping, and natural language dialogue.

Paradox *Trademark* A database management system for personal computers from Borland International.

paradoxical combinator *See* combinator.

parallel Involving the simultaneous transfer or processing of the individual parts of a whole, such as the bits of a character. *Compare* serial.

parallel access Access to a storage device in which a number of bits are transferred simultaneously rather than sequentially. For example, access to semiconductor memory almost invariably yields a number of bytes in parallel; by contrast access to the contents of a disk is usually serial in nature.

parallel adder A binary adder that is capable of forming sum and carry outputs for addend and augend words of greater than one bit in length by operating on corresponding pairs of addend and augend bits in parallel, i.e. at the same time. Parallel adders normally incorporate *carry lookahead logic to ensure that carry propagation between subsequent stages of addition does not limit addition speed. *See also* adder, serial adder.

parallel algorithm An algorithm designed to run "efficiently" on a parallel computer. A parallel algorithm may involve a greater number of arithmetic operations than a serial counterpart. It is designed, however, so that many arithmetic operations are independent and can be performed in parallel, i.e. simultaneously.

parallel arithmetic Operation upon more than one bit or digit of a number at the same time. *See* parallel adder.

parallel composition *See* process algebra.

parallel computer A computer that is capable of *parallel processing.

parallel in parallel out (PIPO) A term used to describe a *shift register that can be loaded in parallel and also read in parallel, in addition to which (by implication) data can enter and leave the device serially.

parallel input/output (PIO) A method of data transfer between devices, typically a computer and its peripherals, in which all the bits associated with a character or byte are presented to the interface simultaneously on separate conductors. There are usually other parallel conductors to carry the control signals. PIO is frequently used since it is compatible with the format used within the processor and enables high rates of data transfer to be achieved. When connection over any significant distance has to be made, the cost of the conductors and the associated drive circuits becomes significant and it is then preferable to convert to a *serial input/output.

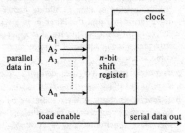

parallel data in: A_1, A_2, A_3 ⋯ A_n → n-bit shift register → clock, load enable, serial data out

Parallel in serial out

parallel in serial out (PISO) A term used to describe a class of digital device that can accept parallel n-bit data words and convert them into serial sequential n-bit data streams. These devices often consist of an n-bit *shift register that is parallel loaded with the data word (see diagram). This data is then clocked out of the register in serial form. Compare serial in parallel out.

parallel interface A connection point that comprises a set of individual electric connections, each having a specified function, usually either data or control. The transfer of data across the interface is achieved by one connection per bit of a data word or byte; for example for 8 bits there would be 8 connections in parallel. The control signals are also carried on individual electric connections in parallel with the data connections. Compare serial interface, serial-parallel.

parallel port An input/output socket on a computer or other device for a *parallel interface. A parallel port on a computer is often used for a parallel printer.

parallel printer A printer with a *parallel interface that connects to a computer by means of a parallel port. The original parallel printer interface (*Centronics) was unidirectional. Most parallel ports on current com-

puters will support data transfers in either direction.

parallel processing A term applied rather loosely to a number of rather similar concepts but with important detailed differences. The essence of parallel processing is that more than one particular *process is active at any given instant; however the term is often applied to a situation in which a large number of processes are potentially active but at any one instant only one is active. Strictly speaking the term parallel processing should only be applied where more than one processor is active among a group of processes at any one instant. In practice it is seldom used with this accurate connotation. See also concurrent programming.

parallel projection A *projection where the eyepoint is an ideal point (see homogeneous coordinates). The lines along which points are projected are all parallel (having the same ideal point), hence the name of the resulting projection.

parallel rewriting system See L-system.

parallel running Another term for parallel processing.

parallel shooting method See shooting method.

parallel transfer Transmission of multiple units of information concurrently. For example, if two computers connected by eight wires wish to communicate an 8 bit unit of information, the sending computer would present all eight bits at the same time, one bit per wire. The receiving computer would accept the bits from the wires, and recreate the 8 bit unit. Compare serial transfer.

parameter 1. Information passed to a subroutine, procedure, or function. The definition of the procedure is written using *formal parameters* to denote data items that will be provided when the subroutine is called, and the call of the procedure includes corresponding *actual parameters*. See also parameter passing. **2.** A quantity in a function or mathematical model whose value is selected or estimated according to the circumstances. Parameters should be distinguished from *constants*, which are fixed for all uses of the function or model, and *variables*, which are the actual recorded measurements involved in the function or model.

Many properties of functions and mathematical models can be deduced from their structural characteristics without reference to particular values; such properties include continuity, differentiality, and linear independence. A function or model for a specific purpose may be formulated by first establishing the appropriate structure (e.g. polynomial, differential equation of a certain form) in which particular values are not yet determined; such values are parameters of the function or model. Various techniques can then be used to find the most suitable value or range of values for the parameters when considering the observed set of data.

For simple models, such as elementary *probability distributions, parameters may be estimated from the *statistics of the sample, such as the mean and the variance. General principles of estimation, in which the criterion is the agreement between model and data, lead to procedures that may require iterative computing to obtain estimates; important examples are the method of *least squares and its generalization, the method of maximum *likelihood.

The *probability distribution of a parameter estimate is often required, and it is usual to compute its standard deviation, known as its standard error (*see* measures of variation), its *correlation with other parameter estimates, and its confidence limits where appropriate (*see* confidence interval).

parameter passing The mechanism used to pass *parameters to a procedure (subroutine) or function. The most common methods are to pass the value of the actual parameter (*call by value*), or to pass the address of the memory location where the actual parameter is stored (*call by reference*). The latter method allows the procedure to change the value of the parameter, whereas the former method guarantees that the procedure will not change the value of the parameter. Other more complicated parameter-passing methods have been devised, notably *call by name* in Algol 60, where the actual parameter is re-evaluated each time it is required during execution of the procedure.

parametric curve A curve defined as a function of independent variables. For example, a curve in 3-space may be thought of as the path of a moving point and can be described by the values of the position vector **r** at successive instants in time t. Adding higher-order terms in t past the linear form gives curves of different complexity. If t^2 appears only, then it is a quadratic; if t^3 appears it is a cubic, and so on.

parametric patch A *patch defined in the same way as a *parametric surface.

parametric surface A surface defined as a function of two parameters. For example, the successive positions and shapes of a deformable curve $\mathbf{r}=\mathbf{r}(u)$ moving in 3-space generate a surface where each point is characterized by the time v at which the moving curve passes through it and the value of the parameter u, which characterizes the point on the moving curve.

parametric techniques *See* nonparametric techniques.

parent A node A is the parent of node B in a *tree if B is the root of one of the subtrees of the tree rooted at A.

parent file (father file) *See* file recovery.

parenthesis-free notation *See* Polish notation, reverse Polish notation.

Parikh's theorem A theorem in formal language theory that concerns the nature of *context-free languages when order of letters is disregarded.

Let the alphabet Σ be the set $\{a_1,\ldots,a_n\}$. The *letter distribution*, $\phi(w)$, of a Σ-word w is the n-tuple

$$\langle N_1,\ldots,N_n\rangle$$

with N_i the number of occurrences of a_i in w. The *Parikh image*, $\phi(L)$, of a Σ-language L is

$$\{\phi(w) \mid w \in L\}$$

i.e. the set of all letter-distributions of words in L. L_1 and L_2 are *letter-equivalent* if

$$\phi(L_1) = \phi(L_2)$$

Letter distributions may be added component-wise as vectors. This leads to the following: a set S of letter distributions is *linear* if, for some distributions d and $d_1,\ldots,d_k$, S is the set of all sums formed from d and multiples of d_i. S is *semilinear* if it is a finite union of linear sets.

Parikh's theorem now states that if L is context-free $\phi(L)$ is semilinear. It can also be shown that $\phi(L)$ is semilinear if and only if L is letter-equivalent to a *regular language. Hence any context-free language is letter-equivalent to a regular language – although not all such languages are context-free.

parity A function that is computed to provide a check on a group of binary values (e.g. a word, byte, or character) by forming the modulo-2 sum of the bits in the group. The generated sum, a redundant value, is called the *parity bit*. The parity bit is 0 if the number of 1s in the original group was even. The parity bit is 1 if the number of 1s in the original group was odd.

The parity computation just defined will cause the augmented group of binary values (the original group plus the parity bit) to have an even number of 1s; this is called *even parity*. In some cases, hardware considerations make it desirable to have an odd number of 1s in the augmented group, and the parity bit is selected to cause the total number of 1s to be odd; this is called *odd parity*. *See also* parity check.

parity bit *See* parity.

parity check (odd-even check) The computation, or recomputation for verification, of a parity bit to determine if a prescribed parity condition is present. *See* parity. *See also* checksum.

parity-check code, parity-check matrix *See* linear code.

Parlog A parallel version of *Prolog.

parser (syntax analyzer) *See* parsing.

parser generator A program that accepts the syntactic description of a programming language and generates a *parser for that language. *See also* compiler-compiler, YACC.

parse tree (syntax tree) A tree defining the syntactic structure of a sentence in a *context-free language. The interior nodes are labeled by nonterminals of the context-free *grammar; the descendants of a node labeled by A, say, spell from left to right the

right-hand side of some production having left-hand side A. The leaf nodes of a parse tree may be terminals or nonterminals. If all the leaves are terminals then they spell from left to right a sentence of the language.

Parse tree

An example of a parse tree is shown in the diagram. It is assumed that the grammar in question has productions

$$A \to BC, B \to b, C \to cc$$

Note that it is conventional for the top of the tree to be its root and the bottom to be its leaves.

An early stage in compiling a program usually consists of generating a parse tree in which the constructs that make up the program are expressed in terms of the *syntax of the programming language.

parsing (syntax analysis) The process of deciding whether a string of input symbols is a sentence of a given language and if so determining the syntactic structure of the string as defined by a *grammar (usually *context-free) for the language. This is achieved by means of a program known as a *parser* or *syntax analyzer*. For example, a syntax analyzer of arithmetic expressions should report an error in the string

$$1-+2$$

since the juxtaposition of the minus and plus operators is invalid. On the other hand the string

$$1-2-3$$

is a valid arithmetic expression with structure specified by the statement that its subexpressions are

$$1,2,3 \text{ and } 1-2$$

(Note that 2–3 is not a subexpression.)

The input to a parser is a string of tokens supplied by a *lexical analyzer. Its output may be in the form of a *parse tree or a *derivation sequence. *See also* bottom-up parsing, top-down parsing, precedence parsing.

partial correctness, proof of *See* program correctness proof.

partial differential equations Differential equations that involve two or more independent variables, which in practice are often space and time variables. Because more than one independent variable is present, the "derivatives" that occur are partial derivatives. Such equations are widespread in science and model physical phenomena; they also arise frequently in the form of systems of equations. Simple examples in space and time are given by the heat conduction (or diffusion) equation,

$$\partial u/\partial t = \alpha\partial^2 u/\partial x^2$$

and the wave equation,

$$\partial^2 u/\partial t^2 = \beta\partial^2 u/\partial x^2$$

where α and β are physical constants. Steady-state phenomena in two space variables are typified by Laplace's equation,

$$\partial^2 u/\partial x^2 + \partial^2 u/\partial y^2 = 0$$

Appropriate initial and boundary conditions must be specified for these equations. The majority of partial differential equations that arise in practice require numerical techniques for their solution, the most successful and widely used being *finite–difference and *finite–element methods.

partial evaluation An *optimization technique. Parts of a program that have just enough data are evaluated, other parts are kept unchanged. For *logic programming languages, *unification and *resolution automatically support mechanisms for partial evaluation such as: unfolding of procedure calls with their bodies, forward and backward propagation of data structures, and evaluation of built-in functions wherever possible. Special techniques, for example *lazy evaluation, are necessary for partial evaluation of *functional languages.

partial function Roughly, a *function

$$f: S \to T$$

that holds for only a proper *subset of S. Strictly, if the subset over which it holds is R, then

$$f: R \to T$$

is a function. However it may be more convenient to work with S rather than with R. The set U,

$$U = S - R,$$

is nonempty, and f has no value (or rather has the *undefined value*) at points in U; f is then said to be *undefined* on U and *defined* for all elements in the subset R of S, i.e. in S but not in U.

Partial functions arise naturally in computing. When recursive definitions of functions are given, the definition can sometimes loop for certain parameters. Definitions of functions can also give rise to overflow or *exception situations. In these cases it is convenient to talk about partial functions. *Compare* total function.

partially ordered set *See* partial ordering.

partial ordering (partial order) A *relation defined between elements of some *set and satisfying certain properties, discussed below. It is basically a convenient generalization of the usual comparison operators, such as > or <, that are typically defined on the integers or the real numbers. The generalization also captures the essential properties of the set operations such as "is a subset of", the alphabetic ordering of strings, and so on. In *denotational semantics, partial orderings are used to express some *approximation relation* between partially defined computational objects.

Two different but equivalent definitions of a partial ordering are possible. The first is a generalization of the usual ≤ operation in which the relation must be a *transitive, *antisymmetric, and *reflexive relation defined on the set S. The second definition is a generalization of the usual < operation in which the relation must be a transitive, *asymmetric, and *irreflexive relation defined on S. A set with a partial ordering defined on it is called a *partially ordered set* or sometimes a *poset*.

partial recursive function A *function on the natural numbers that can be obtained from certain initial functions by a finite number of applications of *composition, *primitive recursion, and *minimization. In general the function may not be defined for certain values of its argument and so is a *partial function. The initial functions used are normally the *zero function, *successor function, and *projection functions. The partial recursive functions can be defined in many ways and, according to the *Church–Turing thesis, are precisely the functions on natural numbers that can be defined by algorithms. *See also* primitive recursive function.

particle system A means of modeling objects without boundaries, such as fire, cloud, smoke, gas, and water. An object is represented by a collection of elementary particles whose trajectories are traced. These individual particles move in three-dimensional space and change such attributes as color, transparency, and size as a function of time. Accurate modeling of the physics of the system is not attempted; instead *heuristic laws are used to approximate the desired effect.

partition 1. The term used in some operating systems to refer to a static area of memory for use by jobs, and also applied by association to the jobs executed in that area.
2. of a set. *See* covering.

partition-exchange sort *Another name for* quicksort.

Pascal A programming language in common though decreasing use. Pascal was designed as a tool to assist the teaching of programming as a systematic discipline. To that end it incorporates the *control structures of *structured programming – sequence, selection, and repetition – and *data structures – arrays, records, files, sets, and user-defined types. It is an austere language, with a minimum of facilities, but what is provided is so well suited to its task that the language is in practice more powerful than its more elaborate competitors.

Pascal was relatively easy to implement on a variety of machines since the Pascal compiler was written in Pascal. Used first as an educational tool, Pascal became a more-or-less standard language for the teaching of computer science. It spread into microcomputing in the form of the UCSD p-System: this is now little used, the dominant version in the micro world now being *Turbo Pascal. In 1982 ISO Standard Pascal was defined, but modern compilers, particularly Turbo

Pascal, implement an extended and nonstandard version of the language.

pass A single scan through a body of data, for example by a compiler reading the program text or a statistical package reading its data.

passband A range of frequencies with a lower limit and an upper limit, such that all frequencies between these limits (but not necessarily excluding other frequencies) are passed, with little attenuation, by a filter or a channel. *See also* bandwidth, band-pass filter, filtering.

pass instruction *Another name for* no-op instruction.

passive-matrix LCD *See* LCD.

passive optical network (PON) A network system of *optical fibers that contains no active (switching) elements.

passive star A network topology in which the outer *nodes connect to a single central node that does not process the message in any way but simply connects the transmission paths between the outer nodes. The central node is unlikely to fail due to its passive operation. It is thus unlikely that the entire network will be disabled during normal operation. *See also* active star, star network, network architecture.

password A unique character string held by each user, a copy of which is stored within the system. During *login an *authentication process takes place; the password entered by the intending user must correspond with the stored value before the user is accepted by the system. A good password should contain at least six to eight apparently random characters. Personal details, such as vehicle license numbers or relatives' names, are too easily guessed to be secure when used as passwords; even dictionary words are susceptible to exhaustive search. *See also* irreversible encryption.

paste To insert the contents of the *clipboard or the paste *buffer into a text or graphics object at a desired point.

patch 1. *Informal* A change to a program – usually to correct some error – that is introduced in a manner that emphasizes convenience and speed of change rather than security, and is intended to effect only a temporary repair. Even where a program is written in some high-level language, the patching might be carried out in machine-code terms on the compiled version of the program. Often during testing a series of minor errors will be corrected by patching in order to permit testing to continue without the delay of recompilation. Subsequently the corresponding changes will all be incorporated into the program source text at a single compilation.

2. (surface patch) A boundary piece of a surface. Patches are descriptions of three-dimensional shapes specified as bounded equations with criteria for joining other patches along their edges; for example, for smooth surfaces the patch equations must be differentiable at the edge. Complex surfaces are often broken down into patches. The whole surface is then described by the collection of patches. There is a wide variety of techniques for defining patches, for example *Coons patches and *Bézier patches. Patches are widely used in computer-aided design to describe curved surfaces and complex smooth geometries.

patchboard (plugboard) A matrix of sockets that can be interconnected manually by means of *patchcords*, i.e. cables with plugs attached to each end. Thus one socket can be *patched* to another. Patchcords are used to make temporary connections between devices, to program *analog computers, and to connect different peripheral devices to computer lines.

patchcord *See* patchboard.

patent A government grant to an inventor assuring him/her the exclusive right to exploit or sell the invention for a limited period (usually 20 years). Under the 1985 Guidelines for Examination in the European Patent Office, patent protection is available to inventive computer programs in Europe if the invention is expressed in terms of a programmed machine. Programs can be patented in the USA if they comply with the originality and other requirements of the US Patent Act. Inventive hardware is patentable in Europe and this leads to a serious flaw in the law; the same task can be performed by both software and hardware but the former is expressly excluded from protection by a clause in the European Patent Convention. The question of whether a program that performs the same task as a piece of patented hardware infringes the patent in the hardware has not yet been decided in Europe, nor has it been decided whether a PROM is a piece of software or hardware. Many of these inventions are now given a special type of copyright protection under new laws protecting chip masks. *See also* trade secrets.

path 1. A route between two vertices of a *graph, passing along edges and, in the case of a directed *graph, with attention paid to the direction along the edges. More formally there is a path between vertices V_0 and V_k if each pair

$$(V_i, V_{i+1}), i = 0,1...,k-1$$

is an edge of the graph and, in the case of a directed graph, is suitably directed.

In typical applications, the existence of paths between vertices indicates physical connections between them or perhaps logical connections or dependencies. *See also* cycle.

2. A sequence of instructions that may be performed in the execution of a program. A path through a program is equivalent to a traversal of the *control-flow diagram for that program from the start node or vertex to the end node of the graph.

3. *See* access path.

path testing A test strategy equivalent to finding all possible *paths through the *control-flow diagram of a program. Testing each path at least once is a typical test strategy, but for much real software complete path *test coverage would require an impracticably large test run/time. Path testing almost always requires more test runs than either *branch testing or *statement testing.

pattern An *equivalence class associated with a special kind of *relation defined on functions. Let

$$F = \{f \mid D \rightarrow A\}$$

be a set of functions mapping elements from some domain D into some set A, which can be regarded as an alphabet. With each function f in F is associated a *weight* $w(f)$, defined as the formal multiplication of all the images $f(x)$ under f. In effect $w(f)$ describes the number of occurrences of the different images in A.

An equivalence relation can then be defined between two functions of F in such a way that equivalent functions have equivalent weights, though the reverse is not in general true. The patterns of F are the equivalence classes that emerge from this equivalence relation.

The weight of a pattern is just the weight of any member of that pattern; the weight of the equivalence class $[f]$ containing f is just $w(f)$. The formal sum of the weights $w(f)$ taken over all the equivalence classes in F gives the *pattern inventory* of the set F. An important theorem due mainly to George Pólya indicates the close link between pattern inventory and *cycle index polynomial.

These ideas are often applied in *combinatorics and *switching theory. For example, a pattern inventory can indicate the number of essentially different wiring diagrams or logic circuits needed to realize the different possible logic functions.

pattern inventory *See* pattern.

pattern matching The technique of comparing two patterns in order to say how similar they are, or of comparing one pattern with a set of patterns in order to say to which member of the set it is most similar. This usually implies that a numerical value can be computed, as a *function of two patterns, by means of a pattern matching algorithm. The patterns concerned may be purely logical (i.e. *data structures) or physical (e.g. one-, two-, or three-dimensional images, represented as arrays). The term is commonly used where the patterns are *expressions represented either abstractly or as *strings. When the patterns are physical images, the term *pattern recognition is more common.

pattern recognition The process of detecting the presence of a specified pattern in a *signal, or assigning a probability to its possible presence. For example, visual pattern recognition involves the identification of two-dimensional patterns in a *gray-level array. The specification of one of more patterns is

done either analytically, or, more usually, by the provision of *templates, which are model patterns for comparison. Pattern recognition employs the techniques of *digital signal processing, *image processing, and *artificial intelligence.

payload of a cell or packet in a network. *Another name for* body.

PC *Abbrev. for* personal computer, most often used to mean an *IBM-compatible computer as opposed to other architectures. The abbreviation is sometimes used however to refer to any variety of personal computer, although the unabbreviated form is more common in this context.

PCB (or pcb) *Abbrev. for* printed circuit board. *See* printed circuit.

PC card *Another name for* PCMCIA card. *See* PCMCIA.

PC clone *See* clone.

PC-compatible *See* IBM-compatible.

PCI *Abbrev. for* personal computer interface. A standardized interface for personal computers that allows their interconnection with a range of peripherals.

PCI bus A *local bus originated by Intel and increasing in popularity for personal computers needing a high-performance local bus.

PCL *Abbrev. for* printer control language. PCL was originally introduced by Hewlett-Packard in their early laser printers and has evolved as the de facto standard for high-quality printers. The commands cover text, formatting, paper handling, and graphics. The language has developed over time and is often used to define the facilities offered by a printer, as in "This printer supports PCL-5".

PCM *Abbrev. for* pulse code modulation.

PCMCIA *Abbrev. for* Personal Computer Memory Card International Association, a body set up in 1989 whose members include hardware and chip manufacturers, software houses, and system integrators. The PCMCIA has defined the specifications for peripherals of credit-card size, known as *PCMCIA cards*, that can be used for a variety of upgrades. Many portable computers now offer *PCMCIA slots* for interfacing external peripherals such as *hard disks, *modems, *flash memory, or network interfaces. PCMCIA slots come in different thicknesses labelled I, II, and III. *See also* add-in card.

PCMCIA card, slot *See* PCMCIA.

p-code An intermediate language designed as the target language for *UCSD Pascal and other languages in the *p-system software.

PCTE *Abbrev. for* portable common tool environment. An international standard (ISO 13719) in three parts. Part 1 defines an abstract specification for a *PTI (public tool interface) that includes access to an *object management system including file contents, and facilities to support distribution, secure access, etc. Part 2 defines a binding to the C programming language. Part 3 defines a binding to the Ada programming language. The same definitions are also contained in the 3rd edition of ECMA standards 149, 158, and 162 respectively.

PCTE was originally developed by an ESPRIT project partially funded by the EEC in the 1980s. The current standard has evolved from the original specification under the influence of several international initiatives, and incorporates ideas from PCTE+ developed by NATO and CAIS–A developed by the US Department of Defense. There are several implementations available on a variety of platforms.

Work is progressing on the definition of several enhancements to the standard, including object-oriented and fine-grain extensions, and a binding to the CORBA interface definition language is planned.

PDA 1. *Abbrev. for* personal digital assistant.
2. *Abbrev. for* pushdown automaton.

PDH *Abbrev. for* plesiochronous digital hierarchy. An interim set of standards and products for data transmission, which allows the combination of a number of lower-speed channels (*tributaries*) into a composite signal transmitted on a synchronous higher-speed bearer. In principle, the data rate on the high-speed channel will simply be the aggregate of the data rates on the lower-speed channels; if the data rates on these channels are the same, or are simple multiples of some common basic rate, this aggregate rate will be a multiple of the data rate on the tributary channels. In practice, the data rates on the tributaries will not be exact, and to allow for this the high-speed channel must have an overall data rate slightly greater than the sum of the data rates on the tributaries. Since the high-speed channel is strictly synchronous, it is necessary to insert "stuffing" bits, which are then subsequently discarded. Further, at each point where data enters or leaves the high-speed channel, the composite signal must be completely broken down into its components, data inserted or extracted, and the composite signal re-created. This adds to the complexity and hence the cost of the system. *See also* SDH.

PDL 1. *Abbrev. for* program design language.
2. *Abbrev. for* page description language.

PDN *Abbrev. for* public data network.

PDP series A family of machines manufactured by *Digital Equipment Corporation.

PE *Abbrev. for* phase-encoded. *See* tape format.

peak-to-average ratio The ratio of the highest value of a quantity to its average value, used as a measure to indicate the variability of the quantity. For example, in a computer network that connects a user's workstation to a file server, the traffic is typically made up of long periods during which very little traffic flows, interspersed with periods of intense activity when the system transfers a large volume of data in a short time. A measurement of the average data rate over a period of many minutes may show a low apparent data rate, and give a misleading impression of the high data rate needed to provide satisfactory response to a request for a file movement or to refresh a user's screen. The peak-to-average ratio indicates the extent to which the traffic consists of bursts of traffic.

Peano arithmetic An axiomatic theory, based on first-order logic, about the natural numbers. Its axioms are first-order statements about the simple arithmetic operations of successor $n+1$, addition $n+m$, and multiplication $n.m$, together with the principle of *induction. A great variety of facts in mathematics and computer science can be reduced to, or can be coded as, statements about natural numbers, and Peano arithmetic is a strong enough theory to express and prove formally the majority of basic results. However, *Gödel's incompleteness theorems show that there are first-order statements that are true of the natural numbers but are not provable in Peano arithmetic, or its extensions. Although many algebras satisfy the axioms of Peano arithmetic, there is only one *computable algebra that satisfies the axioms and that is the so-called *standard model of Peano arithmetic*, namely the algebra

$$(\{0,1,2, \ldots\} \mid 0, n+1, n+m, n.m)$$

peek To examine the contents of an absolute memory location from a high-level language, usually by means of a function of this name whose argument is the address in question. *Compare* poke.

peephole optimization *See* optimization (in programming).

peer-to-peer protocol A *protocol that governs the exchange of information between entities operating at the same level in a protocol stack. *See* seven-layer reference model.

pel *Another name for* *pixel *or* picture element.

penetration A technique of *security evaluation.

Pentium *Trademark. See* Intel.

percentile The value below which an integral percentage of observations lie: the pth percentile is the value below which p% of observations lie. The 50th percentile is the *median and the 25th and 75th percentiles are known as *quartiles*.

perception An interpretation process in which raw sensory signals are converted into meaningful symbols. Human perception is still poorly understood but inspires research into *image understanding, *pattern recognition, and other intelligent systems that attempt to convert complex sensory data into meaningful interpretations of objects and events in the world. Related philosophical problems include the *symbol grounding problem*, which concerns the semantic content of symbols and how they are related to sensation.

perceptron An early type of single-layer *neural network. An input array is covered by a set of *feature detectors whose outputs are weighted, summed, and then thresholded to give a single binary output. A perceptron learning algorithm can be used to adjust the weights during training on examples from pattern classes so that new inputs may be correctly classified. Mathematical analyses of perceptrons in the 1970s exposed severe limitations and halted research on neural networks. Now, however, perceptrons have been superseded by multilayer neural networks that do not suffer from those limitations.

perfect codes *Error-correcting codes in which the Hamming spheres surrounding the codewords entirely fill the *Hamming space without overlap. These spheres all have radius e, where the code can correct e errors, and their centers (codewords) are separated from each other by a distance of $(2e + 1)$; thus the spheres have no points (words) in common where they touch, but their surfaces are separated by unit distance with no points between them. Perfect codes attain the *Hamming bound exactly.

The only *binary *linear perfect codes are the *repetition codes, the *Hamming codes, and the (23,12) *Golay code.

perfective maintenance *See* software maintenance.

perfect matching A term used in graph theory. A matching of a *graph is any subset of its edges such that no two members of the subset are adjacent. A perfect matching is a matching in which every *vertex of the graph is an end-point of some element of the matching.

performance model A model created to define the significant aspects of the way in which a proposed or actual system operates in terms of resources consumed, contention for resources, and delays introduced by processing or physical limitations (such as speed, bandwidth of communications, access latency, etc.). The creation of a model can provide insight into how a proposed or actual system will or does work.

A model will often be created specifically so that it can be interpreted by a software tool that simulates the system's behavior, based on the information contained in the performance model. Such tools provide further insight into the system's behavior, and can be used to identify bottlenecks or hot spots where the design is inadequate. Solutions to the problems identified might involve provision of more physical resources, or change in the structure of the design.

performance monitoring Measurement, by direct observation or by programmed processes, of activity at various points in a computer system to find out where bottlenecks and delays are taking place. Results are used for system *reconfiguration in order to improve overall performance.

performance testing The specification for a system will usually have some requirements for how well the system should perform certain functions, additional to a statement of required functions. Thus while *functional testing* will, for example, demonstrate that the sum and average of a set of numbers will be calculated, *performance testing* will concentrate on how well the calculation is done (speed, accuracy, range, etc.). Typically, performance testing will consist of one or more of the following.

Stress and timing tests, for example measuring and demonstrating the ability to meet peak service demand measured by number of users, transaction rate, volume of data, and the maximum number of devices all operating simultaneously.

Configuration, compatibility, and recovery tests, for example using a combination of the slowest processor, the minimal memory, the smallest disk, and the last version of the operating system, and checking that other valid combinations of processor, memory, disk, communications, and operating systems will interoperate and recover from faults.

Regression tests, showing that the new system will perform all the required application functions of the system it replaces.

period The time required for a *periodic* waveform – i.e. a waveform recurring at fixed intervals – to repeat itself.

periodogram In *time series analysis, a diagram showing the most important cyclical regularity in the data. Peaks in the diagram correspond to periods of cycles that most closely correlate with the data. Interpretation of periodograms is by spectral analysis.

peripheral Any device, including I/O devices and backing store, that is connected to a computer. The term originated in the mainframe era when all the computing was centralized and the input/output functions were attached around the periphery of the installation. Since the advent of smaller cheaper computers, printers, etc., the term peripheral is seldom used.

peripheral processor The name used in CDC systems for a special-purpose processor used to control peripheral units. (These processors go by a variety of names: on IBM systems they are referred to as *channels, and have a much more restricted order code than a CDC peripheral processor.) In all cases the essence of the peripheral processor is that its order code is specifically tailored to the requirements of transferring information between main memory and the peripheral device or devices controlled by the peripheral processor.

PERL *Acronym for* practical extraction and report language. A *scripting language for scanning text files, extracting information, and printing reports. Originally developed in the UNIX environment, implementations for other platforms are now available, including MS-DOS.

permanent error of peripheral storage. *See* error rate.

permanent virtual circuit (PVC) *See* virtual circuit.

permutation of a *set S. A *bijection of S onto itself. When S is finite, a permutation can be portrayed as a rearrangement of the elements of S. The number of permutations of a set of n elements is $n!$

A permutation of the elements of $\{1,2,3\}$ can be written

$$1\ 2\ 3$$
$$2\ 1\ 3$$

indicating that 1 is mapped into 2, 2 into 1, and 3 into 3. Alternatively the above can be written, using a *cycle notation, as (1 2); this implies that the element 3 is unaltered but that 1 is mapped into 2 and 2 into 1.

For collections of elements in which repeated occurrences of items may exist, a permutation can be described as a rearrangement of elements in which each element appears with the same frequency as before.

permutation group A *subgroup of the group that is formed from the set, S_n, of all *permutations of n distinct elements and on which is defined the dyadic operation of *composition of functions. The full group S_n is usually called the *symmetric group* and possesses $n!$ elements. Every finite group is isomorphic to some permutation group.

permutation matrix A square matrix in which each column contains precisely one nonzero element, which is equal to unity. If P is an $n \times n$ permutation matrix and x is a vector of n elements, the vector Px will be a *permutation of the elements of x.

persistence The property of data that continues to exist after a process accessing it has finished. The term is usually used for data that is preserved when the computer is switched off, and when the notation for accessing it is substantially the same as for other data. Persistence shows that the existence of a data item is distinct from its accessibility, which is determined by the *scope of its declaration. By implication, *persistent data* is preserved in *backing store, and special techniques are often needed to store and access the data values and to mark their creation and destruction.

persistent data *See* persistence.

persistent programming The style of programming, with appropriate language and run-time support, that recognizes persistent data (*see* persistence). It is based on the view that persistence is orthogonal to *data type, so that programmers should not be restricted in the types for which persistent data may be created, and that with appropriate *declarations no special statements should be required to handle persistent data; in particular there should be no explicit input/output operations for such data.

A *persistent programming language* has constructs that define the lifetimes of data

objects (as well as their types), without prescribing how they are stored. Programs that are written in such a language reference and use data in the same way whether or not it is persistent. (In contrast, programming using a *database or *filing system requires explicit operations that read the persistent data from backing store into *main memory, and subsequently write it out if it has been modified.)

personal computer A general-purpose single-user *microcomputer designed to be operated by one person at a time (*see also* PC). Personal computers range from cheap domestic or hobby machines with limited memory and program storage and an ordinary TV as the display device, to extremely sophisticated machines with powerful processors, large-capacity disk storage, high-resolution color-graphics systems, high-speed network interfaces, and many other options. In scientific, engineering, and business environments the personal computer is superseding the *terminal connected to a time-sharing system, especially since communication ports and network connections allow transfers of data between the personal computer and other computers as well as *client/server computing. The development of the personal computer is a consequence of the continually increasing ratio of computing power to cost coupled with decreasing weight, size, and power consumption.

personal digital assistant (PDA) A pocketbook-sized computer with a combined touch-sensitive membrane covering an LCD panel as its main input and output device. The user writes on the screen with a penlike stylus, and the objects drawn are echoed on the screen. It is possible to interpret handwriting by means of character-recognition techniques, to store what is written or drawn as images for later retrieval, or for the screen to display menus and check boxes so that selections may be made with the stylus. Applications include calendars, diaries, and personal organizer functions. Communications with other computers are also available.

perspective projection A *projection where the eyepoint is a Euclidean point. The lines along which points are projected all pass through the eyepoint.

PERT *Abbrev. for* performance evaluation and review techniques. Management techniques for planning, scheduling, and controlling projects. Dependencies are drawn as directed *graphs to show the logical sequence of activities that must occur before a project can be completed. *See also* critical path method.

PERT chart A method of expressing the dependence of distinct activities for project management (*see* PERT). The chart is drawn as a *weighted directed *graph where each edge represents a specific activity and its weight is the time required to complete that activity. The activity can only be started when those edges (activities) incident to it have been completed. The chart has one start point and one termination point.

The critical path for time to project completion is calculated together with the float, earliest start, and latest start times on individual activities. Some PERT tools allow different types of resource to be allocated to an activity, with limits on total resource of each type, and for "hammocks" (dummy activities) to be used to monitor project milestones and resource usage. *See also* activity network, critical path method.

PES *Acronym for* programmable electronic system. A term used in certain official guidelines and standards to describe a complete computer-based system. For example in an industrial process-control application, the input sensors, the computer hardware and software, and the output actuators would comprise the PES.

Petri net A model of a concurrent system that is expressed in a specific graphical notation and can be used to explore certain properties of the system. A Petri net consists of a set of *places*, a set of *transition bars*, and a set of directed edges. Each transition bar has an associated set of input places and an associated set of output places. A transition bar is linked to each of its input places by a directed edge from the place to the bar, and to each of its output places by a directed edge from the bar to the place.

States of the concurrent system are represented by the presence of *tokens* at places, with a specific state being represented by a specific allocation of tokens to places. Such an allocation is called a *marking*.

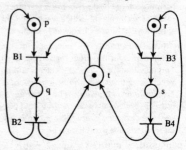

Example of a Petri net

The example net shown in the diagram employs the conventional graphical notation. Places are represented by the circles labeled p ... t, transition bars are represented by the lines labeled B1 ... B4, and the initial marking is shown by the use of dots to represent tokens.

Transition bars represent possible changes of state in the concurrent system. A transition bar can only *fire* (i.e. the change of state occur) when each of its input places holds at least one token. When a bar fires it removes one token from each of its input places and deposits one token at each of its output places. Thus the combination of the input and output places for a transition bar represents both the conditions under which the change of state can occur and the effects of that state change.

The firing of a transition bar is an indivisible event and simultaneous firing of two or more bars is therefore not possible. When the state is such that two or more bars are candidates to fire, each candidate must be considered individually.

By starting from an initial marking that represents an initial state of the system and applying a straightforward procedure that generates other markings that can be reached from this initial marking, it is possible to explore the possible states of the system and the ways in which these states can be reached. For example, both deadlock states and unproductive looping can be readily detected, and in general it is possible to check that the behavior of the system is as expected. However, while the procedure for generating reachable markings is straightforward, attempts at full analysis are often frustrated by the sheer number of such markings, and this can be infinite. Thus the general problem of determining whether a given marking is reachable from a given initial state is undecidable.

With the initial marking shown in the example net, both B1 and B3 are able to fire. Suppose that B1 fires. This removes the tokens from places p and t, and deposits a single token at place q. Now only B2 is able to fire. (B3 is no longer able to fire because there is no longer a token at place t.) When B2 fires, the token is removed from place q and new tokens are deposited at places p and t, thus restoring the initial marking. Should B3 now fire, a single token is deposited at place s, and B4 then fires, again restoring the initial marking. (This net may be viewed as modeling a system in which two processes compete for a shared resource. Availability of the resource is represented by the presence of a token at place t. Relevant states of one process, holding the resource or not holding the resource, are represented by tokens at places p and q respectively. Similarly tokens at places r and s represent relevant states of the other process.) .

Petri nets were devised in the early 1960s by C. A. Petri.

PGA 1. *Abbrev. for* programmable gate array. A form of *PLA that has products (*AND operations), but no *sums of products (*OR operations).

2. *Abbrev. for* pin grid array.

PGP *Abbrev. for* pretty good privacy. A utility that allows an e-mail user to encrypt an outgoing mail message using a version of a public key encryption system (*see* cryptography). Although a PGP encrypted message might be decoded by a user with access to very powerful computing resources, the system offers a more than adequate level of protection for the normal user.

phase of a regularly recurring (periodic)

quantity. The stage or state of development of the quantity. It can be expressed, in the form of an angle, as the fraction of a cycle of the periodic quantity that has been completed, with respect to a fixed datum point. Two sinusoidally varying quantities of the same frequency can be *in phase* (reaching corresponding phases at the same time) or *out of phase*. In the latter case the difference in phase – the *phase difference* – is usually expressed as an angle.

phase change An optical recording technology where the process of writing changes the area of the medium that is to represent a 1 bit from one physical state to another, e.g. from crystalline to amorphous, rather than producing a change in its external configuration or state of magnetization. This technology can be used either reversibly or nonreversibly, in some cases in the same medium by adjustment of the power of the laser beam. Phase change has the potential to produce a low-cost storage medium, but technical difficulties have delayed its introduction.

phase-change inkjet printer *See* inkjet printer.

phase-encoded (PE) *See* tape format.

phase-locked loop (PLL) *See* disk format.

phase modulation (PM) *See* modulation.

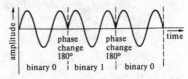

Phase shift keying, 2-phase modulation

phase shift keying (PSK) A method for representing digital data with analog signals by changing the phase of the analog carrier to represent the digital information (*see* diagram). It is a type of *modulation.

There are two ways of detecting the phase information in a signal. *Fixed-reference PSK* assigns a meaning to each phase position. The *demodulator uses a signal source of the same frequency to compare with the incoming signal and detect its phase. *Differential PSK* assigns meaning to phase changes, e.g. a phase change of 180° could be taken to mean a 1, while no phase change means a 0. No comparison with another wave is needed in the demodulator.

The amount of information associated with a phase or phase change depends on the number of discrete phases that the carrier may assume. If the carrier may assume two phases then each phase or phase change represents a single bit. If four phases are used then each phase or phase change represents a different combination of two bits. The greater the number of discrete phases, the more difficult it is to generate, transmit, and detect the analog signal, thus the cost is higher; for this reason, *modems that require eight or more discrete signals usually combine the phase changes with changes in amplitude in order to make the signals more distinct.

See also digital data transmission.

PHIGS *Acronym for* Programmer's Hierarchical Interactive Graphics System, the ISO/IEC 9592 standard. Many of the concepts of *GKS are present in PHIGS (workstations, input model, attribute handling, etc.). However, PHIGS is primarily a three-dimensional standard aimed at providing high-quality views of graphics objects that are hierarchical and made up of many subparts (e.g. a vehicle). Lighting and rendering extensions together with a number of high-level primitives are included in Part 4 of the standard, called *PHIGS PLUS. Part 4 was published some time after the initial three parts. A major revision of PHIGS is in progress (1995).

PHIGS PLUS Part 4 of the *PHIGS standard; PLUS stands for plus lumière und shading. PHIGS PLUS adds lighting and shading calculations to the rendering capabilities of PHIGS, together with a set of primitives to allow surfaces to be rendered realistically or to visualize parameters associated with those surfaces.

phoneme A small element of real speech that is linguistically significant. The transitions between phonemes are acoustically but not linguistically significant. Phonemes may be used by means of concatenation to produce artificial speech. The particular problem with phoneme concatenation is how to actually perform the join since fluent speech requires fluent transitions. *Diphones* are the elements of speech between the centers of adjacent phonemes; they include the transitions, and are more useful for *speech synthesis.

Phong shading A shading model that assumes light sources are points. It allows some of the light hitting a surface to be absorbed. A parameter defines how close a particular surface is to a perfect reflector thus modeling both mirror-like and dull surfaces. *See also* specular reflection.

Photo-CD *Trademark* A system developed jointly by Philips and Kodak for storing high-resolution photographic color images on a compact disk. About 100 35 mm slides can be stored on one disk. Images are stored at five different resolutions, the highest being 3072 by 2048. *See also* CD-ROM format standards.

photorealism Realistic representation in a computer-graphics image so that it looks as though it was produced by photographing a scene.

phototransistor *See* optoelectronics.

phrase-structure grammar (PSG) A *grammar that contains rules which are capable of both generating strings of linguistic elements and providing a constituent analysis of the strings. In their original form, phrase-structure grammars took the form of a set of rewrite rules, for example

$$S \rightarrow NP + VP$$

(which reads rewrite S as NP (noun phrase) + VP (verb phrase)). Various distinctions have been made between different classes of phrase-structure grammar, primarily between *context-sensitive and *context-free grammars.

physical Actual, or involving actual entities, as opposed to logical or conceptual.

physical layer of network protocol function. *See* seven-layer reference model.

pi benchmark A program that uses integer arithmetic to calculate π to some arbitrary accuracy. It is used as a *benchmark to measure the time to complete calculation to a stated accuracy or to measure the number of digits accuracy achieved per second of execution.

pick A type of input to a graphics system that identifies a graphical output primitive or set of primitives that have been indicated by the operator. *See also* logical output device.

Pick An IBM operating system named after its original developer. The system has an integrated database system, and is intended for database applications on workstations and small systems. Pick is designed to be portable between different hardware platforms, and has also been implemented as a subsystem under other operating systems.

pick list A list of choices that can be displayed within a *window and from which normally only one item may be *selected. It may, for example, be a list of files that may be opened within a directory.

pico- (symbol: p) A prefix to a unit, indicating a submultiple of a millionth of a millionth, 10^{-12}, of that unit, as in picosecond.

picture The principal means of defining *data types in *Cobol. The syntax of an elementary data item is defined by means of a character string. Simple examples are "A(20)" defining a string of 20 alphabetic characters, or "9(4)" defining a string of 4 digits. Particularly in the case of numeric items that are to be printed or displayed, the PICTURE clause provides considerable power: it is possible, for instance, to specify the position of the decimal point (explicit or implicit); the presence and position of the sign (+ or –) or of currency symbols; filling out digit strings with zeros or blanks (leading, embedded, or trailing); insertion of commas into long numbers. The MOVE verb, which is used to assign the value of one variable to another, automatically carries out format conversion according to the picture of the receiving item.

picture processing *Another name for* image processing.

PID controller A device used for continuous control of industrial plant, based on combining proportional, integral, and derivative contributions (hence PID) from the discrep-

ancy between an actual value and the desired value. The PID control process is also called *3-term control*.

piecewise continuous Denoting a curve or surface divided into a number of pieces that are continuous to a specified degree across the joins.

piecewise smooth Denoting a surface that can be divided into a number of pieces, each of which satisfies a smoothness constraint.

PIF *Acronym for* program information file. A file used in the *Windows system to hold information as to how a non-Windows application is to be run and what resources are to be allocated to it.

piggyback acknowledgments *Acknowledgments carried in a special field in regular data messages. Thus, as long as there is data ready for both directions of a circuit, no extra messages are needed to carry acknowledgments.

PILOT *Acronym for* programmed inquiry, learning, or teaching. A special-purpose language for developing *computer-assisted learning (CAL) software.

pin (or **PIN**) *Abbrev. for* personal identification number. A number issued to a holder of a *magnetic card, for example a credit card or bank card, that the card holder is required to keep secret. Together with the magnetic card the pin acts as an identifier and password to access computer-based services such as *ATMs, *EPOSs, or *EFTS.

pincushion distortion A distortion that makes a displayed image appear to bulge inward on all four sides.

ping A short message that an application sends from one system on a network to another (or, as a verb, to send such a message), primarily to establish whether the receiver is active, or the network linking sender and receiver is operational. A system receiving a ping will typically respond by immediately retransmitting the incoming message back to the original sender. (The word ping may be an acronym for packet Internet gopher or possibly imitative in origin.)

pin grid array (PGA) A form of *integrated circuit packaging, capable of providing up to several hundred connections to one chip. Connections to the device are made by means of an array of pins underneath the package. The array may be formed as several parallel rows of pins at two opposite sides of the package or around all four sides, depending on the size and complexity of the IC.

pin header A device similar in form to a *DIP but containing no circuitry. Instead each leg is extended vertically through the package allowing pins to be connected together in any configuration by soldering small pieces of wire across the relevant pins. A pin header is more flexible but clumsier than a *DIL switch. It is sometimes used for making external connections to a *printed circuit board.

Pink Book The *coloured book that defines a network service operating over a CSMA/CD bearer network. *See* Ethernet.

pinout A description of the electrical function of each pin on an *integrated-circuit package.

PIO *Abbrev. for* parallel input/output.

pipe A command-line operator available in some operating systems whereby a number of *processes (tasks), whose names are listed sequentially, are activated concurrently so that each process (after the first-named) accepts as its input the output from the immediately previously named process. The operating system provides *buffering of data between the processes, and so the user is relieved of the necessity of specifying temporary files for receiving and delivering the data. Pipes are a notable feature of *UNIX. *See also* command-line interface, filter.

pipeline processing A form of processing – analogous to a manufacturing production line – in which the time required to pass through some functional unit (e.g. a floating point ALU) of a computer system is longer than the intervals at which data may enter that functional unit, i.e. the functional unit performs its process in several steps. When the first step is completed, the results are passed to a second step that uses separate hardware; the first-step hardware is thus free to begin processing new data. This provides

fast throughput for sequential processes, but at the expense of complicating the control unit, which must keep account of operations that are simultaneously in progress. In the past, cost restricted such techniques to supercomputers, which require maximum performance, and to vector processors, which provide long orderly sequences of data as input to pipeline processors. Pipelining is now common in modern microprocessors, providing high performances at a low cost conferred by advances in VLSI circuit technology.

pipelining *Pipeline processing itself, or the use of pipeline processing.

PIPO *Abbrev. for* parallel in, parallel out. *See also* shift register.

P/ISDN *See* ISDN.

PISO *Abbrev. for* parallel in, serial out. *See also* shift register.

pixel (pel) *Derived from* picture element. One of the elements in an *array that is holding pictorial information. It contains data representing either directly or indirectly the brightness and possibly color of a small region of the image. *See also* digital image.

pixel aspect ratio The ratio of width to height of a pixel on a display. Some devices have rectangular pixels, making curve and line drawing more difficult.

pixelblt (pronounced pixelblit) *Short for* pixel block transfer. An operation that can rapidly change the contents of a *pixmap and thus the shade or color of the displayed image. Pixelblt is similar to *bitblt but a number of bits representing a gray-scale or color are used in the operation, rather than a single bit.

pixelization (space quantization) *See* quantization. *See also* discrete and continuous systems.

pixmap An array of elements, with many bits per element, that map one to one to the color or gray-scale image on a *raster display. The elements may not specify the color or grayscale directly but may instead be indices into a lookup table that specifies the color or grayscale. Typically, 24 bits are used for each element to specify three 8-bit indices into color tables that define the *RGB components of the color for that pixel.

pizza-box A piece of equipment, such as a computer system box, whose dimensions are roughly in the same proportions and size as the cardboard boxes used to transport pizzas, i.e. the depth and width approximately equal and very much greater than the height. Such an enclosure can be conveniently placed beneath a *monitor on a desk.

PL/1 *See* PL/I.

PL/360 The first machine-oriented high-level language (or *MOHLL), developed by Wirth as an implementation tool for Algol-W on the IBM System/360.

PLA *Abbrev. for* programmed logic array, or programmable logic array. A read-only device that is a generalized *combinational circuit and may include a *sequential circuit. By means of connections on a semiconductor device, the PLA usually provides a "programmable" *sum of products function that feeds an output register, and sometimes an internal register. When the internal register is used to provide part of the input variables, the PLA is a sequential circuit; otherwise it is a combinational circuit.

The product terms in the function can be thought of as representing values that are to be acted upon when they occur; thus the PLA is a form of fixed *associative memory or a specialized *table lookup device adapted to the situation when the truth table has sparse entries.

Since the PLA is made specific only by the interconnections, it represents a general-purpose building block that requires changes in only one or two steps of the production process to provide different functionality. PLAs can be programmed at the time of manufacture; alternatively they may be programmed by the user, and are then called *field-programmable. See also* programmable device.

plaintext *See* cryptography.

planar graph A *graph that can be drawn on paper (with points representing vertices and lines joining vertices representing edges) in such a way that edges intersect only at vertices.

plasma display *See* plasma panel.

plasma panel (plasma display) A form of *display used in association with computer systems in which light output is produced from the interaction between an electric current and an ionized inert gas such as neon. The display consists of a matrix of individual cells, one per pixel. A typical monochrome or gray-scale display generates red or orange light. Color systems generate ultraviolet radiation, which excites phosphors (red, green, and blue) on the surface of the display; the excited phosphors emit light on return to the ground state.

Plasma panels are rugged, largely immune to external fields, and do not suffer from *flicker, but have proved too expensive for general computer use. Fabrication of large displays is possible. The device is essentially bistable so no special circuitry is required to isolate individual cells from their neighbors.

platform A computer system whose hardware and software make it sufficiently different from all other computers for it to be necessary to generate unique software versions for it. For instance, the Apple Macintosh, PC-compatibles, and Sun SPARC-Stations are all different platforms.

platten The roller, often made of a hard rubber-like substance, used in some impact printers to provide a backing for the stationery. The platten may also drive the paper when feeding between lines or forms (often known as *friction drive*). The platten is sometimes provided with sprockets to drive continuous stationery or may be used with separate paper *tractors.

platter The metallic substrate of a rigid magnetic disk.

plausible reasoning Automatic reasoning techniques in *artificial intelligence that involve some degree of risk or uncertainty and so cannot guarantee absolutely correct solutions. Examples include the use of *probability methods, *abduction, and most *machine-learning techniques. Typical plausible reasoning problems, such as diagnosis, illustrate their differences from the classic algorithmic/logical paradigm.

player *Informal* Usually, the software that will display the contents of an *HTML file; the contents may be text, or digitally encoded audio, images, or video, and the player will present the material using the appropriate hardware. *See also* World Wide Web.

PL/C, PL/CT *See* PL/I.

PLD *Abbrev. for* programmable logic device. A form of *PAL in which the outputs emerge through output cells, an output cell being a *logic circuit that is programmable for a number of characteristics. These characteristics include the choice of *positive or *negative logic, whether the output can be used as an input, whether it is to be fed back into the circuit, whether it is to emerge via a *latch, and whether it is to be *tri-state.

plesiochronous digital hierarchy *See* PDH.

plex A *multilinked structure consisting of a collection of cells of various sizes linked together by pointers into essentially a connected directed *graph, possibly containing cycles. *See also* list processing.

PL/I A programming language designed initially by the IBM users' group SHARE, and adopted by IBM as a major product. PL/I was intended to replace all pre-existing programming languages, incorporating the best features of Cobol, Fortran, and Algol 60. The resulting language is large and complex: it was taken up by only a few other companies, and has had only limited acceptance among IBM users.

PL/I was adopted as a teaching language by a number of universities, notably Cornell, who produced their own versions, PL/C and PL/CT. It was also used as a basis for the microcomputer language *PL/M.

PLL *Abbrev. for* phase-locked loop. *See* disk format.

PL/M A systems programming language for microcomputers in the Intel family. It is based on and bears a strong resemblance to *PL/I. It is now superseded by C.

plotter An output device for translating information from a computer into pictorial or graphical form on paper or a similar medium. There are a wide variety of plotters to match the differing requirements for size,

accuracy, speed, and other attributes such as color.

One of the simplest implementations is a *flat-bed plotter*. One or more pens are mounted on a carriage that can be moved to precise positions on a bar that spans the width of the medium, i.e. the x-axis. The bar is mounted so that it can be moved precisely on tracks that lie parallel to the lengthwise edge of the medium, i.e. the y-axis. It is thus possible to move the pen to any point that lies within the available range of x and y coordinates. The pen can either touch the surface as it moves, thus producing a line, or it can be lifted off the surface as it moves. When drawing a diagonal line the computer generally has to provide only the coordinates of the start and finish points.

Although large flatbed plotters are produced it is often preferable to use the *drum plotter* configuration for large drawings, or for a sequence of drawings. The drum plotter has an arrangement similar to the flatbed plotter for moving the pen across the width of the medium, but the bar is fixed parallel to the axis of a drum. The medium is wrapped around part of the drum surface and is often wound onto take-up spools on either side of the drum axis. The medium has holes punched at its edges that engage with pintles on the drum and thus maintain registration with the rotation of the drum as it translates longitudinal axis coordinates.

plotter font *See* vector font.

plug-and-play Denoting a way in which new devices may be attached to a system. Each different type of device added to a system will require a *device driver. In many cases the user attaching a new type of device must regenerate the operating system and include the appropriate device driver. This is a very error-prone activity. In a plug-and-play system, the underlying operating system will detect the addition of a new type of device, and will automatically enable the appropriate device driver.

Originally the term was descriptive of the early life reliability of products: a product should work when delivered (plug it in and play).

plugboard *Another name for* patchboard.

plug compatible (plug-to-plug compatible) *See* compatibility.

PL/Z The family name for the systems programming languages provided by Zilog for the Z8000 microcomputer. PL/Z–SYS is a variant of *Pascal, while PL/Z–ASM is an assembly language. The languages are no longer used since Zilog went out of business.

PMOS A type of *MOSFET.

PMS *Abbrev. for* processor-memory-switch. A notation consisting of a number of structural primitives, such as memory, M, switch, S, processor, P, etc., connected to form a network that describes the *architecture of a computer system. It allows complex computer systems to be specified at many levels. At the lowest, register transfer, level it is used in conjunction with *ISP.

pneumatic logic *Fluid logic in which the working medium is a gas.

p-n junction *See* junction.

PNO *Abbrev. for* public network operator.

pnp *See* bipolar transistor.

P=NP question One of the major open questions in theoretical computer science at present.

  P is the class of formal languages that are recognizable in *polynomial time. More precisely a language *L* is in *P* if there exists a *Turing machine program *M* and a polynomial $p(n)$ such that *M* recognizes *L* and
$$T_M(n) \le p(n)$$
for all nonnegative integers *n*, where T_M is the time complexity of *M* (*see* complexity measure). It is generally accepted that if a language is not in *P* then there is no algorithm that recognizes it and is guaranteed to be always "fast".

  NP is the class of languages that are recognizable in polynomial time on a nondeterministic *Turing machine.

  Clearly
$$P \subseteq NP$$
but the question of whether or not
$$P = NP$$
has not been solved despite a great amount of research.

  Contained in *NP* is a set *NPC* of languages

that are called *NP-complete*. A language L_1 is in *NPC* if every language L_2 in *NP* can be polynomially reduced to L_1, i.e. there is some function *f* such that

  (a) $x \in L_1$ iff $f(x) \in L_2$

  (b) $f(x)$ is computable by a Turing machine in time bounded by a polynomial in the length of *x*.

  It can be shown that if any NP-complete language is also in *P* then $P = NP$.

  A wide variety of problems occurring in computer science, mathematics, and operations research are now known to be NP-complete. As an example the problem of determining whether a Boolean expression in conjunctive normal form (*see* conjunction) can be satisfied by a truth assignment was the first problem found to be NP-complete; this is generally referred to as the *satisfiability* (or *CNF satisfiability*) *problem*. Despite considerable effort none of these NP-complete problems have been shown to be polynomially solvable. Thus it is widely conjectured that no NP-complete problem is polynomially solvable and $P \ne NP$.

  A language is said to be *NP-hard* if any language in *NP* can be polynomially reduced to it, even if the language itself is not in *NP*.

pocket sorting *Another name for* radix sorting.

point 1. To move the cursor on a screen until it reaches the desired position, item, etc. *See* pointing device. 2. To indicate the storage location of an item of data. *See* pointer. 3. A unit of measurement for type bodies. *See* font.

point and click interface A *graphical user interface where an action is selected by placing a *cursor over its depiction on the display using a *pointing device, and is initiated by *clicking.

pointer 1. **(link)** A value that indicates the storage location of an item of data. Thus when a field of an item A in a data structure contains the address of another item B, i.e. of its first word in memory, it contains a pointer to B; it is said to *point* to B. 2. *Another name for* pointing device.

pointing device (pointer) Any means of

passing spatial information to a computer system. The computer is usually programmed to display the current position by means of crosshairs or a cursor on the screen. The *mouse, *trackerball, *joystick, *data tablet, *digitizer, and *light pen are examples of these input devices.

point of presence *See* PoP.

point-of-sale system (POS system, EPOS system) A system in which *point-of-sale terminals* are used as input to a digital computer. A point-of-sale terminal is a specialized cash register, credit-card recording system, or ticket dispenser that causes all information on the transaction to be relayed to a central computer. Some point-of-sale systems include credit validation. Better stock, cash, and credit control are maintained by having the data entered into a computer as soon as it is available at the point of sale. Point-of-sale systems are also useful in monitoring petty theft of cash and merchandise.

point-to-point control *See* end-to-end control.

point-to-point line A dedicated communication link that joins only two nodes in a network. *Compare* multidrop line.

point-to-point protocol *See* PPP.

Poisson distribution The basic discrete *probability distribution for data in the form of counts of random events. If each event occurs with the same probability and the mean frequency of events is μ, the probability that exactly r events will occur is

$$e^{-\mu}\mu^r/r!$$

The Poisson distribution is discrete, taking the values $r = 0, 1, 2,\ldots$ and it can be obtained as a limiting case of the *binomial distribution as n tends to infinity while np is held fixed. The mean and variance of the Poisson distribution are both equal to μ.

poke To modify the contents of an absolute memory location from a high-level language, usually by means of a procedure of this name whose two arguments are the address in question and the value to be deposited there. *Compare* peek.

Polish notation (prefix notation) A form of notation, invented by the Polish mathemati-

cian Jan Lukasiewicz, in which each operator precedes its operands, e.g.

$$a + b \text{ is expressed as } +ab$$

If all operators take exactly two operands, or if each operator has a specific number of operands, then no brackets are required since the order of evaluation is always uniquely defined; the notation can then be described as *parenthesis-free*. *See also* reverse Polish notation.

polling The process by which one station on a *multidrop line (the primary station) addresses another station (a secondary station), giving the secondary station access to the communication channel. The secondary station is then able to send status information and/or data to the primary. The primary station resumes control of the line and may send data of its own or poll another station.

Polling is a form of *time division multiplexing. The precise polling strategy used depends upon the application. In *roll-call polling* the primary station addresses each secondary station in turn. Some stations may be addressed more often than others if their response-time requirements or traffic loads are heavier. *Hub polling* is used to minimize line turnaround delays on *half duplex multidrop lines. The primary station polls the station at the opposite end of the line, which transmits any data it has and polls the next closest station. This process is repeated until control reaches the primary station again. Since data is flowing in one direction only, from the outermost nodes toward the primary station, the only turnaround delays occur when the primary station wishes to transmit.

Polling is not suitable for situations where the response delay time is fairly large, as is the case in satellite transmission systems.

polyadic operation An *operation that may apply to different numbers of operands on different occasions.

polyalphabetic *See* substitution cipher.

polygon clipping Removal of part of an object outside a polygon (*see* clipping). Efficient algorithms exist that pipeline the sequence of edges that define the polygon to the set of planes to be clipped against. Polygon clipping is particularly difficult because it is necessary that closed polygons remain closed. Clipping a polygon can result in several disjoint polygons. Typical algorithms include the *Sutherland–Hodgman and the *Weiler–Atherton clipping algorithms.

polygon filling *Area filling applied to one or more polygons.

polyline A graphical output primitive consisting of a sequence of connected straight lines.

polymarker A graphical output primitive consisting of a set of points marked with the same shape.

polymorphic Denoting programming languages in which variables and routines can hold, take, and return differently typed values at different times. *See* polymorphism.

polymorphism A feature of some modern high-level programming languages that allows arguments to procedures and functions to vary systematically over a whole class of *data types, rather than being restricted to a single type. A simple example would be a function to find the length of a list. The code for such a function should be the same for lists of integers, lists of Booleans, or lists of anything. In a language like Pascal, however, the argument to such a function must have a single type; hence to handle both lists of integers and lists of Booleans, two functions would have to be defined. This can be avoided in languages (such as *ML) that support *polymorphic types* like "list of alpha", where alpha is a *type variable* standing for an arbitrary type. A *polymorphic function* is one that takes one or more arguments of polymorphic types.

polynomial A formal power series, i.e. a sum of multiples of powers of an independent variable known as the *indeterminate* (often written as x, s, or t), e.g.

$$3x^4 + 7x^2 + 2x + 5$$

or, in general,

$$p(x) = \sum_{i=0}^{\infty} a_i x_i$$

The coefficients (a_i) are elements of some algebraic system, S, having appropriate addition and multiplication operations; the expression is then described as a polynomial

over S. For example, if the coefficients are all integers, the polynomial is said to be over the integers. If $a_r \neq 0$ but $a_i = 0$ for all $i > r$, then r is called the *degree* of the polynomial, usually written

$$r = \deg (p)$$

If $a_r = 1$, the polynomial is *monic*.

Arithmetic on polynomials consists primarily of addition, subtraction, and multiplication of polynomials; in some cases division, factoring, and taking the greatest common divisor are also important operations.

Addition and subtraction are done by adding or subtracting the coefficients of like powers of x.

Multiplication is done by the rule

$$(a_r x^r + \ldots a_1 x + a_0)(b_s x^s + \ldots b_1 x + b_0)$$
$$= (c_{r+s} x^{r+s} + \ldots c_1 x + c_0)$$

where

$$c_k = a_0 b_k + a_1 b_{k-1} + \ldots a_{k-1} b_1 + a_k b_0$$
$$a_i, b_j = 0 \text{ for } i > r, j > s$$

In coding theory, much use is made of polynomials over the *ring of integers modulo q, for some integer $q > 1$. Such polynomials themselves form a commutative *ring with an identity. More particularly, coding theory employs polynomials over the *field of integers modulo p, for some suitable prime number p. (For binary systems, $p = 2$.) These polynomials can be multiplied and divided; in general, they may be factorized. A polynomial (over a field) that can be factorized is said to be *reducible*; otherwise it is *irreducible*. When divided by another, a polynomial over a field gives a unique quotient and remainder. Every such polynomial can be uniquely factorized into irreducible factors.

The set of polynomials (over a field), modulo a given monic irreducible polynomial (over the same field), itself forms a field; this is called an *extension field* of the original *base field* of coefficients (which were integers modulo p). Extension fields of this kind are fundamental to much of coding theory.

The extension field of polynomials modulo G, over the integers modulo p, contains p^g elements, where g is the degree of G. G is called the *generating polynomial* of the extension field. A polynomial that is an element of this field is said to be *primitive* if and only if it does not exactly divide the polynomial $x^c - 1$

(over the field of integers modulo p) for any c less than $p^g - 1$.

A practical problem of some importance is to find all the values of x that satisfy the equation

$$p_n(x) = 0$$

where $p_n(x)$ is a *polynomial equation* of degree n. Such equations have n solutions, called *roots*, which in general are complex. If the given coefficients a_i are real the complex roots occur in conjugate pairs. It is quite common for some of the roots to be very sensitive to small changes in the coefficients, i.e. to have a large *condition number.

A single root α may be found by an iteration such as *Newton's method or the *secant method. The polynomial

$$p_{n-1}(x) = p_n(x)/(x - \alpha)$$

has the same roots as p_n except for α; it may be used to determine the other roots. The process of calculating p_{n-1} is known as *deflation*, and is used after each root is found; thus the polynomials used are of progressively lower degree. Deflation depends on the roots being accurate. If an approximate root is used, the deflated polynomial will have inaccurate coefficients, and possibly very inaccurate roots. To minimize deterioration of the successive polynomials used, it is important to determine each root to the greatest possible precision and, where feasible, to determine the roots in increasing order of magnitude.

polynomial codes A family of *linear *error-correcting or *error-detecting codes whose encoding and decoding algorithms may be conveniently expressed in terms of *polynomials over a base field (and therefore easily implemented in terms of *shift registers with *linear combinational logic).

polynomial equation *See* polynomial.

polynomial interpolation *See* interpolation.

polynomially bounded algorithm *See* complexity measure.

polynomial number A number in a fixed-radix system. *See* number system.

polynomial space A way of characterizing the *complexity of an algorithm. If the space complexity (*see* complexity measure) is poly-nomially bounded, the algorithm is said to be executable in polynomial space. Many problems for which no *polynomial time algorithms have been found, nevertheless can easily be solved in an amount of space bounded by a polynomial in the length of the input.

Formally *PSPACE* is defined as the class of formal languages that are recognizable in polynomial space. Defining *P* and *NP* as the classes of languages recognizable in polynomial time and recognizable in polynomial time on a nondeterministic Turing machine, respectively (*see* P=NP question), it can be shown that *P* is a subset of *PSPACE* and that *NP* is also a subset of *PSPACE*. It is not known, however, whether

$$NP = PSPACE$$

although it is conjectured that they are different, i.e. that there exist languages in *PSPACE* that are not in *NP*.

Many problems associated with recognizing whether a player of a certain game (like GO) has a forced win from a given position are *PSPACE-complete*, which is defined in a similar manner to NP-completeness (*see* P=NP question). This implies that such languages can be recognized in polynomial time only if

$$PSPACE = P$$

Such problems can thus be considered to be even harder than NP-complete problems.

polynomial time A way of characterizing the *complexity of an algorithm or program. If the number $f(n)$ of elementary operations required to apply the algorithm of program to data of size n increases with n no more rapidly than a polynomial $p(n)$,

$$f(n) \leq p(n) \text{ for all } n,$$

then the algorithm or program is said to be executable in polynomial time. Here time is identified with steps in computation, such as invocations of primitive operations, execution of basic instructions, state transitions, etc. *See also* complexity measure, P=NP question.

polyphase merge sort A method of *merging in which the *keys are kept on more than one backing store or file. Items are merged from the source files onto another file. Whenever one of the source files is exhausted, it immediately becomes the destination of the merge operations from the nonexhausted and previous-destination files. When there is only one file left the process stops. The repeated merging is referred to as *polyphase merging*.

PON *Abbrev. for* passive optical network.

pooling block An area of memory used to contain many short records that are to be transferred to or from a device for which the access time is long compared with the actual transfer time. *See also* buffer.

pop *See* stack.

PoP *Acronym for* point of presence. An access point to the Internet, either the geographical location or, as a technical term, the equipment that supports the Internet access hardware and software.

POP *Acronym for* post office protocol. The protocol that defines the communication between a utility that can accept electronic mail on behalf of a user, holding it until such time as the user wishes to recover the messages. *See* message store.

POP-2 A programming language developed by the University of Edinburgh (UK) for research in *artificial intelligence. POP-2 provided the facility to manipulate the linked data structures characteristic of *LISP, but retained a more familiar procedural structure, and was thus more accessible to programmers raised in the Algol environment of the time. *POP-11 is a modern version of POP-2.

POP-11 A programming language for artificial intelligence that claims to combine *LISP and *POP-2.

P operation (down operation) *See* semaphore.

POPL *Acronym for* Principles of Programming Languages. Title of an annual conference organized by the *ACM at which the results of much research in programming languages are announced.

POPLOG A programming environment combining *POP-11 and *Prolog.

population *See* sampling.

pop-up menu A *menu that appears on the

display when the user changes the state of a *button or makes a selection from a *menu bar. The menu item is selected by pointing to the desired entry before changing the button state back to the original state.

pop-up program A program that is permanently resident in memory and "pops up" onto the screen at the touch of a key. The concept has been largely superseded by the advent of *graphical user interfaces, where any program can be made to "pop up".

port 1. **(I/O port)** A connection point with associated control circuitry that allows I/O devices to be connected to the internal bus of a microprocessor. *See also* parallel port, serial port, communication port.
2. A point through which data can enter or leave a *network, either on the network or the *DTE (computer) interface.
3. To move software from one type of computer system to another, making any necessary changes en route. In a simple case little more than recompilation may be required, while in extreme cases the software might have to be entirely rewritten.

portable 1. *Another word for* machine-independent.
2. A word applied to software that can readily be transferred to other machines, although not actually *machine-independent.
3. A computer that can be simply carried from one place to another by one person. They cannot necessarily be used in transit. Examples include *laptop and *notebook computers.

POS *Abbrev. for* point of sale. *See* point-of-sale system.

poset *Short for* partially ordered set. *See* partial ordering.

POS expression *Short for* product of sums expression.

positional system *See* number system.

position-independent code Program code that can be placed anywhere in memory, since all memory references are made relative to the *program counter. Position-independent code can be moved at any time, unlike *relocatable code, which can be loaded anywhere but once loaded must stay in the same position.

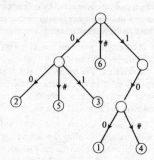

Position tree for 10010 #

position tree Let $\alpha = a_1 a_2 \ldots a_n$ denote a string, or *word, in the set of all Σ-words, Σ^*, and let # be in the alphabet Σ. Then the position tree $T(\alpha)$ for α# is a tree whose edges are labeled with elements of

$$\Sigma \cup \{\#\}$$

and is constructed according to the following rules:

(a) $T(\alpha)$ has $(n+1)$ leaves labeled

$$1, 2, \ldots, n+1$$

(*see* diagram);

(b) the sequence of labels on the edges of the path from the root to the leaf labeled i is the *substring identifier for position i in α#.

positive acknowledgment *See* acknowledgment. *See also* backward error correction.

positive display A display where the image consists of dark symbols on a light background (usually white). Positive displays are claimed by some authorities to cause less eyestrain. *See also* paper white display, negative display.

positive logic 1. A logic system in which logic 1 is assigned to the higher voltage and logic 0 to the lower voltage.

2. A logic system in which all the Boolean variables and Boolean functions behave as described.

Compare negative logic.

POSIX An IEEE trial-use standard (P1003) that defines the behavior of a set of *supervisor calls, basing these closely on those found in *UNIX. However, POSIX is not itself an operating system so much as a formal description of one form of operating system of which UNIX is a specific instance. The intention is that a program written in such a way as to use only those functions defined by the POSIX specifications will be readily *portable between different operating systems, provided that these are all conformant to the POSIX definitions.

Postal, Telegraph, and Telephone Administration *See* PTT.

postcondition of a statement S in some program. An *assertion that characterizes the state of the program immediately after execution of S. The postcondition is expressed in terms of properties of certain program variables and relationships between them. Where a program text is annotated by attaching assertions, a postcondition is attached immediately after the statement to which it relates. *See also* precondition.

postedit *See* postprocessor.

posterization The redefining of an image so that the number of *gray levels or colors is reduced. This enhances the boundaries between different parts of the image.

postfix notation *Another name for* reverse Polish notation.

postmaster The activity at a site that undertakes the management of the electronic-mail service for that site. The management activity includes dealing with the maintenance of e-mail addresses and with errors or failures in the mail services, as well as replying to queries. Some of this work is carried out by computer programs while other aspects demand human intervention. On a large site with many e-mail users, the role of postmaster will usually be a joint activity by several people to ensure continuity of service.

postmortem Analysis of the cause of some undesired system behavior, based upon information recorded at the time that the undesired behavior was detected. For example, *abnormal termination of a program might result in a record of the state of the program at the time of termination, and this record might subsequently be used for postmortem analysis of the reason for termination.

post office protocol *See* POP.

postorder traversal (endorder traversal)
A tour of the nodes of a binary tree obtained by using the following recursive algorithm: visit in postorder the left subtree of the root (if it exists); visit in postorder the right subtree of the root (if it exists); visit the root of the tree. *Compare* preorder traversal, symmetric order traversal.

postprocessor A program that performs some operations on the output of another program, typically formatting the output for some device or filtering out unwanted items. This operation is sometimes called a *postedit*.

Post production system An approach to *effective computability on strings of symbols, formulated by E. L. Post. A *Post production* is a string rewriting rule. A set L of strings is said to be *Post-generable* if there exists a finite set of strings, called axioms, and a finite set P of Post productions such that each string in the set can be obtained from the axiom set by some finite derivation, where each step in the derivation is sanctioned by an application of some production in P. It turns out that the class of Post-generable sets on some fixed *alphabet A is exactly the class of *recursively enumerable sets, order A.

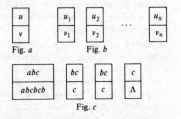

Fig. *a*   Fig. *b*

Fig. *c*

Post's correspondence problem

Post's correspondence problem A well-known algorithmically unsolvable *decision problem. Given a finite set of "dominoes" of the form shown in Fig. *a*, with u and v being *strings, the question is whether or not one can form a sequence, as shown in Fig. *b*, such that reading all the us in order gives the same string as reading all the vs. Fig. *c* shows such

a sequence, where Λ is the empty string. Even though there are only finitely many different dominoes given, there is an infinite supply of duplicates for each one; the same domino can thus be used more than once in the sequence. Dominoes cannot be inverted.

Depending on the dominoes given, it is sometimes obvious that the answer to the question is "no". However there is no algorithm that can discover this in all cases.

PostScript *Trademark* A high-level device-independent *page description language developed by Adobe Systems Inc. It is a de facto *graphical device interface standard. PostScript accurately defines pages of text, which can be rendered at a variety of resolutions. Support for PostScript is often incorporated into the output device.

Powell's algorithm An algorithm that minimizes a function of several variables without calculating derivatives. The method searches to find a direction in which the function decreases and then moves to a new point in that direction. It then searches from this new point. The process continues until no direction can be found that will decrease the function.

power down *See* power off.

power-fail recovery A method of dealing with the effects of a loss of the incoming power supply. The system is equipped with a power-line monitor, which detects any long-term deviation in the supply-line voltage from acceptable limits, and causes a *power-fail interrupt* when deviations occur. The service routine for this interrupt stores the *process descriptors for all processes in *nonvolatile memory and then halts all activity. When the supply-line voltage is restored, the system restarts and can reinstate all processes from the previously stored process descriptors.

power-limited channel A physical transmission channel whose rate of throughput of energy is limited to some value. *See* signal-to-noise ratio, channel coding theorem.

power management Operation of a computer so as to minimize electric power consumption. This is especially important in battery-powered systems, but is increasingly to be found in mains-powered systems. The economies are achieved by shutting down high-consumption components after they have been idle for a short period and starting them up again as soon as any input activity is detected.

power method A method of finding the eigenvalues of a matrix (*see* eigenvalue problems) by successively multiplying a starting vector by the matrix. Convergence depends on the properties of the matrix and in the case of complex eigenvalues further work is needed to find them after convergence.

power off (power down) To switch off an electrical or electronic device.

power on (power up) To switch on an electrical or electronic device.

PowerPC A *RISC microprocessor chip designed in 1991 by a partnership between IBM, Apple, and Motorola. The processor has a 64-bit architecture. The initial 601 chip was followed by the 603 and 620 versions. The chip appears in Apple's PowerMac systems, as well as IBM systems using the AIX operating system.

power routing *See* logic circuit.

power set of a *set S. The set of all *subsets of S, typically denoted by 2^S. It can be described as

$$\{A \mid A \subseteq S\}$$

The number of elements in the power set of S is 2^N, where N is the number of elements in S.

power up *See* power on.

ppm *Abbrev. for* pages per minute.

PPP *Abbrev. for* point-to-point protocol. A protocol allowing *IP (Internet Protocol) traffic to be handled on a serial line.

pragma 1. A statement in a programming language that is intended to convey information to a particular implementation, and can be ignored in other implementations of the language.

2. A statement in a programming language that provides information that may assist the compiler in translating the program, but can

be ignored without affecting the correct working of the program.

preamble sequence The set of signals preceding genuine data in a transmission. The term is most commonly used in connection with Ethernet (CSMA/CD) signaling, where each packet is preceded by a sequence of alternate 1s and 0s to allow the receiving system to synchronize its local clock with that of the transmitter.

precedence The rules determining the order in which operations are carried out, if this is not defined unambiguously by brackets. For example, in most languages the expression

$$a * b + c$$

will be evaluated by doing the multiplication first, and brackets would be used to enforce the alternative order thus:

$$a * (b + c)$$

There is no consensus about precedence of operations in language, particularly when new operators may be introduced. A simple order used in *Pascal is as follows:

unary NOT

multiplying operators

adding operators

relational operators

Other languages may have further operators such as exponentiation and further categories such as logic operators, whose position in the order would be defined. Operators of the same precedence are usually applied in order from left to right, but in some languages the order is undefined.

precedence parsing A *bottom-up parsing technique that exploits precedence relations on the symbols of the grammar to decide when a string of symbols may be replaced, i.e. form a handle. Two precedence parsing techniques, *operator precedence* and *simple precedence*, are in common use.

In simple precedence three relations, $<\!\cdot$ $\cdot\!>$ and $\doteq$, are defined on the symbols (terminal and nonterminal) of the *grammar. If

$$X <\!\cdot Y, X \doteq Y, \text{ or } X \cdot\!> Y$$

then, respectively, X is said to yield precedence to Y, have the same precedence as Y, or take precedence over Y. Note that these relations are not symmetric. By inserting the precedence relations between symbols in a sentential form and then regarding the $<\bullet$ and $\bullet>$ symbols as matching brackets, a handle is determined as the leftmost string delimited by $<\bullet$ at its left end and $\bullet>$ at its right end.

Operator precedence differs from simple precedence in that the three precedence relations are defined on just the terminal symbols of the grammar. Furthermore the grammar must satisfy the property that nonterminals on the right-hand side of a production must always be separated by at least one terminal.

Arithmetic expressions provided the original motivation for operator precedence since conventionally multiplication takes precedence over addition. Simple precedence is a generalization of operator precedence. Both methods are limited in the scope of their application to grammars for which at most one precedence relation exists between any ordered pair of symbols. In addition the right-hand side of productions must be unique.

precision The number of digits to which numbers are represented. For example, if p bits are allocated to the mantissa in the representation of floating-point numbers used in a particular computer, then in that computer floating-point numbers have p bits of precision. In general, the precision of floating-point numbers is proportional to their value (i.e. relative) whereas the precision of fixed-point numbers is absolute (independent of the value).

It is important not to confuse the term precision with *accuracy*. For example, the number

$$3.142\ 8571$$

has eight-decimal digit precision, irrespective of what it represents. If this number represents 22/7 then it is also accurate to eight decimal digits but if it represents the irrational number π then it is accurate only to three decimal digits.

precondition of a statement S in some program. An *assertion that characterizes the state of the program immediately prior to execution of S. The precondition is expressed in terms of properties of certain program variables and relationships between them. Where a program text is annotated by attaching assertions, a precondition is attached immediately before the statement to which it relates. For a consistent annotation the precondition of S must be implied by the *postcondition of any statement whose execution can immediately precede execution of S. *See also* weakest precondition.

predicate A *function from some domain to a truth value. If the domain comprises n variables

where $n = 0,1,2,\ldots$

the function is called an *n-place predicate*. In the special case where $n = 0$, the predicate is a *statement*. Predicates are the fundamental building blocks of the *predicate calculus.

predicate calculus (predicate logic, first-order logic) A fundamental notation for representing and reasoning with logical statements. It extends *propositional calculus by introducing the *quantifiers, and by allowing *predicates and *functions of any number of variables. The syntax involves *terms, *atoms*, and *formulas*. An atom (or *atomic formula*) has the form $P(t_1,\ldots,t_k)$, where P is a *predicate symbol* and $t_1,\ldots,t_k$ are terms. Formulas may be built from these atoms in the following ways:

(a) any atom is a formula;

(b) formulas can be combined by the usual propositional connectives (*negation, *conjunction, *disjunction, etc.);

(c) if F is a formula, then $\forall v.F$ and $\exists v.F$ are also formulas (*see* quantifier).

A *sentence* is a formula with no *free variables. An example of a sentence is

$$\forall x\ .\ G(x,c) \leftrightarrow \forall y\ .\ G(f(x,y),y)$$

where $\leftrightarrow$ signifies the *biconditional and G is a predicate symbol, f is a function symbol, x and y are variables, and c is a constant symbol. The overall meaning of a sentence (true or false) depends on the *interpretation given to the symbols occurring in it. For example, let G be interpreted as the predicate "greater than", f as the operation of multiplication, and c as the number 1. Then the above sentence says that a number x is greater than 1 if and only if it has the property that, for all y, xy is greater than y. This is true if the *domain of interpretation* is the *natural numbers, but not if it is the integers (because of the possibility of negative y).

Predicate calculus can claim to be a fundamental logical language since all the more complicated logics can, in some sense, be reduced to it. A simple but practically important extension is *many-sorted predicate calculus*. Here there are several sorts of variables, and the operations and relations come from a many-sorted *signature.

Another possible extension is *second-order logic*, which allows predicate and function variables, such as P in the following:

$$\forall P . [P(a) \wedge \forall k . P(k) \Rightarrow P(s(k))] \Rightarrow \forall n . P(n)$$

($\wedge$ and $\Rightarrow$ signify *conjunction and *conditional.) This example, given the appropriate interpretation of a and s, expresses a principle of *induction: if P is true for zero, and true for $k+1$ whenever it is true for k, then it is true for all n. Again this sentence holds for natural numbers but not integers.

Applications of predicate calculus in computer science are commonplace and include formal *specification, *program correctness, *logic programming, and *databases. *See also* modal logic.

predicate transformer A function that maps predicates to predicates. Specifically, the predicate transformer for some statement S is a function that maps some predicate R into the *weakest precondition of S with respect to R. The term was introduced by Dijkstra in 1975 in conjunction with a calculus for the derivation of programs; this provides for development of a program to be guided by the simultaneous development of a total correctness proof for the program. *See* program correctness proof.

predictive PCM *See* pulse code modulation.

predictor-corrector methods The standard approach in the implementation of *linear multistep methods for the solution of *ordinary differential equations. Two such formulas are used on each step, one of which is implicit (*see* linear multistep methods). An example of such a formula pair are Euler's method (*see* discretization) and the trapezoidal rule (*see* ordinary differential equa-

tions). A predictor-corrector method based on these formulas has the form

$$y^p_{n+1} = y_n + hf(x_n, y_n) \quad \text{(prediction)}$$
$$y_{n+1} = y_n + \tfrac{1}{2}h(f(x_n, y_n) + f(x_n, y^p_{n+1})) \quad \text{(correction)}$$

This permits the more accurate implicit formula to be used effectively, without solving an equation for y_{n+1}, and provides an estimate for the *local error, namely $y^p_{n+1} - y_{n+1}$. Such estimates are used to control accuracy and *stability.

preemptive allocation An allocation that removes a resource from one *process and transfers it to another. When a process requests use of a resource, the appropriate resource controller will at some stage assign the resource to the process. A resource such as a processor is used for a period of time, during which no other process can use the resource. If during this period of use a second process becomes available to run, the processor scheduler may preempt the processor and transfer it to the second higher-priority process.

A more important type of preemptive allocation arises when a nonsharable resource, such as a tape transport, has been allocated to a process but not yet used by it. If a second process requests a tape transport then use of the transport may be denied the first process, and the transport preempted for use by the second process.

prefix of a string α. Any string β where α is the *concatenation $\beta\gamma$ for some string γ. Thus in coding theory, a word is said to be a prefix of another word if the former word matches the first symbols of the latter. *See also* prefix codes.

prefix codes Codes in which no codeword is a *prefix of any other codeword. The idea is usually applied to *variable-length codes. A prefix code has the property that, as soon as all the symbols of a codeword have been received, the codeword is recognized as such. Prefix codes are therefore said to be *instantaneously decodable*. (They are of necessity *uniquely decodable.)

prefix notation *Another name for* Polish notation.

prefix property The property that no codeword is the *prefix of any other codeword. *See* prefix codes.

PREMO An ISO/IEC standard under development for the PREsentation of Multimedia Objects.

preorder traversal A tour of the nodes of a binary tree obtained by using the following recursive algorithm: visit the root of the tree; visit in preorder the left subtree of the root (if it exists); visit in preorder the right subtree of the root (if it exists). *Compare* postorder traversal, symmetric order traversal.

preprocessor A program that performs modifications to data in order to make it suitable for input to another program, especially a *compiler. The modifications may be simple changes of format, or may include *macro expansions.

presentation graphics A field of computer graphics that is limited to the production of the line graphs, bar charts, and pie charts used as visual aids in the presentation of quantitative information on trends and statistics.

presentation layer of network protocol function. *See* seven-layer reference model.

prestore To store, in advance, data needed by a program, or storage of such data.

preventive maintenance (routine maintenance) Maintenance performed on a regular basis, and intended to prevent failures or to detect incipient failures. An example of the former is routine lubrication and cleaning of devices that have moving magnetic media. An example of the latter is a *marginal check* in which electrical parameters may be varied to induce failures in marginally performing circuits. *Compare* remedial maintenance.

PRF *Abbrev. for* pulse repetition frequency.

PRI *Abbrev. for* primary-rate ISDN. *See* ISDN.

primary index *See* indexed file.

primary memory *Another name for* main memory, specifically the form used as the medium for storing instructions and data that are currently undergoing processing by a CPU.

prime implicant *See* implicant.

primitive 1. Not capable of being broken down into simpler form; nondivisible. The term is used for example with reference to actions requested by a process via supervisor calls, especially the use of P and V operations (*see* semaphore).
2. A primitive operation, action, element, etc. *See also* graphics primitive.

primitive element An element α of a *finite field F whose various powers,
$$\alpha^0 (= 1), \alpha, \alpha^2, \alpha^3, \ldots$$
will ultimately include all the nonzero elements of F. Every finite field contains such an element.

primitive polynomial *See* polynomial.

primitive recursion In the study of *effective computability, a particular way of defining a new function in terms of other simpler ones. The functions involved are functions over the nonnegative integers. Primitive recursion is then the process of defining a function f of $n+1$ variables in the following manner:
$$f(x_1, x_2, \ldots x_n, 0) = g(x_1, x_2, \ldots x_n),$$
$$f(x_1, x_2, \ldots x_n, y+1) =$$
$$h(x_1, x_2, \ldots x_n, y, \ f(x_1, \ldots x_n, y))$$
where g and h are functions of n and $n+2$ variables respectively. *See also* primitive recursive function.

primitive recursive function A *function that can be obtained from certain initial functions by a finite number of applications of *composition and *primitive recursion. The initial functions are normally the *zero function, *successor function, and *projection (or generalized identity) functions, where all functions are defined on the nonnegative integers. Primitive recursive functions are *total functions, defined in a simple way by *induction. There is also a notion of *primitive recursive set*, namely one whose *characteristic function is primitive recursive.

The arithmetic functions of addition and multiplication are examples of primitive recursive functions. Indeed most of the functions and sets on natural numbers that we wish to compute are primitive recursive.

The idea can be generalized: for example, a primitive recursive function on lists satisfies a definition analogous to the one given above, with the successor function adding an element to the front of a list.

See also recursive function.

primitive recursive set *See* primitive recursive function.

primitive type A *data type, such as integer, real, logical, and character, that is made available to the user by the basic hardware. More complex data structures are built up from the primitives, usually by software.

Prim's algorithm A method of finding the minimum-cost *spanning tree of a weighted undirected *graph, developed by R. C. Prim (1957).

principal component analysis *See* multivariate analysis.

printed circuit A physical realization of an electronic circuit design in which the connections between the terminals of individual components are formed from copper conductors laminated onto a flat supporting sheet of an insulating material such as fiber glass. The conductor pattern is normally printed and etched onto the sheet and components are then attached to the copper "lands" by hand or dip soldering. The supporting sheet plus circuit is known as a *printed circuit board (PCB)*.

Double-sided PCBs are commonly produced. These consist of an insulating sheet with a circuit on each side, with interconnections possible between the two circuits. Multilayer printed circuits are also fabricated.

A PCB connects via an appropriate socket to the internal wiring of, say, a computer system. Smaller modular PCBs may be connected to a PCB to enhance its function. *See also* edge connector, motherboard.

printed circuit board *See* printed circuit.

printer An output device that converts the coded information from the processor into a readable or pictorial form on paper or transparent media. There are many types, varying in method, speed, and quality of printing: there are *serial printers, *line printers, and *page printers, and these may be *solid-font or *matrix printers. Many matrix printers, including laser and inkjet printers, can act as *plotters. Printer technology may or may not use mechanical impact to transfer ink (*see* impact printer, nonimpact printer).

printer format (print format) The *format for printed output, defining the character and line spacing and the areas of the page where printing will occur. In some *line and *serial printers the pitch of characters and lines is selected by switches or is not variable. The format aspect that is often different for each job involves the lines on which printing is not required; this is controlled by a *vertical format unit. Recent designs of serial and *page printers allow the host system to control all aspects of the format by the use of control codes.

printout The output of a printer. It may be a stack of fanfolded paper prior to any bursting or trimming operations. Increasingly, desktop printers have the ability to print onto single sheets of paper. *See also* stationery.

print quality The characteristics of the printed characters on a *printout that make them acceptable for their application. These characteristics include degree of conformity with the intended shapes of the characters, uniformity of limb width, uniformity of print density, contrast with the paper, amount of smudging, accuracy of location of the characters compared with their intended positions on the paper, and amount of extraneous ink (or toner in an *electrophotographic printer). The print quality depends on the type of *printer, its age, cleanliness, and condition, the type and amount of previous use of the *ribbon (on impact printers), and the characteristics of the *stationery.

The basic print quality requirement is that all characters must be legible out of context. In the most demanding application, the printed page must have all characters accurately and completely printed with uniform density and high contrast, and no visible flaws. Print quality close to this is known as *letter* (or *correspondence*) *quality*; it is intended to match the quality attainable with a good typewriter. In general, slower impact printers produce higher-quality print but the highest quality is available from *laser printers.

Some printouts are intended for data capture via *OCR equipment; examples are debit and payment slips and cheques. These must conform to the standards specifying font shape (e.g. OCR B) and with the minimum print-quality standards specified for OCR. These are international standards.

print server *See* server.

prioritize To put into an order according to the relative urgency or importance. In a multiprogramming environment the programs should be prioritized so that urgent jobs are not delayed by background processing tasks. Program interrupts should be similarly treated. *See also* interrupt priority.

priority Relative importance or urgency. Priority is the quality of having precedence, i.e. requiring early attention, and can be quantified by numerical value, which is used to determine the order in which several requests for a resource are satisfied. In the situation where several otherwise identical processes are free to run, the one with the highest priority will be run next, hence the term *priority processing*. A *priority interrupt* in a system will be dealt with ahead of standard interrupts that may be awaiting a response. In data transmission a field is allocated to the holding of a code that indicates the relative urgency of the associated message. *See also* interrupt priority, interrupt I/O.

priority encoder *See* encoder.

priority interrupt *See* priority, interrupt priority, interrupt I/O.

priority processing *See* priority.

priority queue A linear *list where each insertion specifies a priority number as well as the element to be inserted, and each removal or access takes the earliest of the elements with highest priority.

privacy Roughly speaking, the right to be left alone. The law on privacy is vague and judgemade in both the USA and the UK. It is complicated by cases on *trade secrets and has been overtaken by the computer-related version of privacy, data protection. *See* data protection legislation.

With regard to protection against unauthorized reading of computer data, i.e. to the privacy of data, there are two concepts.

1. Protection of data about an individual or corporate entity. Where data can be determined to refer to a specific person, or in some cases to a specific organization, there may exist a legal right to limit access to that data and, in many cases, associated rights to guarantee accuracy and completeness. This form of privacy exists only for data about an identifiable individual, and exists to protect the rights of the individual to whom the data refers. *See* data protection legislation, Computer Misuse Act 1990.

2. Protection of data owned by an individual or corporate entity. Where data is deemed to be in some sense the property of someone (or some group) there may exist a right to limit access to that data. This form of privacy exists for data belonging to someone, and exists to protect the rights of the owner of the data. *See* trade secrets. *See also* integrity, security.

privileged instructions Instructions that can only be issued when a computing system is operating in one of the high, or the highest, *execution states.

probabilistic compaction (probabilistic compression) A *data-compaction code in which the *encoding (and therefore *decoding) table is constructed using a previously formed estimate of the *probabilities of the symbols in the messages – files or data stream – intended for future compaction (*compare* statistical compaction).

The decoding table need not be stored or transmitted along with the compacted text, since it need be recorded only once within the filing system, or made known only once to the receiver of the data stream, for all future files or messages. The disadvantage, however, of probabilistic compaction is that no one estimate of probabilities will be a perfect fit with the statistics of any given file or message. A useful compromise is to have a set of probability tables, each tailored to one kind of data (source programs, object programs, plaintext, and so on); this is called *generic compaction*.

probabilistic reasoning Problem-solving techniques based on the use of probability theory for weighing evidence and inferring conclusions. *See* probability, Bayes's theorem, belief systems.

probability A number between 0 and 1 associated with an event (*see* relative frequency) that is one of a set of possible events: an event that is certain to occur has probability 1. The probability of an event is the limiting value approached by the relative frequency of the event as the number of observations is increased indefinitely. Alternatively it is the degree of belief that the event will occur.

The concept of probability is applied to a wide range of events in different contexts. Originally interest was in the study of games of chance, where correct knowledge of probability values allowed profitable wagers to be made. Later the subject was studied by insurance companies anxious to predict probable future claims on the basis of previously observed relative frequencies. Today probability theory is the basis of statistical analysis (*see* statistical methods).

The *probability calculus* is the set of rules for combining probabilities for combinations of events, using the methods of symbolic logic applied to sets.

See also probability distributions.

probability calculus *See* probability.

probability distributions Theoretical formulas for the *probability that an observation has a particular value, or lies within a given range of values.

Discrete probability distributions apply to observations that can take only certain distinct values, such as the integers 0, 1, 2,... or the six named faces of a die. A probability, $p(r)$, is assigned to each event such that the total is unity. Important discrete distributions are the *binomial distribution and the *Poisson distribution.

Continuous probability distributions apply to observations, such as physical measurements, where no two observations are likely to be exactly the same. Since the probability of observing exactly a given value is about zero, a mathematical function, the *cumulative distribution function*, $F(x)$, is used instead. This is defined as the probability that the observation does not exceed x. $F(x)$ increases monotonically with x from 0 to 1, and the probability of observing any value between two limits, x_1 and x_2, is

$$F(x_2) - F(x_1)$$

This definition leads, by differential calculus, to the *frequency function*, $f(x)$, which is the limiting ratio of

$$F(x + h) - F(x) \text{ to } h$$

as h becomes small, so that the probability of an observation between x and $(x + h)$ is $h.f(x)$. The most important continuous distribution is the *normal (or Gaussian) distribution.

Probability distributions are defined in terms of *parameters, whose values determine the numerical values of the probabilities.

probit analysis A statistical technique used to relate the proportion of subjects responding to the strength of an applied stimulus. The stimulus is often applied in a series of increasing amounts in geometrical progression, and the proportion responding is modeled by the cumulative normal frequency distribution (*see* probability distributions). The method estimates the *median effective stimulus* or *LD50* and the *slope* of the response. It is widely used in pharmacology, biology, and in testing the safety of products.

problem definition A precise statement of some problem to be solved, with the emphasis on providing a complete and unambiguous definition of the problem rather than an easy introduction to it.

problem description A self-contained overview of some problem to be solved, perhaps with accompanying information on constraints that the solution must respect, possible approaches to the solution, etc.

problem-oriented language A programming language whose control structures and (in particular) data structures reflect in some measure the characteristics of a class of problems, e.g. commercial data processing or scientific computation. By contrast, the structures of a machine-oriented language reflect the internal structure of the underlying machine.

procedural abstraction The principle that any operation that achieves a well-defined effect can be treated by its users as a single entity, despite the fact that the operation may actually be achieved by some sequence of lower-level operations (*see also* abstraction). Procedural abstraction has been extensively employed since the early days of computing, and virtually all programming languages provide support for the concept (e.g. the SUBROUTINE of Fortran, the **procedure** of Algol, Pascal, Ada, etc.).

procedural cohesion *See* cohesion.

procedural language An *imperative *procedure-oriented language.

procedure A section of a program that carries out some well-defined operation on data specified by *parameters. It can be *called from anywhere in a program, and different parameters can be provided for each call.

The term procedure is generally used in the context of high-level languages; in assembly language the word *subroutine is more commonly employed.

procedure-oriented language A programming language that enables a program to be specified by defining a collection of *procedures. These procedures may call each other, and are called by the main program (which can itself be regarded as a procedure).

process 1. (task) A stream of activity. A process is defined by its code, i.e. the ordered set of machine instructions defining the actions that the process is to take, the contents of its *workspace, i.e. the set of data values that it can read, write, and manipulate, and its *process descriptor, which defines the current status of any resources that are allocated to the process.
2. To carry out the actions defined by the sequence of instructions that make up the code of a program.

process algebra The algebraic study of abstract computing processes. Suppose that there is a set A of basic computational actions (such as assignments, tests, sends, requests), and that these actions can be combined to form finite and infinite processes. There are a number of operations that, given two processes p_1 and p_2, can form new processes; examples are the *sequential composition* $p_1.p_2$ and *parallel composition* $p_1||p_2$ of the

processes. There is a great deal of freedom to define and interpret such operations and the processes they create, especially if the actions and processes may exist concurrently and communicate in various ways. Methods of communication and cooperation between processes are at the heart of process algebra. Process algebra studies semantic ideas using mainly standard algebraic methods, including: axiomatic theories whose axioms are often equations; equivalence relations (e.g. several kinds of bisimulation); algebraic constructions; and computable algebras. An example of a set of axioms for process algebra is the set ACP of J. A. Bergstra and J. W. Klop; this was developed from earlier work on *process calculuses by R. Milner and others, and has subsequently been extended and adapted to express the huge range of semantic phenomena exhibited in modern concurrent communicating systems.

The motivation behind process algebra is to model computing systems using processes and to specify the systems by equations based on appropriate operators on processes. Thus concurrent computing systems are specified by equations and their semantics are obtained by solving fixed-point equations. Various related semantic and logical methods are used, including: *initial algebra semantics; *operational semantics based on transition systems; metric space and topological methods; and *modal and *temporal logics for reasoning about processes.

Process algebra has the potential to become a general theory of computing, relevant to system modeling and parallel-program development. There is much research needed to develop its foundations, tools, and applications.

process calculus The study of abstract computing processes by means of various formal systems and calculuses. An early influential calculus was the calculus of communicating systems (CCS) of R. Milner. This has given rise to many adaptations and new approaches to a theory of processes. For example, it led to the systematic development of *process algebra to which many process calculuses may be said to belong, and it inspired an influential reformulation of the parallel language *CSP as a process calculus by C. A. R. Hoare.

process control Use of a dedicated computer (known as a *process controller*) to control a specific industrial or manufacturing process. Information (sensed) from that process is used as a source of data; computations made upon that data determine control signals to be sent to the process. The computations may involve some statistical properties (such as moving average) for *statistical process control*.

In general there are two forms of process control: *continuous* and *discrete*. Continuous process control is involved with the manufacturing of some form of continuous product, primarily chemicals, an example being the automatic control of a catalytic cracker for petroleum distillation. Although chemicals may be manufactured in batches, this is still considered a continuous process since the variables that control the process can be varied continuously. Discrete control is concerned with the manufacturing of individual (discrete) items, as in the welding of two parts to form a larger assembly. Discrete process control has strong connections with *industrial robotics. See also* numerical control, computer-aided manufacturing, computer-integrated manufacturing.

process descriptor A set of information that defines the status of resources allocated to a *process. When a system contains a number of processes, any of which may be active at any one time, there will be for each process a descriptor defining the status of that process. Within the descriptor the *ready* indicator shows whether the particular process is able to proceed, or whether it must await the completion of some other activity before it can be executed by the CPU. For processes that are unable to run, the process descriptor will indicate the reason for which that process is *suspended* and will contain pointers to relevant queues and semaphores. The process descriptor will also contain a copy of the contents of the processor registers that are to be reinstated when the process is restarted. When a process is running, the process descriptor will contain information (the *resource descriptor*) on the resources allocated to the process and on the permissible operations on these resources.

process model *See* software development process model.

process modeling A form of modeling where the model produced is a *software or *system development process.

processor A computer, usually/often the *central processor. *See also* microprocessor, I/O processor, communication processor.

processor allocation The measure of the amount of processor resource that is available to a *process. Normally the allocation will be expressed as a time, or as a number of instructions to be executed.

processor status word (PSW) A word that describes fully the condition of a processor at each instant. It indicates which classes of operations are allowed and which are forbidden, and the status of all interrupts associated with the processor. It will also contain the address of the instruction currently being executed. The PSW is held in a *register known as the *processor status register. See also* program status word.

processor time (CPU time) The time for which a *process has been receiving service from the processor. *See also* system accounting.

product group *Another name for* direct product.

production *See* grammar, semi-Thue system.

production rule system (production system) A programming language in which the programs consist of *condition* ⇒ *action* rules; these rules are known as *productions* or *production rules*. The programs are interpreted by a repetition of the following operations: all rules whose conditions are satisfied are found, one of them is selected, and its action is called. Such systems are often known as *rule-based systems* in artificial intelligence.

production run Execution of a program in the normal way to produce useful results. *Compare* dry run.

productive time *See* available time.

PROGRAM CORRECTNESS PROOF

product of sums expression (POS expression) A *Boolean function expressed as a product of sum terms, i.e. as an AND of OR terms containing uncomplemented or complemented variables. An example is

$$f = (x \lor y) \land (x' \lor z')$$

The function is also realizable as the NOR of a group of NOR terms. *See also* standard product of sums, sum of products expression.

product term A product (AND) of Boolean variables, uncomplemented or complemented. *See also* sum of products expression.

profiling Production of a histogram (or equivalent) concerning some aspect of a system. For example, an *execution profile* for a program might show the proportion of time spent in each individual procedure during a run of the program, while a *statement profile* might show the distribution of the statements in a program between the different kinds of statement provided by the language.

program A set of statements that (after translation from programming-language form into executable form – *see* compiler) can be executed by a computer in order to produce a desired behavior from the computer. A *procedural program* gives a precise definition of the procedure to be followed by the computer system in order to obtain the required results. By contrast, a *nonprocedural program* specifies constraints that must be satisfied by the results that are produced but does not specify the procedure by which these results should be obtained; such a procedure must be determined by a problem-solving *shell* based on the defined constraints.

program analysis *See* static analysis.

program compatibility A measure of the degree to which programs can effectively be used together in a common environment. Factors affecting program compatibility include machine and operating system dependencies, and the structure of the data that are read and written by the programs.

program control Control of a computer's functioning by a sequence of instructions that comes from a memory and is called the program.

program correctness proof A formal mathematical demonstration that the *semantics of a program are consistent with some specification for that program (*see* program specification). There are two prerequisites to the provision of such a proof: there must be a formal specification for the program, and there must be some formal definition of the semantics of the programming language. Such a definition may take the form of a set of *axioms to cover the semantics of any simple statement in the language, and a set of *inference rules that show how the semantics of any compound statement, including a complete program, can be inferred from the semantics of its individual component statements (simple or compound).

For a typical sequential program written in some *imperative (procedural) language, the program specification can conveniently be given in the form of two *assertions: an *input assertion* and an *output assertion*. These are expressed in terms of properties of certain program variables and relationships between them. The proof then consists of a formal demonstration that the semantics of the program are consistent with the input and output assertions; this demonstration is of course based upon the formal definition of the semantics of the programming language. Interpreted operationally, the assertions characterize program states and the proof shows that if execution of the program is initiated in a state for which the input assertion is "true" then the program will eventually terminate in a state for which the output assertion is "true".

This kind of proof is known as a *proof of total correctness*. Historically, however, such a proof has often been resolved into two parts: first, a *proof of partial correctness*, which shows that if the program terminates then it does so in a state for which the output assertion is "true", and second, a *proof of termination*, which shows that the program will indeed terminate (normally rather than abnormally).

A common approach to the proof of partial correctness begins by attaching the input and output assertions to the program text at the very beginning and very end respectively. Further assertions, called *intermediate asser-

tions, are attached to the program text both before and after every statement (simple or compound). The assertion attached immediately before and immediately after a statement are known respectively as the *precondition and *postcondition of that statement.

The proof of partial correctness consists of a formal demonstration that the semantics of each statement in the program, whether simple or compound, are consistent with its precondition and postcondition. This demonstration can begin at the level of the simple statements and then proceed through the various levels of compound statement until eventually it is demonstrated that the semantics of the complete program are consistent with its precondition and postcondition, i.e. with the input assertion and the output assertion. The semantics of an individual statement are shown to be consistent with its precondition and postcondition by applying to the precondition and postcondition the appropriate axiom or inference rule for that statement. This yields a theorem, called a *verification condition*, that must be proved using conventional mathematics in order to demonstrate the required consistency.

Note particularly that the overall proof of correctness is achieved not by consideration of execution histories, but rather by treating the program as a static mathematical object to which certain axioms and inference rules apply.

The central problem with such a proof is the devising of the intermediate assertions. This requires a full appreciation of the design of the program and of the semantics of the programming language. Often the key lies in finding appropriate intermediate assertions to attach inside the various loops in the program, i.e. loop *invariants. Devising intermediate assertions for some arbitrary program is often extremely difficult and a constructive approach, in which program and proof are developed together, is definitely preferable.

In order to present a proof of termination it is necessary to demonstrate first that the program does not suffer from abortive termination and second that the program does not endlessly repeat some loop. A demonstration

of the former may become very complex, e.g. it may be necessary to demonstrate that arithmetic overflow will not occur. A demonstration that the program will eventually exit from some loop can be based on a *well-ordered set. For example, suppose that for some loop an expression E can be found such that the loop can be shown to terminate immediately if the value of E is negative. Further suppose that the value of E can be shown to decrease on each iteration around the loop. It then follows that the loop must terminate.

Proofs of correctness do not offer a complete solution to the problems of software reliability in practical systems. The sheer size and complexity of proofs presents many difficulties that are only partly alleviated by *mechanical verifier systems. Issues such as the limitations of computer arithmetic, indeterminacy, and parallelism all present additional problems. It may be very difficult to develop a specification against which to verify a program, and impossible to demonstrate that this specification is itself "correct" in that it properly reflects the intentions of the developers (and even more difficult to prove that it satisfies the needs of the intended users).

Work on proofs of correctness has made a major contribution to software engineering in that many advances in the understanding of programming languages, principles, and methods have their origins in this work. In addition the scope for practical applications of program proofs is growing and the formal approach to program correctness is of increasing significance.

program counter (instruction counter; current address register) A counting *register that normally increments in each instruction cycle to obtain the program sequence (i.e. the sequence of instructions) from memory locations. This counter will have its contents changed by branch instructions to obtain the next instruction from the branch target. The program counter forms part of the *processor status word; this enables subsequent restarting of an interrupted program.

program decomposition The breaking down of a complete program into a set of component parts, normally called modules. The decomposition is guided by a set of design principles or criteria that the identified modules should reflect. Since the decomposition determines the coarse structure of the program, the activity is also referred to as *high-level* or *architectural design*. *See also* modular programming, program design.

program design The activity of progressing from a specification of some required program to a description of the program itself. Most phase models of the *software life cycle recognize program design as one of the phases. The input to this phase is a specification of what the program is required to do. During the phase the design decisions are made as to how the program will meet these requirements, and the output of the phase is a description of the program in some form that provides a suitable basis for subsequent implementation.

Frequently the design phase is divided into two subphases, one of coarse *architectural design* and one of *detailed design*. The architectural design produces a description of the program at a gross level; it is normally given in terms of the major components of the program and their interrelationships, the main algorithms that these components employ, and the major data structures. The detailed design then refines the architectural design to the stage where actual implementation can begin. *See also* program design language.

program design language (PDL) A language, used for expressing *program designs, that is similar to a conventional high-level programming language but emphasizes structure and intention rather than the ability to execute programs expressed in the language. PDLs are often employed in conjunction with *structured programming. When not executable they are termed *pseudolanguages.

Typically the formal syntax of a PDL would cover data definition and overall program structure. Facilities in the latter area would include the basic control-flow constructs – sequential, conditional, and itera-tive – plus those for the definition and invocation of subroutines. These facilities would be used to define the overall framework of the program, but individual actions within the framework would be expressed using pseudolanguage – natural English mixed with a more formal semantically rich language. Correspondingly, the PDL facilities for data definition may be expected to be richer than those of a typical programming language, encompassing a broader range of basic types and a more extensive set of data-structuring facilities. A wide variety of PDLs have been defined; normal practice is to select one that is well-matched to the target programming language.

program development system A software system that provides support to the program development phase of a software project. A typical program development system employs a simple database (or perhaps just a basic filing system) as a repository for information, and offers *software tools for editing of program source texts, compiling, link loading, and debugging. Usually some form of command-language interpreter is also available; this may have been produced specifically for the program development system, or may have been inherited from the underlying operating system. *Compare* software engineering environment.

program file A *file containing one or more programs, or program fragments, in *source code or *object code form.

program library (software library) A collection of programs and packages that are made available for common use within some environment; individual items need not be related. A typical library might contain compilers, utility programs, packages for mathematical operations, etc. Usually it is only necessary to reference the library program to cause it to be automatically incorporated in a user's program. *See also* DLL.

program listing (source listing; listing) An output produced by a *compiler or *assembler, consisting of the source program neatly laid out and accompanied by diagnostic information and error messages. In the case of an assembler, the listing may also include a readable version of the object code.

programmable array logic *See* PAL.

programmable devices 1. Devices under the control of a *stored program obeyed by a *fetch-execute cycle. *See* computer, central processor.
2. Integrated circuits whose action is determined by the user either until reprogrammed (*erasable programmable devices*) or for the life of the device (*nonerasable programmable devices*). Erasable devices are usually implemented by the storage of static electric charges, whereas nonerasable devices either employ *fusible links or have their structure determined at the final masking stage of manufacture.

Static charge or fusible-link devices are called *field-programmable*, since they may be programmed by the user "in the field", i.e. on the customer's premises; masked devices are called *mask-programmable*, implying programmability only at the time of manufacture. This terminology is common for *programmed logic. In the case of read-only memory the same distinction often appears as "programmable" (*PROM) and, by implication, as "nonprogrammable" (*ROM).

programmable electronic system *See* PES.

programmable gate array *See* PGA.

programmable logic array *See* PLA.

programmable logic device *See* PLD.

programmable ROM *See* PROM.

program maintenance *See* software maintenance.

programmed I/O A way of controlling input/output activity in which the processor is programmed to interrogate a peripheral or a number of peripherals to see if they are ready for a data transfer. When a number of peripherals are involved the interrogation process is called *polling. *Compare* interrupt I/O.

programmed logic In general, *programmable devices that are more complicated (logical) than read-only memories, thus including programmed logic arrays (*see* PLA), programmed gate arrays (PGAs), pro-

grammed-array logic (PAL), and uncommitted logic arrays (ULAs).

programmed logic array *See* PLA.

programmer 1. A person responsible for writing computer programs. *See* applications programmer, systems programmer.
2. *See* PROM programmer.

programmer unit *Another name for* PROM programmer, and also applied to equipment for programming other field-programmable devices (*see* programmable devices).

programmer workbench *Another name for* software development environment.

programming In the broadest sense, all technical activities involved in the production of a *program, including analysis of requirements and all stages of design and implementation. In a much narrower sense it is the coding and testing of a program from some given design. This narrower usage is most common in the context of commercial programming, where a distinction is often drawn between systems analysts, who are responsible for analysis of requirements and design, and programmers, who are responsible for implementation and testing.

programming language A notation for the precise description of computer programs or algorithms. Programming languages are *artificial* languages, in which the *syntax and *semantics are strictly defined. Thus while they serve their purpose they do not permit the freedom of expression that is characteristic of a natural language.

programming standards A set of rules or conventions that constrain the form of the programs that are produced within an organization. Such rules may range in scope from those that address the high-level design and decomposition of the program to *coding standards*, which govern the use of individual constructs provided by the programming language.

programming support environment *See* PSE (def. 1).

programming theory A general term for a number of interrelated and rapidly developing subjects concerned broadly with the application of formal mathematical methods to the study of programming concepts. Principle areas are: *semantics of programming languages, *program specification, *program correctness, *program transformation, and programming methodology.

program proving *See* program correctness proof.

program specification A precise statement of the effects that an individual program is required to achieve. It should clearly state what the program is to do without making any commitment as to how this is to be done. For a program that is intended to terminate, the program specification can take the form of an input-output specification that describes the desired mapping from the set of input values to the set of output values. For cyclic programs, which are not designed to terminate, it is not possible to give a simple input-output specification; normal practice is to focus attention on the individual functions performed by the program during its cyclic operations.

For both terminating and cyclic programs a variety of notations have been employed for program specifications, ranging from natural language with embedded equations and tables to formal notations such as those based upon first-order *predicate calculus.

program status word (PSW) A collection of information that encapsulates the basic execution state of a program at any instant. It permits an interrupted process to resume operation after the interrupt has been handled. The information is held in the *program status register*, and usually contains the value of the *program counter and bits indicating the status of various conditions in the ALU such as overflow and carry, along with the information on supervisor privileged status. The contents of other processor registers may also need to be preserved in memory after an interruption of a process and recovered when the interrupted process is resumed so that the complete process state is reestablished. *See also* processor status word.

program structure The overall form of a program, with particular emphasis on the individual components of the program and the interrelationships between these components. Programs are frequently referred to as either *well structured* or *poorly structured*. With a well-structured program the division into components follows some recognized principle such as *information hiding, and the interfaces between components are explicit and simple. By contrast, with a poorly structured program the division into components is largely arbitrary (or even nonexistent), and interfaces are implicit and complex. At a finer level, a well-structured program employs appropriate data structures and program units with a single entry point and a single exit point (*see* structured programming, def. 2), while a poorly structured program has arbitrary data structures and flow of control.

program synthesis An *automatic programming technique in which programs are generated from descriptions of input/output relationships. This is a research area in *artificial intelligence.

program testing Checking by means of actual execution whether a program behaves in the desired manner. The program is executed and supplied with test data, and the way in which the program responds to this test data is analyzed. *Compare* program correctness proof.

program transformation The study of systematic ways of transforming a program into another program that has some desirable property and is equivalent to the original program (or, if not equivalent, is related to the original).

Often the aim of such transformation is to produce a more efficient program. It is widely felt that much of the complexity of programming results from the need to produce efficient programs, and that it is therefore desirable to begin with a simple (yet inefficient) program and then transform it to an efficient (but complicated) one. Such transformations may be carried out by hand, by machine, or by both.

Other aims of transformation include expressing certain *language constructs in terms of others (*transformational semantics*). Also, developing algorithms by transformation can serve to verify their correctness, to elucidate their structure, and to provide better understanding of the possible algorithms. *See also* refinement.

program unit A constituent part of a large program, and in some sense self-contained.

program verification Any method that will ensure that a program will do exactly what it is supposed to do. *See also* program correctness proof.

program virus *See* virus.

Prograph An object-oriented dataflow language with a purely graphical interface.

progressive encoding A method of image encoding that uses multiple scans rather than a single scan. (A scan is a single pass through the data of one or more components in an image.) The first scan encodes a rough approximation to the image that is recognizable and can be transmitted quickly compared to the total transmission time of the image. Subsequent scans refine the appearance of the image. Progressive encoding is one of the options in the *JPEG standard.

projection A mapping from one coordinate space to another, possibly of a lower dimension. It takes the points of an object onto the points of a fixed plane (the *view plane) in such a way that each pair of points is collinear with a fixed point, the *center of projection* or *eyepoint*, which lies neither on the object nor the view plane. The main types of projection are *parallel and *perspective projections.

projection function The function U_i^n that extracts the ith coordinate from an ordered n-tuple (*see* ordered pair). More formally

$$U_i^n(x_1, x_2, \ldots x_n) = x_i$$

See also primitive recursive function.

projective transformation Usually, a perspective projection.

project support environment *See* PSE (def. 2).

Prolog A *logic programming language, widely used in artificial intelligence. The basic element of Prolog programs is the *structure*, which expresses a simple relationship among individuals (constants or variables). Examples of structures are:

sister(mary, jane).

ancestor(adam, X).

Words that start with a lower-case letter are constants and words that start with a capital letter are variables, so mary, jane, and adam are constants and X is a variable. Prolog programs consist of clauses, where each is either a simple assertion or an implication. The former consists of a single structure, while the latter takes the form:

"A if B1 and B2 and … and Bn",

where the conclusion A and the conditions Bn are all structures. An example of an implication is

grandfather(X, Y) :-
        father(X, Z), parent(Z, Y).

which means "X is a grandfather of Y if X is the father of Z and Z is a parent of Y".

A Prolog program is invoked by presenting a query in the form of a conjunction of structures, as in

friend(fred, X), father(john, X).

Execution of the program then determines (if possible) a set of values for the variables in the query such that the truth of the query then follows from the assertions and implications in the program. The above example tries to find all the sons of john that are friends of fred.

Prolog was used as the basis of the Japanese *fifth generation project.

PROM *Acronym for* programmable read-only memory. A form of semiconductor read-only memory, *ROM, whose contents are added by a separate process after the device has been manufactured. This process of programming the PROM is accomplished by means of a device known as a *PROM programmer. In general the programming process involves the destruction of *fusible links within the PROM and is irreversible, i.e. the contents of the memory cannot be altered. Certain PROMs, including *EPROMs, can however be reprogrammed numerous times. *See also* EEPROM, EAPROM.

PROM programmer (programmer unit) An item of equipment that establishes the correct conditions for the programming of a *PROM device and thus allows the user to program the PROM. The programming process often requires the physical destruction of fusible links within the PROM using relatively high voltage pulses, hence the jargon terms *PROM zapping*, *blowing*, *blasting*, and *burning*. Such equipment may be capable of programming a number of different types of PROM and/or *EPROM devices.

prompt A change to the contents of a computer display to indicate that input is required from the operator. *See also* acknowledgment, echoing, feedback.

proof Informally, a form of *deduction associated with a deductive logic. More formally, when applied to a formal system *F*, a proof is a sequence of *well-formed formulas with each item in the sequence being either an axiom of *F* or being derived from previous items through the application of an inference rule of *F*.

propagation delay The time required for a change in the input to a *logic gate or *logic circuit to produce a change in the output. It is usually very brief. It is inherent in any gate or circuit, being caused by unavoidable delays in transistor switching and propagation of electric signals through passive components.

proper ancestor *See* ancestor.

proper subset, subgroup, subgraph *See* subset, subgroup, subgraph respectively.

proportional spacing *See* font.

propositional calculus A system of *symbolic logic, designed to study *propositions*. A proposition is a statement that is true or false. There are many alternative but equivalent definitions of propositional calculus, one of the more useful for the computer scientist being given below.

The only terms of the propositional calculus are the two symbols *T* and *F* (standing for true and false) together with variables for logical propositions, which are denoted by small letters $p,q,r,\ldots$; these symbols are basic and indivisible and are thus called *atomic formulas*.

The propositional calculus is based on the study of *well-formed formulas*, or *wff* for short. New wff of the form

$$(\sim A), (A \vee B), (A \wedge B),$$
$$(A \supset B), (A \equiv B),$$
$$(\text{IF } A \text{ THEN } B \text{ ELSE } C)$$

are formed from given wff *A*, *B*, and *C* using logical *connectives; respectively they are called *negation, disjunction, conjunction, implication, equivalence*, and *conditional*. If $\langle atf \rangle$ denotes the class of atomic formulas, then the class of wff, $\langle wff \rangle$, can be described in *BNF notation (*see* Fig. 1).

Proofs and theorems within the propositional calculus are conducted in a formal and rigorous manner: certain basic axioms are

$$\langle wff \rangle ::= \langle atf \rangle | \ (\sim \langle wff \rangle) | \ (\langle wff \rangle \vee \langle wff \rangle) |$$
$$(\langle wff \rangle \wedge \langle wff \rangle) | \ (\langle wff \rangle \supset \langle wff \rangle) |$$
$$(\langle wff \rangle \equiv \langle wff \rangle) |$$
$$(\text{IF } \langle wff \rangle \text{ THEN } \langle wff \rangle \text{ ELSE } \langle wff \rangle)$$

Fig. 1 Class of wff in BNF notation, used in propositional calculus

$$\frac{\Gamma \to A \text{ and } \Gamma \to B}{\Gamma \to A \wedge B}$$

$$\frac{\Gamma \to A \wedge B}{\Gamma \to A} \qquad \frac{\Gamma \to A \wedge B}{\Gamma \to B}$$

Fig. 2 Rule of inference for $\wedge$

assumed and certain rules of *inference are followed. In particular these rules must deal with the various connectives.

The rules of inference are stated using a form such as

$$\frac{\alpha}{\beta}$$

The rule should be interpreted to mean that on the assumption that α is true, it can be deduced that β is then true. Logicians often use the notation $\alpha \vdash \beta$. In writing the rules it is convenient to employ a notation such as

$$\Gamma, A \Rightarrow B$$

Γ is some set of wff whose truth has been established; A and B are some other wff highlighted for the purposes of the rule; $\Rightarrow$ denotes implication (to avoid confusion with the symbol $\supset$). For example, the rules for the introduction and elimination respectively of the $\wedge$ connective are shown in Fig. 2.

protected location A memory location that can only be accessed by an authorized user or process. *See also* memory protection.

protection domain A set of access privileges to protected resources. Where many *processes coexist, each process having differing access permission to a number of protected resources via some form of key, it may be convenient to group together a set of such keys in order to provide a single process with access to the resources that it requires. Access control can then be manipulated independent of the processes concerned. The protection domain is either the set of keys, or equivalently, the set of resources to which the keys give access.

protocol An agreement that governs the procedures used to exchange information between cooperating entities. More specifically, a protocol is such an agreement operating between entities that have no direct means of exchanging information, but that do so by passing information across a local interface to so-called *lower-level* protocols, until the *lowest*, *physical*, *level* is reached. The information is transferred to the remote location using the lowest-level protocol, and then passes upward via the interfaces until it reaches the corresponding level at the destination. In general, a protocol will govern the

format of messages, the generation of checking information, and the flow control, as well as actions to be taken in the event of errors.

A set of protocols, governing the exchange of information between (physically remote) communicating entities at a given level, and the set of interfaces governing the exchange between (physically adjacent) protocol levels, are collectively referred to as *protocol hierarchy* or a *protocol stack*.

See also seven-layer reference model.

protocol hierarchy *See* protocol.

protocol stack *See* protocol.

protocol translation *See* internetworking.

prototype *See* software prototyping.

PSE 1. *Abbrev. for* programming support environment. A software system that provides support for the programming aspects of software development, repair, and enhancement. A typical system contains a central database and a set of *software tools. The central database acts as a repository for all the information related to the programming activities.

PSEs vary in the general nature of their databases and in the coverage provided by, and the degree of cooperative interaction of, the set of tools and the programming languages supported. A programming support environment might be considered as a more technologically advanced form of *program development system.

2. *Abbrev. for* project support environment. A software system that provides support for the full life cycle of software development and also the project control and management aspects of a software-intensive project. The project support environment will have all the features of a programming support environment (see above) plus *software tools to support the earlier phases of software development (*see* CASE (upper)) and tools associated with the management and control of the project. *See also* IPSE.

pseudocode *Another name for* pseudolanguage.

pseudoinstruction (pseudo-operation; directive) An element in an assembly language that is similar to an instruction but provides control information to the assembler as opposed to generating a particular instruction. Examples are:

generate absolute code/generate relative addresses;

start a new segment;

allocate space for constants or variables.

pseudolanguage (pseudocode) A form of representation used to provide an outline description of the *specification for a software module. Pseudolanguages contain a mixture of natural language expressions embedded in syntactic structures taken from programming language (such as IF..THEN..ELSE). The formality of the definition varies from ad hoc (e.g. defined within a project team) to being sufficiently formal to enable automatic parsing and syntax checking (e.g. supported by a *CASE tool). Pseudolanguages are not intended to be executed by computer; they must be interpreted by people.

pseudonoise sequence A sequence of symbols with *pseudorandom properties intended to simulate *noise. Most commonly *m-sequences are used.

pseudo-operation *Another name for* pseudoinstruction.

pseudorandom Mimicking randomness. A *deterministic process, which cannot in principle be random, may nevertheless exhibit properties of randomness. It may therefore serve as a surrogate random process, in which case it is called pseudorandom.

pseudorandom numbers *See* random numbers.

PSG *Abbrev. for* phrase-structure grammar.

PSK *Abbrev. for* phase shift keying.

PSL/PSA *Abbrev. for* problem statement language/problem statement analyzer. A computerized system that can be used for the development and analysis of an *expression of requirements and to provide assistance during system design. The expression of requirements is maintained in a database: PSL is the input language to this database while PSA is the management system and report generator for the database.

The basic database model consists of objects that may have properties and may be interconnected by means of relationships. The types of object and relationship are predefined within PSL, there being more than 20 kinds of object and more than 50 kinds of relationship. The objects and relationships are concerned with various aspects of the system for which requirements are being expressed: system input/output flow, system structure, data structure, data derivation, system size and volume, system dynamics, system properties, and project management. PSA permits the analysis of the database and the production of various kinds of report, e.g. on database modifications, database content, and on unused data objects or breaks in information flow.

PSL/PSA was developed by Daniel Teichroew on the ISDOS project at the University of Michigan. The system has been implemented on a wide range of computers and has been used extensively by many organizations.

PSPACE, PSPACE-complete *See* polynomial space.

PSS 1. *Abbrev. for* packet switching service. A data transmission service, such as BT's Packet SwitchStream, that uses *packet switching techniques.
2. *Abbrev. for* Packet SwitchStream.

PSTN *Abbrev. for* public switched telephone network (as opposed to a leased line).

PSW *Abbrev. for* processor status word, program status word.

P-switch *Short for* printer switch. A hardware switch allowing several users to share a printer. An alternative version allows a user to select one of several printers. The P-switch may be manually operated or automatic. As networking becomes more affordable, P-switches are becoming less common.

p-system A software system for microcomputers developed from *UCSD Pascal. The system provides a number of languages in a uniform manner, using p-code as a common intermediate language.

PTI *Abbrev. for* public tool interface. A concept made necessary as *PSEs – project and programming support environments – increase the degree of and demand for information exchange and interaction between various *software tools, especially tools from different suppliers. A common specification is required for the interface between the tools and the *object management system. Similarly as an increasing number of tools are used within a single development, it becomes desirable to have a common *user interface for the tools (assisting the user to learn the interface and get the best out of the tools). Both these interfaces may be included within a single PTI, but the current trend is to define them in separate PTIs. The user-interface aspects are dominated by the *OSF definitions for *wimp interfaces. The most well-developed standard for object management systems is *PCTE. At a less sophisticated level the OSF file-store definitions can also be used. An alternative approach is offered by *CDIF.

PTIME *See* polynomial time.

PTO *Abbrev. for* public telecommunications operator.

PTT *Abbrev. for* Postal, Telegraph, and Telephone Administration. Each member country of the *CCITT (for all practical purposes every country in the world) has a PTT, which is that country's representative on the CCITT. In those countries where the provision of communications services remains as a government monopoly, the PTT is the agency that delivers the communications services, both internally and for international connections. In countries where there is no longer a government monopoly, the PTT is still responsible for the issue of licenses and may also be one of a number of competing suppliers of communications services.

The image of the PTTs was as suppliers of limited data communications, based on speech-quality circuits operating at low bit rates up to say 9600 bps, and in some countries this persists. However, in response both to competition from other suppliers and to the growing demands of the marketplace, many PTTs are now aggressive suppliers of innovative high-grade services, offering digital services with operating speeds over the full range from a few hundred bps up to tens or hundreds of Mbps, and with extensive interworking with other suppliers for both domestic and international traffic.

p-type semiconductor *See* semiconductor.

public data network (PDN) A data network that is accessible for use by private individuals, or by organizations other than that operating the network. In most countries it is necessary to be licensed to operate a PDN. *See also* PTT, public network operator, public telecommunications operator.

public domain The status of a work, such as a program or document, where the author has irrevocably waived any copyright in the work so that it can be freely copied and used. In countries such as Germany and the USA statutes and government publications are considered to be in the public domain. In the computer industry the term is normally applied to the computer programs and data supplied to computer user groups by its active members for circulation among the group as an aid to the operation of computers or the removal of bugs.

public key encryption *See* cryptography, RSA encryption.

public network operator (PNO) An organization authorized to offer network services to other organizations, or directly to members of the public. In those countries with a government monopoly in the provision of network services the only PNO will be the *PTT. In those countries with a deregulated market in the provision of network services, it is still only appropriately licensed organizations that are allowed to act as PNOs.

public telecommunications operator (PTO) A UK agency licensed to provide data transmission services to organizations or private individuals, where the services cross public rights of way. Within the UK, until the mid-1980s, the only organization able to offer such services was British Telecom (previously the GPO) and, for purely historical reasons, the civic authorities in the city of Hull. At the time of the BT privatization, legislation was enacted that allowed the creation of further PTOs, although for a long time only Mercury took advantage of this.

There are now a large number of organizations taking out licenses to act as PTOs, driven in part by the installation of optical fiber networks in metropolitan areas. *See also* public network operator.

public tool interface *See* PTI.

puck An input device that defines a location by sensing its position on a *data tablet. A lens can be incorporated into the puck if points are being input to give the locations of positions on a detailed drawing.

pull-down menu (drop-down menu) A *menu that appears on a computer screen when its title, often occurring in a menu bar, is selected by means of a *mouse or other *pointing device or an appropriate sequence of keystrokes. One or more of the menu options may then be selected in the same way, after which the menu will normally vanish.

pull-up resistor A resistor that is connected between the power-supply line and a logic line and ensures that the line is normally pulled up to the supply potential. *Open-collector logic devices may be connected to the logic line and each device is then capable of pulling the line low, i.e. to ground.

pulse A transient change in voltage, current, or some other normally constant physical parameter. This transient consists of a fixed-amplitude geometrically defined transition from one level to another, followed, after a fixed time, by an opposite and often equal amplitude transition. The first edge to occur on a pulse is the *leading edge*, the second transition being the *trailing edge*.

For rectangular pulses the transitions should in theory be stepwise, i.e. instantaneous. In reality however they require a finite time in which to occur. For transitions from low to high voltage, current, etc., a convenient measure of this time is the *rise time*,

defined as the time required for the pulse amplitude to rise from 10% to 90% of its maximum value (see diagram). The *fall time* is the time interval between the 10% point and the 90% point on the negative-going edge of the pulse.

The time interval between the leading and trailing edge of a rectangular pulse is called the *pulse width*. The *pulse height* is the amplitude of a pulse, usually its maximum to minimum voltage, current, etc., ignoring any short-duration spikes or low-amplitude ripple superimposed on the main pulse. *See also* ringing.

pulse code modulation (PCM) A technique used by *codecs to convert an analog signal into a digital bit stream. The amplitude (usually) of the analog signal is sampled (8000 samples per second for voice-quality telephone lines with 4000 Hz bandwidth), and a digital code is selected to represent the sampled value. The digital code is transmitted to the receiving end, which uses it to generate an analog output signal. Encoding techniques may be used to reduce the amount of data that is transmitted between the sender and the receiver, based on known characteristics of the analog signal. For example, *mu-law (µ-law) encoding* converts the analog signal to a digital code based on the logarithm of its value, rather than on a linear transformation.

Differential PCM (DPCM) transmits the difference between the current sample and the previous sample. DPCM assumes that the difference requires fewer bits than the signal amplitude.

Delta (Δ) PCM is a version of DPCM in which a single bit is used for each sample, representing a signal change of plus or minus one unit. A constant signal is represented as a series of plus or minus transitions.

Predictive PCM extrapolates from the previous few samples what the next sample should be, and transmits the difference between the actual value and the predicted value.

See also modulation.

pulse generator A circuit or instrument that generates a sequence of *pulses, usually (but

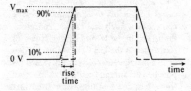

Rectangular voltage pulse

not necessarily) of uniform height, width, and pulse repetition frequency.

pulse height *See* pulse.

pulse repetition frequency (PRF; pulse repetition rate) of a *pulse train. The average number of pulses that occur per second, expressed in hertz. It is equal to the reciprocal of the *period.

pulse shaping Alteration of the shape of a *pulse. Usually pulse-shaping circuits receive pulses that are distorted and convert them into rectangular pulses; sometimes they incorporate a *monostable circuit to set the output pulse width.

pulse stretcher An electronic device that is often included in logic circuitry in order to extend the duration of very short input pulses. This ensures that the pulses are of adequate length, i.e. they are of the minimum duration required for reliable processing by the circuitry. A *monostable is often used for this purpose.

pulse train A repetitive series of *pulses, separated in time by a fixed and often constant interval. The duration of each pulse and its amplitude are also often made constant. This type of waveform may be defined by its *mark-space ratio*, i.e. the ratio of pulse duration, t_1, to pulse separation, t_2, and by its *pulse repetition frequency, which is given by

$$1/(t_1 + t_2)$$

pulse-triggered flip-flop *See* flip-flop.

pulse width *See* pulse.

pumping lemmas Two theorems in formal language theory that express necessary conditions for languages to be *regular or *context-free:

If language L is regular, there exists an integer n such that,

for any *word z in L, $|z| > n$,

there exist u, v, w with

$z = uvw$, v nonempty, $|vw| \le n$,

such that:

$uv^k w \in L$, for all $k \ge 0$

If language L is context-free, there exist integers p and q such that,

for any z in L, with $|z| > p$,

there exist u, v, w, x, y with

$z = uvwxy$, v and x nonempty,

$|vwx| \le q$,

such that:

$uv^k wx^k y \in L$, for all $k \ge 0$

The conditions are used in constructing algorithms for decision problems about regular and context-free grammars, and in proving certain languages are not regular or are not context-free.

punched card (punch card) A rectangular paper card into which data could be encoded by punching patterns of holes. The holes were then sensed by a *punched card reader*, which converted the punched patterns into binary code. Punched cards were used extensively for input, output, and file storage of data on early computer systems but are now obsolete.

The cards were of a uniform size and were notionally divided into a number of *columns* parallel to the short edge and a number of *rows* – usually 12 – parallel to the long edge. The 80 column card, 7.375″ by 3.25″ (18.73 by 8.25 cm) in size, was the most common type; each column was divided into 12 positions at which holes could be punched, a particular combination of holes in a column representing a specific character. Cards could be read column by column (i.e. one character at a time), generally at speeds between 150 and 2000 cards per minute, or they could be read row by row, so reducing the time to read a card. The last type of punched card to be widely used was the 96 column IBM card.

Prior to the development of computers a variety of machines were available that enabled the various activities of data processing, e.g. sorting, collating, and listing or tabulating, to be carried out using data files composed of punched cards. Stout cards with holes punched in them were used by Jacquard to control the weaving of patterns on a loom in about 1800. Charles Babbage saw the possibility of using punched cards to control his *Analytical Engine, conceived in the 1830s. In the 1880s Herman Hollerith, a statistician at the US Census Bureau, developed a machine that electrically sensed holes punched in cards and could sort and accumulate totals; the machines were used in the 1890 census. In 1896 Hollerith formed his own company, which was later to become IBM.

punched card reader *See* punched card.

punched tape Punched *paper tape.

pure BCD *Another name for* natural BCD. *See* binary-coded decimal.

push *See* stack (def. 1).

pushdown automaton (PDA) A *finite-state automaton augmented by a *stack of symbols that are distinct from the symbols allowed in the input string. Like the finite-state automaton, the PDA reads its input string once from left to right, with acceptance or rejection determined by the final state. After reading a symbol, however, the PDA performs the following actions: change state, remove top of stack, and push zero or more symbols onto stack. The precise choice of actions depends on the input symbol just read, the current state, and the current top of stack. Since the stack can grow unboundedly, a PDA can have infinitely many different configurations – unlike a finite-state automaton.

A *nondeterministic PDA* is one that has a choice of actions for some conditions. The languages recognized by nondeterministic PDAs are precisely the *context-free languages. However not every context-free language is recognized by a deterministic PDA.

pushdown stack, pushdown list *Other names for* stack (def. 1).

pushup stack, pushup list *Other names for* queue. *See also* stack (def. 2).

PVC *Abbrev. for* permanent virtual circuit. *See* virtual circuit.

Python A *scripting language incorporating features from C, Modula 3, and Icon.

Q

q-ary (q-valued) Having q values, where q is a positive integer not less than 2. In *logic circuits, the treatment of q values is called *multivalued logic, or binary logic for $q = 2$. In coding theory, some codes are restricted to the binary case; others can operate with arbitrary q or with q a prime number. Throughout switching and coding theory, the binary case is by far the most important. *See also* polynomial.

q-ary logic *Digital logic employing q states. The term is sometimes used to mean digital logic in general, but more usually has the implication that there are more than two states, in which case the term is synonymous with *multivalued logic.

QBE *Abbrev. for* query by example.

QC *Abbrev. for* quality control.

QR factorization A form of matrix factorization widely used in *numerical linear algebra. For A, an $m \times n$, $m \geq n$, real square matrix, the factorization takes the form
$$A = QR$$
where Q is an $m \times m$ *orthogonal matrix and R is an $m \times n$ matrix whose first n rows form an upper (or right) *triangular matrix. An important application is in solving overdetermined linear systems of equations of the form $Ax = b$, $m > n$; b is an m-component column vector and x is a column vector of n unknowns. The QR factorization, under appropriate conditions, reduces the problem to solving a simpler square upper triangular system of the form $Rx = c$.

For a square matrix, $m = n$, a further major application is in computing the eigenvalues and eigenvectors of A. Here a sequence of QR factorizations are carried out in an iteration scheme that ultimately reduces A to a matrix of a particularly simple form whose eigenvalues are the same as those of A. The eigenvalues (and if required, eigenvectors) can now be easily computed.

quad *See* quadtree.

quadratic spline A *spline of degree 2.

quadrature 1. A method of signal modulation involving two carrier waves with a 90° phase difference. This allows better usage of the bandwidth of the communications link. Quadrature is used in higher-speed modems. **2.** *See* numerical integration.

quadtree A space tree in which a square region is recursively divided into four smaller regions, known as *quads*. The quads are usually squares. *See also* octree.

qualifier register (condition-code register) A set of *indicators that record the status or condition of the last result output from the *ALU. It forms part of the *program status word.

qualitative reasoning An *artificial intelligence approach in which precise numerical quantities are avoided in favor of symbolic qualitative values. Variables take values from a quantity space, e.g. {high, low, zero}, and are processed by various qualitative calculi. Based on intuitive ideas about human reasoning (*see* imprecision), this formalism is proving valuable in modeling and reasoning about problems in diagnosis, process control, system verification, and explanation.

quality assurance *See* software quality assurance.

quality control (QC) The use of sampling, inspection, and testing methods at all levels of system production to produce defect-free hardware and software.

quantifier One of the two symbols $\forall$ or $\exists$ used in *predicate calculus. $\forall$ is the *universal quantifier* and is read "for all". $\exists$ is the *existential quantifier* and is read "there exists" or "for some". In either case the reference is to possible values of the variable v that the quantifier introduces. $\forall v . F$ means that the formula F is true for all values of v, while $\exists v . F$ means that F is true for at least one value of v. As an example, suppose that $P(x,y)$ is the predicate "x is less than or equal to y". Then the following expression

$$\exists x . \forall y . P(x,y)$$

says that there exists an x that is less than or equal to all y. This statement is true if values range over the *natural numbers, since x can be taken to be 0. It becomes false however if values are allowed to range over negative integers as well. Note also that it would be false even for natural numbers if the predicate were "x is less than y". Other notations such as $(\forall v)F$ in place of $\forall v . F$ are also found.

quantization The process of constructing a discrete representation of a quantity that is usually regarded as continuous (*see* discrete and continuous systems). For example, the measurement of the amplitude of a *signal at discrete intervals of time, when the signal occurs over continuous time, is called *time quantization*, or *sampling*; the measurement of the brightness of picture elements (*pixels) in a space-continuous picture is called *space quantization*, or *pixelization*.

The term quantization without the predication of time or space usually refers to the quantization of amplitude; the same applies to *digitization, which is nearly synonymous with quantization.

quantization noise The effective continuous noise power, the addition of which to a continuous signal has the same effect as the amplitude *quantization to which the signal is subjected (*see* discrete and continuous systems). The effect of time *quantization may also be described by the addition of noise, but in a more complex way. *See also* Nyquist's criterion.

quantizer An electronic device that can convert an *analog signal into a signal having values that are identical to the analog signal only at discrete instants of time. The action is analogous to observing, i.e. *sampling, the analog signal, approximating it by the nearest preferred value and holding this value until the next observation time. The output signal thus consists of a number of steps between specified levels. *See also* digitizer.

quantum The amount of time allocated to an individual *process in a *time-slicing process-management system. *See also* scheduling algorithm.

quantum computing An area of research that is concerned with the behavior of nanocircuits built from logic gates consisting of only a few atoms (in which there are quantum effects), and the prospect of quantum bits that superpose the states 0 and 1.

quantum-inspired computing The use of computational methods inspired by the principles of quantum mechanics, such as probabilistic universes, interference, and superposition of states. The approach is primarily aimed at problems that are known to be NP-hard (*see* P=NP question) or require large amounts of processing time. A quantum-inspired computation may suggest rather than guarantee a result, which needs to be checked by normal algorithm.

Quantum-inspired sorting, for instance, splits a list of items to be sorted into distinct parallel universes and then sorts the sublists both within and across universes using interference. For quantum-inspired *genetic algorithms, each chromosome evolves in its own universe, with interference between two or more universes implementing crossover.

quartile *See* percentile.

quaternary logic *See* multivalued logic.

Quattro Pro *Trademark* A widely used *spreadsheet supplied by Novell.

query by example (QBE) A screen-based form-filling user interface to a *relational database. The software derives the searches to be made from examples given by the user.

query language Strictly a language for the specification of retrieval criteria against which information is obtained from a database. The term is something of a misnomer when, as with *SQL, a language that originated for this purpose has been extended to include facilities for updating and for schema modification. *See also* query processing.

query processing 1. The retrieval of information from a *database according to a set of retrieval criteria, the database itself remaining unchanged.
2. In the context of a specific *query language, the technique of translating the retrieval criteria specified using the language (*see* def. 1) into more primitive database-access software, including a selection among different methods to choose the most efficient in the particular circumstances.

queue 1. (FIFO list; pushup stack; pushup list) A linear *list where all insertions are made at one end of the list and all removals and accesses at the other. Like a pushdown *stack, a queue can be implemented in hardware as a specialized form of addressless memory, and is most commonly used for speed buffering between a real-time data input/output stream and a form of memory that requires start/stop time.

2. *See* queue management, queuing theory.

queue management A queue is characterized by the way in which customers (i.e. processes) join it in order to wait for service, and by the way in which customers already in the queue are selected for servicing. Both of these activities are controlled by the *queue manager.*

queuing network A network of queues (*see* queuing theory) used to model a system, particularly for performance analysis.

queuing theory The study of systems in which customers, arriving at random and requiring varying periods of service, may have to wait in order to be served. From the number of service points and the *probability distributions of arrival times and service times, the distribution of the length of queue and the waiting time before service may be predicted.

Queuing theory has important applications in any system liable to congestion, where the costs of improved service may be balanced against the costs of congestion.

quibinary code *Another name for* biquinary code.

QuickBasic *See* Basic.

quickersort An algorithm published in 1965 by R. S. Scowen using a method similar to *quicksort. It repeatedly splits the array to be sorted into parts such that all elements of one part are less than all elements of the other, with a third part in the middle consisting of a single element.

quicksort (partition-exchange sort) A form of sorting by exchanging due to C. A. R. Hoare. By comparing sortkeys from the two extremes of the file, and alternately working up the file from the bottom until an exchange is necessary and then working down the file from the top, the original problem can be reduced to two smaller problems. The same process is then applied to each part, and is further repeated until the problems are trivially small. *See also* heapsort.

Quicktime *Trademark* A utility program from Apple for embedding *multimedia, such as audio and video, in a document. It is available for Windows as well as the Macintosh.

quiesce To render a device or system inactive by, for example, rejecting new requests for work.

q-valued See q-ary.

R

RACE *Acronym for* research on advanced communications in Europe. A cooperative venture of a group of organizations, coordinated and part-funded by the European Union.

race condition (race) A condition in *sequential circuits in which two or more variables change at one time. In practice, i.e. with nonideal circuits, there is a possibility of incorrect operation under such a condition. *See also* hazard.

racking See scroll.

radio button One of a set of *buttons in a *dialogue box that, when activated, allows only one of a set of mutually exclusive options to be selected at a time (as when selecting a radio station using a button with a pre-set frequency). For example, there may be a set of radio buttons with the options to print a full document, the current page, or multiple pages.

radiosity A method used in computer graphics for producing photorealistic images but originating from thermal engineers in the 1950s. The scene is divided into many small objects and accurate modeling of diffuse interreflection between objects is calculated (*see* diffuse reflection). This results in a large number of simultaneous equations to be solved, so the method is not the fastest available. The energy input to the system comes from the light sources. *See also* clustering.

radix (base) The number of distinct digits in a fixed-radix *number system. These digits represent the integers in the range zero to one less than the radix. The radix of a number can be indicated by means of a subscript, as in 24_8 or 101_2. *See also* binary system, hexadecimal notation, octal notation.

radix complement (true complement) For an integer represented in a fixed-radix *number system, a number formed by adding one to the *radix-minus-one complement of the given integer. For example, in the decimal system the *ten's complement* of 0372 is 9628 (i.e. 9627 + 1); in the binary system the *two's complement* of 1100 is 0100 (i.e. 0011 + 1). *See also* complement number system.

radix exchange A form of *sorting by exchanging. Instead of comparing two sortkeys, individual bits are compared, starting with the most significant bit. The file is then split into two subfiles, one with keys having 0 as first bit, the other with 1 as first bit. The process continues on the first subfile, comparing the second bits, and similarly on the second subfile, and so on until the file is sorted.

radix-minus-one complement (diminished radix complement) For an integer represented in a fixed-radix *number system, a number formed by replacing each digit d in the integer by its *complement*, i.e. by

$$(R - 1 - d)$$

where R denotes the radix of the system. For example, in the decimal system the *nine's complement* of 0372 is 9627; in the binary system the *one's complement* of 1100 is 0011. *See also* complement number system, radix complement.

radix notation See radix point.

radix point A symbol, usually a dot, used to separate the integral part from the fractional part of a number expressed in a *radix notation*, i.e. in the notation used in a positional *number system.

radix sorting (digital sorting; pocket sorting) A sorting algorithm in which the file is first sorted on the least significant digit of the sortkey, then the next least significant until in the final pass a sort is made on the most significant digit. The algorithm is best implemented using *linked lists. *See also* divide and conquer sorting.

ragged array An array where the numbers of elements in each row (or column) are not equal: such arrays are described as *row-ragged* (or *column-ragged*). A ragged array is usually represented using an *access vector or a vector of pointers, each pointer referring to a row (or column) of the ragged array.

ragged right A method of laying out lines of print such that a new line is started after the last word that fits in before the right margin, and no extra white space is inserted in the line to make the end of the last word reach the margin exactly. *See also* justify.

RAID *Acronym for* redundant array of independent disks (or drives). A storage system based on a *disk array that holds a certain amount of redundant information. The redundant information can be used either to detect or in some cases correct errors. As with any system, the greater the fraction of the information that is redundant, the greater the protection against undetected errors, or the ability to recover from errors when detected.

In 1988, David A. Patterson, Garth Gibson, and Randy Katz of the University of California at Berkeley published a paper entitled *"A Case for Redundant Arrays of Inexpensive Disks"*, which outlined five array models or RAID levels. The levels were named RAID 1 through 5, although no hierarchical relationship was implied. Since the publication of the paper, a sixth RAID level has been described by the authors. In addition, RAID level 0 is used to refer to a stripe set (*see* stripe disk). However, the absence of redundancy in a stripe set makes the term RAID a misnomer. The use of the word inexpensive arose from the belief that arrays of low-cost PC drives offered a significant decrease in storage costs when compared to SLEDs (single large expensive disks), which at the time were used on mainframe systems.

Four RAID levels – 0, 1, 3, 5 – have been found to be commercially attractive; however, each has drawbacks when applied in products. RAID product developers frequently improve upon the data mapping and redundancy protection models outlined in the original paper. This is achieved by combining RAID levels and/or combining RAID data mapping with other technologies such as caching. The RAID level 0 and the Berkeley RAID levels are as follows.

RAID 0 or *Disk Striping* Data is distributed uniformly in *chunks* across the *member disks of the array; no redundant information is generated. If there are N disks in the array, its *MTBF is $1/N$ times the MTBF of a single disk. The data transfer capacity and I/O rate is very high for both reads and writes.

RAID 1 or *Mirroring* All data is duplicated across the N disks of the array so that the *virtual disk has a capacity equal to that of one physical disk. For $N > 3$ this configuration has the highest data reliability. The data transfer rate is higher than a single disk for reads and slightly less than a single disk for writes. The I/O rate is up to twice that of a single disk for reads and similar to a single disk for writes.

RAID 2 Each sector of data is divided into small *chunks* and is distributed across the k data disks. The virtual sector size is thus k times that of a physical disk. Data is protected by a *Hamming code; the N disks of the array comprise k data disks and m redundant disks such that

$$N \le 2^m - 1 \text{ and } k = N - m$$

Data reliability is comparable to RAID 3, 4, or 5 while the data transfer capacity and I/O rate is comparable to RAID 3.

RAID 3 or *Parallel Transfer Disks with Parity* Each sector of data is divided into small *chunks* and distributed across the $N - 1$ data disks. The virtual sector size is thus $(N - 1)$ times that of a physical disk. The redundant information is stored on a dedicated parity disk. Data reliability is comparable to RAID 2, 4, or 5 while the data transfer capacity is the highest of all.

RAID 4 or *Independent Access Array* Data is striped to *chunks* on the data disks, which are very much larger than the data sectors. Redundant information is stored on a dedicated parity disk. Data reliability is much higher than for a single disk – comparable to RAID 2, 3, or 5. Data transfer capacity and I/O rate is similar to disk striping for reads but significantly lower than single disk for writes.

RAID 5 or *Independent Access Array with Rotating Parity* Data is distributed as in RAID 4 but to all the disks of the array. Redundant information is interspersed with user data. Data reliability is comparable to

RAID 2, 3, or 4. Data transfer capacity and I/O rate is similar to disk striping for reads but lower than a single disk for writes.

RAID 6 is as RAID 5 but with an additional parity disk. The additional parity is independently computed such than *any* two disks in the array can simultaneously fail and the array will still provide user data. Data reliability is the highest except for RAID 2 with more than three member disks. Data transfer capacity and I/O rate is similar to disk striping for reads and lower than RAID 5 for writes.

RAM *Acronym for* random-access memory.
1. The *main memory of a computer. It is fabricated using semiconductor technology and allows the computer user to access (read from) or alter (write to) individual storage locations within the device (see def. 2).
2. A semiconductor memory device in which the basic element consists of a single cell that is capable of storing one bit of information. Large-capacity memories are formed as two-dimensional arrays of these cells. An individual cell is identified uniquely by row and column addresses, which are derived by decoding a user-supplied address word. A typical organization is shown in the diagram. Each cell in a RAM is thus independent of all other cells in the array and can be accessed in any order and in the same amount of time, hence the term *random access; data can be both read from and written to the cells in the array. RAM is usually *volatile memory and is used for temporary storage of data or programs.

RAM devices can be classified as *static* or *dynamic*. Static RAM (SRAM) is fabricated from either bipolar or MOS components (*see* bipolar transistor, MOSFET); each cell is formed by an electronic *latch whose contents remain fixed until written to or until the power is removed. Dynamic RAM (DRAM) cells, which comprise MOS devices, utilize the charge stored on a capacitance as a temporary store (*see* bucket); due to leakage currents, the cell contents must be *refreshed at regular intervals, typically every millisecond. Static and dynamic RAMs are well suited to fabrication in integrated-circuit form. Compared with static RAMs, dynamic RAMs have larger cell densities, lower power consumption, but slower access times. *Compare* ROM.

RAM disk (RAM drive, virtual disk) A portion of a computer's *RAM memory made to behave as though it were a disk. It can be written to and read from as though it were a real disk but it is very much faster. However

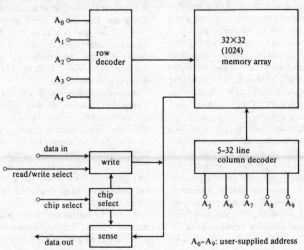

Typical organization of a RAM

it will generally have a lower capacity than a hard disk. The contents of the RAM disk are not preserved when the computer is switched off.

RAM drive *Another name for* RAM disk.

Ramp-C benchmark A *benchmark that measures the limiting capacity of a computer system by a combination of an increasing number of transactions from a standardized mix and an increasing number of terminals, until no more transactions or terminals can be added. This is represented for a number of configurations of the computer until the highest capacity is reached. A percentage (typically 70%) of the highest capacity is then taken as the benchmark result.

random access 1. A type of memory access in which storage locations can be accessed in any order. The term is applied primarily to the *main memory of a processor where the *access time to any word or byte is fixed, i.e. the access time to any item of information is independent of the address of that item and of the address of any previous item referred to. Main memory is fabricated from semiconductor *RAM or *ROM, and the access time is typically of the order of 10–100 nanoseconds.

The term random-access memory has also been used to describe memory implemented on *magnetic disk to distinguish it from serially accessed devices such as magnetic tape.

See also RAM disk.

2. A method of access to a *file (especially a data file): a file is said to be randomly accessed if the sequence of transactions submitted to it does not match any sequence in which records may be organized.

random-access file A file that is organized to support *random access. The most common random-access methods are *hashing, *indexed sequential, and *B-tree based methods. *See also* ISAM, VSAM.

random-access memory *See* RAM. *See also* random access.

random-access stored-program machine A general-purpose computer in which the program and data are contained in (usually the same) read-write random-access memory. *See also* von Neumann machine.

random algorithms Algorithms that are fast but instead of always giving the correct answer give the correct answer with high probability. They have been devised because of the difficulty (impossibility?) of finding *polynomial time algorithms for some problems (*see* P=NP question).

An example is that of trying to test whether or not a number is prime. Given an integer n there is a test that uses a "guess" i, chosen at random between 1 and n, that takes $O(\log_2 n)$ time to perform. If the test is successful n is known to have factors; on the other hand if n has factors then the test will be successful for at least half of the integers in the range 1 to n. Thus if the test fails k times it can be said that n is prime with probability $1 - 2^{-k}$.

Several other examples of problems amenable to a similar approach have now been found. However, such examples are either already known to be solvable in polynomial time anyway (although the random algorithms are an order of magnitude faster) or, like prime-testing, under suspicion of so being.

random logic A term generally used to describe a relatively nonuniform digital logic circuit. For example, a control unit will contain random logic; an ALU, having a regular structure, will not.

random numbers Numbers that are drawn using a random *sampling technique from a set of permissible numbers. True random numbers are difficult to obtain, and programs using them are difficult to debug.

Attempts to produce random numbers using the arithmetic properties of a computer result in *pseudorandom numbers*, since in principle the numbers generated depend on their predecessors. However, their *frequency distribution may be assumed to correspond to a given theoretical form, and they may be assumed to be independent of each other. Basic pseudorandom numbers are uniformly distributed in the range (0,1), and may be transformed to provide other distributions.

Many methods for their generation have been proposed over the years, one of the earliest being the *middle square method* proposed by von Neumann: the previous random number is squared and the middle digits extracted from the result to form the next number in the sequence. More successful methods are based upon the linear congruential method in which a sequence of numbers is generated using the formula

$$X_{n+1} = aX_n + c \pmod{m}$$

for particular choices of a, c and m.

Pseudorandom numbers are used in a number of applications: in *Monte Carlo methods of numerical integration, to sample a large set and so gain insight into the set, and to simulate natural phenomena such as the collision of nuclear particles.

random sampling *See* sampling.

random variable A quantity that may take any of a prescribed set of values with *relative frequency determined by its *probability distribution.

range 1. of a binary *relation R, a subset of $S_1 \times S_2$, say. The *subset of S_2 consisting of all elements to which some element of S_1 is related. If R is the relation "is the wife of" defined from men to women, the range of R is the set of married women.

Since a *function is a special kind of relation, the range of

$$f: X \to Y$$

can be written as

$\{y \mid y \in Y \text{ and } y = f(x) \text{ for some } x \text{ in } X\}$

2. *See* measures of variation.

range image An image defined by a regular array of values that describe a surface. A *range scanner* is a device that automatically generates range images either in Cartesian or cylindrical coordinates.

rank 1. The number of linearly independent rows or columns of a matrix of numbers.

2. of a graph. *See* connected graph.

rank correlation *See* correlation.

rank correlation coefficient *See* nonparametric techniques.

RARE *Acronym for* Réseaux Associés pour la Recherche Européenne. A loose association of private or semiprivate packet networks

operated by a number of European countries for the use of their academic and research communities. *JANET is one such network. RARE was formed to foster cooperation on matters of common interest. It is not intended that RARE shall operate a network itself.

raster A predetermined pattern of scanning lines that provides substantially uniform coverage of a display area.

raster display A display that consists of a regular grid of *pixels and is normally driven from a *frame buffer. How the image is generated on a raster display will depend on the display technology used, the *raster-scan display being a particular example.

raster image file format (RIFF) An *image file format used to specify the graphical image to be printed on a raster printer such as an electrostatic plotter.

rasterizer A special device situated between a graphics system and a raster device to convert line drawings to a raster form.

rasterop *Another name for* bitblt.

raster-scan display 1. A widely used method of presenting graphical or pictorial images in which the electron beam of a *cathode-ray tube is swept across the screen, one row at a time and from top to bottom. As the electron beam sweeps, the beam intensity is turned on and off dependent on information defining the picture to be created. It is similar to the definition of a TV picture. *Compare* vector display.

2. A physical device operating in this way.

rate 1. of a code. For any (n, k) *block code or *convolutional code, the value defined as

$$R = k/n$$

It is a measure of "efficiency" in the sense that the more *redundancy there is in the code, the lower the rate. On the other hand, high redundancy may bring about greater efficiency in detecting or correcting errors. Thus the rate measures only one aspect of the overall efficiency.

2. *See* data transfer rate.

rational language *Another name for* regular language.

rational number (rational) Mathematically, a number that is *fractional and is defined as the ratio of two whole numbers: the *numerator* (an *integer) and the *denominator* (a strictly positive integer). In *a/b*, *a* is the numerator and *b* the denominator. *See also* rational type, real numbers.

rational type In a programming language, a range of *rational number values.

In computer representations of rational numbers, there are problems with the sizes of the numerator (to provide the range required) and of the denominator (to retain the precision). Consequently, *floating-point notation is often preferred even though it brings problems of its own. Also, it is harder to provide hardware support for strict rational operations (which never lose precision) than for floating-point (which is a limited-precision rational notation often used for approximating *real numbers). While most programming languages provide floating-point notation, only a few provide a rational type.

raw data Data in the form in which it reaches a computer system from the outside world: data that has not been vetted for correctness, nor sorted into any sequence, nor processed in any other way.

raw error rate of peripheral storage. *See* error rate.

ray casting A *rendering technique in which, for each pixel, a ray is traced from the eye position (in image space) through the pixel to find the intersection with all the objects in the scene. The intersection with the nearest object determines the color of the pixel. *Ray tracing is more complex.

Rayleigh–Ritz method *See* finite-element method.

ray tracing A *rendering technique in which a ray is cast from each pixel on the screen: these rays are followed into the scene, and the first surface to be struck is determined. *Secondary rays* may be generated to determine whether the point is in shadow, and also to follow reflections back toward their sources. Some limit is usually placed on the number of rays to be traced. In *adaptive ray tracing* the number of rays generated is dependent

on the objects and the illumination encountered by previous rays.

RBT *Abbrev. for* remote batch terminal.

RDBMS *Abbrev. for* relational database management system.

reachability A concept from graph theory concerned with whether there is a *path between two vertices in a directed *graph. Vertex *V* is said to be *reachable* from vertex *U* provided that there is a path from *U* to *V*. There may be several different paths from one vertex to another, the shortest being called a *geodesic*. The set of points that can be reached from a given vertex *V* is called the *reachable set* of *V*.

A directed graph is *unilaterally connected* when, for any pair of vertices, at least one vertex is reachable from the other.

reachability matrix *Another name for* adjacency matrix.

read To sense and retrieve (or interpret) data from a form of storage or input medium. The word is often used to qualify the meaning of a noun, as in read head.

read clock *See* disk format.

reader A device for holding or moving a data medium and sensing the data encoded on it. *See* card reader, document reader.

read error *See* error rate.

read head *See* magnetic tape.

read instruction A program step that causes data to be retrieved from a defined storage location and written into a register or buffer.

read-mostly media *See* write-once.

read-only file A file that can be read or copied, but not erased or modified. The protection is maintained by the operating system and in multiuser systems can be made to depend upon the category of the user. A file might be writeable by its owner, read-only to the owner's colleagues, and inaccessible to everyone else. *See also* file protection.

read-only memory *See* ROM.

read-only optical media Optical storage media that cannot be written by the user but that carry data imprinted during manufacture, usually by pressing from a master disk. *See* optical storage.

readout 1. Information retrieved from computer memory after processing and displayed on a screen or copied into backing store.
2. The operation of reading data from a storage device.

read time The period between the availability of the first and last bits of data concerned in a single read operation. It does not include any latency or waiting time or any regenerative action that may be associated with a destructive read operation. *See also* access time.

read-while-write check *See* magnetic tape.

read/write head A component of a *disk drive that records and retrieves data from magnetic disks. Read/write heads are also used sometimes to record and retrieve data from *magnetic tapes. In the case of disk drives the assembly consists of a head, often known as a *slider*, and a mounting arm, known as a *flexure*. There are two categories of head: those used in floppy drives in which the slider is in contact with the media, and those used in "rigid drives" in which the head flies above the surface of the media. The flying height of the latter depends upon the slider geometry, the flexure loading force, and the rotational speed of the disk.

Early drives (e.g. the IBM 3330–11) employed a flexure with a high load force, typically 350 grams, and the heads were withdrawn from the disk surface before rotation stopped. The 3340 Winchester drive first delivered by IBM in 1973 employed a radically new head design. Heads of this type are now known as *Winchester heads*, and have the following characteristics:
the read/write head is supported by a trimaran structure, with two outriggers supporting a narrow inner "hull", i.e. the slider; before drive operation, and when it ceases, the heads rest on the disk surface, which is lubricated;
the loading force was reduced to 10 grams;
the flying height was reduced to 0.25 micrometers (10 microinches) compared to 0.8 μm in the 3330.

With the introduction of the IBM 3370 (Whitney drive) in 1979 the head design was again changed. The size of the slider was made smaller and was fabricated using "thin film" technology; also the flexure was made much simpler. The result of this was a much more stable head that can be loaded, although not in the 3370, toward the media while it is rotating. Winchester heads cannot be so loaded. The term *Whitney* is now used to describe the type of head and flexure outlined above even if it is not manufactured by thin film techniques, in which case it is sometimes called a *minicomposite head*.

read/write memory A type of memory that, in normal operation, allows the user to access (read from) or alter (write to) individual storage locations within the device. The choice of read or write operation is normally determined by a read/write signal applied to the device. *RAM devices are typical read/write memories. *Compare* ROM.

ready signal A signal from a device indicating that it can accept new commands or data. *Compare* busy signal.

realism *See* photorealism.

real numbers (reals) The numbers that allow a numerical quantity to be assigned to every point on an infinite line or continuum. Real numbers are thus used to measure and calculate *exactly* the sizes of any continuous line segments or quantities. The development of a number system that meets these requirements has proved to be a long and complex process that reached a conclusion only in the 19th century. Establishing theoretical foundations for mathematical developments such as the calculus have involved sorting out subtle, conflicting, and inconsistent ideas about the reals (such as infinitesimals). The set of reals is infinite and not countable: there does not exist a method of making finite representations or codings of real numbers. Research on the foundations of the continuum continues – for instance on computation with the reals and on the uses of infinitesimals.

The real numbers, like the *natural numbers, are one of the truly fundamental data types. Unlike the natural numbers, however, reals cannot be represented exactly in computations. They can be approximated to any degree of accuracy by *rational numbers.

A real number can be defined in several ways, for example as the limit of a sequence of rational numbers. A real x is represented by a sequence $q(0), q(1), \ldots$ of rational numbers that approximates x in the sense that for any degree of accuracy ε there exists some natural number n such that

for all $k > n$, $|q(k) - x| < \varepsilon$

A real number is a *computable real number* if there is an algorithm that allows us to compute an approximation to the number to any given degree of accuracy. A real x is computable if (a) there is an algorithm that lists a sequence $q(0), q(1), \ldots$ of rational numbers that converges to x, and (b) there is an algorithm that to any natural number k finds a natural number $p(k)$ such that

for all $n > p(k)$, $|q(n) - x| < 2^{-k}$

Most of the real numbers that we know and use come from solving equations (e.g. the algebraic numbers) and evaluating equationally defined sequences (e.g. e and π) and are computable. However, most real numbers are noncomputable.

The approximations to real numbers used in computers must have finite representations or codings. In particular, in practise, there are gaps and separations between adjacent pairs of the real numbers that are represented (*see* model numbers). The separation may be the same between all numbers (*fixed-point) or may vary and depend on the size of the adjacent values (*floating-point). Some programming languages ignore this difference, describing floating-point numbers as "real". Calculations with real numbers on a computer must take account of these approximations.

real-time clock A clock that runs regardless of whether *processes that refer to the clock are running or not. The clock may take two forms, either as a peripheral device that can be read by a process when the process chooses or as a source of interrupts that occur at precisely determined intervals. A real-time clock measures *elapsed time. *See also* relative-time clock.

real-time language A programming language designed for programming systems in which the response time of the computer to stimuli is time critical. For instance, if a computer is controlling an elevator, then the computer must be able to respond quickly to the movements of the cage. *Ada, *Modula, *CORAL 66, and RTL-2 are real-time languages to various degrees.

real-time system Any system in which the time at which output is produced is significant. This is usually because the input corresponds to some movement in the physical world, and the output has to relate to that same movement. The lag from input time to output time must be sufficiently small for acceptable timeliness. Timeliness is a function of the total system: missile guidance requires output within a few milliseconds of input whereas scheduling of steamships requires responses measured in days. Real-time systems are usually considered to be those in which the response time is of order milliseconds; interactive systems are those with response times of order seconds and batch systems are those with response times of hours or days. Real-time systems may be subdivided into *hard* and *soft*, depending on the severity of failure to meet a deadline for output.

Examples of real-time systems include process control, embedded computer systems, point-of-sale systems, and computer-aided testing.

real type (type real) A *data type comprising values that have a fractional part and approximate to the mathematical *real numbers. They can be operated on by real-number arithmetic operations such as addition, subtraction, multiplication, division, and square root. Usually the representations do not include transcendental real numbers but are limited to a subset of *rational numbers. *See also* floating-point notation.

reason-maintenance system *See* truth-maintenance system, belief systems.

reboot To *restart a computer after it has been operating for some time, usually in an attempt to clear an error condition. *See* bootstrap, cold boot, warm boot.

recognize (accept) a formal language. *See* automaton, finite-state automaton.

reconfiguration The process of redefining and in some cases reconnecting the units of a multiple-unit computer system. This procedure may be accomplished automatically, manually, or by a combination of both. The purpose may be to provide different system functionality or continued operation after the failure of one unit. If done automatically the latter case would represent a *fail-soft situation. *See also* configuration.

reconstitute To rebuild, generally used to denote the recovery process necessary to restore a system to an operational state after some error. It usually involves resorting to a backup state and running appropriate programs.

record 1. A collection of data handled together in transfers to and from peripheral devices. Files held on backing store are frequently treated as sequences of records. The collection of data transferred as a unit is called a *physical record*. In contrast, the collection of data relating to one subject is then called a *logical record*. The number of logical records in a physical record is the *blocking factor*.
2. A *data structure in which there are a number of named components, called *fields, not necessarily of the same type. It may have variants in which some of the components, known as *variant fields*, are absent; the particular variant for a given value would be distinguished by a discriminant or *tag field. The record is widely recognized as one of the fundamental ways of aggregating data (another being the *array) and many programming languages offer direct support for data objects that take the form of records (*see* structured variable). Such languages permit operations upon an entire record object as well as upon its individual components.
3. *Another term for* write, used particularly when writing the value of data that may change or disappear.

recording density *See* packing density.

record locking A method of ensuring that if one *process is altering part of the contents of a file, other processes cannot alter that part of the file until the updating activity has been successfully completed. The actual operation of the record-locking mechanism will usually require cooperation between the operating system and the user applications program. Because the lock is applied only to the record(s) that are being updated, the use of record locking allows other processes to operate in other parts of the file, which can be guaranteed not to be affected by the updating process. *See also* file locking.

recoverable error of peripheral storage. *See* error rate.

recovery The process of restoring normal operation after the occurrence of a *failure. *See* failure recovery, power-fail recovery, file recovery, database recovery, error recovery.

recovery data Data saved during execution of a system to enable *error recovery. The data includes *recovery points, and information allowing all data to be restored to the values that existed prior to the recovery point. Thus for data changed by operations following the recovery point, the value of the data prior to this change must be saved as recovery data at the time that the change is being made.

recovery log A file created to permit *database recovery (or *file recovery). The log contains information about all changes made to a database or file since it was last established as being correct and a *backup copy was last taken. The form in which changes may be recorded in a recovery log may vary considerably, depending on the recovery algorithms to be used. In general, a recovery log may be used in one of two ways: (a) to redo all changes since the last backup (if the database or file has been corrupted); (b) to undo all incorrect changes (if the source of error is in the changes). *See also* log file.

recovery point Points in a computation for which the (then) current state can be restored. *See* recovery data, backward error recovery, forward error recovery, atomic action.

recurrence A statement describing some quantity such as $f(n)$ (where f is some *function and n is a positive integer) in terms of values of $f(m)$, where m is a nonnegative integer smaller than n; initial values such as $f(0)$

or $f(1)$ can be assumed to be defined. The concept can be extended to include functions of several variables. A recurrence will then involve defining $f(m,n)$, say, in terms of $f(m',n')$ where in some sense (m',n') is smaller than (m,n); again initial values can be assumed. The numbers in the *Fibonacci series can be defined by a recurrence.

In general, a recurrence can be considered as an equation connecting the values of the function at a number of related points. It has the form

$$g(n, f(n), f(n-1), \ldots, f(n-k)) = 0$$
$$n = k, k+1, \ldots, N$$

Assuming initial values for $f(0), f(1), \ldots, f(k-1)$, values for other points n can be calculated.

Equations of this type arise naturally in the *discretization of continuous problems, and in a slightly different form, known as a *difference equation, appear repeatedly in *combinatorics.

recursion The process of defining or expressing a function, procedure, language construct, or the solution to a problem in terms of itself, so producing a *recursive function, a *recursive subroutine, etc. *See also* primitive recursion.

recursion theorem A theorem of S. C. Kleene: a recursive operator, mapping functions to functions, has a *least fixed point that is a *partial recursive function.

recursive *Often another word for* computable, especially when discussing *effective computability on the set of natural numbers. *Recursive sets and *recursive functions are thus also called computable sets and computable functions. *Recursively enumerable sets are often described as semicomputable.

recursive descent parsing *See* top-down parsing, LL parsing.

recursive doubling A method in which a total computation is repeatedly divided into two separate computations of equal complexity that can be executed in parallel. Recursive doubling is used in *parallel computers and works best when the operation on pairs of operands is *associative.

recursive function 1. In mathematics, a

*function whose usual or natural definition is in terms of itself.
2. In a program, a function *procedure that calls itself.
3. **(general recursive function, total recursive function)** In the study of *effective computability, a *partial recursive function that happens to be *total. For some authors, however, the terms recursive and general recursive are synonymous with partial recursive. It is useful here to summarize the various terms used in this area:

The term partial recursive function is often used in a general sense to mean any computable function on the natural numbers defined by a model of *computation. However, to be precise, a partial recursive function is simply a function defined by *primitive recursion and Kleene's μ-recursion scheme (*see* minimization). Not all such functions are *total functions since the use of the μ-operator allows the possibility of nontermination.

A *primitive recursive function, however, cannot involve the μ-operator and is hence guaranteed to be total. The *Ackermann function is the standard example of a total recursive function that is not primitive recursive.

recursive list (self-referent list) A *list that contains itself as a sublist element or is a sublist element of one of its sublists.

recursively decidable problem *Another term for* decidable problem. *See* decision problem.

recursively enumerable set A subset A of a set B is said to be recursively enumerable, relative to B, if there is an effective procedure that, given an element b in B, will output "yes" if and only if b is an element of A. If b is not in A then, in general, the procedure will never terminate. This is a weaker notion than that of a *recursive set. A set can be recursively enumerable without being recursive. The set A is also said to be *semidecidable* or *semicomputable*.

The set of *Ada programs that terminates (for a given input) is recursively enumerable (with respect to the class of all Ada programs) but it is not recursive.

recursively solvable problem *Another term for* solvable problem. *See* decision problem.

recursively undecidable, unsolvable *Other terms for* undecidable, unsolvable. *See* decision problem.

recursive real number *Another name for* computable real number. *See* real numbers.

recursive relation A *relation whose *characteristic function is recursive.

recursive set A subset *A* of a set *B* is said to be recursive, relative to *B*, if there is an algorithm or effective procedure that, given an element *b* in *B*, will output "yes" if *b* is an element of *A* and "no" if *b* is not an element of *A*. The set *A* is thus also said to be *decidable* or *computable*.

Strictly speaking the sets *A* and *B* should be sets of natural numbers, and the algorithm is a definition of the total *recursive function that is the *characteristic function of *A* in *B*. The concept and terminology is transferred to other data sets using a *Gödel numbering.

Post's theorem says that a set *A* is recursive iff *A* and *B*–*A* are *recursively enumerable.

recursive subroutine A *subroutine that calls itself. Such a self-referential call must occur as one branch of a conditional statement, otherwise there would be an infinite series of calls. As an example, a recursive subroutine to calculate factorial (*n*) would call itself to calculate factorial (*n* – 1), unless *n* = 1 when the value 1 will be returned.

Red Book 1. The *coloured book defining the job submission protocol used within the UK academic community. It is sometimes referred to as *JTMP, Job Transfer and Manipulation Protocol*.
2. Part of the defining documentation for the *ISDN standard, covering the protocol reference model for the ISDN together with numbering and addressing and the functional descriptions of connection types.
3. A National Computer Security Center (*NCSC) publication that discusses the security aspects of *trusted computer systems, with special emphasis on the networking implications.
4. The proprietary format standard common

to all CD disks. *See* CD-ROM format standards.

redline A method of enhancing text on a color screen by displaying characters in red. The characters may be printed with a shaded background when a noncolor printer is used.

reduced instruction set computer *See* RISC.

reducible polynomial *See* polynomial.

reduct An *algebra formed by removing some of the operations, and possibly carriers, of another algebra. Let *A* be an algebra of *signature Σ_0 and let Σ be a subsignature of Σ_0. Then the reduct $A|_{\Sigma}$ of *A* with respect to Σ is the algebra formed by removing from *A* the carriers, constants, and operations of *A* not named in Σ.

reduction machine A machine that evaluates expressions by successively reducing all component subexpressions until only simple terms representing data values remain. For each expression that is not a simple data value, a set of rules define what should be substituted when that expression appears. The machine operates by matching each subexpression of the expression currently being evaluated with its appropriate rule, and substituting as specified by that rule. This process of expression substitution continues until only simple data values remain, representing the value of the original expression.

All subexpressions can be matched and substituted concurrently, and thus there is the potential for a high degree of parallelism. A major objective of reduction machines is to exploit this parallelism.

Reduction machines represent one of the major examples of *non von Neumann architecture, and are of considerable research interest. Traditional *imperative programming languages are unsuited to reduction machines, so *declarative languages are employed.

reduction system *Short for* abstract reduction system.

redundancy The provision of additional components in a system, over and above the minimum set of components to perform the functions of the system, for purposes of *reliability or *robustness. For example, with *triple modular redundancy* three components are deployed in parallel, all performing the same function. Their outputs are compared, and when one component produces a different result from the other two, this item is assumed to be faulty and is ignored. Redundancy covers not only the incorporation of duplicate or triplicate hardware for backup in case of *failure, but also the inclusion of excess symbols in messages sent through communication systems in order to combat the effects of noise (*see* error-correcting code, error-detecting code).

redundancy check A check made with redundant hardware or information that can provide an indication that certain errors have occurred. *See* redundancy, cyclic redundancy check.

Reed–Muller codes (RM codes) A family of *binary *cyclic $(2^m, k)$ *error-correcting *block codes.

Reed–Solomon codes (RS codes) An important and practical family of *linear *error-correcting *block codes, especially suited to the correction of *burst errors. They can be regarded as a generalization of *Bose–Chaudhuri–Hocquenghem (BCH) codes, and as a special case of *Goppa codes. RS codes can be arranged to be *cyclic.

re-engineering The reimplementation of an existing design to exploit technological advances. The usual reason is to improve competitiveness with regard to cost and performance while maintaining compatibility with previous versions.

re-entrant program A program whose instructions are invariant, hence it can be used again without being reloaded. Re-entrant programs consist of logically separate code and data segments, and two instances of such a program can share the same code.

referent 1. The subject of a *model.
2. The data item to which a pointer or indirect address refers.

referential integrity The internal consistency of intrarecord references in a database, ensuring that if a record contains the key of, or a pointer to, another record in the database

then this second record must actually exist and cannot in isolation be deleted. In the context of the *relational model, it means that the set of values held for a *foreign key must always be a subset of the set of values held in the relation of which it is the key.

referential opacity The opposite of *referential transparency.

referential transparency A property of a function signifying that evaluation of the function with a particular set of arguments always returns the same value, whatever the context in which evaluation takes place. In programming terms this means that the function must not exhibit any side effects, i.e. it must not reference or change variables defined outside the function, except for the variables passed as parameters.

refinement The process in programming whereby higher-level or abstract ideas are progressively reexpressed in terms of lower-level or concrete ones. This can involve both the implementation of procedures in terms of lower-level procedures, and also the representation of abstract data in terms of more concrete data. Both kinds of refinement can involve *specifications, with each step of refinement being shown to preserve the specified behavior of the procedure or data type being refined. Although both terms are rather fluid in meaning, there is a possible distinction to be made between refinement and *program transformation, with the latter involving the replacement of one program fragment by an equivalent one at the same level of abstraction rather than its representation in terms of a lower level of abstraction.

Refinement and transformation are two of the main ideas in the increasingly important study of the systematic derivation of correct programs from specifications.

reflectance function A function that defines the spatial distribution and the wavelength composition of the light reflected from an object's surface.

reflectance model A mathematical model of how light is reflected from a surface based on a *reflectance function. The basic reflectance model assumes that all surfaces are perfect mirrors. More realistic models use reflectance functions that more accurately represent the properties of real surfaces (*see also* specular reflection, Cook–Torrance model).

reflexive closure *See* transitive closure.

reflexive relation A *relation R defined on a set S and having the property that

$$x R x$$

for all elements x in S

The relation "is the same age as" defined on the set of people is reflexive. *Compare* irreflexive relation.

refresh (regenerate) **1.** To replenish the charge on the storage capacitors used in *dynamic memory cells and other similar devices. Some devices are provided with internal circuitry that automatically refreshes dynamic cells whenever these cells are read. The word refresh is also used as a noun. **2.** To repeat at regular intervals the display of digital information on a *cathode-ray tube or television monitor in order that the display can appear persistent. *See also* refresh frequency.

refresh frequency The frequency with which a display on a cathode-ray tube is regenerated. To avoid *flicker this must be made as high as possible. *See* CFF.

refutation A method of reasoning used in logic to refute statements, i.e. to prove them false.

regenerate *Another term for* refresh.

register A group of (usually) *bistable devices that are used to store information within a computer system for high-speed access. A register of n bistables can store a word of length n bits, which can represent any n bits of information. Different interpretations can be given to the bit configuration stored in the register; for example, the configuration could represent an instruction, a binary number, an alphanumeric character, etc. A register is often the same size as the computer word; it may also be byte- or character-size or some other size as required. Some registers can behave as *counters as well, or they may behave as *shift registers. *See also* memory hierarchy.

register insertion ring *See* ring network.

register optimization *See* optimization.

register transfer language (RTL) Any of several programming languages that allow the declaration of *register configurations within a structure to perform a computation. The timing of transfers between registers, to describe the behavior, is specified by the order in which such transfers are interpreted during the execution of the program. *See also* CHDL.

regression analysis A statistical technique that is concerned with fitting relationships between a dependent variable, y, and one or more independent variables, $x_1, x_2, \ldots$, usually by the method of *least squares.

A *linear regression model* is one in which the theoretical mean value, μ_i, of the observation y_i is a linear combination of independent variables,

$$\mu = \beta_0 + \beta_1 x_1 + \ldots + \beta_k x_k$$

when k x-variables are included in the model. The multiples $\beta_0, \beta_1, \ldots \beta_k$ are parameters of the model and are the quantities to be estimated; they are known as *regression coefficients*, β_0 being the *intercept* or *constant term*. A model with more than one x-variable is known as a *multiple regression model*.

Nonlinear regression models express μ as a general function of the independent variables. The general functions include curves such as exponentials and ratios of polynomials, in which there are parameters to be estimated.

Various procedures have been devised to detect variables that make a significant contribution to the regression equation, and to find the combination of variables that best fits the data using as few variables as possible. *Analysis of variance is used to assess the significance of the regression model. *See also* generalized linear model, influence.

regression testing Following maintenance to a system, tests performed to demonstrate that the system still performs all the functions required prior to the maintenance. Regression testing is additional to tests made to ensure that the modifications work satisfactorily. *See also* performance testing.

regula falsi *Another name (Latin) for* false position method.

regular expression An expression built from finite *formal languages (i.e. finite sets of strings) using the operations of *union, *concatenation, and *Kleene star. For example, the following two regular expressions each denote the set of all strings of alternating as and bs:

$$\{a, \Lambda\} \{ba\}^* \{\Lambda, b\}$$
$$\{ba\}^* \cup \{a\}\{ba\}^* \cup \{ba\}^*\{b\} \cup$$
$$\{a\}\{ba\}^*\{b\}$$

where Λ is the empty string. A language is *regular if and only if it is representable by a regular expression. Thus the class of regular languages is the smallest one that contains all finite languages and is closed under concatenation, union, and star – the so-called *regular operations*. These three operations correspond to "sequence", "choice", and "iteration" in structured iterative programs.

regular grammar A *grammar in which each production has one of the forms

$$A \to b$$
$$A \to bC$$

where b is a terminal and A, C are nonterminals. Like the right-linear and left-linear grammars (*see* linear grammar) regular grammars generate precisely the *regular languages.

regular language (regular set; rational language) A language recognized by a *finite-state automaton. Of the language classes commonly studied, the class of regular languages is the smallest and mathematically the simplest. Its importance is shown by the existence of several alternative definitions; for some of them *see* regular grammar, linear grammar, regular expression, Myhill equivalence, Nerode equivalence, tree grammar.

regular operations *See* regular expression.

regular set *Another name for* regular language, since in formal language theory a language is simply a set of strings.

relation (defined on sets $S_1, S_2, \dots S_n$) A *subset R of the *Cartesian product

$$S_1 \times S_2 \times \dots \times S_n$$

of the n sets $S_1, \dots, S_n$. This is called an n-ary relation. When a relation R is defined on a single set S the implication is that R is a subset of

$$S \times S \times \dots \times S \quad (n \text{ terms})$$

The most common situation occurs when $n = 2$, i.e. R is a subset of $S_1 \times S_2$. Then R is called a *binary relation* on S_1 to S_2 or between S_1 and S_2. S_1 is the *domain* of R and S_2 the *codomain* of R. If the *ordered pair (s_1, s_2) belongs to the subset R, a notation such as

$$s_1 \, R \, s_2 \quad \text{or} \quad s_1 \, \rho \, s_2$$

is usually adopted and it is then possible to talk about the relation R or ρ and to say that s_1 and s_2 are related.

An example of a binary relation is the usual "is less than" relation defined on integers, where the subset R consists of ordered pairs such as $(4,5)$; it is however more natural to write $4 < 5$. Other examples include: "is equal to" defined on strings, say; "is the square root of" defined on the nonnegative reals; "is defined in terms of" defined on the set of subroutines within a particular program; "is before in the queue" defined on the set of jobs awaiting execution at a particular time.

The *function is a special kind of relation. *Graphs are often used to provide a convenient pictorial representation of a relation.

Relations play an important part in theoretical aspects of many areas of computing, including the mathematical foundations of the subject, databases, compiling techniques, and operating systems. *See also* equivalence relation, partial ordering.

relational database management system (RDBMS) A *database management system that supports the *relational model.

relational model A *data model that views information in a database as a collection of distinctly named tables. Each table has a specified set of named columns, each column name (also called an *attribute*) being distinct within a particular table, but not necessarily between tables. The entries within a particular column of a table must be atomic (that is, single data items) and all of the same type. The logical *records held in a relational database are viewed as rows in these tables. Each logical record is thus constrained to contain only a set of elementary data items each of a prespecified type. The model is, in consequence, also known as the *flat file model*.

The model, first proposed by Codd in

1969 and used exclusively in the context of *database management systems, takes its name from an analogy that can be drawn between a table as described and the mathematical concept of a *relation. In this analogy table corresponds to relation, row (in a table) to tuple (of a relation), and the column names (of the table) to the domain ordering (in the relation). Using this analogy Codd developed various sets of operations on which languages for the manipulation of such tables might be based and from which the now widely used data sublanguage *SQL is derived.

In spite of its name, which can be a source of confusion, the model makes no provision for maintaining relationships between rows in different tables and the only constraint on the rows within a particular table is that no two rows are identical. Each row, from the viewpoint of the model, is thus an independent entity. It can only be related to other rows by correspondences between contained data items, which is a matter for the user.

See also normal forms, foreign key, ERA model.

comparison	operator
less than	<
less than or equal to	<=
equal to	=
greater than or equal to	>=
greater than	>
not equal to	<> ¬ = != #

Relational operators

relational operator An operator representing a comparison between two operands that returns a truth value. The common comparisons are shown in the table, together with the relational operators normally used in computing; "not equal to" has many denotations.

relative addressing Usually either of two ways to expand a short specified address. The first is *self-relative addressing* where the specified address is added to the address of the instruction (generally the current contents of the program counter) that contains the self-relative reference to produce a direct address. The second is *base addressing* in which the specified address is added to the contents of a *base register* containing a base address to produce a direct address. *See also* addressing schemes.

relative complement *Another name for* set difference.

relative frequency The number of occurrences of a particular event, E, divided by the total number of observed events. An *event* is a particular instance of a class of observations, such as the result of the throw of dice, the recording of a man's height, or the survival of a patient given a particular treatment. Relative frequency should be distinguished from *probability. For example, the probability that a fair coin when tossed lands heads up is 0.5, whereas the relative frequency in a particular run of 100 tosses might be 47/100 or 0.47.

The set of relative frequencies for all the events that are possible is called a *frequency distribution. It may be displayed graphically as a *histogram.

relatively prime *See* greatest common divisor.

relative product *Another name for* composition.

relative-time clock A free-running clock that raises an interrupt at regular intervals, often associated with the period of the incoming supply of electricity. These interrupts allow the supervisory system to track the passage of real time, and also guarantee that if a process does not call the supervisor explicitly, the supervisor will nevertheless be entered.

relay In networking, a means of passing information between two or more networks, each offering a similar network function but each using a different *protocol. In general a relay differs from a *gateway or *bridge in offering a *store-and-forward service rather than a real-time service. As an example, a *mail relay* may be used to pass mail messages between networks using different mail protocols. *See also* cell relay, frame relay.

The term relay is used in some communities as synonymous with bridge or gateway. These three terms have meanings that vary between different communities at the same time, and within a given community at different times.

release Transfer of a system from the development stages into wider usage, e.g. into operational use. *See also* software life cycle.

reliability 1. The ability of a computer system to perform its required functions for a given period of time. It is often quoted in terms of percentage of *uptime, but may be more usefully expressed as MTBF (mean time between failures). *See also* hardware reliability, repair time.

2. of software. *See* software reliability.

relocatable code Program code that can be loaded anywhere in memory. Typically the code is divided into *control sections* and all memory addresses are expressed relative to the start of a control section. The compiler/assembler produces a table of all such memory references, and the *loader converts them into absolute addresses as part of the loading process. *See also* position-independent code.

remedial maintenance (corrective maintenance) Maintenance that is performed after a fault, in hardware or software, has been found, in order to correct that fault. *Compare* preventive maintenance.

remote A term used to describe a process or system that uses a communications link, as in remote job entry, remote sensing, and remote procedure call.

remote batch terminal (RBT) A computer terminal attached by means of a communications link to a remote processor for *remote job entry.

remote job entry (RJE) A system by which a communications link is used to submit work from an input device and to receive results on a printer or other output medium. Strictly RJE refers only to the entry of jobs, but the term is commonly applied to cover both input and output. Early computer systems had all their input/output devices in the same room or at best in a room adjacent to the computer mainframe. In the early 1960s the introduction of long-distance telecom-

munications made it possible to site card readers and line printers at a distance from the computer center. It was this that led to the concept of remote job entry.

remote operations service (ROS) A set of definitions of protocols and interfaces designed to support applications in a distributed processing environment. The overall effect is very similar to that of a *remote procedure call.

remote procedure call (RPC) A procedure call in which the actual execution of the body of the *procedure takes place on a physically distinct processor from that on which the procedure call takes place. In general the system invoking the procedure call is separate from the one executing it. Further the two systems and the communication channel linking them are all liable to fail in the period between the start of the procedure call and the final completion of execution and return of any results from the processor executing the procedure body to that executing the procedure call.

These factors have given rise to a number of different proposals for the course of action to be followed in the event of one or other of the systems failing; essentially to have the procedure body executed either at least once (by *retry) or at most once. These proposals tend to reflect the different priorities attached to the effect on the total system in the event of part of it failing.

remote sensing The technique whereby sensors located remotely from a computer are used to produce inputs for a digital system. These inputs are then transmitted either by wire or radio techniques to the computer. An example is the use of digital thermometers and humidity detectors in large buildings: the sensors transmit their readings to a central computer that optimizes energy use by regulating heat and air conditioning.

rendering The part of computer graphics that is concerned with getting from a three-dimensional scene (possibly containing moving objects) to a picture or animated sequence, with more or less sophistication in terms of the effect achieved.

rendezvous A method of synchronizing concurrent tasks in *Ada.

repair time The (sometimes average) time required to diagnose and repair a computer failure, either hardware or software. In combination with MTBF (mean time between failures) the MTTR (mean time to repair) provides a figure-of-merit for system *reliability and/or *uptime.

repeated measures In statistical analysis of data, successive observations obtained from the same source (such as an instrument, operator, animal, etc.). Theoretical models must take account of the *correlations between the successive observations. In some circumstances the changes between successive observations may be regarded as statistically independent.

repeater In general, a device that amplifies a signal to allow it to transmit over greater distances than might otherwise be possible. For free-space signaling systems in which the signal is presented as a modulated carrier, the repeater may also move the signal to a different carrier frequency.

repeat-until loop See do-while loop.

repertoire *Short for* instruction repertoire. *See* instruction set.

repetition codes A trivial family of *cyclic *perfect *error-correcting *block codes, in which the codewords are formed merely by repeating the message words r times. Considered as (n, k) codes (*see* block code), these codes have $n = rk$ for some k.

report generator See generator, RPG.

representation Storage and *data values used to carry information.

request input Input in computer graphics that is initiated by the application. The application waits until the input is entered by the operator before resuming.

requirements analysis The analysis that is necessary for the production of an *expression of requirements, or a *user, a *software, or a *system requirements specification.

requirements specification *See* user requirements specification, software requirements specification, system requirements specification.

requirements specification phase The phase in the *software or *system life cycle where the *user, *software, or *system requirements specification is produced. The phase activities include elicitation, capture, *expression, and *review of requirements.

rerun To run a program again, usually due to a machine malfunction. (The word is also used as a noun.) Some languages allow the programmer to specify restart points: at such points a memory image is preserved so that in the event of a rerun the program does not need to be restarted from scratch.

resampling Use of repeated sampling from an original data set to obtain certain statistical properties of the data. Methods such as the statistical *bootstrap, the *jackknife, and *cross-validation come under this general heading.

rescue dump A copy of the workspace associated with a *process, taken with a view to allowing the process to be restarted following a system failure. *See* dump.

reserved word A word that has a specific role in the context in which it occurs, and therefore cannot be used for other purposes. For example, in many programming languages the words 'IF' 'THEN' 'ELSE' are used to organize the presentation of the written form of statements (between 'THEN' and 'ELSE' and following 'ELSE') whose execution is governed by the value of the Boolean expression between 'IF' and 'THEN'. The use of if, then, else as *identifiers is thus not permitted in these languages since they are reserved words. *See also* keyword.

reset To set a variable, register, counter, or complete processing system back to a prescribed state.

resident Permanently present in main memory, as opposed to transient material that is loaded from disk when required.

residual The difference between a data observation and its corresponding fitted value obtained by *regression analysis. The *residual mean square* is the sum of squared residuals divided by the appropriate *degrees of freedom, and is an estimate of *variance of random variation about the fitted model. Plots of residuals against data variables may suggest important modifications to the model. Plots of ranked residuals against percentage points of the *normal distribution provide a check on the assumptions used in *significance tests in regression analysis. Large residuals identify observations as *outliers*, whose exclusion from the analysis will make a large difference to the conclusions.

residual mean square *See* residual.

residue arithmetic *Another name for* modular arithmetic.

residue check *Another name for* checksum.

resistor-transistor logic *See* RTL.

resolution 1. The amount of graphical information that can be shown on a visual display. The resolution of a display device is usually denoted by the number of lines that can be distinguished visually per inch.

Resolution is often confused with *addressability*. The addressability of a computer-graphics system is defined by the number of displayable lines, or alternatively by the number of points or pixels (picture elements) that can be displayed in the vertical and horizontal directions. Computer graphics systems are now capable of addressing over 16 000 pixels horizontally and vertically but the resolution is likely to be nearer 400 lines per inch.

2. *See* A/D converter, D/A converter.

3. A rule of inference in mathematical *logic, used to deduce a new logical formula from two old ones. It has been used extensively in the automatic derivation of mathematical theorems since it is an efficient alternative to traditional rules of inference. *See also* unification.

resource Any of the component parts of a computer system and the facilities that it offers. All computer systems must include one or more processors, which actually manipulate the stored information, some form of memory in which to store both instructions for the processors and data awaiting manipulation, and input/output devices capable of reading information from the outside world and writing results to the outside world.

resource allocation Either the act of making a resource available to a *process, or the amount of a particular resource that has been allocated. The context almost invariably makes clear which meaning is intended. The amount allocated in the second form of usage may either be a period of time if the entire resource is allocated, as with a processor, or it may be a number of subunits in the case of a resource, such as memory, that is made up of a large number of essentially identical subunits, of which some are allocated to the process.

resource descriptor *See* process descriptor.

response function *See* sequential machine.

response time Usually the elapsed time between an action by a computer-system user and the receipt of some form of response or feedback from the system.

restart To set running again after a temporary halt. The term (also used as a noun) applies particularly to the situation in which a transient hardware error has caused the entire operating system (and all the *processes running under its control) to halt. In such cases it is often found that only processes that were actively running at the time of the error have suffered damage. The damaged processes must be *aborted, but all other processes can be restarted since the resources allocated to them are unaltered, and their *process descriptors are still an accurate reflection of their behavior up to the time of the system error.

restore To reset to an earlier value. For example, when a *process is about to be *restarted on a processor, the contents of the working registers of the processor must be restored to the values they last held when the process was previously running.

restriction of a *relation R or *function f. A relation or function obtained by restricting the domain of R or f. If "is the son of" is a relation defined on all the males in a certain country, a restriction would be this same relation defined on the males of a particular city.

retry *See* error recovery.

return *See* carriage return, hard return.

return channel In a *duplex transmission channel, it is sometimes the case that the main channel operates only in one direction (i.e. *simplex), but that a channel of much lower capacity (and much lower cost) operates in the opposite direction: this is the return channel. It is chiefly used for monitoring the main channel, and for notifying the transmitter of errors detected by the receiver on the main channel. *See also* backward error correction.

return instruction An instruction used to effect the return to the regular program from a *subroutine or an *interrupt. A return instruction must restore the *program counter to the correct value; in the case of a return from interrupt, certain status bits must also be restored. *Compare* call instruction.

reusable resource A resource, such as a CPU or tape transport, that is not rendered useless by being used. A magnetic disk or tape can be used often indefinitely and are to be regarded as reusable resources. *Compare* consumable resource.

reusable software A software module or product designed to provide a function or facility that other designers may require, and is capable of being easily embedded (possibly with some *localization or *own coding) in the reusing design structure.

reversal function The *function $r : L \to L$, where L denotes strings of characters from some *alphabet, defined in such a way that r reverses the order of the elements in its parameter. If & denotes *concatenation of strings, then

$$r(s) = s$$

if s is null or a single character and

$$r(s \& t) = r(t) \& r(s)$$

The idea can be extended to include reversing of items in a *list, of items in some *sequence, or of items in an arbitrary one-dimensional *array. Reversal is an *involution operation.

reverse authentication *See* authentication.

reverse bias The applied d.c. voltage that prevents or greatly reduces current flow in a diode, transistor, etc. For example, a negligible current will flow through a diode when its cathode is made more positive than its anode; the diode is then said to be *reverse biased*. *Compare* forward bias.

reverse Polish notation (RPN; postfix notation; suffix notation) A form of notation, invented by the Polish mathematician Jan Lukasiewicz, in which each operator follows its operands. Thus, for example,

$$a + b \text{ is written } ab+$$
$$a + b * c \text{ is written } abc*+$$

If each operator has a specific number of operands (e.g. if all operators take exactly two operands), then no brackets are required since the order of evaluation is always uniquely defined; the notation can then be described as *parenthesis-free*.

The importance of RPN is that an expression in this form can be readily evaluated on a *stack. Thus translation to RPN, followed by stack evaluation, is a simple but effective strategy for dealing with arithmetic expressions in a programming language. *See also* Polish notation.

reverse video A display attribute in which one or more characters are displayed in the opposite contrast to the surrounding information. For example, in a display that has bright characters on an apparently black screen the reverse video characters appear as black characters within a bright rectangle.

reversible execution *See* recovery point, backward error recovery.

review An important and effective method for verifying the output from a particular phase of a *software life cycle. The phase output is scrutinized by a team of reviewers against the documentation (*specification) available at the start of that phase and against general review criteria for the particular phase completed. These criteria may be defined by a particular method adopted, by the application domain of the proposed software, or by local conventions within a development organization (or any combination of these). The purpose of the review is to evaluate the emerging software in order to discover faults as early as possible.

Reviews can be conducted at most life-cycle phases and at different levels of detail, hence for example:

> user requirements specification review
> software requirements specification review
> system design review
> module design review
> module coding review
> module test procedure review
> integration test plan review
> acceptance test review

Informal reviews are usually conducted on the documented output of an individual by fellow (technical) members of the project team. For example, in a module design review the module author will guide the reviewers through the design, and differences between the module specification and the design will be recorded for later analysis and reworking of the design. Project verification and validation plans, together with the quality plan, will give guidance on procedure, and acceptance levels for unresolved differences.

Formal technical reviews may be conducted by project staff, by independent reviewers from other projects, or by independent third parties. They are usually planned as milestones in verification and validation activities.

rewritable Denoting storage media, especially optical media, on which the user can write data, and can also erase or overwrite so that new data replaces the old (*compare* write-once). *See* optical storage.

rewrite rule *See* term rewriting system, grammar.

rewriting system (or rewrite system) *See* term rewriting system, graph rewrite system, abstract reduction system.

REXX *Short for* restructured extended executor. A procedural programming language with a simplified structure, designed to facilitate rapid prototyping, and available on a wide variety of systems. The name derives from the fact that it was originally developed to simplify the writing of control procedures (known as EXECs) for the IBM mainframe operating system. The IBM mainframe version is called *System Product Interpreter*.

RFC *Abbrev. for* request for comments. A document soliciting input from a community, such as Internet users, during the development of an emerging standard.

RFI *Abbrev. for* radio-frequency interference. Disturbance of a signal usually involving frequencies above 100 kilohertz.

RGB color model A *color model that defines color in terms of its red, green, and blue components, known collectively as *RGB components*. Red, green, and blue light are a set of primary colors: when mixed in equal proportions they produce white light and when mixed in other proportions they produce light of a range of different colors. The RGB model is the usual method of defining color on a *cathode-ray tube.

RGB monitor A raster-scan color *cathode-ray tube that incorporates three electron guns (or one gun divided into three) where each gun is directed at a separate array of red, green, or blue phosphor dots or stripes on the screen.

RGB signal Three separate display signals that are, in effect, monochrome signals directed at just one set of the red, green, or blue phosphors on the display screen. A *composite* RGB signal is one where the sync pulses are added to only one of the display signals (usually green).

ribbon 1. The means by which an *impact printer forms the printed characters on the top copy of printer *stationery, ink being transferred from ribbon to paper. The characteristics of a ribbon depend mainly on the printer for which it is intended. There may however be two or three varieties of ribbon available for one printer type, depending for example on whether maximum utilization of the ribbon (and thus minimum ribbon cost) is important at the expense of *print quality, or vice versa. Black ribbons are usually used but other colors are available.

Ribbon materials are normally nylon fabric, in various thicknesses and thread types, or polyester film. Fabric is soaked with ink, film is coated with ink-bearing wax. Thinner fabrics give better print quality, usually at the expense of ribbon life. Nylon ribbons can be continually reused until print quality is unacceptable due to ink depletion. The printer recycles such a ribbon continuously, either by use of a continuous loop or by reversing it at each end. With film ribbons a much greater proportion of the ink is transferred at each strike, leading to shorter ribbon life. They can however provide much better print quality than fabric ribbons. Degree of inking in a ribbon is a carefully controlled parameter.

Ribbon dimensions depend on the printer type. Wide ("towel") ribbons may be up to 17″ wide, and travel vertically through the printer. Narrow ribbons, 0.2–2″ wide, traverse across the printing area. Narrow fabric ribbons may be on open spools or contained in purpose-designed cartridges to facilitate ribbon handling. All narrow film ribbons are in cartridges. Fabric ribbons in cartridges are often "stuffed" (packed in concertina fashion) in continuous loops rather than being on spools.

*Thermal transfer printers also require a ribbon, in this case a film ribbon coated with a thermoplastic or wax-based ink.

2. In some graphical applications, a horizontal row of control *icons that can often be redefined to suit the user's requirements.

ribbon cable An electric *cable in which a number of individual cables are formed into a flat ribbon, frequently color-coded to facilitate identification.

Richardson extrapolation (deferred approach to the limit) *See* extrapolation.

rich text format *See* RTF.

RIFF *Acronym for* raster image file format.

right-linear grammar *See* linear grammar.

right shift *See* shift.

rightsizing *Informal* Selecting a computer configuration appropriate to an organization's current and future requirements within the lifetime of a system. *See also* downsizing.

right subtree *See* binary tree.

ring 1. An *algebraic structure R on which there are defined two *dyadic operations, normally denoted by + (addition) and • or juxtaposition (multiplication). With respect to addition, R is an abelian *group,

$$\langle R, + \rangle$$

i.e. + is *commutative and *associative. With respect to multiplication, R is a *semigroup,

$$\langle R, \cdot \rangle$$

i.e. • is associative. Further, multiplication is *distributive over addition.

Certain kinds of rings are of particular interest:

(a) if multiplication is commutative the ring is called a *commutative ring*;

(b) if $\langle R, \cdot \rangle$ is a *monoid, the ring is called a *ring with an identity*;

(c) a commutative ring with an identity, and having no nonzero elements x and y with the property that $x \cdot y = 0$, is said to be an *integral domain*;

(d) a commutative ring with more than one element, and in which every nonzero element has an inverse with respect to multiplication, is called a *field.

The different identity elements and inverses, when these exist, can be distinguished by talking in terms of additive identities (or zeros), multiplicative identities (or ones), additive inverses, and multiplicative inverses.

The concept of a ring provides an algebraic structure into which can be fitted such diverse items as the integers, polynomials with integer coefficients, and matrices; on all these items it is customary to define two dyadic operations.

2. *Another name for* circular list, but more generally applied to any list structure where all sublists as well as the list itself are circularly linked.

ring counter *See* shift counter.

ringing A damped oscillation that occurs in many electrical circuits when signals change rapidly, and is due often to unwanted capacitance and inductance in devices and connecting wires.

ring network A network constructed as a *loop of unidirectional links between network stations (*nodes). It generally uses a bit-serial medium such as twisted pairs or coaxial cable. A master clock may be used to tell each station when to read and write bits, or the timing information may be encoded into the data as long as certain restrictions are met to prevent the ring from overflowing.

Each station receives messages on its incoming link. Address and control information is present at the beginning of the message. Based on this information and the control procedure being used on the ring, the station must make two decisions: whether or not to make a copy of the message in its local memory, and whether to pass the message on via its outgoing link or delete the message from the ring. If a station determines that no message is being received on its incoming link, then it may have the option of inserting a message on its outgoing link.

Several different control structures have been used on ring networks:

(a) *token ring – a special bit pattern identifies control information: a station, upon receiving the control token, may insert a message into the ring and reissue the token;

(b) *slotted ring* – a series of "slots" are continuously transmitted around the ring: a station detecting an unused slot may mark it "in use" and fill it with a message;

(c) *register insertion ring* – a station loads a message into a shift register, then inserts the register into the ring when the ring is idle or at the end of any message; the register contents are shifted onto the ring. When the message returns to the register, the register may be removed from the ring.

ripple-carry adder (ripple adder) A binary *adder in which the carry at each stage of addition must propagate or ripple through the succeeding stages of addition in order to form the result. *See also* carry lookahead.

ripple counter An *n*-stage *counter that is formed from *n* cascaded *flip-flops. The clock input to each of the individual flip-flops, with the exception of the first, is taken from the output of the preceding one. The count thus ripples along the counter's length due to the *propagation delay associated with each stage of counting. *See also* cascadable counter, synchronous counter.

RISC *Acronym for* reduced instruction set computer. A computer based on a processor or processors designed to execute a small number of simple register-based instructions extremely fast, preferably one instruction for every cycle of the system clock. (Hence RISC

also stands for reduced instruction set complexity.) RISC processors employ *pipelining and on-chip instruction and data *cache memory among other techniques. Various RISC architectures have been developed by manufacturers, including Hewlett-Packard's HP-PA (precision architecture), ARM RISC processors from Advanced RISC Machines Ltd, Digital Equipment's *Alpha AXP, Sun Microsystem's *SPARC (scalable processor architecture), and the *PowerPC produced by a partnership between IBM, Apple, and Motorola.

rise time of a pulse. *See* pulse.

risk A quantity derived both from the probability that a particular *hazard will occur and the magnitude of the consequence of the undesirable effects of that hazard. The term risk is often used informally to mean the probability of a *hazard occurring. *See also* tolerable risk.

risk analysis A systematic and disciplined approach to analyzing *risk – and thus obtaining a measure of both the probability of a *hazard occurring and the undesirable effects of that hazard.

risk assessment 1. A systematic and disciplined approach to assessing the significance in terms of safety of the complete set of *risks that may occur with a system.

2. An assessment in quantitative or qualitative terms of the damage that would be sustained if a computer system were exposed to postulated *threats. A quantitative risk analysis may ascribe a probable financial loss if each specified threat successfully exploited each possible *vulnerability of the system.

risk evaluation The process of determining the significance of a given measure of *risk.

risk management The collection of processes and procedures involved in analyzing, identifying, evaluating, controlling, and monitoring on an ongoing basis the *risks in a given system.

RJE *Abbrev. for* remote job entry.

RLL *Abbrev. for* run-length limited. Denoting an *NRZ code where the minimum time and maximum time between magnetic flux transitions is carefully controlled. *See* disk format.

RM code *Short for* Reed–Muller code.

robotics A discipline overlapping *artificial intelligence and mechanical engineering. It is concerned with building *robots*: *programmable devices consisting of mechanical actuators and sensory organs that are linked to a computer. The mechanical structure might involve manipulators, as in *industrial robotics, or might concern the movement of the robot as a vehicle, as in *mobile robotics. Robotics research is used in artificial intelligence as a framework for exploring key problems and techniques through a well-defined application.

robustness A measure of the ability of a system to recover from error conditions, whether generated externally or internally; for example, a robust system would be tolerant to errors in input data or to failures of internal components. Although there may be a relationship between robustness and reliability, the two are distinct measures: a system never called upon to recover from error conditions may be reliable without being robust; a highly robust system that recovers and continues to operate despite numerous error conditions may still be regarded as unreliable in that it fails to provide essential services in a timely fashion on demand.

robust statistics Statistical methods insensitive to the effects of *outliers (which may be mistakes or contaminated data). The methods rely on *medians rather than *means, and use more information from the central than from the outlying observations. The ideas are associated with *exploratory data analysis.

rogue value (terminator, sentinel) A value added at the end of a table and that can be recognized as a termination signal by a *table lookup program.

rollback A process that restarts a running program or software system at a *checkpoint. The word is also used as a verb: to restart at a checkpoint.

roll-call polling *See* polling.

roll-in roll-out A method of handling memory

in a system dealing with a number of simultaneously active *processes. When a process becomes active, all its associated workspace and code is brought into main memory. As soon as the process is unable to continue for any reason, typically because the user associated with the process is providing input, the entire workspace and code of the process is copied out onto backing store, retaining only a small buffer capable of receiving input from the user. When user input ceases and the process is able to continue running, the workspace and code are rolled back into main memory. When the process requires to output results to the user or is awaiting further input from the user, it is rolled out onto backing store. *See also* swapping.

roll stationery *See* stationery.

ROM *Acronym for* read-only memory. A *nonvolatile semiconductor memory device used for the storage of data that will never require modification: the memory contents are permanently built into the device during its manufacture according to a specially created pattern or mask. It is thus sometimes called *mask ROM* to distinguish it from programmable ROM, i.e. *PROM. Although it is possible only to read data from the memory locations of a ROM, the locations can be accessed in any order with equal speed. Hence there is *random access to any of the locations in ROM. *See also* EAROM, EEROM. *Compare* RAM.

Romberg method An *extrapolation method for *numerical integration, based on the *trapezium rule.

ROM cartridge (ROM pack) A module containing software that is permanently stored in *ROM. The module can easily be plugged into and later removed from a personal computer or other equipment without the integrated circuitry being handled. ROM cartridges are used for example to provide extra programs to a home computer or extra fonts to a printer (*see* font cartridge).

ROM optical disk (ROM OD) An *optical disk carrying information that is inserted at the time of manufacture and cannot subsequently be altered. Manufacture is usually by pressing copies from a master; copies are therefore cheap although the master is expensive. The predominant format is *CD-ROM.

romware Software (machine instructions) stored more-or-less permanently in a *ROM, *PROM, *EPROM, etc.

root 1. of a tree. The unique node in the tree with no parent. *See* tree.

2. of a polynomial equation. *See* polynomial.

root directory *See* directory tree.

rooted tree *See* tree.

ROS *Acronym for* remote operations service.

rotated dither Rotation of the dither pattern in a *halftone image to remove artefacts. *See also* dithering.

rotation position sensor A feature of some disk drives that allows the central processor to be made aware that a required sector is about to come under the read head of the drive.

rough surface In computer graphics, a surface where the neighboring *facets making up an object are significantly different in orientation.

roundoff error The error caused by truncating numbers in a calculation, usually necessitated because registers in a computer can only hold numbers of a fixed length, say t binary digits. Arithmetical operations on such numbers often give results requiring more than t digits for their representation, which must then be reduced to t digits for further calculation. The nearest t-digit approximation may be used (rounding) or digits after the tth may be dropped (chopping or truncation). The repeated reduction to t digits can cause systematic buildup of error in certain types of calculation.

round robin A method of allocating CPU time in a multiuser environment. Each user is allocated a small amount or quantum of processor time. Once a user's quantum is exhausted, control passes to the next user. The round robin scheduler bears many resemblances to the *feedback queue, which can be thought of as a refinement of the simple round robin scheduler.

route The path used to move information from one place to another. In a packet switching network it is the list of nodes that a particular packet or class of packets is to follow or has followed.

router A unit that supports the low-level linking of several regions of a single network. In any network it is helpful to subdivide the network into a number of regions in which most traffic is between pairs of nodes within that region, with only a small amount of traffic leaving the region. A router links several regions: interregion traffic will be forwarded to the correct region but traffic addressed to a destination in the same region as the sender will not be forwarded. A router must be capable of interpreting the sender and receiver addresses in the data, and must be able to determine where to forward traffic. It must therefore be capable of interpreting the network protocol, must store tables that assist in managing the routing activity, and will probably need to store an entire packet before forwarding it. The router is designed so as to function at the lowest possible level within the protocol stack, consistent with achieving correct partitioning of the network and correct routing of traffic. Despite the complexity of the unit and the delay it introduces, large networks almost invariably include routers. *See also* bridge.

routine *Another name for* subroutine, used usually in combinations, as in input routine.

routine maintenance *Another name for* preventive maintenance.

routing The procedure used to determine the *route taken by a packet in a packet switching computer network. Routing may be *fixed* (computed once at system starting or session initiation) or *dynamic* (recomputed periodically or on a packet-by-packet basis). Routing may be centralized or *distributed* (computed by different nodes independently).

row-major order One way of mapping the elements of a two-dimensional array onto a vector. If a two-dimensional array, A, with m rows and n columns is mapped in row-major order onto a vector b with $m \times n$ elements then

$$a_{ij} = b_k$$
$$\text{where } k = n(i - 1) + j$$

See also column–major order.

row-ragged *See* ragged array.

row vector *See* matrix.

RPC *Abbrev. for* remote procedure call.

RPG *Acronym for* report program generator. A programming language used in commercial data processing for extracting information from files. The input to an RPG consists of a description of the file structure, a specification of the information required, and of its layout on the page. From this information, the RPG constructs a program to read the file, extract the desired information, and format it in the required manner. The best-known example is RPG II.

RPN *Abbrev. for* reverse Polish notation.

RSA encryption A method of public key encryption (*see* cryptography) devised by Rivest, Shamir, and Adleman. A message is encrypted by mapping it onto an integer, M say, raising M to a (publicly known) power e and forming the remainder on division by a (publicly known) divisor, n, to give the encrypted message S. Decryption is achieved by similarly raising S to a (secret) power d, and again forming the remainder on division by n; the result will be the value of M. The method relies on the choice of n as the product of two large secret prime numbers, p and q. The values of e and d are chosen such that
$$e * d \equiv 1 \bmod ((p-1) * (q-1))$$
Security is achieved largely by the difficulty of finding the prime factors of n.

RS232C interface A widely used standard interface that covers the electric connection between data communication equipment, such as a *modem, and data terminal equipment, such as a microcomputer or computer terminal. The RS232C interface standard was developed by the EIA (Electronic Industries Association) and is essentially equivalent to the CCITT's *V24 interface; RS232A and RS232B were earlier superseded versions of the specification.

In 1975 the EIA introduced two new specifications in order to upgrade system capabilities; these are the RS423 interface, which closely resembles RS232C, and the RS422 interface, both of which allow higher transmission rates.

RS code *Short for* Reed–Solomon code.

RS flip-flop (SR flip-flop) *See* flip-flop.

RSI *Abbrev. for* repetitive strain injury. A painful injury that can be caused by prolonged use of badly designed or installed keyboards, though it is found in other unrelated activities involving repetitive muscular movements over a long period of time.

RSL A *specification language for time-critical real-time systems. Statements in RSL are machine processed to produce an abstract semantic model of the system. RSL has four language primitives: elements, relationships, attributes, and structures. Users may define new elements, relationships, and attributes to the set predefined in RSL.

RTD Programme in IT *See* ESPRIT.

RTF *Abbrev. for* rich text format. A *file format for encoding graphics and formatted text to permit easy transfer between different applications and operating systems. Developed by Microsoft, RTF supports graphics, different fonts, highlighting, and paragraph and table formatting. Most word processors will accept and generate RTF files.

RTL 1. *Abbrev. for* resistor-transistor logic. An early *logic family, usually produced in integrated-circuit form, whose principal component parts consist of integrated resistors and *bipolar transistors. Despite its low power dissipation, RTL is now little used since it has a relatively slow switching speed and small *fan-out.
2. *Abbrev. for* register transfer language.

RTM *Abbrev. for* read the manual. The response to a question that ought never to have been asked if the questioner had taken the trouble to read the documentation. More vehement variants include RTBM and RTFM.

rubber-banding Specifying a new input coordinate position by echoing a line stretching from some defined position (often the last position) to the current one. The line appears to stretch like a rubber band from the origin to the current position.

rule-based system (production-rule system) A programming language in which the programs consist of *condition* $\Rightarrow$ *action* rules;

these are known as *production rules*. The programs are interpreted by a repetition of the following operations: all rules whose conditions are satisfied are found, one of them is selected, and its action is called. Such systems have been extensively used in *expert systems. Rule-based systems are a kind of *inference engine.

ruled surface A surface generated by a family of straight lines. Ruled surfaces are obtained by linear interpolation between a pair of boundary curves.

Runge–Kutta methods A widely used class of methods for the numerical solution of *ordinary differential equations. For the initial-value problem

$$y' = f(x,y), y(x_0) = y_0,$$

the general form of the m-stage method is

$$k_i = f(x_n + c_i h, y_n + h \sum_{j=1}^{m} a_{ij} k_j)$$
$$i = 1, 2, \ldots, m$$
$$y_{n+1} = y_n + h \sum_{i=1}^{m} b_i k_i)$$
$$x_{n+1} = x_n + h$$

The derivation of suitable parameters a_{ij}, b_i, and c_i requires extremely lengthy algebraic manipulations, except for small values of m.

Some early examples were developed by Runge and a systematic treatment was initiated by Kutta about 1900. Recently, significant advances have been made in the development of a general theory and in the derivation and implementation of efficient methods incorporating error estimation and control.

Except for stiff equations (*see* ordinary differential equations), explicit methods

with $a_{ij} = 0, j \geq i$

are used. These are relatively easy to program and are efficient compared with other methods unless evaluations of $f(x,y)$ are expensive.

To be useful for practical problems, the methods should be implemented in a form that allows the stepsize h to vary across the range of integration. Methods for choosing the steps h are based on estimates of the *local error. A Runge–Kutta formula should also be derived with a local interpolant that can be used to produce accurate approximations for all values of x, not just at the gridpoints x_n. This avoids the considerable extra cost caused by artificially restricting the stepsize when dense output is required.

run-length encoding A *lossless compression technique where a sequence of pixels with the same value is replaced by a value and count. *See also* image compression.

run-length limited encoding *See* RLL, disk format.

running (active) Currently being executed, usually on a CPU. The *process descriptor for a process that is running will contain an indication that this is the case. Clearly, once the process becomes suspended for any reason, the "running" bit in the process descriptor will be reset.

run time The time at which a program begins to execute, in contrast to the time at which it may have been submitted, loaded, compiled, or assembled. The amount of time – elapsed time or processor time – used in executing a program is called the *execution time* or sometimes the *run time*.

run-time system A collection of procedures that support a high-level language at run time, providing functions such as storage allocation, input/output, etc.

Russell's paradox A contradiction originally formulated by Bertrand Russell and phrased in terms of *set theory. Let T be the set of all sets that are not members of themselves, i.e.

$$T = \{S \mid S \notin S\}$$

Then it can be shown that T is a member of T if and only if T is not a member of T.

The paradox results from certain kinds of recursive definitions. It arises for example in the following situation: the barber in a certain town shaves everyone who does not shave himself; who shaves the barber?

S

SA *Short for* structured systems analysis.

SAA *Abbrev. for* Systems Applications Architecture. IBM's family of standard interfaces that enable software to be written independently of hardware and operating systems.

SADT *Trademark, abbrev. for* structured analysis and design technique. A method for modeling complex problems and systems, developed by Douglas Ross in the mid-1970s. Although SADT is a general-purpose modeling tool, it is particularly effective for requirements definition for arbitrary systems problems and is widely used for this purpose in the software engineering field. SADT can be viewed as having three main parts: a set of methods that can assist an analyst in gaining an understanding of a complex system, a graphical language that can be used to record and communicate that understanding, and administrative guidelines that contribute to the orderly progress of the analysis and early detection of problems.

The methods of SADT are based upon several concepts. Top-down decomposition allows information to be dealt with at progressive levels of detail. Model-building both assists understanding and permits communication of that understanding. Adoption of a variety of complementary viewpoints allows all relevant aspects of a system to be considered while limiting consideration at any time to one well-defined topic. The dual "things" and "happenings" aspects of any subject are used to reinforce understanding and promote consistency. Review and iteration procedures ensure the quality of the model that is developed.

The graphical language of SADT consists basically of boxes and arrows that are used to construct SADT diagrams. The language is concerned only with the structured decomposition of the subject matter, and any other language (e.g. natural language) can be used within the boxes and to label the arrows. A single SADT diagram may model either processes or data. A diagram that models processes, called an *actigram*, uses boxes to show the individual processes and uses arrows to show dataflows between processes, any constraints that apply, and the mechanisms for carrying out the processes. The arrows entering and leaving a box serve to bound the context of the process, and this can then be decomposed on further actigrams through successive levels of detail to any level required. Similarly the corresponding data decomposition is presented in *datagrams* and consideration proceeds from highly abstract data objects through successive levels of decomposition and definition.

The administrative guidelines of SADT provide among other things for independent review of the diagrams as they are produced and for configuration control of the emerging model.

A nonproprietary form of *SADT developed by the US Air Force is now available and is known as *IDEF*.

safety Freedom from *risk. The term is also used in the context of safety level to provide a quantitative measure of the level of safety.

A safe system is one that will never do anything bad. The definition of what is "bad" is application-dependent: the safety requirements for a system controlling an aircraft would obviously be more stringent than those for, say, a stock control system. *Compare* liveness.

safety case The detailed arguments and reasoning that justify claims about the safety *integrity of a given system.

safety-critical system A system in which any failure or design error has the potential to lead to loss of life.

safety integrity *See* integrity.

safety plan The management activities – the set of technical procedures and processes – as well as the people to be employed in ensuring that the requisite safety *integrity levels of a system will be achieved.

safety-related system A *system whose malfunction, either directly or indirectly, has the potential to lead to *safety being compromised.

sampled-data system *See* discrete and continuous systems. *See also* sampling.

sample input Input in computer graphics where the input device continually updates the required input value and the application samples it when it requires it. An example of the use of sample input would be a dial that the operator rotates to define the orientation of a molecule. The application is in a loop whereby it updates the molecule position, samples the new dial position, and repeats the drawing of the molecule.

sampling 1. (time quantization) A process by which the value of an analog, or continuous, signal is "examined" at discrete fixed intervals of time. The resulting *sampled value* will normally be held constant until the next sampling instant, and may be converted into a digital form using an *A/D converter for subsequent processing by a computer.

The *rate* at which a given analog signal is sampled must be a certain minimum value, dependent upon the bandwidth of the analog signal; this ensures that none of the information in the analog signal is lost. The sampling rate may also affect the stability of an analog system if the system is to be controlled by a computer. *See also* Nyquist's criterion.

2. The act of selecting items for study in such a way that the measurements made on the items in the sample will provide information about similar items not in the sample. Items can be people, machines, periods of time, fields of corn, games of chance, or whatever is being studied. *Sample size* is the number of items included in the sample. If the variance of the measurement (*see* measures of variation) is approximately known, the variance of its mean in a sample is the population variance divided by the sample size. This formula can then be used to indicate an appropriate sample size.

A *population* is a complete set of items about which information is required. It must be defined before selecting the sample or results may be ill-defined. The sample is the basis for inference about *probability distributions of measurements on the population. Problems of sampling include avoidance of

*bias and selection of enough samples to ensure adequate precision.

Random sampling is the process that results in each item having the same probability of inclusion in the sample. Items may be selected with the aid of tables of random numbers or with mechanical devices such as cards or coins.

Systematic sampling selects items in some regular manner. It is valid when the order in which items are encountered is irrelevant to the question under study, but can be an unintentional source of bias.

sanitization The erasure of sensitive material from a system, especially its storage media, for example by overwriting or degaussing magnetically.

SA/RT *Short for* structured systems analysis for real time. *See* Ward–Mellor, Hatley–Pirbhai.

satellite computer A computer that forms part of a computing system but is generally much less capable than the mainframe. It is located at a distance from the main system and serves auxiliary functions such as remote data entry or printing. It is now often nearly synonymous with *terminal.

satisfiability The property exhibited by any logical expression or well-formed formula for which it is possible to assign values to variables in such a way that the expression or formula is true. *See also* propositional calculus, predicate calculus, P=NP question.

satisfiability problem *See* P=NP question.

SatStream *Trademark* British Telecom's satellite digital leased-circuit service. SatStream circuits are available as a fully digital service, at speeds ranging from 2.4 Kbps to 2.048 Mbps.

saturation 1. A psycho-physiological measurement of the degree to which a color appears to be free of white.

2. of a transistor. *See* bipolar transistor.

sawtooth waveform A periodic repetitive waveform that is constrained to lie between a maximum and a minimum value. Between these limits the waveform alternately rises and falls linearly with time. The slope of one of the edges of the waveform is made very much steeper than the other, and the waveform thus appears as a repetitive series of linear ramps. *Compare* triangular waveform.

S-100 bus An early backplane bus (IEEE-696) designed for microprocessor system interconnection. It supported 8- and 16-bit data transfers and 24-bit addresses and employed a complex set of control signals.

SCA *Abbrev. for* synchronous concurrent algorithm.

scalability The ability for something designed to operate at one measure of size to operate successfully at other sizes. The term is commonly used in relation to the development of shared computer applications that are intended to be used by large numbers of users. Of necessity, developments take place with a small number of test users. Unless the application is carefully designed to take account of the interactions that will arise when it is called on to service a large number of users, it may well fail to operate at all, or to operate only with an unacceptable level of service. An application that successfully expands its numbers of supported users is said to be *scalable*.

scalable *See* scalability.

scalable font *See* font.

scalable processor architecture *See* SPARC.

scalar A number comprising a single value (such as an *integer or *real number), as opposed to a *complex number (containing two scalars) or a *vector (which is a scalar only in the special case of its containing one number).

scaling The adjustment of values to be used in a computation so that they and their resultant are within the range that can be handled by the process or equipment. The scaling factor is reapplied to correct the result before output or – if this is not possible – it is output as a qualifier with the result.

scan A single pass through the data of one or more components in an image.

scan-line A horizontal line of pixels across a *raster-scan display. Many algorithms proceed scan-line by scan-line. Initially this was

tied in with display performance but it is now a common software technique to reduce dimensionality.

scanner 1. A device that can capture an image and convert it into a unique set of electric signals. The image scanned may be a pattern that is directly related to a code, such as *bar codes on retailed products, or it may be a picture, page, or portion of text. *See also* drum scanner, flatbed scanner, bar code scanner, document scanner.

2. *Another name for* lexical analyzer.

scatter read A process in which data from a single record may be collected into (or for the process of *scatter write* written into) several noncontiguous areas of memory.

sccs *Abbrev. for* source code control system. A utility program, developed initially to run under UNIX, that keeps track of a set of versions and variants of a text file (usually *source language). Sccs can retrieve any one of the set of versions and variants it holds, and can receive new versions or variants together with a commentary concerning who made the change and what has changed from the previous version or variant. An important feature of sccs is that it does not keep the full source text of each version or variant. Instead it keeps one full text and a set of differences between that version and all the other versions and variants. Hence sccs provides a more economical means of storing a module with many versions and variants than, for example, storing them all in separate files.

scheduled maintenance Periodic *preventive maintenance.

scheduler The code responsible for controlling use of a shared *resource. Access to a shared resource must be subject to two requirements. It is essential to ensure that any *process about to be granted use of a resource will not itself suffer damage, and that it will not cause damage to other processes. This can be thought of as establishing the correctness of the scheduling. Quite separately from this, where it is feasible to allow any of several processes to access a resource, then it is necessary to make a choice between them. This choice will generally have a bearing on the efficiency with which system resources are utilized, and is determined by the *scheduling algorithm.

When used without further qualification, the word scheduler refers to controlling the use of the processors. Scheduling of jobs is usually carried out in two stages. The *high-level scheduler* collects together a particular job mix that is to be executed at any one time, according to criteria that are thought to allow the system to be optimally used. The scheduling among these jobs on a very fine time scale is the province of the *low-level scheduler* (or *dispatcher*), which thus allocates processors to processes.

scheduling algorithm The method used to determine which of several *processes, each of which can safely have a *resource allocated to it, will actually be granted use of the resource. The algorithm may take into account the priority of the user associated with the process, the requirement to maintain high utilization of system resources, and deadlines for the job.

For example, in a priority *time-slicing system, the processes awaiting execution are organized in several queues with the higher-priority queues having a smaller time *quantum. Whenever a processor becomes available for scheduling, the oldest process that is free to run in the highest-priority queue is started.

If this process runs to the end of its quantum without generating an interrupt then it will be rescheduled into a lower-priority queue with a larger quantum. If, before the quantum has expired, the process generates an interrupt then it will be returned either to the same queue or possibly to a higher-priority queue with a shorter quantum. If the process is itself interrupted by some external event that allows the rescheduling of a higher-priority process (with a shorter quantum) then again the interrupted process is returned to the queue from which it originated.

The net effect is that low-priority processes, with long quanta, are likely to be interrupted by the completion of input/output transactions on behalf of higher-priority processes, which will thus be freed for further processing.

schema of a database. *Short for* logical schema. *See also* storage schema, user view.

SCHEME A dialect of *LISP, used particularly in teaching computer science.

Schmitt trigger A discrete or integrated circuit whose output has two stable states, i.e. two sustainable values of output voltage, to which it is driven by the movement of its input voltage past two well-defined trigger values. A rise in input voltage above one trigger level causes the output to switch to one state. A fall in input voltage below the other trigger level causes the output to switch to the other state.

Logic signals become corrupted as they travel through a system; the switching edges become *exponentials, *ringing can occur, and *noise may be added. Feeding such a signal through a Schmitt trigger restores the rising and falling edges to a fast transition between the voltages corresponding to the 0 and 1 logic states.

Schonhage algorithm An algorithm that multiplies large numbers very rapidly, based on the ideas of *modular arithmetic. *See* Chinese remainder theorem.

Schonhage–Strassen algorithm A development of the *Strassen algorithm that was published in 1970 and avoids the explicit use of complex numbers. It multiplies two n-bit numbers in steps of

$$O(n \log n \log \log n)$$

Schottky TTL A relatively fast bipolar *logic family, normally produced in integrated-circuit form, whose internal configuration is similar to normal *TTL except that *Schottky transistors* are used. These transistors can be considered as equivalent to a normal *bipolar transistor with a *Schottky diode* connected across the base-collector junction. The Schottky diode is a semiconductor-metal diode that has a low cut-in voltage (*forward bias voltage drop), typically 300 millivolts, compared with 600 mV for other common semiconductor diodes. It also has a relatively high switching speed. In Schottky TTL the low cut-in voltage of the diode limits the base-collector voltage to about 400 mV, which prevents the transistor falling into saturation. This results in faster switching times for the transistors constructed in this way.

scissoring Removing the portion of an image that lies outside a specified region. *See also* clipping.

scope That part of a program in which a particular *declaration applies.

Scott–Ershov domain *See* domain.

scratchpad A type of semiconductor memory that usually has small capacity but very fast access. It is used for temporary storage of intermediate results or other information that is required during the course of a computation.

screen 1. The surface of a cathode-ray tube or other *display device on which information can be displayed.
2. To select and display information in response to an instruction or an inquiry.

screen dump A way of transferring the entire graphical or textual contents of a display screen to a printer. Each *pixel of the display appears as a dot of suitable density on the printer. Color screens can be dumped to color printers.

screened cable *See* cable.

screen editor *See* text editor.

screensaver A program that is initiated after a display has remained unchanged for a definable period of time, usually a few minutes, to prevent a permanent pattern being physically burnt into the screen. In its simplest form the program merely blanks the screen, but screensavers have become something of a subculture and can range from complex moving abstract shapes to colorful animated stories with many variations. It is also possible to have a whole set of screensavers and have one chosen at random on each occasion.

script 1. (command file) A file containing commands or other actions that could have been entered from the keyboard. This is a useful way of replaying often-used sequences of actions. In fact the *scripting languages usually have extra commands not available for direct use such as branches, loops, and procedure calls. There are also usually optional

*parameters that allow the script to be made more general.
2. *See* script theory.

scripting language A programming language that can be used to write programs to control an application or class of applications, typically interpreted. It may for example be a language, such as AppleScript, Script-X, or HyperTalk, for defining multimedia presentations. *See also* PERL, Python, Tcl.

script theory A representation for modeling sequential series of events. Originally designed for *natural language processing, *scripts* capture the main events and themes in a story. A script can be seen as a stereotype and matched against other scripts or situations.

scroll To move the information displayed on a screen in a vertical or horizontal direction: as information disappears at one edge new information becomes visible at the other edge, or alternatively space is provided for the entry of new data. The scrolling action is perceived as a smooth movement. In some displays the movement is in discrete increments of one line pitch and this is referred to as *racking*. Scrolling is technically more difficult to achieve but eases simultaneous reading.

scroll bar, scroll box *See* slider bar.

SCSI (pronounced skuzy) *Acronym for* small computer systems interface. A standard way of connecting peripheral devices, such as disk storage units, to small and medium-sized computers. It is widely used to couple CD-ROM drives to personal computers. Up to seven disk units and one computer can be connected to each SCSI. The interface is specified in a document from the ANSI committee X3.31. The first SCSI standard, SCSI-1, was specified in 1986, SCSI-2 came in 1992, and SCSI-3 is under development.

SDH *Abbrev. for* synchronous digital hierarchy. A set of CCITT standards, and products that implement those standards, intended to support high-speed wide area networking; the intention is to support bit rates from the 100 Mbps range upward. The basic unit within the SDH is the *synchronous transport module*, of which at present (Spring 1995) only the first, STM-1, is finally defined.

A major problem for large-scale WANs is that of allowing relatively low-speed links (*tributaries*) to insert data into the high-speed bearer, or recover data from it, caused by timing problems relating to the large difference in clock rates between the tributary and the high-speed bearer – typically 100–1000 orders of magnitude. STM-1 uses a fixed-size module conceptually made up of 9 rows each of 270 bytes. Modules are transmitted at 125 microsecond intervals, row by row and byte by byte, to give a total transmission rate of 155 Mbps. Within each module, specific rows are assigned to specific types of traffic. The first 9 bytes of each row are assigned for timing and control for the contents of the other 261 bytes. The system is designed to allow tributaries to insert or extract data through a series of units, each of which can accept (or deliver) self-timing data at relatively low clock rates, up to about 8 Mbps, or can accept the output from (or deliver input to) such units at speeds that are submultiples of that for the STM-1 system. The "hierarchy" defines the operations and protocols for all the units needed.

SDLC *Abbrev. for* synchronous data link control. A data link control *protocol originally developed by IBM, based on the use of *frames to delimit message boundaries, providing only link-layer functions. Frames consist of an 8-bit frame delimiter (or "flag"), an 8-bit address, an 8-bit control field, a variable-length user information field, a 16-bit frame check sequence, and a final 8-bit frame delimiter. The flag consists of the special character

          0 1 1 1 1 1 1 0

and is the only occasion on which six successive ones appear. *Bit stuffing is used to ensure that where the user's information contains five contiguous '1's, the system inserts an additional '0', which is removed at the receiver.

The end-stations are designated as either a primary or a secondary station. There is only one primary station, which initiates and terminates link activity and is responsible for

error recovery and for link sharing among multiple secondary stations. The address field has two special values: 0, which is reserved for testing, and 255, which indicates that this is a broadcast frame. The control field is used to carry acknowledgments that frames have been received correctly, or that an error has occurred and that a designated frame is to be retransmitted.

SDPM *Abbrev. for* software development process model.

SEAC *Acronym for* Standards Eastern Automatic Computer. The first stored-program electronic digital computer to become operational in the USA, in 1950. (*Compare* Manchester Mark I, EDSAC, EDVAC.) It was one of two different pioneer machines developed by the National Bureau of Standards: SEAC was installed in Washington, and the other, called SWAC (Standards Western Automatic Computer), in Los Angeles. Like EDSAC and EDVAC, SEAC used mercury *delay line memory.

search 1. To locate a specified piece of information in a table or file (*see* searching).

  2. (find) In word processing, to locate the next occurrence of a specified piece of text. The *search string* may be set to be *case-sensitive or case-insensitive, and also to find the string as a whole word or when embedded in a word. The search string may include *wildcards, and the scope of the search may be the entire document, the current selection (*see* select), or the text forward or backward from the cursor. There is usually a "search again" or "search next" command that searches for the next occurrence of the string previously defined so that multiple occurrences can be located without having to retype the search string.

  3. The locating of a specified piece of information or text.

search and insertion algorithm *See* searching.

search and replace (find and change) In word processing, to *search for a text string and then replace it with another one. The process may be stopped after a single replacement, it may replace all occurrences of the search string without asking, or it may ask for confirmation at each potential replacement. When replacing all occurrences of the search string in an entire document, a *global search and replace*, it is good practice to ask for confirmation.

search engine A program that when initiated by a search command from a user interface examines a body of data for items satisfying the search criteria and returns the items or their locations to the interface. The data could be, say, a literary database or information about very large numbers of *World Wide Web sites. Alta Vista and Yahoo are examples of Web search engines.

searching Locating information in a *table or *file by reference to a special field of each record, called the *key*. The goal of the *search* is to discover a record (if any) with a given key value. There are many different algorithms for searching, principally depending on the way in which the table or file is structured.

If a record is to be inserted in the file, and it is important to ensure that keys are unique, then a search is necessary: the insertion may take place as soon as the search has discovered that no existing record has the new key. Such an algorithm is known as a *search and insertion algorithm*.

See also table lookup, sequential search algorithm, binary search algorithm, breadth-first search, depth-first search, trie search, heuristic search.

search tree *See* binary search tree, multiway search tree.

secant method An *iterative method for finding a root of the *nonlinear equation $f(x) = 0$. It is given by the formula

$$x_{n+2} = x_{n+1} - (x_{n+1} - x_n)[f(x_{n+1})/(f(x_{n+1}) - f(x_n))]$$
$$n = 0, 1, 2, \ldots$$

where x_0 and x_1 are given starting values. This formula is derived by replacing $f(x)$ by a straight line based on the last two iterates. Convergence is ultimately less rapid than for *Newton's method, but it can be overall more efficient on some problems since derivatives are not required.

secondary index *See* indexed file.

secondary memory *Another name for* backing store.

secondary ray *See* ray tracing.

second generation of computers. Machines whose designs were started after 1955 (approximately) and are characterized by both vacuum tube (valve) and discrete transistor logic. They used magnetic core main memory. By this time a wider range of input/output equipment was beginning to be available, with higher-performance magnetic tape and the first forms of online storage (magnetic drums and early magnetic disks). Models of such online storage devices include magnetic drums in the UNIVAC LARC and 1105, and early disks in the IBM 1401–1410. During the second generation, initial efforts at *automatic programming produced B0, Commercial Translator, FACT, Fortran, and Mathmatic as programming languages, these in turn influencing the development of the *third generation languages – Cobol and later versions of Fortran. *See also* Atlas.

second normal form *See* normal forms.

second-order logic *See* predicate calculus.

sector A subdivision of a track on a magnetic disk that represents the smallest portion of data that can be modified by overwriting. Each sector has a unique address, which contains the location of the track and the sector number. In order to read an address or data the drive decoding electronics must be synchronized to the data stream. To achieve this a special pattern, the *preamble*, is written. Following the preamble comes the *address mark or data mark as appropriate.

A disk may be *soft-sectored* or *hard-sectored*. In soft-sectoring, the size and position of the sectors is determined by the control electronics and software: disk drives generate an index signal once per revolution of the disk, and when this is received from the drive unit all the sectors of a track are written in one continuous operation. On a hard-sectored disk, the start of each sector is related to a sector signal generated by the disk drive and is positively related to the position of the disk. Hard-sectoring can achieve higher packing of sectors since it is not necessary to have large intersector gaps to accommodate speed variations.

security Prevention of or protection against (a) access to information by unauthorized recipients or (b) intentional but unauthorized destruction or alteration of that information. Security may guard against both unintentional as well as deliberate attempts to access sensitive information, in various combinations according to circumstances. The concepts of security, integrity, and privacy are interlinked. *See* integrity.

security accreditation Formal authorization that a particular computer installation or network can be used operationally in recognition that all features of the *security policy have been implemented.

security certification A statement by a recognized authority that a *security evaluation has been undertaken competently and in accordance with appropriate regulations.

security classification A classification of the sensitivity of information, e.g. "secret" or "medical records to be inspected only by doctors".

security clearance A categorization associated with a subject, e.g. a user, to describe the *security classification of information to which he or she is entitled to have access.

security evaluation The examination of a system to determine its degree of compliance with a stated *security model, *security standard, or specification. The evaluation may be conducted (a) by analyzing the detailed design, especially of the software, often using *verification and validation, (b) by observing the functional behavior of the system, or (c) by attempting to penetrate the system using techniques available to an "attacker".

The US National Computer Security Center has published *Department of Defense Trusted Computer System Evaluation Criteria*, generally known as the "Orange Book". This has commonly been used to evaluate commercially available systems. More recently, *Information Technology Security Evaluation Criteria (ITSEC)* has been published by the European Union.

security kernel A *trusted process that mediates all information flows within a system in accordance with a specified *security model. *See also* kernel.

security label A representation of the *security classification directly associated with the information to which it relates, e.g. as part of a transmitted protocol.

security model A formal statement of the intrinsic security features to be provided by a system. The statement usually includes a detailed specification, often in mathematical notation, of the allowed and prohibited relationships between subjects and objects according to their respective *security clearance and *security classifications. It may furthermore specify the events that must be recorded in the *audit trail.

security policy A statement of the measures, especially operational, to be taken in order to defend a system against the postulated *threats. The policy may specify the *security processing mode together with the *security model and their relationship with physical and personnel security controls. For example, the security policy will usually specify the way in which *passwords will be allocated and the arrangements for audit, etc.

security processing mode A description of the *security clearances of the entire set of users of a system in relation to the classification of all the information to be stored or processed by the system. *See* dedicated mode, multilevel security.

security standard 1. A statement of the extent of evaluation necessary before a particular security feature can be considered for *security certification as *trusted.
2. A set of security features to be provided by a system before it can be deemed to be suitable for use in a particular *security processing mode, or in accordance with a generalized *security policy.

seeding (error seeding; bug seeding) The deliberate addition of errors to a program. Normally the errors seeded are semantic rather than syntactic, and are usually selected and located in a way that is representative of the normal distribution of error type and positioning. For example, a variable name spelling could be altered, or a branching statement condition changed from "less than" to "less than or equal". The program is then subjected to test and the errors revealed in the test are analyzed into seeded and nonseeded forms. A test or series of tests should successfully reveal all the seeded faults: the technique has been used as a means of checking the effectiveness (and efficiency) of various test strategies.

It is however difficult to be certain that the seeded errors are truly representative both of the occurrence and the effect of real errors. It is particularly difficult to seed nontrivial errors.

seek time The time taken for a particular track on a storage disk or drum to be located. The average seek time is defined as the sum of all single track seek times plus the sum of two track seek times and so on…, divided by the sum of all possible seeks. Typical average seek times for disks are in the range 8–20 milliseconds. *See also* latency, access time.

segment 1. Originally, a clearly identifiable set of data, or code, that was moved between backing store and main memory under the control of the user. Later the term was applied to a set of data, still clearly visible to the user, that was managed by the operating system as part of the *virtual-memory system. A segment differs from a *page in that its size is not fixed, and the user has a measure of direct control over its management.
2. Part of a program. The word is usually used in the context of storage allocation, as in code segment, data segment.
3. A region of near-uniform intensity in a *gray-level image that represents a distinct entity. *Segmentation* is the *image-processing stage that locates and divides up an image into segments.
4. of an Ethernet. A part of an Ethernet that consists of a single length of cable, usually coaxial cable. There are strict limits on the total length of cable that can be used. *See* Ethernet, thick wire.

select 1. To initiate an action or enable a data path.
2. To choose one of several possible control

paths at a particular point in a program. The *selection* operation is usually made by a *case statement, though if there are only two alternatives an *if then else statement can be used.
3. To mark out a section of a document before performing an operation on it, such as *copy, *move, or *cut, or before changing its attributes, such as *font, color, margins, or line spacing. The selection process can be done using the keyboard or *dragging the cursor with a pointing device such as a mouse. The marked text is known as the *selection*.
4. To indicate an item in a menu, menu bar, button bar, etc., with the selection cursor before initiating an action.

selector 1. A device that can switch a signal path or initiate some other action on receipt of a predetermined signal. The actioning signal can be on the path to be switched or from a separate path.
2. *Short for* selector channel. *See* channel.

selector channel *See* channel.

self-adapting process (self-learning process) An *adaptive process that can be "trained" on representative data to provide a best model for that data and that can "recognize" similar data. *See also* artificial intelligence.

self-checking code An *error-correcting or *error-detecting code.

self-compiling compiler A compiler that is written in the language it compiles. Such a compiler makes it relatively easy to transfer a language to another machine, since the compiler can be compiled on a machine on which it has already been implemented.

self-defining A term applied to a programming language, implying that the compiler for the language can be written in the language. *See* self-compiling compiler.

self-documenting program A program whose function and working can be obtained from a reading of the program text, without additional documentation. Structured design, the use of a high-level language, careful choice of identifiers, and judicious use of comments all contribute to this end.

self-dual *See* duality.

self-extending A term applied to a programming language, denoting the ability to add new features to the language by writing programs in that language.

self-learning process *Another term for* self-adapting process.

self-organizing system A computing system that is capable of developing information and structure out of sets of natural data that are presented to it. *See also* artificial intelligence.

self-referent list *Another name for* recursive list.

self-relative addressing *See* relative addressing.

semantic analysis *See* static analysis, symbolic execution.

semantic error A programming error that arises from a misunderstanding of the meaning or effect of some construct in a programming language. *See also* syntax error, error diagnostics.

semantic network (associative network) A means of representing relational knowledge as a labeled directed *graph. Each vertex of the graph represents a concept and each label represents a relation between concepts. Access and updating procedures traverse and manipulate the graph. A semantic network is sometimes regarded as a graphical notation for *logical formulas. *See also* knowledge representation.

semantics That part of the definition of a language concerned with specifying the meaning or effect of a text that is constructed according to the *syntax rules of the language. *See also* denotational semantics, operational semantics, axiomatic semantics, interpretation.

semaphore A special-purpose *data type introduced by Edsger Dijkstra (1965). Apart from creation, initialization, and annihilation, there are only two operations on a semaphore: *wait* (*P operation* or *down operation*) and *signal* (*V operation* or *up operation*). The letters P and V derive from the Dutch words used in the original description.

A semaphore has an integer value that cannot become negative. The signal operation increases the value by one, and in general

indicates that a resource has become free. The wait operation decreases the value by one when that can be done without the value going negative, and in general indicates that a free resource is about to start being used. This therefore provides a means of controlling access to *critical resources by cooperating sequential processes.

semicomputable algebra *See* computable algebra.

semicomputable set *See* recursively enumerable set.

semiconductor A material, such as silicon or germanium, whose electrical conductivity increases with temperature and is intermediate between metals and insulators. In pure semiconductors this effect is due to the thermal generation of equal numbers of negative charge carriers (electrons) and positive charge carriers (holes). These materials are called *intrinsic* or *i-type semiconductors*.

The introduction of specific types of impurity atoms into a pure semiconductor can significantly increase its conductivity: *donor impurities*, which belong to group 5 of the periodic table, greatly increase the number of conduction electrons and produce an *n-type semiconductor*; *acceptor impurities*, which belong to group 3, greatly increase the number of holes and produce a *p-type semiconductor*. These materials are called *extrinsic semiconductors*. The conductivity of an extrinsic semiconductor depends on the type and the amount (or *doping level*) of impurity present.

Semiconductors of different conductivity (n-type, p-type, highly doped n- and p-type, i-type) can be brought together to form a variety of *junctions, which are the basis of semiconductor devices used as electronic components. The term semiconductor is frequently applied to the devices themselves.

semiconductor memory (solid-state memory) Any of various types of cheap memory device, normally produced in *integrated-circuit form, that are used for storing binary data patterns in digital electronic circuits. They consist internally of arrays of *latches constructed of semiconductor devices such as *bipolar transistors or *MOSFETs. The memory *capacity of a single chip is increasing by a factor of four every few years: the 16 megabit chip of dynamic *RAM is now (1995) on the market.

semicustom A technique used for the design of *integrated circuits that is based on the use of fully characterized libraries of circuit elements produced by the manufacturer of the device. The designer is therefore not concerned with low-level details of semiconductor material electrical properties, and can instead concentrate on the functional behavior of the design. Most *ASIC circuit designs (for instance *gate arrays) are produced by this method. *See also* full custom.

semidecidable *See* decision problem.

semidecidable set *See* recursively enumerable set.

semidecision procedure *See* decision problem.

semigroup A very simple *algebraic structure comprising a *set S on which there is defined an *associative operation denoted by $\circ$ (*compare* group). The operator $\circ$ is assumed to take operands from the set and produce results that are also in S. When the set S is finite a semigroup can be described by giving the *Cayley table of the operation $\circ$; otherwise it can be described by giving a rule for $\circ$.

Examples of semigroups include: strings with the operation of *concatenation (joining together); the set of $n{\times}n$ matrices together with the operation of multiplication; the set of transformations of a set and the operation of composing functions; the integers and the operation of choosing the maximum (or minimum) of two elements. The set of integers together with subtraction does not constitute a semigroup.

Semigroups play a major role in the theory of *sequential machines and *formal languages. If M is a sequential machine then any input string induces a function over the state-set of M. The set of all such induced functions forms a *semigroup of the machine* under function *composition (*see* Myhill equivalence, Nerode equivalence). Semigroups are also used in certain aspects of computer arithmetic. *See also* free semigroup, transformation semigroup, monoid.

semiring A *set S (containing a 0 and a 1) on which there are defined two *dyadic operations that are denoted by $+$ and $\cdot$ and that obey certain properties: the set S, regarded as a set with a zero on which the operation $+$ is defined, is a *monoid; the set S, regarded as a set with a unit on which $\cdot$ is defined, is a monoid; the operation $+$ is *commutative; the operation $\cdot$ is *distributive over $+$. A semiring is said to be *unitary* if the operation $\cdot$ possesses a unit. A semiring is *commutative* if the operation $\cdot$ is commutative.

The set of polynomials in x whose coefficients are nonnegative integers constitutes an example of a semiring (which is not a ring), the two operations being addition and multiplication. Other uses of semirings occur in *fuzzy logic. *See also* ring, closed semiring.

semi-Thue system An important concept in formal language theory that underlies the notion of a *grammar. It was defined and investigated by Axel Thue from about 1904. A semi-Thue system over the alphabet Σ is a finite set of ordered pairs of Σ-words:

$$\{\langle l_1, r_1 \rangle, \ldots, \langle l_n, r_n \rangle\}$$

Each pair $\langle l_i, r_i \rangle$ is a rule, referred to as a *production*, with *left-hand side* l_i and *right-hand side* r_i; it is usually written

$$l_i \to r_i$$

Let u and v be Σ-words, and $l \to r$ be a production, then the word ulv is said to *directly derive* the word urv; this is written

$$ulv \Rightarrow urv$$

So w directly derives w' if w' is the result of applying a production to some substring of w. If

$$w_1 \Rightarrow w_2 \Rightarrow \ldots \Rightarrow w_{n-1} \Rightarrow w_n$$

then w_1 is said to *derive* w_n; this is written

$$w_1 \overset{*}{\Rightarrow} w_n$$

So w derives w' if w' is obtained from w by a sequence of direct derivations.

As one example, let Σ be $\{a, b\}$ and let the productions be

$$\{ab \to ba, ba \to ab\}$$

then $aabba$ derives $baaab$ by the sequence

$$aabba \Rightarrow ababa \Rightarrow baaba \Rightarrow baaab$$

It is clear that w derives any permutation of w.

As a second example, with productions

$$\{ab \to ba, ba \to \Lambda\}$$

w derives Λ (the empty word) if and only if *w* has the same number of *a*s as *b*s.

The question of whether *w* derives *w'* is algorithmically undecidable.

sense To determine the condition or content of a signal or storage location. When used in reference to a storage location the word has the same meaning as read.

sensitivity analysis Investigation of the degree to which the behavior of a system is affected by a change in the value of some (explicit or implicit) parameter or variable, or by a combination of changes. For example, a simple analysis might determine how the performance of a system is impacted by changing the number and sizes of the storage buffers that are allocated to that system.

sensor *Another name for* transducer.

sensor-data fusion The idea that data from multiple sensors should be combined so as to remove or reduce noise and uncertainty and increase confidence in the result. Redundancy, majority voting, and probability methods can be used for sets of simple sensors of the same modality, but major research issues are involved where the sensors are complex, as in vision, or operate across different modalities.

sentence *See* predicate calculus.

sentence symbol (start symbol) *See* grammar.

sentential form *See* grammar.

sentinel A *datum that indicates some important state, usually in the context of input or output. For example, an end-of-data sentinel means all the data has been read. *See also* rogue value, flag.

separator A symbol that separates statements in a programming language, e.g. the semicolon in Algol-type languages.

SEQUEL A database *query language, precursor of *SQL.

sequence 1. A *function whose domain is the set of positive integers (or sometimes the set of nonnegative integers). The image set can thus be listed $s_1, s_2, \ldots$ where s_i is the value of the function given argument *i*. A *finite sequence* (or *list*) is a function whose domain is $\{1, 2, \ldots, n\}$ for $n \geq 1$

and hence whose image set can be listed

$$s_1, s_2, \ldots, s_n$$

2. The listing of the image set of a sequence. Hence it is another name for *string.

sequence control register A part of the *control unit that causes the steps of the fetch and execute processes to occur in the correct sequence/timing. *See* program counter.

sequence generator A digital logic circuit whose purpose is to produce a prescribed sequence of outputs. Each output will be one of a number of symbols or of binary or *q-ary *logic levels. The sequence may be of indefinite length or of predetermined fixed length. A binary *counter is a special type of sequence generator. Sequence generators are useful in a wide variety of coding and control applications.

sequencer 1. In computer music, either a computer program or hardware that allows a composer to arrange a sequence or sequences of musical notes. These may then be replayed as continuous loops or on receipt of some trigger event. Often the anchor note for the sequence may be input by means of a conventional *MIDI keyboard. Early sequencers were monophonic hardware solutions, often custom-built. Many modern computer programs for music composition can be viewed as sequencers, but it is the ability to loop, be triggered, and to alter the anchor note that gives the composer the ability to use sequencer technology in live performance.
2. A logic circuit that produces outputs that are intended to provide coordination stimuli for other logic circuits. The exact timing and sequence of these control outputs is dependent on the sequencer circuitry and may depend on a set of input control signals provided by external devices.

sequencing 1. The procedure by which ordered units of data (octets or messages) are numbered, transmitted over a communications network (which may rearrange their order), and reassembled into the original order at their destination.
2. Proceeding through a program in its ordinary order, normally from sequential memory locations. *See also* loop.

sequency The number of positive-going zero crossings (and therefore half the total number of zero crossings) that the amplitude of a *signal makes per unit time, or, in the case of a spatial signal (a picture), per unit of distance. The term is used mainly with regard to signals capable of taking only one positive and one negative value of amplitude, especially the simple case of +1 unit and –1 unit. Although the amplitude is usually discrete, the time (or space) coordinate may be regarded as discrete or continuous, depending on the application and the mathematical methods to be employed.

The term was originally applied to *Walsh functions. In the case of Walsh functions, or any similar functions which are periodic but in which there are several zero crossings per period at unequal intervals, the number of zero crossings per period is called the *normalized sequency*.

Many concepts such as *bandwidth, and processes such as *filtering, which were originally defined in terms of *frequency, can equally well be defined in terms of sequency. The sequency formulation is often handled more simply and more rapidly by discrete devices such as computers.

See also discrete and continuous systems.

sequential (serial) Involving the occurrence of two or more events or activities such that one must finish before the next begins. If one event or activity immediately follows another then they are said to be *consecutive*.

sequential access A method of access to a file, especially a data file: a file is said to be sequentially accessed if the sequence of transactions presented to it matches a sequence in which *records are organized.

sequential algorithm In general, any algorithm executed sequentially, but, specifically, one for decoding a *convolutional code.

sequential circuit (sequential machine) A *logic circuit whose outputs at a specified time are a function of the inputs at that time, and also at a finite number of preceding times. In practice, any physically realizable sequential circuit will have a finite transit time, or delay, between the inputs changing and the outputs changing (one or more of

these inputs may be clock signals); the intention of the term sequential is to include not only *combinational circuits but also (explicitly) *memory elements such as flip-flops. Analysis and synthesis of sequential circuits is facilitated by *state diagrams.

sequential cohesion *See* cohesion.

sequential composition *See* process algebra.

sequential encoding A method of image encoding that uses a single scan through the data, as compared to *progressive encoding, which uses multiple scans. Sequential encoding is one of the options in the *JPEG standard.

sequential file A file organized to support *sequential access.

sequential function Let I and O be alphabets. A function

$$f : I^* \to O^*$$

(*see* word) is sequential if it is the response function of a *sequential machine.

sequential machine 1. A *finite-state automaton with output (in some contexts including machines with infinite state set). Thus there is a function f from the *Cartesian product $I \times Q$ to the product $Q \times O$, with Q a set of states and I, O finite sets of input and output symbols respectively. Suppose, for example,

$$a, q_0 \mapsto q_1, x$$
$$b, q_1 \mapsto q_1, y$$
$$c, q_1 \mapsto q_2, z$$

Then, if the machine is in state q_0 and reads a, it moves to state q_1 and outputs x, and so on. Assuming the starting state to be q_0, it can be seen for example that the input string $abbbc$ is mapped to the output string $xyyyz$. This mapping from the set of all input strings to the set of all output strings, i.e. I^* to O^*, is called the *response function* of the machine. The function f comprises a *state-transition function* f_Q from $I \times Q$ to Q and an *output function* f_O from $I \times Q$ to O.

What is described here is sometimes called a *Mealy machine* to distinguish it from the more restricted *Moore machines*. In a Moore machine, the symbol output at each stage depends only on the current state, and not on the input symbol read. The example above is therefore not a Moore machine since

$$f_O(b,q_1) = y$$

whereas

$$f_O(c,q_1) = z$$

Any Moore machine can be converted to an equivalent Mealy machine by adding more states.

A *generalized sequential machine* is an extension of the notion of sequential machine: a string of symbols is output at each stage rather than a single symbol. Thus there is a function from $I \times Q$ to $Q \times O^*$. *See also* gsm mapping.

2. *Another name for* sequential circuit.

sequential quadratic programming A widely used and successful approach to solving constrained *optimization problems, that is

$$\text{minimize } F(x), x = (x_1, x_2, \ldots, x_n)^T,$$

where $F(x)$ is a given objective function of n real variables, subject to the t nonlinear constraints on the variables,

$$c_i(x) = 0, i = 1,2,\ldots,t$$

Inequality constraints are also possible. A solution of this problem is also a stationary point (a point at which all the partial derivatives vanish) of the related function of x and λ,

$$L(x,\lambda) = F(x) - \Sigma\lambda_i c_i(x),$$
$$\lambda = (\lambda_1, \lambda_2, \ldots, \lambda_t)$$

A quadratic approximation to this function is now constructed that along with linearized constraints forms a quadratic programming problem – i.e., the minimization of a function quadratic in the variables, subject to linear constraints. The solution of the original optimization problem, say x^*, is now obtained from an initial estimate and solving a sequence of updated quadratic programs; the solutions of these provide improved approximations, which under certain conditions converge to x^*.

sequential search algorithm The most simple *searching algorithm in which the keys are searched sequentially from the top of the file until a match is found.

sequential transducer A nondeterministic version of a generalized *sequential machine.

serial 1. Involving the sequential transfer or processing of the individual parts of a whole, such as the bits of a character. *Compare* parallel.

2. *Another word for* sequential.

serial access A method of access to data in which blocks are read from the storage medium in the physical order in which they occur, until the required item is reached.

serial adder A binary *adder that is capable of forming sum and carry outputs for addend and augend words of greater than one bit in length. The individual bits of the addend and augend, starting with the least significant bit, are presented in sequence, together with a carry, to the adder, which then forms sum and carry outputs. The carry must then be stored so that it can be used with the next most significant pair of input bits. A serial adder affords a saving in component count when compared with a *parallel adder, but is generally slower.

serial arithmetic Operation upon one bit or digit of a number at a time.

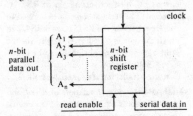

Serial in parallel out

serial in parallel out (SIPO) A term used to describe a class of digital device that can accept serial sequential n-bit data streams and convert them into parallel n-bit data words. These devices often consist of an n-bit *shift register that is serial loaded with n bits of data from the input stream under the control of an external clock (*see* diagram). The n-bit data word can then be read in parallel form from the shift register. *Compare* parallel in serial out.

serial input/output (SIO) A method of communicating data between devices, typically a computer and its peripherals, the individual data bits being sent sequentially. Serial communication may be *asynchronous*, where the data characters include start and stop bits to delimit the data, or *synchronous*, where such additional bits are omitted and the delimiting of the data depends purely on timing. Asynchronous serial communication is more flexible whereas synchronous serial communication makes better use of available bandwidth. Asynchronous methods are generally used with dial-up modems or for general connection of simple serial peripherals. Synchronous methods are usually to be found where *leased lines or proprietary interfaces are used.

serial in serial out (SISO) A term used to describe a *shift register that, by implication, cannot be loaded in parallel and cannot be read in parallel: data can only enter or leave the device serially.

serial interface A connection point through which information is transferred one digital bit at a time. The rate may be high, e.g. 10 megabits per second as in Ethernet, or as slow as 110 bits per second via an RS232C interface. The term is sometimes applied to interfaces such as the RS232C and RS422 in which the data is transferred serially via one path, but some control signals can be transferred simultaneously via parallel paths. *Compare* parallel interface, serial-parallel.

serial-parallel A combination of serial and parallel processing; for example, a decimal string is often processed as 4 bits in parallel, and successive 4-bit units are processed serially.

serial port An input/output socket on a computer or other device that is used for *serial input/output, often making use of the *RS232C standard. The physical port may have a 25- or 9-pin subminiature D connector or an RJ45 connector (which looks like a telephone connector). From the software, a serial port is usually treated as a *device rather than a file.

serial printer A printer that prints one character at a time in the sequence in which they appear in the line of text. The sequence may be taken from left to right, or it may be in alternate directions for alternate lines thus avoiding an unproductive carriage-return

movement. All serial printers have an arrangement in which a print head moves parallel to the paper and along the line to be printed. The print may be formed by impacting an inked ribbon against the paper, as in the case of *dot matrix printers, or by one of the nonimpact marking technologies such as *inkjet or *thermal printers. In some designs the productivity is increased when printing other than complete lines by arranging for the head to move at high speed when passing blank areas. The direction in which the line is to be printed is also optimized.

The speed of a serial printer appears slow compared to the equivalent character per second rate for a *line printer printing full lines. However, the serial printer's ability to print short lines more quickly improves its performance on applications with short lines, such as addresses and amounts on preprinted forms. A 200 cps serial printer can print some types of consumer bills at a rate equivalent to 300 lines per minute.

serial process A *process in which stages in the process are executed in a strictly serial manner, one stage completing before the next starts, and with only one stage active at any one instant.

serial programming *See* single threading.

serial transfer Transmission of information as sequential units. For example, if two computers connected by a single wire wish to communicate an 8-bit unit of information, the sending computer would transmit each of the eight bits in sequence over the wire, while the receiving computer would reassemble the sequential bits into the original 8-bit units. *Compare* parallel transfer.

serpentine recording A method of recording on magnetic tape (usually in cartridge form) where each track is recorded separately and alternate tracks are recorded in opposite directions, so that it is not necessary to rewind the tape after recording each track.

server A system on a network that provides a service to other systems connected to the network. The term was originally restricted to the case where both the server and the systems it served were on the same local area network, and where the server was likely to be expensive in comparison with the systems it served. The term is now used much more generally, applying to systems where the server and the system to which it provides a service (the client) may be linked by a metropolitan area network or wide area network, and where the server may be much less costly than the client. *See also* client/server, file server, compute server.

service bit A bit in an *X25 *packet that indicates whether the packet is formatted to contain primarily data or control information.

service engineering Any maintenance, *preventive or *remedial.

service level agreement (SLA) An agreement between the supplier of a service and the users of that service that sets out the levels of service that will be offered, preferably in quantitative terms, and the obligations on the user of the service. A typical agreement for a computing service or network service will set out the expected levels of service measured in terms of one or more of the following: availability, fault reporting, recovery from breakdowns, traffic levels, throughput, response times, training and advisory services, and similar measures of the service quality as seen by the end-user. The agreement will also set out user costs and charges, the provision of access to premises for service contractors, and standards of training to be achieved by users. The agreement may form part of a legal contract, yet is equally likely to be found within a single large organization where one unit within the organization offers services to other units, but where a legally enforceable contract would not be appropriate.

session layer of network protocol function. *See* seven-layer reference model.

set 1. A collection of distinct objects of any sort. The objects in the set are called its *members* or *elements*. An element can occur at most once in a set and order or arrangement is unimportant. If x is a member of the set S it is customary to write

$$x \in S$$

If x is not a member of S this can be expressed as

$$x \notin S$$

and is equivalent to

$$\text{NOT } (x \in S)$$

i.e. $\in$ and $\notin$ can be regarded as operators. When any element in set S is also in set T, and vice versa, the two sets are said to be *identical* or *equal*.

A *finite set* has a fixed finite number of members and a notation such as

$$\{\text{Ada, Pascal, Cobol, C}\}$$

is possible; the members are separated by commas and here are just the names of various programming languages. When the number of elements is not finite, the set is said to be *infinite* and explicit enumeration of the elements is not then possible.

Infinite and finite sets can be described using a *predicate or statement such as $p(x)$ that involves x and is either true or false, thus

$$\{x \mid p(x)\}$$

This is read as "the set of all elements x for which $p(x)$ is true", the elements being characterized by the common property p. Examples of sets described in this way are (letting R be the set of real numbers):

$$\{(x,y) \mid x \in R, y \in R, \text{ and } x + y = 9\}$$

$$\{n \mid n \text{ is a prime number}\}$$

$$\{l \mid l \text{ is the name of a language}\}$$

There is an implicit assumption here that there is some algorithm for deciding whether $p(x)$ is true or false in any particular case.

The idea of a set is fundamental to mathematics. It forms the basis for all ideas involving *functions, *relations, and indeed any kind of *algebraic structure. Authors differ considerably in the way they define sets. A mathematical logician will distinguish carefully between classes and sets, basically to ensure that paradoxes such as *Russell's paradox cannot occur in sets. However, the informal definition is adequate for most purposes.

See also operations on sets.

2. Any data structure representing a set of elements. One example is a *characteristic vector.

3. To cause the condition or state of a switch, signal, or storage location to change to the positive condition.

set algebra The *algebra that consists of the *set of *subsets of some *universal set U

together with the associated operations of *union, *intersection, and *complement. The set of subsets associated with set algebra is sometimes described as the *power set of U.

set difference The *dyadic operation between two sets S and T, say, resulting in the set $S - T$ consisting of those elements that are in S but not in T. Formally

$$S - T = \{s \mid s \in S \text{ and } s \notin T\}$$

Set difference is a generalization of the idea of the *complement of a set and as such is sometimes called the *relative complement* of T with respect to S. The *symmetric difference* between two sets S and T is the *union of $S - T$ and $T - S$.

set-up time The period of time during which binary data must be present or "set up" at the input to a digital device before the device enters or samples the data. It is commonly specified for memory devices.

seven-layer reference model The standard model for communications *protocols that is formally approved by the International Standards Organization acting in concert with the *CCITT. The ISO approach identifies the functionality required in terms of seven separate layers, as summarized in the table; the two systems that are to communicate each support an implementation of these seven layers. The layers are conceptually organized with the "lowest" layer representing the physical link between the two systems, and with successive "higher" layers progressively being concerned less with the details of the network traffic, and more with the details of the end-user applications that wish to communicate. Each local implementation of these layers is often referred to as a *protocol stack*. Each layer can communicate only with the layers immediately above and below it in the stack. The set of permissible messages and responses in this local "vertical" communication is defined by the corresponding *interface. The lowest, physical layer, communicates downward with the physical link, and information passes via the link to the corresponding lowest layer in the remote system. The highest layer communicates upward with the local end-user application.

By passing a message down through the lower layers at the transmitting end, across the link, and up through the layers at the receiving end, each layer can communicate with the corresponding layer in the remote system. The set of permissible messages and responses in this remote, "horizontal" communication is defined by the corresponding protocol. The entire system is therefore defined by the information that can pass vertically via the interface between adjacent layers in a given stack, and horizontally between corresponding layers in the two remote stacks.

The primary objective of the seven-layer model is to provide a flexible means of describing the behavior of communications systems, capable of dealing with all existing and future technologies, rather than to provide a specific set of protocols and interfaces. The process of reaching international agreements that meet the conflicting requirements of different groups of end-users, accommodate the interests of competing commercial suppliers, and define technically sound products is slow, often taking several years to reach a final set of recommendations. When agreement on proposals has been achieved, the development of commercially viable products conforming to the proposals is again time-consuming. It is then necessary to test the products for conformance, to demonstrate successful interworking between products from different suppliers, and to resolve discrepancies where systems that each separately appear to conform with the proposals do not interwork correctly.

Inevitably during this time, individual users or suppliers will have made their own systems, and in this sense the international standards will always lag behind the ad hoc or proprietary systems. Despite this, the model has itself been used as the basis for networks themselves (X25 for packet networks, ISO 8802.3 for CSMA/CD, ISO 8802.7 for slotted rings, ISO 8802.5 for token rings, ISO 8802.4 for token bus, and X75 for internetwork communication), and for some applications such as electronic mail (X400), directory services (X500), and manufacturing automation (*MAP and *TOP).

Layer	Layer Name	Functional Description
1	Physical Layer	Provides mechanical, electrical, functional, and procedural characteristics to establish, maintain, and release physical connections.
2	Data Link Layer	Provides functional and procedural means to establish, maintain, and release data lines between network entities (e.g. terminals and network nodes).
3	Network Layer	Provides functional and procedural means to exchange network service data units between two transport entities (i.e. devices that support transport layer protocols) over a network connection. It provides transport entities with independence from routing and switching considerations.
4	Transport Layer	Provides optimization of available communication services (supplied by lower-layer implementations) by providing a transparent transfer of data between session layer entities.
5	Session Layer	Provides a service of "binding" two presentation service entities together logically and controls the dialogue between them as far as message synchronization is concerned.
6	Presentation Layer	Provides a set of services that may be selected by the application layer to enable it to interpret the meaning of the data exchanged. Such services include management of entry exchange, display and control of structured data. The presentation layer services are the heart of the seven-layer proposal, enabling disparate terminal and computer equipment to intercommunicate.
7	Application Layer	Provides direct support of application processes and programs of the end user and the management of the interconnection of these programs and the communication entities.

ISO/OSI seven-layer reference model

S-gate *Another name for* ternary threshold gate.

SGML *Abbrev. for* standard generalized mark-up language. An international standard *metalanguage (ISO 8859) used for defining the syntax of textual *mark-up languages. This enables both sender and receiver of the text to identify its structure (e.g. title, author, header, paragraph, etc.).

shading model *See* lighting model.

shadow buffer A shadow-testing acceleration scheme where each point light source is sur-rounded by a direction cube, which contains a list of the objects visible through each cell. The direction of an illumination ray is first looked up in the light buffer associated with that light source as a means of fast shadow testing.

shadowed text *See* font.

shadow-mask cathode-ray tube A type of *cathode-ray tube that has a perforated mask between the electron guns and the phosphor-coated surface to ensure that each electron gun can only hit phosphor spots of the appropriate color.

shaft of light The light component in a liquid that is generated by the diffraction of direct sunlight by the surface of the liquid and may cause light to be concentrated.

Shannon diagram of a *communication sys-tem. A diagram illustrating *Shannon's model of such a system, embodying the source, encoder, channel, noise source, decoder, and destination of information.

Shannon–Fano coding (Fano coding) *See* source coding.

Shannon–Hartley law *See* channel coding theorem.

Shannon's model of a *communication sys-tem. A widely accepted model, set down by Claude Elwood Shannon in 1948, that has an *information source* sending a *message* to an *information destination* via a medium or mechanism called the *channel*. According to Shannon, "the fundamental problem of com-munication is that of reproducing at one point either exactly or approximately a mes-sage selected at another point."

In general, the channel will distort the message and add *noise to it. In order to avoid the distortion, and to reduce the effect of the noise to any desired degree, an *encoder is placed between the source and the channel, and a *decoder is placed between the channel and the destination. Now, the source sends the *transmitted mes-sage*, which is encoded as the *transmitted sig-nal*; this is sent through the channel. It emerges as the *received signal*, which is decoded to give the *received message*; this arrives at the destination.

The channel is considered to have a *noise source* that inputs "information" in addition to that in the transmitted signal. The aim of the encoder and decoder is to make the received message resemble, as closely as required, the transmitted message, in spite of the "information" from the noise source.

See also source coding theorem, channel coding theorem.

Shannon's theorems *See* source coding theorem, channel coding theorem.

Shannon text A short standardized text often used for specifying or comparing the perfor-mance of document-quality printers. It is believed to have the characteristics of "aver-age English text" and is taken from work done by Claude Shannon on the *Mathemati-cal Theory of Communication*. The text con-sists of 128 characters, including spaces, as follows: The head and in frontal attack on an english writer that the character of this point is therefore another method for letters

shape blending *See* blending.

shared logic system A term sometimes used to refer to a system where several terminals share a CPU simultaneously.

shared memory The use of the same portion of memory by two distinct *processes, or the memory so shared. Shared memory is used for interprocess communication and for pur-poses, such as common subroutines, that lead to compactness of memory. *See also* multi-port memory, concurrency.

shareware Software freely distributed with the expectation that anyone wishing to use it on a long-term basis will send a fee to the author. The method of payment and magnitude of the license fee normally forms part of the accompanying documentation. The incentive to register the software may be the promise of future versions, documentation, or extensions to the software.

SHE *Abbrev. for* safety, health, and ergonomics.

sheet feeder A device that may be attached to a printer allowing individual sheets of paper to be fed into the printer without operator action. This device is often available as an add-on feature with impact printers, but is usually incorporated into the mechanism with modern nonimpact printers.

shell A program that provides the *user interface of an *operating system and is often considered to be part of it. The main inner part of the operating system, the *kernel, is thus enclosed by the shell, as in a nut. Some operating systems have a choice of shells.

Shell's method (diminishing increment sort) A sorting algorithm proposed in 1959 by Donald Shell and published as *shellsort*. It is a variant of *straight insertion sort that allows records to take long leaps rather than move one position at a time. It does this by sorting each group $G^{(i)}_j$ of records a distance h_i apart within the file. (The $G^{(i)}_j$ are *disjoint and together contain all the information in the file.) This is repeated for a decreasing sequence of values h_i, and consequently increasing number of groups $G^{(i)}_j$, finally ending with $h_i = 1$.

shellsort *See* Shell's method.

shielded twisted pair (STP) *See* twisted pair.

shift 1. To change the interpretation of characters. The term is commonly met on normal typewriters as a change from lower to upper case.

2. Any complete set of characters obtainable without shifting. Hence *change shift* is a synonym for shift (def. 1).

3. The movement of a bit pattern in a bit string. A *left shift* of m ($<n$) bits will move the bit pattern in a string

$$b_1 b_2 \ldots b_n$$

leftward, giving

$$b_{m+1} \ldots b_n ? \ldots ?$$

Similarly, a *right shift* of m bits converts

$$b_1 b_2 \ldots b_n$$

to $? \ldots ? b_1 b_2 \ldots b_{n-m}$

The bits that are introduced (shown here as question marks) and the use of the bits that are shifted off the end of the string depend on the kind of shift: *arithmetic*, *logical*, or *circular*. In an arithmetic shift the bit strings are regarded as representations of binary integers; if the leading m bits that are lost are all zero, a left shift of m bits is equivalent to multiplication by 2^m and a right shift can be interpreted as integer division by 2^m. In logical shifts the bits introduced are all zero. In circular shifts the bits shifted off at one end are introduced at the other.

shift character Any character used in a stream of characters to change *shift, i.e. to change the interpretation of the characters. *Compare* escape character.

shift counter A *synchronous counter that consists of clocked *flip-flops arranged as a *shift register. Data is propagated from left to right (or from right to left) between the flip-flops by the application of a clock or count pulse. Counting is achieved by setting the contents of the shift register to logic 0 (or logic 1) and loading the leftmost (rightmost) flip-flop with a logic 1 (logic 0). An m-bit counter, which has m flip-flops, will then require m clock pulses to shift this 1 (or 0) to the rightmost (leftmost) flip-flop. The position in the register of the 1 (or 0) thus acts as a count of the number of pulses received since application of the load.

The counter may be made to count continuously by arranging that the output of the rightmost (leftmost) flip-flop sets the input of the leftmost (rightmost) flip-flop. The counter is then known as a *ring counter*.

shift instruction An instruction specifying that the contents of a shiftable register (occasionally concatenated registers) are to be shifted either to the left or to the right a specified number of register positions. *Shifts can be circular or they can be open at both ends. In the latter case there is usually a specification of what happens to bits being shifted out of the register (often they are discarded) and what bits are to be shifted into the register (most often 0s).

shift keying *See* modulation, frequency shift keying, phase shift keying.

shift lock A mode of keyboard operation whereby the characters produced by a keyboard are all constrained to those produced when the shift key is pressed. *See also* caps lock.

shift-reduce parsing *Another name for* bottom-up parsing.

shift register A *register that has the ability to transfer information in a lateral direction. It is an *n*-stage clocked device whose output consists of an *n*-bit parallel data word (*see* diagram). Application of a single clock cycle to the device causes the output word to be shifted by one bit position from right to left (or from left to right). The leftmost (or rightmost) bit is lost from the "end" of the register while the rightmost (or leftmost) bit position is loaded from a serial input terminal. The device may also be capable of being loaded with parallel *n*-bit data words, these then being shifted out of the device in serial form. *See also* serial in parallel out, parallel in serial out, parallel in parallel out, serial in serial out.

Shift registers with parallel outputs, and with combinational logic fed from those outputs (*see* combinational circuit), are of great importance in *digital signal processing, and in the encoding and decoding of *error-

correcting and *error-detecting codes. Such registers may be implemented in hardware or in software, and may be binary or *q*-ary. (Hardware implementation is usually convenient only for binary and sometimes ternary logic.) *See* feedback register, feed-forward (shift) register, Good–de Bruijn diagram.

Shlaer–Mellor An object-oriented development method invented by Sally Shlaer and Stephen Mellor.

shooting method An iterative method for the solution of boundary-value problems in *ordinary differential equations. Consider the problem

$$y'' = f(x, y, y'), y(a) = \alpha, y(b) = \beta$$

Let $y(x; t)$ denote the solution of this differential equation from initial conditions

$$y(a) = \alpha, y'(a) = t$$

This solves the above problem if $F(t) = 0$ where

$$F(t) = y(b; t) - \beta$$

The equation $F(t) = 0$ is solved iteratively, usually by some variant of *Newton's method. Each iteration therefore requires the numerical integration of an initial-value problem.

The method is applicable to all types of boundary-value problems, whatever the form of the boundary conditions. Apart from the problem of obtaining good estimates to start the iteration, difficulties can arise due to severe *error propagation in the integration of the initial-value problem. A useful

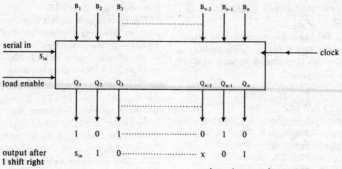

An *n*-bit shift register

improvement is to guess the missing conditions at both ends of the range, matching the two solutions so defined at an interior point. In difficult cases estimates and matching can be used at several interior points to reduce error propagation; this is known as the *parallel-shooting method.*

shortest-path algorithm An algorithm that is designed essentially to find a *path of minimum length between two specified vertices of a *connected *weighted graph. A good algorithm for this problem was given by E. W. Dijkstra in 1959.

shrink-wrap license In the computer industry the terms of the software license are usually printed clearly on a sticky seal or are readable on the box, which is covered with a shrink-wrap film. Within the box are the disks and manuals and there is usually a notice that says that if you need to return the software the packages must be unopened with the shrink-wrap intact and that software with broken seals will not be refunded. The contention is that, once you have broken the seal or stripped off the shrink-wrap, you have entered into a license agreement upon the terms stated in the license. Legally this is very doubtful under English law although there are amendments to the laws of certain US states that make this an enforceable contract under their local laws.

shrink-wrapped product A software product sold as a commercial readily available item. The name is meant to indicate that the buyer obtains a complete package with no possibility of influencing the requirements for or the design of the product. These products are usually sold in large numbers, often by mail order or high-street retailers, and come complete with software, installation instructions, and user manuals.

sibling Either of two nodes in a *tree that are both *children of the same parent.

side effect An effect of a *program unit that is not apparent from its *parameters, for example altering a nonlocal variable or performing input/output.

Siemens Nixdorf Information Systems The IT arm of the German-based Siemens engineering conglomerate. It produces both hardware and software, and acts as a *systems integrator. It is active in a wide range of markets and is number 11 in terms of revenue in the list of the world's top IT suppliers (1993 figures).

sieve benchmark A program that calculates the prime numbers within a specified range in order to obtain a *benchmark timing to complete execution. It is easy to use and is often employed to tune the optimization algorithms in compilers; however its coverage of language features is limited to arrays, simple variable types, looping, and comparison.

sifting technique *Another name for* straight insertion sort.

sig *Short for* signature (def. 2).

sigma algebra (Σ-algebra) *See* signature.

sigma language (Σ-language) *See* formal language.

sigma tree (sigma term; Σ-tree; Σ-term) *See* tree language, term.

sigma word (Σ-word) *See* word.

sign A means used to distinguish between positive and negative numbers. In a computer there are a number of ways of representing the sign of a number, each of which makes use of a single bit called the *sign bit.* The most obvious way of representing positive and negative integers in computer words is by means of the *signed-magnitude* (or *sign-and-magnitude*) *representation.* Here, the leftmost bit in a word is used to denote the sign (0 for + and 1 for –) and the remaining bits in the word are used to represent the magnitude of the integer. It is more usual, however, for a computer to use the two's complement representation of integers. *See* radix complement, complement number system.

signal A form of data that is usually envisaged as a sequence of values of a scalar quantity – the *amplitude* – recorded (i.e. measured, tabulated, or plotted) against time. The amplitude is most often, but by no means always, an electric potential. *See also* discrete and continuous systems, space domain.

signal conditioning *Filtering a continuous signal.

signal operation *See* semaphore.

signal processing The processing of *signals by means of hardwired or programmable devices, the signals being regarded as continuous or discrete and being approximated by analog or digital devices accordingly (*see* discrete and continuous systems). *Filtering and *image processing are examples of signal processing. *See also* digital signal processing.

signal-to-noise ratio The ratio of the *signal power to the *noise power in a physical transmission channel; it is often measured in decibels (dB). The definition is best applied to statistically well-behaved noise such as *white *Gaussian noise. *See also* channel coding theorem.

signature 1. A collection of symbols intended to be associated with *sets and with *functions on and elements from the sets. Signatures provide names for the carrier sets, operations, and constants of *algebras. They are central in the precise treatment of the syntax of many computer science concepts, including (a) *abstract data types, (b) *algebraic specifications, and (c) classes, *modules, and *objects. Typically, headers of modules are signatures. The specification of an Ada *package is in effect a signature.

In its simplest form a signature is a set Σ of symbols with, for each $\sigma \in \Sigma$, a natural number $\rho(\sigma)$ called the *arity of σ. A Σ-*algebra* consists of a set A (called the *carrier* of the algebra) together with, for each $\sigma \in \Sigma$, an n-argument function over A, where $n = \rho(\sigma)$. As an example, suppose

$\Sigma = \{$'zero', 'one', 'plus', 'times'$\}$
with $\rho($'zero'$) = \rho($'one'$) = 0$
and $\rho($'plus'$) = \rho($'times'$) = 2$

Then one Σ-algebra results from taking the set of all integers as carrier, and associating the number 0 with 'zero', 1 with 'one', addition with 'plus', and multiplication with 'times'. As indicated by ρ, addition and multiplication are 2-argument functions while zero and one, being constants, expect no arguments and their arity is 0.

Note that the above example describes only one Σ-algebra. For example, the carrier could be the real numbers; or perversely multiplication could be associated with 'plus' and addition with 'times'; equally sets could be considered instead of numbers, associating, say, *union and *intersection with 'plus' and 'times'. The point is that an algebra can involve arbitrary sets and arbitrary functions: any choice is as much an algebra as any other and it need not reflect in any obvious way the names chosen for the symbols in the signature. Indeed the whole point of signatures is to make a distinction between the names and symbols and their possible interpretations.

In computer science the more complex notion of *many-sorted signature* is used. This allows algebras to have many carriers. A signature now, in addition to function symbols, includes a set of *sorts*. These are symbols that, in an algebra, are associated with carrier sets. Instead of a natural number, $\rho(\sigma)$ is a sequence of sorts indicating which sets the arguments come from, together with an additional sort giving the set in which the result lies.

Signatures are often displayed as shown in the diagram. Here real numbers and Booleans are equipped with their usual operations.

signature	real numbers
sorts	reals
	bools
constants	$0 :\ \rightarrow$ real
	$1 :\ \rightarrow$ real
	tt $:\ \rightarrow$ bool
	ff $:\ \rightarrow$ bool
operations	$+ :$ real $\times$ real $\rightarrow$ real
	$- :$ real $\rightarrow$ real
	$\times :$ real $\times$ real $\rightarrow$ real
	$^{-1} :$ real $\rightarrow$ real
	$\sqrt{} :$ real $\rightarrow$ real
	$\wedge :$ bool $\times$ bool $\rightarrow$ bool
	$\neg :$ bool $\rightarrow$ bool
	$< :$ real $\times$ real $\rightarrow$ bool
	$= :$ real $\times$ real $\rightarrow$ bool
end	

A signature for real numbers

2. That part of an e-mail message in which the originator states his or her identity and claims authenticity.

3. A bit pattern believed to be specific to a particular program and used to identify virus programs or unlicensed copies of proprietary software.

4. *See* signature analysis.

signature analysis A method of determining the location and/or nature of a fault in a digital system by input of test sequences and inspection of the resulting output sequences (*signatures*). The theory is that of *sequential circuits. *See also* convolution, sequence generator.

signature scanning The most common technique of specific *virus detection in which code is scanned for the signatures of any of a set of known viruses. *See* signature (def.3).

sign bit *See* sign digit.

sign digit (signed field) A single digit used to indicate the algebraic sign of a number. If the binary system is being used, the sign digit is called a *sign bit*. *See also* sign, floating-point notation.

signed Containing a *sign: a signed whole-number representation is one whose *bit pattern is interpreted as an *integer type (whose value may be positive, negative, or zero). Numbers of *rational type and in *floating-point notation are almost always signed.

signed field *Another name for* sign digit.

signed-magnitude representation *See* sign.

significance test A statistical procedure whereby a quantity computed from data samples is compared with theoretical values of standard *probability distributions. Formally it is a comparison between a *null-hypothesis*, H_0 (for example that there is no difference between the means of two *populations), and an *alternative hypothesis*, H_1, (that a real difference exists). If H_0 is assumed to be true, the probability distribution of the test statistic can be computed or tabulated. If the test statistic exceeds the *critical value* corresponding to a probability level of α per cent, the null-hypothesis is rejected at the α per cent significance level. The most commonly used levels of significance are 5%, 1%, and 0.1%. Care must be taken to specify exactly what alternative hypothesis is being tested. Tests involving both tails of the probability distribution are known as *two-tailed tests*; those involving only one tail are *one-tailed tests*. *See also* analysis of variance, goodness-of-fit tests, Student's t distribution, chi-squared distribution, multiple-range tests.

sign off *Another term for* log off.

sign on *Another term for* log in.

SIL devices *Short for* single in-line devices. *Integrated circuit devices in which the terminal pins lie in a single line, typically of 0.1 inch pitch. This is in contrast for instance to the layout used for many ICs where the pins lie on two parallel lines – so called dual in-line (*DIL) devices.

silicon chip *See* chip.

silicon disk *Another name for* RAM disk.

SIMD processor *Short for* single instruction (stream), multiple data (stream) processor. *See* concurrency.

similar trees Trees that have the same structure or shape. More formally, two trees are similar if they both comprise exactly one node or, if not, the corresponding subtrees of the two roots are equal in number and are pairwise similar. For ordered trees, the pairwise correspondence is that given by the ordering imposed upon the subtrees of the two trees.

SIMM *Acronym for* single in-line memory module. A memory IC (*integrated circuit) whose pin-out corresponds to the *SIL format. Because the pins lie along one edge of the device package, it can be mounted on a PCB in a perpendicular plane, minimizing the board area occupied and maximizing the packing density. *See also* memory card.

simple parity check (simple parity code) *See* cyclic redundancy check.

simplex 1. Denoting or involving a connection between two endpoints, either physical or logical, that can carry data in only one direction with no possibility of data flow in the opposite direction. *See also* duplex, half duplex.

2. A finite graph of k points (the vertices), or a geometric figure, in which every vertex is connected to every other vertex (e.g. a triangle or tetrahedron).

simplex codes A family of *linear *error-correcting or *error-detecting *block codes, easily implemented as *polynomial codes (by means of *shift registers). Considered as (n, k) codes (*see* block code), they have codeword length

$$n = q^k - 1$$

Binary simplex codes have a minimum *Hamming distance equal to 2^{k-1}. They can be regarded as *Reed–Muller codes shortened by one digit, and are identical with the *m-sequences of length $2^k - 1$, together with the *zero word. They are so-called because their codewords form a *simplex in *Hamming space.

simplex method *See* linear programming.

Simpson's rule The approximation

$$\int_{x_i}^{x_{i+2}} f(x)dx \approx \tfrac{1}{3}h \left(f(x_i) + 4f(x_{i+1}) + f(x_{i+2}) \right)$$

where $h = x_{i+1} - x_i$

It is used in *numerical integration.

SIMULA A programming language based on Algol 60, with extensions to make it suitable for writing *simulation programs. The major innovation in SIMULA was the concept of the *class*, which was a precursor of the *abstract data type.

simulated annealing A powerful enhancement for *hill climbing search in which there is a small probability that random moves will be allowed in directions different from the preferred up-hill direction. This permits occasional moves to occur which can allow the hill climber to escape from local maxima. Initially large moves are allowed but a "cooling" regime continuously lowers the probability of random directions during the search and thus the solution tends to settle on the best local maximum.

simulation Imitation of the behavior of some existing or intended system, or some aspect of that behavior. Examples of areas where

simulation is used include communication network design, where simulation can be used to explore overall behavior, traffic patterns, trunk capacity, etc., and weather forecasting, where simulation can be used to predict likely developments in the weather pattern. More generally, simulation is widely used as a design aid for both small and large systems, and is also used extensively in the training of people such as airline pilots or military commanders. It is a major application of digital computers and is the major application of analog computers.

From an implementation viewpoint, a simulation is usually classified as being either discrete event or continuous. For a *discrete event simulation* it must be possible to view all significant changes to the state of the system as distinct events that occur at specific points in time; the simulation then achieves the desired behavior by modeling a sequence of such events, treating each individually. By contrast, a *continuous simulation* views changes as occurring gradually over a period of time and tracks the progress of these gradual changes. Clearly the choice between these two in any particular case is determined by the nature of the system to be simulated and the purposes that the simulation is intended to achieve.

Although the distinction between simulation and emulation is not always clear, an emulation is normally "realistic" in the sense that it could be used as a direct replacement for all or part of the system that is emulated. In comparison, a simulation may provide no more than an abstract model of some aspect of a system.

simulation language A programming language that is specialized to the implementation of simulation programs. Such languages are usually classified as either discrete event simulation languages or continuous simulation languages. *See* simulation.

simulator Any system that performs a *simulation. It is normally a system dedicated for some period to performing a specific simulation, as distinct from, say, the case where a simulation program is executed as a normal job on some general-purpose computer. Simulators often employ either special-purpose hardware or hardware components from the system that is simulated.

simultaneous equations A set of equations that together define an unknown set of values or functions. The term is normally applied to *linear algebraic equations.

single-address instruction An instruction that makes explicit reference to only one operand location; the source of any required second operand is implied. *See also* accumulator, instruction format, addressing schemes.

single-assignment languages A class of programming languages. These languages have the appearance of traditional *imperative languages in that they incorporate the *assignment statement and typical control flow constructs such as if statements and loops. They impose the limitation, however, that no variable may be assigned a value more than once. (Special provision must be made for assignment statements within loops.) This limitation significantly alters the nature of the assignment statement, which can then be viewed as statically associating a name with a value rather than as a dynamic destructive operation. This static nature allows the normal ordering restrictions of imperative languages to be relaxed, and assignment statements can be executed as soon as the expression on the right-hand side can be evaluated. Because of this property, single-assignment languages are closely associated with dataflow computing (*see* dataflow machine).

single attach *See* fiber distributed data interface.

single in-line devices *See* SIL devices.

single instruction, multiple data (SIMD) *See* concurrency.

single-step operation Proceeding through the execution of a program either by single instructions or by single steps (clock times) within an instruction. This method is used during program and/or hardware debugging.

single threading A property of a body of code that activates more than one processor, but

does so in such a way that at any one time no more than one processor is active. This results in what is termed *serial programming*. For example, code that initiates peripheral transfers may be so written that while a transfer is in progress the processor will not be active, and vice versa. *See also* multithreading, threading.

singly linked list (one-way linked list) A *linked list in which each item contains a single link to its successor. By following links it is possible to access the entire structure from the first item.

singular matrix A square matrix, A, of numbers whose *determinant is zero. A is singular if and only if it is not invertible (*see* inverse matrix).

sinking technique *Another name for* straight insertion sort.

SIO *Abbrev. for* serial input/output.

SIPO *Abbrev. for* serial in, parallel out. *See also* shift register.

SISD processor *Short for* single instruction (stream), single data (stream) processor. *See* concurrency.

SISO *Abbrev. for* serial in, serial out. *See also* shift register.

sister *Another name for* sibling, rarely used.

site license The practice of granting an extended license to a business to allow it to make and use a number of copies of a particular computer program at a particular location or site. This has been a popular way of getting a large company to standardize on particular software packages. The software house thereafter obtains its regular income from support and upgrade fees rather than individual licenses on a per workstation basis.

site network A network constrained to the boundaries of a single site. For many purposes the term is synonymous with *local area network.

situation semantics An approach to natural-language *semantics built upon the ontological framework of situation theory (Barwise and Perry 1983). The theory is built on the notion of *situations*, which are parts of the world – either concrete or abstract – that the speaker or listener individuates or discriminates. Situation semantics tries to capture the meaning of an utterance by constructing formal relations between the *utterance situation* (the situation that the actual utterance is made in), the *discourse situation*, the wider embedding situation (consisting of elements of the world in which the discourse takes place), and *resource situations* (for example, situations in another time and place referred to by the utterance).

SI units The system of units of measurement adopted internationally for scientific and technical use under the *Système International d'Unités*. There are seven fundamental units (the meter, second, kilogram, ampere, kelvin, candela, and mole) of seven dimensionally independent physical quantities. Other units are derived algebraically from these base units without the use of numerical factors, or are dimensionless (like the radian). The symbols for all units are standardized, as are the prefixes (and their symbols) that represent decimal multiples (e.g. nano-, micro-, milli-, kilo-, mega-, giga-) of the units.

sizing 1. Preparing an estimate of the likely size of a program or software system. This estimate may subsequently be used, for example, to determine the amount of memory required on a computer system that is to execute the program.
2. *See* downsizing, rightsizing.

skeletal strokes A way of defining complex drawings based on a path and a deformable picture. The picture is deformed to generate the required drawing relative to the path. It provides a richer brush and stroke metaphor for *paint programs.

skew In a *sequential circuit, the arrival of a signal at two or more places at significantly different times, when it should have arrived at more nearly the same time. Skew is said to be present when the difference in arrival times is great enough to cause or threaten malfunction of the circuit; this difference (usually measured in nanoseconds) is called the amount of skew. Most commonly, concern is expressed about *clock skew* – the skew in *clock signals – for which the phenomenon has usually the most serious conse-

quences. Skew may be caused by component malfunction, or bad physical construction, but most often by bad logic design of the circuit. *See also* race condition.

skewed tree (unbalanced tree) Any tree that is not *balanced.

skew-symmetric matrix A square matrix, A, such that $a_{ij} = -a_{ji}$ for all a_{ij} in A.

SLA *Abbrev. for* service level agreement.

slave machine (direct-coupled machine) A large processor used to handle large jobs in a *master-slave system.

slice of an array. **1.** The array of lower dimension that is obtained by fixing one or more of the indexes of the original array. For example, if A is a 3×4 two-dimensional array then the slice $A[2,]$ denotes the one-dimensional row vector comprising the second row of A while $A[,3]$ denotes the column vector comprising the third column.
2. (trim) The array that is obtained from a larger array of dimension n by restricting the range of an index. For example, if A is a 3×4 two-dimensional array then the 2×4 two-dimensional array comprising the first two rows only of A is a slice of A.

slice architecture *See* bit-slice architecture.

slider bar A control object that belongs to a *window in a *graphical user interface (GUI). It normally consists of a long thin rectangle with a square marked off at each end containing an outward-pointing arrow; within the rectangle is marked a small box that can be moved along the rectangle by *clicking on the arrows or inside the rectangle, or by *dragging the small box. A numerical value corresponding to the box's position within the rectangle is available to the program and can be used in various ways. If it is used to move text up and down behind the window then the slider bar is known as a *scroll bar*, and the interior box is the *scroll box*. The appearance and mode of operation of the slider bar varies slightly with each GUI.

SLOC *Acronym for* source lines of code. A *metric that is a count of the number of lines of source-language statements of a software module, package, or complete software system. There is no defined standard for determining which lines should be counted. Most organizations will exclude blank lines and include lines containing executable statements, but differ on whether to include comment lines and data-definition lines. Many software cost-estimation approaches are based on estimating the number of SLOC in a proposed project (*see* COCOMO).

slot reader *See* card reader.

slotted ring *See* ring network.

Smalltalk *Trademark* An *object-oriented language, an object-oriented programming development environment, and a library of *objects. Smalltalk was the first language to bring together all the features that characterize an *object-oriented programming system. The language was developed at the Xerox Palo Alto Research Center, went through many versions during the 1970s (Smalltalk-74, Smalltalk-76, Smalltalk-78), and finally matured as Smalltalk-80. At first it was only implemented on Xerox workstations, but a version of Smalltalk-80 is now available for Sun workstations, and PC versions (Smalltalk V) can be purchased.

smart card A plastic card similar to a credit card but having memory and a microprocessor (or specialized logic) embedded in it. Originally intended for electronic funds transfer systems with better security than that possible with normal credit cards, it is gradually being used for applications in medicine, road toll charging, access to secure areas, and any application where the data embedded within the card should travel with the user rather than being held centrally.

smart machine *Informal. See* mechatronics.

smart terminal *Informal name for* intelligent terminal.

SMDS *Abbrev. for* switched multimegabit data service. A switched broadband service that is being introduced by a number of *public network operators (PNO). The intention is that SMDS will support data services at a range of bit rates from 1.536 Mbps (2.048 Mbps in Europe) up to 45 Mbps (34 Mbps in Europe) and subsequently at higher speeds, certainly as high as 155 Mbps. SMDS is a *connectionless system, based on variable-

length *packets with a payload of up to 9188 bytes. Each packet contains both the source and destination addresses, the addresses being the same as *ISDN addresses and globally unique.

SMDS offers the end-user access at a range of predetermined bit rates (e.g. 2, 4, 10, 16, and 25 Mbps), treating these as average bit rates that cannot be exceeded, while using a fixed bit rate *bearer (in this case of 34 Mbps) between the SMDS access points. A control algorithm in the access unit ensures that the average rate at which the end-user can submit data for transmission cannot be exceeded. There are no restrictions on the rate at which the user can receive data, since it is possible for data to arrive from a number of separate subscribers at a rate that would exceed the average rate at which a user can transmit. This allows the PNO to offer a service tailored to the end-users' overall needs, together with the ability to upgrade between one bit rate and the next by simply resetting the values of the control parameters in the access unit.

smiley *See* emoticon.

SML *Abbrev. for* standard ML.

smoothing A means by which a table of values $f(x_0), f(x_1), \ldots, f(x_m)$ at the distinct points $x_1, x_2, \ldots, x_m$, can be approximated (represented) by a function, say

$$\sum_{i=1}^{n} c_i \phi_i(x),$$

where $\phi_i(x)$, $i = 1, 2, \ldots, n$, are chosen, and the coefficients c_i, $i = 1, 2, \ldots, n$, are to be determined. Typically $m > n$. The objective is to choose a fit that reduces the effect of random errors in the data combined with producing a curve that is smooth (no rapid changes or oscillations) between the data points. This is generally referred to as smoothing. The smoothing is often achieved by using low-degree polynomials (with suitable $\phi_i(x)$) and the coefficients c_i are frequently determined by the least-squares criterion (*see* approximation theory). *Compare* interpolation.

smooth shading A class of shading methods that give a continuous appearance over functions and structures. The fairness, or overall smoothness, of curves and surfaces is of particular interest. Definitions of smoothness may be based on extreme or average quantities (e.g. curvature) or on subjective assessment. They may also be linked to fluid-dynamics considerations.

SMP *Abbrev. for* symmetric multiprocessing. A form of supercomputing based on *RISC technology. Compared with traditional supercomputers, SMP systems are relatively easy to program, inexpensive, and can be used for a greater range of applications. They are scalable systems.

SMTP *Abbrev. for* simple mail transfer protocol. A *protocol used to control the transfer of e-mail messages between systems on the Internet.

SNA *Acronym for* Systems Network Architecture. A *network architecture developed by IBM for use with large mainframe computers.

snapshot dump A *dump that shows the state of a program at some particular point in its execution. It is usually obtained during testing or debugging and indicates the point in the program that has been reached and the values of some subset of the program variables.

sniffer program A program written to monitor all messages flowing on a network, with the intention of capturing legitimate usernames and passwords or for the illicit identification of other confidential information.

SNMP *Abbrev. for* simple network management protocol. A *protocol used to allow the transmission of *network management information across a network, between a network management center and the devices that constitute the active *switches within the network. The active devices must therefore be able to act as addressable entities on the network. *See also* managed device.

SNOBOL A programming language designed primarily for the manipulation of textual data. It incorporates powerful pattern-matching and string-searching operators. The current version, SNOBOL IV, also includes facilities for processing other kinds of data, and is in fact a general-purpose language with a special capability in text manipulation.

snowflake *Informal* A network made up of nodes that can each support a number of end-user devices, with the nodes themselves connected in an arbitrary configuration. A number of Ethernet hubs each supporting end-user systems connected by twisted pairs, with the hubs interconnected by coaxial cable or optical fiber, might be described as a snowflake.

SO *Abbrev. for* small outline. An alternative package for *integrated circuits offering a higher packing density on *printed circuit boards. *VSO (very small outline)* packages offer even higher packing densities.

soft copy A nondurable form of data output, such as text or graphical information on a VDU or the output from an audio response unit.

soft fill (tint fill) The act or process of changing the color of an area, taking into account the initial background color.

soft font A *font that is not permanently resident in a printer or VDU but is downloaded from the host.

soft keyboard A keyboard in which the function or code to be generated by each key can be allocated and changed by program control. Keyboards on terminals for applications such as industrial data collection or point-of-sale applications frequently have keyboards in which some keys – usually the numeric and certain essential functions – are hard-wired and the others are soft keys. The soft keys may have a meaning that is allocated to them at the time of initial installation and remains unchanged, or they may have their meaning changed during the course of a single transaction.

soft object *See* blobby model, metaballs.

soft return *See* hard return.

soft-sectored disk *See* sector.

soft shadow A shadow produced by a light source that is larger than a single point. The resulting umbra and penumbra of the shadow can either be modeled accurately or suggested by various approximations.

software A generic term for those components of a computer system that are intangible rather than physical. It is most commonly used to refer to the programs executed by a computer system as distinct from the physical hardware of that computer system, and to encompass both symbolic and executable forms for such programs. A distinction can be drawn between *systems software, which is an essential accompaniment to the hardware in order to provide an effective overall computer system (and is therefore normally supplied by the manufacturer), and *applications software specific to the particular role performed by the computer within a given organization.

Software Best Practice *See* ESSI.

Software Capability and Maturity Model *See* Capability and Maturity Model.

software component specification A precise statement of the effects that the software component of a system is required to achieve. When developing a system, production of the *software requirements specification is typically followed by a period of preliminary investigation and high-level design. It is then possible to identify any necessary hardware components of the system and to produce the software component specification for the software component.

A software component specification should be detailed, focusing on what the software is to do rather than how this is to be done. The traditional use of natural language for this purpose is being superseded by use of more formal notations.

software development environment (programmer workbench) The set of *software tools collected together (sometimes using a common database or user interface as in an *IPSE) for use by a software developer, or team of developers, when developing software.

software development process model (SDPM) A model that indicates a set of software processes – manual or automated – to be used in a software development project. The model should indicate the interdependencies that exist between the development processes including the products generated by each process, and the information (including products generated by other processes) required by each process.

software engineering The entire range of activities used to design and develop software, with some connotation of "good practice". Topics encompassed include user requirements elicitation, software requirements definition, architectural and detailed design (*see* program design), *program specification, program development using some recognized approach such as *structured programming, systematic *testing techniques, *program correctness proofs, *software quality assurance, software project management, documentation, performance and timing analysis, and the development and use of *software engineering environments. Further, software engineering is generally expected to address the practical problems of software development, including those encountered with large or complex systems. Thus, while there is some emphasis on formal methods, pragmatic techniques are employed where necessary. In its entirety, software engineering addresses all aspects of the development and support of reliable and efficient programs for the entire range of computer applications.

software engineering environment A software system that provides support for the development, repair, and enhancement of software, and for the management and control of these activities. A typical system contains a central database and a set of *software tools. The central database acts as a repository for all information related to a project throughout the lifetime of that project. The software tools offer support for the various activities, both technical and managerial, that must be performed on the project.

Different environments vary in the general nature of their databases and in the coverage provided by the set of tools. In particular, some encourage (or even enforce) one specific software engineering methodology, while others provide only general support and therefore allow any of a variety of methodologies to be adopted. All environments, however, reflect concern for the entire *software life cycle (rather than just the program development phase) and offer support for project management (rather than just technical activities). These two features normally differentiate a software engineering environment from a *program development system. *See also* PSE (def. 1).

Software Engineering Institute An organization founded by the US government in 1983 to develop the discipline of software engineering and to increase industrial awareness of it. The institute is part of Carnegie Mellon University, Pittsburgh; it is financed partly by the US government and partly by private industry. Its best-known development is the *Capability and Maturity Model.

software environment 1. The set of facilities, such as operating system, windows management, database, etc., that is available to a program when it is being executed by a processor. 2. *See* software development environment.

software house A company whose primary business is to produce software or assist in the production of software. Software houses may offer a range of services, including hiring out of suitably qualified personnel to work within a client's team, consultancy, and a complete system design and development service.

software library *Another name for* program library.

software life cycle The complete lifetime of a software system from initial conception through to final obsolescence. The term is most commonly used in contexts where programs are expected to have a fairly long useful life, rather than in situations such as experimental programming where programs tend to be run a few times and then discarded. Traditionally the life cycle has been modeled as a number of successive phases, typically:

    user requirements
    system requirements
    software requirements
    overall design
    detailed design
    component production
    component testing
    integration and system testing
    acceptance testing and release
    operation and maintenance

Such a breakdown tends to obscure several important aspects of software production, notably the inevitable need for iteration around the various life-cycle activities in order to correct errors, modify decisions that prove to have been misguided, or reflect changes in the overall requirements for the system. It is also somewhat confusing to treat operation and maintenance as just another life-cycle phase since during this period it may be necessary to repeat any or all of the activities required for initial development of the system. There has therefore been a gradual movement toward more sophisticated models of the software life cycle. These provide explicit recognition of iteration, and often treat the activities of the operation and maintenance period simply as iterations occurring after rather than before release of the system for operational use. *See also* spiral model, V-model, waterfall model.

software maintenance The process of modifying a software system or component. There are three classes.

Perfective maintenance incorporates changes demanded by the user; these may, for example, result from changes in requirements or legislation, or be for embedded applications in response to changes in the surrounding system. *Adaptive maintenance* incorporates changes made necessary by modifications in the software or hardware (operational) environment of the program, including changes in the maintenance environment. *Corrective maintenance* is the successful repair of faults discovered in the software.

Maintenance for software always involves a change in the software. This may be effected at the coding level, or may require significant changes in design. *Regression testing of the software follows maintenance as part of a reverification and revalidation activity. Software maintenance is a prodigious source of new software faults, so good quality control through software engineering is essential.

software metric *See* metric.

software monitor *See* monitor (defs. 2 and 3).

software package *Another name for* application package.

software piracy Unauthorized copying and resale of software for commercial purposes in breach of *intellectual property rights.

software process 1. *See* software development process model.
2. *See* process.

software prototyping Development of a preliminary version of a software system in order to allow certain aspects of that system to be investigated. Often the primary purpose of a prototype is to obtain feedback from the intended users; the requirements specification for the system can then be updated to reflect this feedback, and so increase confidence in the final system. Additionally (or alternatively) a prototype can be used to investigate particular problem areas, or certain implications of alternative design or implementation decisions.

The intention with a prototype is normally to obtain the required information as rapidly as possible and with the minimum investment of resources, and it is therefore common to concentrate on certain aspects of the intended system and completely ignore others. A prototype may for example be developed with no concern for its efficiency or performance, and certain functions of the final system may be entirely omitted. It must however be realistic in those aspects specifically under investigation.

software publisher An imprecise term used to describe a company that acts toward software authors in the same way as a publisher of books acts toward the authors of books. It may thus commission software from authors or receive unsolicited contributions. It may then market these in a variety of ways and pay royalties to the authors.

software quality assurance (SQA) The process of ensuring that a software system and its associated documentation are in all respects of sufficient quality for their purpose. While a quality assurance team may be involved in all stages of a development project, there is typically a recognized quality assurance activity following completion of development and prior to release of the system for operational use.

The checks performed by the quality assurance team (which should be independent of the development team) vary between organizations and also depend on the nature and purpose of the software system. However they typically include functional testing of the software, checks that *programming standards have been respected, that the program documentation is complete and of an adequate standard, and that the user documentation for the system is of the desired quality. The team would also probably explore the reliability of the software system, and attempt to ensure that the software system and its associated documentation are so organized as to promote system maintainability.

software reliability A measure of the extent to which a software system can be expected to deliver usable services when those services are demanded. Software reliability differs considerably from program "correctness" (*see* program correctness proof). Correctness is the static property that a program is consistent with its specification, while reliability is related to the dynamic demands that are made upon the system and the ability to produce a satisfactory response to those demands.

A program that is "correct" may be regarded as unreliable if, for example, the specification against which the program is shown to be correct does not capture all of the users' expectations of the program. Conversely, a program that is not completely correct may be regarded as reliable if the errors are insignificant, occur infrequently at noncritical times, or can simply be avoided by the users.

software requirements specification A document that defines what a program or software system is required to do and the constraints under which this required functionality must be provided. These constraints are often referred to as *nonfunctional* requirements; they may affect the way in which the software is developed (e.g. for safety-critical or security-critical software) or may impose physical limits on the space, size, and performance of the software to be developed. A software requirements specification will usually be based upon an abstract model, which leaves open the design and implementation decisions; this model is developed using a recognized requirements-analysis method and is possibly supported by the use of a *CASE tool.

software technology A general term covering the development methods, programming languages, and tools to support them that may be used in the development of software.

software tool A program that is employed in the development, repair, or enhancement of other programs or of hardware. Traditionally a set of software tools addressed only the essential needs during program development: a typical set might consist of a *text editor, *compiler, *link loader, and some form of *debug tool. Such a set concentrates solely on the program production phase and is that normally provided by a *program development system.

It is now recognized that software tools can assist in all activities of all phases of the *software life cycle, including management and quality-assurance activities. Thus a comprehensive set would address such issues as requirements specification, design, validation, configuration control, and project management. Such tools would frequently form part of an integrated *software engineering environment.

solid color In computer graphics, an area of color with the same value.

solid-font printer Any type of *impact printer in which the complete shape of each character of the repertoire is engraved or molded onto a font carrier. The font carrier may be one of a number of forms including a molded wheel, as in a *daisywheel printer, or an etched band of metal, as in a *band printer. *Compare* matrix printer.

solid inkjet printer *Another name for* phase-change inkjet printer. *See* inkjet printer.

solid models Three-dimensional structures that are valid models of solids irrespective of how this is to be ensured.

solid-state device An electronic component fabricated principally or entirely from solid material, usually semiconducting, and depending for its operation on the movement of charge carriers.

solid-state memory *Another name for* semiconductor memory.

solid texture An approach to *texturing an object's surface by defining a *space-filling curve function that is only evaluated at the surface of the object. This avoids the conformance problems of *texture mapping but results in a more limited range of textures. It is effective at simulating substances, such as marble, in which a grain actually occurs throughout and is unrelated to the shape of the object.

solvable problem *See* decision problem.

SONET *Acronym for* synchronous optical network. A network standard designed by collaboration between the members of the CCITT and the vendors of WAN products, and intended primarily for the transport of *ATM over long distances. The SONET standard is defined for operation over *optical fibers at a minimum bit rate of 51.84 Mbps (OC-1 in North America) or 155.52 Mbps (SDH-1 in Europe). Both standards allow for speeds up to 2.48 Gbps.

SOP expression *Short for* sum of products expression.

sort generator *See* generator.

sorting Rearranging information into ascending or descending order by means of *sortkeys. Sorting may be useful in three ways: to identify and count all items with the same identification, to compare two files, and to assist in searching, as used in a *dictionary. An *internal sorting* method keeps the information within the computer's high-speed RAM; an *external sorting* method uses backing store. There are a wide variety of methods.

sortkey (key) The information, associated with a record of information, that is to be compared in a *sorting process. It follows that the sortkeys must be capable of being ordered, i.e. two keys k_1 and k_2 are such that
$$k_1 < k_2, \quad k_1 = k_2, \quad \text{or } k_1 > k_2$$

sort merge *See* merge exchange sort.

sound card (audio card) A plug-in module

that adds sound input and output capabilities to a computer; it is a type of *add-in card. Some systems have the module as part of their original design. The sound card takes digitized audio signals from the processor and converts them into an analog audio signal used to drive headphones or as input to an audio amplifier or active speakers. The majority of sound cards are designed for the IBM PC. The input and output resolution of the *D/A converters on these are typically 8 or 16 bit; some are monophonic but most are stereophonic. The input and output sample rates available may vary from 8 kHz through to the CD rate of 44.1 kHz. Some have built-in amplifiers and mixing capabilities. Most sound cards have some form of digital synthesizer while the higher-end systems use *digital signal processing technology and can perform *wave-table synthesis from samples of real instruments loaded onto either *RAM or *ROM. *See also* multimedia.

soundex code A method of encoding words that sound alike. An application is surnames that are spelled differently but pronounced virtually the same. All names with similar sounds are given the same *key, while some secondary algorithm is used to match the names. A soundex code for a name is in the form *addd* where *a* is the initial character of the name and *ddd* are three digits that are derived from the remaining consonants. For example, "Johnson" becomes J523 while "Johnstone" is J525.

soundness theorem A theorem about a logical system *L* and a semantics *S* for the formulas of *L* stating that if a formula is provable in the logic *L* then it is valid in the semantics *S*. A soundness theorem confirms that the logic is actually expressing and deriving properties that are valid according to the semantics. *See also* completeness theorem.

source alphabet (source set) *See* code.

source code The form of a program that is input to a *compiler or *translator for conversion into equivalent object code.

source coding (source compression coding) The use of *variable-length codes in order to reduce the number of symbols in a message to the minimum necessary to represent the information in the message, or at least to go some way toward this, for a given size of alphabet. In source coding the particular *code to be used is chosen to match the source (i.e. the relative probabilities of the symbols in the source alphabet) rather than any channel through which the message may ultimately be passed.

The main problem in source coding is to ensure that the most probable source symbols are represented by the shortest *codewords, and the less probable by longer codewords as necessary, the weighted average codeword length being minimized within the bounds of *Kraft's inequality. The most widely used methods for ensuring this are *Huffman coding* and *Shannon–Fano coding*; the former is more efficient for a given *extension of the source but the latter is computationally simpler. In either case, a large extension of the source may be necessary to approach the limiting compression factor given by the *source coding theorem.

See also Shannon's model. *Compare* channel coding.

source coding theorem In *communication theory, the statement that the output of any information source having *entropy H units per symbol can be encoded into an alphabet having N symbols in such a way that the source symbols are represented by codewords having a weighted average length not less than $H/\log N$ (where the base of the logarithm is consistent with the entropy units). Also, that this limit can be approached arbitrarily closely, for any source, by suitable choice of a *variable-length code and the use of a sufficiently long *extension of the source (*see* source coding).

The theorem was first expounded and proved by Claude Elwood Shannon in 1948.

source compression coding *Another name for* source coding.

source compression factor The ratio of message lengths before and after *source coding (which is generally intended to make messages shorter). *See also* source coding theorem.

source language The language in which the input to a *compiler or *translator is written.

source-level compatibility *Compatibility that exists when a program may be executed on two or more different computer systems by moving the *source code and recompiling it on each system without any changes. *See also* binary-level compatibility.

source lines of code *See* SLOC.

source listing *Another name for* program listing.

source program The original high-level-language program submitted to a *compiler.

source route bridge (SRB) A form of *routing used to allow connection to be established between pairs of nodes on different *token rings. A node wishing to establish a connection issues a special explorer *packet that is broadcast to all nodes on all rings until it is recognized by the specified destination node. The specified node then returns a specific reply packet that returns to the original node, acquiring routing information as it does so, and thus presenting the source node with a complete route between the two nodes. This technique presents a *dynamic choice of route at the time of establishing the connection, but all subsequent traffic must follow the path determined at that time.

source set *Another name for* source alphabet. *See* code.

spaceball A graphical input device that is based on a fixed spherical ball. It inputs six different values defined by the orientation of the ball and the pressure together with the direction that is applied to it. It allows complex objects to be positioned and rotated in three-dimensional space using the single input device. Internally a spaceball is normally made from a set of strain-gauges.

space character A nonprinting character that causes the active position to be moved one position to the right. The space character occupies a position in memory. *Compare* blank character.

space complexity *See* complexity measure, polynomial space.

space-division switch Any switching mechanism that is based on the through connection of a set of input lines selectively to a set of output lines. Space-division switches are implemented either by electromechanical or electronic means. Prior to the advent of time-division switching, all telephone and telegraph switching machines were implemented using a variety of space-division switching techniques, particularly Strowger (step-by-step) switches and crossbar switches.

space domain A term used to refer to a situation in which the amplitude of a *signal varies with position (usually in two dimensions, as in a picture) rather than with time. *See also* time domain, filtering.

space-filling curve A curve of infinite length that encloses a finite area. The curve is nowhere differentiable and between any two points of the area there is a curve of infinite length. Most space-filling curves exhibit a degree of self-similarity.

space quantization (pixelization) *See* quantization. *See also* discrete and continuous systems.

spacetime A formulation of 3-dimensional space and time as a 4-dimensional space. In computer graphics spacetime is used, for example, in constraining object positions in space and time in a consistent way.

spam *Informal* To send an e-mail message in an indiscriminate way (or, as a noun, the actual mail message). Many systems have publicly accessible distribution lists, typically holding the e-mail addresses of a group of users who share a common interest and wish to distribute material to colleagues on the list. A large system will have many such lists, often with overlapping membership, and on occasions spamming will occur: unwanted mail messages, such as sales literature, have been sent to every member of every mailing list on every system attached to a network, regardless of the extent to which the same person may be on several lists, or whether the recipients have any interest in the contents of the message. This activity is a breach of *netiquette. The recipients of spam may respond by *flaming. (The word derives from a Monty Python sketch concerned with excessive offerings of cooked spam.)

spanning subgraph *See* subgraph.

spanning tree A *subgraph of a *connected graph *G*; this subgraph is a *tree and includes all the nodes of *G*. A *minimum-cost* spanning tree is a weighted spanning tree, formed from a *weighted graph, such that the real numbers assigned to each edge, when summed, total not greater than the corresponding sum for any other weighted spanning tree.

SPARC *Trademark*; *acronym for* scalable processor architecture. Sun Microsystems' *RISC architecture intended for multiple implementations with differing cost/performance requirements for workstations, compute servers, etc. The SPARC processor design is based on the early fundamental RISC processor design at the University of California, Berkeley. The architecture provides a 24-register window into a larger register set as local space for a procedure, plus an additional 8 global registers. The 24-register window is moved by 16-register positions on procedure call leaving an 8-register overlap with the window of the calling procedure. This technique normally avoids the reuse of a procedure's register set and hence the need to preserve register contents prior to procedure call; the overlap provides efficient parameter passing between calling and called procedures. If the depth of procedure nesting exceeds the number of register windows, then the oldest window is preserved in memory prior to procedure entry and its reuse; it must be recovered from memory before a return is made to this oldest procedure. The number of overlapping windows comprising the register set will determine the frequency of the need to preserve and recover register windows from memory. The number is a cost/performance design decision; eight is typical.

sparse matrix A matrix usually arising in the context of *linear algebraic equations of the form $Ax = b$ in which A is of large order and has a high proportion of zero elements (greater than, say, 90%). Special techniques are available that exploit the large number of zeros and reduce considerably the computational effort when compared to a general full matrix. Examples of such methods are variants of Gaussian elimination (*see* linear algebraic equations) and *iteration methods. Large sparse systems can arise in the numerical solution of *ordinary and *partial differential equations. *See also* numerical linear algebra.

spatial coherence The extent to which a property exhibits a similar value over some spatial region. Spatial coherence is exploited in some illumination calculations in which a scene is broken down into discrete cells that can each be treated as a single entity. The scene is spatially coherent over each cell. The proximity of objects is usually in terms of their positions in object space.

spatial reasoning Techniques in *artificial intelligence that attempt to emulate human reasoning during navigation and other spatial tasks. Current research involves enhanced forms of *logic and *qualitative reasoning. Spatial reasoning has applications in computer-aided design, robotics, and other forms of engineering application, as well as in *cognitive science where models of spatial skills help to explain human performance.

SPDL *Abbrev. for* standard page description language. Part of the *ODA standard that makes it possible to map to and from the leading *page and *document description languages.

special character *See* character set.

specialization/generalization A particular form of association between entities found in object-oriented approaches to design, programming, etc. The association is used to indicate a hierarchy of *objects such that objects lower in the hierarchy inherit properties from those higher in the hierarchy. Thus objects lower in the hierarchy are more specialized, whereas objects higher in the hierarchy are more generalized.

specification A formal description of a system, or a component or module of a system, intended as a basis for further development. The expression of the specification may be in text in a natural language (e.g. English), in a *specification language, which may be a formal mathematical language, and by the use of specification stages of a methodology that includes a *diagrammatic technique. Characteristics of a good specification are that it should be unambiguous, complete, verifiable, consistent, modifiable, traceable, and usable after development.

specification language A language that is used in expressing a *specification. It has a formally defined syntax and semantics, and its design is based on a mathematical method for modeling or defining systems (e.g. set theory, equations and initial algebras, predicate logic). Examples include *SADT, *RSL, *VDM, *OBJ, and *Z.

spectral analysis *See* time series.

specular reflection Reflection from a glossy surface. Many real surfaces are not matt but reflect light, i.e. are glossy; the surfaces of billiard balls, apples, and china are glossy while mirrors are an extreme case, being perfect specular reflectors. If the surface is not a perfect mirror, the reflected light will occur in a cone centered around the perfect reflection direction. The amount of light reflected will be some fraction of the incident light. The result is a *highlight that has the color of the light source rather than of the object. An empirical formula suggested by Bui-Tuong Phong in 1975 is often used in *computer graphics to define specular reflection. *Compare* diffuse reflection.

speech compression Any technique to compress speech in order to use less bandwidth when transmitting. Various standardized techniques are used in Europe and the US, most of which employ *lossy compression.

GSM 06.10 is used by European wireless telephones. It uses residual pulse excitation/long-term prediction (RPE/LTP) coding and compresses 160 frames of 13-bit samples into 260 bits. A sample rate of 8 kHz is used. *CELP 3.2a* is the US Department of Defense's code excited linear prediction voice coder; it is based on Federal Standard 1016, which operates at 4800 bps.

speech-generation device A means for producing spoken messages in response to signals from a data-processing or control system. The selection of messages is produced by assembling speech sounds from a set of

fundamentals that may be artificial in origin or may have been extracted by processing human speech.

speech recognition The process of recognizing elements of speech by analysis of the acoustic signal. Many systems may be trained to a particular operator's voice and can build up dictionaries/vocabularies to enable faster and more accurate recognition.

Typically speech recognition is a many-stage process, starting with the digital *sampling of the acoustic signal followed by some form of *spectral analysis, such as linear predictive coding (LPC), cochlear modeling, etc. The next stage is to recognize the elements of speech – *phonemes, groups of phonemes, and words; many systems employ hidden Markov model (HMM) algorithms, dynamic time warping (DTW), or neural networks (NN) for the recognition phase. In addition most systems utilize some knowledge of the language.

See also voice input device.

speech synthesis The production of artificial speech for output by a *D/A converter. The input is typically a file of ASCII text. The synthesis may be performed either by hardware or software, the *Klatt synthesizer being an example. The methodology employed to produce the speech signal may be by concatenation of prerecorded words or of elements of real speech (such as *phonemes), or by pure synthesis driven by data derived from a complex analysis of the input text.

The quality of the speech produced depends greatly on the techniques employed at both the lexical analysis phase and the synthesis phase. The particular problem with phoneme concatenation is how to actually perform the join since fluent speech requires fluent transitions. Other commonly used elements of speech are demisyllables, syllables, words, and word systems. As the units become longer, so the quality increases, but then so does the storage requirement and the processing overhead.

speech understanding The processing of speech that involves the mapping of the acoustic signal, usually derived from some form of *speech recognition system, to some form of abstract meaning of the speech. *See also* natural language understanding.

speed of a computer. A rather vaguely defined term that is often used to indicate the relative processing power of a given computer system, since the power of a computer is largely governed by the ability of the central processing unit to execute instructions rapidly. The CPU's speed is itself dependent on numerous factors such as word length, instruction set, technology of implementation, and memory access times.

speedup theorem A theorem in complexity theory that, like the *gap theorem, can be expressed in terms of abstract complexity measures (*see* Blum's axioms) but will be more understandable in the context of time. Given any total *recursive function $r(n)$, there exists a recursive language L such that for any Turing machine M recognizing L, say within time bound $S(n)$, there exists another Turing machine M′ that also recognizes L but within a time bound $S'(n)$ that satisfies

$$r(S'(n)) \leq S(n)$$

for all but a finite number of values of n. Thus for this language there can be no fastest program.

spelling checker (or **spell checker)** A program, often a component of a word processing system, that will check any or all of the words in a document against a set of dictionaries; this set consists of a base dictionary and optional extra dictionaries specific to the subject of the document or created by the user. On finding a word not known to it the spelling checker may suggest alternative spellings and ask if the word is to be added to the dictionary. Spelling checkers cannot of course detect errors that are themselves valid words, while their attempts to find alternatives to proper names can be distinctly amusing.

sphere-packing bound *Another name for* Hamming bound.

spiral model A *software life-cycle model devised by Barry Boehm that encompasses a management strategy, a life-cycle development model, and *risk assessment. The model takes its name from the spiral repre-

sentation as shown in the diagram overleaf. Beginning at the center of the spiral, where there is limited detailed knowledge of requirements and small costs, successive refinement of the software is shown as a traverse around the spiral, with a corresponding accumulation of costs as the length of the spiral increases. Interaction between phases is not shown directly since the model assumes a sequence of successive refinements coupled to decisions that project risks associated with the next refinement are acceptable. Each 360° rotation around the center of the spiral passes through four stages: planning, seeking alternatives, evaluation of alternatives and risks, and (in the lower right quadrant) activities equivalent to the phases represented in *waterfall or *V-models.

spline In its simplest form a spline function (of degree n), $s(x)$, is a piecewise polynomial on $[x_1, x_N]$ that is $(n-1)$ times continuously differentiable, i.e.

$$s(x) \equiv \text{polynomial of degree } n$$
$$x_i \leq x \leq x_{i+1}, i = 1, 2, \dots, N-1$$

These polynomial "pieces" are all matched up at points (called *knots*):

$$x_1 < x_2 < \dots < x_N$$

in the interior of the range, so that the resulting function $s(x)$ is smooth. The idea can be extended to functions of more than one variable. *Cubic splines* – spline curves of degree 3 – provide a useful means of approximating data to moderate accuracy. Splines are often the underlying approximations used in *variational methods. *See also* B-spline.

split One of the basic actions applicable to a set S on whose elements a *total ordering $\leq$ is defined; when applied in the form

$$split(a, S)$$

where a is a member of S, S is partitioned into two *disjoint sets S_1 and S_2: all the elements in S_1 are less than or equal to a and all those in S_2 are greater than a. *See also* operations on sets.

split screen A display screen in which the top and bottom areas of the screen face may be treated as separate screens for the purpose of data manipulation. The split is usually into two parts, not necessarily equal, but there may be more. One part may be used for

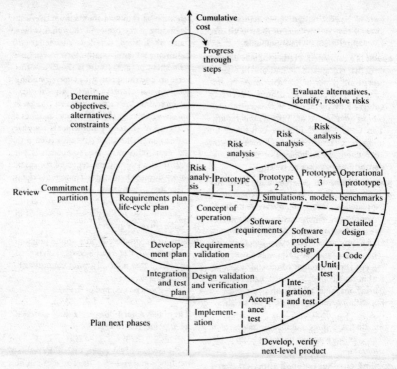

Spiral model [from *Computer*, May 1988, page 62. © 1988 IEEE]

entering data from the attached keyboard while the other part displays instructions or prompts. The entered data may be manipulated by *scrolling or erasing without affecting the other part of the screen. *See also* window.

spoofing A deliberate attempt to cause a user or resource to perform an incorrect action. *See also* threat.

spool 1. The reel or former on which magnetic tape or printer ribbon is wound.

2. To transfer data intended for a peripheral device (which may be a communication channel) into an intermediate store, either so that it can be transferred to the peripheral at a more convenient time or so that sections of data generated separately can be transferred to the peripheral in bulk. Spooling is therefore a method of handling virtual input and output devices in a *multiprogramming system.

For simplicity consider the case of output. Normally a program wishing to output to a page printer will claim a printer, use it to produce its results, and then release the printer. In a multiprogramming environment this is a potent source of delay since the speed at which a printer operates is typically slow compared with the speed of the process driving the printer; it would therefore be necessary to provide a number of printers approximately equal to the number of processes active in the system.

Spooling is commonly used to overcome this problem. Output destined for a printer is diverted onto backing store. A *process wishing to use a printer will be allocated an area of backing store, into which the results destined for the printer are written, and a *server process, which acts as a virtual printer and transfers information destined for the printer into the backing store area. When the process has no more data to send to the printer, it will inform the server process, which will terminate the information written into backing store. Subsequently a system utility will be used to copy the contents of the backing store for this process onto the printer. Similar arrangements can be established for dealing with the input to processes.

spread *See* measures of variation.

spreadsheet A program that manipulates tables consisting of rows and columns of *cells*, and displays them on a screen; the cells contain numerical information and formulas, or text. Each cell has a unique row and column identifier, but different spreadsheets use different conventions so the top left-hand cell may be A1, 1A, or 1,1. The value in a numerical cell is either typed in or is calculated from a formula in the cell; this formula can involve other cells. Each time the value of a cell is changed by typing in a new value from the keyboard, the value of all other cells whose values depend on this one are recalculated. The ability of the cells to store text is used to annotate the table with column headings, titles, etc.

The spreadsheet is particularly suited to the personal computer since it requires the fast and flexible display handling that is a feature of such systems. The common characteristic of all spreadsheets is the way the screen of the computer acts as a *window onto the matrix of cells; if there are more rows and columns than will fit on the screen, then the spreadsheet can be scrolled horizontally or vertically to bring into view previously hidden rows or columns. To change a value it is only necessary to move the cursor into the required cell displayed on the screen and type in the new value.

Spreadsheets can be used for storing and amending accounts, "what if?" financial projections, and many other applications involving tables of numbers with interdependent rows and columns. A spreadsheet is often a component of an *integrated office system.

Examples include Excel, Lotus 1-2-3, and Quattro Pro. *See also* multidimensional spreadsheet.

spread spectrum signaling A form of *modulation in which the frequency of the *carrier for the modulated signal is switched rapidly between a number of predetermined possible frequencies. This has several advantages over signaling using a fixed allocation of frequencies. Its use may allow a number of transmitters to share the same range of frequencies. Successive frequencies may be determined in a way known only to the transmitter and the receiver, making it very difficult for an eavesdropper to detect the resulting signal.

sprite A user-definable pattern of *pixels that can be moved about as an entity on a display screen by program commands. For example, the screen cursor in a windows system that takes on different appearances in different situations is a sprite.

SQA *Abbrev. for* software quality assurance.

SQL (Formerly known as SEQUEL, acronym for structured English query language) The de facto standard language for database access and update for *relational database management systems. It is not a complete programming language and is generally used in association with a host language (*see* database language). Originating from the research at IBM that led to its *DB2 group of products, the name was changed from SEQUEL to SQL, then said to stand for structured query language, for legal reasons. There was wide interest in the further development of the language, leading to an ANSI standard in 1986, an ISO standard in 1988, and to the "International Standard Database Language SQL (1992)" generally known as *SQL2*, the definition of which in document ISO/IEC 9075:1992 runs to some 600 pages.

SQL/DS The version of *DB2 that runs under the IBM operating systems VSE and VM.

square matrix A matrix in which the number of rows is equal to the number of columns. An $n \times n$ matrix is sometimes called a matrix of *order n*.

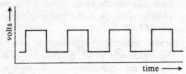

Square wave

square wave A signal consisting of alternate binary ones and zeros. The diagram shows how such a signal, when displayed on an *oscilloscope, may appear. A square wave can be considered as a *pulse train in which pulse separation is equal to pulse duration. When such a waveform is used to operate an electronic switch, it is described as a *switching waveform.

SRAM *Abbrev. for* static RAM. *See* RAM.

SRB *Abbrev. for* source route bridge.

SR flip-flop *Another name for* RS flip-flop. *See* flip–flop.

SSADM *Abbrev. for* structured systems analysis and design method. The standard UK government analysis and design methodology, originated by *CCTA; it is the subject of British Standard BS 7738. The latest version (1995) is SSADM 4+.

SSADM covers the data (information), processing (function), and events (logical) views of a system. The methodology has six phases covering analysis, requirements specification, logical design, and physical design of data and processes down to the program specification. Notations provided are for entity life history diagrams, dataflow diagrams, and process outline specifications. Tools support is available. SSADM is also compatible with the PROMPT II project management methodology.

SSI *Abbrev. for* small-scale integration, i.e. integration of generally less than 100 transistors on a single chip. *See* integrated circuit.

SSU *Abbrev. for* session support utility. An extension of the basic ANSI communication protocols providing for dual screen operation. SSU was developed by Digital Equipment Corporation and widely emulated by other vendors.

stability A multidiscipline term with a variety of (related) meanings. In *numerical analysis it is used with what appears to be a bewildering array of possible prefixes. There are, however, two important basic usages.

Given a well-defined numerical procedure it is important that roundoff errors do not seriously influence the accuracy of the results. This is referred to as *numerical stability* and depends on the *error-propagation properties of the procedure.

*Discretization methods for the solution of integral and differential equations are based on a subdivision of the region in which the solution is required. Stability here means that perturbations in the data (initial or boundary conditions) have a bounded effect on the solution obtained (ignoring roundoff error) for a given subdivision. The existence of a uniform bound on this effect over all sufficiently fine subdivisions is a necessary condition for the convergence of the method as the subdivision is refined.

In the solution of *ordinary differential equations much of the stability theory has been developed in the study of stiff systems of equations. Of great importance to this development was the concept of *A-stability* introduced by Dahlquist in 1963. A method is A-stable if it produces bounded solutions for the test problem

$$y' = qy, y(0) = 1, \text{Re}(q) < 0$$

for *all* stepsizes. The trapezoidal rule (*see* ordinary differential equations) is an example of an A-stable method. Much of the later theory has investigated similar properties for more general test problems.

stable sorting algorithm A sorting algorithm that preserves the relative ordering of records with equal sortkeys.

stack 1. (pushdown stack; pushdown list; LIFO list) A linear *list where all accesses, insertions, and removals are made at one end of the list, called the *top*. This implies access on a last in first out (LIFO) basis: the most recently inserted item on the list is the first to be removed. The operations *push* and *pop* refer respectively to the insertion and removal of items at the top of the stack. Stacks occur frequently in computing and in particular are closely associated with *recursion.

2. Loosely, a linear *list where accesses, insertions, and removals are made at one end or both ends of the list. This includes a pushdown stack, described above. When the earliest inserted item on the linear list is the first to be removed (first in first out, FIFO), it is a *pushup stack*, more properly known as a *queue. When insertions and deletions may be made at both ends, it is a double-ended queue, or *deque.

A stack may be implemented in hardware as a specialized kind of addressless memory, with a control mechanism to implement any of the insertion/removal regimes. *See also* stack processing.

stack algorithm In general, any algorithm that employs a *stack, but, specifically, one for decoding a *convolutional code.

stack architecture An architecture in which *stack processing is used.

stack frame In a *block-structured language, storage required by a block (procedure) is allocated on entry to the block and is deallocated at the exit from the block. Since blocks are nested, storage can be allocated on a last in first out basis on a *stack, and the area of the stack containing data for a particular block is called the stack frame for the block.

stack manipulation *Another name for* stack processing.

stack processing (stack manipulation) Use of a pushdown *stack or *LIFO implemented in hardware as a data memory. This permits the use of *zero-address instructions where both operand sources and result destinations are implicitly the top locations of the stack, thus making programs more compact. Stack mechanisms are also used to provide a way of keeping track of multiple interrupts in which the stack serves as a way of "nesting" the interrupts so that those of lesser priority are pushed down until those of higher priority can be attended to.

staging A form of *spooling associated with the use of magnetic tape. The contents of a tape that is to be operated upon by a process may be staged onto magnetic disk. In this form, tape-winding time is virtually eliminated since it is possible to locate a particular part of the "tape" much more rapidly if it is entirely held on disk.

staircase waveform A waveform that is generally constrained to lie between maximum and minimum voltage values. Between these extremes the waveform can only take on discrete and constant values of voltage for fixed periods of time. The waveform thus consists of a number of small step changes in voltage level, hence the term staircase. The height of each step will normally be made constant but may be variable, as may the period of time over which the waveform resides at a given voltage level.

stand-alone Denoting hardware or software that is capable of performing its function without being connected to any other component.

standard 1. A publicly available definition of a hardware or software component, resulting from international, national, or industrial agreement.
2. A product, usually hardware, that conforms to such a definition.

standard deviation *See* measures of variation.

standard error *See* measures of variation.

standard function A *function provided as part of a programming language, in particular to evaluate the standard mathematical functions (sin, cos, exp, etc.). The term is sometimes used more generally as a synonym for library program (*see* program library).

standard interface A point of interconnection between two systems or parts of a system, e.g. that between a processor and a peripheral, at which all the physical, electric, and logical parameters are in accordance with predetermined values and are collectively used in other instances. An interface may be classed as standard on the basis of manufacturer, industry, or international usage. The I/O channels of a processor may be classed as standard interfaces because they are common to all processors of that type, or common to more than one type of peripheral, but they may be specific to a manufacturer. Some interfaces are de facto industry standards and can be used to connect devices from different vendors. Other interfaces are standardized by agreement within trade associations or international committees such as the *CCITT.

Although a peripheral and its host may comply with the specification, this does not guarantee functional *compatibility.

standardization 1. The establishment of an international, national, or industrial agreement concerning the specification or production of components – electric, electronic, or software – or equipment in general, or of procedures for the use or testing of equipment or software.

2. The act of committing an organization to use specific standards to meet particular needs whenever they arise within the organization. Typically an organization might standardize upon use of a specific compiler for some language, some specific application package, or a particular database management system.

standard ML (SML) A popular *functional programming language derived from *ML. Unlike other functional languages, standard ML also supports some aspects of the procedural programming style, in particular for input and output. In consequence it is a general-purpose programming language.

standard product of sums One of the two canonical (i.e. standard or normal) forms of a *Boolean function, useful in comparing and simplifying functions. This form contains one *standard sum term, or maxterm, for each "zero" (false) entry in the *truth table for the expression. This form can be represented as the AND (product) of a group of ORs (the sum terms) of Boolean variables, uncomplemented or complemented. It can also be shown to be the NOR of a group of NORs of the identical variables. *Compare* standard sum of products.

standard product term (minterm) A product (AND) of n Boolean variables, uncomplemented or complemented but not repeated, in a function of n variables. With n variables, 2^n different standard product terms are possible. The complement of any standard prod-

uct term is a *standard sum term, or maxterm.

standard sum of products One of the two canonical (i.e. standard or normal) forms of a *Boolean function, useful in comparing and simplifying functions. This form contains one *standard product term, or minterm, for each "one" (true) entry in the *truth table for the expression. This form can be represented as the OR (sum) of a group of ANDs (the product terms) of Boolean variables, uncomplemented or complemented. It can also be shown to be the NAND of a group of NANDs of the identical variables. *Compare* standard product of sums.

standard sum term (maxterm) A sum (OR) of n Boolean variables, uncomplemented or complemented but not repeated, in a function of n variables. With n variables, 2^n different standard sum terms are possible. The complement of any standard sum term is a *standard product term, or minterm.

standby time *Another name for* idle time. *See* available time.

STAR One of the early *vector processors, manufactured by CDC and unique on several grounds: it is one of the large machines built by CDC but not designed by Seymour Cray (the architect was Jim Thornton); it was noted for having very wide words that can be processed in parallel; it was the first machine marketed that was aimed at very rapid processing of vectors.

star closure *See* Kleene star.

star-height The maximum depth to which the *Kleene-star operator is nested in a given *regular expression. The star-height of a *regular language L is the smallest star-height of any regular expression for L. There is no known algorithm for determining the star-height of a regular language. It is however known that there are regular languages of arbitrary star-height.

If complement and intersection are allowed, the class of *generalized* regular expressions is obtained. For these it is not known if there are languages of star-height greater than one.

star network A simple network topology with

all links connecting directly to a single central *node. Star networks work well when traffic consists of multiple secondary nodes communicating with a single primary node, e.g. computer terminals connected to a time-sharing host.

The main disadvantages of a star network are:

(a) central switch failure disrupts the entire network;

(b) circuit failures between the central switch and the terminals result in loss of user communication (no alternate paths);

(c) the cost of having every user directly connected to the central site may be very high for geographically distant (dispersed) nodes;

(d) total communication capacity is often limited by the speed of the central switch.

The main advantage of a star network is that the design of the end terminals may be very simple. *See also* network architecture.

STARTS A UK initiative, begun in 1982 and relaunched in 1994, to promote and disseminate best practice in software development. In its later phase, it is a self-financing technology transfer program sponsored by the Department of Trade and Industry, managed by the National Computing Centre, and funded by subscribing companies. It deals with the major issues posed by industry's increasing dependence on software, concentrating on the practical rather than the theoretical, and including consideration of how to implement change. It provides information through publications, workshops, and seminars, which in its first phase included widely used advice on method and tool selection and purchasing practice.

start symbol (sentence symbol) *See* grammar.

start time *Another name for* acceleration time.

startup The initialization of a computer system when switched on or restarted after some error has occurred. *See* bootstrap.

starvation *Informal* A situation occurring when the rate at which a *process can proceed is sharply reduced by its inability to gain access to a particular resource.

statecharts A development of state-transition diagrams that introduces hierarchical states and concurrent states. In a statechart a concurrent state can indicate that a modeled item must be in several parallel states simultaneously. This is useful where an object can have several independent behaviors while in a given operating mode. For example, an aircraft in flight will simultaneously have a navigation state (e.g. manual control or autopilot control) and this will be independent of which radio is being used to communicate with air-traffic controllers (and at which frequency).

state diagram 1. A graphical version of a *state table.

2. *See* state-transition diagram.

statement The unit from which a high-level language program is constructed: a program is a sequence of statements. It is analogous to an *instruction at the machine-code level. *See also* declaration.

statement label *See* label.

statement testing A test strategy in which each statement of a program is executed at least once. It is equivalent to finding a *path (or set of paths) through the *control-flow graph that contains all the nodes of the graph. It is a weaker testing strategy than *path testing or *branch testing because it (usually) requires the least number of test cases.

state space A method of problem representation used in *search and in *machine learning. The N independent variables in a problem description can be imagined as axes of an N-dimensional hyperspace. Problems can then be viewed as the task of finding a path from a given start state to some desirable goal state.

state table 1. A table describing the behavior of a *sequential circuit as a function of stable internal conditions – *states* – and input variables. For each combination of these, the next state of the circuit is specified together with any output variables.

2. *See* finite-state automaton.

state-transition diagram (STD) A diagram that indicates the possible states of a *finite-state automaton and the allowable transitions between such states. There are several different dialects of STDs. Each one depicts the states, transitions, and event(s) that can cause each transition. STDs may also indicate conditions that control whether a legal transition is allowable, or actions that are undertaken either during a transition or on entry to a new state. Because an STD defines a finite-state automaton, the object being modeled may be only in one state at a time. STDs can be used to define the control structure of a software module, or to define the modes of operation of large systems. *See also* statecharts.

state-transition function *See* finite-state automaton.

state variable A (generally) binary variable describing the state of each memory element within a *sequential circuit.

static Not changing, incapable of being changed, or unable to take place during some period of time, usually while a system or device is in operation or a program is running. *Compare* dynamic.

static allocation An allocation that cannot be changed while a process is running.

static analysis Analysis of a program that does not require the program to be executed, as in dynamic *testing. A *software tool is used to check syntax and to construct one or more of
  a *control-flow graph,
  a *dataflow graph,
  an information flow graph.
Information flow analysis identifies the relationships between outputs and the input variables, and a *semantic analysis* provides formulas for these relationships. Comparing the results of semantic analysis with a formal *program specification reveals inconsistencies between specification and implementation.

Early work (1975–76) led to analyzers (DAVE, AUDIT, FACES) for single languages such as Fortran. Later work led to analyzers for C (e.g. LINT, 1978). There are now analysis tools (e.g. MALPAS, SPADE) that are multilanguage and have facilities for comparing specification and code.

static data structure A data structure whose organizational characteristics are invariant throughout its lifetime. Such structures are well supported by high-level languages and familiar examples are *arrays and *records. The prime features of static structures are

(a) none of the structural information need be stored explicitly within the elements – it is often held in a distinct logical/physical header;

(b) the elements of an allocated structure are physically contiguous, held in a single segment of memory;

(c) all descriptive information, other than the physical location of the allocated structure, is determined by the structure definition;

(d) relationships between elements do not change during the lifetime of the structure.

Relaxation of these features leads to the concept of a *dynamic data structure.

static dump A dump, usually of the workspace of a *process, taken at a time when the process can be guaranteed to be inactive, such as at the end of a job step.

static RAM (SRAM) *See* RAM.

station in a communication network. *Another name for* node.

stationery The paper used in *printers. It is one type of *data medium and is available in a number of forms.

Continuous stationery consists of an unbroken length of paper that has transverse perforations dividing the length into identical sheets. The perforations allow the paper to be provided in fanfold form and to be easily separated into shorter lengths or single sheets after printing a job. There are sprocket holes at ½″ pitch, ¼″ from both edges, by which the stationery is driven accurately through a printer by a *tractor or pin-wheel mechanism. Continuous stationery may be up to 20″ wide and may have additional transverse or longitudinal perforations to enable the sheets to be separated into smaller forms.

Roll stationery is provided in roll form for applications where ease of filing the *printout is not important. It is commonly friction-fed through the printer, but some rolls have sprocket holes as on continuous stationery. Printers that use roll stationery usually have a tear-off facility. Rolls may be typically 2″–3″ wide as used on *point of sale terminals, or 8″–10″ as used on other printers.

Single-sheet stationery consists of a pack of identical separate sheets that may be fed manually into a printer, or may be loaded as a pack into a printer attachment – a *cut-sheet feed* – designed to feed them automatically one sheet at a time.

Single-part stationery has only one layer of paper passing through the printer. *Multipart stationery* consists of two or more layers of paper crimped together to pass through the printer so that multiple simultaneous copies of printout can be obtained on an *impact printer. The papers may be interleaved with carbon to form the copies, or *NCR* (*no carbon required*) paper may be used. NCR paper has a coated surface that under pressure releases ink locally. Multipart stationery can be in continuous, roll, or single-sheet form.

Label stationery consists of a suitable backing in continuous single-part form on which are mounted self-adhesive labels. These are used to print addresses, for example, the labels being subsequently removed from the backing and applied to envelopes.

Stationery is provided in a number of special forms, e.g. *carrier stationery*, which has custom-designed forms or envelopes mounted onto a backing, which in turn may be single-sheet or continuous form. Stationery can also be *preprinted* according to the needs of the user.

Stationery specifications consist of two main parts. There is the specification of the paper, which states the characteristics required of the paper in order to withstand the stresses of the types of printer for which it is intended and to give the required printing performance; such characteristics include strength, thickness, porosity, smoothness, density, and material content. A coating may also have to be defined for use with certain printer types, e.g. *thermal printers. There is also the specification of the conversion requirements, which state what form the finished stationery must take, including dimensions, preprinting, and any

special requirements. Stationery is subject to international standards.

statistical analysis *See* statistical methods.

statistical compaction (statistical compression) A *data-compaction code in which the *encoding (and therefore *decoding) table is formed from the statistics of the particular file (or data stream) being compacted. This may happen either *incrementally*, or, if feasible, during a preliminary pass over the input data. The decoding table must be stored or transmitted along with (i.e. following or interspersed within) the compacted text, so that the message can be decompacted when required (*compare* probabilistic compaction).

In the incremental case, if the gathering of statistics (and formation of the table) is recommenced (wholly or partly) whenever the performance falls below some limit, then the code is said to be *adaptive*.

statistical methods Methods of collecting, summarizing, analyzing, and interpreting variable numerical data. Statistical methods can be contrasted with *deterministic methods, which are appropriate where observations are exactly reproducable or are assumed to be so. While statistical methods are widely used in the life sciences, in economics, and in agricultural science, they also have an important role in the physical sciences in the study of measurement errors, of random phenomena such as radioactivity or meteorological events, and in obtaining approximate results where deterministic solutions are hard to apply.

Data collection involves deciding what to observe in order to obtain information relevant to the questions whose answers are required, and then making the observations. *Sampling involves choice of a sufficient number of observations representing an appropriate population. Experiments with variable outcomes should be conducted according to principles of *experimental design.

Data summarization is the calculation of appropriate *statistics (def. 2) and the display of such information in the form of tables, graphs, or charts. Data may also be adjusted to make different samples more comparable, using ratios, compensating factors, etc.

Statistical analysis relates observed statistical data to theoretical models, such as *probability distributions or models used in *regression analysis. By estimating *parameters in the proposed model and testing hypotheses about rival models, one can assess the value of the information collected and the extent to which the information can be applied to similar situations. *Statistical prediction* is the application of the model thought to be most appropriate, using the estimated values of the parameters.

More recently, less formal methods of looking at data have been proposed, including *exploratory data analysis.

statistical multiplexing A technique of *time division multiplexing of a number of subchannels onto a common wider bandwidth channel, where the total *bandwidth required by the individual subchannels exceeds the bandwidth of the multiplex channel. Since the maximum rate required by any one channel is seldom used, due to breaks in transmission, this technique is possible through judicious use of buffering. In this system bandwidth is not allocated permanently to each subchannel but only as required.

statistical prediction *See* statistical methods.

statistics 1. Numerical data relating to sets of individuals, objects, or phenomena. It is also the science of collecting, summarizing, and interpreting such data.

2. Quantities derived from data in order to summarize the properties of a sample. For example, the mean of a sample is a statistic that is a *measure of location, while the standard deviation is a *measure of variation.

status of a process. *See* process descriptor.

status bar (status line) In many kinds of display, including text and *graphical user interfaces, a line of usually textual information about current status. A word-processor status bar may tell the user what line and page is currently in use, if typeover or insert mode is in force, and which font is currently

selected, while a database status bar might have the current record number and field name and whether the display may be edited.

status register *See* program status word, processor status word.

status signal A *busy signal or *ready signal.

STD *Abbrev. for* state-transition diagram.

Steffenson iteration A method that combines the functional iteration scheme $x_{n+1} = G(x_n)$ with *Aitken's Δ^2 process to solve the equation $x = G(x)$.

STEP The international standard, ISO 10303: Standard for the Exchange of Product Model Data, covering all aspects of product life cycle in all industries. It is a neutral way of representing product data throughout its life, independent of any particular computer-aided system. STEP includes a textual *logical schema language, *EXPRESS*, which is based on the *ERA (entity-relationship-attribute) model.

stepped index fiber *See* fiber optics.

stepsize *See* finite-difference method.

stepwise refinement An approach to software development in which an initial highly abstract representation of some required program is gradually refined through a sequence of intermediate representations to yield a final program in some chosen programming language. The initial representation employs notations and abstractions that are appropriate for the problem being addressed. Subsequent development then proceeds in a sequence of small steps. Each step refines some aspect of the representation produced by the previous step, thus yielding the next representation in the sequence. Typically a single step involves simultaneous refinement of both data structures and operations, and is small enough to be performed with some confidence that the result is correct. Refinement proceeds until the final representation in the sequence is expressed entirely in the chosen programming language. The approach is normally associated with N. Wirth, designer of the *Pascal and *Modula languages. *Compare* structured programming.

stiff equations *See* ordinary differential equations.

STM *Abbrev. for* synchronous transfer module. *See* SDH.

stochastic matrix A matrix, much used for example in simulation, modeling, and communication theory, in which every row is a probability distribution, i.e. every element lies between 0 and 1, and the sum of the elements of each row is unity. A *doubly stochastic matrix* is a stochastic matrix whose transpose is a stochastic matrix.

stochastic model *See* stochastic process.

stochastic process A set of *random variables whose values vary with time (or sometimes in space). Examples include populations affected by births and deaths, the length of a queue (*see* queuing theory), or the amount of water in a reservoir. *Stochastic models* are models in which random variation is of major importance, in contrast to *deterministic models. Stochastic processes give theoretical explanations for many *probability distributions, and underly the analysis of *time-series data.

storage (memory, store) A device or medium that can retain data for subsequent retrieval. *See* storage device. *See also* memory.

storage allocation 1. The amount of storage allocated to a *process.
2. The act of allocating storage to a *process. In a multiprogramming system it is necessary to control the use of storage to ensure that processes do not interfere with one another's workspace, except where they do so intentionally in order to cooperate. This represents one instance of the resource control activities within the system.

storage device A device that can receive data and retain it for subsequent retrieval. Such devices cover a wide range of capacities and speeds of access. The semiconductor devices used as the *main memory for the processor may take only a few nanoseconds to retrieve data but the cost of storing each bit is very high by comparison with the devices used as *backing store, which may take milliseconds or even many seconds to retrieve data. *See*

also memory hierarchy, memory management.

storage element *See* memory element.

storage hierarchy *See* memory hierarchy.

storage location *See* location.

storage oscilloscope An instrument that is used to measure fast nonrepetitive signals. It does this by capturing the signal on demand and continuing to display it until reset. This can be achieved in two ways: a digital storage oscilloscope samples the incoming signal, stores these samples, and displays them; other storage oscilloscopes use a special storage *cathode-ray tube that retains the image by mapping it as a charge pattern on an electrode behind the screen; the pattern then modulates the electron beam to give a picture of the captured signal.

storage pool Those areas of storage that are not allocated to *processes and are used by the storage allocation system as the source from which to meet requests. When a process releases storage it will be returned to the pool for subsequent reallocation.

storage protection The mechanisms, both hardware and software, ensuring that *processes access storage in a controlled manner. For storage in the high-speed levels of the *memory hierarchy, protection is implemented by hardware in order to maintain speed; for slower devices the protection may be entirely by software. In all cases, the intention is to ensure that the type of access made by a process to the storage is in accordance with that indicated when the storage was allocated to the process. For example, in a system with paged memory management a process may be granted access to an area of memory, but only for the purpose of executing the code in that page. Attempts to read from the page or to write to it would be prohibited by the (hardware) protection mechanism.

storage schema (internal schema) A specification of how the data relationships and rules specified in the *logical schema of a database will be mapped to the physical storage level in terms of the available constructs, such as aggregation into records, clustering on pages, indexing, and page sizing and caching for transfer between secondary and primary storage. Storage schema facilities vary widely between different DBMS.

storage structure The mapping from a *data structure to its implementation (which may be another data structure). Thus a date may be represented as a vector of three integers (with six permutations to choose from), directly as a string of characters, or, in more recent high-level languages, as a record with three selectors – day, month, and year. A good choice of storage structure permits an easy and efficient implementation of a given data structure.

storage tube A vacuum tube that can receive and retain information. The data can be erased and new data entered as required. The data may be graphical and visible on the face of the tube or it may be retrieved as an electric signal. *See also* electrostatic storage device.

store 1. *Another name for* storage, or memory, used especially in the UK.
2. To enter or retain information for subsequent retrieval.

store and forward A method in which information is passed from node to node in a communication network, pausing in each node until sufficient resources (bandwidth, buffer pools, etc.) are available for the next leg of the journey – called a *hop*. In computer networks the information being passed may be *messages, *packets, or *cells (small fixed-structure packets), and may be self-contained with regard to the store-and-forward network (*datagrams), or may depend upon the maintenance of state information (*flow control, *routing paths, etc.) from previous messages or packets. A store-and-forward network is based upon the tradeoff between the cost of memory and computational resources in the store-and-forward nodes, and the cost of the transmission lines between the nodes. *See also* message switching, packet switching.

stored program A *program that is stored in the *memory of a computer. The execution of the program then requires the use of a *control unit – to read instructions from the

memory at appropriate times and arrange to carry them out.

The memory used to store the program may be the same as or different from memory used to store the data. There are advantages in using the same (read-write) memory, allowing programs to be modified, but there may be advantages in limiting opportunities for program modification, either by using physically read-only memory or by restricting access to the part of the memory containing programs.

The concept of program and data sharing the same memory is fundamental to what is usually referred to as a *von Neumann machine or a von Neumann architecture. Although there is some disagreement as to whether the stored-program concept was originated by John von Neumann or by the team of John W. Mauchly and J. Presper Eckert, the first documentation was written by von Neumann in 1945 in his proposal for the *EDVAC.

storyboard An outline specification of an animated film or a report.

STP *Abbrev. for* shielded twisted pair. *See* twisted pair.

straight insertion sort (sifting technique; sinking technique) A sorting algorithm that looks at each sortkey in turn, and on the basis of this places the record corresponding to the sortkey correctly with respect to the previous sortkeys.

straight selection sort A sorting algorithm based upon finding successively the record with the largest sortkey and putting it in the correct position, then the record with the next largest key, etc.

Strassen algorithm An algorithm developed in 1968 by V. Strassen to multiply large numbers. It uses the properties of *Fourier transforms. *See also* Schonhage–Strassen algorithm.

stream 1. A flow of data characterized by relatively long duration and constant rate. When the rate is known ahead of time then communication resources may be reserved for the stream. For example, stream traffic may be carried using low-overhead synchronous

*time division multiplexing (TDM), while other traffic on the same channel is carried by higher-overhead asynchronous TDM. This is particularly important in satellite transmission systems, where overhead differences between synchronous and asynchronous traffic are very great. It is also important in applications, such as packet speech, that require a low variation in *network delay.

2. A finite or infinite sequence of elements of a nonempty set A indexed by time. If T is a set of time instants, or clock cycles, then the stream can be represented by a function

$$a : T \rightarrow A,$$

where $a(t)$ is the element in the stream at time t in T. Usually, in modeling computing systems, the elements of A are data or instructions, and time is assumed to be discrete, in which case $T = \{0,1,2, \ldots\}$.

stream cipher A cipher in which a relatively small quantity of data is encrypted (or decrypted) at each iteration of the algorithm – perhaps just one character or byte – but in which the algorithm contains memory that retains message-dependent information between iterations.

streamer *Informal name for* streaming tape transport.

streaming A mode of operation of a tape transport, introduced in 1978 by IBM, in which the length of *magnetic tape passing the head while stopping and restarting exceeds the length of the interblock gap. After a stop, therefore, the tape has to be *repositioned* (i.e. backed up) in order to be in the correct position for the next start. The alternative to streaming mode is *start/stop mode*.

Streaming allows a tape transport with only moderate acceleration to handle tape at a considerably higher speed than it could in start/stop mode. However, the average data rate is only improved if substantial quantities of data (typically tens to thousands of kilobytes) are transferred between stops, because of the considerable repositioning time (typically 0.1–2 seconds). The most common application is disk *backup.

Streaming also allows the interblock gap to be very short, increasing the amount of data

that can be stored on a given length of tape; this is not compatible with the currently used international format standards for open-reel tape, but most cartridge-tape standards define a short or zero interblock gap.

streaming tape transport A tape transport capable of operating in *streaming mode, and of automatically repositioning the magnetic tape when it stops. Some versions are also capable of operating in start/stop mode at a lower tape speed (or with extended interblock gaps).

Streaming tape transports can use simpler, and hence cheaper and more reliable, mechanisms than those designed for start/stop mode at similar tape speeds. In particular, they usually operate without the *capstan and tape *buffers of conventional tape transports, tape motion and tension being controlled entirely from the reels. Most cartridge tape transports operate only in the streaming mode.

streams interface In *object-oriented programming, a means of transferring different objects to and from backing store without having to detail the data structure of the object. The streams interface uses methods that form part of the object itself.

stream transformer A function that maps *streams to streams. If $[T \rightarrow A]$ is the set of all streams of elements of set A indexed by time T then, for example, a stream transformer that maps a pair of streams into one stream is a function of the form

$$F : [T \rightarrow A]^2 \rightarrow [T \rightarrow A]$$

Stream transformers are often defined in the equivalent but logically simpler form

$$G : [T \rightarrow A]^n \times T \rightarrow A$$

where $G(a,t) = F(a)(t)$ for stream a and time t, i.e. $G(a,t)$ is the element on the output stream $F(a)$ at time t.

Stretch A monster computer chartered by the US Government and built in the late 1950s by IBM as their IBM 7030; it was designed to "stretch the technique of computer building to its limits." It had a pipelined instruction unit with address lookahead, and a 64-bit word length with double precision arithmetic if required. Addressing was down to the bit over a two-million word memory. It was capable of variable word length working and, in fact, almost anything that could be expected of hardware. A limited number of 7030s were built for atomic energy and similar research establishments.

strictness A term applied to functions. A function that always requires the value of one of its arguments is said to be *strict* in that argument. *See also* lazy evaluation.

stride *See* dope vector.

strikeout A method of leaving a deleted section of printed or displayed text visible but clearly marked with a horizontal line through it.

string 1. A *flexible one-dimensional array, i.e. a flexible vector, of symbols where the lower bound of the vector is fixed at unity but the upper bound, i.e. the string length, may vary.
2. A type of input to a graphics system consisting of a sequence of characters. The usual input device is a keyboard. *See also* logical input device.
3. Any one-dimensional array of characters. In formal language theory a string is often referred to as a *word. *See also* sequence.

string manipulation The action of the fundamental operations on strings, including their creation, *concatenation, the extraction of *string segments, *string matching, their comparison, discovering their length, replacing *substrings by other strings, storage, and input/output.

string matching Searching within a string for a given substring.

string segment A *substring of a character string that can usually only be replaced by an array of the same size.

stripe disk A real or *virtual disk drive that forms part of a *stripe set. A stripe set is so-named because user data is interleaved over two or more *member disks. A stripe set forms a single virtual disk drive whose capacity is approximately the sum of its real or virtual members. *See also* RAID, mirror disk.

strobe A pulse used to sample the occurrence of an event in time, at a specified point in relation to the event.

stroke A type of input to a graphics system

consisting of a sequence of positions, possibly with other information. *See also* logical input device.

stroke textures A paradigm where the path of a pen and its pressure is used to define both the tone and texture of an image.

strongly terminating (strongly normalizing) *See* abstract reduction system.

strong typing A feature of some programming languages that requires the type of each data item to be declared, precludes the application of operators to inappropriate data types, and prevents the interaction of incompatible types.

structural induction The principle of *induction defined as follows. Let S be a set on which the *partial ordering $\leq$ is defined and which contains no infinite decreasing sequences (where decreasing is defined by the ordering relation). If P is some *predicate and if the following two conditions hold:

(a) let a be a smallest element of S, i.e. there is no x in S such that $x \leq a$, then $P(a)$ is true,

(b) for each element s in S, if $P(x)$ is true for each x in S with $x \leq s$, and from this it follows that $P(s)$ is true,

then $P(s)$ is true for all s in S. Structural induction tends to be used in proving properties of recursive programs.

structure 1. of a program. *See* program structure.
2. The relationship between parts of a compound data object.
3. *See* data structure, control structure, storage structure.

structured analysis *Short for* structured systems analysis.

structured coding *See* structured programming (def. 2).

structured English A form of process logic representation, similar to *pseudolanguage, used in *structured systems analysis.

structured programming 1. A method of program development that makes extensive use of *abstraction in order to factorize the problem and give increased confidence that the resulting program is correct. Given the specification of a required program, the first step is to envisage some "ideal" machine on which to implement that program. This ideal machine should offer both an appropriate set of *data structures and an appropriate set of operations on those data structures. The required program is then defined as a program for the specified ideal machine.

By this means the original problem has been reduced to one of implementing the specified ideal machine, and this problem is itself tackled in the same way. A second ideal machine is envisaged, this machine being ideal for implementing the data structures and operations of the first machine, and programs are produced to effect the implementation. This process continues until eventually a level is reached at which the specified data structures and operations of the ideal machine can conveniently be implemented directly in the chosen programming language. Thus the eventual program is based upon "levels of abstract machine", where the top-level machine is ideally suited to the specific application and the lowest-level machine directly executes the chosen programming language. The development process is not, however, simply one of "subroutinization", since both operations and data structures are refined simultaneously at each level.

The overall method of structured programming, which is largely due to E. W. Dijkstra, is heavily influenced by a concern for *program correctness. The intention is that at any level the implementation machine should be so well suited to the problem at hand that the programs for that machine will be small and simple. It should therefore be possible at each level to provide a convincing rigorous argument that the programs are correct.

2. An approach to *coding in which only three constructs are employed for governing the flow of control through the program. These three constructs allow for sequential, conditional, and iterative control flow. Arbitrary transfer of control (i.e. the *GOTO statement) is expressly forbidden. As a direct result, for each compound statement within the program there is precisely one entry point and one exit point, and reasoning about the program is thereby made easier.

structured systems analysis A specific technique for *systems analysis that covers all activities from initial understanding of the problem through to specification and high-level design of the software system. The technique embodies four main concepts: *dataflow diagrams*, a *data dictionary*, *data store structuring*, and *process logic representations*.

The *dataflow diagrams show the various processing elements in the system, and the dataflows between these processing elements and the major stores of data within the system. The processing elements are described in nonprocedural terms, typically using natural language, and a processing element from one diagram may be decomposed onto further diagrams to show greater levels of detail. A *data dictionary is used to record all the various data items in the system, the constraints upon these data items, and the processing elements by which they are accessed. As the decomposition proceeds so both the data stores and the actions of the processing elements are defined in more detail. The data store structuring techniques are based upon the *relational model of data and show how each data store is accessed and organized. The algorithms employed by the processing elements are defined by use of process logic representations, typically *program design languages, *decision tables, or "structured" natural language.

Two similar versions of structured systems analysis were developed separately by Gane and Sarson and by De Marco. The technique is intended primarily for use in traditional DP system development.

structured variable A variable in a programming language that is a composite object, being made up of components that are either simple data items or are themselves structured objects; these components are identified by *names.

In many programming languages, especially Pascal, the word *record* is used for a structured variable; in C the term *struct* is used.

stub **1.** A substitute component that is

employed temporarily in a program so that progress can be made, e.g. with compilation or testing, prior to the genuine component becoming available. To illustrate, if it is required to test the remainder of a program before a particular procedure has been developed, the procedure could be replaced by a stub. Dependent upon circumstances, it might be possible for this stub always to return the same result, return values from a table, return an approximate result, consult someone, etc.

2. *See* decision table.

Student's t distribution An important *probability distribution used instead of the *normal distribution when the standard deviation is estimated from data. Discovered by W. S. Gosset ('Student') in 1908, the t distribution gives wider *confidence intervals than the *normal distribution because of the uncertainty in the estimate of the standard deviation (*see* measures of variation). The probability values depend on an integer f, the number of *degrees of freedom, which is the number associated with the estimate of the standard deviation. Tables of the t distribution are widely available, but algorithms for direct computation are relatively lengthy.

The most common applications are

(a) testing differences between *means of two samples;

(b) testing differences from zero of estimated parameters in *regression analysis and *experimental design;

(c) evaluation of *confidence intervals for means and other estimated quantities.

STX A *control character indicating start of text.

subdirectory A *directory that is itself pointed to by an entry in a directory. The entries in a subdirectory may point either to further directories or to files. *See also* access path.

subgraph A portion of a *graph G obtained by either eliminating edges from G and/or eliminating some vertices and their associated edges. Formally a subgraph of a graph G with vertices V and edges E is a graph G' with vertices V' and edges E' in which V' is a subset of V and E' is a subset of E (edges in E' joining vertices in V').

If V' is a proper *subset of V or E' is a proper subset of E then G' is a *proper subgraph* of G. If all the vertices of G are present in the subgraph G' then G' is a *spanning subgraph* of G. *See also* spanning tree.

subgroup A subset T of a *group G on which the dyadic operation ∘ is defined; T contains the identity, e, of G, the inverse x^{-1} for any x in T, and the quantity $x \circ y$ for any x and y in T. For any group G the set consisting of e alone is a subgroup; so also is the group G itself. All other subgroups are *proper subgroups* of G.

sublist *See* list.

submatrix of a given matrix, A. Any matrix derived from A by deleting one or more of its columns and/or one or more of its rows. *See also* trim.

submenu A menu that appears as a result of the selection of a menu item. Menu items that cause further menus to appear rather than cause an immediate action to be performed are often indicated by ellipsis, by a right-pointing arrow, or by some other device, as in SAVE... or SEARCH ▶.

subnet *Short for* communication subnetwork.

subnotebook A computer that is smaller than a *notebook but larger than a *palmtop or *personal digital assistant. A full-size keyboard cannot be accommodated but a certain amount of typing is possible, and lack of mechanical disk drives coupled with a monochrome LCD screen and components with low power consumption lead to considerable battery life and low weight. The advent of the *PCMCIA accessory slots have added to the flexibility of such computers.

sub-Nyquist sampling *See* Nyquist's criterion.

subprogram Part of a program that may be executed by a *call from elsewhere. The term covers *subroutines, *procedures, and *functions.

subrecursive hierarchy *See* hierarchy of functions.

subroutine A piece of code that is obeyed "out of line", i.e. control is transferred to the subroutine, and on its completion control reverts to the instruction following the *call. (The instruction code of the CPU usually provides *subroutine jump* and *return* instructions to facilitate this operation.) A subroutine saves space since it occurs only once in the program, though it may be called from many different places in the program. It also facilitates the construction of large programs since subroutines can be formed into libraries for general use. (The same concept appears in high-level languages as the *procedure.)

In the early days of programming, what is now called a subroutine was known as a *closed subroutine*. This was in contrast with the *open subroutine*, which was a piece of code that appeared in several places in a program, and was substituted "in line" by the assembler for each call appearing in the program. The open subroutine was just a convenient shorthand for the programmer: the same facility is now known as a *macro.

subschema of a database. *Another name for user view.*

subscript A means of referring to particular elements in an ordered collection of elements. For example, if R denotes such a collection of names then the *i*th name in the collection may be referenced by R_i (i.e. R subscript i). This printed form is the origin of the term but it is also used when the "subscript" is written on the same line, usually in parentheses or brackets: R(i) or R[i]. *See also* index, array.

subsemigroup A *subset T of a *semigroup S, where T is *closed under the dyadic operation $\circ$ defined on S. Let x be an arbitrary element of S. Then the set consisting of

$$x, x \circ x, x \circ x \circ x, \ldots$$

i.e. all powers of x, is a subsemigroup of S.

subsequence 1. A *function whose domain is a subset of the positive integers and hence whose image set can be listed:

$$s_{i1}, s_{i2}, \ldots s_{im}$$
where $i1 < i2 < \ldots < im$

2. The listing of the image set of a subsequence. Hence a subsequence of a string $a_1 a_2 \ldots a_n$ is any listing of the form

$$a_{i1}, a_{i2}, \ldots a_{im}$$
where $1 \leq i1 < i2 \ldots < im \leq n$

See also sequence.

subset of a *set S. A set T whose members are all members of S; this is usually expressed as $T \subseteq S$. A subset T is a *proper subset* of S if there is some element in S that is not in T; this is expressed as $T \subset S$.

substitution 1. A particular kind of mapping on *formal languages. Let Σ_1 and Σ_2 be alphabets. For each symbol a in Σ_1 let $s(a)$ be a Σ_2-language. The function s is a substitution. A *homomorphism occurs where each $s(a)$ is a single word. s is Λ-*free* if no $s(a)$ contains the empty word.

The function s can be extended to map Σ_1-words to Σ_2-languages:

$$s(a_1 \ldots a_n) = s(a_1) \ldots s(a_n)$$

i.e. the *concatenation of the languages $s(a_1), \ldots, s(a_n)$. s can then be further extended to map Σ_1-languages to Σ_2-languages:

$$s(L) = \{s(w) \mid w \in L\}$$

where $s(L)$ is called the *substitution image* of L under s.

2. *See* substitution cipher.

substitution cipher A *cipher, or a component of a more complicated cipher, that involves the symbol at each place in the *plaintext being (effectively) looked up in a table, and replaced by the substitute symbol found there. Since a cipher must be invertible (for *decryption), the table must contain a *permutation of the alphabet (*compare* transposition cipher).

The size of the table can be increased (to strengthen the cipher) by using an *extension of the plaintext source. If the table remains constant for the entire plaintext, the substitution is *monalphabetic*; if it changes with each advance of one symbol position in the plaintext, possibly repeating a fixed schedule, it is *polyalphabetic*.

substring of a string of symbols, $a_1 a_2 \ldots a_n$. Any string of symbols of the form

$$a_i a_{i+1} \ldots a_j$$
where $1 \leq i \leq j \leq n$

The *empty string is regarded as a substring of any string.

substring identifier Let $\alpha = a_1 a_2 \ldots a_n$ denote a string in Σ^* and let $\# \notin \Sigma$. The substring identifier for position i in $\alpha\#$ is the shortest substring in $\alpha\#$ starting at position i that identifies position i uniquely. The existence of such a substring is guaranteed since

$$a_i a_{i+1} \cdots a_n \#$$

will always identify position i uniquely. *See also* position tree.

subsurface scattering *Diffuse reflection caused by light entering a material, being absorbed, scattered, and eventually exiting the material.

minuend	0	0	1	1
subtrahend	0	1	0	1
difference	0	1	1	0
borrow	0	1	0	0

Modulo-two subtraction

subtractor An electronic *logic circuit for calculating the difference between two binary numbers, the minuend and the number to be subtracted, the subtrahend (*see* table). A *full subtractor* performs this calculation with three inputs: minuend bit, subtrahend bit, and borrow bit. It produces two outputs: the difference and the borrow. Full subtractors thus allow for the inclusion of borrows generated by previous stages of subtraction when forming their output signals, and can be cascaded to form n-bit subtractors. Alternatively the subtract operation can be performed using two *half subtractors*, which are simpler since they contain only two inputs and produce two outputs.

Neither of these devices is commonly encountered since modulo-two subtraction is more conveniently accomplished using two's complement arithmetic and binary *adders.

subtree *See* tree.

subtype A *subset of a *data type, obtained by constraining the set of possible values of the data type. The same operations can be applied to subtype as to type.

successive approximation *Another name for* iteration.

successive over-relaxation *See* iterative methods.

successor function 1. The *function $SUCC$ that occurs in programming languages such as Ada or Pascal and produces the next element of an enumeration type. Typically

$SUCC(4)$ produces 5

$SUCC(`A`)$ produces `B`

2. The *function

$$S : N \rightarrow N$$

for which $S(n) = n + 1$

where N is the nonnegative integers. S plays a crucial role in recursive function theory, particularly in the definition of *primitive recursive functions.

suffix of a string α. Any string β where α is the *concatenation $\gamma\beta$ for some string γ. *Compare* prefix.

suffix notation *Another name for* reverse Polish notation.

suite 1. A set of programs or modules that is designed as a whole to meet some specified overall requirement, each program or module meeting some part of that requirement. **2.** A collection of PC applications (spreadsheet, word processor, database, etc.) that are designed to work together.

sumcheck *See* checksum.

sum of products expression (SOP expression) A *Boolean function expressed as a sum of product terms, i.e. as an OR of AND terms containing uncomplemented or complemented variables. An example is

$$f = (x \wedge y') \vee (x' \wedge z)$$

The function is also realizable as the NAND of a group of NAND terms. *See also* standard sum of products, product of sums expression.

sum term A sum (OR) of Boolean variables, uncomplemented or complemented. *See also* product of sums expression.

Sun Microsystems Inc. A US manufacturer of high-performance *workstations. It is the largest manufacturer of workstations in the world in terms of revenue (1993 figures) and number 18 in the list of the world's top IT companies in terms of revenue. Sun workstations are most commonly found in *CAD and *CASE applications but they have increasingly started to penetrate more commercial markets.

SuperCalc *Trademark* A *spreadsheet program for PCs and compatibles from Computer Associates.

supercomputer A class of very powerful computers that have extremely fast processors, currently capable (1995) of performing 10–30 Gflops, i.e. 10–30 billion floating-point operations per second (*see* flops); most are now multiprocessor systems (*see also* SMP, MPP). Large main-memory capacity – tens or hundreds of thousands of words – and long word lengths – typically 64 bits – are the other main characteristics. Supercomputers are used, for example, in meteorology, engineering, nuclear physics, and astronomy. Several hundred are in operation worldwide at present. Principal manufacturers are *Cray Research and NEC, Fujitsu, and Hitachi of Japan.

superconducting memory A memory made up of components whose function depends on the phenomenon of superconductivity. *See also* Josephson technology.

superconducting technology A logic construction technique depending on the phenomenon of superconductivity. *See also* Josephson technology.

superconductivity The physical phenomenon that causes some materials to have zero electric resistance when held at very low temperatures. Superconductivity is of interest to computer engineers since it points to the possibility of great computing power with little or no heat generation. This is especially so since the recent demonstration of superconductivity in certain complex metallic oxides at relatively high temperatures.

superhighway *See* information superhighway.

SuperJANET The high-speed successor to the UK Joint Academic Network (*JANET). SuperJANET is intended to provide access at speeds of at least 2 Mbps to all UK Universities and Research Council sites, and at speeds at the limit of what is practically available at any time for the larger sites.

supermini A medium-sized multiuser computer whose systems and architecture have evolved from the minicomputers of a few years ago. A supermini may have as much or more power than a small *mainframe, but it has a different ancestry.

super-Nyquist sampling *See* Nyquist's criterion.

supersampling The *sampling of an image at a higher resolution than the display followed by an averaging down to the true pixel level. The averaged values contain more information about the true image than if the sampling had been performed at display resolution. This technique is used to reduce *aliasing effects in images.

superscalar An architectural approach for high-performance computation where a number of instructions are simultaneously accessed from memory and, where *data dependency constraints allow, are issued for simultaneous execution by multiple independent pipelines, thus giving an enhanced instruction execution rate. RISC processors employing 2- and 4-issue superscalar pipelines are currently available (1995). Optimized compilation is needed to minimize data dependencies between consecutive instructions in order to maximize multiple-issue opportunities and hence performance. *See also* VLIW.

supertwisted nematic display *See* LCD.

SuperVGA *See* SVGA.

supervisor (monitor; executive) The permanently resident part of a large operating system, dealing most directly with the physical components of the system as distinct from the virtual resources handled by most *processes. Within the supervisor different parts handle different physical components (*see* kernel, memory management, I/O supervisor).

The term has also been used as another name for the entire operating system.

supervisor call (SVC) *See* interrupt.

supervisor state (executive state) *See* execution states.

support programs Programs that do not make a direct contribution to performing the primary function of a computer system but rather serve to assist in the operation of the system. A typical example is a program that serves to archive the contents of a filing system. *See also* software tool.

suppress To prevent the output or sensing of selected data or signals. *See also* zero suppression.

surface-accessibility shading The *rendering of a surface that takes account of such effects as dust collecting, oxidation, polishing, etc., which depend on how accessible parts of the surface are.

surface-color map The combination of illumination with texture map to give the color of points on a surface.

surface-mount technology A form of IC (*integrated circuit) packaging where the pins are bent so that they lie in approximately the same plane as the bottom of the IC package. This means that the pins lie along the surface of PCB tracks leading up to the IC and this removes the need to drill holes in the PCB to accept the pins, as is necessary in other forms of packaging. The pins are usually spaced more closely together and along all edges in surface-mount devices, enabling a more compact PCB layout.

surface patch *See* patch.

surface reconstruction The combining of multiple views of an object to give a better definition of an object than provided by any one view.

surface reflection The reflection of an environment by an object.

surface subdivision Division of patched surfaces into smaller *patches usually in order to make enough shape freedom available to meet given fairness constraints.

surfing *Informal* Dipping into the information available from the services on a large network, especially the Internet, with no definite objective in mind. Surfing is closely allied to *browsing.

surjection (onto function) A *function whose *range and codomain coincide. If

$$f : X \to Y$$

is a surjection then for each y in the codomain Y there is some x in X with the property that

$$y = f(x)$$

A function that is not surjective is sometimes said to be *into*.

suspended process *See* process descriptor.

Sutherland–Hodgman clipping algorithm A *polygon-clipping algorithm in which the fundamental idea is to clip the original polygon and each resulting intermediate polygon against each edge of the clipping region in succession. The algorithm allows any planar or nonplanar polygon to be clipped to a convex clipping volume.

SVC *Abbrev. for* supervisor call. *See* interrupt.

SVGA (SuperVGA) A color *graphics adapter that is the upgrade of the original 800×600 pixel *VGA (video graphics array) standard. It generates 1024×768 or 1280×1024 pixels with 16 or 256 colors. It is designed so that a graceful degradation to VGA is possible.

swapping A method of handling main memory by writing information to backing store during periods when it is not in use, and reading it back when required. *See also* paging, roll-in roll-out, memory hierarchy.

sweeping Moving a geometric element along a given path so as to form a new element as its locus; for example, a circle sweeping along a straight line creates a cylinder. The dimensionality of the resulting sweep surface is often higher than that of the generator, even though they are both embedded in the same space.

sweep surface A surface defined by *sweeping.

SWIFT *See* electronic funds transfer system.

swipe reader *Informal term for* slot reader. *See* card reader.

switch 1. Usually an electronic or electromechanical device that is used to connect or disconnect an electric current to an electric circuit (*see also* optical switch). An electronic switch can present either an effective open circuit or closed circuit depending on the status of an applied "select" signal. These switches are often used to provide isolation between low- and high-voltage switching circuits or to allow remote control of electric systems.

The word is also used as a verb, followed by a suitable preposition.

2. A type of branch with a choice of many places to which control may be passed. The destination of the branch is determined by the value of some variable. Most high-level languages have a means of doing this: Algol 60 has switch variables, Fortran has computed GOTOs, and several other languages, such as C, Pascal, and Ada, have case statements.

3. To undergo or cause to undergo *switching.

switched multimegabit data service *See* SMDS.

switching Any of various communication techniques that provide point to point transmission between dynamically changing data sources and sinks. *See also* packet switching, message switching, circuit switching.

switching algebra A term that is virtually synonymous with *Boolean algebra when applied to the analysis and synthesis of *logic (switching) circuits.

switching circuit *Another (largely obsolete) name for* logic circuit. Before the availability of low-cost electronic components, logic circuits were commonly implemented using relays and other switching devices. An AND function was implemented using a series connection of two switches; an OR function used a parallel combination of two switches.

switching speed (toggling speed) A measure of the rate at which a given electronic logic device is capable of changing the logic state of its output in response to changes at its input. It is a function of the delay encountered within the device, which in turn is a function of the device technology.

switching theory The theory of and manipulative methods for *switching algebra. It includes *Boolean-algebra and *state-table or *state-diagram methods of description, as well as *minimization methods.

switching waveform A waveform or signal that is capable of exhibiting one of two possible distinct states, often corresponding to logic 1 and logic 0, and that may be used to change the status of an active switching element between two distinct conditions such as on and off or open and closed.

SYBASE *Trademark. See* database management system.

Sylvester matrices *See* Hadamard matrices.

symbol 1. One of a set of distinct elements in the alphabet of a *formal language. *See* signature, word.

2. An *identifier in a program.

symbolic addressing An addressing scheme whereby reference to an address is made by some convenient symbol that (preferably) has some relationship to the meaning of the data expected to be located at that address. It serves as an aid to the programmer. The symbolic address is replaced by some form of computable/computed address during the operation of an assembler or compiler.

symbolic execution A form of semantic analysis/proof of a program in which symbols are used as input variables. The program is viewed as having an input state determined by the input data and the initial state of the program. For each line of the program a test is made to see if the state has changed. Each state change is recorded. A logical path through the program is converted into an ordered set of state changes. The final state for each path should be an output state or program termination. The program is proved correct if each sequence of inputs generates only the required output states.

The technique has been automated, but the size of program that can be handled is limited and manual assistance may be needed to handle loops correctly and efficiently. *See also* static analysis, program correctness proof.

symbolic logic The treatment of *formal logic involving the setting up of a formalized language. The *propositional calculus and *predicate calculus are two of the more common areas of interest.

symbol manipulation The manipulation of characters rather than numbers, as occurs in symbolic mathematics, text preparation, and finite-state automata simulation.

symbol table A list, kept by a language *translator, of *identifiers in the source program and their properties. Before the translator processes any of the source program, the symbol table contains a list of predeclared identifiers; for example, the value of π or the largest integer that a system can hold might be associated with particular names by the translator. As translation proceeds, the translator will insert and remove symbols from the table as necessary. The properties of entries in the symbol table vary with both language and implementation.

symmetric difference *See* set difference.

symmetric function A *function $f(x_1, x_2, \ldots x_n)$ whose value is unaltered by any *permutation of its n variables. Such functions arise repeatedly in *switching theory.

symmetric group *See* permutation group.

symmetric list *Another name for* doubly linked list.

symmetric matrix A square matrix A such that $a_{ij} = a_{ji}$ for all a_{ij} in A. Thus a symmetric matrix is equal to its *transpose.

symmetric order traversal (inorder traversal) A tour of the nodes of a binary tree obtained by using the following recursive algorithm: visit in symmetric order the left subtree of the root (if it exists); visit the root of the tree; visit in symmetric order the right subtree of the root (if it exists). *Compare* postorder traversal, preorder traversal.

symmetric relation A *relation R defined on a set S and having the property that

whenever $x R y$

then $y R x$

where x and y are arbitrary elements of S. The relation "is equal to" defined on the integers is symmetric. *See also* antisymmetric relation, asymmetric relation.

symmetry group A *group consisting of all those *functions that transform a rigid plane figure into itself; the *dyadic operation on the elements of the group is that of *composition of functions. The larger and more complex a symmetry group the greater the symmetry associated with the underlying geometric figure.

synchronization A relationship between *processes such that one process cannot proceed beyond a particular point until another

process has reached a particular point. For example, when one process is writing data in a buffer to be read by another process, the two processes must be synchronized so that the reading process does not attempt to read the buffer beyond the point at which the writing process has written data in the buffer. Synchronization can be achieved by using a *semaphore.

synchronizer A storage device with a wide range of operating speeds that is used in an intermediate capacity when transferring data between devices that cannot operate at the same rate.

synchronous Involving or requiring a form of computer control operation in which sequential events take place at fixed times, usually determined by a *clock signal of fixed frequency. This requires predetermination of the length of time required by each class/set of events; it requires no acknowledgment that preceding events have been completed. *Compare* asynchronous.

synchronous bus A bus used to interconnect devices that comprise a computer system where the timing of transactions between devices is under the control of a synchronizing clock signal. A device connected to a synchronous bus must guarantee to respond to a command within a period set by the frequency of the clock signal or a transmission error will occur. Such buses are usually employed in closely controlled processor backplane environments where device characteristics and interdevice signal delays are known.

synchronous circuit An electronic logic circuit in which logic operations are performed under the control of and hence in synchronism with an externally generated clock signal.

synchronous concurrent algorithm (SCA) An algorithm that consists of a network of processors computing and communicating in parallel and synchronized by means of a global clock, or possibly a family of clocks. The algorithm operates continually in discrete time, processing infinite *streams of input data; its behavior can be represented by a *stream transformer. SCAs are *deterministic, and can be considered as special types of timed deterministic *dataflow algorithms. Hardware systems, such as systolic arrays or microprocessors, are made from SCAs. Other examples of SCAs include certain neural networks, cellular automata, spatially extended discrete-time dynamical systems, and finite-element algorithms. Through the concept of an SCA, a wide variety of deterministic parallel algorithms can be given a common mathematical theory and programming methodology. The theory is based on the use of *equational specifications and *abstract computability theory, and the programming tools on imperative languages using *concurrent assignments.

synchronous counter A *counter consisting of an interconnected series of *flip-flops in which all the flip-flop outputs change state at the same instant, normally on application of a pulse at the counter input. These counters have advantages in speed over asynchronous *ripple counters, in which the output must propagate along the chain of flip-flops after the application of a pulse at the count input. *See also* cascadable counter, shift counter.

synchronous digital hierarchy *See* SDH.

synchronous optical network *See* SONET.

synchronous TDM *See* time division multiplexing.

synchronous transmission A method of data transmission in which the time interval between individual bits is accurately determined by some form of *clock signal. The clock signal may either be generated locally at both the transmitter and the receiver, with a separate channel that provides a means of maintaining accurate synchronization between the two clocks, or the actual data signal may be encoded by the transmitter in such a way that a clock signal can be recovered from it at the receiver. Synchronous transmission has the advantage that it is not necessary to insert start and stop indications between successive bytes, and is normally used for higher data rates. *See also* asynchronous transmission.

syndrome In coding theory, a symbol vector (ordered set of symbols) generated at an intermediate stage of the decoding algorithm for an *error-correcting code. The syndrome depends only on the error pattern and not on the transmitted codeword. A further stage of the decoding algorithm will use the syndrome to correct the errors in the received message. The details of how the syndrome is found and how it is used, and indeed whether all the errors can be corrected, will depend on the particular error-correcting code that is being employed. If no errors occurred, the syndrome will usually be the *zero word.

syntactic error *See* syntax error.

syntactic monoid of a formal language L. The *semigroup of the *minimal machine for L.

syntax (syntax rules) The rules defining the legal sequences of symbolic elements in a language. The syntax rules define the form of the various constructs in the language, but say nothing about the meaning of these constructs. Examples of constructs are: expressions, procedures, and programs (in the case of programming languages) and terms, well-formed formulas, and sentences (in the case of logical languages). *See also* parsing, BNF, extended BNF.

syntax analysis *Another name for* parsing.

syntax analyzer (parser) *See* parsing.

syntax diagram A diagrammatic representation of the *syntax rules of a programming language; a pictorial equivalent of *BNF.

syntax error A programming error in which the grammatical rules of the language are broken. Syntax errors can be detected by the compiler, unlike *semantic errors, which do not become apparent until run-time. *See also* error diagnostics.

syntax tree *Another name for* parse tree.

synthetic camera A type of *rendering technique that seeks to replicate the characteristics – especially the distortions (e.g. out of focus, aberration) – of a real camera or the human eye, rather than the perfectly sharp achromatic pictures usually produced by computer graphics.

system Anything we choose to regard (a) as a whole and (b) as comprising a set of related components. More formally a system $S =$

(C, R), where C is the set of its components and R is the set of relationships (or interfaces) that combine them into a coherent whole. In computing the word is freely used to refer to all kinds of combinations of hardware, software, data and other information, procedures, and human activities. An airline reservation system, for instance, comprises all those things, distributed and connected worldwide. At the other end of the spectrum, an *operating system just comprises software components. *See also* systems engineering, engineering of computer-based systems.

system accounting Recording the use of system *resources. On a *multiprogramming system the apportioning of the use of system resources among the active *processes can only be done by the system. For resources such as processors, which are allocated in their entirety to an individual process for a large number of short intervals of time, the appropriate measure is found by recording the real time at the start and finish of each interval to give the length of each interval; accumulating these through the life of the process yields the processor time.

For resources such as memory, in which a number of subunits is allocated to the process (which will subsequently return them to the *resource allocation mechanism), the usually accepted measure is to determine the elapsed time for which the subunits are allocated to the process and to charge a "rent" for each subunit. For nonreusable resources the normal practice is to charge on a unit-cost basis for the amounts used.

In a bureau, which relies for its revenue on real money charges made to clients, the implementation of the accounting system is a nontrivial problem, especially in regard to decisions concerning spoilt work, or delays experienced by one client because of other clients' activities.

systematic code An (n, k) *block code in which every codeword can be separated into k *information symbols* and $(n - k)$ *check symbols*. The information symbols are identical with those of the source message before encoding. Thus the process of encoding a systematic code involves the insertion of $(n - k)$ check symbols into (i.e. among, before, or, most usually, after) the information symbols. The insertion positions must be the same for all the codewords in the code. Every *linear code can be arranged to be systematic.

system box *See* desktop.

system building tools A suite of programs and utilities designed to simplify the development and maintenance of a large system. Most system building tools allow the user to specify the components that need to be brought together to generate a version of the system, and maintain information that shows how the content of any one component relies on other components. The tools also keep track of any alteration to any components. If, following alterations to system components, a new version of the system is generated, the tools will ensure that the latest version of each component is used and that the newly generated version is internally consistent.

system bus Any *bus used to connect together system components such as processors, memory systems, disk controllers, etc. *See also* VME bus.

system crash *See* crash.

system definition The document(s) giving the most authoritative available description of some existing or envisaged system. The term is usually used as a synonym for *system requirements specification.

system design The activity of proceeding from an identified set of requirements for a system to a design that meets those requirements. A distinction is sometimes drawn between *high-level* or *architectural design*, which is concerned with the main components of the system and their roles and interrelationships, and *detailed design*, which is concerned with the internal structure and operation of individual components. The term system design is sometimes used to cover just the high-level design activity. *See also* system requirements specification, review.

system development *See* system life cycle.

system dictionary *See* data dictionary.

system generation The construction of a

version of an operating system. Any large system is almost invariably constructed from a number of separate modules of code, each dealing with specific aspects of the system or with specific types of device. Where it is known that a facility or device will not be supported, it is possible to omit the corresponding modules and to generate a version of the system that contains only modules that are known to be required. This is achieved during system generation.

systemic grammar A *grammar in which a set of categories and levels are used to account for the formal aspects of language. The three levels are FORM (grammar and lexis), SUBSTANCE (phonic and graphic material), and CONTENT (semantics). The four fundamental categories are UNIT (e.g. a sentence), STRUCTURE (the syntagmatic arrangement of patterns), CLASS, and SYSTEM.

system life cycle The phases of development through which a computer-based system passes. Life cycle phases have been defined in very many different ways and in varying degrees of detail. Most definitions, however, recognize broad phases such as initial conception, requirements definition, outline design, detailed design, programming, testing, implementation, maintenance, and modification. Some include additional activities such as manual procedures design and staff training.

Most life cycle definitions arose as a result of analysis of the tasks of system development, with the objective of making those tasks more amenable to traditional techniques of management planning and control. In some cases, elaborate planning and control systems have been designed on the basis of the life-cycle analysis, with highly formalized documentation and clearly defined managerial decision points.

system requirements specification A detailed statement of the effects that a system is required to achieve. A good specification gives a complete statement of what the system is to do, without making any commitment as to how the system is to do it: it constrains only the externally observable behavior and omits any design or implementation bias.

A system requirements specification is normally produced in response to a *user requirements specification or other *expression of requirements, and is then used as the basis for *system design. The system requirements specification typically differs from the expression of requirements in both scope and precision: the latter may cover both the envisaged system and the environment in which it will operate, but may leave many broad concepts unrefined. Traditionally, system requirements specifications took the form of natural-language documents. However, both the need for precision and problems with the increasing size of specification documents have led to the development of more formal notations. These are capable of being mathematically manipulated so as to show that the system as designed and implemented actually meets the specification. This may be especially important in connection with *safety-critical systems.

A system requirements specification may also be used in contract negotiations during and after the purchase of the system, which must meet the specifications that the contractor has agreed to accept. This is especially important where the purchaser sets out the requirements in terms of a range of functions and performance levels that the contractor commits to supplying and meeting, rather than as an inventory of components (hardware and software) that the contractor undertakes to supply.

systems analysis The analysis of the role of a proposed system and the identification of a set of requirements that the system should meet, and thus the starting point for *system design. The term is most commonly used in the context of commercial programming, where those involved in software development are often classed as either systems analysts or programmers. The systems analysts are responsible for identifying a set of requirements (i.e. systems analysis) and producing a design. The design is then passed to the programmers, who are responsible for actual implementation of the system.

system security An (operating) system is responsible for controlling access to system resources, which will include sensitive data. The system must therefore include a certain amount of protection for such data, and must in turn control access to those parts of the system that administer this protection. System security is concerned with all aspects of these arrangements.

systems engineering A form of engineering that addresses systems at a high level of abstraction prior to determining the particular engineering disciplines that will be appropriate in satisfying the system's requirements. This is a very wide topic, ranging much wider than computer-based systems; it includes, for example, the study of social systems, economic systems, and ecological systems. *See also* engineering of computer-based systems.

systems house A term used rather loosely to describe a company that designs and produces complete bespoke systems, containing both hardware and software. While some of the components will be bought in, the use of the term implies that the company has a serious capability in both hardware and software.

systems integrator A term that is similar to *systems house but implies less emphasis on bespoke systems and more emphasis on putting together existing components.

system software *See* systems software.

system specification *See* system requirements specification.

systems programmer A person who specializes in systems programming and low-level *software, such as *operating systems, *compilers, *communication systems, and *database management systems. *Compare* applications programmer.

systems programming Work carried out by *systems programmers, i.e. the production of systems software.

systems software (system software) The totality of software required to produce a system acceptable to end users. *See also* systems programming.

systems theory The study of *systems in themselves, usually to find characteristics common to all systems or to classes of systems. Systems theorists may be most concerned with the development of theory for its own sake (most often called *general systems theory*), or they may be more concerned with the applications of systems ideas within particular disciplines or problem areas in order to solve problems that are not amenable to traditional "reductionist" approaches. Systems theory has been called the study of organized complexity.

There have been a number of attempts to categorize systems. Perhaps the simplest and most useful is by P. Checkland, who proposes four categories: natural systems, designed physical systems, designed abstract systems, and human activity systems. He also proposes four concepts that are central to systems thinking:

"the notion of whole entities which have properties as entities (emergent properties ...); the idea that the entities are themselves parts of larger similar entities, while possibly containing smaller similar entities within themselves (hierarchy ...); the idea that such entities are characterized by processes which maintain the entity and its activity in being (control ...); and the idea that, whatever other processes are necessary in the entity, there will certainly be processes in which information is communicated from one part to another, at the very minimum this being entailed in the idea 'control'."

system tables The data that collectively defines the status of all *resources and all *processes within the system. Although such data may be represented as tables, it may be more conveniently represented internally as linked lists with pointers back to associated semaphore variables in some cases.

system testing *See* testing.

System V A version of *UNIX.

systolic array An extension of the *pipelining approach to processor design where a number of processing elements, usually arranged as a one- or two-dimensional array, form a compound processing unit capable of high throughput. The configuration may be programmable to be optimal for a specific computing requirement and available memory or I/O bandwidth. Such arrays communicate with memory or I/O only at their boundaries. Data is "pulsed" from the memory into processor(s) at an array boundary and then pulses through the array, undergoing processing by each element, until it exits at another boundary and is returned to memory. Each element of the array can contribute to the overall processing required and hence a high data throughput is achievable. The name derives from the systolic (pumping) action of the heart.

T

T 1. *Symbol for* tera-.
2. A dialect of LISP, similar to *SCHEME.

tab *Short for* tabulate, i.e. to lay out data, *and for* tabulation character, a control character used when laying out data to control the movement of a print or display mechanism. Most keyboards have a tab key, which may initiate the tabulation function or may be used for other control purposes.

table A collection of *records. Each record may store information associated with a key by which specific records are found, or the records may be arranged in an *array so that the index is the key. In commercial applications the word table is often used as a synonym for matrix or array.

table-driven algorithm An algorithm that uses *table lookup.

table lookup (TLU) A fast method of transforming one set of data values into another. The target data are stored in the form of a *table. In order to perform the transformation, a source datum is used to index into or search the table of target data. The resulting target datum is the result of the table lookup. *See also* hashing.

tablet *Short for* data tablet.

tabular documentation A method to assist with the *documentation of computing systems using tables. For millennia tables have

been used to store and display large quantities of information. It is possible to develop the conception and theory of tables beyond the usual idea of a *table with the needs of displaying formal information about software and hardware.

tag 1. To mark in some distinctive fashion any node in a data structure that has been traversed. Using this technique precautions can be taken against revisiting nodes, e.g. in a circular list.
2. *Short for* tag field. A field that is used to discriminate between variants of the same type.

tagged architecture A computer architecture in which extra data bits are attached to each word to denote the *data type, the function of the word, or both. Tagged architecture can represent a powerful form of *memory protection, and has formed a foundation for certain secure computer systems based on *hardware security.

tagged image file format *See* TIFF.

tail of a list. **1.** The last item in a *list.
2. The list remaining when the *head has been removed.

tape Either *magnetic tape or *optical tape; *paper tape is now obsolete.

tape backup system (TBS) The software, tape drives, and media that form a system to back up information held usually on disks. Backups are performed according to a number of more or less complex regular schemes to ensure maximum possibility of restoration in case of a breakdown of the primary data store. *See also* dump.

tape-bounded Turing machine *See* multitape Turing machine.

tape cartridge *Short for* magnetic tape cartridge (generally).

tape deck *Another name for* tape transport. *See* magnetic tape.

tape drive *Another name for* tape transport. *See* magnetic tape.

tape format The format of information recorded on magnetic tape, allowing a system to recognize, control, and verify the data. Tape format is defined at two levels.

The *high-level format* defines the data as it is presented to the magnetic tape subsystem by the host computer. This data stream consists of user data and *labels, divided into sections (usually corresponding to files) by *tape marks. The tape subsystem need not distinguish between user data and labels, but it recognizes tape marks. The data at this level may be divided into *blocks, usually of equal length – typically a few kilobytes. This is done for physical convenience and has no logical significance. In some tape subsystems the data is continuous at this level, and division into blocks is done within the subsystem.

The *low-level format* defines what is actually recorded, as a pattern of reversals of magnetism, on the tape. The subsystem divides the data into blocks if this is not already done, and adds its own control information to each block and also at each end of the tape and each file mark. All formats include a degree of redundancy so that errors can be detected, and usually corrected, without reference to the host computer. In many formats an *interblock gap* (an area with no reversals of magnetization, typically half an inch long) is inserted between blocks so that the tape can, if necessary, be stopped and restarted between one block and the next (*but see* streaming). Where different formats are permitted on the same type of reel or cartridge, each format may include an *identity burst* or other means at the beginning of the tape to allow the subsystem to recognize the format.

Open-reel tape has been widely used for data interchange, so there are only a few accepted formats; all use ½ inch tape with nine tracks recorded in parallel. *NRZ* (*nonreturn to zero*) has a density of 800 bits per inch (bpi) which, with typical block lengths, allows about 20 megabytes of user data on a standard 2400 foot tape; it was introduced in the 1950s and is now virtually obsolete. *PE* (*phase encoded*), introduced in the 1960s, doubles this density and capacity. *GCR* (*group code recording*), introduced in the 1970s, uses a format in which data is recoded to give more powerful error correction, and packs 6250 data bits to the inch or typically 140 megabytes on a 2400 foot tape. All these formats are covered by ISO standards.

*Cartridge tape was introduced after open-reel tape; it is used more for backup than for interchange, so standards are less essential. There is therefore a much wider range of formats. Some are defined as ISO standards, but others remain proprietary. Capacities vary from a few megabytes to tens of gigabytes per cartridge.

tape header A *header label written at the beginning of a volume of magnetic tape. *See also* label.

tape label *See* label.

tape library 1. An area in which reels of magnetic tape are stored when not actually in use on a tape transport. Each reel is normally stored in a protective case and is visibly labeled, in addition to any *label that may be recorded on the tape.
2. An *automated tape library.

tape mark A signal recorded on magnetic tape that does not represent data but is used to delimit sections of data – usually individual files, hence the alternative term *file mark*. The tape mark is written at the direction of the host system but its form is determined by the magnetic tape subsystem in accordance with the standard for the relevant *tape format. Most formats allow the tape mark to be recorded as a separate *block, but in formats that provide for the insertion of block headers by the subsystem it is usual for the tape mark to take the form of a flag in one of these headers.

If the subsystem encounters a tape mark during a read operation, the host system is informed. In most magnetic tape subsystems there is a *skip to tape mark* (or *tape-mark search*) command that causes the tape to be run to the next tape mark without transferring any data to the host; sometimes there is also a *multiple-skip* command containing a parameter *n*, which causes the tape to skip to the *n*th tape mark. Skip operations are sometimes performed at a higher speed than that used for reading.

It is conventional to write a double tape mark after the last file in a volume.

tape marker *See* BOT marker, EOT marker.

tape punch, tape reader *See* paper tape I/O.

tape transport (tape drive; (magnetic) tape unit; tape deck) A peripheral device that moves magnetic tape past sensing and recording heads. *See* magnetic tape.

tape unit *Another name for* tape transport. *See* magnetic tape.

Targa (TGA) An uncompressed *image file format for 24 bit color images, defined by Truevision Inc., that can easily be decoded. It has a random-access version. Color is specified by three independent color tables for red, green, and blue.

target alphabet *See* code.

target computer *See* host computer.

task 1. *Another name for* process.
2. *Another name for* job.
When each job consists of only one process, the above difference is not significant. The concurrent execution of a number of tasks is referred to as *multitasking. See also* parallel processing.

tautology A law of logic, in the form of a proposition, that describes a universal truth; no matter what values are assigned to the variables in the proposition the result is always true. An example from the *propositional calculus is

$$(P \vee Q)' = P' \wedge Q'$$

where $\vee$ and $\wedge$ are the *or* and *and* operators and P' is the negation of P. In the *truth table for a tautology the final result column contains only the value true. If the final column contains only the value false, then a *contradiction* has been identified.

TB (or Tb) *Symbols for* terabyte. *See* tera-, byte.

TBS *Abbrev. for* tape backup system.

Tbyte *Abbrev. for* terabyte. *See* tera-, byte.

Tcl *Abbrev. for* Tool command language. An *extensible *scripting language that can be embedded in applications that are written in C.

TCO Central Organization of Salaried Employees in Sweden, a trades union group that presses the authorities for tighter standards of safety, health, and ergonomics to be applied to the office environment.

TCP *See* TCP/IP.

TCP/IP *Trademark; abbrev. for* Transmission Control Protocol/Internet Protocol. The obligatory standard to be used by any system connecting to the *Internet. The two *protocols were originally developed on the DARPA net. They were devised to optimize the performance of networks that are based on unreliable data-transmission systems operating at relatively low data rates.

The Internet Protocol, IP, is the lower of the two protocols. It provides a *connectionless *datagram service, and a managed address structure for data transmission. An IP address can take one of four forms, class A to class D, which always occupy a total of 32 bits (see table): the first bits define the class of the address; the next group of bits defines the identity of the subnetwork attached to the Internet; the final group defines the address of the host system within the subnetwork. Class A addresses are for large subnetworks with many hosts, and classes B and C are for progressively smaller networks with progressively fewer hosts; class D addresses are used for *multicasting. IP allows a long datagram to be fragmented into numbered *packets, which can then be transmitted and reassembled in their correct sequence at the destination system. It is intended to be used in conjunction with the Transmission Control Protocol, TCP.

class	class definition	network identity	host address
A	bit 31 = 0	7 bits	24 bits
B	bits 31–30 = 10	14 bits	16 bits
C	bits 31–29 = 110	21 bits	8 bits
D	bits 31–28 = 1110	28 bits	not used

Summary of Internet address classes

TCP provides error-free delivery of arbitrarily long messages, known as *segments*, with the data being released to the host system in the same order as the original transmission. It achieves this by a "sliding window" mechanism. As data are transmitted, they are accompanied by a *checksum; at the receiving end the checksum is verified and an acknowledgment is returned to the transmitter, which indicates the position of the last data to be successfully received. The transmitter will not send data beyond a certain point, determined by the size of the window, i.e. the gap between the last data to be sent and the last data for which an acknowledgment has been received. If the checksum fails at any point, the transmitter will retransmit data from the point immediately following the latest acknowledgment of correct receipt.

t distribution *See* Student's t distribution.

TDM *Abbrev. for* time division multiplexing.

TDR *Abbrev. for* time domain reflectometer.

TDS *Abbrev. for* tabular data stream. A data format *protocol that refers to messages between an *SQL client and an SQL server.

tear-off menu A *pull-down menu that can be moved from the place where it was first displayed to another part of the screen that may be more convenient, and from where any of its options may be selected at a later time.

TECO A powerful but difficult to use *text editor at one time much favored by systems programmers on Digital Equipment machines.

telebanking Remote access to banking services using computers and telecommunication.

telecommuting *Another name for* teleworking.

teleconferencing A computer-based system enabling users to participate in an activity, such as the management of a complex project, despite being separated in space and/or time. Users will typically be provided with access to a computer terminal, which will allow them to communicate with other members of their team, often but not necessarily simultaneously. Data communication lines are used to transmit the conference information between participants. The system is controlled by a "manager" whose function is to organize the participants and allow them access to the conference and to transmit their inputs to other members.

Some teleconferencing systems enable conference participants to "see" each other (*see* videoconferencing), but other systems use very simple terminals and can only com-

municate using the written word. A conference log will be maintained by the system to keep a record of all activity in the conference, and can be displayed for reference by the participants.

teleprinter *UK term for* teletypewriter.

teleshopping Remote access to shops, stores, etc., using computers and telecommunication.

telesoftware Software distributed from supplier to customer by *downloading.

teletex A means of low- to medium-speed text transmission, from keyboard to printer, over public data networks. Transmission speeds can range from 2.4 Kbps (using *circuit switching) to 48 Kbps (using *packet switching), as against 50 bps for telex. It permits a more extensive character set than telex, and permits line and paragraph formatting as in normal correspondence. Teletex standards are the responsibility of CCITT. Teletex was expected to replace telex by about 1990 but has so far had limited market acceptance; its future is in some doubt because of the rapid spread of fax.

teletext A system for one-way broadcast transmission of information, primarily in text form but with primitive graphics capability, using spare television channel capacity and adapted domestic TV receivers. On a channel offering teletext, a number of "pages" of information (up to about 100) are transmitted in a continuous cycle, concurrently with the normal TV signal and leaving it unaffected while the receiver is used for normal viewing. Having selected teletext mode on the control pad, it is then possible to select any page number; when the selected page next arrives in the transmission cycle, it is stored in local memory in the set and displayed indefinitely (until the user selects another page or exits from teletext mode). *Compare* videotex.

teletypewriter (typewriter terminal, teleprinter (*UK*)) An obsolete device similar to an electric typewriter but with a signal interface by means of which it could communicate with a computer: it could receive messages for printing or could send messages generated on its keyboard. Often a paper tape punch and reader were attached or integrated into the unit. Teletypewriters were once extensively used as interactive *terminals (especially the *Teletype* model) but have been superseded by *VDUs.

teleworking (telecommuting) Working (usually with information) remote from the office, using computers and telecommunication.

TELNET *Acronym for* teletype network. The protocol developed for the *ARPANET to allow users on one host computer to connect to the time-sharing resources of another host. The TELNET protocol specifies a standard terminal type, the *network virtual terminal (NVT)*, including its character set (a modified form of ASCII) and standard control sequences for terminal functions such as "move to the next line". Standard control sequences are also defined for host functions such as "interrupt process". It is the responsibility of the programs at each end of the TELNET connection to perform a suitable mapping between the NVT's character set and control functions, and the conventions of the local system. Many of the parameters of the NVT can be modified through option negotiation, in which both ends of the TEL-NET connection must agree to a proposed change before it can take place.

The name TELNET is also used for similar protocols in networks other than the ARPANET.

template A pattern that specifies a structure – i.e. a relationship between parts of a compound data object – from which *instances may be made. The term is a convenient means of differentiating the structure specification from the declaration of individual instances of the structure.

temporal cohesion *See* cohesion.

temporal logic A *modal logic in which the modal operators express notions of time such as "always", "sometimes", "strong next", "weak next", "next-time", "last-time", "interval chop", "since", "until", and "while". The logical study of reasoning about time has provided new insights and practical techniques for handling time in computations.

ten's complement *See* radix complement.

ter *See* CCITT.

tera- (symbol: T) A prefix indicating a multiple of one million million, 10^{12}, as in terahertz and teravolt. When the binary number system is involved in a structure or process (as in semiconductor RAM or ROM), the prefix indicates a multiple of 2^{40}, i.e.

$$1\ 099\ 511\ 627\ 776,$$

as in terabyte or terabit. The context usually clarifies which meaning is intended.

term An expression formed from symbols for functions, constants, and variables. An example is

$$f(a, g(h(b), c, d))$$

Terms are defined recursively as follows: a term is either a variable symbol, a constant symbol, or else has the form $\phi(\tau_1, \ldots, \tau_k)$, where ϕ is a function symbol and each of $\tau_1, \ldots, \tau_k$ is itself a term. The example above thus has the overall form $f(\tau_1, \tau_2)$: in this case $\phi = f$ and $k = 2$. Another constraint is that different occurrences of the same symbol ϕ cannot occur with different values of k, i.e. each ϕ must have a fixed *arity* (number of arguments). Thus

$$f(a, f(h(b), c, d))$$

would not be a term since the first f has arity 2 while the second has arity 3; neither would

$$f(a, g(h(b), c, h)),$$

since the first h has arity 1 while the second has arity 0.

Terms are often built using *signatures. A Σ-*term* is a term in which each constant and function symbol used is in a signature Σ, and has the arity associated with it by Σ and, if Σ is a many-sorted *signature, all the sorts match properly. A Σ-term is also called a *term over signature Σ*. Often a Σ-term is allowed to contain variables (of arity 0) in addition to symbols in Σ. Terms containing variables are called *open terms*; terms containing only symbols of the signature are called *closed* or *ground terms*. Terms can also be viewed as trees (*see* tree language). Terms (whether as expressions or as trees) are important in the construction of virtually all syntactic concepts. Terms as defined here are sometimes called *first-order terms*, to distinguish them from the *higher-order terms* (such as those involved in *lambda calculus). *See also* predicate calculus, initial algebra, equation.

term algebra *See* initial algebra.

terminal 1. A data input and/or output device that is connected to a controlling processor to which it is subservient and usually remote. There are a very wide range of terminal types. The *VDU is frequently used as a terminal by which a user can input queries or instructions and receive instructions. The information may be in the form of text or it may be mainly graphical. Terminals designed for a particular environment and business activity come under a general heading of *application terminals. If the terminal has a built-in capability to store and manipulate data it is classed as an *intelligent terminal; without this capability terminals are classed as dumb.

2. (terminal symbol) *See* grammar.

terminal controller A device capable of controlling the transfer of data, in both directions, between a *server and a number of terminals. In this context terminal usually means a graphics device of rather limited flexibility.

terminal node *Another name for* leaf node.

terminal server A system capable of supporting the data-processing requirements of terminals. In this context terminal usually means a graphics device of rather limited flexibility. *See* server, enterprise server.

terminal symbol *See* grammar.

termination 1. The end of execution of a *process. A process that reaches a successful conclusion terminates normally by issuing a suitable supervisor call to the operating system. *See also* abnormal termination.

2. of an Ethernet. The device attached to the end of an *Ethernet segment that suppresses any reflection from the end of the cable. The terminator is a simple resistor, whose resistance is equal to the characteristic impedance of the cable to which it is attached, standardized as being 50 ohms. The termination totally absorbs any incoming signal, and eliminates reflections back into the segment. *See also* bus terminator.

termination, proof of *See* program correctness proof.

terminator 1. A symbol that marks the end of a statement in a programming language (frequently a semicolon).

2. *Another name for* rogue value.

term language *Another name for* tree language.

term rewriting system (TRS) A formal system for manipulating *terms over a *signature by means of rules. A set R of rules (each a *rewrite rule*) creates an *abstract reduction system $\rightarrow_R$ on the algebra $T(\Sigma, X)$ of all terms over signature Σ and variables X. Usually, the rules are a set E of *equations that determine a reduction system $\rightarrow_E$ using rewrites based on equational logic.

Let E be a set of equations such that, for each $t = t' \in E$, the left-hand side t is not a variable. The pair (Σ, E) is called an *equational TRS*. The equations of E are used in derivations of terms where the reduction $t \rightarrow_E t'$ requires substitutions to be made in some equation $e \in E$ and the left-hand side of e is replaced by the right-hand side of e in t to obtain t'.

The first set of properties of a term rewriting system (Σ, E) is now obtained from the properties of abstract reduction systems. The following are examples.

(1) The term rewriting system (Σ, E) is *complete* if the reduction system $\rightarrow_E$ on $T(\Sigma)$ is Church–Rosser and strongly terminating.

(2) Let $\equiv_E$ be the smallest congruence containing $\rightarrow_E$ and $T(\Sigma, E)$ be the factor algebra $T(\Sigma) \mid \equiv_E$. Then $T(\Sigma, E)$ is the initial algebra of $Alg(\Sigma, E)$. If (Σ, E) is a finite equational TRS specification that is complete, then $T(\Sigma, E)$ is a *computable algebra.

See also orthogonal term rewriting system.

ternary logic *See* multivalued logic.

ternary selector gate (T-gate) A *combinational ternary logic gate that is important as a building block in the synthesis of ternary logic circuits (*see* multivalued logic). A T-gate has four inputs

$$\{a_0, a_1, a_2, s\}$$

and one output $\{t\}$, all of which can take values represented by elements of the set $\{0,1,2\}$. The function of the T-gate is given by $t = a_s$. It thus acts as a ternary selector, the choice from

$$\{a_0, a_1, a_2\}$$

being selected by the value taken by the s input.

ternary threshold gate (S-gate) A *combinational ternary logic gate that is important as a building block in the synthesis of ternary logic circuits (*see* multivalued logic). An S-gate may have any number of inputs $\{a_i\}$ and one output $\{s\}$, all of which can take values represented by elements of the set $\{0,1,2\}$. The function of the S-gate is given by

$$
\left. \begin{array}{l} s = 0 \\ s = 1 \\ s = 2 \end{array} \right\} \text{ iff } \sum_i (a_i - 1) \left\{ \begin{array}{l} < 0 \\ = 0 \\ > 0 \end{array} \right.
$$

The reason for the name S-gate is because the French for threshold is *seuil*. The S-gate should not be confused with the *ternary selector gate (T-gate). More complicated versions of the S-gate have been defined in various ways. *See also* threshold element.

tessellation (tiling) A complete covering of the Euclidean plane by nonoverlapping regions.

test and set A single indivisible instruction that is capable of testing the value of the contents of a register and altering them. The instruction is used to implement more powerful indivisible operations (such as *lock, *unlock, or *semaphore operations) when the process executing the operation is capable of being interrupted and where the servicing of the interrupt may cause another process to be restarted.

test bed Any system whose primary purpose is to provide a framework within which other systems can be tested. Test beds are usually tailored to a specific programming language and implementation technique, and often to a specific application. Typically a test bed provides some means of simulating the environment of the system under test, of test-data generation and presentation, and of recording test results.

test coverage An estimate of the thoroughness of *testing of a program, usually measured as the proportion of the total actually tested by one or more of *path testing, *branch testing, *statement testing.

test data *See* testing.

test-data generator Any means for the automatic or semiautomatic production of data for use in the *testing of some system. Typically both valid and invalid input data for the system under test will be generated in order to test responses to both valid and erroneous inputs. Some generators effectively produce a pseudorandom data stream, recognizing only constraints on the formats of the data. More advanced generators might attempt to produce data that will give good test coverage.

testing (dynamic testing) Any activity that checks by means of actual execution whether a system or component behaves in the desired manner. This is achieved by one or more *test runs* in which the system is supplied with input data, known under these circumstances as *test data*, and the responses of the system are recorded for analysis.

Tests can be categorized according to the conditions under which they are performed and the purposes they serve. *Module testing* (or *unit testing*) is performed on individual components in isolation. At the time that components are brought together to form complete subsystems or systems, *integration testing* is performed in order to check that the components operate together correctly. Integration testing typically pays particular attention to the interfaces between components. By contrast, *system testing* normally treats the complete system as a "black box" and investigates its behavior without concern for individual components or internal interfaces. *Acceptance testing* is normally under the control of the procurers of the system, and is designed to ensure that the system is suitable for operational use.

See also beta test, branch testing, path testing, performance testing, regression testing, statement testing, black-box testing, glass-box testing. *Compare* static analysis.

test run *See* testing.

TeX or strictly T_EX (pronounced tek: the letters are Greek) A computer typesetting system designed by Donald E. Knuth that aims to produce results as good as "hot metal" setting when using a modern raster-image laser typesetter. Knuth was particularly concerned to produce high-quality setting of mathematical material, but TeX is equally suited to textual material. The system includes many innovative techniques, particularly its algorithm for breaking paragraphs into lines in an optimal manner. The source code for TeX is in the public domain, and as a result it is widely used in academic institutions throughout the world.

The input language of TeX provides a very low-level control over the placing of marks on the printed page, and it is generally used via an intermediary macro language. The "Plain TeX" macros provided as part of the system are still at quite a low level, and many users employ higher-level packages such as AMS-TeX and *LaTeX.

The output from TeX is in a device-independent form, and separate drivers are needed to convert this into the appropriate code for a particular printer. While output normally goes to a laser printer or phototypesetter, it is possible to write a driver for a dot-matrix printer operating in graphics mode. Knuth designed a whole new family of typefaces called Computer Modern Roman to go with TeX using his *META-FONT system, but these do not reproduce well at low resolutions; many users therefore prefer to use *PostScript fonts, using a conversion program to translate the device-independent output from TeX into PostScript code.

Texas Instruments A large US electronics corporation. IT sales account for only about 10% of its revenue but this nevertheless makes it number 71 in terms of revenue in the list of the world's top IT suppliers (1993 figures). It produces computers of all sizes from notebook computers to large-scale systems. In the software field, its *electronic data interchange software and its Information Engineering Facility, a *CASE tool, are well known.

text editor A program used specifically for entry and modification of data that is in a textual format. Such data may be a program written in a high-level language, a report or book written in a natural language, or numerical input for, say, a statistical program.

Text editors form an essential part of the user interface of all interactive systems. They may be *line-oriented*, where the text is considered to be a series of lines separated by end-of-line markers, *character-oriented*, where the text is considered to be a stream of characters with any end-of-line or page markers counting as characters, or *screen editors*. With screen editors, the display screen forms a movable *window into the text, within which the cursor may be positioned at points where insertions, deletions, and other editing functions are to be performed.

There is a considerable overlap in function between text editors and *word processing systems.

text formatter *See* formatter.

text mode (character mode) A way of using a computer display such that the basic unit is the *character cell* – the space taken up by a single character. The only images that can be displayed are those that can be built from character-sized blocks; surprisingly complex images can however be built in text mode. A display device can be operated in a number of different text modes. The coarsest is probably the 40 characters by 24 lines used in some *teletext systems, while some text modes have 132 characters per line. Each character has attributes such as color, boldface type, blink, underline, or reverse video. *Compare* graphics mode.

text processing All forms of text manipulation including word processing.

text-to-speech (TTS) The method of converting ASCII text to a speech waveform. *See also* speech synthesis.

texture mapping (decal) A method of changing the surface representation of an object to give the impression that the surface is patterned in a defined way without explicitly modeling it as part of the surface geometry. It allows complex surface rendering without the enormous computation needed if the geometric surface was defined and then rendered. The texture may determine or modify any surface characteristic, including color, reflectivity, transparency, or even surface normals.

texture placement The deformations to be applied to a texture before it is applied to the geometry of an object.

texturing The simulation of uneven surfaces and unevenly colored surfaces, both regular and irregular, such as those of bricks or stone. This is usually done by techniques that do not require modification of the underlying model.

TFEL *Acronym for* thin-film electroluminescent display.

T flip-flop A clocked *flip-flop whose output "toggles", i.e. changes to the complementary logic state, on every active transition of the clock signal (*see* clock). The device acts as a divide-by-two *counter since two active transitions of the clock signal generate one active transition of the output. It can be considered as being equivalent to a *JK flip-flop whose J and K inputs are held at logic 1.

Tflops (TFLOPS, teraflops) A million million floating-point operations per second. *See* flops.

TFT *Abbrev. for* thin-film transistor.

TGA *See* Targa.

T-gate *Another name for* ternary selector gate.

theorem proving The formal method of providing a proof in *symbolic logic. It uses deductive *inference. Each step in the proof will (a) introduce a premise or axiom and (b) provide a statement that is a natural consequence of previously established results using only legitimate rules of inference.

Such formal proofs are often long and tedious. Sophisticated programs known as *theorem provers* can be used to automate much of the process. *See also* mechanical verifier.

theory In logic, a set of sentences that are true under a particular interpretation.

theory of types *See* hierarchy of functions.

thermal inkjet A type of *inkjet printer.

thermal printer A type of printer in which the image is produced by localized heating of paper that has a very thin thermosensitive coating containing two separate and colorless components. When heated the color former melts and combines with the previously colorless dyestuff to make a visible mark. Various colors are possible but blue and black are the most common. Blue toning paper allows higher print speeds but the image fades with time and is not compatible with some photocopiers. Black toning paper requires higher temperatures and pressure at the print head, thus causing greater wear, but fades less quickly and has a longer shelf life. The printers can be either *serial or *line printers. *See also* thermal transfer printer, electrothermal printer.

thermal transfer printer A printer in which thermoplastic ink is transferred to paper from a donor roll or thin backing material by localized heating. This type of printer, introduced in 1982, is very quiet in operation, produces a good contrast image, and is mechanically simple in design. The print head is similar to that used in the earlier *thermal printers that use sensitized paper, but the heating elements are usually smaller and thus allow the formation of a better character shape.

The printers may be *serial or *page printers. A speed of 100 characters per second has been achieved for good-quality serial printers and 4 pages per minute for line printers. The page printer can have a print head with as many as 3200 elements spanning an 8″ width. A donor film, the same size as the page to be printed, is laid over the paper and they are passed beneath the print head. Successive donor films of different colors can be used to print full-color pictures.

thesaurus A feature of word processing systems whereby similes and synonyms may be displayed on screen and incorporated into the text. *Full text retrieval systems may have *thesaurus searching* as an option whereby terms similar in meaning to those sought will also be located. A thesaurus can be used to define a set of allowed terms for use as key-words during the entry of data into text retrieval systems.

thick Ethernet Standard *thick wire cabling used for Ethernet network connections.

thick wire One of the two forms of standard *coaxial cable specified for use as the physical medium for *Ethernet (or CSMA/CD) network connections; the other form is *thin wire*. The original CSMA/CD standard specified a coaxial cable with an overall diameter of about 10 mm; this allowed data to be presented as a baseband signal at 10 Mbps, with a range of 500 yards, and is referred to as thick wire or *10base5 cable*. A subsequent standard specified a coaxial cable with an overall diameter of about 5 mm; this allowed data to be presented as a baseband signal again at 10 Mbps, but with a reduced range of 200 yards, and is referred to as thin wire or *10base2 cable*. The outer layer of insulator in thick Ethernet cabling is usually made of a yellow plastic while in thin Ethernet cabling it is usually made of black plastic, and the two cables are sometimes referred to as *yellow* and *black Ethernet* respectively.

thin Ethernet Standard thin wire cabling used for Ethernet network connections. *See* thick wire.

thin-film electroluminescent display (TFEL) An *electroluminescent display that has an active matrix associated with it using thin-film transistor technology to ensure no sneak currents cause neighboring pixels to be partially illuminated.

thin-film transistor (TFT) A transistor fabricated from an extremely thin film of amorphous (noncrystalline) silicon, or sometimes from a more responsive material. TFT technology is employed, for example, in active-matrix *LCDs where the thin-film circuitry is deposited on a glass substrate in the screen and is used to control individual pixels.

thin wire *See* thick wire.

third generation of computers. Machines whose design was initiated after 1960 (approximately). Probably the most significant criterion of difference between *second and third generations lies in the concept of computer *architecture. Generally, second generation machines were limited to what the engineers could put together and make work. Advances in electronic technology – the development of *integrated circuits and the like – made it possible for designers to design an architecture to suit the requirements of the tasks envisaged for the machines and the programmers who were going to work them. With the development of the experimental machines – the IBM *Stretch and the Manchester University *Atlas – the concept of computer architecture became a reality. Comprehensive *operating systems became, more or less, part of the machines. *Multiprogramming was facilitated and much of the task of control of the memory and I/O and other resources became vested in the operating system or the machine itself.

third normal form *See* normal forms.

third-party maintenance *See* TPM.

thrashing A phenomenon that may arise in *paging or other forms of *virtual-memory system. If the page-turning rate for a paging system becomes high, usually because the amount of real memory available for holding pages is small compared with the total *working set of all the *processes currently active, then each process will find itself in a situation in which, on attempting to reference a page, the appropriate page is not in memory. In trying to find space to hold the required page, the system is likely to move out onto backing store a page that will very shortly be required by some other process. As a consequence the paging rate rises to very high levels, the fraction of CPU cycles absorbed in managing page-turning overheads becomes very high, processes become blocked as they wait for page transfers to complete, and system throughput falls sharply.

One method by which thrashing may be alleviated is by an increase in the bandwidth between main memory and backing store, i.e. by providing sufficient interchange capacity to allow the thrashing to take place without inducing unduly long waits for paging-drum transfers. A more effective cure is to reduce the ratio between the total working-set size and the amount of space available for holding the active pages, thus increasing the hit rate on pages in memory, either by reducing the size of the working set or by increasing the amount of memory on the system.

threaded list A list in which additional linkage structures, called *threads*, have been added to provide for traversals in special orders. This permits bounded workspace, i.e. read-only traversals along the direction provided by the threads. It does presuppose that the list and any sublists are not recursive and further that no sublist is shared.

threading A programming technique used in some code generators in which the "code" consists of a sequence of entry points of routines. The threaded code is interpreted by executing an unconditional branch to the destination indicated by a word of the code; on completion the routine thus activated terminates by again executing an unconditional branch to the entry point indicated by the next code word. *See also* single threading, multithreading.

threat Any action intended to breach the *security of information stored in a system by (a) gaining unauthorized access to that information usually without alerting the authorized user, (b) *denial of service to the authorized user, (c) *spoofing, which aims to confuse by introducing false information, usually as to the identity of the user. Some threats are with premeditated malicious intent but others are opportunistic, e.g. *browsing, or occur during a *crash. *See also* vulnerability.

three-address instruction *See* instruction format. *See also* multiple-address machine.

three-dimensional array *See* array.

three-state output *Another name for* tri-state output.

three-term (or 3-term) control *See* PID controller.

threshold element (threshold gate) A *logic element whose output is determined by comparing a weighted sum of inputs with a predetermined/prescribed threshold value. If the threshold is exceeded, the output is a logic 1; if not, the output is logic 0. If the

number of inputs is odd, if the weights are all equal, and the threshold is equal to half of the number of inputs, then the threshold element behaves as a *majority element.

A system of threshold elements is described by or as *threshold logic*. *See also* ternary threshold gate.

throughput A figure-of-merit for a computer system in which some description of operating rate such as instructions per minute, jobs per day, etc., is used.

Thue-system A *semi-Thue system in which, for each production $l \rightarrow r$, the reverse production $r \rightarrow l$ is also present (as in the first example under semi-Thue system). Clearly then

$$w \Rightarrow w' \text{ iff } w' \Rightarrow w$$

TIFF *Acronym for* tagged image file format. An *image file format developed by a set of companies chaired by Aldus and currently being standardized by ISO (TIFF/IT). It is widely used in the desktop publishing industry for representing color or gray-scale pictures.

tile To arrange open *windows on a display such that no window overlaps any other window. Conversely when the windows are arranged in an echelon one on top of the other such that each one reveals a little of the one beneath it, they are said to be *cascaded*.

tiling *See* tessellation.

tiling structure *See* iterated function system.

time-bounded Turing machine *See* multitape Turing machine.

time complexity *See* complexity measure, P=NP question.

time division multiplexing (TDM) A method of sharing a transmission channel among multiple sources by allocating specific time slots to each source. Both synchronous and asynchronous TDM is used.

Synchronous TDM does not require identity bits to be included in a message since the receiving device knows which device is transmitting at all times. The two main methods used in synchronous TDM to identify when a device's time slot occurs are *polling and *clocking. Polling requires a central device to interrogate each sending device when its time slot occurs. Clocking requires each device to have a synchronized clock and a prearranged sending sequence known to all devices. Polling and clocking waste time slots if a device has no data to send. More refined methods require devices to reserve their time slots ahead of time or allow devices to use time slots of other devices if they were unused on the previous cycle.

Asynchronous TDM allows devices to send data as it is ready, without a prearranged ordering. Data must carry with it the identity of the sending device. Since devices may send data at the same time, collisions may occur, making the messages unreadable. Many networks that utilize asynchronous TDM use *CSMA/CD (carrier sense multiple access with collision detection) to sense when messages have collided and must be retransmitted.

TDM is used in *baseband networking, and may also be used on channels of a *broadband networking system.

See also multiplexing, frequency division multiplexing.

time division switch An all-electronic switching system based on *time division multiplexing (TDM) principles: an input digitized signal from a source is connected to an output trunk by assigning a group of bits from the input data stream to a time slot in a high-speed TDM output data stream. Time-division switches are commonly also used as tandem switches where time slots from an input TDM trunk are selectively connected to time slots in an output TDM trunk.

time domain A term used to refer to a situation in which the amplitude of a *signal varies with time. *See also* space domain.

time domain reflectometer (TDR) A system used in the characterization of cables employed as transmission lines. A very short pulse ($\approx$100 picoseconds) is launched into the cable at one end and the reflections of it are measured to obtain the position and impedance of any discontinuities along the length of the cable.

time-of-day clock A digital device that provides time-of-day information. It is typically used as a means of scheduling control applications or data collection activities.

timeout A condition that occurs when a process which is waiting for either an external event or the expiry of a preset time interval reaches the end of the time interval before the external event is detected. For example, if the process has sent a message and no acknowledgment has been detected at the end of the preset time period, then the process may take appropriate action, such as retransmitting the message.

The word is also used as a verb.

time quantization (sampling) *See* quantization, discrete and continuous systems.

timer clock A timing device that can generate a *timeout signal after a fixed period of time. These devices are often made programmable, i.e. presetable, so that various timing durations can be obtained. In addition the timeout signal may be generated continuously, i.e. after every timing period, or on a one-shot basis.

time series A set of observations ordered in time and usually equally spaced; each observation may be related in some way to its predecessors. Time-series problems arise in economics, commerce, industry, meteorology, demography, or any fields in which the same measurements are regularly recorded.

Time-series analysis is based on models of the variability of observations in a time series, by postulating trends, cyclic effects, and short-term relationships, with a view to understanding the causes of variation and to improving forecasting (*see also* periodogram).

Autoregression is the use of *regression analysis to relate observations to their predecessors. *Moving-average methods* use the means of neighboring observations to reveal underlying trends. Autoregression and moving averages are combined in *ARMA* (or *Box-Jenkins*) forecasting techniques.

Cyclic influences may be of known period (months in a year or days in a week) and data may be seasonally adjusted on the basis of long-term means. Cyclic influences of unknown period may be studied by *spectral analysis*.

Analogous techniques may be used for data regularly ordered in space rather than time.

time sharing A technique, first advocated by Christopher Strachey, for sharing the time of a computer among several jobs, switching between them so rapidly that each job appears to have the computer to itself. *See also* multiaccess system.

time slicing Process scheduling in which a *process is allowed to run for a predefined period of time, now called a *quantum, before rescheduling. *See also* scheduling algorithm.

timestamp The time and date of an operation or event when automatically added to a screen display, log file, or output file of a computer procedure. It is a valuable aid to the tracking down of errors and can be used as part of an auditing process. The time and date are derived from the computer's internal *real-time clock.

timing analysis The use of structural information of a program and a knowledge of the processor instruction or module execution times to synthesize the temporal behavior of a software system. For sequential systems this is a simple analysis. For highly concurrent systems the use of simulation techniques or queuing models may be necessary, and system performance/time response becomes stochastic rather than deterministic. *See also* performance testing.

timing diagram A graphical description of the operation of a *sequential circuit; the state(s) of all the relevant variables (inputs, internal memory, and outputs) are shown as functions along the time dimension.

tint fill *See* soft fill.

TIP *Acronym for* terminal interface processor. A specially configured *IMP that was the ARPANET equivalent of a *PAD.

tip node *Another name for* leaf node.

Tk A toolkit of windowing functions added to *Tcl that simplifies the production of X Window system interfaces to applications.

T²L *See* TTL.

TLB *Abbrev. for* translation look-aside buffer.

TLU *Abbrev. for* table lookup.

TM *Abbrev. for* Turing machine.

toggle 1. Anything that can be set to one of two states. It usually conveys meaning, as in "printer on/printer off", or at a lower level "direct address/indirect address", or perhaps in a word-processing system "bold on/bold off".
2. To change the state of a toggle.

toggling speed *Another name for* switching speed.

token 1. One of the meaningful units (names, constants, reserved words, etc.) in the input to a compiler. The *lexical analyzer breaks up the input, which is a stream of characters, into a sequence of tokens.
2. A unique sequence of bits granting send permission on a network. *See* token ring, token bus.
3. *See* Petri net.

token bus A form of network (usually a *local area network) in which access to the transmission medium is controlled by a *token. The network stations (nodes) are interconnected by a *bus, i.e. signals are placed on the transmission medium by one station and can be read by all the other stations. If the signal is a token, indicating that the station that was last transmitting has now finished, the token is passed from station to station in a strict sequence. In a *token ring this sequence is determined by the order in which stations are physically connected to the transmission medium. A station wishing to transmit will start to do so by removing the token from the bus and replacing it with the data to be transmitted; when transmission is complete, the transmitting station will reinitiate the token passing process.

A token bus system has the advantage that the priority of stations can be redefined by redefining the order in which stations are permitted to acquire the token.

token ring A *ring network architecture configured on the basis that each station (node) on the ring awaits the arrival of a *token from the adjacent upstream node, indicating that it is allowed to send information toward the downstream node. The network is configured in a manner that ensures that only a single token is present on the ring at one time. When a sending node intercepts the token, it first sends its message to the downstream node followed by the token, which is then passed to each succeeding node until it is again intercepted by a node with a message awaiting transmission. Token rings are defined by ISO standard 8802.5.

tolerable risk A level of *risk deemed acceptable by society in order that some particular benefit or functionality can be obtained, but in the knowledge that the risk has been evaluated and is being managed.

tool *See* software tool.

toolbox A set of *software tools, probably from several vendors, not necessarily as closely related or providing as full coverage of the *software life cycle as a *toolkit*. The set of tools in a toolkit is usually from a single vendor. *See also* PSE, CASE, IPSE, software engineering environment.

toolkit *See* toolbox.

TOP *Acronym for* Technical Office Protocol. A project that operates in a similar field to the *MAP set of protocols but concentrates on the management of the design process and the associated activities such as costing inventory, rather than on the automation of the machining and assembling of components.

top-down development An approach to program development in which progress is made by defining required elements in terms of more basic elements, beginning with the required program and ending when the implementation language is reached. At every stage during top-down development each of the undefined elements from the previous stage is defined. In order to do this, an appropriate collection of more basic elements is introduced, and the undefined elements are defined in terms of these more basic elements ("more basic" meaning that the element is closer to the level that can be directly expressed in the implementation language). These more basic elements will in turn be defined at the next stage in terms of still more basic elements, and so on until at some stage the elements can be defined directly in the implementation language.

In practice, "pure" top-down development

is not possible; the choice of more basic elements at each stage must always be guided by an awareness of the facilities of the implementation language, and even then it will often be discovered at a later stage that some earlier choice was inappropriate, leading to a need for iteration. *Compare* bottom-up development.

top-down parsing A strategy for *parsing sentences of *context-free grammars that attempts to construct a *parse tree from the top down. The term includes techniques that may or may not involve backtracking.

Beginning with a parse tree consisting of just the start symbol of the *grammar, a top-down parser attempts to expand those leaf nodes labeled by nonterminals from left to right using the productions of the grammar. As leaves labeled by terminals are created they are matched against the input string. Should the match fail, new alternatives for the interior nodes are tried in a systematic way until the entire input string has been matched or no more alternatives are possible. A top-down parser without backtracking uses the information contained in the portion of the input string not yet matched to decide once and for all which alternatives to choose. The *LL parsing technique is the most powerful example of the top-down strategy.

Top-down parsing is often implemented as a set of recursive procedures, one for each nonterminal in the grammar, and is then called *recursive descent parsing*.

topological sort A sorting process over which a partial ordering is defined, i.e. ordering is given over pairs of items but not between all of them. An example is given by a dictionary. If a word v is defined in terms of word w, this is denoted by $w < v$. Then a topological sort of the dictionary implies an ordering of the terms so that there will be no forward references.

topology 1. The study of those properties of *sets that are shared by all images (homeomorphic images) of the sets under certain mappings that might be described as deformations. Topology is sometimes described as geometry done on a rubber sheet; this sheet can be pulled or stretched into different shapes. Topological properties are unaltered by distortions of this kind. Topological properties can be attributed to *graphs, *grammars, and even *programs themselves.

2. (interconnection topology) *See* network architecture.

total correctness, proof of *See* program correctness proof.

total function A *function

$$f : S \to T$$

whose value is defined for all elements x in the set S; thus for each x, $f(x)$ produces some value in T. *Compare* partial function.

totally ordered structure *Another name for* linear structure.

total ordering A *partial ordering with the added property that there is always order between any two elements. The usual "less than" ordering between integers is a total ordering. The relation "is a subset of" defined on the *algebra of sets is not.

total recursive function *See* recursive function.

totem-pole output The output stage of a TTL gate that acts as a power amplifier. *See* TTL.

touchpad *See* touch-sensitive device.

touch screen An input device that responds to the touch of a stylus, which may be a finger, so that the stylus position on the screen may be estimated. It is thus a touch-sensitive *locator. The stylus could be used, say, to make selections from a number of displayed options. The touch screen often operates by using a continuous resistive layer as a variable resistor.

touch-sensitive device A flat rectangular device that responds to the touch of, say, a finger by transmitting the coordinates of the touched point to a computer. The touch-sensitive area may be the screen itself, which is then called a *touch screen. Alternatively it may be integral with the keyboard or a separate unit that can be placed on a desk: movement of the finger across the so-called *touchpad* can cause the cursor to move around the screen.

tournament A directed *graph in which there

is precisely one directed edge between any pair of *vertices.

tournament method A method of finding a specific element in some set (e.g. largest of a set of numbers), so called because it involves pairing elements and comparing them to find which one goes through to the next stage, leaving just one element at the end that has not lost.

tower A piece of equipment, such as a computer system box, whose dimensions are such that height > depth > width. A large tower might be free-standing on the floor, while a smaller one might be a *deskside* unit and the smallest ones stand on the desktop. *See also* midi-tower.

Towers of Hanoi An ancient problem supposedly devised by a Vietnamese emperor to help with the selection of an advisor. It may be stated as follows. Three poles (labeled A, B, and C) stand vertically on the ground. Pole A holds a set of circular disks all of differing radii; from the ground up these disks are positioned in decreasing order of radius size. The problem is to move the disks to pole C by means of a series of moves, each involving the transfer of a disk from one pole to another, with the constraint that at any time all disks on any one pole are situated in decreasing order of radius when viewed from the ground up. This problem has a solution that has a particularly appealing recursive solution.

TPM *Abbrev. for* third-party maintenance. Any maintenance carried out by an organization that is neither the supplier nor the owner of equipment. An advantage of TPM is that systems consisting of items from different suppliers can be maintained from a single point. However, expertise and access to spares and manuals may not be as good as when the originator of the equipment does the work.

TP monitor *Abbrev. for* transaction processing monitor. *See* transaction processing.

trace program A program that monitors the execution of some software system and provides information on the dynamic behavior of that system in the form of a *trace*, i.e. a report of the sequence of actions carried out. Typically a trace program will offer several options as to the kind of trace produced. For example, there may be options to produce a statement-by-statement trace, or to trace just those statements that alter the flow of control, or to trace changes to the value of a specific variable.

track The path followed by the *head over the surface of a recording medium (usually magnetic or optical). The tracks on magnetic disks are circular and concentric. On optical disks they may be similar but are more often turns of a continuous spiral path. Most magnetic tapes carry several tracks running the length of the tape; these may be written or read simultaneously (parallel recording) or, for other tape formats, one at a time (serial recording, or *serpentine recording if alternate tracks are recorded in opposite directions). In *helical scan recording the tracks run diagonally across the axis of the tape.

On *CD-ROM optical disk, the word track is also used (as it is on compact audio disk) to define an item of the contents, of variable length, which may occupy many turns of the spiral path.

tracker See MOD.

trackerball (or trackball) A *pointing device that consists of a ball supported on bearings so that it is free to rotate in any direction but is restrained within a socket so that less than half of its surface is exposed. In use, the ball is rotated by the operator's fingers and sensors on two of the support bearings generate trains of pulses related to the rotation of the ball about two axes at right angles. In the late 1970s such devices were expensive and were only used in applications such as Air Traffic Control; by the mid-1980s they had reduced significantly in price and become popular for personal computer applications. *Laptop and *notebook computers often incorporate trackerballs into their keyboards.

tractor A device for moving continuous *stationery through a printer and maintaining good registration relative to the page boundaries. The technique by which this is achieved is known as *tractor feed*. The trac-

tors are used in pairs and consist of loops of light chain or bands on which are mounted pegs (also known as pintles or sprockets) that engage with holes that have been punched along both edges of the stationery. The tractors are usually driven by a d.c. servo or stepper motor that is controlled by the printer electronics. In high-speed printers there may be pairs of tractors above and below the print line but in lower-speed devices there is usually only one pair and friction is relied upon to keep the paper tensioned. In printers for transaction documents the tractors are arranged immediately below the print line so that the document may be torn off close to the last line of print.

trade secrets Pieces of confidential information given in circumstances of confidence that enable the recipient to short-circuit an otherwise necessary course of development. Thus a source listing containing debugged code for one or more algorithms, if given in circumstances of confidence, may be protected by the law as a trade secret and the recipient (and any person who knowingly received the information) barred from using the algorithms in programs of his own. Like *privacy, the law on trade secrets is not at all clear. See also copyright, patent.

traffic A measure of the quantity of data or other messages taking place between points of a communication network.

traffic control A term sometimes used in reference to the control of input and output. It covers both the hardware (channels and interrupts) and software (resource allocation and process synchronization) necessary to achieve the orderly and correct movement of data in a multiprogramming system.

trailer label A *sentinel that occurs at the end of data organized in sequential form, e.g. on magnetic tape. Trailer labels typically include summary statistics of the data, e.g. the total number of records in the file.

trailer record A record that follows a group of related records and contains data relevant to those records. For example, a trailer record may appear at the end of a file and contain a total of monetary fields held on that file, which may be used as a security check.

trailing edge of a pulse. *See* pulse.

train printer An obsolete type of *impact *line printer in which the type font was etched or engraved upon metal slugs that were pushed around a guide track. It was introduced by IBM in 1965 to supersede the *chain printer. The track guided the slugs around a loop, one section of which ran parallel to the line to be printed. The use of slugs in a track enabled greater accuracy of print to be achieved and also yielded flexibility of character repertoire. Heavily used characters could be easily replaced and special symbols substituted for other characters. Speeds of up to 3000 lpm were achieved.

Train printers dominated the high-speed printer market up to 1982, when the *band printer offered superior performance at lower cost and nonimpact printers with superior print quality and versatility became financially viable.

transaction An input message to a system that, because of the nature of the real-world event or activity it reflects, requires to be regarded as a single unit of work and must either be processed completely or rejected. Where the processing of a transaction involves several changes to be made to a database, and for some reason the activity is interrupted and not completed, then any changes made to that point must be reversed (*backed out*) and a DBMS must provide facilities to ensure this happens. When the processing of a transaction has been completed satisfactorily the changes to the database are *committed* – made permanent.

transaction file (movement file) A file, especially a *data file, containing transaction records, prior to the updating of a *master file. Transaction files are only used in *batch processing systems. Once updating has been carried out, the transaction file may be kept in order to permit subsequent recovery of the master file (*see* file recovery) or for auditing purposes but is otherwise redundant.

transaction processing A method of organizing a data-processing system in which *transactions are processed to completion as they arise. A *transaction processing monitor* (*TP monitor*) is a software system that facilitates the handling of transactions in such circumstances. *Compare* batch processing.

transceiver A device that can both transmit and receive signals on a communication medium. Many communication devices, including *modems, *codecs, and *terminals, are transceivers.

transducer 1. (sensor) Any device that converts energy in the form of sound, light, pressure, etc., into an equivalent electrical signal, or vice versa. For example, a semiconductor laser converts electrical energy into light, and a piezoelectric device converts mechanical stress into electrical energy (and vice versa).

2. In formal language theory, any *automaton that produces output.

transfer rate *See* data transfer rate.

transformation 1. *Another name for* function, used especially in geometry.

2. of programs. *See* program transformation.

3. of statistics data. A change of scale used to improve the validity of statistical analyses. For data in which small values have smaller *variance than large values a logarithmic or square-root transformation is often recommended. For data in the form of proportions, a transformation from the scale (0,1) to an infinite scale is advisable before performing *analysis of variance or *regression analysis. Several transformations exist for proportions, such as the *logistic or log-odds-ratio that is used in the analysis of *generalized linear models. Appropriate transformations may be suggested by studying *residuals in a regression analysis.

transformational grammar A grammar that makes essential use of transformation rules to convert the *deep structures of sentences into their surface structures. *See also* generative grammar.

transformational semantics *See* program transformation.

transformation matrix An $m \times n$ matrix of numbers used to map vectors with n elements onto vectors with m elements.

transformation monoid *See* transformation semigroup.

transformation semigroup A *semigroup

consisting of a collection C of transformations of a *set S into itself (*see* function), the *dyadic operation $\circ$ being the *composition of functions; it is essential that the set C should be *closed with respect to composition, i.e. if c_1 and c_2 are in C then so is $c_1 \circ c_2$.

If the identity transformation (*see* identity function) is included in the transformation semigroup, a *transformation monoid* results. Every monoid is isomorphic to a transformation monoid.

transform domain *See* filtering.

transient error An error that occurs once or at unpredictable intervals. *See also* error rate.

transistor A semiconductor device having, in general, three terminals that are attached to electrode regions within the device. Current flowing between two of these electrodes is made to vary in response to voltage or current variations imposed on the third electrode. The device is capable of current or voltage amplification depending on the particular circuit implementation employed. It can also be used as a switch by driving it between its maximum and minimum of current flow.

The transistor was invented in 1948 by Shockley, Brattain, and Bardeen at Bell Telephone Labs. As performance and manufacturing techniques improved, the transistor enabled a huge growth in computer technology.

See also bipolar transistor, field-effect transistor, MOSFET.

transistor-transistor logic *See* TTL.

transitive closure of a *transitive *binary relation R. A relation $R^\star$ defined as follows:
$$x \, R^\star \, y$$
iff there exists a sequence
$$x = x_0, x_1, \ldots, x_n = y$$
such that $n > 0$ and
$$x_i \, R \, x_{i+1}, \, i = 0, 1, 2, \ldots, n-1$$
It follows from the transitivity property that
$$\text{if } x \, R \, y \text{ then } x \, R^\star \, y$$
and that R is a subset of $R^\star$.

Reflexive closure is similar to transitive closure but includes the possibility that $n = 0$. Transitive and reflexive closures play important roles in parsing and compiling techniques and in finding paths in graphs.

transitive relation A *relation R defined on a set S and having the property that, for all x, y, and z in S,
$$\text{whenever } x \, R \, y \text{ and } y \, R \, z$$
$$\text{then } x \, R \, z$$
The relations "is less than" defined on integers, and "is subset of" defined on sets are transitive.

translation (protocol translation) *See* internetworking.

translation look-aside buffer (TLB) A specific component of some implementations of a *cache, especially in conjunction with paged memory management (*see* paging). A cache is a high-speed memory, occupying a position in the *memory hierarchy between the high-speed registers of a processor and the main random-access memory (RAM) of the system. The cache holds copies of small areas of the RAM, each area being labeled with both the physical address of the area of RAM of which it is a copy and with the address by which it is known to the process owning it. The process form of the address, which typically contains segment and page information, is translated to the corresponding physical address by the hardware of the address management system; a TLB is an *associative memory that indicates whether this address corresponds to one held in the cache, and so can be accessed by using the cache, or whether it is necessary to fetch the corresponding area of memory from RAM into the cache.

translation table A table of information stored within a processor or a peripheral that is used to convert encoded information into another form of code with the same meaning. There are a variety of codes used within the field of computing and sometimes more than one code may be used within a single system. For output devices such as printers the *ASCII code is widely used but the code used within the processor may be *EBCDIC. A translation table is used to make the required conversion.

translator A program that converts a program written in one language to the equivalent program in another language. A *compiler is a specific example of a translator: it takes a program written in a high-level language such as Fortran or Algol and converts it into machine code or assembly language.

translator writing system A set of *software tools that are designed to aid the production of new language translators. A *compiler-compiler is an example of one such tool.

transmission channel *See* channel.

Transmission Control Protocol *See* TCP/IP.

transmission control unit *See* communication processor.

transmission line Any physical medium that conveys information between remote points. It may, for example, be a telephone line, a coaxial cable, a waveguide, or an optical fiber. *See also* multiplexing.

transmission rate The speed at which information may be transferred from a device or via a circuit. The unit used is usually related to the amount of information transferred per cycle, e.g. characters per second or bits per second. With data transmission circuits the *baud rate is sometimes used.

transparency In computer graphics the simulation of transparency includes both unrealistic but cheap techniques in which only the surface of the "transparent" object modifies the color of the light, and more complex methods in which the distance traveled through the transparent object is accounted for and refractions and so on may be modeled. More advanced techniques include the modeling of internal scattering, which gives a more realistic impression of translucency.

transparent 1. Denoting a property or a component of a computer system that provides some facilities without restrictions or interference arising from the way it is implemented. For example, if a machine with 32-bit wide words has an 8-bit wide ALU yet performs correct 32-bit arithmetic, then the ALU size is transparent in such use.
2. Denoting or using a transmission path that passes a signal, or some particular feature of a signal, without restricting or changing it. Note that nontransparent systems would not allow particular signals to be transmitted as

data, reserving them for special purposes. *See also* data transparency.

transport 1. A mechanism for transporting an information storage medium past an access station. The word is most frequently used to refer to either a document or a tape transport.
2. A service provided by a (local or wide area) communication network, or the architectural layer or interface with this service.

transportable *See* portable.

transport layer of network protocol function. *See* seven-layer reference model.

transpose of an $m \times n$ matrix A. The $n \times m$ matrix, symbol A^T, given by interchanging rows and columns. Thus the i,jth element of A^T is equal to the j,ith element of A.

transposition cipher A *cipher, or a component of a more complicated cipher, that involves the symbol at each place in the *plaintext being moved to a newly decided (and often different) place, i.e. within each block of plaintext the positional indices of the symbol places are changed according to some plan. Since a cipher must be invertible (for *decryption), the plan must be a *permutation of the range of positional indices. *Compare* substitution cipher.

transputer A high-performance microcomputer, devised and manufactured by the UK company INMOS, designed to facilitate interprocess and interprocessor communication. The transputer comprises a 32-bit *RISC processor with fast on-chip static *RAM, process scheduling in hardware with a submicrosecond context switch, external memory controller, and high-speed serial links. The latest T9000 processor provides a 32-bit integer processor, a 64-bit floating-point processor and a 16 Kbyte cache memory as well as a communications processor and four high-bandwidth serial links. Implementation of advanced packet switched communication structures can be accomplished by employing other special support components.

A single transputer is a powerful processor in its own right: the serial links allow an architecture in which transputers are arranged in an array, each communicating with its four nearest neighbors. With suitable algorithms this permits very high performance on complex numerical problems.

The transputer is programmed in *occam: the program architecture of processes communicating through channels can be implemented by time-slicing a single computer, or by using multiple transputers, when the serial links provide the channels. Applications of the transputer in pipelines and arrays have demonstrated that it is a successful low-cost approach to achieving a high parallel-processing rate.

trap A system state similar to that caused by an *interrupt but synchronous to the system rather than asynchronous as in the case of an interrupt. There are a variety of conditions that can cause a trap to occur. Examples of such conditions include the attempted execution of an illegal instruction, or an attempt to access another user's resources in a system that supports multiuser protection. The attempted operation is detected by the hardware and control is transferred to a different part of the system, usually in the operating system, which can then decide on what action to take.

trapezium rule The approximation

$$\int_{x_i}^{x_{i+1}} f(x)\mathrm{d}x \simeq \tfrac{1}{2}h(f(x_i) + f(x_{i+1})),$$

$$h = x_{i+1} - x_i$$

used as the basis for an *extrapolation method in *numerical integration.

trapezoidal rule *See* ordinary differential equations.

traveling salesman problem (TSP) A well-known *graph-searching problem. In practical terms the problem can be thought of as that of a salesman who wishes to perform a circular tour of certain cities, calling at each city once only and traveling the minimum total distance possible. In more abstract terms, it is the problem of finding a minimum-weight *Hamiltonian cycle in a *weighted graph. The problem is known to be NP-complete (*see* P=NP question).

traversal A *path through a *graph in which every vertex is visited at least once. Traversals are usually discussed in connection with special kinds of graphs, namely *trees.

Examples include *preorder traversal, *postorder traversal, and *symmetric order (or inorder) traversal. When parse trees for arithmetic expressions are traversed, these tree traversals lead to prefix (*Polish) notation, postfix (*reverse Polish) notation, and *infix notation respectively.

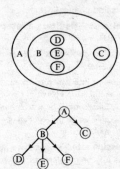

Sample tree represented as a Venn diagram (top) and as a directed graph

tree 1. Most commonly, short for *rooted tree*, i.e. a finite set of one or more *nodes such that firstly there is a single designated node called the *root* and secondly the remaining nodes are partitioned into $n \geq 0$ *disjoint sets, $T_1, T_2, \ldots, T_n$, where each of these sets is itself a tree. The sets $T_1, T_2, \ldots, T_n$ are called *subtrees* of the root. If the order of these subtrees is significant, the tree is called an *ordered tree*, otherwise it is sometimes called an *unordered tree*.

A tree corresponds to a *graph with the root node matching a vertex connected by (directed) arcs to the vertices, which match the root nodes of each of its subtrees. An alternative definition of a (*directed*) tree can thus be given in terms from graph theory: a tree is a directed *acyclic graph such that firstly there is a unique vertex, which no arcs enter, called the root, secondly every other vertex has exactly one arc entering it, and thirdly there is a unique path from the root to any vertex.

The diagram shows different representations of a tree.

2. Any *connected acyclic graph.

3. Any data structure representing a tree (def. 1 or 2). For example, a rooted tree can be represented as a pointer to the representation of the root node. A representation of a node would contain pointers to the subtrees of the node as well as the data associated with the node itself. Because the number of subtrees of a node may vary, it is common practice to use a *binary-tree representation.

The terminology associated with trees is either of a botanic nature, as with *forest, *leaf, root, or is genealogical, as with *ancestor, *descendant, *child, *parent, *sibling. *See also* binary tree.

tree automaton A generalization of the notion of a *finite-state automaton, applying to trees rather than strings (*see* tree language). There are two versions. A *top-down* machine begins at the root of the tree; having read the symbol at a node it changes state accordingly and splits into n machines to process separately the n descendants. A *bottom-up* machine begins with several separate activations of itself – one at each leaf node of the tree. Whenever all the subtrees of a particular node have been processed, the machines that have processed them are replaced by a single one at that node. Its state is determined by the symbol at the node and the final states of the descendant machines.

tree grammar A generalization of the notion of *grammar, applying to trees (often called *terms* in this context) rather than strings (*see* tree language). A *regular tree grammar* is the corresponding generalization of the notion of *regular grammar. Productions have the form

$$A \to t,$$

where A is a nonterminal and t a term, e.g.

$$S \to h(a,g(S),b) \mid c$$

trees:

frontiers: c acb $aacbb$ etc.

Language generated by a tree grammar

These productions generate the *regular tree language* shown in the diagram. Note that the *frontiers* of these trees are the strings shown below each tree in the diagram. A set of strings is *context-free if and only if it is the set of frontiers of the trees in a regular tree language.

The notion of *context-free grammar can be similarly generalized. This time nonterminals can themselves be function symbols having an arbitrary number of arguments, e.g.

$$F(x_1,x_2) \to$$
$$f(x_2,F(x_1,g(x_2))) \mid h(x_1,x_1,x_2)$$

This means, for example, that $F(a,b)$ could be rewritten to

$$f(b,F(a,g(b))),$$

and then to

$$f(b,f(g(b),F(a,g(g(b))))),$$

and then to

$$f(b,f(g(b),h(a,a,g(g(b)))))$$

tree language (term language) In *formal language theory, a generalization of the notion of language, applying to trees (often called *terms* in this context) rather than strings. Alphabets are extended to give each symbol an *arity*, the arity of each symbol dictating the number of subterms, or descendants in the tree, that it has.

trees:

terms: $f(a,b)$ $f(g(a),g(b))$ $g(f(a,g(g(b)))$

Examples of Σ-trees and Σ-terms

For example, let Σ be the alphabet $\{f,g,a,b\}$ and give arities 2,1,0,0 to f,g,a,b respectively. Then examples of Σ-*trees* and their equivalent representations as Σ-*terms* (or *well-formed expressions over* Σ) are shown in the diagram. A Σ-language is now any set of Σ-terms. *See also* tree grammar, tree automaton.

treelike network *See* network architecture.

tree search Any method of searching a body of data structured as a tree. *See* breadth-first search, depth-first search.

tree selection sort A refinement of *straight selection sort that makes use of the information gained in the first step to save on the subsequent number of comparisons required. It was proposed in 1956 by E. H. Friend and modified by K. E. Iverson in 1962. *See also* heapsort.

tree walking *Traversal of a tree.

trial function *See* finite-element method.

triangle inequality *See* inequality.

triangular matrix A square matrix in which every element lying to one side of the main diagonal is equal to zero. Thus for a *lower triangular matrix*, L,

$$l_{ij} = 0 \text{ if } i < j$$

and for an *upper triangular matrix*, U,

$$u_{ij} = 0 \text{ if } i > j$$

If, in addition,

$$l_{ii} = 0 \text{ or } u_{ii} = 0$$

then L or U is said to be *strictly lower* or *strictly upper triangular* respectively. The inverse of a lower (or an upper) triangular matrix, if it exists, is easy to calculate and is itself lower (or upper) triangular.

triangular patch A *patch that is a triangle. *See also* triangulation.

triangular waveform A periodic repetitive waveform that takes on its peak positive and negative excursions at fixed points in time. Between these peaks the waveform alternately rises and falls linearly with time. The rates of rise and fall determine the repetition rate or frequency of the waveform and in general are made equal. *Compare* sawtooth waveform.

triangulation A collection of triangles such that any pair of triangles intersect at most at one common vertex or along a common edge, whose union describes a surface in space.

tridiagonal matrix A band matrix A in which

$$a_{ij} = 0 \text{ if } |i - j| > 1$$

trie search A searching algorithm that examines data stored in a *trie* (name derived from information re*trie*val). A trie is essentially an n-ary tree with nodes that are n-place vectors, the components of which correspond to digits or characters.

trigger To initiate the operation of an electric circuit or device. Thus a signal supplied to the trigger input of a circuit may cause the circuit's output signal to be synchronized to this input.

trim of an array. The array obtained by constraining the subscripts to lie in some specified subrange. For example, the trim of a vector

$$v = (v_1 \ v_2 \ ... \ v_{10})$$

obtained by constraining the index i so that $3 \le i \le 7$ is the vector

$$(v_3 \ v_4 \ v_5 \ v_6 \ v_7)$$

See also slice.

triple precision The use of three times the usual number of bits to represent a number. It is seldom required. *See also* double precision.

tri-state output (three-state output) An electronic output stage consisting of a logic gate, commonly an inverter or buffer, that exhibits three possible *logic states: logic 1, logic 0, and an inactive (high-impedance or open-circuit) state. The inactive state allows the device outputs to be combined with other similar outputs in a busing structure such that only one device is active on the bus at any one time.

tristimulus values Three values defining a color in a specific trichromatic *color model.

trivial graph A *graph with just one vertex.

Trojan horse (trojan) An apparently innocent program designed to circumvent the security features of a system. The usual method of introducing a Trojan horse is by donating a program, or part of a program, to a user of the system whose security is to be breached. The donated code will ostensibly perform a useful function; the recipient will be unaware that the code has other effects, such as writing a copy of his or her username and password into a file whose existence is known only to the donor, and from which the donor will subsequently collect whatever data has been written.

Trojan horses can be particularly effective when offered to systems staff who can run code in highly privileged modes. Two remedies are effective: no code should be run unless its provenance is absolutely certain; no code should be run with a higher level of privilege than is absolutely essential. *See also* virus.

Tron *Acronym for* the real-time operating-system nucleus. A project begun in 1984 at Tokyo University to create a framework for the design of microprocessor systems for *workstations, *personal computers, and industrial embedded applications. The project has developed Tron architectures on silicon, now manufactured by Hitachi, and three operating systems: *BTron, CTron,* and *ITron.*

BTron is a business-oriented operating system for personal computers with English, Japanese, and other character set capabilities. CTron is a (network) communications-oriented operating system. ITron is a real-time operating system, designed to give rapid response to external events and intended for applications ranging from ATMs (automatic teller machines) to aircraft landing systems.

trouble shooting The resolution of a particular problem associated with a project or system. This activity is exceptional rather than part of the planned life of the project or system.

TRS *Abbrev. for* term rewriting system.

true complement *Another name for* radix complement.

truncation *See* roundoff error.

truncation error The error incurred in cutting short an infinite process after finitely many terms or iterations, or by not proceeding to the limit. It represents one of the main sources of error in *numerical methods for the algorithmic solution of continuous problems. Its analysis and methods for its estimation and control are central problems in *numerical analysis. In the numerical solution of differential equations it is closely related to the concept of *discretization error.

trunk *Another (US) name for* bus.

trunk circuit An interconnecting transmission channel between a switching machine in one location and a switching machine in an adjacent node.

trusted Having, involving, or denoting a security feature that is necessary to uphold a *security policy. Such features, when granted *security certification, may be considered "trustworthy".

truth-maintenance system (reason-maintenance system) A collection of techniques in *artificial intelligence recording dependencies between assertions in a logical database. Given a query and a database, a truth-maintenance system will return a set of statements, called an *explanation*, that supports the query; hence the query statement can be derived from the statements in the explanation. Applications are found in diagnosis, where a complete model of the working system is used to reason from symptoms to causes; an explanation, generated by a fault query, defines the steps from symptoms to cause. This is different from *heuristic *rule-based systems and *probabilistic systems, which mainly use reasoning rules that relate cause to symptom.

truth table 1. A tabular description of a *combinational circuit (such as an *AND gate, *OR gate, *NAND gate), listing all possible states of the input variables together with a statement of the output variable(s) for each of those possible states.
2. A tabular description of a *logic operation (such as *AND, *OR, *NAND), listing all possible combinations of the truth values – i.e. *true* (T) or *false* (F) – of the operands together with the truth value of the outcome for each of the possible combinations.

TSP *Abbrev. for* traveling salesman problem.

TSR *Short for* terminate and stay resident program. A type of program normally found on microcomputer systems. After the program has been loaded into memory and executed it does not release the memory but remains there, ready to be reactivated when required, often by a single keystroke (*see* hot key). The advantage is that it is not necessary to terminate one program before starting another; however, the maximum amount of memory available for other programs is reduced.

TTL *Abbrev. for* transistor-transistor logic. A widely used family of logic circuits that is produced in integrated-circuit form and whose principal switching components are *bipolar transistors. It is available in low power and high switching speed versions (*see* Schottky TTL), in addition to the standard form.

The diagram shows the equivalent circuit of a TTL two-input *NAND gate. The basic circuit uses a multiemitter bipolar transistor, Q_1, which is easily fabricated in integrated-circuit form. Each base-emitter junction of Q_1 effectively acts as a *diode, in a similar manner to a *DTL input stage. Thus if all inputs are at a high voltage (logic 1), all input "diodes" are reverse biased; the collector voltage of Q_1 rises to V_{cc}, turning on Q_2 (which acts as a phase splitter). The emitter voltage of Q_2 rises while its collector voltage falls, turning Q_3 on and Q_4 off. The output thus falls to logic 0, i.e. zero volts.

If any one of the Q_1 inputs is returned to logic 0, 0 volts, then Q_1 is turned hard on, turning off Q_2 whose collector voltage rises; this turns on Q_4. No current is available via Q_2 for Q_3's base, and so Q_3 turns off. The output thus increases to +5 volts, i.e. logic 1. Diode D_1 is included to establish the correct bias conditions for Q_4. The output stage, consisting of Q_3, D_1, Q_4, and R, acts as a power amplifier and is often termed a *totempole output*.

TTL is the most commonly used technology for SSI and MSI devices due to its low cost, high speed, and ready availability.

TTS *Abbrev. for* text-to-speech.

TTY *Abbrev. for* Teletype. *See* teletypewriter.

T-type flip-flop *See* T flip-flop.

tuple *See* n-tuple, relational model.

Turbo languages Implementations of popular programming languages by Borland for the IBM PC and equivalents (and in some cases for the Apple Macintosh). They included Turbo Basic, Turbo C, Turbo C++, Turbo Pascal, and Turbo Prolog. They were characterized by extremely fast compile speed and an integrated environment comprising editor, compiler, and debugger; in addition, the language as implemented included many enhancements over the "standard" language. The Turbo languages were very popular and sold in large numbers, making the version of the language they implemented a de facto standard.

Borland have since changed their marketing strategy and moved toward the professional market. Of the Turbo languages, only Turbo Pascal and Turbo C++ remain.

Turing computability *See* Turing machine.

Turing machine (TM) An imaginary computing machine defined as a mathematical abstraction by Alan Turing to make precise the notion of an effective procedure (i.e. an algorithm). There are many equivalent ways of dealing with this problem; among the first was Turing's abstract machine, published in 1936.

A Turing machine is an *automaton that includes a linear tape that is potentially infinite (in both directions), divided into boxes

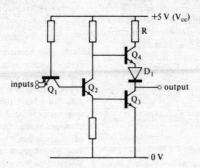

TTL NAND gate

or cells, and read by a read-head that scans one cell at a time. Symbols written on the tape are drawn from a finite alphabet:

$$s_0, \ldots, s_p$$

The control or processing unit of the machine can assume one of a finite number of distinct internal states:

$$q_0, \ldots, q_m$$

The "program" for a given machine is assumed to be made up from a finite set of instructions that are quintuples of the form

$$q_i s_j s_k X q_l$$

where X is R, L, or N

The first symbol indicates that the machine is in state q_i while the second indicates that the head is reading s_j on the tape. In this state the machine will replace s_j by s_k and if $X = R$ the head will move to the right; if $X = L$ it will move to the left and if $X = N$ it will remain where it is. To complete the sequence initiated by this triple the machine will go into state q_l.

The machine calculates functions on the natural numbers as follows: a function f,

$$f: \mathbf{N}^k \to \mathbf{N}$$

where $\mathbf{N} = \{0, 1, 2, \ldots\}$,

$\mathbf{N}^k = \mathbf{N} \times \ldots \times \mathbf{N}$ k times

is (*Turing*) *computable* if for each x in $\mathbf{N}^k$, when some representation of x in $\mathbf{N}^k$ is placed on the tape (with the machine in the initial state of q_0 say), the machine halts with a representation of $f(x)$ on the tape. *See also* effective computability.

It is customary in the study of abstract computation models to make a distinction between deterministic and nondeterministic algorithms. In a *deterministic Turing machine* the overall course of the computation is completely determined by the Turing machine (program), the starting state, and the initial tape-inputs; in a *nondeterministic Turing machine* there are several possibilities at each stage of the computation: it can execute one out of possibly several machine instructions. The class of problems solvable by deterministic Turing machines in *polynomial time is the class *P*; the class of problems solvable by nondeterministic Turing machines in polynomial time is the class *NP*. *See also* P=NP question.

Turing's thesis The hypothesis, analyzed by Alan Turing in 1936, that any function on strings or the natural numbers that can be computed by an algorithm can be computed by a *Turing machine. *See also* Church–Turing thesis.

Turing test A test proposed by the mathematician and *artificial-intelligence pioneer Alan Turing to decide whether an intelligent system has reached a level of competence comparable to that of human beings. The essential idea is to communicate with an unknown entity – by means of a keyboard and/or screen – and decide, on the basis of answers to questions, whether the responding agent is another person or a computer system. Many artificial-intelligence programs can pass the Turing test if restricted to a very severely limited domain, but asking general questions about the wider world of human experience soon exposes their shortcomings. Several variations of the test exist and it is still a topic of philosophical debate.

turnaround time (turnround time) 1. The time that elapses between the submission of a job to a computing facility and the return of results.

2. In data communications, the time taken to reverse the direction of transmission on a channel.

turnkey operation The delivery and installation of a complete computer system plus application programs so that the system can be placed into immediate operational use.

turtle graphics A method for translating information from a computer into pictures or patterns. The original drawing device was a simple pen-plotter known as a *turtle*, a motorized carriage carrying one or more pens and connected to its controller and power source by a flexible cable. The drive wheels of the carriage could be precisely controlled to steer it in any direction across a floor or other flat surface covered in paper or similar material; the pens could be raised and lowered by control signals.

The action of the turtle can now be simulated by graphics on the display of a small computer: the *screen turtle* usually has the form of a triangular arrow that may or may not produce a line as it is made to move across the screen. *See also* LOGO.

twisted pair A form of *cable used to carry electric signals. An electric circuit must always contain an outward and a return path. For high-frequency signals, the outward and return paths consist of conducting wires that must be kept close together so that the outward current in one conductor is balanced by the corresponding inward current in the other, thus reducing the amount of energy lost by radiation. This is achieved in twisted-pair cabling by twisting the two wires together. The resulting pair of wires may either be placed inside an outer conducting screen to give a *shielded twisted pair (STP)*, or left uncovered as an *unshielded twisted pair (UTP)*; the screen of an STP provides additional isolation from external sources of electric interference, and is usually formed from an interwoven fine wire mesh. Many pairs can be further twisted together.

Much of the cabling installed within buildings to provide *local loops for speech and low-speed data traffic is in the form of twisted pairs. There is emphasis on providing equipment capable of signaling in the multi-megabit range over distances of up to 100 meters over these cabling installations.

two-address instruction *See* instruction format. *See also* multiple-address machine.

two-dimensional array *Another name for* matrix. *See also* array.

two-level grammars (VW-grammars, van Wijngaarden grammars) A generalization of *context-free grammars that enables non-context-free aspects of a language to be specified. Developed by A. van Wijngaarden, they were used in the formal definition of Algol 68. The productions of a two-level grammar are split into two parts: those in the first part are called *hyperrules* and act as templates for context-free productions; those in the second part are called *metaproductions*. The metaproductions are context-free productions and they define the set of nontermi-

nals to be used in the hyperrules. The power of two-level grammars comes from the fact that the hyperrules can be templates for an infinite set of productions. It is in this way that they are used to define non-context-free aspects of a language.

two-level memory A memory system with two memories of different capacities and speeds. *See* multilevel memory, memory hierarchy.

two-norm (Euclidean norm) *See* approximation theory.

two-plus-one address *See* instruction format.

two's complement *See* radix complement.

two-way linked list *Another name for* doubly linked list.

two-way merge An algorithm that merges two ordered files into one single sorted file. It may be viewed as a generalization of sorting by insertion, and was proposed by John von Neumann in 1945.

type *Short for* data type, used especially in combination, as in logical type (or type logical) and integer type (or type integer).

type 0 (1, 2, 3) language (or grammar) *See* Chomsky hierarchy.

typeahead A feature of keyboard use such that when the user hits the keys faster than the computer can process them the computer stores up the key presses and eventually catches up without losing any. The unprocessed characters are stored in the *typeahead buffer*.

type-insensitive code A program for the numerical solution of *ordinary differential equations that attempts to be efficient, irrespective of whether the problem is stiff or nonstiff. This is usually achieved by switching automatically in the code between different classes of methods.

typewriter terminal *Another name for* teletypewriter.

U

UART *Acronym for* universal asynchronous receiver/transmitter. A *logic circuit, usually an integrated circuit, that will convert an asynchronous serial data stream into a byte-parallel form and vice versa. The normal application is in the interfaces for data transmission lines and peripherals.

UCS *Short for* Universal Multiple-Octet Coded Character Set. A 16-bit code, defined in ISO/IEC 10646, intended to redress the deficiencies and restrictions of the *ISO-7 code in a worldwide context. UCS is closely similar to *Unicode. It contains an 8-bit subset that is backward-compatible with ISO-7.

UCSD Pascal A version of *Pascal developed at the University of California San Diego, and later marketed by Softech Inc. UCSD Pascal was developed as a portable system to run on a variety of personal computers; this was achieved by compiling into *p-code, an interpretive code for a hypothetical machine that could be implemented on many target systems. UCSD Pascal introduced a number of extensions to the language, particularly in the areas of string handling and independent compilation (*see* interface); it is thus not compatible with the ISO Standard for Pascal. UCSD Pascal has been superseded by *Turbo Pascal.

UI *Abbrev. for* user interface.

UIMS *Acronym for* user-interface management system.

UKERNA *See* JANET.

ULA *Abbrev. for* uncommitted logic array.

ULTRIX A version of *UNIX designed and implemented by Digital Equipment Corporation to run on their VAX series of processors.

unary operation (monadic operation) defined on a set S. A *function from the domain S into S itself. The *identity function is unary. Other examples are the operations of *negation in arithmetic or logic and of taking *complements in set theory or in *Boolean algebra. Although basically functions, unary operations are frequently represented using a special notation, e.g. $\neg A$ or A'. When the set S is finite, a *truth table can be used to define the meaning of the operation.

unbundling The separation of system software charges from hardware charges in the marketing of computer systems. Historically, when system software was minimal and represented a small part of total system cost, it was included without additional charge. Unbundling was a natural result of system hardware becoming less expensive while software was becoming a much larger proportion of the cost.

uncertainty 1. The uncertainty about a piece of knowledge in a *knowledge base can be represented in a variety of ways. The most popular is to attach a number to the fact or rule, e.g. 1 for complete truth, 0 for complete falsity, ¾ for likely. Sometimes these numbers are intended to be the probability of the knowledge being true. Reasoning systems must assign an inferred uncertainty value to an inferred piece of knowledge. *See also* certainty factor.
2. *See* entropy.

uncommitted logic array (ULA) A form of programmable logic array. *See* PLA.

unconditional jump (unconditional branch) A *jump that causes the program sequence to start at a new address; the instruction address becomes the contents of the *program counter.

undecidable *See* decision problem.

underflow The condition that arises when the result of an arithmetic operation is smaller than the allowable range of numbers that can be represented, or the result so obtained.

undirected graph *See* graph.

undo A feature of some *applications that allows the user to reverse the effect of the last action or actions. This allows recovery from unintentional actions, and could prevent major damage resulting from a very simple but incorrect command. *See also* rollback, user-friendly.

unfolding *See* folding.

Unibus *Trademark* A minicomputer *bus structure devised by Digital and used originally in their PDP 11 series of computers. It is a single bus structure that has 56 bidirectional lines and is common to peripherals, memory, and the processor. The maximum transfer rate is one 16 bit word every 750 nanoseconds. All transfers are initiated by a master device and acknowledged by the receiving or storage device. The allocation of the role of master device is dynamic and the processor can grant control of the bus in response to a request from a peripheral.

Unicode A 16-bit code, defined by the Unicode Consortium, intended to redress the deficiencies and restrictions of the *ISO-7 code in a worldwide context. Unicode is closely similar to *UCS. It contains an 8-bit subset that is backward-compatible with ISO-7.

unification An operation on well-formed formulas, namely that of finding a *most general common instance*. The formulas can be *terms or atomic formulas (*see* predicate calculus). A *common instance* of two formulas A and B is a formula that is an *instance* of both of them, i.e. that can be obtained from either by some consistent substitution of terms for variables. As an example let A and B be the following:

$$A = p(f(u),v)$$
$$B = p(w,g(x))$$

Let u, v, w, x, y, z be variables, and c, d constants. Consider the substitution that replaces u, v, w, x respectively by the terms y, $g(z), f(y)$, z. This substitution, when applied to A and B, transforms them both into the same formula I_1, where

$$I_1 = P(f(y), g(z))$$

Hence the above is a common instance of A and B. It is however only one of infinitely many: other common instances of A and B include

$$I_2 = P(f(z),g(y))$$
$$I_3 = P(f(y),g(y))$$
$$I_4 = P(f(f(y)),g(g(z)))$$
$$I_5 = P(f(c),g(d))$$

Note that I_2, I_3, I_4, I_5 are themselves instances of I_1. In fact any common instance of A and B is an instance of I_1 and therefore I_1 is called a *most general common instance* of A

and B. Of the formulas above, the only other one that is a most general common instance is I_2. I_5 would also be one if c and d were variables rather than constants; indeed the y and z of I_1 could be any two distinct variables. In some cases A and B have no common instance; two examples of this are

$$A = P(f(u),v)$$
$$B = P(g(w),x)$$

and

$$A = P(f(u),u)$$
$$B = P(w,f(w))$$

If A and B do have a common instance however, they must have a most general one. There are algorithms (the original one being Robinson's, 1965) for deciding whether a given A and B have a common instance, and if so finding a most general one. Robinson's motivation for describing unification was its role in *resolution theorem proving. Resolution was at one time associated with "general problem-solving" techniques in artificial intelligence. More recently it has provided the conceptual basis for the logic programming language *Prolog. Another use of unification is in compile-time type-inference, especially for *polymorphic types.

unilaterally connected graph *See* reachability.

uninterruptible power supply (UPS) A power supply that is guaranteed to provide correct working voltages to the circuits of a computer in spite of interruptions to the incoming electrical power supply from the grid. Short-duration interruptions may be dealt with by a device that takes energy stored in a battery and supplies it to the computer at the correct AC voltage, using a fast switchover from the incoming to the battery power supply. For longer-duration interruptions other means may be employed.

union 1. of two *sets. The set that results from combining the elements of two sets S and T, say, usually expressed as

$$S \cup T$$

$\cup$ is regarded as an *operation on sets, the *union operation*, which is *commutative and *associative. Symbolically

$$S \cup T = \{x \mid x \in S \text{ or } x \in T\}$$

The union of S and the *empty set is S. *See also* set algebra.

2. of two *graphs, G_1 and G_2. The graph that includes all the vertices and edges of G_1 and G_2, i.e. that contains the union of the two sets of vertices and of the two sets of edges as its vertices and edges.

unipolar signal A signal whose signaling elements are constrained to lie either between zero volts and some arbitrary positive voltage or less commonly between zero volts and some negative voltage. Unipolar signals are used in data-communication systems. *Compare* bipolar signal.

uniquely decodable (uniquely decipherable) A term usually applied to *variable-length codes: unique decodability ensures that codewords can be recognized unambiguously in the received signal so that the decoding process is the exact inverse of the encoding process.

Unisys A US corporation formed from Sperry and Burroughs in 1987. It is second only to IBM in revenue among suppliers of mainframes and is also an important supplier of software and services; like many similar companies, it is trying to project itself as a solution provider rather than simply a supplier of hardware. It is number 12 in the list of the world's largest IT companies (1993 figures).

unitary semiring *See* semiring.

unit matrix *Another name for* identity matrix.

unit testing (module testing) *See* testing.

UNIVAC *Short for* Universal Automatic Computer. The US's first commercially available computer system, delivered in 1951 slightly later than the *Ferranti Mark I. Its memory was in the form of mercury *delay lines. It was the product of the Eckert–Mauchley Computer Corporation, formed in 1948 by the designers of *ENIAC. From 1951 through the mid-1950s over 40 machines were produced. The company was acquired by Remington–Rand Inc., which merged with Sperry Corporation in 1955 to form Sperry Rand Corp. Sperry later merged with Burroughs Corp. to form *Unisys.

Universal Character Set *See* UCS.

universal flip-flop *See* flip-flop.

universal quantifier *See* quantifier.

universal set A *set that, in a particular application, includes every other set under discussion. Such sets give a more definite meaning to notions like *complement and *membership: in asking whether or not x is in S, where S is some set, it is assumed that x is a member of some universal set.

universal Turing machine A *Turing machine M that, given any input x and a suitable encoding of any Turing machine K, outputs the result of applying the Turing machine K to the input x. A universal Turing machine therefore can perform all the computations for the class of Turing machines. The existence of such a machine was discovered by A. Turing in 1936. It lead to the concept of the stored-program computer.

UNIX *Trademark* (or Unix) An operating system that originated in Bell Laboratories in 1971. The system was initially written to run on Digital Equipment's PDP11 minicomputer, and was primarily intended to provide a working environment for a group of users cooperating on a small number of related projects; the group thus had considerable shared interests over and above the fact that they all used the same computer system. In the intervening years UNIX has become very popular and is now the effective standard for workstations and mid-range systems.

UNIX provides a consistent approach to multitasking, with built-in operations for the creation, synchronization, and termination of *processes either from the system environment or from within an existing process. This allows the extension and customization of the UNIX command set. There is also a consistent file-management system that provides a structured means of directory control and of file naming, with the ability to control access to files, including mechanisms for shared access. The output from any process can be directed to a file, or can itself serve as the input to some other process, with the operating system ensuring that the producing and consuming process remain correctly synchronized.

UNIX has been implemented by a wide

range of workers and on a wide range of hardware platforms. Versions have been written by individual workers through to large software houses and major hardware manufacturers, for computer systems from desktop computers through to enterprise servers. As an almost inevitable consequence there has been a bewildering number of restrictions and/or extensions to the facilities offered by the system, as well as differing implementations of what are apparently the same features. There have been repeated efforts at standardization, and several versions have been defined, incorporated in the Single Unix Specification of *X-OPEN.

unlock (unlock primitive) An indivisible operation by which a process indicates that it has completed its access to a particular resource. *See also* lock, semaphore.

unordered tree *See* tree.

unpack To convert from a packed format to a form in which individual items are directly accessible. *See* pack.

unshielded twisted pair (UTP) *See* twisted pair.

unsigned Not containing a *sign: an unsigned whole-number representation is one whose *bit pattern is interpreted as a natural type (whose value may be zero or strictly positive), possibly as a subset of an integer type.

unsolvable *See* decision problem.

up *Informal* Denoting a system or component that is operational and in service and either busy or idle; it has passed all its tests and is in a condition during which random faults may be predicted to give an *MTBF.

UPC *Abbrev. for* Universal Product Code. *See* bar code.

upline The direction from a remote node toward a central or controlling node in a hierarchical network. The word may also be used as a verb: to upline or to *upline load*, i.e. to send data from a remote end-user's node to a central node. Upline loading may be used for the storage of data that were created or modified at the remote node, but cannot be stored there permanently. Upline loading may also be used to transmit data collected at a remote

node to a more central node for further processing. *Compare* downline.

upload To load *upline, i.e. to send data from a remote end-user's node to a central node in a network.

up operation *Another name for* V operation. *See* semaphore.

upper bound 1. of a set S on which the *partial ordering < is defined. An element u with the property that $s < u$ for all s in S. Also u is a *least upper bound* if, for any other upper bound v, $u < v$.

Since numerical computing demands the truncation of infinite arithmetic to finite arithmetic, the computation of least upper bounds of real numbers, indeed of any limit, can only be achieved to a machine tolerance, usually defined to be machine precision: the smallest epsilon eps, such that

$$1.0 + \text{eps} > 1.0$$

in computer arithmetic. *See also* lower bound.

2. of a matrix or vector. *See* array.

UPS *Abbrev. for* uninterruptible power supply.

uptime The time or percentage of time during which a computer system is actually operating correctly.

up vector A vector used to specify the y-direction of a string of text or the y-axis of a coordinate system.

upward compatibility *See* compatibility.

URL (or url) *Abbrev. for* universal (or uniform) resource locator. The address system used to specify the location of multimedia documents in the *World Wide Web. For example,

http://www.eit.com/web/www.guide/

is the URL of a starting point for new Web users.

Usenet (Netnews) The name given to a number of similar services that provide a means of allowing users to access information on a network. Most Usenet services rely on cooperative action by a number of *server systems; these transfer newly entered information on one server to other distributed servers, where it will be accessed by users. The news items, usually referred to as *messages* or *articles*, are indexed to allow rapid searching for information relating to a specific topic. A *newsgroup* is a collection of Usenet messages that have been indexed as referring to a common theme, and are probably all held on a single server. The Usenet approach allows users to access information generated in other countries without the need to make international network connections.

user agent An entity that offers services to the user as both a sender and a receiver of electronic-mail messages. When preparing to send a mail message, the user agent allows the user to construct the message. The message is then passed by the user agent to the *MTA (message transfer agent), which is responsible for passing the message to the recipient. At the point of delivery, the user agent allows the user to determine what messages await collection. The user agent may also be able to access a *message store, which can act as a buffer for incoming mail.

user area The part of the main memory of a computer that is available for use by the users' programs. A significant portion of the main memory may be dedicated to the operating system and the facilities that it requires, such as buffers.

user-friendly A qualitative term applied to *interactive systems (hardware plus software) that are designed to make the user's task as easy as possible by providing feedback. Ways that help to make a system user-friendly include:
• list of valid commands available on request;
• use of a *graphical user interface;
• ability to *undo actions made in error or by accident;
• use of graphics and color to indicate what's going on;
• availability of a *help system giving information appropriate to the current situation;
• choice of interaction methods to suit personal preference and level of expertise;
• immediate verification of data input, such as checking that a number is in the correct range or word-by-word *spell checking.

As computers and terminals become available to many more people with no previous experience in the computer industry, it becomes important that only the simplest interactions should be necessary for them to start making practical use of the systems.

The term user-friendly is acquiring a wider ranging application, e.g. to other types of *human-computer interfaces, catalogues, and training manuals.

user interface (UI) The means of communication between a human user and a computer system, referring in particular to the use of input/output devices with supporting software. Examples include the *graphical user interface (GUI) and *command-line interface (CLI).

user-interface management system (UIMS) A computer system sitting between the application and the user that takes over responsibility for the user interaction. Some systems allow old *legacy applications to be updated to a modern window-based environment with little or no change to the original application.

user manual (user guide) *See* documentation.

user requirements specification A document that defines what a proposed system must be capable of doing to solve the problems of a defined set of potential users of such a system. The user requirements specification should be completely independent of any solution-oriented bias and must use terminology from the problem domain of the users. It must be understandable by the intended users who must "buy in" to it. Therefore it is most unlikely to be created using a conventional requirements-analysis method, since these introduce solution bias, representations, and concepts that are rarely understood by (and are irrelevant to) the users.

user state *See* execution states.

user view (external schema, subschema) A view of part or all of the contents of a database specified to facilitate a particular purpose or user activity. It is a partial and/or redefined description of the *logical schema of the database.

utility programs (utilities) The collection of programs that forms part of every computer system and provides a variety of generally useful functions, including file copying and deleting, text preparation, and program cross-referencing.

UTP *Abbrev. for* unshielded twisted pair. *See* twisted pair.

uvwxy lemma *Another name for* the *pumping lemma for context-free languages.

V

V The letter used by the *CCITT to categorize standards relating to data communications over telephone (analog) circuits; the number following the letter identifies a particular standard. Some of the more important standards in the V-series are listed:

V21	300 bps data transmission;
V23	multispeed operation, with differing bit-rates on the incoming and outgoing circuits, at speeds up to 1200 bps;
V24	functions of the circuits, and operating procedures for 25-pin serial interfaces;
V28	further details relating to V24;
V35	standards for data transmission at speeds up to 48 Kbps.

vaccine *See* inoculation.

vacuum fluorescent display (VFD) A small cathode-ray tube displaying individual characters or messages. VFDs are used, for example, in retail POS terminals.

VADS *Abbrev. for* value-added data service. A network service in which the service provider offers end-users additional services over and above the simple movement of data from one location to another. For example, a service offering end-users the ability to create and maintain mailing distribution lists as well as simple electronic mail might be classed as a VADS.

validation *See* verification and validation.

validity check Any check that some entity respects the constraints applying to that entity. For example, when the value of a data item is input by a program, a validity check is normally performed to ensure that this value is within the acceptable range.

valuator A type of input to a graphics system consisting of a real value. Actual input devices that readily provide input to valuators are dials, rheostats, etc. *See also* logical input device.

value-added *See* VADS, VAN, VAR.

VAN *Abbrev. for* value-added network. *See* VADS, managed data network service.

V&V *See* verification and validation.

van Wijngaarden grammar *Another name for* two-level grammar.

VAR *Abbrev. for* value-added reseller. VARs form a class of business operation that adds value to basic PCs and other computing equipment by configuring it with additional hardware and/or software.

variable 1. A unit of storage that can be modified during program execution, usually by *assignment or read operations. A variable is generally denoted by an *identifier or by a *name.
2. The name that denotes a modifiable unit of storage.
3. *See* parameter.
4. In logic, a name that can stand for any of a possibly infinite set of values.

variable bit rate (VBR) A stream of data in which the data arrives at a variable number of bits per second. For example, where data are to be transferred out of the memory of one computer system, across a network, and into the memory of a second computer system, it is perfectly feasible to suspend the transfer at some stage and to restart it later, without any detriment to the transfer. Such changes in the rate of delivery of data are not tolerable when transmitting digitally encoded speech. *See also* codec, constant bit rate.

variable delay in a network. *See* network delay.

variable-length code A *code in which a fixed number of source symbols are encoded into a variable number of output symbols. This variable number (the *code length) may be made to depend on some property of the source symbols input to the encoder, often their relative frequency of occurrence. If a variable-length code is to be instantaneously decodable (i.e. a *prefix code), it must obey *Kraft's inequality. *See also* source coding theorem. *Compare* fixed-length code.

variable-length vector A *vector, i.e. a one-dimensional array, that usually has a fixed lower bound but its upper bound may vary according to values assigned to the array. *See also* string.

variable word length computer A computer that does not have a *fixed word length but operates on data of different word lengths; this may also apply to instruction sizes. The lengths of data words that can be handled are usually in units of *characters or *bytes, so that the computer handles strings of characters or bytes. It is then known as a *character machine* or *byte machine* respectively. A variable word length computer is particularly important where data is itself of varying lengths (e.g. strings of characters) as well as cases where natural data lengths do not fit word (hardware-restricted) boundaries.

variance *See* measures of variation.

variant field An optional part of a *record.

variation 1. *See* measures of variation.

2. (contractual variation) The process of changing a contract to supply goods or services, and the results of any change to the contract as represented in a contract amendment.

variational method A technique for the solution of certain classes of *ordinary and *partial differential equations that involves the use of a *variational principle*. That is, the solution of the differential equation is expressed as the solution of a minimization problem that involves an integral expression. The equation is then solved by carrying out an approximate minimization. Variational principles arise naturally in many branches of physics and engineering. As an example, the solution of

$$y'' + q(x)y = f(x), 0 \leq x \leq 1$$
$$y(0) = y(1) = 0$$

is also the solution of the problem

$$\underset{v \in V}{\text{minimize}} \int_0^1 \{v'(x)^2 - q(x)\, v(x)^2$$

$$- 2f(x)\, v(x)\} \ dx$$

where V is a class of sufficiently differentiable functions that are zero at $x = 0$ and $x = 1$. An approximate minimization can be carried out by minimizing over the subspace of functions

$$\sum_{j=1}^{n} c_j \phi_j(x)$$

When the trial functions $\phi_j(x)$ are *splines, the resulting method is an example of the *finite-element method.

VAX *See* Digital Equipment Corporation.

VAX/VMS *Trademark* The operating system offered by Digital Equipment Corporation as the standard system for their VAX range of processors. The system functions by producing a *virtual machine for each user of the VAX hardware.

VBA *Abbrev. for* Visual Basic for Applications.

VBR *Abbrev. for* variable bit rate.

VDI *Abbrev. for* virtual device interface. *See* CGI.

VDM *Abbrev. for* Vienna Development Method. A notation and methodology for writing formal specifications, based on the Vienna Definition Method developed at the IBM Laboratory in Vienna in the 1960s for the definition of programming languages. *See* constructive specification.

VDT *Abbrev. for* visual display terminal, *another term for* visual display unit. *See* VDU.

VDU *Abbrev. for* visual display unit. A device that consists of a *display, *keyboard, and computer connection. Many VDUs also provide a selection of display attributes that can be used to emphasize or differentiate items of information, for example:

(a) blink or flash – in which the items are intermittently displayed at a rate that can be readily perceived;

(b) brilliance – in which a noticeable difference in illumination is applied in a steady state;

(c) reverse video – in which the character is displayed in the opposite contrast to the surrounding information, e.g. by substituting black for white and vice versa;

(d) underline – in which a line, usually displayed at the same brilliance or blink rate as the associated character, is drawn beneath the character;

(e) color – the color of the item and its background may be controlled individually.

vector A one-dimensional *array. Vectors are widely used in computing since the memory is essentially a vector of words. The notation for vectors is determined by the programming language. In this dictionary a bold italic lower-case letter, e.g. v, is used to denote a vector in its entirety, and the corresponding plain italic lower-case letter indexed by a subscript, e.g. v_i, is used to denote an element of the vector.

A vector may also be used to express a deficient *matrix, in which case it is necessary to distinguish between a row vector and a column vector.

vector display 1. A method of presenting graphical or pictorial images in which the beam of a *cathode-ray tube (CRT) is turned on as it moves from one position to another, thus creating a line. (The pen of a pen plotter may sometimes be operated in this way.) In a CRT the complete picture is created from a sequence of lines, which need to be regularly *refreshed to ensure a flicker-free picture. The amount of information that can be displayed depends on the number of lines that can be drawn before the image needs to be refreshed. *Compare* raster-scan display.
2. A physical display operating in this way.

vectored interrupts An efficient method implemented in hardware for dealing with many different devices, each of which is capable of interrupting and each different type of device requiring a unique *interrupt handler. The *interrupt vector* is an array of interrupt handler locations. When a device successfully interrupts the processor, it supplies the processor with a reference to its entry in the interrupt vector. The processor then uses this to transfer control to the appropriate interrupt handler.

vector font (plotter font) A *font created as a series of dots connected by lines that can be scaled to different sizes. It is used by plotters.

vector norm *See* approximation theory.

vector processing Processing of sequences of data in a uniform manner, a common occurrence in manipulation of matrices (whose elements are vectors) or other arrays of data. A vector processor will process sequences of input data as a result of obeying a single vector instruction and generate a result data sequence. This orderly progression of data can capitalize on the use of *pipeline processing. *See also* array processor.

Veitch diagram *Another name for* Karnaugh map.

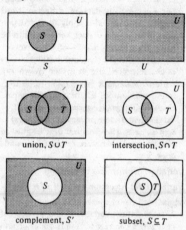

union, $S \cup T$ intersection, $S \cap T$

complement, S' subset, $S \subseteq T$

Venn diagrams

Venn diagram A schematic representation of a *set, first used in the 19th century by John Venn. A universal set U will typically be represented by a rectangle, and a subset S of U by the interior of a circle (or another simple closed curve) lying wholly within the rectangle. Some examples are shown in the diagram. Where appropriate, the shaded areas represent the sets indicated beneath each figure.

verification The process of checking the accuracy of transcription of information. It is generally applied to data that has been encoded via a data-preparation machine by an operator reading from a document. The documents are subsequently read by another operator and entered into a machine that compares the input with that prepared by the first operator. Any differences are signaled and a correction or confirmation action is made by the second operator.

Data may also be verified when it is copied to a storage peripheral from the main store or another storage peripheral. In this case the data is normally coded in a way that allows *error detection, and verification only involves checking the written data for consistency: it is not compared with the source data.

verification and validation (V&V) A generic term for the complete range of checks that are performed on a system in order to increase confidence that the system is suitable for its intended purpose. This range might include a rigorous set of functional tests, performance testing, reliability testing, and so on, in which case the term *verification, validation and testing (VV&T)* is more appropriate. Although a precise distinction is not always drawn, the verification aspect normally refers to completely objective checking of conformity to some well-defined specification, while the validation aspect normally refers to a somewhat subjective assessment of likely suitability in the intended environment.

verification condition *See* program correctness proof.

Veronica *Acronym for* very easy rodent oriented network index to computerized archives (the reference to rodents being related to the *Gopher system). An information-retrieval tool on the *Internet. A Veronica server holds an index of Gopher server systems, which can be accessed using Gopher on a workstation; the result of a search of the index is a menu of Gopher server systems that contain relevant information, and this menu can then be used by the workstation to connect directly to the Gopher servers.

version control Control of the creation and usage of the various versions of a given entity. For a recognizable entity, e.g. a software component, there may be various reasons for developing several distinct versions of the entity. A later version may represent an improvement over an earlier one, in that cer-

tain errors have been corrected or new capabilities added, or it may use an alternative approach to meeting the same requirements.

Version control promotes correct usage of the various versions, perhaps by restricting access to existing versions and creation of new versions. For example, the "current release" version of some software component may be protected against modification or deletion, while access to (or even knowledge of) a version under development may be limited to the development team.

version number A number attached to a specific version of a software item and used to distinguish this version from other versions. Simple version numbers are usually allocated in sequence so that successive version numbers will correspond to successive versions. Version numbers can also be composite, consisting of several parts often separated by periods. This numbering scheme allows a hierarchical identification of versions and is one way of distinguishing potential subsets among a set of versions. Configuration management approaches and configuration management tools must define a strategy for numbering versions.

vertex An element of the set of points that underlies the concept of a *graph. Edges are obtained by joining together pairs of vertices.

vertical check *See* cyclic redundancy check.

vertical format unit (VFU) The part of the control electronics of some early printers, governing the vertical format of the document to be printed. Information about the desired format was encoded into a loop of paper tape, or a disk, that moved in synchronism with the paper. In modern printers this has been superseded by a system in which the formatting information is downloaded from the host computer and stored in the printer.

vertical microinstruction *See* microprogramming.

vertical recording *See* magnetic encoding.

very large-scale integration *See* VLSI, integrated circuit.

VESA Video Electronics Standards Association, a US-based organization set up to define standards for many aspects of display technology and their interfaces. It defined the *VGA and *SVGA standards and is also involved in standards relating to acceptable flicker-free levels.

VFD *Abbrev. for* vacuum fluorescent display.

VFU *Abbrev. for* vertical format unit.

VGA *Abbrev. for* video graphics array. A color *graphics adapter that is available for some models of the IBM PS/2 series. Adapters to the VGA standard are produced by other manufacturers to fit into non-IBM computers. The VGA can generate a 640×480 16-color screen in addition to all the modes of the now-obsolete EGA and MCGA adapters, including a 16-color screen of 640×350, 640×200, or 320×200 pixels and a 320×200 256-color screen. Multiple graphics pages are available so that a range of animation techniques are possible. VGA is analog in composition: each of the three colors that constitute the image can take on a range of intensities between zero and a maximum value. *See also* SVGA.

VHDL A *CHDL (computer hardware description language) developed as part of the very high speed integrated circuit (VHSIC) project. It embodies many of the principles of *CONLAN and (as IEEE-1076) has become the accepted standard CHDL.

video 1. Relating to the storage or broadcasting of information that contains both pictures and sound. 2. The process of storing, reproducing, or broadcasting video information.

videoconferencing A system in which two or more sites, each equipped with a video camera and TV screen, are interconnected by a network so that participants at each site can both see and hear their opposite numbers at the other sites. There are now a number of commercial services offering videoconferencing facilities that can operate over digital networks.

videodisk A form of *read-only optical disk, devised for recording TV programs but also used for education and training. A write-once version is also available. Videodisks have been used for recording data, particularly when it is in image form, for computer systems; *CD-ROM is now preferred for most such applications.

video scanner (image grabber) A device that allows a single TV frame (or multiple frames) to be stored in memory for analysis or processing by a computer. These can be simple monochrome devices for low-cost applications or can be very fast real-time units that with powerful processor support can handle image manipulation or TV standards conversion in full color.

video terminal A VDU that is used as a *terminal.

videotex A system that provides interactive dial-up access to one or more remote services providing information. The user communicates with the information source by means of the keyboard of a personal computer, or a special videotex terminal, that is linked to the telephone through a modem. The information-providing capacity of a videotex service is limited only by the amount of online file store that the operator of the service can provide with reasonable response times, and by the effectiveness of the indexing facilities provided to enable users to find the information they want. Although initially conceived as a domestic service, the take-up of videotex has been mainly by businesses; in some cases, companies use it as a straightforward means of providing a data communication network linking geographically dispersed locations. *Compare* teletext.

Vienna Development Method *See* VDM.

viewing The mapping of scenes defined in a world-coordinate system to pictures seen from a particular view point, possibly with *culling of the original scene and *clipping of the area viewed.

view plane The plane onto which an object is projected in a *parallel or *perspective projection.

viewport The area of a display that receives a particular view of the world scene. *See* viewing.

VIPER A 32-bit validated computer implemented in silicon on sapphire, originally devised by the Royal Signals and Radar

Establishment, UK. The top-level design was simulated in *Algol 68 and was formally proven between two levels of *HOL specifications using pencil and paper algebra and a HOL theorem prover. The major state-design level was simulated in the *CAD toolset ELLA, and was also formally proven using the HOL theorem prover. A block-level model was also simulated in ELLA. The gate and chip levels were tested, and conventional *VLSI CAD checks were performed. It is believed that the VIPER microprocessor has been proved correct to the highest level practicable in the late 1980s.

virgin medium Material such as a magnetic tape or disk that is suitable for the recording of data, but has not been used or preformatted for that purpose. *Compare* empty medium.

virtual call service In a *packet switching network, a technique of setting up a *virtual circuit between terminals prior to the transmission of user data.

virtual circuit A connection that to the end-user behaves like a *circuit but is actually realized in some other way, typically by the use of some form of *packet switching system. A virtual circuit must be brought into existence or *created* before it can be used, and after use it will normally be dismantled or *cleared*. Usually this creation and clearing will be undertaken by the users of the system, by means of an appropriate *protocol. A *permanent virtual circuit (PVC)* is created by the operator of the network system and cannot be cleared down by the user. Use of virtual circuits is usually associated with *connection-oriented network services. Virtual circuits tend to be favored by agencies that charge for the use of telecommunications systems, such as *PTTs and *PNOs, as the appropriate charging can be driven by the actions of creating and clearing the virtual circuit.

virtual connection *See* virtual circuit.

virtual disk drive An abstract entity realized by array management software (*see* disk array) whose functionality is the same as a physical disk drive. Its cost, *MTBF, and performance may well be very different. *See* RAID.

virtual machine A collection of resources that emulates the behavior of an actual machine. The virtual machine concept originated in Cambridge, Mass., in the late 1960s as an extension of the *virtual memory system of the Manchester *Atlas computer.

A *process is defined in its totality by the contents of the workspace to which it has access. Provided that the behavior of the workspace is consistent with the expected behavior, there is no means by which a process can determine whether a resource that it manipulates is realized by a physical resource of that type, or by the cooperative actions of other resources that jointly present the same changes in the contents of the process' workspace. As an example, a process cannot determine whether its output is passed directly to a printer or is sent via some form of *spooling system. Similarly it cannot determine whether it has sole use of a processor or is *multiprogramming with other processes. In a virtual machine environment no particular process has sole use of any system resource, and all system resources are regarded as being potentially sharable. In addition, use of virtual machines provides *isolation between multiple users of a single physical computer system, giving some level of computer security.

The virtual machine approach forms the basis of a number of commercially produced operating systems, especially of IBM's VM/CMS and of Digital's VAX/VM products.

virtual memory A system in which a *process's workspace is held partly in high-speed memory and partly on some slower, and cheaper, backing-store device. When the process refers to a memory location the system hardware detects whether or not the required location is physically present in memory, and generates an interrupt if it is not; this allows the system supervisor to transfer the required data area from backing store into memory. For this purpose the address space is subdivided into *pages typically holding 4 kilobytes of data. Addresses within a page are defined by the 12 low-order bits in the address. The high-order bits can be thought of as the page number; they are used to search an *associative memory that shows either the physical location within memory of word zero of the page, or indicates that the page is not present in memory – at which point an interrupt is generated. The system supervisor then locates the page on backing store and transfers it into memory, updating the associative memory as it does so.

virtual reality (VR) The creation and experience of environments. The central objective is to place the participant in an environment that is not normally or easily experienced. *Augmented reality* is similar to virtual reality but the virtual image is superimposed on a real-world image often using see-through *head-mounted displays.

virtual screen Some VDUs can support more than one session at one time. A virtual screen is seen by the host as a unique application resource, but is invisible to the user. The user is able to switch, at will, between virtual screens, viewing the chosen screen as a physical screen.

virtual terminal A nonphysical terminal that is defined as a superset of characteristics of a class of physical terminal types. The virtual terminal idea is analogous to defining a non-real-world language into which some set of real-world languages can be translated bilaterally.

In some *packet switching networks, attempts have been made to use the virtual terminal concept as a means of performing protocol translation between dissimilar terminals. At the input node the message is translated into the virtual terminal format, and at the output node it is retranslated into the receiving terminal's protocol. The generality of the concept is somewhat limited because of nontranslatable characteristics of certain types of terminals with respect to others.

virus Program code written to replicate by attaching copies of itself to other objects within the system, and normally also having a detrimental effect. This may range from generation of irritating messages, through *denial of service, to corruption or complete destruction of data. A *program virus* will seek

out and copy itself into other program files whenever a previously infected program is run. A *boot sector virus* copies itself into that sector of a disk and spreads whenever a system is boot loaded from an infected disk. Viruses are spread when infected programs or disks are transferred to previously clean systems. *See also* logic bomb, Trojan horse, worm.

virus detection The systematic pursuit of *viruses. Techniques of virus detection may be either *specific*, checking for a set of known viruses, or *generic*, exploiting characteristics common to all viruses and aimed at detecting both known and previously unknown viruses. Techniques may be further classified into *dynamic procedures*, in which a permanently resident program is constantly checking the running system for viruses, or *static procedures*, which are invoked at regular intervals, typically daily, to detect viruses introduced since their last activation. *See* immunization, inoculation, signature scanning.

VisiCalc *Trademark* An early innovative *spreadsheet program developed by Visi-Corp for the Apple microcomputer system.

Visual Basic A system for rapid development of Microsoft *Windows applications. The user designs a visual interface by selecting "controls" (e.g. menus, dialog boxes) from a predefined palette, and then provides code in a dialect of Basic to specify the actions for each control in response to user input. Because the code is interpreted, the run-time performance of applications produced in this way is inferior to that of an application coded in C or C++.

Visual Basic for Applications (VBA) A common control language for Microsoft applications, in which Basic control structures and variables are supplemented by procedures and functions specific to the application. It was first implemented for the Excel spreadsheet. *See also* Word Basic.

Visual C++ A C++ program development system marketed by Microsoft, combining a C++ compiler with an integrated development environment based on a visual interface. Its *AppWizards*, which generate skeleton code for a *Windows application, make it a particularly powerful tool for development in the Windows environment.

visual display unit (visual display terminal) *See* VDU.

visualization The display of data with the aim of maximizing comprehension rather than photographic realism.

Viterbi decoding The decoding of a *convolutional code by Viterbi's algorithm.

VLB *Abbrev. for* VESA local bus. A fast 32-bit parallel bus used to interface graphics accelerator cards and other fast interface cards to the computer bus. *See also* VESA, local bus.

VLFMF *Abbrev. for* very low-frequency magnetic field. CRT displays, transformers, fluorescent lights, etc., can emit magnetic fields at low frequency (50 Hz to 100 kHz) that some allege can be harmful to humans. There is currently no consensus as to the levels or exposure limits that might be harmful.

VLIW *Abbrev. for* very long instruction word. A VLIW machine is one in which a number of normal instructions are combined and are capable of simultaneous execution using parallel functional units. The instruction may be hundreds of bits long. A compiler must ensure that operations packaged in a VLIW do not have *data dependencies that would be violated by their parallel execution. *See also* superscalar.

VLSI *Abbrev. for* very large-scale integration, i.e. integrated-circuit fabrication technology that allows over 100 000 transistors to be integrated on a single chip. *See* integrated circuit.

VM/CMS *Trademark, acronym for* virtual machine, conversational monitor system. An operating system originally produced in Cambridge, Mass. (On its first introduction the C stood for Cambridge.) The original system ran on a specially modified IBM 360/44, and was the first to make formal use of the concept of a *virtual machine, as distinct from a *virtual memory. The basis of the system is a supervisory level that creates a number of virtual machines (VMs); in each of these VMs a user can run his or her own program, using a terminal to control the VM and also to provide the route by which the

user passes input to, or receives output from, this VM. Most users run a copy of CMS, the monitor system, which in turn actually controls the running of the jobs.

VME bus *Trademark; acronym for* Versa Module Eurocard, originally Motorola Versabus. A highly versatile asynchronous backplane bus (IEEE-P1014) that facilitates construction of digital systems from system modules such as processor, memory, disk controller, and external interfacing cards. Data transfers are made by way of a 16- or 32-bit data bus nonmultiplexed with a 32-bit data bus. Transfers are controlled by *handshaking interaction of request and acknowledge signals between the current bus master and the addressed slave device. Any intelligent connected device may request bus mastership, which then enables it to initiate data transfers; contention between requesting devices is resolved by a two-level priority *bus arbitration system. A flexible prioritized *interrupt-handling scheme is also included to enable devices to demand attention from the processor or other designated interrupt-handling device.

V-model A *software life-cycle model that is a development of the *waterfall model. The diagram shows the STARTS V-model in which successive phases are displayed in a V formation with square-corner boxes representing the activities performed in a phase and with rounded-corner boxes representing the outputs from a phase. Outputs become the inputs to the next phase. The left leg of the V includes phases in which the detail of the design and the implementation of the software are gradually increased. In ascending the right leg of the V, the software is progressively assembled from its modules and testing proceeds from single modules through to the full system and eventual acceptance of the system.

Across-phase activities such as project and quality management are included; some links to contractual procedures are also included, for example invitation to tender (ITT). The model shares the weakness of waterfall-type models in omitting a diagrammatic representation of iteration between life-cycle phases.

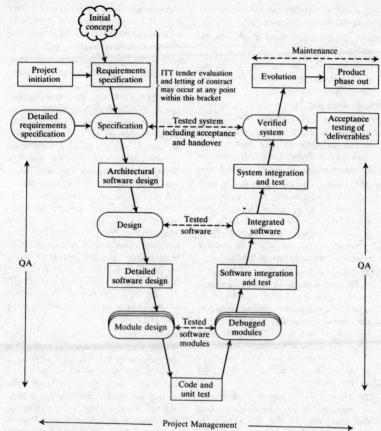

V-model [Reproduced from the STARTS Guide 1987, by permission of the Department of Trade and Industry, with acknowledgments to the National Computing Centre and for help given by representatives of UK industry]

tation of iteration between life-cycle phases. *See also* spiral model.

VMS *See* VAX/VMS.

voice activation The binding of spoken commands to commonly used system commands. It is often more efficient to speak a command rather than type on a keyboard or click on a mouse. It is also a way to avoid *RSI (repetitive strain injury). *See also* speech recognition.

voiceband *See* bandwidth.

voice coil *See* actuator.

voice input device A device in which speech is used to input data or system commands directly into a system. Such equipment involves the use of *speech recognition processes, and can replace or supplement other input devices.

Some voice input devices can recognize spoken words from a predefined vocabulary, some have to be trained for a particular speaker. When the operator utters a vocabulary item, the matching data input is displayed as characters on a screen and can then be verified by the operator. The speech recognition process depends on the comparison of each utterance with words appearing in a stored vocabulary table. The table is created or modified by using the voice input equipment together with a keyboard. A data item or system command is typed and the related spoken word is uttered, several times. The spoken word is then analyzed and converted into a particular bit pattern that is stored in the vocabulary table.

voice mail *See* voice messaging.

voice messaging (voice mail) A message system closely related to *electronic mail but in which the body of the message is presented as speech. Such systems may be implemented as extra features on a PABX system, using the tone-dialing features of the handset to control the addressing, storing, and accessing of the recorded speech. Alternatively they may be implemented as an extension to e-mail by allowing the sender to present the body of the message as digitized speech, for later recovery by the recipient who will reconvert the stored form to an audio signal.

voice recognition The process of recognizing a specific voice or speaker. Many of the processes involved are the same as those used in *speech recognition.

void set *Another name for* empty set.

volatile memory A type of memory whose contents are destroyed on the removal of power to the memory. When volatile memories are used for crucial applications, they can be backed up with temporary battery-power supplies. *Compare* nonvolatile memory.

Volterra integral equation *See* integral equation.

volume A removable unit of any data storage medium, e.g. a reel or cartridge of magnetic tape or a demountable disk.

volume label *See* label.

volume visualization A *visualization technique based on splitting the projected picture into three-dimensional voxels (volume equivalents of pixels) and applying *rendering techniques to the voxels before the mapping to two dimensions.

von Neumann machine Any computer characterized by the following concepts:

(a) the main units are a *control unit, *ALU, *memory, and input and output facilities;

(b) programs and data share the same memory, thus the concept of a *stored program is fundamental;

(c) the control unit and ALU, usually combined into a *central processor (which may contain internal storage – accumulators and other registers), determine the actions to be carried out by reading instructions from the memory.

It follows that a program for a von Neumann machine consists of a set of instructions that are examined one after another; a *program counter in the control unit indicates the next location in the memory from which an instruction is to be taken. It also follows that the data on which the program operates may include *variables: storage locations can be named so that the stored value may be subsequently referenced or changed during execution of the program.

The vast majority of present-day computers are von Neumann machines. The name is taken from that of the American, John von Neumann. *Compare* non von Neumann architecture.

V operation (up operation) *See* semaphore.

Voronoi diagram A breakdown of a plane into *Voronoi regions* (also called *Dirichlet regions*) based on a set of points. For each point P in the set, the corresponding Voronoi region consists of the set of points closer to P than to any other point in the set.

voting logic *See* comparator.

voxel The three-dimensional equivalent of a *pixel. It is an axis-aligned box, typically an element in a space-subdivision structure.

VR *Abbrev. for* virtual reality.

VSAM *Acronym for* virtual storage access method. An *access method for data files, supporting both *sequential access and indexed access (*see* indexed file), and based on primary indexes that are structured as B+

trees (*see* B-tree). It is specific to IBM machines and operating systems using *virtual memory techniques, and improves on *ISAM.

V-series *See* V.

VSO *Abbrev. for* very small outline. *See* SO.

VTFL code *Short for* variable-to-fixed-length code. A *code in which the data input to the *encoder may vary in length between iterations of the encoding algorithm, but the data output is always of the same length. The *decoding of a VTFL code is *FTVL. Also, VTFL is the decoding scheme for data that were encoded by a FTVL code (e.g. a *Huffman code).

VTVL code *Short for* variable-to-variable-length code. A *code in which both the data input to the *encoder and the data output from it may vary in length between iterations of the encoding algorithm. The *decoding of a VTVL code is also VTVL.

vulnerability Any mechanism that could lead to a breach of the security of a system in the presence of a *threat. Vulnerabilities may arise unintentionally due to inadequacy of design or incomplete debugging. Alternatively the vulnerability may arise through malicious intent, e.g. the insertion of a *Trojan horse.

VV&T *See* verification and validation.

VW-grammar *Short for* van Wijngaarden grammar, *another name for* two-level grammar.

W3 (or W³) *Abbrev. for* World Wide Web.

wafer A large single crystal of semiconductor, usually silicon, that is used as the substrate on which *integrated circuits are manufactured. *Wafer-scale integration* is a technique that utilizes a very large area of the silicon wafer to implement a *VLSI circuit.

wafer-scale integration *See* wafer.

WAIS *Abbrev. for* wide area information service. A service designed to provide ready access to information of interest to users based at widely separated locations, typically in a *wide area network. The term is used both to refer to a database server holding indexed information, and also to a software utility that runs on a network-connected workstation and allows a user at the workstation to carry out searches of documents held in remote databases. The documents have full-text indexing, which allows all documents containing either a keyword, or combinations of keywords, held in any of the document-holding servers to be located and retrieved. The system also allows the use of nontext data. *See also* gopher, World Wide Web.

wait list A list of the processes that are awaiting the completion of some activity before they can again run on a processor. Typically the activity is associated with input or output, but may in theory be associated with any activity that can cause a process to be suspended while awaiting the freeing of a *semaphore (or an equivalent mechanism that may be in use to control process synchronization).

wait operation *See* semaphore.

wait state A situation in which one component of a system is unable to proceed until some other component has completed an operation. As a commonly occurring example, the basic operating time of many processors is less than the time needed to read data from the memory subsystem. In general, the processor is unable to proceed further until information that is requested from the memory has been received. To cater for this, when the processor passes the address of the data to be read to the memory controller and requests information to be read from the memory, the processor enters a wait state, performing no operations of any kind, until the memory controller signals that the data is available to the processor. *See also* zero-wait state.

walkthrough A product review performed by a formal team. A number of such reviews may be held during the lifetime of a software project, covering, for example, requirements specification, program specifications, design, and implementation. The review is formally constituted; there is a clear statement of the contribution that each member of the review team is required to make, and a step-by-step procedure for carrying out the review. The person responsible for development of the product under review "walks through" the product for the benefit of the other reviewers, and the product is then openly debated with a view to uncovering problems or identifying desirable improvements.

wallpaper In a *graphical user interface (GUI), the pattern on those parts of the screen outside the *desktop. The wallpaper can be chosen from those supplied with the GUI or can be provided by the users. Small repeated patterns or screen-filling pictures can be used. *Compare* screensaver.

Walsh analysis One of the many forms of orthogonal analysis (especially of *signals); it employs the *Walsh functions as its orthonormal basis. Walsh analysis is especially suited to *digital signal processing since the Walsh functions themselves, and the operations based upon them, are easily represented and rapidly carried out by simple digital systems. The analysis of a signal in terms of Walsh functions is called its *Walsh transform*. *See also* discrete and continuous systems, filtering, sequency, bandwidth.

Walsh functions A complete set of functions that form an *orthonormal basis for *Walsh analysis: they take only the values $+1$ and -1, and are defined on a set of 2^n points for some n. For purposes of computer representation, and also for their use in coding, it is usual to represent "$+1$" by "0", and "-1" by "1". As an example, the 8-point Walsh functions are then as follows:

$$wal(8,0) = 00000000$$
$$wal(8,1) = 11110000$$
$$wal(8,2) = 00111100$$
$$wal(8,3) = 11001100$$
$$wal(8,4) = 10011001$$
$$wal(8,5) = 01101001$$
$$wal(8,6) = 01011010$$
$$wal(8,7) = 10101010$$

Note that the Walsh functions (usually denoted *wal*) consist alternatively of even and odd functions (usually denoted *cal* and *sal* by analogy with *cos* and *sin*). Furthermore, within the set of 2^n functions there is one function of zero *sequency, one of (normalized) sequency 2^{n-1}, and one pair (odd and even) of each (normalized) sequency from 1 to $2^{n-1} - 1$.

A set of Walsh functions corresponds, with some permutation of columns, to a *Reed–Muller code and, with a column deleted, to a *simplex code. *See also* Hadamard matrices.

Walsh transform *See* Walsh analysis.

WAN *Acronym for* wide area network.

wand A small hand-held device that can be used to read printed *bar codes or characters. The device may have a shape similar to a pen, but is usually larger in diameter or may be designed to be grasped in the palm of the hand. In use it is stroked over the surface of the printing at a steady speed and an audible and/or visual signal is actioned to indicate if a satisfactory sensing of data was achieved. The wand usually only contains the sensors and the minimum of electronics and is connected to the control electronics by a flexible cable. In some devices the wand is only a plastic enclosure and handle for guiding the end of an array of optical fibers.

Ward–Mellor A particular variant of *structured systems analysis developed by Paul Ward and Stephen Mellor for use in real-time systems development. In addition to the techniques used in structured systems analysis, Ward–Mellor introduces the concept of control processes in dataflow diagrams described by state-transition diagrams.

warm boot (warm restart) A method of restarting a computer without switching it off and then on again or using an equivalent technique (*see* cold boot). The implication is that not all parts of the operating system are reinitialized; there is some carry-over from the environment before the reboot. However, a warm boot will normally be quicker and often simpler than a cold boot and may well serve whatever purpose was intended by the restart.

Warnock's algorithm A *hidden-line removal algorithm that is based on recursive subdivision of the scene until areas are obtained that are trivial to compute. The algorithm works because of *area coherence. It solves the general problem by avoiding it. If the scene is simple enough to render then it is rendered; otherwise it is divided into smaller parts and the process is repeated.

warping Distorting an image or texture to achieve some desired effect.

Warshall's algorithm An algorithm for *transitive closure that saves computational time or storage space by doing computations in a particular order.

watchdog timer A timing device used to guard against errors caused by the lack of an expected response to a processor action within some maximum permitted time. One example would be if no acknowledgment is received to the transmission of a message from one processor to another. After some time interval it would be assumed that the transmission had failed and should be repeated. *See also* timeout.

waterfall model A *software life-cycle model that represents the successive phases as boxes and the onward progression of partially worked software as connecting arcs. Typically the first phase, whatever its name, is shown as the highest box, and the outputs of this and other phases appear to flow into the

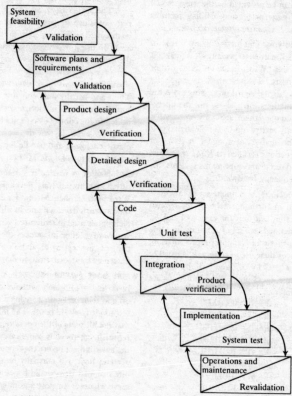

Waterfall model [from *Computer*, May 1988, page 62. © 1988 IEEE]

subsequent phases. Sometimes the flow is only shown from first phase toward the last phase and no iteration around phases is conceived. Other versions of the model show a reverse flow as in the example shown in the diagram.

It is rare for the waterfall style of model to show the various activities that occur across all life-cycle phases. For example, the diagram omits important activities such as project management, quality management, and configuration control. A further weakness of many waterfall models is the treatment of maintenance. Maintenance in this example is shown as a single box: this is the view of a system as perceived by the supplier, and particularly a supplier who has no responsibility for software maintenance. In reality each maintenance action will follow the full life cycle from feasibility through to implementation. *See also* spiral model, V-model.

WATFIV An improved version of *WATFOR.

WATFOR A fast load-and-go *Fortran compiler developed at the University of Waterloo in Canada (hence WATerloo FORtran) and widely used for the teaching of programming in the Fortran era.

wavelet A basis function, W, that yields the representation of a function $f(x)$ of the form:
$$f(x) = \sum b_{jk} W(2^j x - k)$$
Wavelets are based on two fundamental ideas: dilation and translation. The construction of wavelets begins with the solution to a dilation equation:
$$\phi(x) = \sum c_k \phi(2x - k)$$
$\phi(x)$ is called the *scaling function*. W can then be derived from $\phi(x)$:
$$W(x) = \sum (-1)^k c_{1-k} \phi(2x - k)$$
Wavelets are particularly useful for representing functions that are local in time and frequency. The idea of wavelets grew out of seismic analysis and is now a rapidly developing area in mathematics. There are elegant recursive algorithms for decomposing a signal into its wavelet coefficients and for reconstructing a signal from its wavelet coefficients.

wavelet image compression An approach to image compression based on *wavelets.

The image is represented by a collection of quantized wavelet coefficients.

wavelet radiosity The use of hierarchical basis functions (*wavelets) in *radiosity calculations.

wavelet transform A decomposition of a signal in terms of a *wavelet basis.

wave-table synthesis A technique for reproducing a wide frequency range from a small number of original samples at selected base frequencies. It is often used to create in a more accurate way the sounds of real musical instruments by means of a number of *sound cards. Data is either held in ROM or loaded into RAM. The specialized hardware then performs interpolation from various base notes held in RAM or ROM. The technique is often used by on-board *MIDI systems.

WC *Abbrev. for* world coordinates.

weakening (monotonicity) A rule of reasoning that implies that from a clause such as $P \Rightarrow Q$ (where $\Rightarrow$ should be interpreted as "implies" and P and Q are atoms) one can deduce both $P \vee R \Rightarrow Q$ and $P \Rightarrow Q \vee R$ (where $\vee$ signifies "or"). In other words, additional antecedents can always be added to a clause in a *deduction.

weakest precondition For some given program statement S and some *postcondition R there is a (possibly empty) set of program states such that if execution of S is initiated from one of these states then S is guaranteed to terminate in a state for which R is true. The weakest precondition of S with respect to R, normally written

wp (S,R)

is a predicate that characterizes this set of states. Use of the adjective weakest explicitly indicates that the predicate must characterize all states that guarantee termination of S in a state for which R is true.

The term was introduced by Dijkstra in 1975 in conjunction with a calculus for the derivation of programs; this provides for development of a program to be guided by the simultaneous development of a total correctness proof for the program. *See* program correctness proof, predicate transformer.

weakly terminating (weakly normalizing)
See abstract reduction system.

Web *See* World Wide Web.

WEB *See* literate programming.

weighted code A *block code in which a weight has been assigned to each of the symbol positions in a codeword. *See also* 8421 code, excess-3 code.

weighted graph A *graph that has weights associated with the edges of the graph. The weight can be regarded as a *function from the set of edges into some appropriate codomain. This function is sometimes called a *cost function*. For example, in graphs with geographical origins, weight might represent distance or cost of travel.

weighted least squares *See* least squares, method of.

weighted mean *See* measures of location.

Weiler–Atherton clipping algorithm A *polygon-clipping algorithm that is capable of clipping a concave polygon with interior holes to the boundaries of another concave polygon also with interior holes. (A concave polygon has an interior angle greater than 180°.) It is thus more general, though more complex, than the *Sutherland–Hodgman clipping algorithm.

well-formed formula (wff) *See* propositional calculus.

well-founded relation A particular kind of *partial ordering, used in termination proofs (*see* program correctness proof). A well-founded relation on a set S consists of a partial ordering

$$R \subseteq S \times S$$

such that there does not exist any infinite sequence $x_1, x_2, x_3, \ldots$ of members of S for which each pair $\langle x_i, x_{i+1} \rangle$ belongs to R. As an example, if S consists of the natural numbers, then the "greater than" relation, containing all pairs $\langle m,n \rangle$ such that $m > n$, is well-founded, since there are no infinite descending sequences of natural numbers. On the other hand "greater than or equal to", and "less than" are not well-founded. On the set of integers, none of these relations are well-founded. As another example, if S is the set of all finite sets of natural numbers, then "proper superset of" is well-founded.

In the application to terminate proofs it is shown that, whenever a certain point in the program is visited during execution, the current value of some quantity lies within S and also that, if x is the value of that quantity at one such visit, and x' its value at a later visit, the pair $\langle x,x' \rangle$ belongs to R. It then follows that that point in the program cannot be visited infinitely often. By considering enough such points it can be concluded that any execution must have finite length.

well-ordered set A set S on which the relation $<$ is defined, satisfying the following properties:

(a) given x,y,z in S,
  if $x < y$ and $y < z$, then $x < z$

(b) given x,y in S, then exactly one of the following three possibilities is true:

$$x < y, \ x = y, \ \text{or} \ y < x$$

(c) if T is any nonempty subset of S, then there exists an element x in T such that

$$x = y \ \text{or} \ x < y,$$

i.e. $x \leq y$ for all y in T

This relation $<$ is said to be a *well ordering* of the set S.

wff *Abbrev. for* well-formed formula. *See* propositional calculus.

W grammar *Another name for* two-level grammar.

whetstone benchmark A *benchmark program built up from a carefully selected mix of computer instructions and data types selected to be "typical" for scientific calculations. The whetstone metric so obtained has been widely used to measure comparative processing performance of hardware/software systems. The metric was developed by ICL at Whetstone, England.

while loop *See* do-while loop.

while program *See* while programming language.

while programming language A small imperative programming language whose programs are based on a *signature Σ and are made from assignments, sequential composition, conditional statements, and while statements. Programs in the language are defined, using an abbreviated BNF notation, by

$$S ::= x := t \mid S_1; S_2 \mid$$

if b then S_1 else S_2 fi $\mid$ while b do S od where x is any *variable, t is any *term over the signature Σ, b is a Boolean term, and S, S_1, and S_2 are while programs. The role of the signature is to define the data types (and hence the types of variables needed) and the basic operations on data (and hence the terms that appear in assignments). The while programming language can compute functions and sets on any algebra with signature Σ. When applied to the simple algebra

$$(\{0,1,2,\ldots\} \mid 0, n+1)$$

of natural numbers, the while programs compute all partial *recursive functions. The while language is an important language for the theoretical analysis of ideas about *imperative programming. It is easily extended by adding constructs, such as the *concurrent assignment, **repeat** and **for** statements, and nondeterministic constructs (like the random assignment $x := ?$).

Whirlwind The first real-time computer, built at the Massachusetts Institute of Technology and capable of calculating at high speed. The Whirlwind project had its origins in wartime defense and was officially launched in December 1944. The first version, operational in 1950, used *electrostatic storage tubes but a ferrite *core store was in use (its first appearance) by 1953. *See also* Digital Equipment Corporation.

whiteboard (electronic blackboard) A common area between applications and users in which mutually useful information is stored in a standard form that all can access.

white-box testing *Another name for* glass-box testing.

white noise Noise occurring in a channel and regarded as continuous in time and continuous in amplitude, the noise being uniform in energy over equal intervals of *frequency. (Note that, by contrast, white light is uniform in energy over equal intervals of wavelength.) *Compare* impulse noise.

white pages *See* yellow pages.

Whitney read/write head *See* read/write head.

whois An online *directory service relating primarily to people responsible for administering, managing, and operating networks, and for network-accessible services.

whole number A number that is not *fractional or *real. It is an *integer or a member of some subset of the integers such as the *natural numbers.

wide area information service *See* WAIS.

wide area network (WAN) A *network with communications often over large distances and, like a *local area network (LAN), generally operated by a single organization. In the case of a WAN, however, this organization may be active in commerce or industry and have plant or offices at a number of widely dispersed sites. Alternatively the principal activity of the organization may be the operation of the WAN, as with a *public network operator. In both cases the WAN will interconnect the LANs at the dispersed sites. *See also* metropolitan area network.

wideband (broadband) *See* bandwidth.

widget An element of a user interface that behaves in a particular way. The term is associated with the *X Windows system, where a widget in general corresponds to an X window together with the functions and rules that determine its input and output behavior. Examples of widgets include *buttons and *scroll bars. Widgets are therefore components from which user interfaces can be constructed. Different widget sets are available on X windows and these provide the elements for constructing user interfaces. Different widget sets will usually provide different styles of interface.

width of a bus. The number of signal lines in the *bus.

wildcard A character that can stand for a number of different characters. In a search, for instance, if $ is a wildcard meaning any number of characters, then find **compute$** will find *compute, computer, computers, computed,* etc. Again if % is a wildcard meaning any single character in, say, a command to delete some files, then **delete fred%** will cause *fred1*, *fred2*, *fred3* to be deleted, but not *fred23* (more than one character) nor *fred* on its own (no character to match). Wildcards are widely used in commands and text searches. *See also* pattern matching.

Williams-tube store *See* electrostatic storage device.

wimp *Acronym for* windows, icons, menus, pointers. An informal term used to identify the main advantages claimed for a windows system.

Winchester technology The name given to the design approach used in the IBM 3340 disk drive, which was introduced in 1973. It demonstrated a significant advance in technology, allowing an increase in recording density to 300 tracks per inch and 5600 bits per inch. The technology has been adopted by many manufacturers.

The read/write heads and the carriage assembly that supports them are enclosed with the disks in a hermetically sealed enclosure called a *data module*. When the data module is mounted in the drive unit it is automatically coupled to a system that supplies it with filtered cooling air. An entirely new head design was also introduced (*see* read/write head). The surface of the disk has an oxide coating of only 1.12 micrometers, compared to 4.7 µm of previous designs, and a lubricant coating to prevent damage during head take-off and landings.

Most recent designs using aspects of Winchester technology have the disk pack permanently fixed within the drive. The capacity of these disks ranges from a few tens of megabytes to approaching a gigabyte.

winding number The number of times the sequence of points defining a polygon winds around a particular point. This value may be used to implement an efficient polygon inside/outside test: points for which the winding number is nonzero are defined as inside the boundary. The test gives a different result from the *odd–even rule.

window 1. A rectangular area on a display screen inside which part of an image or file is displayed. A *windows system* is a means of presenting users with views of the state of a number of separate *processes, each carrying out a task. The user is able to initiate, monitor, and terminate processes, each process having an associated window. The window for each process is assigned to a specific area of the display and can be moved and often resized. It may overlap or be overlapped by the windows associated with other processes (i.e. more than one window can be displayed at once). As each process runs, it updates the contents of its window, and the user can direct input to the process by placing the cursor in the window and typing or otherwise generating input. This is of value where a user with a workstation is managing a number of different related activities.

The windows system was originally conceived at Rank Xerox and was first used commercially on the Apple Macintosh computer. It is now available on most types of computer. *See also* windows manager, Windows, X Windows.

2. A source region in one coordinate system that is mapped into a destination region (called a *viewport) by a window-to-viewport transformation. Both window and viewport are normally rectangular regions, thus a window-to-viewport transformation consists of translation and scaling components only.

3. An allocation of messages, data units, or both, given by a receiver to a sender in a data communication protocol. It controls how much data the sender may transmit before it receives an *acknowledgment from the receiver. The window is used for *flow control by the receiver, to prevent the sender from transmitting more rapidly than the receiver can process. The window is also used for *error management, by establishing the range of data that is unacknowledged and thus may need to be retransmitted. The selection of a proper window size is dependent upon the properties of the path between the sender and receiver: bandwidth, delay, and network congestion are important factors.

Windows *Trademark* A *graphical user interface developed by Microsoft for the Intel family of microprocessors; it is also known as *Microsoft Windows* or *MS Windows*. Versions of Windows prior to *Windows 95 ran in conjunction with *MS-DOS and concealed many of the innate limitations of MS-DOS by allowing a form of virtual memory, unified management of peripheral devices, and multitasking. Windows permits easy transfer of information between applications, which may be running in separate *windows on the screen simultaneously. A style guide for application developers ensures that all Windows applications work in a similar way, markedly reducing the time taken to learn new applications.

Windows 95 *Trademark* A version of Microsoft *Windows that was released in August 1995 and superseded Windows and *Windows for Workgroups. The result of a major development project, Windows 95 no longer requires MS-DOS as it incorporates its functions. It uses the 32-bit capabilities of the latest *Intel processors and is much more aware of its environment in terms of networks and peripherals. The user interface has been changed as a result of trials with a very large number of users of all kinds.

Windows for Workgroups *Trademark* A version of Microsoft *Windows designed to facilitate working in small groups.

windows manager (window manager) A program for organizing the *windows of a graphical user interface. The position, size, and contents of a window can be controlled by an application. There may be many applications active at any one time, and each application may have more than one window active at any one time. Windows are created, managed, and closed down by requests from the applications to the windows manager; the applications are *clients while the windows manager is the *server. All changes to all windows are controlled by the windows manager, which will check the validity of a request from an application and then update the contents of the application's window in accordance with the request, returning a message to the client on the outcome of the request. In addition, the windows manager continuously monitors the position of the mouse cursor, reporting the position of the *mouse to an application at any time when the cursor is positioned within a window associated with that application, and generating an "event" when a mouse button is pressed or released. The application can use information about the state of the mouse button, and the cursor position within the window, to control the running of the application. The windows manager also offers some common functions, such as the ability to resize a window, to drag the entire window, and to iconize the window – shrinking its size to the minimum possible. When the windows manager changes the size of a window the client application is informed, and can then redraw the contents of the window appropriately.

Windows NT *Trademark* A later version of *Windows, sometimes referred to as simply *NT* (NT stands for new technology). It comes in standard and *server versions, and is particularly aimed at the *file-server market. Versions of Windows prior to Windows 95 ran over *MS-DOS as the underlying operating environment. Although the non-NT versions of Windows largely concealed many of the innate limitations of MS-DOS, they could not fully exploit some of the hardware advances in the later versions of the Intel architecture, such as wider address and data buses. Windows NT overcomes this by embedding the basic operating system directly into the Windows product. Another major difference between Windows NT and its predecessors is the appearance of versions running on non-Intel processors, such as Digital's Alpha.

windows system (window system) *See* window.

Winograd's algorithm A method, due to S. Winograd, for multiplying matrices that requires fewer multiplications than a straightforward calculation as a result of "pre-processing" the two matrices concerned. This involves storing vectors that are used several times in the calculation.

wired logic A form of digital logic in which some logic functions are implemented by directly connecting together the outputs of one or more logic gates. The success of this technique depends on the electronic characteristics of the gates involved. The technique is commonly used in bus communication systems with *tri-state output or with *open-collector devices.

wired-program computer A digital computer, usually a special-purpose one, in which the sequence of operations is fixed and cannot be easily altered. The sequence may take different paths in accordance with data-dependent conditions. Speed of operation and reliability may be gained at a cost in flexibility.

wireframe model A presentation of a scene made up of lines, with no attempt not to draw lines defining objects that may be obscured by other objects.

wireless LAN (WLAN) A *local area network in which (some of) the physical links are carried by a free-space signaling system. Much of the cost of a LAN lies in the final flexible link between the network outlet, which is wired in as a fixed part of the fabric, and the actual end-user device such as a PC or workstation. The presence of this link also places restrictions on the location of equipment. A WLAN replaces this final link by a free-space link, using either infrared or microwave as a carrier, allowing freedom of movement for the user and a simplified wiring installation for the fixed wiring.

wire wrapping A technique for connecting components into *circuit boards by tightly wrapping wires around specialized terminals instead of soldering wires to them.

WLAN *Abbrev. for* wireless local area network. *See* wireless LAN.

word 1. (machine word; computer word) A vector of bits that is treated as a unit by the computer hardware. The number of bits, referred to as the *word length* or *word size*, is now usually 16 or 32. The memory of a computer is divided into words (and possibly subdivided into *bytes). A word is usually long enough to contain an *instruction or an integer. *See also* memory hierarchy.

2. (string) In *formal language theory, a finite sequence of *symbols* drawn from some set of symbols Σ. This is then a *word over the alphabet* Σ or a Σ-*word*. The elements of Σ are also called *letters*. Common notation includes:

$|w|$ – the length of the word w,

w_i – the ith symbol in w,

Λ, the *empty word* – the unique word of length 0,

Σ^* – the set of all Σ-words.

Σ^* is infinite unless Σ is empty, in which case

$$\Sigma^* = \{\Lambda\}$$

Word *Trademark* A major *word-processing system developed over many years by the Microsoft Corporation. There are versions for MS-DOS, Windows, and Macintosh operating environments.

Word Basic A Basic-like control language for writing *macros in Microsoft *Word. The control structures and variables of Basic are supplemented by a collection of procedures and functions that constitute the Windows *API.

word length (word size) *See* word.

WordPerfect *Trademark* A major *word-processing system acquired in 1994 by Novell Inc. There are versions for MS-DOS, Windows, Macintosh, and UNIX operating environments.

word processing A facility that enables users to compose documents using a computer with facilities to edit, re-format, store, and print documents with maximum flexibility. A typical word-processing system consists of a personal computer running a word-processing program, and an associated printer, such as an *inkjet printer, capable of producing high-quality output of many different text *fonts as well as diagrams and pictures.

The systems available today fall into three main categories: stand-alone systems supporting one operator; networked systems enabling several operators to share printers and files; hybrid systems attached to a central mainframe or minicomputer and able to perform additional functions. The following features are generally provided.

• Document creation and editing, including the ability to
• insert, delete, copy and move text around in a document;
• include text and/or graphics from other files;
• search for and replace strings in the document.

- Checking of spelling according to general and specialist dictionary files.
- Document formatting and printing using a choice of paper sizes and formats with multiple copies as required.
- Text justification to specified margins with automatic hyphenation.
- Ability to create a document from a standard template, e.g. one containing a company letter heading.
- Use of alternative character sets such as bold, italic, underlined.
- Layout of tables, figures, etc.
- Substitution of variable information when printing the document for easy production of form letters, etc.

word processor 1. A computer program to perform *word processing.
2. A system designed specifically for word processing.

word size (word length) *See* word.

word wrap *See* wraparound.

work area *Another name for* workspace.

workbench *Another name for* software development environment.

work file *See* file.

working set The set of *pages currently in use by a process. A process running in a *virtual memory environment can be regarded as having a subset of its total address space actually in use over any short period of time. The objective of the *memory management system is to ensure that for each process those pages, and only those pages, that are actually in use are retained in memory, thus maximizing the *hit rate for these pages.

workspace (work area) A block of locations within the main memory that are used for the temporary storage of data during processing. The user of an application such as a spreadsheet, word processor, or statistical package perceives the workspace as the space containing, and hence limiting, the tables, graphics, documents, data matrices, etc., that are currently being operated upon.

workstation A position for an operator that is equipped with all the facilities required to perform a particular type of task. A satisfactory workstation must take into account desk, seating, media-handling, and storage facilities and also lighting and other environmental factors such as noise, drafts, and glare.

A workstation is often a powerful computer system that has excellent graphics and a very fast processor, is highly interactive, and is usually part of a network. Such systems are much used in engineering, electronics, energy, and aerospace industries, and in universities. Applications include *CAD, *desktop publishing, and *AI research. In data processing and office systems the basic electronic equipment would normally be a visual display and keyboard; however there may also be ancillary electronic equipment such as magnetic storage devices, printer, OCR, or bar-code scanner.

world coordinates (WC) The preferred coordinate system used by an application.

World Wide Web (Web, WWW, W3, W³) A distributed information service that was developed at CERN, the European Laboratory for Particle Physics, Geneva, in the early 1990s. The Web is a large-scale distributed *hypermedia system that is based on cooperating *servers attached to a network, usually the *Internet, and allows access to "documents" containing "links". It is accessed using a workstation that is connected to the network and is running a suitable utility program.

Within the Web, documents are presented in *hypertext mark-up language (HTML), and may consist of textual material or a number of other forms, such as graphics, still or moving video images, or audio clips. Each form of document has associated with it a *player, a means of displaying that document on a suitably configured workstation. Within a document there will be material to be displayed and usually one or more links, which in a text document appear as highlighted words or phrases, or as icons. The links hold embedded pointers to other documents located elsewhere on the Web by the use of a *URL. A URL contains information specifying the network protocols to be used, the network address of the server holding the document, and the local index entry for that document. Activating a link, typically by positioning the mouse pointer over the highlighted text and clicking, will cause the workstation to connect via the network to the corresponding server, load the document and the means of presenting the document, and display the document. Most workstation implementations also allow the workstation to initiate file transfers or to act as a *gopher station.

worm 1. (or **WORM**) *Acronym for* write once, read many (times). A class of storage device in which information, once written, cannot be erased or overwritten. The write-once CD-ROM is an example. *See* optical storage. **2.** A virus-like program that seeks out other connected hosts in a computer network and, by exploiting a *vulnerability, transfers itself to them.

worst-case analysis *See* algorithm.

worst fit A method to map *segments to holes (spaces) in *virtual memory. It selects the largest available hole in memory that can fit a needed segment, so as to leave a large hole for other segments.

wp (or **WP**) *Abbrev. for* word processing or word processor.

wraparound A facility of a VDU, allowing it to display lines of text that would otherwise be too long to be displayed completely: the line appears on the screen as two or more successive lines. This division into shorter lines that can fit within the available screen size is a function of the VDU electronics and there is no need for a format character to be included in the data stream. Wraparound may occur when a given number of characters has been received or, in word-processing applications, at word boundaries – when it is known as *word wrap*.

write (often followed by *to*) To cause data to be recorded in some form of storage. The word is often used to qualify the meaning of a noun, as in write head.

writeable control store (WCS) *See* microprogramming.

write error *See* error rate. *See also* write error recovery.

write error recovery An *error recovery process used if an error is detected when data is being written to a storage peripheral or is being verified (*see* error detection). The first step is to check that it is not simply a reading error. If the error persists, it is usual either to overwrite the block or else to write the data again in another location. Often several attempts are made, and both methods may be used in turn. Some devices, such as certain optical disk drives, use such powerful *error-correcting codes that write error recovery is considered unnecessary.

write head *See* magnetic tape.

write instruction A program instruction that causes an item of data to be recorded in some form of storage.

write-once Denoting optical media on which the user can write data, which is then permanent: the media cannot be erased and reused. It is often called *worm* media, standing for *write once read many times*, or *read-mostly* media. *See* optical storage.

write protect To prevent a disk drive from writing to a disk. *See* floppy disk.

write ring (write-permit ring) A ring that is attached to the hub of a reel of magnetic tape to permit its content to be overwritten or erased. When the reel is mounted on a tape transport the ring actuates a switch that permits the writing process. An interrupt is normally sent to the system if writing is attempted without the write ring.

write time The elapsed time during which a given amount of data is being recorded in some storage device. It does not include any latency or check read time.

WWW *Abbrev. for* World Wide Web.

wysiwyg *Acronym for* what you see is what you get, a catch phrase coined by Flip Wilson in his 'Geraldine Jones' impersonation in 1969. In computer systems it has come to mean a system where the screen displays text and graphics almost exactly as it would be printed. There may be minor differences in resolution and fonts used. Wysiwyg is considered to be a desirable feature of *word processing, *desktop publishing, and other programs where the appearance of the final printed product is important.

X

X The letter used by the *CCITT to categorize standards relating to data communications over digital circuits; the number following the letter identifies a particular standard. Some of the more important standards in the X-series are listed.

X3	*PAD control;
X25	data signaling between the equipment associated with the *PTT and the user;
X28	communication between a PAD and an *ASCII device;
X29	communication between two PADs;
X75	communication between networks using X25;
X121	standards for *addressing in an X25 network;
X400	message handling services: all standards in the range X400 to X499 relate to various aspects of message handling;
X500	directory services: all standards in the range X500 to X599 relate to various aspects of directory services.

Xerox Corporation A US-based company, best known for its reprographic equipment. Less than 25% of its revenue comes from IT sales but it is still number 22 in terms of revenue in the list of the world's top IT suppliers (1993 figures). While much of this revenue comes from printers, it has a significant presence in the PC, workstation, and software markets. The *Smalltalk object oriented development system was developed in its research laboratories at Xerox Park as was the *Ethernet local area network.

XGA *Abbrev. for* extended graphic array. An upgrade by IBM in 1991 of its old 8514A standard. It offers an image of 1024×768 pixels with 256 colors. It can thus be regarded as a subset of *SVGA.

XModem One of the *protocols used to control the transfer of information over a *modem. The protocol is primarily intended for modems on a dialed connection, although there are variants for use with privately owned or leased circuits, and for networks. XModem is intended for transfers from one personal computer to another, rather than between PCs and large servers or between mainframe systems.

XMS memory *See* extended memory.

X-ON/X-OFF A method of *flow-control based on the exchange of specific control characters over a *duplex channel. The sending device will assume that the receiver is able to accept characters at any time, and will transmit on that basis. If the receiver is unable to accept further characters it will transmit an 'X-OFF' character to the sender, which must then cease transmission until an 'X-ON' character is transmitted by the receiver.

X-OPEN A joint initiative by some of the world's leading computer manufacturers to endorse and integrate evolving standards in order to encourage applications *portability, and to give a seal of approval to conforming products. Common standards have been defined for UNIX (incorporated in the Single Unix Specification), languages (C, Cobol, Fortran, Pascal), and data management (ISAM, SQL). Coverage of standards by X-OPEN is being extended to include networking, *X Windows, and the *POSIX user interface.

XOR or **xor** *See* exclusive-OR operation.

XS3 code *Short for* excess-3 code.

X-series *See* X.

X Terminal A dedicated graphical terminal supporting the *X Windows protocol and incorporating a powerful processor. It operates over a *local area network using resources from its host.

XUI *Abbrev. for* X user interface.

X user interface (XUI) The user interface to the *X Windows system.

X Windows A seminal *client/server system originally developed at MIT in the 1980s to allow a workstation, running under *UNIX and equipped with keyboard, screen, and *mouse, to support an interactive graphics environment.

A *window is a rectangular area on the display screen whose position, size, and contents can be controlled by an application. There may be many applications active at any one time, and each application may have more than one window active at any one time. Windows are created, managed, and closed down by requests from the applications or clients, to a server, the *windows manager.

The definition of the X Windows system covers both the behavior of the windows manager, and the form and content of messages that pass between the windows manager and the client applications. The windows manager and the client applications may either coexist on a single workstation (typically a small UNIX system), or some of the client applications may reside on other systems connected by a network to the workstation that runs the windows manager. Somewhat confusingly, some of the client applications may well run on a server; for example an application requiring the completion of an extensive arithmetic calculation may well use a compute server.

Y

YACC *Acronym for* yet another compiler-compiler. A widely used *compiler-compiler provided as part of the *UNIX operating system environment.

Yahoo *See* search engine.

Yellow Book 1. The *coloured book defining the *transport service within the UK academic community.
2. *See* CD-ROM format standards.

yellow Ethernet *Another name for* thick Ethernet. *See* thick wire.

yellow pages Indexing information providing an online directory of services on a network. In contrast, the information of the *white pages* provides an online index of users on a network. In both cases the services or users indexed will normally be those of local interest, typically those on a local area network. As the yellow pages are used directly by the computer systems on the network to access services provided by other systems, there is a high premium on accuracy.

Yourdon A proprietary software design method devised by Ed Yourdon. It was one of the first methods in the group known collectively as *structured systems analysis. Yourdon has diagram notations for *ERA diagrams, *dataflow diagrams, structure charts (module calls), and *state-transition diagrams. Also supported are *review techniques such as structured *walkthrough, and guidelines for analysis and design that include qualitative assessment of the good and bad characteristics of a design. The method is supported by tools and used for real-time and data-processing applications.

Z

Z A formal notation, based on *set algebra and *predicate calculus, for the specification of computing systems. It was developed at the Programming Research Group, Oxford University. Z specifications have a modular structure. *See also* constructive specification.

Z3 An electromechanical programmed calculator built in Berlin by Konrad Zuse and fully operational in 1941. Like the earlier (nonprogrammed) calculators, Z1 (mechanical) and Z2 (electromechanical), constructed by Zuse, it did not survive the war. An improved machine, the Z4, was completed by 1945.

Z-buffer (depth buffer) A method for *hidden-surface removal. For each object in a scene, pixels are generated with color and depth information. The Z-buffer is an array that stores the current Z-depth of each pixel. As objects are sent to the Z-buffer only those nearest the viewer are retained. Each pixel is set to the new light intensity only if the depth of the point is less than the value stored at the corresponding position in the Z-buffer. The method is simple but costly in processing and storage, hence hardware or low-level implementations are common. *See also* A-buffer.

zero-address instruction An instruction that contains no address fields; operand sources and destination are both implicit. It may for example enable *stack processing: a zero-address instruction implies that the *absolute address of the operand is held in a special *register that is automatically incremented (or decremented) to point to the location of the top of the stack.

zero function The *function whose value is zero for every element in its domain. The term is usually applied more specifically to the function

$$Z : N \rightarrow N$$
for which $Z(n) = 0$

for all n in N, the set of nonnegative integers. This function is basic to the theory of *recursive and *primitive recursive functions.

zero matrix *Another name for* null matrix.

zero suppression The elimination of nonsignificant zeros. While numerical data is being processed it may be expanded to a uniform number of digits by the addition of nonsignificant zeros to the left of the most significant digit. For printout or display these nonsignificant zeros are suppressed.

zero-trip loop *See* do-while loop.

zero-wait state A situation in which the time taken by the memory controller from receipt of an address, and a request for data to be read from or written to that address, is sufficiently short that the device making the request will not need to enter a *wait state.

zero word In coding theory, a word consisting entirely of zero digits. It lies at the origin of *Hamming space. *See also* Hamming weight.

ZIF socket *Short for* zero insertion force socket. A *chip socket into which it is possible to place a chip with no downward force. Electric contact is then made by moving a small lever that causes each leg of the chip to be firmly gripped. A ZIF socket is used where chips are regularly moved in and out of a socket, e.g. in a *PROM programmer.

Ziv–Lempel compaction *Another name for* Lempel–Ziv compaction.

zone in a network. *Informal* A subnetwork within a larger network. *See* domain.

UK Data Protection Legislation

The UK has now enacted the Data Protection Act 1984 to comply with the Council of Europe Convention. The Act establishes an independent public register, and is concerned only with "personal data" as defined in the Act.

The definitions are as follows:

data means information recorded in a form in which it can be processed by equipment operated automatically in response to instructions given for that purpose.

personal data means data consisting of information that relates to a living individual who can be identified from that information (or from that and other information in the possession of the data user), including any expression of opinion about the individual but not any indication of the intentions of the data user in respect of that individual.

data subject means an individual who is the subject of personal data.

data user means a person who holds data.

The Act came into effect in stages:

• **From 12 September 1984:** Under sections 23 and 24(3) an individual has been entitled to compensation from a data user for any damage or distress suffered by reason of the loss, damage, destruction, disclosure, or access to his personal data, provided the damage has been suffered after 12 September 1984. It is a defence to an action of this kind if the data user can prove that he had taken such care as in all the circumstances was reasonable to prevent the damage or distress.

This is in effect a right of action for damages caused by inadequate computer security.

• **From 11 November 1985:** Data users have been able to register their activities with the Data Protection Registrar.

The registration form requires the data user to give:
• its name and address;
• a description of the personal data it holds and the purpose or purposes for which the data is held;
• a description of the source or sources from which it intends or may wish to obtain the data or the information to be contained in the data;
• a description of any person or persons to whom it intends or may wish to disclose the data;
• the names or a description of any countries or territories outside the UK to which it intends or may wish directly or indirectly to transfer the data;
• one or more addresses for the receipt of requests from data subjects for access to the data.

The Registrar is using a classification system to assist data users in filling in the registration forms so that, in most cases, a small business would be able to indicate by the use of code numbers the type of data it holds, the type of sources it uses, and the type of person to whom it intends to disclose the data. Registration forms and notes concerning registration are available from Post Offices.

• **From 11 May 1986:** If a data user who is holding personal data fails to register then under Section 5 of the Act the data user will be guilty of the new criminal offence of failing to register. A data user is also not entitled to process personal data after registration except in accordance with the terms of its registration.

• **From 11 November 1987:** Under Section 24 of the Act if a court is satisfied on the application of a data subject that personal data held by a data user concerning him is inaccurate it may order the rectification or erasure of the data. Additionally it may order the rectification or erasure of any data held by the data user that contains an expression of opinion that appears to the court to be based on the inaccurate data. However the section contains provisions that will, alternatively, allow the data user, in certain circumstances, to supplement the data by a statement of true facts as approved by the court.

- **From 11 November 1987:** Under Section 11 the Registrar is allowed to strike a data user off the register. Additionally prior to that date he was entitled to take action against a data user relying on information on misuse of data having taken place since September 1984 and was entitled to indicate to a data user his intention to strike a data user off the register the moment his powers to do so came into effect.

  In practice he has to indicate specific requirements to a data user and failure to comply will lead to an "enforcement notice" requiring the data user to take within a time limit particular steps to comply with the Data Protection Principles (see below). Only as a last resort will the Registrar issue a deregistration notice.

- **From 11 November 1987:** A data subject has been entitled to obtain a printout from a registered data user of any personal data held by him. The details and the consequences of this provision are referred to in Subject Access Provisions (below).

  It is now possible for a person to apply for and, on payment of a fee, obtain copies of any criminal convictions recorded against him on the UK Police National Computer. Standard forms are available to do this from Scotland Yard. No prosecutions have been brought under the Act and little use has been made of it by legal practitioners in the UK.

Data Protection Principles

The eight principles of data protection legislation are fundamental statements of good practice that have behind them the criminal and civil penalties of the Data Protection Act 1984. They are:

1. The information to be contained in personal data shall be obtained, and personal data shall be processed, fairly and lawfully.

2. Personal data shall be held only for one or more specified and lawful purposes.

3. Personal data held for any purpose or purposes shall not be used or disclosed in any manner incompatible with that purpose or those purposes.

4. Personal data held for any purpose or purposes shall be adequate, relevant, and not excessive in relation to that purpose or those purposes.

5. Personal data shall be accurate and, where necessary, kept up to date.

6. Personal data held for any purpose or purposes shall not be kept longer than necessary for that purpose or those purposes.

7. A data subject shall be entitled

   (a) at reasonable intervals and without undue delay or expense

      (i) to be informed by any data user whether he holds personal data of which that individual is the subject; and

      (ii) to access to any such data held by a data user; and

   (b) where appropriate, to have such data corrected or erased.

8. Appropriate security measures shall be taken against unauthorized access to, or alteration, disclosure, or destruction of personal data and against accidental loss or destruction of personal data.